Algebraic Theory of

Machines, Languages, and Semigroups

List of Contributors

MICHAEL A. ARBIB

E. F. ASSMUS, JR.

JANE M. DAY

J. J. FLORENTIN

SEYMOUR GINSBURG

KENNETH KROHN

ROBERT McNAUGHTON

SEYMOUR PAPERT

JOHN L. RHODES

ELIAHU SHAMIR

BRET R. TILSON

H. PAUL ZEIGER

Algebraic Theory of Machines, Languages, and Semigroups

Edited by MICHAEL A. ARBIB
Stanford University
Stanford, California

With a Major Contribution by
KENNETH KROHN
and JOHN L. RHODES

1968

ACADEMIC PRESS New York and London

ACADEMIC PRESS INC.
111 Fifth Avenue, New York, New York 10003

United Kingdom Edition published by
ACADEMIC PRESS INC. (LONDON) LTD.
Berkeley Square House, London W.1

LIBRARY OF CONGRESS CATALOG CARD NUMBER: 68-18654

PRINTED IN THE UNITED STATES OF AMERICA

To Our Parents,
Without Whom

Contributors

Numbers in parentheses indicate the pages on which the authors' contributions begin.

MICHAEL A. ARBIB (37, 127) Stanford University, Stanford, California

E. F. ASSMUS, JR. (15), Mathematics Department, Lehigh University, Bethlehem, Pennsylvania

JANE M. DAY† (269), The Institute for Advanced Study, Princeton, New Jersey

J. J. FLORENTIN (15), Centre for Computing and Automation, Imperial College, London, England

SEYMOUR GINSBURG (313), System Development Corporation, Santa Monica, California

KENNETH KROHN (81, 191, 233), Krohn-Rhodes Research Institute, Washington, D. C.

ROBERT MCNAUGHTON (297), Rensselaer Polytechnic Institute, Troy, New York

SEYMOUR PAPERT (297), Massachusetts Institute of Technology, Cambridge, Massachusetts

JOHN L. RHODES (1, 81, 127, 147, 191, 233), University of California, Berkeley, California, and Krohn-Rhodes Research Institute, Berkeley, California

ELIAHU SHAMIR (329), The Hebrew University, Jerusalem, Israel

BRET R. TILSON (1, 81, 127, 147, 191, 233), University of California, Berkeley, California

H. PAUL ZEIGER (55), Department of Aerospace Engineering, University of Colorado, Boulder, Colorado

† *Present address*: College of Notre Dame, Belmont, California.

Preface

This book is an integrated exposition of the algebraic, and especially semigroup-theoretic, approach to machines and languages. Designed to carry the reader from the elementary theory all the way to hitherto unpublished research results, it can be used as a text, as a reference book for workers in the field, and as a chance for readers with an interest in any subset of {machines, languages, semigroups} to extend their interest to the whole set.

This book has two parents: a series of expository lectures given by eight of the authors at a conference on the Algebraic Theory of Machines, Languages, and Semigroups held at Asilomar, California, from August 30 to September 7, 1966[†] and a seminar conducted by John Rhodes since 1964 in the Mathematics Department of the University of California at Berkeley. The material has been edited, rearranged, and rewritten to provide a book that is both introductory and sophisticated and has perhaps as much cohesion as any volume with one editor and eleven contributors may hope to achieve!

The chapters have been arranged in an order in which I believe the novice will find it most profitable to read them, save that the chapters by McNaughton, Ginsburg, and Shamir form a unit that may be read any time after Chapter 1. The first six and last three chapters would provide the basis for an excellent course on automata theory, with the remaining material suitable for an advanced course.

Chapters 1, 5, and 7–9 were written by Bret Tilson on the basis of John Rhodes' lectures. With chapter 6, they form a self-contained unit and may be read independently of all the other chapters. However, the reader will find that the interstitial chapters, besides providing extra material, will give him a much better feel for the machine-

[†]Besides this expository material, some 52 research papers were presented at the Asilomar Conference. These have been published elsewhere; some details are given in the Appendix.

algebraic material. Chapters 5, 6, 8, and 9 are devoted to a treatment of the research on the algebraic theory of decomposition of machines and semigroups by Kenneth Krohn and John Rhodes, which research, in fact, is the dominant theme of the first nine chapters.

The reader may find the following information useful in deciding in which order it will be best for him to read the chapters.

Chapter 1 contains the basic definitions and examples on semigroups which constitute the algebraic terminology required for the discussion in following chapters, and with which every reader should be familiar.

Chapter 2, although not a prerequisite for what follows, should prove valuable to the reader with a background in engineering or logical design, in helping him get a feel for those problems of logical design which are most amenable to algebraic treatment.

Chapter 3 makes explicit the basic relationships between machine concepts and semigroup concepts, and provides a diagrammatic approach to the cascade composition of machines which will help the reader provide elegant proofs of known results, and should also prove valuable in the discovery of new ones.

Chapter 4 provides Zeiger's proof of the Krohn–Rhodes theorem on automaton decomposition. It uses covers, a technique that should prove most appealing to readers who are familiar with the Hartmanis and Stearns lattice-theoretic approach to automaton decomposition.

Chapter 5 provides a lengthy treatment of the semigroups of machines, and two proofs of the Krohn–Rhodes theorem, which says, roughly speaking, that any machine can be built from "flip-flops" and machines whose semigroups are simple groups "contained in" the semigroup of the original machine, using repeated cascade composition. Just which "building-blocks" are necessary is also discussed, as are machines that are "combinatorial" in that they can be built from "flip-flops" alone.

Chapter 6 gives an elementary discussion of the minimal number of group machines (i.e., machines whose semigroup is a group) required to build a given machine from group machines and combinatorial machines. This number [the (group) complexity of the machine] is well defined by the results of Chapter 5.

Chapter 7 continues the exposition of Chapter 1 on standard semigroup theory giving the material required for Chapters 8–10. The main results are those of Green on the ideals of a semigroup, and the representation theorems of Rees and Schützenberger.

Chapter 8 builds on these well-known results to explore the semilocal theory and the structure of homomorphisms of finite semigroups.

Chapter 9 applies the results of Chapter 5, 6, 7, and 8 to give an axiomatic characterization, and many equivalent definitions with certain computational advantages, of the notion of complexity introduced in Chapter 6. The analysis is only carried through for semigroups that are unions of groups, but extensions to other cases are indicated.

Chapter 10 provides an exposition of recent research on topological semigroups, in the hope of hastening the day when many of the results developed for finite semigroups and machines in previous chapters will be extended to topological semigroups and machines.

Chapter 11 provides our transition to the study of formal languages, showing the way in which we may associate languages with finite-state machines, and relating these to their semigroups.

Chapter 12 discusses the way in which formal languages may be characterized, be they generated by grammars, accepted by finite-state machines with auxiliary storage, or built up from basic sets by algebraic operations. Of particular interest are the context-free languages.

Chapter 13 closes our book, showing how the algebraic methods of Schützenberger may be used to study context-free languages by using formal power-series in noncommuting variables.

One note of caution to the reader. Each author has his own prejudices about notation. I have made only minor changes toward uniformity, my rationalization being that many readers will wish to read an author's papers, for the notation of which readers may as well be prepared. However, each author carefully defines his own choice of symbolism, and so the reader who starts each chapter at the beginning should encounter no difficulties on this score.

The Asilomar Conference was organized by the Krohn–Rhodes Research Institute, with the cooperation of the Department of Mathematics, University of California, Berkeley, and sponsored by the United States Air Force Office of Scientific Research, Applied Mathematics Division (Lt. Col. B. R. Agins, Chief), under Contract No. AF49(638)-1714.

My own work has been partially supported by the Air Force Office of Scientific Research, Information Sciences Directorate, under Contract AF-AFOSR-1198-67.

Finally, I should like to thank the authors for their cooperation in revising their material to make it fit in better with the other contributions, and their general promptness—a rare and valued commodity.

MICHAEL A. ARBIB

Stanford, California
March 1968

Contents

CONTRIBUTORS vii
PREFACE ix

Chapter 1. **Semigroups: Elementary Definitions and Examples** **1**
John L. Rhodes and Bret R. Tilson

1. Elementary Definitions and Examples 2

Chapter 2. **Algebraic Machine Theory and Logical Design** **15**
E. F. Assmus, Jr., and J. J. Florentin

1. Introduction 15
2. The Machine Model 16
3. State Transition Maps 20
4. Group Machines 21
5. Series-Parallel Decomposition of Group Machines 22
6. Decomposition of Semigroup Machines 25
7. The Algebraic Machine Model and Design Requirements 30

References 35

Chapter 3. **Automaton Decompositions and Semigroup Extensions** **37**
Michael A. Arbib

1. Background 37
2. Cascades, Wreath Products, and Irreducibility 40
3. Semigroup Extensions and Automaton Cascades 49

References 54

Chapter 4. **Cascade Decomposition of Automata Using Covers** **55**

H. Paul Zeiger

1. Automata 55
2. Independence of Coordinates 60
3. Assignment of Coordinates 62
4. Covers 70
5. Permutation Automata 75
6. Discussion 79
References 80

Chapter 5. **The Prime Decomposition Theorem of the Algebraic Theory of Machines** **81**

Kenneth Krohn, John L. Rhodes, and Bret R. Tilson

1. Basic Definitions 81
2. Elementary Properties of Machines; Relations between Machines and Semigroups 86
3. A Proof of the Prime Decomposition Theorem (Krohn-Rhodes) for Finite Semigroups and Machines 101
4. The Prime Decomposition Theorem: A More Algebraic Proof 113
5. Some Results on Combinatorial Semigroups; An Application of the Prime Decomposition Theorem 120
References 125

Chapter 6. **Complexity and Group Complexity of Finite-State Machines and Finite Semigroups** **127**

Michael A. Arbib, John L. Rhodes, and Bret R. Tilson

1. Definitions of Group Complexity 127
2. Definition of Complexity; Existence of Semigroups of Arbitrary Complexity 133
3. Complexity and Ideals 140
Notes and References 145

Chapter 7. **Local Structure Theorems for Finite Semigroups** **147**

John L. Rhodes and Bret R. Tilson

1. Local Coordinates: Rees Theorem 147
2. Applications of Rees Theorem and the Schützenberger Group; Local Homomorphisms and Translations; Local Properties of Semigroups 160
3. Subsemigroups 183
References 189

Chapter 8. **Homomorphisms and Semilocal Theory** **191**
Kenneth Krohn, John L. Rhodes, and Bret R. Tilson

1. Homomorphisms 191
2. Semilocal Theory 197
3. Decomposition of Homomorphisms 213
References 231

Chapter 9. **Axioms for Complexity of Finite Semigroups** **233**
Kenneth Krohn, John L. Rhodes, and Bret R. Tilson

1. The Axioms 234
2. The Theorem 235
3. Corollaries of the Theorem 262
Notes and References 266

Chapter 10. **Expository Lectures on Topological Semigroups** **269**
Jane M. Day

1. Arcs and Semigroups 271
2. Constructing New Semigroups from Old 279
3. Some Useful Tools of Compact Semigroups 284
4. Relative Green Relations 290
References 294

Chapter 11. **The Syntactic Monoid of a Regular Event** **297**
Robert McNaughton and Seymour Papert

Text 297
References 312

Chapter 12. **Lectures on Context-Free Languages** **313**
Seymour Ginsburg

1. Grammars and Ambiguity 314
2. Acceptors and Languages 318
3. Operations 324
4. Decision Problems 326

Chapter 13. **Algebraic, Rational, and Context-Free Power Series in Noncommuting Variables** **329**

Eliahu Shamir

1. Introduction 329
2. Algebraic and Rational Power Series 330
3. Transductions and Assignments 334
4. A Representation Result and Some Consequences 336
References 341

Appendix **343**

Glossary of Symbols 345

Author Index 349

Subject Index 352

Algebraic Theory of
Machines, Languages, and Semigroups

CHAPTER 1

Semigroups: Elementary Definitions and Examples[†]

JOHN L. RHODES[‡]
University of California, Berkeley, California
Krohn-Rhodes Research Institute, Berkeley, California

BRET R. TILSON
University of California, Berkeley, California

In this chapter, we provide the basic notions about semigroups required in the following chapters. Throughout this book, we assume of the reader no knowledge of semigroup theory which we do not explicitly provide. However, we do assume that the reader is familiar with the elements of group theory, or at least has access to one of the standard texts which contains all the material needed for an understanding of the Jordan-Hölder theorem.

Most of the semigroup theory contained in Chapters 1 and 7 is standard, although we believe that it contains some novelties of presentation. Clifford and Preston's two volumes on "The Algebraic Theory of Semigroups"[§] contain a wealth of material for the reader who wishes to go further. However, by restricting ourselves mainly

† The authors wish to thank Richard Mateosian for his work on an earlier version of this chapter. This work was sponsored by the United States Air Force, Office of Scientific Research, Grant Numbers AF–AFOSR–848–66 and AF 49(638)–1550; the United States Air Force, Air Force Systems Command, Contract Number AF 33(615)–3893; and the Office of Naval Research, Information Systems Branch, Contract Number Nonr 4705(00).

‡ Alfred P. Sloan Research Fellow, 1967–1968.

§ Am. Math. Soc., Providence, Rhode Island, 1961.

to finite semigroups, we have been able to present results in a compact yet readable form more suitable to the reader whose interest in semigroups is attuned to the research problems of automata theory.

1. Elementary Definitions and Examples

1.1 Definition. A *semigroup* is an ordered pair $(S, \cdot)$, where S is a nonempty set and the dot is an associative binary operation, i.e., a function $(s_1, s_2) \to s_1 \cdot s_2$ from $S \times S$ into S such that for all $s_1, s_2, s_3 \in S$, $(s_1 \cdot s_2) \cdot s_3 = s_1 \cdot (s_2 \cdot s_3)$. $(S, \cdot)$ will usually be abbreviated to S and $s_1 \cdot s_2$ to $s_1 s_2$.

The *order* of the semigroup S, denoted $|S|$, is the cardinality of the set S. *All semigroups considered will be of finite order* unless the contrary is explicitly stated.

The element $e \in S$ is an *idempotent* iff $e^2 = e$; it is a *left* (*right*) *identity* iff, for all $s \in S$, $es = s$ $(se = s)$; it is a *left* (*right*) zero iff, for all $s \in S$, $es = e$ $(se = e)$. If e is a left identity and f is a right identity, then $e = ef = f$. Any left (right) identity or zero is an idempotent.

The element $e \in S$ is an *identity* iff, for all $s \in S$, $se = s = es$; it is a *zero* iff, for all $s \in S$, $se = e = es$. S has at most one identity or zero, for, if e_1 and e_2 are two such, then $e_1 = e_1 e_2 = e_2$. We shall often denote identities and zeros generically by 1 and 0, respectively.

A *monoid* is a semigroup with an identity, and a *group* is a monoid S such that, for each $s \in S$, there is an element $s^{-1} \in S$ called the *inverse* of s such that $ss^{-1} = e = s^{-1}s$, where e is the identity of S. An element of a monoid can have at most one inverse, for, if s_1 and s_2 are inverses of s, then $s_1 = s_1 s s_2 = s_2$.

A semigroup is *commutative* or *abelian* iff $s_1 s_2 = s_2 s_1$ for all $s_1, s_2 \in S$.

If $s_1, \ldots, s_n$ are elements of a semigroup S, then we define $s_1 s_2 \ldots s_n = s_1(s_2 \ldots (s_{n-1} s_n) \ldots)$, and all other meaningful products formed by inserting parentheses in the sequence $s_1, \ldots, s_n$ are equal to $s_1 \ldots s_n$. Furthermore, if S is commutative, then, for any permutation π of $\{1, \ldots, n\}$, $s_1 \ldots s_n = s_{\pi(1)} \ldots s_{\pi(n)}$. These facts, known respectively as the generalized associative and commutative laws, can be proved by induction on n.

If s is an element of a semigroup S, we define *powers* of s as follows. Let $s^1 = s$; for $n > 1$, let $s^n = s^1 s^{n-1}$. If S is a group with identity e, let $s^0 = e$ and let $s^{-n} = (s^{-1})^n$ for $n > 0$, where s^{-1} is the inverse of s.

1.2 Definition. Let S be a semigroup. Then $T \subseteq S$ is a *subsemigroup* of S iff $T \neq \varnothing$ and, for all $t_1, t_2 \in T$, $t_1 t_2 \in T$. T is a *subgroup* of S iff T is a subsemigroup of S, and T is a group. T is a *maximal proper subsemigroup* of S iff $T \neq S$ and, whenever $T \subseteq V \subseteq S$ with V a subsemigroup of S, then $T = V$ or $V = S$. T is a *maximal subgroup* of S iff T is a subgroup of S, and $T \subseteq V \subseteq S$ with V a subgroup of S implies $T = V$.

If X is a nonempty subset of S, then $\langle X \rangle$, the *subsemigroup generated* by X, is the smallest subsemigroup of S containing X, i.e., the intersection of all subsemigroups of S containing X. Clearly, the intersection of subsemigroups of a semigroup is empty or is another subsemigroup. $\langle X \rangle$ is easily seen to be the set of all finite products $x_1 x_2 \ldots x_n$ of elements of X.

We say X *generates* S iff $\langle X \rangle = S$. Clearly, $\langle S \rangle = S$. Let $a \in S$. Then $\langle a \rangle$ is the *cyclic subsemigroup* of S generated by a, where $\langle a \rangle$ denotes $\langle \{a\} \rangle$. S is a *cyclic semigroup* iff $S = \langle a \rangle$ for some $a \in S$.

We say S is a *torsion* semigroup if $\langle a \rangle$ is finite for every a in S.

1.3 Definition. Let S_1 and S_2 be semigroups. Then $\varphi : S_1 \to S_2$ is a *homomorphism* iff $\varphi(s_1 s_2) = \varphi(s_1)\,\varphi(s_2)$ for all $s_1, s_2 \in S_1$. If $X \subseteq S_1$, we denote by $\varphi(X)$ the set $\{y \in S_2 : y = \varphi(s) \text{ for some } s \in X\}$. If $\varphi(S_1) = S_2$, then φ is an *onto* homomorphism or *epimorphism*, and we write $\varphi : S_1 \twoheadrightarrow S_2$ and call S_2 a *homomorphic image* of S_1. If, for all $s, t \in S_1$, $s \neq t$ implies $\varphi(s) \neq \varphi(t)$, then φ is a *one-to-one* (written $1:1$) homomorphism or *monomorphism*.† An *isomorphism* is a $1:1$ and onto homomorphism. We say S_1 is *isomorphic* to S_2, written $S_1 \cong S_2$ iff there is an isomorphism $\varphi : S_1 \twoheadrightarrow S_2$. If $\varphi : S_1 \twoheadrightarrow S_2$ is an isomorphism, we can define the *inverse* of φ, $\varphi^{-1} : S_2 \twoheadrightarrow S_1$, where, for each $s \in S_2$, $\varphi^{-1}(s)$ is the unique element of S_1 such that $\varphi[\varphi^{-1}(s)] = s$. Clearly, φ^{-1} is an isomorphism. Thus, it is easy to show that $(\cong)$ is an equivalence relation on the class of semigroups.

1.4 Examples (Definitions, Notation, and Extensions).

We now give a large number of examples of semigroups. The reader will find it useful to keep a number of these in mind as he studies the subsequent theory. All of them will be important in the sequel, but *the reader need not master them before continuing.*

† Readers acquainted with categorical algebra should note that we do *not* use epi- and mono- in the categorical sense.

1.4a. Let A be a nonempty set. Then A^r (respectively A^l) denotes the semigroup $(A, \cdot)$ with $a_1 \cdot a_2 = a_2$ (respectively $a_1 \cdot a_2 = a_1$) for all $a_1, a_2 \in A$. When $|A| > 1$, A^r and A^l are examples of semigroups that are not groups.

Thus, A^r (respectively A^l) is the set A turned into a semigroup by letting each element act as a right (respectively left) zero.

1.4b. Let X be a set, and let 2^X be the set of all subsets of X. Then $(2^X, \cap)$ is an abelian semigroup. $(2^X, \cup)$ is isomorphic to $(2^X, \cap)$ under the isomorphism $A \to X - A = \{x \in X : x \notin A\}$.

1.4c. Let S be a semigroup, and let A and B be subsets of S. Let $A \cdot B = \{ab : a \in A, b \in B\}$ (usually abbreviated to AB). Then $s \to \{s\}$ is a monomorphism of S into $(2^S, \cdot)$. We make the convention that $A \cdot \varnothing = \varnothing \cdot A = \varnothing$, where $\varnothing$ denotes the empty set.

1.4d. Let X be a set. A *relation* R on X is any subset $R \subseteq X \times X$. We write $x_1 R x_2$ or $x_1 \equiv x_2 \pmod{R}$ iff $(x_1, x_2) \in R$. Then $(2^{X \times X}, \cdot)$, the semigroup of all relations on X, has composition defined by

$$R_1 \cdot R_2 = \{(x, y) : \text{for some } z \in X, (x, z) \in R_1, (z, y) \in R_2\}.$$

If R is a relation, let $R^{-1} = \{(y, x) : (x, y) \in R\}$. Then $(R \cdot S)^{-1} = S^{-1} \cdot R^{-1}$ for all relations S, R on X. The *identity* relation on X, $\Delta(X) = \{(x, x) : x \in X\}$. A relation R is an *equivalence relation* iff (1) $\Delta(X) \subseteq R$ (R is *reflexive*); (2) $R = R^{-1}$ (R is *symmetric*); (3) $R \cdot R \subseteq R$ (R is *transitive*).

Inclusion is a partial ordering on the set of all relations on X. This partial ordering forms a lattice when restricted to the equivalence relations. [A lattice is a partial ordering for which any pair of elements has a least upper bound (LUB) and greatest lower bound (GLB).] If R_1 and R_2 are equivalence relations,

$$\mathrm{GLB}(R_1, R_2) = R_1 \cap R_2, \text{ and } \mathrm{LUB}(R_1, R_2) = \cup\{(R_1 \cup R_2)^n : 1 \leqslant n < \infty\},$$

the *transitive closure* of $R_1 \cup R_2$. Thus, x is equivalent to y in $\mathrm{LUB}(R_1, R_2)$ iff there exists $x = x_0, x_1, x_2, \ldots, x_n = y$, so that $x_i R_1 x_{i+1}$ or $x_i R_2 x_{i+1}$ for $i = 0, \ldots, n-1$. If R_1 and R_2 are equivalence relations for which $R_1 \cdot R_2 = R_2 \cdot R_1$, then it is easy to see that $R_1 \cdot R_2$ is an equivalence relation, and so $R_1 \cdot R_2 = \mathrm{LUB}(R_1, R_2)$.

1.4e. Let S be a semigroup. A *congruence* on S is an equivalence relation $\equiv$ such that, if $s_1 \equiv s_2$, then, for all $s \in S$, $ss_1 \equiv ss_2$ and

$s_1 s \equiv s_2 s$. The relation $\equiv$ is a *left* or *right congruence* if the first or second, respectively, of the preceding congruences always holds. If $\equiv$ is a congruence on S, let $[s]$ denote the equivalence class of $s \in S$. Let $S/\equiv$ denote the set of these equivalence classes, and let $\eta_{\equiv} : S \twoheadrightarrow S/\equiv$ be defined by $\eta_{\equiv}(s) = [s]$. Then $[s] \cdot [t] = [st]$ is a well-defined semigroup multiplication on $S/\equiv$, and $\eta_{\equiv}$ is an epimorphism.

Conversely, if $\varphi : S \twoheadrightarrow S_1$ is an epimorphism, then let $(\text{mod } \varphi)$ be the congruence on S given by $s_1 \,(\text{mod } \varphi)\, s_2$ iff $\varphi(s_1) = \varphi(s_2)$. Then $\varphi^* : S/(\text{mod } \varphi) \to S_1$, where $\varphi^*([s]) = \varphi(s)$ is an isomorphism, and $\varphi = \varphi^* \eta_{(\text{mod}\varphi)}$, with φ^* an isomorphism.

1.4f. Let A be a nonempty set. Then ΣA, the *free noncommutative semigroup without identity on the generators* A is the set of all finite nonempty ordered sets of elements of A with the semigroup operation given by *concatenation*, i.e.,

$$(a_1, \dots, a_n) \cdot (b_1, \dots, b_m) = (a_1, \dots, a_n, b_1, \dots, b_m).$$

ΣA is an infinite semigroup.

ΣA is called the free semigroup on A because any mapping φ of the set A into a semigroup S has a unique extension φ^Γ to a homomorphism of ΣA into S, given by $\varphi^\Gamma(a_1, \dots, a_n) = \varphi(a_1) \dots \varphi(a_n)$. In particular, if A is a set of generators of S and φ the identity map, then $\varphi^\Gamma : \Sigma A \to S$ is an epimorphism, so that every semigroup is a homomorphic image of a free semigroup.

1.4g. $\mathbf{Z}$ denotes the integers $\{0, \pm 1, \pm 2, \dots\}$. $(\mathbf{Z}, +)$ is the group of integers under ordinary addition. $\mathbf{Z}^+$ denotes the nonnegative integers. $(\mathbf{Z}^+, +)$ is a subsemigroup of $(\mathbf{Z}, +)$. Let (n) denote the congruence on $(\mathbf{Z}, +)$ given by $z_1(n)\, z_2$ [usually written $z_1 \equiv z_2 \,(\text{mod } n)$] iff $z_1 - z_2 = kn$ for some $k \in \mathbf{Z}$. $\mathbf{Z}_n = \mathbf{Z}/(n)$ is called the *cyclic group of order n* or the additive group of *integers modulo n*.

1.4h. Let S be a semigroup.

(1) We define the semigroup S^1 as follows. If S is a monoid, $S^1 = S$. If not, $S^1 = S \cup \{1\}$, where $1 \notin S$, multiplication in S is unchanged, and 1 acts as an identity for $S \cup \{1\}$.

(2) Define the semigroup S^0 as follows. If S has a zero and $|S| > 1$, then $S^0 = S$. Otherwise, $S^0 = S \cup \{0\}$, where $0 \notin S$, multiplication in S is unchanged, and 0 acts as a zero for $S \cup \{0\}$.

(3) Define the semigroup S^I to be $S \cup \{I\}$, where $I \notin S$, multiplication in S is unchanged, and I acts as an identity for $S \cup \{I\}$. Notice $S \neq S^I$, even when S is a monoid. Notice that S is a subsemigroup of S^1, S^0, and S^I.

We shall identify the 1 of $(\Sigma A)^1$ with the empty set. Most other authors in this volume denote $(\Sigma A)^1$ by A^*.

1.4i. Let A and B be nonempty sets. Then $F(A, B)$ is the set of all functions from A into B. Write $F(A, A)$ as $F(A)$. $F_L(A)$ is the semigroup $[F(A), \cdot]$, where, for $a \in A$, $(fg)(a) = f[g(a)]$. $F_R(A)$ is the semigroup $[F(A), \circ]$, where $(f \circ g)(a) = g[f(a)]$. When working with $F_R(A)$, we sometimes write $(a)f$ instead of $f(a)$. Hence, $(a)(f \circ g) = [(a)f]\, g$. $\mathrm{SYM}_L(A) \subseteq F_L(A)$ and $\mathrm{SYM}_R(A) \subseteq F_R(A)$ are the subgroups consisting of the $1:1$ and onto functions on A, i.e., the permutations of A.

Let S be a semigroup, and let $L : S \to F_L(S^1)$ be given by $L(s)(r) = sr$ for $s \in S$, $r \in S^1$. L is a $1:1$ homomorphism, since $L(s_1 s_2)(r) = s_1 s_2 r = L(s_1)[L(s_2)(r)] = L(s_1)\, L(s_2)(r)$ and $L(s)(1) = s$ for all $s, s_1, s_2 \in S$, $r \in S^1$. The monomorphism L is the *left regular representation* of S. Thus, every semigroup is isomorphic with a subsemigroup of $F_L(A)$ for some set A.

Similarly, $R : S \to F_R(S^1)$, given by $(r)R(s) = rs$ for $r \in S^1$, $s \in S$, is a monomorphism called the *right regular representation* of S.

Notice that $F_R(X)$ is isomorphic with the subsemigroup of $(2^{X \times X}, \cdot)$, consisting of all relations R with the property that, for each x, $(x, y) \in R$ for exactly one y. Similarly, $F_L(X)$ is isomorphic with the subsemigroup consisting of all R for which, for each y, $(x, y) \in R$ for exactly one x.

1.4j. Let X be a finite set. The *symmetric inverse semigroup* on X, denoted $\mathrm{SIS}_L(X)$, is the set of all $1:1$ and onto functions whose range and domain are subsets of X. If $f : A \to B$ and $g : C \to D$, then gf has domain $f^{-1}(B \cap C)$ and range $g(B \cap C)$ and satisfies $gf(a) = g[f(a)]$. $\mathrm{SIS}_R(X)$ is defined dually.

1.4k. Let S be a semigroup. Then $r(S)$ is the semigroup $(S, \cdot)$, where $s_1 \cdot s_2 = s_2 s_1$ for $s_1, s_2 \in S$. Clearly, $r[r(S)] = S$, and $r(S) = S$ iff S is abelian. If S is a group, $x \to x^{-1}$ is an isomorphism of S with $r(S)$, since $(xy)^{-1} = y^{-1}x^{-1}$. However, for $|A| \geqslant 2$, A^l is not isomorphic with $r(A^l) = A^r$.

Given a definition, theorem, construction, etc., involving a semigroup S, its *dual* is its analog for $r(S)$, i.e., the definition, theorem, etc., applied to $r(S)$. We do not propose to define this concept precisely, but its meaning will always be clear when it is used. For example, the left and right regular representations are dual constructions.

1.41. Let A be a nonempty set, and for each $a \in A$, let X_a be a set. Then the *cartesian product* of the X_a's, denoted $\prod \{X_a : a \in A\}$, is the set of functions $f : A \to \bigcup \{X_a : a \in A\}$ such that, for all $a \in A$, $f(a) \in X_a$. This is more easily visualized as the set of all "$|A|$-tuples" in which entries in the "ath spot" are elements of X_a. If $X_a = B$ for all $a \in A$, then $\prod \{X_a : a \in A\} = F(A, B)$ (see 1.4i). If S_a is a semigroup for each $a \in A$, we define a semigroup structure on $\prod \{S_a : a \in A\}$ by $(f \cdot g)(a) = f(a) \cdot g(a)$. This is called the *direct product* of the S_a's. For example, if S is a semigroup, $F(A, S)$ is a semigroup under the foregoing law of composition by taking $S_a = S$ for all $a \in A$. This law of composition is often called *pointwise multiplication* or *coordinatewise multiplication.*

The ath coordinate map or projection $p_a : \prod \{S_a : a \in A\} \to S_a$ given by $p_a(f) = f(a)$ is an epimorphism. We usually write $\prod \{S_a : a \in \{1, \ldots, k\}\}$ as $S_1 \times \cdots \times S_k$, in which case an element $f \in S_1 \times \cdots \times S_k$ is written $[f(1), \ldots, f(k)]$. Then $p_j(s_1, \ldots, s_k) = s_j$.

1.4m. Let A and B be nonempty sets. Let G be a group, and let $C : B \times A \to G^0$ be a function. Then $\mathcal{M}^0(G; A, B; C)$, the *Rees* $|A| \times |B|$ *matrix semigroup* with structure group G and structure matrix C, is the semigroup $[(G \times A \times B) \cup \{0\}, \cdot]$, where 0 is the zero of the semigroup and

$$(g_1, a_1, b_1) \cdot (g_2, a_2, b_2) = \begin{cases} (g_1 C(b_1, a_2) g_2, a_1, b_2) & \text{if } C(b_1, a_2) \neq 0 \\ 0 \quad \text{if } C(b_1, a_2) = 0. \end{cases}$$

Thus $(g_1, a_1, b_1)(g_2, a_2, b_2) = 0$ iff $C(b_1, a_2) = 0$. It follows that, for $m_1, \ldots, m_k \in \mathcal{M}^0(G; A, B; C)$, $m_1 \ldots m_k = 0$ iff $m_i m_{i+1} = 0$ for some $i = 1, \ldots, k - 1$.

It is sometimes convenient to regard (g, a, b) as an $|A| \times |B|$ matrix over G^0 with g in the (a, b) position and 0 elsewhere and to regard 0 as the $|A| \times |B|$ zero matrix. Then, if C is thought of as a $|B| \times |A|$ matrix over G^0, the matrix product $(g_1, a_1, b_1)\, C(g_2, a_2, b_2)$ makes sense (where the indicated addition of elements of G^0 is determined by $x + 0 = x = 0 + x$ for all $x \in G^0$), and is exactly the product $(g_1, a_1, b_1) \cdot (g_2, a_2, b_2)$ given previously. In this context, (g, a, b) is often denoted by $(g)_{ab}$, and $\mathscr{M}^0(G; A, B; C)$ is denoted by $S_{mn}(G, C)$, where $m = |A|$ and $n = |B|$.

Thus, $S_{mn}(G, C)$ is the semigroup consisting of all $m \times n$ matrices with coefficients in G^0 with at most one nonzero entry and multiplication given by

$$(g)_{ab} \cdot (g')_{a'b'} = (g)_{ab} C(g')_{a'b'} .$$

When $m = |A|$ and $n = |B|$, then of course $S_{mn}(G, C)$ and $\mathscr{M}^0(G; A, B; C)$ are isomorphic.

The set $\mathscr{M}^0(G; A, B; C) - \{0\}$ is a subsemigroup of $\mathscr{M}^0(G; A, B; C)$ iff $0 \notin C(B \times A)$, i.e., iff C has no zero entries. In this case, we denote $\mathscr{M}^0(G; A, B; C) - \{0\}$ by $\mathscr{M}(G; A, B; C)$. Then $[\mathscr{M}(G; A, B; C)]^0 = \mathscr{M}^0(G; A, B; C)$.

A Rees matrix semigroup is *regular* iff its structure matrix is nonzero at least once in each row and column. Regular Rees matrix semigroups play an important role in the structure of finite semigroups (see Chapter 7).

1.4n. $E(S)$ is the set of idempotents of S, and $IG(S) = \langle E(S) \rangle$. $IG(S) = E(S)$ if S is commutative.

If $e_1, e_2 \in E(S)$, we say $e_1 \leqslant e_2$ iff $e_1 e_2 = e_1 = e_2 e_1$. S is a *band* iff $S = E(S)$. The semigroups A^l and A^r are bands. $(2^X, \cap)$ is a commutative band. An example of a semigroup in which $IG(S) \neq E(S)$ is (see 1.4m) $S_{22}(\{1\}, C)$, where $C(2, 2) = 0$ and $C(a, b) = 1$ for $(a, b) \neq (2, 2)$.

1.4o. Let G be a group. Let $\mathscr{CM}(n, G)$ denote the set of $n \times n$ matrices over G^0 which are nonzero at most once in each column. Then $\mathscr{CM}(n, G)$, the $n \times n$ *column monomial* matrices over G^0, form a semigroup using the ordinary rules of matrix multiplication and the convention $x + 0 = x = 0 + x$ for all $x \in G^0$. Similarly, $\mathscr{RM}(n, G)$, the semigroup of $n \times n$ *row monomial* matrices over G^0, consists of those $n \times n$ matrices over G^0 which are nonzero at most once in each row. Note that $\mathscr{RM}(n, G)$ acts faithfully on the right of $S_{mn}(G, C)$ for any m, n, G, C by formal matrix multiplication on the right by elements of $\mathscr{RM}(n, G)$, and $\mathscr{CM}(m, G)$ acts faithfully on the left of $S_{mn}(G, C)$ by formal matrix multiplication on the left by elements of $\mathscr{CM}(m, G)$.

We now introduce the important notion of an ideal, and present a few properties. A more detailed analysis is deferred to Chapter 7.

1.5 Definition. Let S be a semigroup. An *ideal* is a nonempty subset $I \subseteq S$ such that, for all $i \in I$, $s \in S$, $is \in I$, and $si \in I$. Thus, I is an ideal iff $IS \subseteq I$ and $SI \subseteq I$. I is a *right* or *left* ideal if the first or second, respectively, of these conditions holds. Notice ideals, left and right ideals, are subsemigroups.

An ideal of S is *minimal* if it properly contains no ideal of S. An ideal I of S is 0-*minimal* if $I \neq \{0\}$ and I properly contains no ideal of S different from $\{0\}$. Notice that a minimal ideal is 0-minimal *except* in the case $I = \{0\}$. Hence, in general, minimal does not imply 0-minimal. Minimal and 0-minimal left and right ideals are defined analogously.

A semigroup S is *null* if $S^2 = \{0\}$.

A semigroup S is *simple* iff it has no ideals other than itself. S is 0-*simple* if S is not null and S has no ideals other than $\{0\}$ and itself. Notice that a simple semigroup is 0-simple *except* in the case $S = \{0\}$. Hence, in general, simple does not imply 0-simple. Left simple, left 0-simple, right simple, and right 0-simple semigroups are defined analogously.

1.6 Remark. The sets of ideals, left ideals and right ideals, of a semigroup S are closed under the operations of union and nonempty intersection. If I_1 and I_2 are ideals of S, then I_1I_2 is an ideal of S, and $I_1I_2 \subseteq I_1 \cap I_2$. Furthermore, if $I_1, \ldots, I_n$ are all the ideals of S, then $I_1 \ldots I_n = I_1 \cap \ldots \cap I_n$, and this ideal is the *kernel* of S, denoted $K(S)$. Since $K(S)$ is contained in each ideal of S, it is the unique minimal ideal of S. $K(S) = \{0\}$ iff S has a zero. The proof of these remarks is left to the reader.

1.7 Fact. Let S be a semigroup.

(a) S is simple iff $SaS = S$ for all $a \in S$.

(b) S is 0-simple iff $S \neq \{0\}$ and $SaS = S$ for all $a \in S$, $a \neq 0$.

(c) Let I be a minimal ideal of S. Then I is a simple semigroup. Thus, in particular, $K(S)$ is simple.

(d) Let I be a 0-minimal ideal of S. Then I is either a null or 0-simple semigroup.

PROOF. (b) Let S be 0-simple. Then S^2 is a nonzero ideal of S. Hence, $S^2 = S$, and $S^n = S$ for all $n > 0$. For each $a \in S$, SaS is an ideal, and so $SaS = S$ or $SaS = \{0\}$. Let $I = \{a \in S : SaS = \{0\}\}$.

I is an ideal of S, and so $I = \{0\}$, since $S^3 = S$ implies $I \neq S$. Thus, $0 \neq a \in S$ implies $SaS = S$.

Conversely, if $SaS = S$ for $0 \neq a \in S$, let I be a nonzero ideal of S, and let $0 \neq a \in I$. Then $S = SaS \subseteq$ SIS $\subseteq I$, so that $S = I$ and S is 0-simple.

(a) The proof is similar to (b).

(d) Let I be a 0-minimal ideal of S. If $I^2 = \{0\}$, I is null. If not, $I^2 = I$, since I^2 is a nonzero ideal of S contained in I. Hence, $I^n = I$ for all $n > 0$. Let $0 \neq a \in I$. Then S^1aS^1 is a nonzero ideal of S contained in I; hence it equals I. Thus, $IaI = (IS^1)a(S^1I) = I^3 = I$, and so I is 0-simple, by (b).

(c) The proof is similar to (d). ∎

1.8 Remark. A 0-minimal left ideal or right ideal of a 0-simple semigroup need not be 0-simple. For example, let $S = S_{22}(\{1\}, I)$, I the 2×2 identity matrix (see Example 1.4m). Then $L = \{(1)_{11}, (1)_{21}, 0\}$ is a 0-minimal left ideal of S, and $\{(1)_{21}, 0\}$ is an ideal of L. Note that $L^2 \neq \{0\}$.

We say that a subsemigroup T of a semigroup S *breaks off* iff $S - T$ is a subsemigroup of S. The foregoing example shows that $\{0\}$ need not break off in a 0-simple semigroup. However, if S is left 0-simple or right 0-simple, it is easy to see that $\{0\}$ breaks off and $S = T^0$, where T is, respectively, left simple or right simple.

1.9 Fact. Let S_1 and S_2 be semigroups, and let $\varphi : S_1 \twoheadrightarrow S_2$ be an epimorphism.

(a) Let S_1' be a subsemigroup, subgroup, ideal, left ideal, right ideal, simple subsemigroup, left simple subsemigroup, right simple subsemigroup, minimal ideal, minimal left ideal, minimal right ideal, kernel, or null subsemigroup of S_1. Then $\varphi(S_1')$ has the same property in S_2. If S_1' is a 0-minimal ideal (hence 0-simple), then $\varphi(S_1') = \{0\}$ or $\varphi(S_1')$ is a 0-minimal ideal (hence 0-simple). If e is the identity (respectively zero) of S_1, then $\varphi(e)$ is the identity (respectively zero) of S_2.

(b) Let S_2' be a subsemigroup, ideal, left ideal, or right ideal of S_2. Then $\varphi^{-1}(S_2')$ has the same property in S_1. $T \to \varphi^{-1}(T)$ is a $1:1$ inclusion-preserving map of the sets of left, right, and two-sided ideals of S_2 *into* the corresponding sets for S_1.

(c) Let S_2' be a simple, right simple, left simple, or left and right simple (i.e., a group) subsemigroup of S_2. Then there exists a subsemigroup S_1' of S_1 having the same property as S_2' such that $\varphi(S_1') = S_2'$. In fact, any subsemigroup T of S_1 minimal (under inclusion) with respect to the property $\varphi(T) = S_2'$ can be taken for S_1'.

PROOF. The proof of the fact is left to the reader. ▮

In the remainder of this section, we prove a number of basic facts.

1.10 Fact (classification of cyclic semigroups). Let $S = \langle s \rangle$ be the cyclic semigroup generated by $s \in S$. Then either (1) $S \cong (\mathbf{Z}^+, +)$ under the isomorphism $n \rightarrow s^n$; or (2) S is finite and there exist unique integers r and m, the *index* and *period*, respectively, of S, such that $S = \{s, s^2, \ldots, s^{m+r-1}\}$, with $K_s = \{s^r, \ldots, s^{m+r-1}\}$ a cyclic subgroup of order m.

For any two integers r and m, there exists a unique (up to isomorphism) finite cyclic semigroup of index r and period m.

PROOF. If all powers of s are distinct, then case 1 clearly holds. If not, let r be the smallest positive integer such that $s^r = s^{r+x}$ for some positive integer x. Let m be the smallest such x. Then $s, s^2, \ldots, s^r$ are distinct, and distinct from $s^{r+1}, \ldots, s^{r+m-1}$. If $k \geqslant m$, then $s^{r+k} = s^{r+jm+n} = s^{r+n}$, where $0 \leqslant n < m$. Thus, $S = \{s, s^2, \ldots, s^{r+m-1}\}$. Finally, $s^{r+p} \rightarrow (r + p)(\text{mod } m)$ is an isomorphism of $\{s^r, \ldots, s^{r+m-1}\}$, with $(\mathbf{Z}_m, +)$, and case 2 holds.

Let r and m be given, and consider $f \in F_L(\{0, \ldots, r + m - 1\})$ given by $f(i) = i + 1$ for $i = 0, 1, \ldots, r + m - 2$ and $f(r + m - 1) = r$. Then $\langle f \rangle \subseteq F_L(\{0, \ldots, r + m - 1\})$ has index r and period m. The assertion of uniqueness is easily verified. ▮

A semigroup S is a *torsion semigroup* if $|\langle s \rangle| < \infty$ for each $s \in S$. A *torsion group* is a torsion semigroup that is a group. In particular, every finite semigroup is a torsion semigroup. Although we are only concerned with finite semigroups in this work, the proofs of certain important facts are also valid for this wider class of semigroups.

We now state some useful consequences of Fact 1.10.

1.11 Fact. (a) Let S be a torsion semigroup. Let $s \in S$. Then among the powers of s there is a unique idempotent.

(b) G is a torsion group iff every subsemigroup of G is a subgroup of G. In particular, subsemigroups of finite groups are subgroups.

PROOF. (a) The identity of the cyclic subgroup of $\langle s \rangle$ is the unique idempotent.

(b) If G is not a torsion group, then it has a cyclic subsemigroup isomorphic with $(\mathbf{Z}^+, +)$, which is not, of course, a group. Conversely, if S is a subsemigroup of the torsion group G, let $s \in S$, and let r and m be its index and period. Then $s^r s^m = s^r$, and so $1 = s^m \in S$. If $m = 1$, then $s^{-1} = s \in S$, and, if $m > 1$, $s^{-1} = s^{m-1} \in S$. Thus, S is a group. ▌

1.12 *Fact.* Let S_1 be a torsion semigroup and let $\varphi : S_1 \twoheadrightarrow S_2$ be an epimorphism. Then S_2 is a torsion semigroup and φ is an order-preserving map of $E(S_1)$ onto $E(S_2)$ (see Example 1.4n).

PROOF. If $s \in S_1$, $\varphi(\langle s \rangle) = \langle \varphi(s) \rangle$, so that S_2 is a torsion semigroup. Clearly, $\varphi[E(S_1)] \subseteq E(S_2)$. Conversely, if $e \in E(S_2)$, take $x \in S_1$ such that $\varphi(x) = e$, and let f be the unique idempotent such that $x^n = f$ for some n. Then $\varphi(f) = e^n = e$, so that $\varphi[E(S_1)] = E(S_2)$. Finally, if $e_1 e_2 = e_1 = e_2 e_1$, then $\varphi(e_1)\, \varphi(e_2) = \varphi(e_1) = \varphi(e_2)\, \varphi(e_1)$, so that φ is order-preserving. ▌

Exercises and Extensions

X1.1. If S is a monoid and $xy = 1$ for $x, y \in S$, then x is a *left inverse* of y and y a *right inverse* of x.

(a) Construct a semigroup with n left identities and no right identities. If an element of a monoid has a left inverse and a right inverse, then they are equal.

(b) Let S be a semigroup with the property that there is an element $x \in S$ which "divides" each element of S, i.e., for each $s \in S$, there exist l, $r \in S$ such that $lx = s = xr$. Then S is a monoid.

X1.2. (a) Let $\psi : A \to S$ be a function from the set A into the semigroup S. Then ψ has a unique extension to a homomorphism $\psi^\Gamma : \Sigma A \to S$, and $\psi^\Gamma(\Sigma A) = \langle \psi(A) \rangle$.

(b) Let T be any semigroup such that $T = \langle A \rangle$ and such that for any semigroup S and function $\theta : A \to S$ there exists a unique extension of θ to a homomorphism $\theta^\Gamma : T \to S$. Then T is isomorphic with ΣA by an isomorphism that leaves each element of A fixed.

X1.3. Let S be a semigroup. Let $e \in E(S)$, and define $H_e = \{s \in S\colon es = s = se$ and $sr = e = rs$, some $r \in S\}$. Then H_e is the maximal subgroup of S containing e. In fact, if G is a subgroup of S and $G \cap H_e \neq \phi$, then $G \subseteq H_e$. Thus, for $f \neq e$, $H_f \cap H_e = \phi$, and $\{H_e : e \in E(S)\}$ is the set of maximal subgroups of S.

X1.4. Let S be a finite cyclic semigroup. Find all homomorphic images and all subsemigroups of S. Are they all cyclic semigroups?

X1.5. (a) Let T be a torsion semigroup, and let $s_1, \ldots, s_m \in T$. Then for any integer $N \geqslant 1$ there exists $n \geqslant N$ such that $s_j^n \in E(S)$ for $j = 1, \ldots, m$.

(b) Let S be a finite semigroup, and let $t_1, t_2 \in S$. Let r_1, r_2, m_1, m_2 be, respectively, the indices and periods of $\langle t_1 t_2 \rangle$ and $\langle t_2 t_1 \rangle$ [so that r_1, r_2, m_1, m_2 are the smallest integers such that $(t_1 t_2)^{r_1+m_1} = (t_1 t_2)^{r_1}$ and $(t_2 t_1)^{r_2+m_2} = (t_2 t_1)^{r_2}$]. Then $m_1 = m_2$, and $| r_2 - r_1 | \leqslant 1$. Is a sharper statement about r_2 and r_1 possible?

X1.6. For the semigroups of 1.4a, b, i, and j, determine the following: (a) the maximal subgroups (up to isomorphism); (b) $IG(S)$; and (c) the maximal subsemigroups (this is more difficult and is completely solved in Chapter 7).

X1.7. If a Rees matrix semigroup $S = \mathscr{M}^0(G; A, B; C)$ is regular, prove the following:

(a) If $s, t \in S$, and $x \in S^1$ are such that $sx = t$, then $t = 0$ or there exists $y \in S^1$ such that $ty = s$.

(b) If $s, t \in S$, and $x \in S^1$ are such that $xs = t$, then $t = 0$ or there exists $y \in S^1$ such that $yt = s$.

(c) If $s, t \in S - \{0\}$, then there exist $x, y \in S^1$ such that $xsy = t$.

CHAPTER 2

Algebraic Machine Theory and Logical Design

E. F. ASSMUS, JR.
Mathematics Department, Lehigh University, Bethlehem, Pennsylvania

J. J. FLORENTIN
Centre for Computing and Automation, Imperial College, London, England

1. Introduction

Algebraic machine theory is a branch of the theory of computation. In applications, it is best suited to model the overall action of specific pieces of logical hardware rather than programs or computer systems. It does not, however, model the action of electronic devices directly, but only through the movements of abstract "states."

For logical designers, algebraic machine theory answers some questions but not others. It does not deal with hazards and races, which are the result of badly timed electrical pulses, because these are determined by detailed electronic action. Its main contribution is to settle completely the relation between the input-output behavior of a finite machine and the motions of its internal states. All the different state representations of a machine with specific input-output action can by systematically derived and related; in particular, machines can be broken down into fundamental components. It also shows the importance of coding the input and output signals of a logical unit.

This chapter shows intuitively how finite machine action can be represented algebraically. Emphasis is laid on the insights that a logical designer can gain from the theory.

Algebraic machine theory is very powerful in discussing the structure of classes of machines. This is illustrated by considering linear machines.

2. The Machine Model

The machine model used is idealized to the extent that fixed transitions occur in response to each possible input. Poorly timed signals cannot cause false state transitions, and internal feedback effects within the electronic circuitry are ignored. However, two kinds of circuit units are distinguished, first, combinational logical units without memory (these recode input and output signals), and second, units with memory which are directly associated with semigroups.

The machine has a finite set of memory states $Q = \{q_1, q_2, \ldots, q_k\}$, a finite input alphabet $X = \{a_1, a_2, \ldots, a_m\}$, and a finite output alphabet $Y = \{\alpha_1, \alpha_2, \ldots, \alpha_n\}$. Its action is given by the next state function $\delta : Q \times X \to Q$, and the output function $\lambda : Q \times X \to Y$.

2.1 Specifying Machine Action. The next state and output function can be given in the following ways:

(i) In a state diagram. Each node in the diagram represents a memory state, and the edges going between nodes are labeled with the input causing the transition and the corresponding output. There may be several edges between the same two nodes; in that case, each would correspond to a different input letter.

(ii) By state transition and output tables.

(iii) Boolean matrices and output vectors. This method can be used only for the state output form of machine described later. For each input symbol, there is a matrix. The matrix has one row and column for each machine state. If the input being considered causes a transition from state i to j, then the i-j entry in the matrix is 1; otherwise, it is zero. There is an initial state row vector; if a machine starts in state i, this vector has a 1 in the i position and zeroes elsewhere. There is also an output column vector; if state i has output α_i, then this vector has α_i in the ith place. The state resulting from a particular input sequence and initial state can be found by multiplying the initial state vector by the matrices corresponding to the input sequence symbols; and the corresponding output can be found by further multiplying by the output vector.

(iv) Input sequence to output symbol functions for each initial state. To specify input-output behavior, the input sequence to output sequence function is not needed. An input sequence to final output symbol function is enough. For initial state i, we have $f_i : \Sigma X \rightarrow Y$, where ΣX is the set of all sequences over X. The next state function is not given; however, it will be seen later that there is a state transition function that can be naturally associated with input-output functions. In practice, this is the likely way to specify a machine. It is so basic that Krohn-Rhodes [1] take the function $\Sigma X \rightarrow Y$ as the definition of a machine.

Figure 1 exemplifies these machine action specifications.

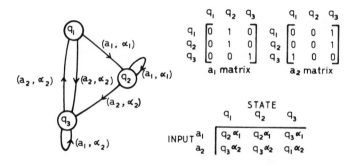

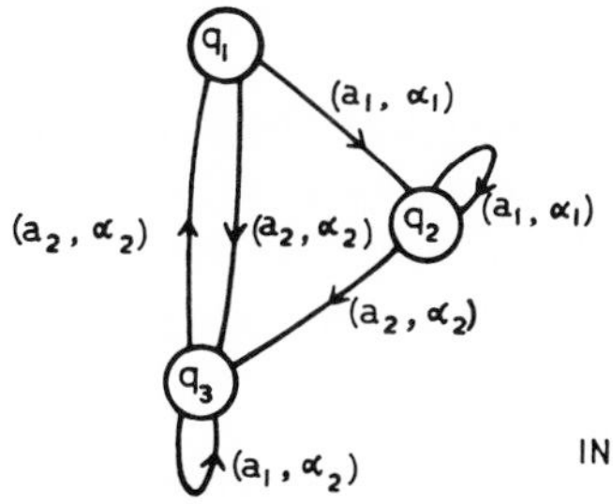

$$\begin{array}{c|ccc} & q_1 & q_2 & q_3 \\ \hline q_1 & 0 & 1 & 0 \\ q_2 & 0 & 1 & 0 \\ q_3 & 0 & 0 & 1 \end{array} \qquad \begin{array}{c|ccc} & q_1 & q_2 & q_3 \\ \hline q_1 & 0 & 0 & 1 \\ q_2 & 0 & 0 & 1 \\ q_3 & 1 & 0 & 0 \end{array}$$

a_1 matrix $\qquad$ a_2 matrix

	STATE q_1	q_2	q_3
INPUT a_1	$q_2\alpha_1$	$q_2\alpha_1$	$q_3\alpha_1$
a_2	$q_3\alpha_2$	$q_3\alpha_2$	$q_1\alpha_2$

FIG. 1. State diagram transition table and matrices of example machine.

2.2 General Output and State Output Machines. The aforementioned machine is of general output, or Mealy, type; its output depends on both current state and current input in a general way. As a special case of output specification, the output may depend on the next state only. Thus, each state is associated with a particular output symbol, although several states might map onto the same output. Given the state to output symbol map, the output may be found from the state transition function. This special machine is the Moore, or state output, machine.

A state output machine may always be constructed to imitate the input-output behavior of an arbitrary general output machine. Given the arbitrary machine, we form a new, state output machine with state set $Q^1 = \{(q_i, \alpha_j) | \, q_i \in Q, \alpha_j \in Y\}$. The new state transition function is

δ', where $\delta'[(q_i, \alpha_k), a_j] = [\delta(q_i, a_j), \lambda(q_i, a_j)]$, and the new output function is λ', where $\lambda'[(q_i, \alpha_k), a_j] = \alpha_k$.

States in the new machine which cannot be reached from other states may be discarded. States that cannot be reached from other states in the original machine lead to states with a choice of labeling in the new machine; any ambiguity here can always be resolved.

The state output machine gives a clear separation between the next state transition and output actions. It is worth noting the timing in a state output machine; an input in one time interval has its associated output appear in the next time interval.

2.3 Consequences of the Finite Machine Specification. The finite machine specification has several consequences:

(i) The input-output function set is closed under left translation by any input sequence. Consider the input-output function for initial state q_i in some machine. Take an input sequence x, made up of two subsequences x_1 and x_2, so that $x = x_1x_2$. Start the machine in state q_i and first apply x_1 only. The machine must arrive at some state q_j. Restart the machine and apply x_2. The final state cannot be affected by the restart, and so $f_j(x_2) = f_i(x_1x_2)$. This is true for all x_2, and so we can construct the input-output function for q_j from $f_j(x) = f_i(x_1x)$. We write f_j as $f_iL_{x_1}$, where L_x is the left translation operator $L_x(x') = xx'$. By choosing all possible sequences for x, we find a finite set of functions f_iL_x. Each new function found by left translation means that a new state is needed in the machine. When a set of functions is closed under left translation, a minimal state machine is automatically specified, and its state transition function can be found from left translation by single symbol inputs. In principle, this construction solves the problem of finding a minimal state machine to realize a given input-output behavior, but in practice only a small number of input-output pairs will be given, and the remainder will be "don't cares." Completing the function so as to achieve economy of states is still an unsolved problem.

(ii) A finite machine defines a right invariant, finite, equivalence relation on the set of input sequences. Given a machine and a fixed initial state q_i, we apply each input sequence and note the final state. Sequences producing the same final state are equivalent. If sequences x, y are equivalent, then for any other sequence z, $\delta(q_i, xz) = \delta(q_i, yz)$. Thus, $xz \equiv yz$, showing right invariance. Conversely, given a right-invariant, finite equivalence relation over the set of input sequences, we can construct the minimal state machine that would produce this classification of inputs. A state in the machine is allocated for each equivalence class. However, we must identify the initial state; this can be done by adding the null sequence to the set of input sequences. The null sequence is denoted by Λ, and the set of input sequences plus the null sequence by X^*. The equivalence class containing the null sequence identifies the initial state. It may be necessary to add a new equivalence class especially to hold the null sequence. The state transition function is found from $\delta([x], a_i) = [xa_i]$, where $[x]$ is the state corresponding to the class containing x. These right-invariant equivalence classes are closely linked to the set of functions obtained by left translation and can be used to find a minimal state machine from an input-output specification. As an example of the effect of "don't cares," consider the recognition of the sequence 111 over $x = \{0, 1\}$. The four equivalence classes $\{1\}$, $\{11\}$, $\{111\}$ plus the class of remaining sequences will produce the required machine. On the other hand, if the machine final state is checked after exactly three symbols are input, then the classes $\{0, 00, \ldots, 111, \ldots\}$, $\{1, 01, \ldots\}$, $\{11, 101, \ldots\}$ are adequate. Here all sequences of length other than 3 are "don't care."

(iii) A finite machine defines a finite congruence relation over the set of input sequences. This set of equivalence classes is a refinement of that just produced. For each input sequence, the machine is started from each state in turn and the final state noted. Sequences are equivalent when they cause the same transition from each initial state. If sequences x, y are equivalent in this sense, then for any other sequences u, v, $\delta(q_i, uxv) = \delta(q_i, uyv)$ for all $q_i \in Q$. Hence, $uxv \equiv uyv$, and the equivalence relation is both left and right invariant, i.e., a congruence relation. Because of the left and right invariance, the equivalence classes may be multiplied together, as $[x][y] = [xy]$. The set of equivalence classes with multiplication forms a finite semigroup. The set of congruence classes may also be found from input-output behavior rather than from machine action. Using the input-output functions, we say sequences x and y are equivalent if $f_i(uxv) = f_i(uyv)$ for all f_i in the given set. Again a machine may be produced from a given congruence relation over X^*. The states correspond to classes, and the state transition function is as before. This classification of inputs represents the essential behavior of a finite machine. All tasks performed by a finite machine can be viewed as the construction of certain of these classes.

3. State Transition Maps

In a state output machine, we may study the state transitions separately from the outputs they cause. We study the pattern of state transitions by considering all the transitions caused by each input symbol, that is, the state-set-to-state-set map produced by each input symbol. These maps are the basic elements in the algebraic theory of machines.

3.1 The Semigroup of State Transition Maps. The state transition maps corresponding to single input symbols may be multiplied together to find the state transition maps produced by input sequences. Since there are a finite number of states, the set of maps which is closed under multiplication is finite. The set of maps is a representation of an abstract finite semigroup. This semigroup is the fundamental connection between algebra and machines, and all the basic properties of machines are reflected in it. Furthermore, the semigroup of state transition maps is the same as that found by forming congruence classes over the set of input sequences. The sequences in each class produce the state transition map corresponding to the class.

Algebraic machine theory uses the semigroup in several ways:

(i) It is used to form a standard version of any machine.

(ii) It leads to different realizations of a required machine action over different state sets.

(iii) Certain methods of decomposing the semigroup lead to decomposition of the machine into series-parallel connected components.

(iv) The methods of semigroup decomposition allow the definition of irreducible component machines from which all machines are built.

3.2 Standard Semigroup Machines. Given an arbitrary machine, we may construct a standard version of it which has the same input-output behavior. First, the set of congruence classes over X^* is derived and, hence, the semigroup of the arbitrary machine. This semigroup S_M contains an identity. Now form the machine with state set S_M, input alphabet S_M, and output alphabet Y, the same as the original machine. The state transition function is $\delta(s_1, s_2) = s_1 \cdot s_2$. It is a state output machine with output function $i_M : S_M \to Y$.

Both machines have the same input applied, but the input to the semigroup machine passes through a coding function $h_M : X \to S_M$, which takes input symbol a_i to the semigroup element associated with its congruence class. The machines are made equivalent only when started from special initial states; the semigroup machine must start in the identity state, and the original machine from a chosen state. The output map, i_M, is then constructed by applying one input sequence from each congruence class and noting the output of the original machine.

Many machines have the same semigroup, and their relationship is important in considering how different machines may do the same job. This will be examined after distinguishing different types of machines.

3.3 Types of State Transition Maps. There are two basic kinds of state transition maps: (i) permutations, where the map is a 1-1 onto function of the state set; a machine that has only such maps has a semigroup that is a group; and (ii) collapsers; here two distinct states go into the same state under the input.

It is a major achievement of the Krohn-Rhodes decomposition theory to show that after proper decomposition of any machine we arrive at components that are either group machines or are amongst four elementary collapser machines.

4. Group Machines

The state motions of a group machine are permutations of the state set which represent the group. There are many sets of permutations which can represent a particular group, but it is clear that only transitive ones are useful, i.e., those in which any state can be reached from any other state. Permutations may be found by first finding any subgroup, then forming the right cosets. Each coset now corresponds to a state element; however, the difficulty arises that the representation may not be faithful. The condition that the representation be faithful is that the chosen subgroup must contain no nontrivial, normal subgroups of the original group.

Every subgroup of an abelian group is normal; hence, every abelian group machine has only one transitive state set in which each state corresponds to a group element.

4.1 Group Machines with Output. There may be many transitive permutation representations of a group and, thus, many possible state sets for a machine with given group. However, the state set cannot usually be chosen freely, because the required output behavior limits the choice. In a state output machine, this can be seen by first considering the standard machine with a state corresponding to each group element. Each state has a known output symbol derived from the initial specification of the machine action. Now the states may be collected into right cosets just so long as all the states in each coset have the same output.

As a simple example, take the noncyclic group of order 6. It can have two generators A, C that serve as binary inputs to the standard machine; the state and output tables are then

State		I	A	A^2	C	CA	CA^2
Input	A	A	A^2	I	CA	CA^2	C
	C	C	CA^2	CA	I	A^2	A

State	I	A	A^2	C	CA	CA^2
Output	a	b	c	a	b	c

with output alphabet $\{a, b, c\}$. It is seen that the cosets $\{I, C\}$, $\{A, CA\}$, $\{A^2, CA^2\}$, are consistent with the output requirements and allow the machine to be represented on three states.

5. Series-Parallel Decomposition of Group Machines

Group machines may be broken up into a series-parallel connected pair whenever the group contains a subgroup. What is actually broken up is the motion of the states, and the output action can only be retained by reproducing the state motion of the standard machine and using the output map from the full group to the output alphabet. A key idea is to parameterize the group elements, and thus parameterize the states in the standard machine. The state transition is then found separately for each parameter in a separate machine.

Consider, then, a standard group machine with one state for each group element. The group G contains a subgroup H. We may therefore write the group as $G = H + Hc_1 + Hc_2 + \cdots + Hc_n$, where the c_i are the coset leaders. Each group element is now parameterized as $g = hc$. When the group machine is in state g and receives input g_1, it moves to the new state $g' = gg_1$. If the standard machine state is parameterized, we have $h'c' = hcg_1$. We multiply in the following way: first we put $c' = \overline{cg_1}$, where $\bar{x}$ is the coset leader of the coset containing x. Then we have $h' = hcg_1(\overline{cg_1})^{-1}$.

Now cg_1 is a group element that can be written $h''c''$, so that $cg_1(\overline{cg_1})^{-1} = h''$. So the multiplication for h' may be carried out entirely in the subgroup H. The process of finding the new coset leader is carried out only with the old coset leader and the input, and so it may be done in a machine having one state for each coset leader. The state transition table for this, front, machine is found by considering the coset motions for each group element input. The second multiplication for h' needs the output of the front machine, c, as well as h. This machine has one state for each element in H and is the standard machine for H.

There is just one problem in the preceding two-machine scheme: the output of the front machine, cg_1, is not available when required for the second machine; hence the product $cg_1(\overline{cg_1})^{-1}$ must be produced from a coding function. This coding needs only the current c and g_1, and does not need any memory. It is therefore not a machine but is a combinational logic circuit.

The output of the series-parallel pair passes through an output coder that takes an output from each machine and forms the product to get the group element, and then codes this to the output symbol. The inputs to the series-parallel pair are group elements. Figure 2 shows the series-parallel decomposition of a group machine.

The nature of the equivalence between the series-parallel machines and the original standard group machine should be noted; the series-parallel machines can be set at any state pair, (c, h), to match any state of the group machine. The equivalence is thus independent of

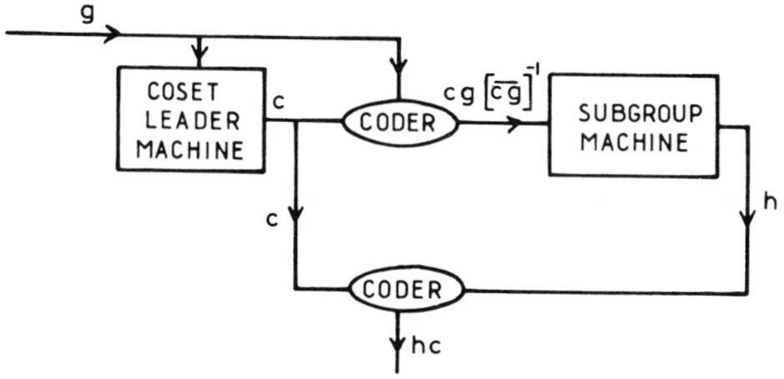

FIG. 2. Series-parallel decomposition of group machine.

the initial state, in contrast to that between the standard group machine and its original arbitrary machine. It is also worth noting that the unit time delay across each machine is kept, while also having unit delay across the two series-parallel machines from input to output.

The decomposition may be continued. The second machine is a standard group machine and can be broken up as before. The first machine will not usually be in group form, and before it can be broken up it must be replaced by its standard group machine. From the discussion in Sect. 4, it will be seen that the group of the first machine is a homomorphic image of G. If K is the largest subgroup in H which is normal in G, then the group of the first machine will be G/K, the factor group of G by K. Now if G has no nontrivial, normal subgroups, i.e., it is *simple*, then the first machine will have group G. Thus, no matter how far the breakup is taken, the simple groups persist. As the process of breakup is continued, the simple groups that appear will be homomorphic images of all the subgroups of the original group G. When the breakup has reached the stage at which all the simple groups that are homomorphic images of subgroup G have been extracted, no new groups will appear. These simple groups are the fundamental components from which the original machine was made.

The foregoing breakup into simple groups justifies regarding machines with simple groups as the basic component machines from which all group machines may be constructed.

When the decomposing subgroup, H, is normal in G, the first machine is a standard group machine with group G/H. The input to the series-parallel pair may be coded for input to the first machine by going through a coding function that is the homomorphism from G to G/H.

5.1 Examples of Group Machine Decomposition

(i) Cyclic group of order 6: $G = \{I, A, A^2, A^3, A^4, A^5\}$. Choose subgroup $H = \{I, A^2, A^4\}$. The cosets are $\{I, A^2, A^4\}$, $\{A, A^3, A^5\}$.

The resulting first machine is the group machine of order 2, and the second is the group machine of order 3.

Choosing I and A as coset leaders, we find the coding function between the machines in terms of (c, g) pairs:

$$(I, I),\quad (I, A),\quad (A, I),\quad (A, A^5) \qquad \text{go to } I$$

$$(I, A^2),\quad (I, A^3),\quad (A, A^2),\quad (A, A) \qquad \text{go to } A^2$$

$$(I, A^4),\quad (I, A^5),\quad (A, A^3),\quad (A, A^4) \qquad \text{go to } A^4$$

(ii) Noncyclic group of order 6: $G = \{I, A, A^2, C, CA, CA^2\}$. Choose subgroup $H = \{I, A, A^2\}$. The cosets are $\{I, A, A^2\}$, $\{C, CA, CA^2\}$. The resulting first machine is again the group machine of order 2, and the second is the group machine of order 3.

With I and C as coset leaders, the coding between machines is

$$\begin{array}{rl} (I, I),\quad (I, C),\quad (C, I),\quad (C, C) & \text{go to } I \\ (I, A),\quad (I, CA^2),\quad (C, CA),\quad (C, CA^2) & \text{go to } A \\ (I, A^2),\quad (I, CA),\quad (C, A),\quad (C, CA^2) & \text{go to } A^2 \end{array}$$

These two examples show how the coding between machines plays an essential part in reconstructing the group of the original machine.

6. Decomposition of Semigroup Machines

6.1 Resets. When a machine has a semigroup that is not a group, some of its state transition maps must be collapsers. We first discuss a special case of collapsers.

A state transition map that takes all states into one new state has been called a reset by Zeiger [2]. If r is a reset in a semigroup of state transition maps, S, then $sr = r$ for all $s \in S$, so that r is a right zero in the abstract semigroup. Also, $rs = r'$, where r' is a reset in S. A machine whose state transition maps are either permutations or resets Zeiger calls a permutation-reset machine.

6.2 Decomposition of Permutation-Reset Machines. A permutation-reset machine will have a semigroup, S, which is the union of a group G, and a set of resets R. The standard semigroup machine for S can be decomposed into a series-parallel connected standard group machine for G, and a standard semigroup machine for R^1, which is R with a two-sided identity added.

Each state in the standard semigroup machine for S is parameterized as $s = rg$, with $r \in R^1$, $g \in G$, and thus one parameter is held in each component machine. When the S machine is in state rg and an input s is applied, the new state $r'g'$ is found from $r'g' = rgs$. We consider two cases:

(i) $s \in R$, $r'g' = rgs = s$. We arbitrarily set $g' = g$, and then $r' = rgsg^{-1} = sg^{-1}$. Only the R^1 machine needs to be changed, and so the input coder passes an identity to the group machine and passes the product sg^{-1} to the R^1 machine. Thus, the R^1 machine needs the state of the G machine and can be taken as the second machine of the series-parallel connection.

(ii) $s \in G$. Arbitrarily put $g' = gs$, and leave $r' = r$, so that $r'g' = r(gs)$. Here the input coding function passes the identity to the R^1 machine, and s to the G machine.

The scheme of state changes involves arbitrary choices, but always gives a correct result. The output coder takes the outputs of the G and R^1 machines and multiplies them together. Figure 3 illustrates this.

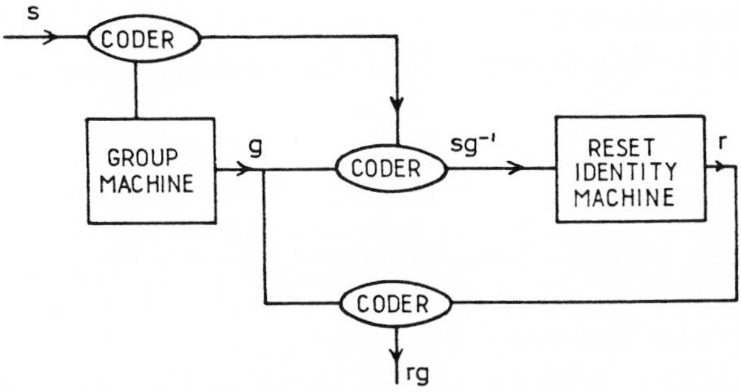

FIG. 3. Series-parallel decomposition of permutation-reset machine.

6.3 Reset-Identity Machines. The simplest reset-identity machine has two states, and a semigroup with three elements. Its semigroup is $\{r_0, r_1, I\}$, with r_0 reset to state zero, r_1 reset to state 1, and I the identity.

The action of any reset-identity machine can be reproduced by parallel-connected two-state reset-identity machines. Each input to the arbitrary machine is coded to a binary sequence of appropriate length, and one digit is passed to each two-state machine which is reset to 0 or 1. The identity input is treated differently and is coded to the identity input on each two-state component machine.

Thus, permutation-reset machines may further be decomposed to a group machine and a set of parallel-connected two-state reset-identity machines.

6.4 General Semigroup Machines. Zeiger has shown† how any general semigroup machine may be broken down into permutation-

† See his chapter on "Cascade Decomposition of Automata using Covers" in this volume.

reset components. As in the decomposition of group machines, the states are placed in blocks that are chosen so that under any input the blocks move into each other. The movement of blocks is reproduced in the state movement of the first of the series-parallel machines. In the group case, the blocks of states are nonoverlapping, but the general semigroup blocks are allowed to overlap.

To break a machine down into permutation-reset components, usually more than two series-parallel components are needed, the sequence of machines varying in each case. First a set of blocks is produced, and then it is successively refined to give the state set of subsequent machines.

To start the decomposition, take the standard semigroup machine with state set S. Take all the semigroup elements, c_i, which act as collapsing inputs. Form the subsets Sc_i, and discard any subsets that are wholly contained in another. If there are any elements of S not contained in the Sc_i, add them to the subsets as singleton subsets. These subsets form the first set of blocks. Under a collapsing input c_j, Sc_i moves to Sc_ic_j, which is contained in Sc_j, so that every block moves into the same new block. Thus, a collapser input to the original machine becomes a reset input to the first machine. A permuting element, $p \in S$, moves Sc_i to Sc_ip, which will be different for all Sc_i that are retained in the preceding construction. Thus a permuting input to the original machine is a permuting input to the first machine. If permuting inputs p_1, p_2, p_3 have $p_1 \cdot p_2 = p_3$, then $Sc_ip_1p_2 = Sc_ip_3$, so that the permutations in the first machine are a homomorphic image of a set of permutations in S, i.e., a subgroup.

If the first set of blocks is refined, each block being subdivided into a new set of overlapping blocks, then a second machine may be placed in series parallel with the first. The second machine has enough states to indicate the subdivision of the blocks of the first machine. The input to the second machine is the pair of the input to the original machine and the state of the first machine. The reader is referred to Zeiger's chapter for details of the construction, which shows how a sequence of permutation-reset machines may be derived, all the permutation groups involved being homomorphic images of subgroups of the original semigroup.

6.5 The Krohn-Rhodes Result. The aforementioned decompositions are special examples of the general Krohn-Rhodes result, which says, broadly, that the basic machines are the two-state reset-identity machines, and all the machines whose semigroups are simple groups. Furthermore, any machine may be reconstructed as series-parallel connections of two-state identity-reset machines and simple group machines, the simple group machines required being those having simple groups which are homomorphic images of all possible subgroups of the original semigroup. There may be very many different ways of series-parallel connecting the required simple group machines and two-state identity-resets. Many copies of the simple group machines may be used, and an arbitrary number of two-state identity-resets may be used.

6.6 Some Decomposition Methods of Krohn-Rhodes. [†] In order to show some decomposition methods alternative to those in the foregoing, we briefly describe some due to Krohn-Rhodes which form an essential step in the proof of the general result. Krohn-Rhodes divide all finite semigroups into three classes: cyclic semigroups, left simple semigroups, and semigroups with a proper left ideal and a proper subsemigroup whose union is the whole semigroup. They decompose the corresponding machines in different ways:

(i) Cyclic semigroup machines. A cyclic semigroup has elements $a, a^2, \ldots, a^n, a^{n+1}, a^{n+2}, \ldots, a^{n+m} = a^n, a^{n+m+1} = a^{n+1}$, etc. It can be realized as a state transformation by the transitions shown in Fig. 4. The state set is divided into two subsets, one called progressive collapsing and the other a cyclic permutation. The two-state subsets can be put in separate, parallel machines. Thus, the cyclic group and resets are separated.

(ii) Left simple semigroup machine. A left simple semigroup S has $SI = S$ for every subset $I \subset S$. Two obvious left simple semigroups are a group and a set of left zeros. A set of state transition

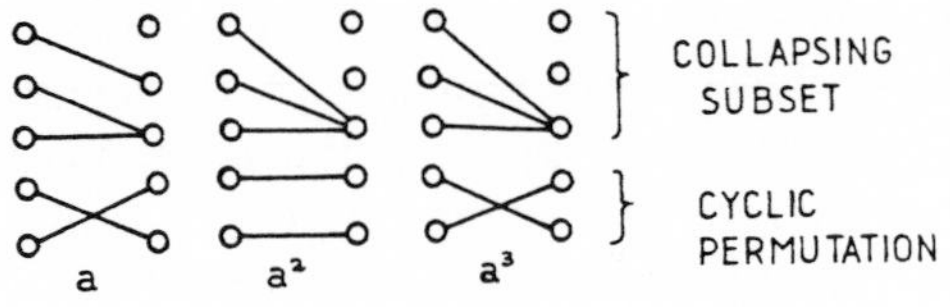

FIG. 4. State transition for cyclic semigroup.

† A complete algebraic treatment of this material appears in Sect. 3 of Chapter 5 of the present volume.

maps that represent a set of left zeros has the following structure. The state set has two subsets. One subset has an identity transformation in every map; the other subset collapses into the first subset. This is illustrated in Fig. 5. The most general left simple semigroup

FIG. 5. State transitions for left zeros.

has the form group × left zeros semigroup, and it can be reconstructed as a parallel left zero and group machines. Again, the group and resets are separated.

(iii) Left ideal and subsemigroup machines. After i and ii, the only remaining class of semigroups is that where the semigroups have a proper left ideal, T, and a proper subsemigroup, V, such that $S = T \cup V$.

The elements of S are parameterized by $s = tv$, where $t \in T'$, $v \in V'$, and T', V' are modified versions of T and V. In the series-parallel machine pair, the V' machine is first, and the T' machine is second. The input coding treats the input in either of two ways. Suppose the input is s:

(a) $s \in S - T$. The input is passed to the V' machine and an identity input passed to the T' machine. The new state is found from the old by $t'v' = tvs$, the multiplication vs being done in the v' machine.

(b) $s \in T$. A coder between the machines passes vs into the T' machine. The V' machine is sent to a special clear state.

The modifications to the T, V machines to get the T', V' machines are now evident. The T' machine has an identity added. The V' machine has the element of V as states plus a special state c. The clear input resets all states to c. When the machine is in state c, an input $v_i \in V$ causes a state transition to v_i.

This breakup is followed by further breakups on the T', V' machines. Eventually, the breakups of either type a or b terminate the process, so that finally the group and reset components are separated. There may be choices in T at each stage, so that different sequences of machines may be produced.

6.7 Significance of the Series-Parallel Connection. The series-parallel connection of machines is the most general one that excludes feedback from output to input. To see the kind of effects introduced by feedback, take a two-counter with its input passing through an "and" gate, as shown in Fig. 6. When the counter is set to "0," input

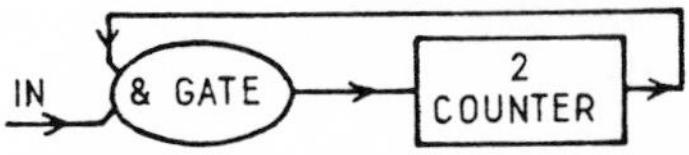

FIG. 6. A collapser machine.

ceases, and the counter is fixed. Thus, a group machine has produced a collapser action. As another example, take a delay carrying two parallel bits with input and feedback passing through a combinational logic circuit. The logic carries out multiplication for the group of order 4. Now a delay is a collapser machine, and so here a collapser has produced a group machine action.

In the series-parallel connection, group component machines always produce group machines, and a collapser component must be added to get collapser action. With feedback, state mapping properties are not preserved; in fact, *any* state transition map may be produced. What the series-parallel decomposition does is to decouple the states of different machines as far as possible, whereas feedback cross-couples the states of different machines.

7. The Algebraic Machine Model and Design Requirements

Engineers are constantly designing finite machines as parts of computing, communications, and automation equipment. Present design techniques are largely empirical, and any methods that would lead more surely to a better end product would be welcome; yet, at the present time, no practical use appears to have been made of the algebraic theory of machines. There are a number of possible reasons for this. We now discuss these and go on to suggest that the algebraic theory of machines will come to be applied when the overall work a machine has to do is specified algebraically from the beginning. At the moment, there is one applications area that is considered algebraically; it is the design of error correcting codes.

When a code is described algebraically, the accompanying encoding and decoding machines are also described algebraically. These encoding and decoding machines have not yet been treated in quite the way used in the algebraic theory of machines, and so an analysis of a linear machine, typically used in decoding, will be outlined.

Algebraic machine theory models only limited aspects of the action of finite machines. It considers solely the abstract states of the machine, and the way in which the state changes under the action of successive inputs. It does not consider the way in which the state is made up from the settings of electronic hardware, like flip-flops or delay lines. Still less does it attempt to model the way in which individual hardware elements change their settings in response to each input.

Logical designers work through three stages of design. They usually start with an input-output specification, and first produce a purely logical design. Essentially, they produce a set of states, a state transition table, and an output for each state. Then they go on to hardware. Each state has to be represented through chosen settings of memory devices like flip-flops; this is the state assignment problem. The main aims here will be speed of operation, economy, and the use of standard, available devices. After finding a hardware version of the machine, they must go on to check that the wanted state transitions are not marred by faulty timing of fast electrical pulses, or slight delays in the responses of gating devices. Algebraic machine theory can help directly only with the first stage, although it might indirectly help with the second and third stages by allowing alternative machines to be produced which have the same input-output behavior. In practice, speed is often an overriding requirement, and the avoidance of faulty state transitions can dominate design work.

7.1 Producing an Abstract Machine from an Input-Output Specification. Algebraic machine theory can provide the link between a required input-output behavior and the initial abstract machine design. It is worth following through how, in principle, this could be done, so as to make clear the severe difficulties.

We recall from Sect. 2.3 that, if a complete input-output specification is given, it can be made into a function $f: X^* \to Y$, where X is the input alphabet, X^* is the set of all strings over the input alphabet plus the null string, and Y is the output alphabet. $f(x)$ is the final output symbol produced by the input string x when the machine is started in a given initial state.

The machine semigroup may then be found by forming equivalence classes over X^* with the relation $x \equiv y$ if $f(uxv) = f(uyv)$ for all u, v in X^*. The set of equivalence classes with multiplication of concatenation of representative strings corresponds to the machine semigroup. Every representation of this semigroup by a set of mappings on a finite set of states is potentially a state set and state transition table for a machine realization. When an output map from the state set to the output alphabet is added, the function f is reproduced. Now, only a few of the potential machines produced from state transition considerations will satisfy the extra output requirements.

There can be practical difficulties in starting the preceding process because the engineer often has only a partial specification of the input-output behavior. Very few of the input-output pairs of f will be given, and the remaining entries can be filled in arbitrarily. Completing the function in some useful way is still an unsolved problem.

Suppose, however, the semigroup can be found. Then, if it is not a simple group, or a reset/identity semigroup, it can be decomposed. The decomposition gives the semigroups of the appropriate series-parallel component machines. At this point, further significant difficulties come up. The semigroup will probably need to be given by its multiplication table. This table will be substantially larger than the state transition table. For instance, a machine with 10 states and 2 inputs will have a state transition table with 20 entries; on the other hand, the semigroup may have up to 10^{10} elements, and so the multiplication table may have up to 10^{20} entries. It is this size problem that virtually prohibits a direct use of the semigroup; it can only be used through its general properties.

7.2 Systematic Approaches to Machine Design. A systematic approach to machine design is possible when the input-output task is defined in some general way. One possibility is to have the task defined as a calculation, perhaps over a finite field. Parity checking in decoding is an example. The simplest approach here is to turn the calculation into an algorithm, and then write a program. The resulting machine is then a special-purpose computer that runs this program. This approach has important practical advantages in repair and maintenance, because the machine action is broken down into a series of easily understood steps. However, the finite memory aspect of the problem is lost.

Sometimes, the machine state transitions can be defined directly by an equation. This is the situation to be aimed at, and it occurs in designing encoders and decoders. These coding machines are often linear.

7.3 Linear Machines. In coding theory, code elements are represented by polynomials over a finite field, and the decoding process involves addition and multiplication of these polynomials. Such arithmetic leads to linear machines.

A linear machine [3] has memory devices that store the element values from a finite field and has logic units that add and also multiply by constants. A linear machine with n memory devices has states corresponding to the finite set of n-vectors over the finite field, F. The input at time i, X_i will also be an n-vector over F. If V_i is the state vector at time i, then the next state is given by

$$V_{i+1} = AV_i + BX_i ,$$

where A, B are given $n \times n$ matrices over F. At the next time instant,

$$\begin{aligned} V_{i+2} &= AV_{i+1} + BX_{i+1} \\ &= A^2V_i + ABX_i + BX_{i+1} . \end{aligned}$$

From the state transition equations, it will be seen that the elements of the machine semigroup are (A^r, X), with X an n-vector over F. The semigroup multiplication is

$$(A^r, X) \times (A^p, X') = (A^{r+p}, X') = (A^{r+p}, A^pX + X').$$

The multiplication shows that the machine semigroup, S_M, is the semidirect product of the finite cyclic semigroup, $A^r = S_A$, and the additive group of the vector space, G_V. The machine can be made up from the series-parallel connection of component machines corresponding to S_A and G_V. The operation of the series-parallel machine is easily visualized when A is nonsingular, and so S_A is a group. The S_A machine stores A^r, and the G_V machine stores X. A new input X' is coded to (A, X'), and A is passed into the S_A machine, which goes to A^{r+1}. The G_V machine receives input $A^{-(r+1)}BX'$, and goes to $A^{-(r+1)}(AX + BX')$. The G_V machine needs to have the state of the S_A machine.

It is possible to go on and decompose the S_A and G_V machines. Since S_A is a cyclic semigroup, it can be imitated by parallel machines.

If S_A has index m and period n, one parallel machine will have period 1 and index m semigroup, and the second parallel machine will have a cyclic group of order n. This cyclic group machine can again be decomposed into series-parallel counters. G_V is an additive group, and so it can be decomposed into the direct product of cyclic groups of prime order. Hence, the G_V machine can be imitated by parallel-connected prime counters.

This decomposition of a linear machine would lead to realizations rather different from those currently used.

7.4 Further Possible Applications of the Algebraic Theory of Machines. In the standard machine realization shown in Fig. 7, the

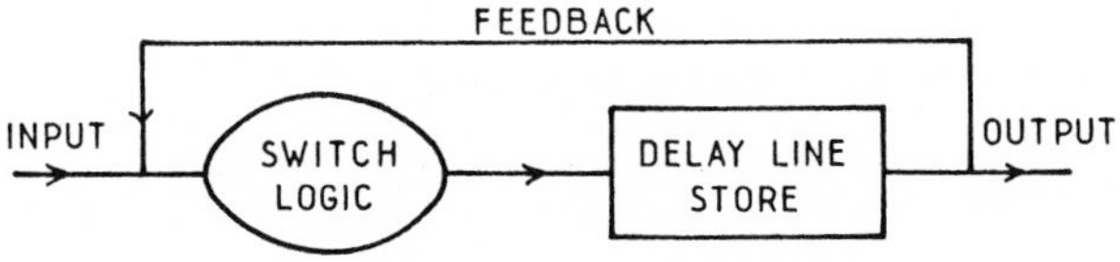

FIG. 7. Standard machine realization.

switch logic contains a coding of the machine semigroup multiplication table. The design of the switch circuit should be based on this, although no method of using this information is known at the moment.

Errors in machines are errors in state transitions. These can be caused by intermittent faults in devices or by hazards and races due to the finite acting time of devices. Hazards and races are sometimes eliminated by studying the state transitions in detail and then choosing a state assignment with sufficient states to ensure that troublesome transitions do not occur. Such detailed studies are difficult to make, and more general schemes are needed.

General schemes for eliminating errors actually correct errors soon after they occur in various subunits of the memory and switching circuitry [4]. The schemes are based on the principles of error-correcting codes; they correct errors no matter how they are caused.

The connections between error correction and the machine semigroup are not yet clear; however, certain remarks can be made:

(i) If there is a right zero in the semigroup, and it occurs reasonably often in the input, then the machine will be reset, and error conditions will not persist. With an incomplete input-output specification, it may be possible to introduce a right zero deliberately for this purpose.

(ii) Simple group machines might be natural self-contained units for error correction. Within the simple group machines, further error correction will take place.

REFERENCES

1. K. B. Krohn and J. L. Rhodes, Algebraic theory of machines, I, *Trans. Am. Math. Soc.* **116**, 450–464 (1965).
2. H. P. Zeiger, Cascade synthesis of finite-state machines, *Proc.* 1965 *IEEE Sixth Ann. Symp. Switching Circuit Theory Logical Design.* IEEE, New York, 1965.
3. W. H. Kautz, "Linear Sequential Switching Circuits." Holden-Day, San Francisco, 1965.
4. S. Winograd and J. D. Cowan, "Reliable Computation in the Presence of Noise." M.I.T. Press, Cambridge, Massachusetts, 1963.

CHAPTER 3

Automaton Decompositions and Semigroup Extensions†

MICHAEL A. ARBIB

Electrical Engineering Department, Stanford University, Stanford, California

Our main aim is to make explicit those relationships between machine concepts and semigroup concepts which have been known in various stages of exactness for years to workers in automata theory but which have received little careful attention in the literature and, simultaneously, to provide intuitively appealing approaches to standard material. Our diagrammatic approach to the cascade composition of machines will help the reader to provide elegant proofs of known results and should also prove valuable in the discovery of new ones.

1. Background‡

One focus of our interest in the algebraic theory of machines is the state-output automaton (or machine) abstractly described by a quintuple $M = (X, Y, Q, \delta, \beta)$, where X is a finite set of inputs, Y is a finite set of outputs, Q is a (not necessarily finite) set of states, $\delta : Q \times X \to Q$ is the next-state function, and $\beta : Q \to Y$ is the output function. The interpretation of an automaton is as a system such that if, at time t, it is in state q, its output will be $\beta(q)$; furthermore, if at time t it also receives input x, then at time $t + 1$ it will be in state $\delta(q, x)$.

† This research was supported in part by the U. S. Air Force Office of Scientific Research, Information Sciences Directorate, under Grant No. AF-AFOSR-1198-67.

‡ Some of this material is covered in more detail in Chapter 2.

We introduce X^*, the set of all finite sequences of input symbols, and include in it Λ, the "empty string" of 0 symbols. X^* is a semigroup under concatenation, i.e., concatenation is associative ($(x_1x_2)\,x_3 = x_1(x_2x_3)$), and has identity Λ. We then extend the applicability of δ so that it maps $Q \times X^*$ into Q, by repeated application of the equalities

$$\delta(q, \Lambda) = q$$
$$\delta(q, x'x'') = \delta[\delta(q, x'), x'']$$

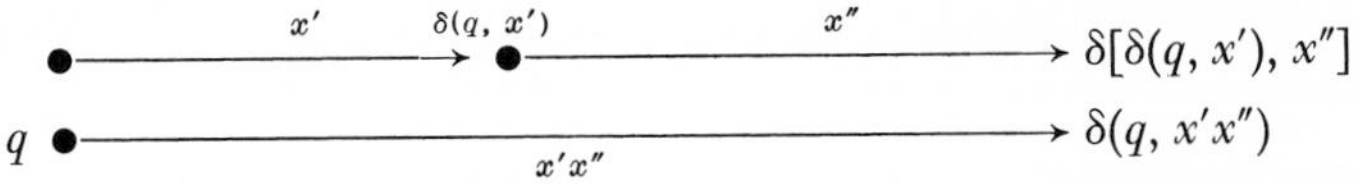

We may associate with each state q of a machine M the way it produces an output for each input string. This is expressed by the function $M_q : X^* \to Y$, where $M_q(x) = \lambda(q, x)$, where henceforth we write $\lambda(q, x)$ for $\beta[\delta(q, x)]$. Clearly, M behaves the same if started in two states q, q', with the same input-output function, i.e., if $M_q(x) = M_{q'}(x)$ for all input strings x. So if our interest in M is in its external behavior, we may replace it by its reduced form, which has one state for each *distinct* function M_q. Let M in state q have input-output function f, and let q' be a state *reachable* from q, i.e., we can find $x \in X^*$ such that $\delta(q, x) = q'$. Then q' has function

$$M_{q'}(x') = M_{\delta(q,x)}(x') = \lambda[\delta(q, x), x'] = \lambda(q, xx') = f(xx') = fL_x(x'),$$

where $L_x : X^* \to X^*$ is the "left multiplication by x" function: $L_x(x') = xx'$. L_x is *not* a homomorphism. Then, in our reduced form for M, we replace each state reachable from q by its input-output function fL_x, and the reduced form (restricted to states reachable from q) has finitely many states just in case there are only finitely many distinct functions fL_x (so that infinitely many strings $x \in X^*$ must yield the same fL_x). Thus, our interest centers on machines of the form

$$M(f) = (X, Y, Q_f, \delta_f, \beta_f),$$

where f is a given function mapping X^* to Y, and where

$$Q_f = \{g : X^* \to Y \mid g = fL_x \text{ for some } x \in X^*\},$$
$$\delta_f(g, x) = gL_x$$
$$\beta_f(g) = g(\Lambda),$$

especially in the case when f is such that Q_f is a finite set. We may often refer to the function $f : X^* \rightarrow Y$ as a machine itself, with $M(f)$ in mind if we need to think of machines as quintuples.

With such a machine $M(f)$, we associate a semigroup f^S, namely, the collection of transformations of the state set Q_f induced by the input strings to $M(f)$, i.e.,

$$f^S = \{s: Q_f \rightarrow Q_f \mid \exists\, x \in X^* \text{ such that } s(q) = \delta(q, x) \text{ for all } q \in Q\}.$$

We write $[x]_f$ for the state transformation induced by x. Our semigroup is finite if and only if Q_f is finite. If M is not in reduced form, we associate with it (and some specified starting state q) the semigroup of the reduced machine $M(f)$, where f is just M_q.

We may introduce a function $i_f : f^S \rightarrow Y$ by the definition $i_f(s) = f(x)$ if $s(q) \equiv \delta(q, x)$. This does not depend on the choice of x. We may then define a new "semigroup machine" with "state-output" i_f as

$$M(f^S, i_f) = (f^S, f^S, Y, \delta, i_f),$$

where $\delta(s, s') = s \cdot s'$ (semigroup multiplication).

We write S^M for the machine of the semigroup S, namely, $(S, S, S, \delta, 1)$, where $\delta(s, s') = s \cdot s'$, and $1(s) = s$.

We say that the machine M *simulates* the machine M' if, provided we encode and decode the input and output appropriately, M can process strings just as M' does. We require the encoder and decoder to be memoryless (i.e., operate symbol by symbol) in order to make M do all the computational work involving memory (see Fig. 1). If M

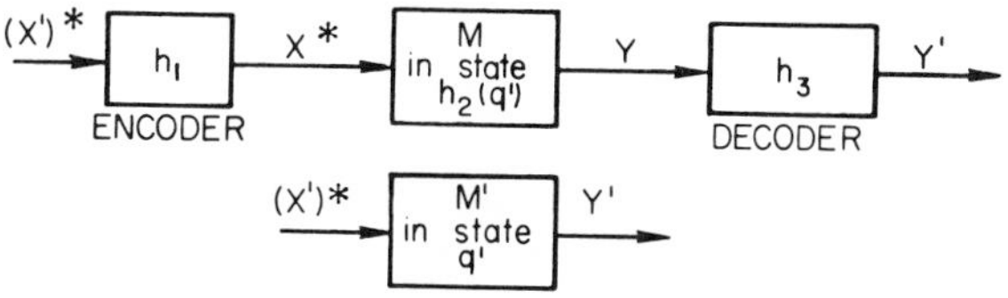

FIG. 1

simulates M', we write $M' \mid M$ and say that M' *divides* M. If both $M \mid M'$ and $M' \mid M$, we say that M and M' are *weakly equivalent*. The utility of semigroups in finite automata theory is emphasized by the result that $M(f^S, i_f)$ is weakly equivalent to $M(f)$. In fact, if we define $j_f : X \rightarrow f^S$ by $j_f(x) = [x]_f$, then the two machines are

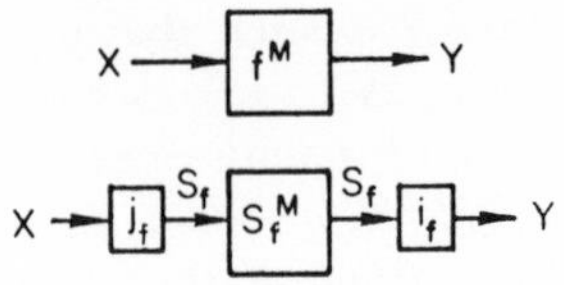

FIG. 2

identical in their input-output behavior, when their initial states are matched (see Fig. 2).

It turns out that semigroups, as well as machines, have a natural concept of divisibility. We say a semigroup S *divides* a semigroup S' if there is a subsemigroup S'' of S of which S' is the image under a homomorphism Z:

$$S' \supseteq S'' \xrightarrow{Z} S,$$

i.e., if the multiplication of S can be "simulated" by multiplication in S'. If S and S' have associated maps $i : S \to Y$, $i' : S' \to Y'$, then we say that (S, i) *divides* (S', i') if the foregoing situation holds, and there is, further, a mapping $H : Y \to Y'$ such that

$$i[Z(s)] = H[i'(s)] \qquad \text{for all} \quad s \in S.$$

The important tieup between the machine and semigroup concepts of divisibility is that the machine $M(g)$ started in state g may be simulated by the machine $M(f)$ started in state f if and only if the pair (g^S, i_g) divides the pair (f^S, i_f).† Henceforth we shall only consider state-output machines with finitely many states.

2. Cascades, Wreath Products, and Irreducibility

The composition of machines in series and parallel may be subsumed in the following portmanteau way of combining machines.

2.1 *Definition*. Given state-output machines M' and M and a map $Z : \tilde{X} \times Y \to X'$, and a map $\eta : \tilde{X} \to X$, we define the *cascade of M' and M with connecting map Z* to be $M' \times_Z{}^\eta M =$

† Further details are given in Chapter 5.

$(\tilde{X}, Y' \times Y, Q' \times Q, \delta_Z, \beta_Z)$, where we may read δ_Z and β_Z from Fig. 3:

$$\delta_Z[(q', q), \tilde{x}] = [\delta'\{q', Z(\tilde{x}, \beta(q))\}, \delta(q, \eta(\tilde{x}))\}],$$
$$\beta_Z(q', q) = [\beta'(q'), \beta(q)].$$

We usually omit η from explicit mention.

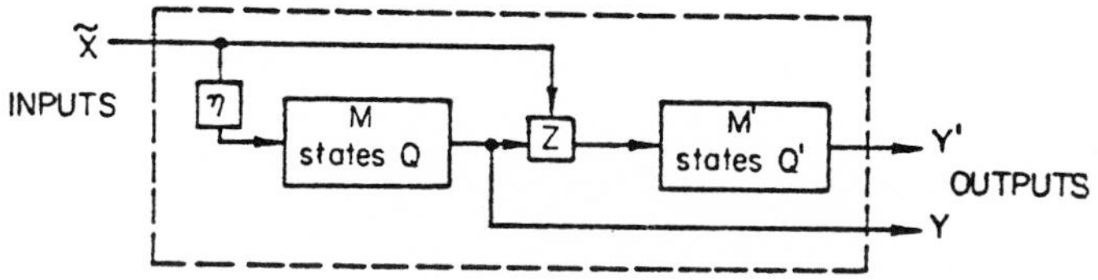

FIG. 3. $M' \times_{Z^\eta} M$ with states $Q' \times Q$.

2.2 Definition. A machine M is *irreducible* if for each cascade $M' \times_Z M''$ that is divided by M we must have

$$M \mid M' \qquad \text{or} \qquad M \mid M'',$$

i.e., M cannot be broken down into a cascade of "smaller" parts.

We may build up cascades of cascades repeatedly. The end result will always be some linear ordering of n machines, such that the input to the jth machine at time t only depends on the overall system input at time t and the outputs of the first $(j - 1)$ machines at time t. To reinforce this observation, the reader may compute the appropriate choiçes for $\hat{Z}'$, $\hat{Z}''$, and $\hat{\eta}$ which ensure that a given $M_3 \times_{Z''} (M_2 \times^{\eta}_{Z'} M_1)$ is equivalent to $(M_3 \times_{Z}^{\hat{\eta}} M_2) \times^{\hat{\eta}}_{Z'} M_1$ (see Fig. 4).

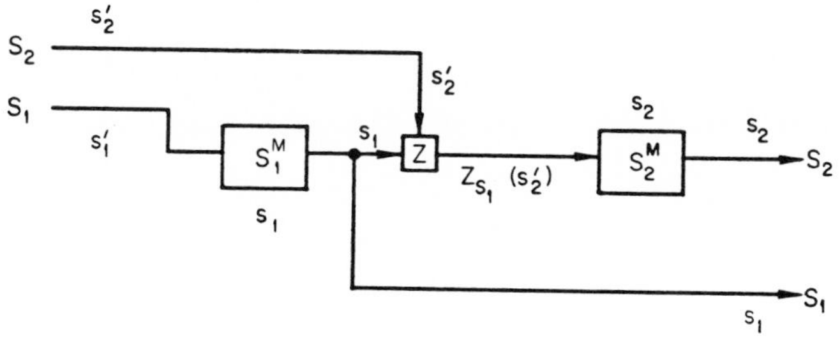

FIG. 4

Now suppose that, in Definition 2.1, we take $\tilde{X} = S_2 \times S_1$, $\eta(s_2, s_1) = s_1$ and have Z independent of the s_1 of $\tilde{x}$, so that we may write $Z_{s_1}(s_2')$ for $Z[(s_2', s_1'), s_1]$.

Furthermore, let machine M be replaced by the semigroup machine $S_1{}^M$ while M' is replaced by $S_2{}^M$. We then have

$$\delta_Z[(s_2, s_1), (s_2', s_1')] = [s_2 Z_{s_1}(s_2'), s_1 s_1'].$$

The operation δ_Z becomes *associative* if we require that Z enjoy the properties

$$Z_{s_1 s_1'}(s_2) = Z_{s_1}[Z_{s_1'}(s_2)],$$

$$Z_{s_1}(s_2 s_2') = Z_{s_1}(s_2)\, Z_{s_1}(s_2'), \qquad s_1, s_1' \in S_1, s_2, s_2' \in S_2.$$

This leads us naturally to consider the semidirect product of S_1 and S_2.

2.3 Definition. Let S_1 and S_2 be semigroups, and Z a homomorphism of S_1 into Endo (S_2) (i.e., the monoid of endomorphisms of S_2 under composition): $s_1 \to Z_{s_1}$.

Then, *the semidirect product of S_1 and S_2 with connecting homomorphism Z* is the semigroup $S_2 \times_Z S_1$ with elements the cartesian product set $S_2 \times S_1$ and multiplication

$$(s_2, s_1)(s_2', s_1') = [s_2 Z_{s_1}(s_2'), s_1 s_1']$$

Correspondingly, we have the definition:

2.4 Definition. A semigroup S is *irreducible* if, for all semidirect products $S_2 \times_Z S_1$ such that $S \mid S_2 \times_Z S_1$, we must have

$$S \mid S_2 \qquad \text{or} \qquad S \mid S_1.$$

Our definitions have been so worded as to render highly plausible the result that a machine is irreducible if and only if its semigroup is irreducible. However, we shall see that this is not true!

Given a cascade machine $M' \times_Z M$ with semigroup $\tilde{S}$, it is tempting to believe that we can always find a suitable homomorphism $\tilde{Z}$ such that

$$S \mid S' \times_{\tilde{Z}} S,$$

where S' is the semigroup of M', and S that of M.

However, this is usually impossible, since the original map Z may so completely "cut across" the multiplicative structure of the semigroups that no $\tilde{Z}$ can be found with the desired homomorphism properties.

Simulating M with S^M, and M' with S'^M, we may represent $M' \times_Z M$ by Fig. 5.†

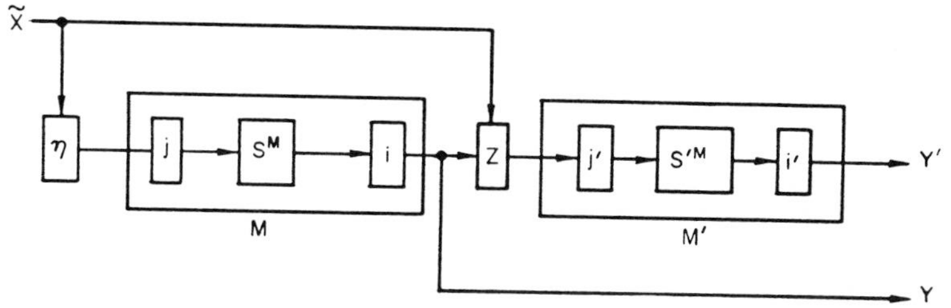

FIG. 5

The (not necessarily reduced) state-space of this cascade is $S' \times S$. We consider $\hat{S}$, the semigroup of transformations of $S' \times S$ induced by input sequences.

Let t be an input sequence, i.e., an element of $\tilde{X}^*$. The action of t on the S^M machine is simply multiplication by an appropriate element, $I_S(t)$, of S. However, the action of t on the *second* machine, S'^M, will depend on the state of S^M at the beginning of the operation: if the latter is s, then let us denote the former by $I_{S'}(t)(s)$. Thus, $I_{S'}(t)$ is an element of $F(S, S')$, the semigroup of *maps* (not just homomorphisms) of S into S', with composition defined by $(f_1 \cdot f_2)(s) = f_1(s) \cdot f_2(s)$.

Thus, $\hat{S}$ is obtained by replacing the element t of the input free semigroup by the element $[I_{S'}(t), I_S(t)]$ of the *set* $F(S, S') \times S$. What is the semigroup multiplication induced on this set by the input action? The action of t_1 followed by t_2 yields

$$[I_{S'}(t_1), I_S(t_1)] \cdot [I_{S'}(t_2), I_S(t_2)] = [I_{S'}(t_1 t_2), I_S(t_1 t_2)]. \tag{1}$$

But the action of $t_1 t_2$ on S^M is simply that of t_1 multiplied by that of t_2:

$$I_S(t_1 t_2) = I_S(t_1)\, I_S(t_2), \tag{2}$$

† Exercise: Given that $\tilde{M} \mid M' \times_x{}^\eta M$, find η' and Z' such that $\tilde{M} \mid S'^M \times^{\eta'}_{Z'} S^M$.

whereas the action of t_1t_2 on S'^M when S^M is started in state s is that of t_1 on S'^M when S^M is started in state s, multiplied by that of t_2 on S'^M when S^M is started in state $s \cdot I_S(t_1)$:

$$I_{S'}(t_1t_2)(s) = [I_{S'}(t_1)(s)] \cdot [I_{S'}(t_2)(s \cdot I_S(t_1))]. \tag{3}$$

2.5. If the reader will refer back to the definition of the semidirect product and consider the map

$$W : S \to \text{Endo}\,[F(S, S')]$$

defined by

$$W_s(l')(s_1) = l'(s_1 s),$$

he will see that the multiplication defined on $F(S, S') \times S$ is that of the semidirect product $F(S, S') \times_W S$. This suggests that the latter semigroup deserves our special attention; we call it the *wreath product* of S and S', and denote it S' w S.

Note that W is completely defined when we give S and S', and so need not be mentioned explicitly.

We have that $\hat{S}$ is a subsemigroup of the wreath product of S and S'. But the semigroup of $M' \times_Z M$ is a homomorphic image of $\hat{S}$, being simply the action of $\tilde{X}^*$ on the reduced state-space. So the semigroup of $M' \times_Z M$ must divide the wreath product of the semigroups of M' and M.

Thus, although in general there is no semidirect product of S' and S which is divisible by $\tilde{S}$, it is always true that $\tilde{S}$ divides that semidirect product of $F(S, S')$, with S known as the wreath product.

The converse is almost true. We may construct $(S' \text{ w } S)^M$ from S^M and S'^M, though not necessarily from M and M', and it is then easy to simulate any reduced machine whose semigroup divides S' w S

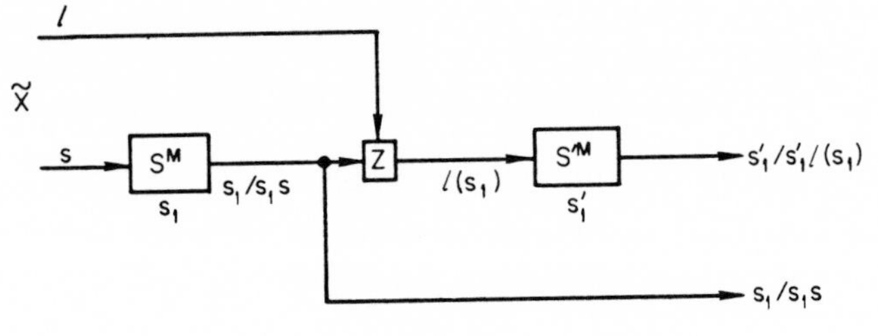

FIG. 6

with this cascade. In fact, consider the cascade $S'^M \times_Z S^M$ with $\tilde{X} = S \times F(S, S')$ and $Z_s(s', l') = l'(s)$ (see Fig. 6). The action of (l, s) followed by (l', s') on (s_1, s_1') yields $[s_1' l(s_1)\, l'(s_1 s), s_1 s s']$, and so inputs do indeed compose under wreath product multiplication.

We thus have the following crucial result.

2.6 Theorem. Consider the finite semigroups S and S'. Then, a semigroup $\tilde{S}$ is the semigroup of $S'^M \times_Z S^M$ for some connecting map Z, iff $\tilde{S}$ divides the wreath product $S' \text{ w } S$. ▮

In fact, the converse half of Theorem 2.6 may be given a form that is simultaneously stronger (using only semidirect products) and weaker (using more machines).

2.7 Theorem. For any semigroups S_1 and S_2, the machine $(S_2 \text{ w } S_1)^M$ of their wreath-product may be obtained from copies of $S_1{}^M$ and $S_2{}^M$ using only semidirect products.

PROOF. We must use the fact that $S_2 \text{ w } S_1 = F(S_1, S_2) \times_W S_1$ and $F(S_1, S_2) = S_2 \times S_2 \times \cdots \times S_2$ [$\#(S_1)$ times]. In Fig. 7, we

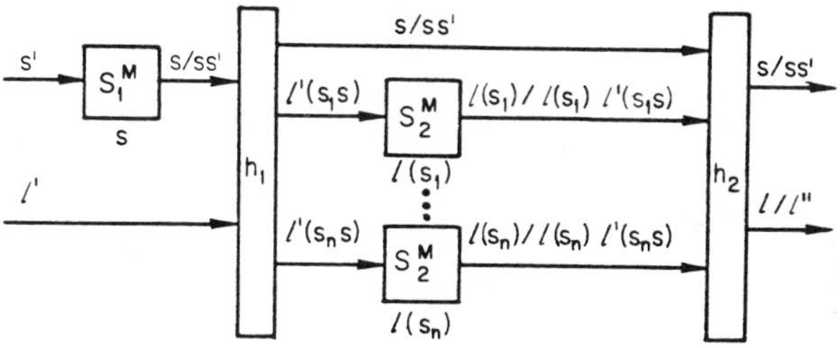

FIG. 7

label each machine with its state at time t. s on a line means that the line carries signal s at time t; s/ss' on a line means that the line carries signal s at time t and signal ss' at time $t+1$. h_1 and h_2 are defined by diagram, e.g., $h_1(s, l') = [s, l'(s_1 s), \ldots, l'(s_n s)]$, where $S_1 = \{s_1, s_2, \ldots, s_n\}$. We have that $(S_2 \text{ w } S_1)^M$ may be constructed as shown in Fig. 7, where $s' \in S_1$, $l' \in F(S_1, S_2)$, $(l', s') \in S_2 \text{ w } S_1$, and $l''(s_k) = l(s_k)\, l'(s_k s)$, the wreath multiplication. The output l'' amounts to a table of values describing a member of $F(S_1, S_2)$. An input of (l', s') at time t results in the required output of (l'', ss') at time $t+1$. ▮

We now prove the following theorem.

2.8 Theorem. If M is irreducible as a machine, its semigroup S is irreducible as a semigroup.

PROOF. Suppose M is irreducible. To say that S divides the semidirect product $S_2 \times_Z S_1$ is just another way of saying that S^M is simulable by the cascade of machines $S_2{}^M \times_Z S_1{}^M$. Since $M \mid S^M$, we have $M \mid S_2{}^M \times_Z S_1{}^M$, and by irreducibility $M \mid S_1{}^M$ or $M \mid S_2{}^M$. But divisibility of machines implies divisibility of their semigroups, and so $S \mid S_1$ or $S \mid S_2$. Thus, S is irreducible. ▮

2.9 Theorem. If M is a machine whose semigroup S is irreducible as a semigroup, then M is *s*-irreducible, in the sense that, if

$$M \mid M_2 \times_Z M_1,$$

where M_1 has semigroup S_1, and M_2 has semigroup S_2, then either $M \mid S_1{}^M$ or $M \mid S_2{}^M$.

PROOF. Let S be irreducible. Now, if $M \mid M_2 \times_Z M_1$, then S must divide $S_2 \text{ w } S_1$ and so divides S_1 or $F(S_2, S_1)$. If S divides S_1, then S^M divides $S_1{}^M$. But $F(S_2, S_1) \cong S_2 \times \cdots \times S_2$ [$\#(S_1)$ times]. So if S divides $F(S_2, S_1)$, then S must divide S_2, by irreducibility, in which case S^M divides $S_2{}^M$. Thus, $M \mid S_1{}^M$ or $M \mid S_2{}^M$. ▮

2.10. Thus *a machine is s-irreducible if and only if its semigroup is irreducible.* Krohn and Rhodes [1] give the theory of irreducible semigroups (respectively *s*-irreducible machines) and how other semigroups (respectively machines) may be built up from them by semidirect products and division (respectively cascades and simulation). This theory is re-presented in Chapter 5.

The reader may share the disconcertion I felt on first realizing that irreducibility of machines was not equivalent to irreducibility of semigroups.† The reason for this inequivalence is simply that the output maps of M_1 and M_2 may make their output sets so small that neither M_1 nor M_2 alone can simulate M, although one of $S_1{}^M$ and $S_2{}^M$ is big enough to simulate M.

† I am grateful to Don Stanat for aiding the awakening.

2.11 Example. Consider the machine M that does addition mod 3; its output always equals its state, and the state transitions are given by the following table:

	1	2	3
1	2	3	1
2	3	1	2
3	1	2	3

Now let M_1 be the machine M with an output coder adjoined, whose function h is given by

$$h(1) = 1, \qquad h(2) = s, \qquad h(3) = s.$$

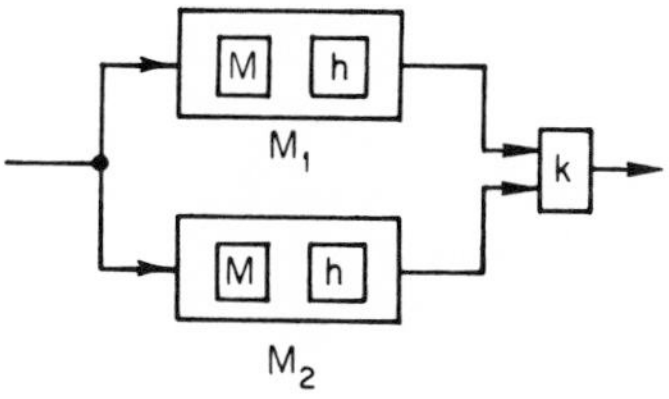

FIG. 8

Let us simulate M, started in state 1, by a cascade of M_1 started in state 1 and M_2, which is just M_1 started in state 2 (see Fig. 8). The reader may verify that, if we define k by

$$k\binom{1}{s} = 1, \qquad k\binom{s}{s} = 2, \qquad k\binom{s}{1} = 3,$$

then this cascade behaves exactly as M. In short, $M \mid M_2 \times M_1$, and $s = s_1 = s_2$, but it is not possible that $M \mid M_2$ or $M \mid M_1$, since the output set of M_1 alone is too small to encode all the outputs of M. While on the topic of clarifications, note that we can only be sure of simulating a machine M by the machine S^M of its semigroup if M is *cyclic*, i.e., all states are reachable from some initial state q. [We use "cyclic" in the *algebraic* sense of having a single generator, $Q = \delta(q, X^*)$, rather than implying that the state graph consists only of cycles.] For then, if state $q' = \delta(q, x)$, we may encode it as $[x]$, and several choices may be available. But if S has several orbits on the state-space of M, we may only be able to code up the states of one orbit; in general, we need one copy of S^M for each orbit, and a selector switch that keys in the machine with a state that encodes the appropriate initial state.

We have used the cascade as the rule for loop-free composition of machines. Krohn and Rhodes [1] use series and parallel composition. We have seen that series and parallel connections are special cases of cascade connections. The converse is not quite true (see Fig. 9).

The trouble with the cascade of M_2 and M_1 is that M_1 receives the output of M_1 and the input for X simultaneously, whereas in a series connection M_2 cannot be placed in series with M_1 with a direct through path from X to M_2. A resolution of this problem is seen in Fig. 9, where the series-parallel combination of (b) has the same input-output function as in (a), albeit with an extra delay of one time unit. The boxes marked D_X and D_{Q_2} are delay boxes, with state sets X and Q_2 (the state set of M_2), respectively. They emit an input one

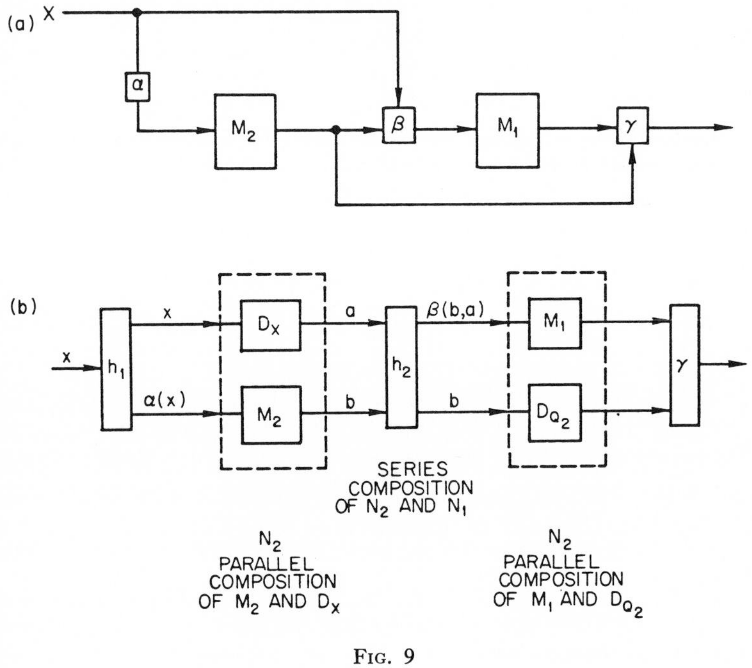

FIG. 9

time unit after receiving it; they are just reset or basic combinational machines, to use the terminology of other chapters.

In fact, it can be proved that delay machines may be necessary in going from cascades to series-parallel compositions. (The reader may see this by reworking material in Chapter 5, Sect. 2.)

In my experience [2, 3] it is far easier to realize a machine by cascade compositions of given machines than by series-parallel compositions. If one then desires a series-parallel composition (and it is not clear that one often would), one may then apply the technique of Fig. 9 to obtain the deserved representation. The reader is invited to apply this simplifying technique to the material of Chapter 5.

3. Semigroup Extensions and Automaton Cascades

A congruence ρ on a semigroup S is an equivalence relation with the additional property that, if $x \rho x'$ and $y \rho y'$, then $xy \rho x'y'$. The set of equivalence classes then becomes a semigroup S/ρ with multiplication well defined by $[x][y] = [xy]$. Note that, if S is a monoid, with identity 1, then $[1]_\rho$ is a submonoid of S, and S/ρ is a monoid.

We say that the semigroup S is an *extension of the semigroup* T *by the congruence* ρ if ρ is a congruence on S and there is a t in S with $[t]_\rho \cong T$. If $\Sigma = S/\rho$, we may also say that S is an *extension of the semigroup* T *by the semigroup* Σ.

Now suppose that G is a group, and ρ is any congruence on G. It is then easy to verify that $H = [1]_\rho$ is a normal subgroup of G and is the only subsemigroup of G of the form $[g]_\rho$, and that $K = G/\rho$ is just the factor group G/H. Our notion reduces, for groups, to the familiar: A group G is an extension of H by K if $H \lhd G$ and $G/H \cong K$.

Let us briefly recall Schreier's characterization of all extensions of a group H by a group K.

Suppose $K \cong G/H$. Then each element of K has $|H|$ representations as $[g]$ for $g \in G$. Let us choose one member $\bar{g}$ from each $[g]$, and keep that choice fixed.

Since H is normal, $\bar{g}h \in H\bar{g}$ for every $g \in G$ and $h \in H$. Thus the mapping

$$h \to \bar{g}h\bar{g}^{-1} = h^{[g]} \tag{4}$$

is an automorphism of H.

Since $\bar{g}_1\bar{g}_2$ lies in $[g_1][g_2] = [g_1g_2]$, we may define $([g_1], [g_2])$ by

$$\bar{g}_1 \cdot \bar{g}_2 = ([g_1], [g_2])\, \overline{g_1g_2}\,. \tag{5}$$

We may then reconstitute the multiplication of G by

$$\begin{aligned}(h_1\bar{g}_1)(h_2\bar{g}_2) &= h_1h_2^{[g_1]}\bar{g}_1\bar{g}_2\\ &= h_1h_2^{[g_1]}([g_1], [g_2])\, \overline{g_1g_2}.\end{aligned} \tag{6}$$

If we define

$$\beta(h_2\bar{g}_2\,, [g_1]) = h_2^{[g_1]}([g_1], [g_2]),$$

this rule yields the construction† of G^M as a cascade of H^M and K^M (see Fig. 10)

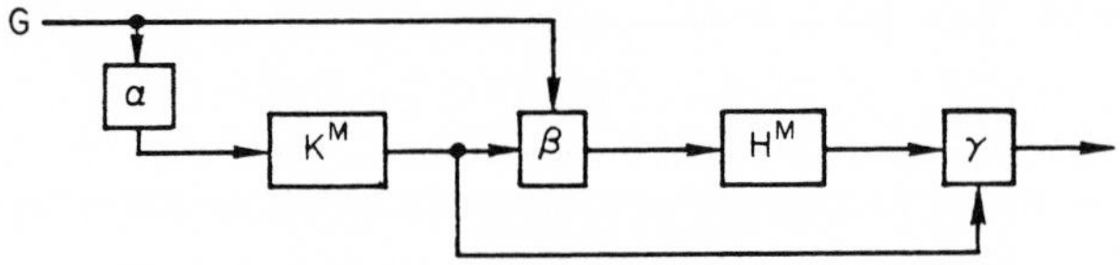

FIG. 10

with

$$\alpha : G \to K : g \to [g],$$

$$\beta : G \times K \to H : (g_2\,, [g_1]) \to (\bar{g}_2 g_1)[\overline{\bar{g}_1 g_2}]^{-1},$$

$$\gamma : H \times K \to G : (h, [g]) \to h\bar{g}\,.$$

The discussion of (4)–(6) yields, after a certain amount of computation, the following characterization, where condition (7) is required to ensure associativity of the extension.

3.1 Schreier's Theorem. If a group G has normal subgroup H and factor group $K = G/H$, and we choose coset representatives $u \in K \to \bar{u} \in G$, then automorphisms of H, $h \to h^u$ for each $u \in K$, and a factor set (u, v) for $u, v \in K$ are determined satisfying

$$(h^u)^v = (v, u)\, h^{vu}(v, u)^{-1},$$

$$(v, w)^u(u, vw) = (u, v)(uv, w). \tag{7}$$

† This construction can be obtained directly, of course, and has been so presented by Assmus and Florentin in Chapter 1, as well as by Rudolf Bayer of the Boeing Company, Seattle, Washington.

Conversely, if for every $u \in K$ there is given an automorphism $h \to h^u$ of H, and if for these automorphisms and a factor set $\{(u, v) \in H \mid u, v \in K\}$ conditions (7) hold, then elements $h\bar{u}$, $u \in K$, $h \in H$, with the product rule

$$h_1\bar{u}_1 \cdot h_2\bar{u}_2 = h_1 h_2^{u_1}(u_1, u_2)\, \overline{u_1 u_2},$$

define a group G with a normal subgroup (isomorphic to) H and $G/H \cong K$.

For further details, the reader may consult Chapter 15 of Hall [4]. The apparent discrepancy in formulas is caused by the group theorists' use of $\bar{u}h$ as the typical element of G (i.e., left cosets), whereas the machine theorist finds the form $h\bar{u}$ more convenient.

Now we would like to transfer this discussion to the extension of semigroups. But group extensions have a crucial property not preserved for most semigroup extensions, namely, that elements of G can be uniquely labeled by an element of H and an element of K, and that there is an element of G for each such labeling pair.

3.2 Example. Let $S = \{1, r_1, \ldots, r_n\}$ be the $n + 1$ element semigroup with n right zeros, and identity 1. Let ρ be the congruence with equivalence classes $[1] = \{1\}$; $[r_1] = \{r_1, \ldots, r_n\}$. Then $S/\rho \cong \{1, r_1\}$, and the pair $T = [1]$ and $\Sigma = \{1, r_1\}$ gives us no clue as to the size of the extension S of T by Σ. T and Σ give us too few labels for S. Or should we consider it as an extension of $[r_1]$ by Σ with too many labels?

3.3 Example. Let S be a semigroup, and I a proper ideal of S (i.e., $I \subsetneq S$, $SIS \subset I$). Define the congruence ρ on S by

$$[s] = \{s\} \qquad \text{if } s \in S - I,$$

$$[s] = I \qquad \text{if } s \in I.$$

S/ρ is usually called the Rees factor semigroup S/I. S is an extension of $T = I$ by $\Sigma = S/I$, and we have too many labels. The theory of this type of extension, "ideal extensions," has been developed by Clifford and by Munn [5, Sects. 4.4 and 4.5].

It is thus only for a restricted class of semigroup extensions that the Schreier theory generalizes. Redei [6] characterized such a class and gave the appropriate generalization. We present a modified version, tailored to fit our present demands.

3.4 Definition. The monoid S is said to be a *Schreier extension* of the monoid T by the monoid Σ iff

(i) T is a submonoid of S;

(ii) there is a map (not necessarily a homomorphism) $\sigma \to \bar{\sigma}$ of Σ into S such that the map $(t, \sigma) \to t\bar{\sigma}$ is a one-to-one map of $T \times \Sigma$ onto S (if $s = t\bar{\sigma}$, we may write $\bar{s}$ for $\bar{\sigma}$); and

(iii) the relation ρ with $s_1 \rho s_2$ iff $\bar{s}_1 = \bar{s}_2$ is a congruence on S with $S/\rho \cong \Sigma$, the isomorphism being given by $\eta(s) = \sigma$ iff $\sigma = \bar{s}$, $[1]_\rho = T$.

The reader may easily verify the following lemma.

3.5 Lemma. Any semidirect product $S_2 \times_Z S_1$ of two monoids S_2 and S_1 is a Schreier extension of S_1 by S_2.

Let S be a Schreier extension of T by Σ. Then for each σ_1 in Σ, $s = t\bar{s}$ in S, $\bar{\sigma}_1 t\bar{s}$ is in $T\overline{\sigma_1 s}$, and so there is a unique $\beta(\sigma_1, s)$ such that

$$\bar{\sigma}_1 s = \beta(\sigma_1, s)\, \overline{\sigma_1 \bar{s}}\,.$$

Thus, if $s_1 = t_1\bar{s}_1$ and $s_2 = t_2\bar{s}_2$, then

$$s_1 s_2 = t_1 \beta(\bar{s}_1, s_2) \cdot \overline{s_1 s_2}\,.$$

This yields a machine that realizes S^M as a cascade of Σ^M and T^M, which the reader may visualize from Fig. 10 by changing K to Σ and H to T, with

$$\alpha : S \to \Sigma : s \to [s],$$

$$\beta : \Sigma \times S \to T : (\sigma, s) \to \beta(\sigma, s),$$

$$\gamma : \Sigma \times T \to S : (\sigma, t) \to t\sigma.$$

Now, let us, without loss of generality, henceforth assume $\bar{1} = 1$.

By condition (iii), for each σ, τ in Σ, $\bar{\sigma}\bar{\tau} \in T\overline{\sigma\tau}$, so there must exist a unique $(\sigma, \tau) \in T$ such that

$$\bar{\sigma}\bar{\tau} = (\sigma, \tau)\, \overline{\sigma\tau}.$$

Since $\bar{1} = 1$, it is clear that $(\sigma, 1) = (1, \sigma) = 1$.

Again, for any t in T and σ in Σ, $\bar{\sigma}$ is in $T\bar{\sigma}$ and t is in $T\bar{1}$, and so $\bar{\sigma} \cdot t$ is in $T\bar{\sigma}$.

Thus there is a unique element t^σ of T such that

$$t^\sigma \bar{\sigma} = \bar{\sigma} t.$$

Note that $1^\sigma = 1$ for all σ in Σ, and $t^1 = t$, since $\bar{1} = 1$. We may then reconstitute the multiplication by

$$\begin{aligned}(t_1\bar{\sigma}_1)(t_2\bar{\sigma}_2) &= t_1 t_2^{\sigma_1} \bar{\sigma}_1 \bar{\sigma}_2 \\ &= t_1 t_2^{\sigma_1} (\sigma_1 , \sigma_2)\, \overline{\sigma_1 \sigma_2} \,.\end{aligned}$$

Associativity implies

$$t_1 t_2^{\sigma_1} (\sigma_1 , \sigma_2)\, t_3^{\sigma_1 \sigma_2} (\sigma_1 \sigma_2 , \sigma_3) = t_1 [t_2 t_3^{\sigma_2} (\sigma_2 , \sigma_3)]^{\sigma_1} (\sigma_1 , \sigma_2 \sigma_3). \tag{8}$$

Setting $t_1 = t_2 = t_3 = 1$, we get

$$(\sigma_1 , \sigma_2)(\sigma_1 \sigma_2 , \sigma_3) = (\sigma_2 , \sigma_3)^{\sigma_1} (\sigma_1 , \sigma_2 \sigma_3). \tag{9}$$

Setting $t_1 = t_2 = 1$, $\sigma_3 = 1$, we get [recalling $(\sigma, 1) = (1, \sigma) = 1$]

$$(\sigma_1 , \sigma_2)\, t_3^{\sigma_1 \sigma_2} = (t_3^{\sigma_2})^{\sigma_1} (\sigma_1 , \sigma_2). \tag{10}$$

Finally, setting $\sigma_2 = \sigma_3 = 1$, $t_1 = 1$, we obtain

$$t_2^{\sigma_1} t_3^{\sigma_1} = (t_2 t_3)^{\sigma_1}, \tag{11}$$

i.e., t^σ is an endormorphism of T for each σ. In fact, (9)–(11) suffice to reconstitute (8). We may thus verify, in a routine fashion, our version of

3.6 Redei-Schreier Theorem. Given a Schreier extension S of the monoid T by the monoid Σ, with $\sigma \to \bar{\sigma}$ (and $\bar{1} = 1$) being our choice of representatives for Σ-classes in S, then endomorphisms of T, $t \to t^\sigma$, for each $\sigma \in \Sigma$, and a factor set (σ, σ') for $\sigma, \sigma' \in \Sigma$ are determined satisfying

$$\begin{aligned}(\sigma_2 , \sigma_3)^{\sigma_1} (\sigma_1 , \sigma_2 \sigma_3) &= (\sigma_1 , \sigma_2)(\sigma_1 \sigma_2 , \sigma_3), \\ (t_3^{\sigma_2})^{\sigma_1} (\sigma_1 , \sigma_2) &= (\sigma_1 , \sigma_2)\, t_3^{\sigma_1 \sigma_2}, \\ (\sigma_1 , 1) &= (1, \sigma_2) = 1.\end{aligned} \tag{12}$$

Conversely, if for every $\sigma \in \Sigma$ there is given an endomorphism $t \to t^{\sigma}$ of H, and if for these endomorphisms and a factor set $\{(\sigma, \sigma') \in T \mid \sigma, \sigma' \in \Sigma\}$ conditions (12) hold, then elements $t\bar{\sigma}$, $\sigma \in \Sigma$, $t \in T$ with the product rule

$$t_1\bar{\sigma}_1 \cdot t_2\bar{\sigma}_2 = t_1 t_2^{\sigma_1}(\sigma_1, \sigma_2)\,\overline{\sigma_1\sigma_2}$$

define a monoid S that is a Schreier extension of T by Σ.

REFERENCES

1. K. Krohn and J. Rhodes, Algebraic theory of machines, I, *Trans. Amer. Math. Soc.* **116**, 450–464 (1965).
2. M. A. Arbib, Chapters on automata theory, *in* "Topics in Modern System Theory" (R. E. Kalman, P. L. Falb, and M. A. Arbib, authors). McGraw-Hill, New York, 1968.
3. M. A. Arbib, "Theories of Abstract Automata." Prentice-Hall, Englewood Cliffs, New Jersey (1968).
4. M. Hall, "The Theory of Groups." Macmillan, New York, 1961.
5. A. H. Clifford and G. B. Preston, "The Algebraic Theory of Semigroups," Vol. I. Am. Math. Soc., Providence, Rhode Island, 1961.
6. L. Redei, Die Verallgemeinerung der Schreierschen Erweiterungstheorie, *Acta Sci. Math.* (Szeged) **14**, 252–273 (1952). (For an English translation of the portions relevant to our discussion, see L.A.M. Verbeek, On Schreier's extension theory as generalised for monoids by L. Redei, EURATOM Rept. EUR/C-15/1043/63e, Ispra, June 1963, 11 pages.)

CHAPTER 4

Cascade Decomposition of Automata Using Covers

H. PAUL ZEIGER

Department of Aerospace Engineering, University of Colorado, Boulder, Colorado

1. Automata

We shall discuss abstractions of certain problems that arise when designing devices like vending machines, counters, computers, and telephone switching networks. As an example, we automate a toll booth. The attendant posts a sign that reads "stop" until three nickels have been deposited and then posts a sign that reads "go" until the car passes; if a car passes against the stop sign, the attendant sounds an alarm. More explicit instructions for the attendant are

	Nothing happening	A nickel is being deposited	A car is passing
0	Post stop; go to row 0.	Post stop; go to row 1.	Sound alarm; go to row 0.
1	Post stop; go to row 1.	Post stop; go to row 2.	Sound alarm; go to row 0.
2	Post stop; go to row 2.	Post go; go to row 3.	Sound alarm; go to row 0.
3	Post go; go to row 3.	Post go; go to row 3.	Post stop; go to row 0.

FIG. 1. To run the toll booth, scan row 0 for the entry whose column heading describes the situation you face, and take the action given by that entry; next, scan the row to which it sends you for the entry whose column heading describes the situation you now face, and so on. Perform one such instruction every $\frac{1}{2}$ sec. (The row number is just the number of nickels deposited, if we interpret 3 as 3 or more.)

given in Fig. 1; to execute these he need not count, but merely observe the situation, read, act, and remember to which row he is going. Whatever condition in the brain of the attendant determines which row he is scanning we call the *state* of the attendant. To avoid confusion about timing, we establish a unit of time ($\frac{1}{2}$ sec) and require that the attendant execute one instruction every time unit.

Stimulus of electrical automaton in volts on a pair of lines	Stimulus of original automaton
00	Nothing is happening
01	A nickel is deposited
10	A car passes

(a)

State of electrical automaton in volts on a pair of lines	State of original automaton in row numbers from Figure 1
00	0
01	1
10	2
11	3

(b)

Response of electrical automaton in volts on a pair of lines	Response of original automaton
00	Post stop.
01	Post go.
10	Sound alarm.

(c)

FIG. 2. Let each of the electrical stimuli in (a) correspond to the original stimulus next to it, and similarly for the states in (b) and the responses in (c).

The reader may suspect that we have just turned the attendant into an automaton: that is correct; indeed, we define an automaton as any agent that has some stimuli, some states, some responses, and an operation (like that programmed in Fig. 1) that transforms each state-stimulus pair into a next response and a next state. If this operation transforms the state-stimulus pair (x_1, u) into the next response-next state pair (y, x_2), we call y the *response to u given x_1*, and we call x_2 the *successor of x_1 under u*. Sometimes the description of an automaton requires that we specify, in addition, an initial state (like row 0 in Fig. 1).

We next replace the human automaton just described with an electrical automaton. In an electrical device, it is convenient to let each stimulus, response, or state be a row of voltages on a bundle of lines, each line carrying one of two possible voltages. Figures 2 and 3 show a translation of the original description into such electrical terms. To simulate the human operation described in Fig. 1, we need an electrical device that (1) transforms each pattern of state and stimulus voltages into a pattern of next response and next state voltages, and (2) carries forward the latter patterns for use one time unit later. Such a device is shown schematically in Fig. 4. A discussion of possible contents for the boxes in Fig. 4 can be found in any text on logical design.

Although reluctant to introduce any abstraction, we must give a name to and a definition for the kind of relation that exists, via Fig. 2 and 3, between the electrical automaton and the human one. A *homomorphism* from an automaton A to an automaton A' is an operation h that transforms each stimulus, state, response, and operation of A into a stimulus, state, response, or operation (respectively) of A' so that, for each stimulus and state of A, the next state

		Stimulus		
		00	01	10
State	00	00, go to 00	00, go to 00	10, go to 00
	01	00, go to 01	00, go to 10	10, go to 00
	10	00, go to 10	01, go to 11	10, go to 00
	11	01, go to 11	01, go to 11	00, go to 00
		next response, next state		

FIG. 3. Under the correspondence shown in Fig. 2, this operation will correspond to the operation shown in Fig. 1.

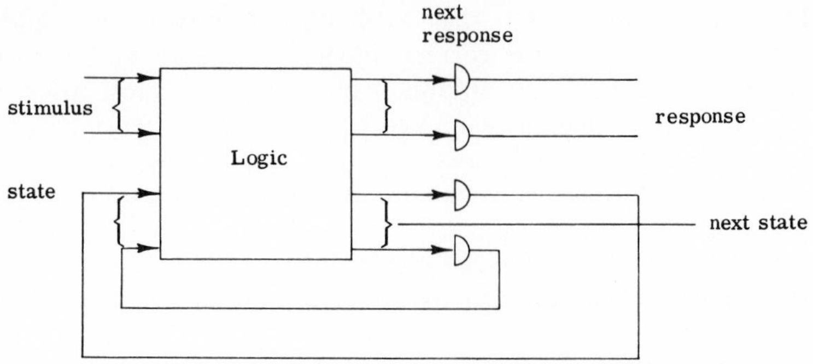

FIG. 4. The box marked "Logic" instantaneously produces next-response and next-state voltages in response to present state and present stimulus voltages as required by Fig. 3. Each half-round box is a delayor that guarantees that *one time unit hence* the state or the response voltage pair is the one called (at present) *next* state or *next* response.

and next response of A' got by applying first h and then the operation of A' are the same as those got by applying first the operation of A and then h. Pictorial versions of this verbal definition are shown in Figs. 5 and 6. (The reader is hereby challenged to find a simpler definition that still captures the right intuitive notion.) The homomorphism from the electrical automaton to the human one described in Figs. 2 and 3 can be inverted to give a homomorphism from the human automaton to the electrical one; any homomorphism with this special property is called an isomorphism.

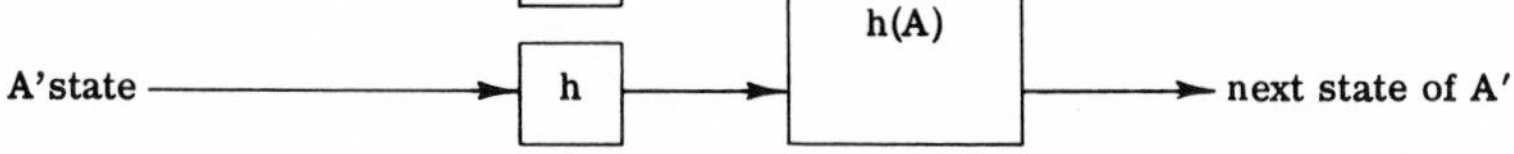

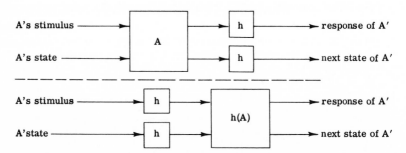

FIG. 5. The box marked A denotes the operation of an automaton A; the box marked $h(A)$ denotes the operation of an automaton A'. The boxes marked h denote an operation that transforms each stimulus, state, response, or operation of A into a stimulus, state, response, or operation of A'. h is a homomorphism if and only if the two operations separated by the dotted line are equal.

Symbol	Denotes
A→B	an operation that transforms each element of the set A into some element of the set B
A→B→C	the operation got by first applying A→B, then B→C.
A × B	the set of all rows (a, b) for which the first coordinate a belongs to the set A and the second coordinate b belongs to the set B.
A × B ↓ ↓ C × D	the operation that transforms each element of A × B into the element of C × D got by using A→C on first coordinates and B→D on second coordinates.

(a)

$$\begin{array}{ccccccc} X & \times & U & \rightarrow & Y & \times & X \\ \downarrow & & \downarrow & & \downarrow & & \downarrow \\ X' & \times & U' & \rightarrow & Y' & \times & X' \end{array}$$

Symbol	Denotes
X	the set of states of automaton A
U	the set of stimuli of A
Y	the set of responses of A
X × U→Y × X	the operation of A
and similarly for automaton A′	

(b)

FIG. 6. The notation given in (a) will be used from now on. The (vertical) transformations from unprimed sets to primed sets in diagram (b) constitute a homomorphism from A to A' if and only if the diagram (b) commutes, i.e.,

$$\begin{array}{ccc} X \times U \rightarrow & Y \times X & \\ & \downarrow \quad \downarrow & \\ & Y' \times X' & \end{array} = \begin{array}{c} X \times U \\ \downarrow \quad \downarrow \\ X' \times U' \rightarrow Y' \times X' \end{array}$$

In what follows, operations will be composed (apply f, and then apply g) much more often than they are evaluated (take the image of x under f); seldom will two operations defined on the same set take values in the same set. Consequently, we can reduce the burden on the reader's memory by denoting an operation defined on A and taking values in B by $A \rightarrow B$.

Later we shall have to consider noninvertible homomorphisms in which several states of A correspond to one state of A'. This is because every design problem starts with an automaton A' and ends with an automaton A having certain desired properties (like binary electrical internal variables) and a homomorphism h from A *onto* A'. (Here "onto" means that every stimulus, state, response, and operation of A' is the image under h of some stimulus, state, response or operation of A.) Often the desired features are not possessed by *any* A that is *iso*morphic to A' but are possessed by some *larger* A from which there is a (noninvertible) homomorphism onto A'.

2. Independence of Coordinates

In this section, we pursue further the search for an automaton A isomorphic to a given automaton A' and having certain desired properties: this time the independence of some state coordinates from other state coordinates. An illustration of what we mean by independence of state coordinates is given in Figs. 7–9 and a detailed definition for it in Figs. 10 and 11.

		Stimulus		
		00	01	10
State	000	00 ; 000	00 ; 100	10 ; 000
	100	00 ; 100	00 ; 110	10 ; 000
	110	00 ; 110	01 ; 111	10 ; 000
	111	01 ; 111	01 ; 111	00 ; 000
		next response, next state		

FIG. 7. Here is still another automaton isomorphic to that described in Sect. 1. Note that the first coordinate of the next state is determined by the stimulus and the first coordinate of the present state; the second coordinate of the next state is determined by the stimulus and the first two coordinates of the present state, and, trivially, the third coordinate of the next state is determined by the stimulus and the first three coordinates of the present state.

In Fig. 12, we see that a dependence relation among coordinates of A is reflected in a relation between partitions on the state set of A'. The best-understood decomposition techniques use this correspondence in reverse; we first seek appropriate partitions on the state set of A', and then try to construct from them the coordinates for each state of A. For a more detailed discussion of this technique,

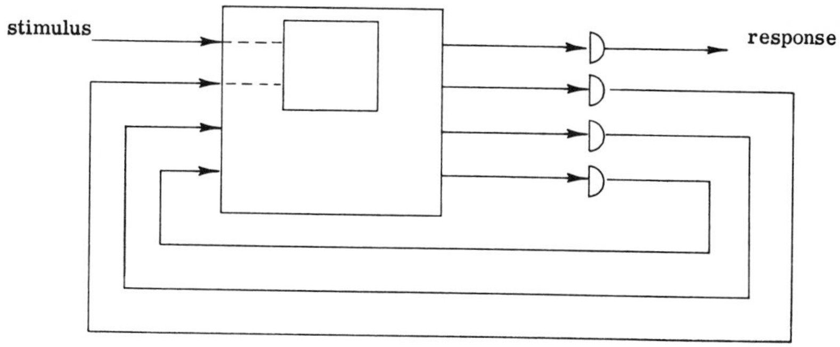

(a)

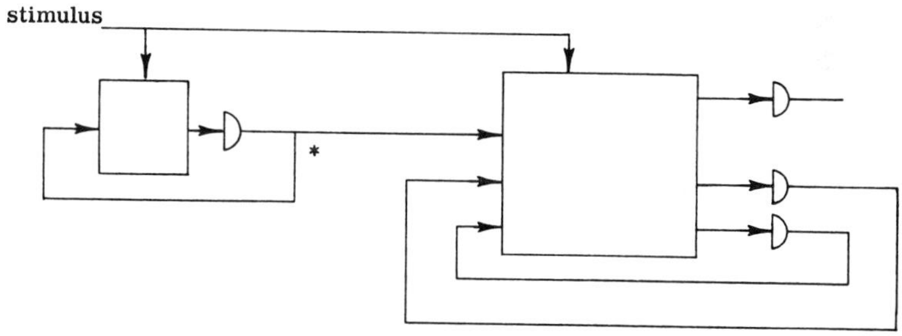

(b)

FIG. 8. Since the first coordinate of the next state is determined by the stimulus and the first coordinate of the present state, the first coordinate can be produced by the small inner box shown in (a). This box can then be pulled outside as shown in (b). The line marked with an asterisk is needed because other next-state coordinates may depend on the first coordinate of the present state.

see Hartmanis and Stearns [1]. We shall use this technique to seek an automaton A having a special kind of coordinate independence: the cascade form illustrated in Figs. 7–9. In this case, Fig. 13 demonstrates that the thing to look for is a *nested sequence of preserved partitions*. (The definitions are in Fig. 13.) For example, to find the cascade form given in Fig. 7 for the human automaton described in Fig. 1, the first preserved partition of the state set is $\{\{0\}, \{1, 2, 3\}\}$, and the second is $\{\{0\}, \{1\}, \{2, 3\}\}$.

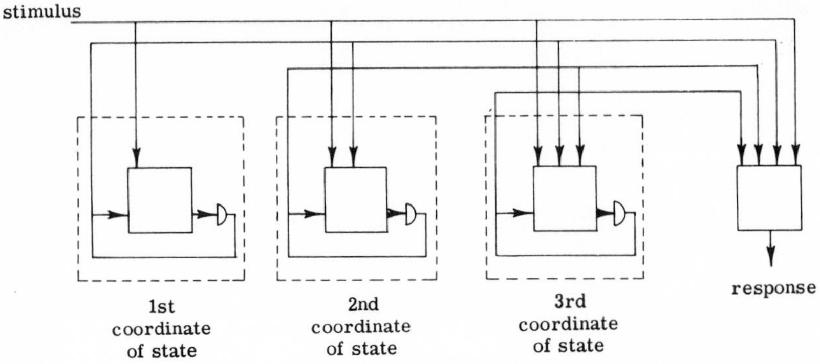

FIG. 9. Continuing the reasoning of Fig. 8, we get this form for the automaton of Fig. 7. Each part enclosed in dotted lines is itself an automaton, called a *component*. Each stimulus for a component is composed of an external stimulus, together with the states of all previous components; each next response of a component is its next state. This is what we mean by *cascade form.*

n	f(n)
1	5
2	2
3	4
4	2
5	5
6	2

FIG. 10. Henceforth, $\{a, b, c\}$ denotes the set having a, b, and c as elements. The *partition*, $\{\{1, 5\}, \{2, 4, 6\}, \{3\}\}$, of the operation f given above is the set of all inverse images under f of sets containing one element; the inverse image under f of a set B is the set of all x for which $f(x)$ is in B.

We are thus led to the following problems: (1) find a nested sequence of preserved partitions; and (2) construct a cascade automaton A whose coordinate projections correspond to these partitions as shown in Fig. 13. We shall postpone consideration of the first of these problems and devote Section 3 to the second.

3. Assignment of Coordinates

Suppose we are given an automaton A' and a nested sequence of preserved partitions; we wish to construct an automaton A, with a

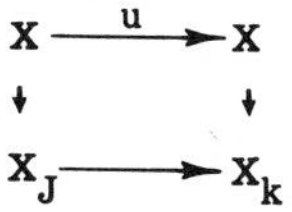

Symbol	Denotes
u	any stimulus of an automaton A
X	the set of all states of A
$X \xrightarrow{u} X$	the operation that transforms each state into its successor under stimulus u
$X \longrightarrow X_k$	the projection that transforms each state into its k-th coordinate
$X \longrightarrow X_J$	the projection that transforms each state into the row of those coordinates specified by the row J of integer indices

FIG. 11. The kth coordinate of the next state of A is determined by those coordinates indexed by the set J of the present state, which means that for each stimulus u there exists an operation $X_J \dashrightarrow X_k$ for which the diagram commutes (i.e., $X \to X_J \dashrightarrow X_k = X \xrightarrow{u} X \to X_k$). Thus, for each u, the image under u of any block of the partition (see Fig. 10) of $X \to X_J$ is a subset of some block of the partition of $X \to X_k$.

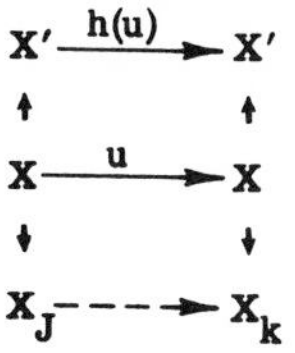

Symbol	Denotes
$X' \xrightarrow{h(u)} X'$	the operation that transforms each state (of A′) into its successor under stimulus h(u). (h is a homomorphism from A to A′.)
$X \longrightarrow X'$	the operation that takes each state of A into its image under h in A′.
others	see Figure 11

FIG. 12. If h is an isomorphism, then we can invert it. Then, as in Fig. 11, the image under any $h(u)$ of any block of the partition of $X' \to X \to X_J$ is a subset of some block of the partition of $X' \to X \to X_k$. Thus, *we can seek an A, isomorphic to A', having independence of some coordinates from other by seeking pairs of partitions of X' for which the image under any state transformation $X' \xrightarrow{h(u)} X'$ of any block of the first partition is a subset of some block of the second partition.*

homomorphism onto A', so that the projections $X \to X_1{}^k$ correspond to the given partitions. We temporarily restrict our attention to the case where there is just one partition, and therefore two components of A. Note first that there is no trouble with the stimuli and responses of A; we just let them equal the stimuli and responses of A' and let the homomorphism be the identity transformation on them. With the states, however, we face problems: (1) it is easy to set up $X \to X_1$ to fit the first partition, but how do we choose an $X \to X_2$ so that

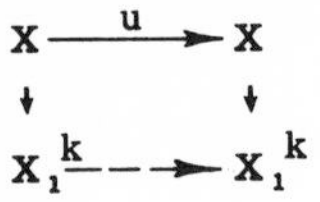

Symbol	
$X \longrightarrow X_1^k$	the projection that transforms each state of A into its first k coordinates
others	See Figure 11

FIG. 13. The first k state coordinates move independently of the remaining coordinates if and only if the image under $X \xrightarrow{u} X$ of any block of the partition of $X \to X_1^k$ is a subset of some block of the same partition. In this case, we say that the partition of $X \to X_1^k$ is *preserved* by the state transformation $X \xrightarrow{u} X$. An automaton is in *cascade form* if for each k and for each u the partition of $X \to X_1^k$ is preserved by $X \xrightarrow{u} X$. Incidentally, for each k the partition of $X \to X_1^{k+1}$ is finer than that of $X \to X_1^k$. Thus, as in Fig. 12, *we can seek an A, isomorphic to A', that is in cascade form by seeking a nested sequence of preserved partitions of the state set of A'.*

$X \to X_1^2$ has the desired partition? (usually there are many possible choices); and (2) if the partition blocks are of unequal size, the operation of A will be incompletely specified; how do we fill in the "don't care" conditions? These problems are illustrated in Fig. 14.

We need some definitions. If U is the set of stimuli of an automaton, let U^* denote the set of all (finite) sequences of stimuli. Note that U^* has an associative operation $U^* \times U^* \to U^*$ got by following one sequence with another to build a larger sequence. If A is an automaton, X its state set, and U its set of stimuli, a *state transformation* of A is an operation $X \xrightarrow{v} X$ (where v is in U^*) that transforms each state s into the state that results when A' is started in state s and fed the sequence v. If B is a subset of X mapped into itself by $X \xrightarrow{v} X$, then we denote this transformation of B by $B \xrightarrow{v} B$.

Returning to our two problems, we note that, if B is a subset of the state set of A made up of all states having a given, fixed, first coordinate, then the homomorphic image, B', of B is a block of the preserved partition. If $X' \xrightarrow{v} X'$ maps B' into itself, then $X \xrightarrow{v} X$ must leave the corresponding first coordinate fixed, and so *the action of $X \xrightarrow{v} X$ on second coordinates must be at least as complicated as $B' \xrightarrow{v} B'$*. Thus, it would seem rather optimistic to pick a block of the preserved partition and ask that each state transformation of the second component be isomorphic to some transformation, $B' \xrightarrow{v} B'$, of that block in the original machine; for the rest of this section, we consider when and how this ideal can be reached.

In the situation illustrated in Fig. 14, it is clear that the second component of A is going to require one state transformation corre-

stimulus

	1	2
1	2	3
2	4	4
3	5	1
4	5	6
5	6	1
6	2	4

next state

(a)

state of A′	first coordinate of A	second coordinate of A
1	0	1
3	0	3
4	0	4
6	0	6
2	1	x
5	1	y

(b)

		stimulus 1	stimulus 2
state	01	1x	03
	03	1y	01
	04	1y	06
	06	1x	04
	11	0	0
	13	0	0
	14	0	0
	16	0	0

(c)

		state of 1st component, stimulus			
		0, 1	0, 2	1, 1	1, 2
state of 2nd component	1	x	3		
	3	y	1		
	4	y	6		
	6	x	4		
		next state of second component			

(d)

FIG. 14. The operation of A' is given in (a); the next response entries, irrelevant to the problem, have been omitted. We want a two-component cascade automaton A with a homomorphism onto A' and a first coordinate projection that corresponds to the partition $\{\{1, 3, 4, 6\}, \{2, 5\}\}$. The innocent part of the assignment of coordinate projections has been done in (b); it is clear that it does not matter what values we use for the binary assignment of first coordinates nor does it matter which four values we use for the second coordinate assignment within *one* block; that leaves the x and y entries, which we must choose from the set $\{1, 3, 4, 6\}$. On the basis of (b), we can fill out a partial table for the operation of A as shown in (c). How we complete this table determines the operation of the second component shown, in part, in (d).

sponding to each state transformation of A' which transforms the set $\{1, 3, 4, 6\}$ into itself. In Fig. 15, we arranged things so that *no more* state transformations were required by the second component. A criterion for when and how we can do this is given by the lemma below.

We adopt the following notation:

A' = an automaton

X' = its set of states

U = its set of stimuli

U^* = the set of all sequences of stimuli

P = a partition of X' preserved (see Sect. 2) by each stimulus

D = a subset of X'

B = a block of P (B may have subscripts)

$D \xrightarrow{v} B$ = the operation that takes each state s in D into the state that results when A' is started in state s and fed the sequence v.

retract = B_i is a retract of D if there exist two sequences, w_i and v_i, in U^* for which $B_i \xrightarrow{w_i} D \xrightarrow{v_i} B_i$ equals the identity transformation of B_i

Retract Lemma. If there exists a D for which each block of P is a retract of D, then there exists a homomorphism onto A' from a two-stage cascade automaton A whose action on first coordinates matches the action of A' on P and whose second-component state transformations match the action on D of those state transformations of A' which transform D into itself.

PROOF. Let the stimulus set of A be U and the state set of A be $P \times D$. Let h be the identity operation on U together with the operation $P \times D \to X'$ that takes each pair (B_k, s) into the image of s under $D \xrightarrow{v_k} B_k$. Now we must complete, for each u, the diagram

$$\begin{array}{ccc} P \times D & \dashrightarrow & P \times D \\ \downarrow & & \downarrow \\ X' & \xrightarrow{\quad u \quad} & X' \end{array}$$

so that it commutes.

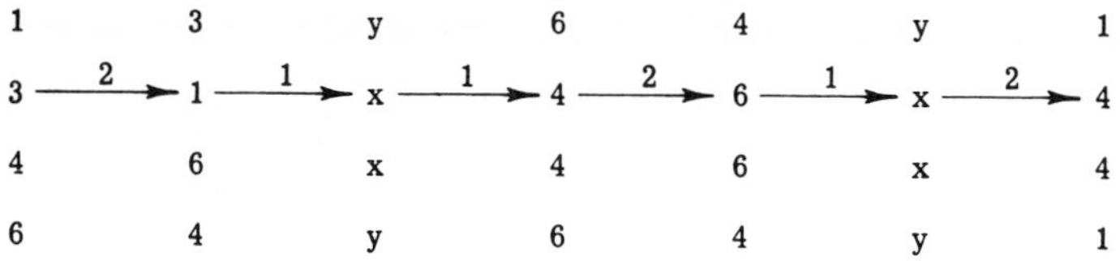

(a)

		state of 1st component, stimulus			
		0, 1	0, 2	1, 1	1, 2
state	1	4	3	(6)	(1)
of	3	6	1	(4)	(4)
2nd	4	6	6	4	4
component	6	4	4	6	1
		next state of second component			

(b)

FIG. 15. Shown in (a) are some of the state transformations of the second component produced by sequences of inputs. These transformations are generated regardless of what values we give x and y; no *new* transformations will be generated if we set $x = 4$, $y = 6$. The resulting operation for the second component is shown in (b).

First coordinates are no problem; we just let the action of $P \times D \to P \times D$ on first coordinates match that of $X' \xrightarrow{u} X'$ upon P. Then we consider the action on second coordinates (one first-coordinate block B_j at a time) via the restricted diagram:

$$\begin{array}{ccc} \{B_j\} \times D & \dashrightarrow & \{B_k\} \times D \\ \downarrow & & \downarrow \\ B_j & \xrightarrow{\quad u \quad} & B_k \end{array}$$

Here $X' \xrightarrow{u} X'$ maps B_j into B_k. By definition of the operation $P \times D \to X'$, when we further restrict this diagram to second coordinates, we get

$$\begin{array}{ccc} D & \dashrightarrow & D \\ {\scriptstyle v_j}\downarrow & & \downarrow{\scriptstyle v_k} \\ B_j & \xrightarrow{\quad u \quad} & B_k \end{array}$$

which we must complete so that it commutes, using only a state transformation of A' which transforms D into itself. We see immediately that $D \xrightarrow{v_j} B_j \xrightarrow{u} B_k \xrightarrow{w_k} D$ does the job.

If each block of P is finite, we can improve the lemma by requiring only that $B \xrightarrow{w} D \xrightarrow{v} B$ be a permutation, rather than an identity, for there will then be an integer n for which $(B \xrightarrow{w} D \xrightarrow{v} B)^n$ is an identity. We can meet the hypotheses of the lemma with a new $B \xrightarrow{w'} D = (B \xrightarrow{w} D \xrightarrow{v} B)^{n-1} (B \xrightarrow{w} D)$. ▮

The reader may have noticed that in this section the responses of the automata were irrelevant to the assignment of coordinates; also irrelevant was the distinction between a stimulus and a sequence of stimuli. In this context, it is convenient to replace an automaton A with a *transformation automaton* $\mathbf{A}$ that is just like A except that (1) the next response of $\mathbf{A}$ to stimulus u given state s is the successor of s under u (i.e., next response $=$ next state), and (2) the stimuli of $\mathbf{A}$ are all *sequences* of stimuli of A. (The appropriate extension of the operation of A to handle the new stimuli is obvious.) The advantage of transformation automata is that the operation that transforms each element of U^* into itself, each state of $\mathbf{A}$ into the block P that contains it, and the operation of $\mathbf{A}$ into the operation $P \times U^* \to P$ that completes the commutative diagram

$$\begin{array}{ccc} P \times U^* & \longrightarrow & X \\ \downarrow \quad \downarrow & & \downarrow \\ P \times U^* & \longrightarrow & X \end{array}$$

is a homomorphism. We shall call the image of $\mathbf{A}$ under this homomorphism the *quotient automaton* $\mathbf{A}/P$ (read "$\mathbf{A}$ mod P").

Now consider an automaton A' and a nested sequence of preserved partitions $P_1, P_2, \ldots, P_k$. To produce (if we can) a cascade automaton A with homomorphism onto A', we do the following:

(1) Pass to the transformation automaton $\mathbf{A}'$.

(2) Construct the *last* component $\mathbf{A}_k$ by applying (if possible) the retract lemma to $\mathbf{A}'$ and P_k.

(3) $\mathbf{A}_k$ is now preceded by $\mathbf{A}'/P_k$; again apply (if possible) the retract lemma to $\mathbf{A}'/P_k$ and P_{k-1} to get the *next-to-last* component $\mathbf{A}_{k-1}$.

(4) Continue until you reach the first component $\mathbf{A}_0 = A'/P_1$.

(5) Pass from the resulting cascade transformation automaton back to the original form by restricting stimuli and adjoining response logic. To describe more succinctly the components that arise in this construction, we assign to each transformation automaton **A** and subset D of the state set of **A** the *subautomaton* $\mathbf{A}_D$ whose state set is D, whose stimuli are those of **A** which transform D into itself, and whose operation is the obvious restriction of that of **A**. Let P_i/P_{i+1} be the partition of the blocks of P_{i+1} induced by P_i. Then, if D_i is the subset of P_{i+1} of which each block of P_i/P_{i+1} is a retract, then the component $\mathbf{A}_i$ is $(\mathbf{A}'/P_{i+1})_{D_i}$. Notice that we can now find any $\mathbf{A}_i$ independently of all the other components.

So far, if given an automaton A' and a nested sequence $P_1, \ldots, P_k$ of preserved partitions, we can construct, in any order, the components of a cascade automaton that has a homomorphism onto A', provided each partition P_i/P_{i+1} for each quotient automaton $\mathbf{A}'/P_{i+1}$ satisfies the hypotheses of the retract lemma. Our position is unenviable

(a)

state	next state, stimulus 1	next state, stimulus 2
1	3	2
2	2	1
3	1	4
4	2	5
5	3	4

(b)

inverse images, stimulus 1	inverse images, stimulus 2	state sets
3	2	1
24	1	2
15	-	3
-	35	4
-	4	5
15	-	3
24	135	24
3	24	15
3	2	1
24	1	2
15	4	35
-	35	4
135	24	135
24	135	24

FIG. 16. The partitions of the state transformations of the automaton in (a) are computed by the backward table (b). Intersecting partitions generated from {{1, 3, 5}{2, 4}} gives the preserved partition {{1, 3, 5}{2, 4}}; intersecting partitions generated from {{1, 5}, {2, 4}, {3}} gives the preserved partition {{1, 5}, {2, 4}, {3}}.

because, given only A', it is usually difficult or impossible to find *any* preserved partitions, much less a nested sequence satisfying the appropriate hypotheses. In the next section, we shall remedy this situation by dropping the requirement that A be strictly isomorphic to A'; we close this section with a method that is occasionally helpful in finding preserved partitions; for more exhaustive procedures, refer to the text by Hartmanis and Stearns [1].

Consider a transformation machine **A** with state set X and stimulus set U^*. Start with the partition of any state transformation $X \xrightarrow{v} X$ (see Fig. 11); generate the set of all partitions of transformations $X \xrightarrow{w} X \xrightarrow{v} X$, where $X \xrightarrow{v} X$ is fixed and w ranges over all of U^*; intersect all these partitions. The resulting partition is preserved, for, if a block B of states is collapsed to a singleton by $X \xrightarrow{w} X \xrightarrow{v} X$ for all w, so is the image of B under $X \xrightarrow{u} X$ for each u in U^*. (If not, there would be trouble with $X \xrightarrow{u} X \xrightarrow{w} X \xrightarrow{v} X$.) An example is given in Fig. 16. Liu [2] has shown that, if an automaton can be built as a cascade of unit delays, partitions of this type will provide the construction. In other cases, the method usually produces the (useless) partition of X into singletons.

4. Covers

For the next two sections, we shall consider only transformation automata (this incurs no loss in generality); nevertheless, we shall, as a reminder, retain the asterisk on U, the set of input sequences, and depict in operation tables only the generating set of stimuli for U^*. We wish to extend our capabilities for finding a cascade automaton, with a homomorphism onto a given automaton, to cover the situation shown in Fig. 17. The example and the definitions given there suggest that we extend our existing procedures to preserved *covers* instead of preserved partitions. We observe with delight that the retract lemma carries over without change to the more general situation; we observe with alarm that, although each state transformation induces a unique transformation of the blocks of a preserved partition, the same is *not* necessarily true for a preserved cover (see Fig. 18). The following lemma provides a modicum of protection against this possibility.

Uniqueness Lemma. If G is a group of permutations of a set X and C is a cover of X preserved by G and no block of C is a

	0	1
0X	0Y	1X
0Y	0Z	1Z
0Z	0Y	1Z
1X	0Z	1Z
1Y	0Z	1X
1Z	0X	1Y

A

0X	A
0Y	B
0Z	D
1X	B
1Y	C
1Z	E

X→X′

	0	1
A	B	B
B	D	E
C	D	B
D	B	E
E	A	C

A′

FIG. 17. The homomorphism that operates on states by the $X \to X'$ shown transforms the cascade automaton A onto the automaton A'. If, as in Sect. 3, we pull the partition of the first coordinate map $X \to X_1$ through the homomorphism, we get, not a partition, but the overlapping collection of blocks $C = \{\{A, B, C\}, \{B, C, E\}\}$. Observe that (1) since $X \to X'$ is onto, each state in X' is an element of some block of C, and (2) since

$$\begin{array}{ccc} X' & \xrightarrow{u} & X' \\ \uparrow & & \uparrow \\ X & \xrightarrow{u} & X \\ \downarrow & & \downarrow \\ X_1 & \xrightarrow{u} & X_1 \end{array}$$

commutes (recall Fig. 12), the image under any state transformation of any block of C is a subset of some block of C. Any collection of blocks of states satisfying point 1 will be called a *cover*. Any cover that also satisfies point 2 will be called a *preserved cover* (like the preserved partitions in Fig. 13).

1	5
2	4
3	3
4	3
5	2

(a)

{1, 2, 3}	{3, 4, 5}
{2, 3, 4}	{3, 4, 5}
{3, 4, 5}	{1, 2, 3}

(b)

{1, 2, 3}	{3, 4, 5}
{2, 3, 4}	{2, 3, 4}
{3, 4, 5}	{2, 3, 4}

(c)

FIG. 18. If C is a preserved cover on a state set X, we say the transformation $C \to C$ *corresponds to* the state transformation $X \to X$ if $C \to C$ transforms each block B of C into a block that includes the image of B under $X \to X$. *Both* the block transformations (b) and (c) correspond to the state transformation (a). In diagrams, we write $C \to C \sim X \to X$ for $C \to C$ corresponds to $X \to X$.

proper subset of any other block of C, then, for each g in G, just one transformation g' of C corresponds to g, and g' is also a permutation.

PROOF. It suffices to show that, for each B in C, $g(B)$ is actually an element of C, not merely a subset of one. Suppose not, i.e., $g(B)$ is a proper subset of B'; then $B = g^{-1}g(B)$ is a proper subset of $g^{-1}(B')$. But, since C is preserved, $g^{-1}(B')$ is a subset of some B'', and so B is a proper subset of B'', in contradiction to our final hypothesis. The reader can adapt the same reasoning to show g' is a permutation. ▌

Although preserved partitions frustrate the investigator by their scarcity, preserved covers embarrass him by their profusion. In fact, any collection C of blocks can be converted to a preserved cover by appending to it the images under all state transformations of all of its blocks plus singletons of any states not yet covered, and then discarding those blocks that are subsets of other blocks. Our program is to find among the preserved covers something analogous to a nested sequence of preserved partitions, and from it produce a cascade automaton having components that are as simple as possible. One type of component to aim for is suggested by Fig. 17; there each state transformation of the first component takes all its states, 0 and 1, into one state, 0 or 1. Such a state transformation will be called a *reset.* Although components having only reset state transformations are not sufficient to build (under cascade connection) even counters, components (henceforth called permutation-reset components) having only permutations and resets for state transformations are sufficient to build *any* finite-state automaton. We shall devote the rest of the section to proving this fact.

As with partitions, we call cover C_1 *coarser* than a cover C_2 (and C_2 finer than C_1) if each block of C_2 is a subset of some block of C_1; if, in addition, C_2 is *not* coarser than C_1, we call C_1 *properly coarser* than C_2. Here is the concept analogous to a quotient automaton: if A is a transformation automaton, C is a preserved cover for it, and A^0 is a transformation automaton having the same stimuli as A; we say *A^0 tells where A is in C* if there is an operation $X^0 \to C$ from the state set of A^0 onto C for which, for each stimulus v,

$$\begin{array}{ccc} X^0 & \xrightarrow{\quad v \quad} & X^0 \\ \downarrow & & \downarrow \\ C & \dashrightarrow & C \end{array}$$

can be completed so it commutes by a $C \dashrightarrow C$ that corresponds to the state transformation $X \xrightarrow{v} X$ of A—in diagrammatic summary

$$\begin{array}{ccc} X^0 & \xrightarrow{\quad v \quad} & X^0 \\ \downarrow & & \downarrow \\ C & \dashrightarrow & C \\ & \wr & \\ X & \xrightarrow{\quad v \quad} & X \end{array}$$

Once again the reader is challenged to find a simpler definition that does the job.

Having thus completed the preliminaries, we now assault:

The Main Theorem: For each finite-state automaton A', there is a homomorphism onto A' from a cascade automaton A having only permutation-reset components; furthermore, for each component the permutation group got by discarding the resets is a homomorphic image of a subgroup of the semigroup of state transformations of A'.

PROOF. (The assertion preceding the semicolon is much easier to prove; the reader should be able to supply a proof using the sequence of covers $C_k =$ the set of all subsets of X containing k fewer states than X; or see Lemma 7.5 on p. 199 of the text by Hartmanis and Stearns [1]. To get the hard half of the theorem, we have to get into a position where we can use the retract lemma to control the permutation groups; this seems to require that we pick covers in the somewhat intricate way described below.) Although we surely must proceed by induction, all the obvious induction steps run into technical difficulty, and we are forced to adopt a curiously indirect induction step: we show that, for each automaton A' with preserved cover C_1 and automaton A_1 that tells where A is in C_1, we can follow A_1 with a permutation-reset automaton A_2, whose group is a homomorphic image of a subgroup of the semigroup of state transformations of A', to form a two-stage cascade automaton A that tells where A' is in some preserved cover C_2 properly finer than C_1 (provided C_1 does not already consist entirely of singletons). Our program will be, first, to construct a C_2 only very slightly finer than C_1, second, to specify the state set of A_2 and an operation $X \rightarrow C_2$ by which A is to tell where A is in C_2, and, third, to specify the operation of A_2, using only permutation and reset state transformations, so that A does tell where A is in C_2.

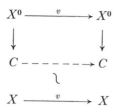

We construct C_2 by discarding blocks from C_1. To find which blocks to discard, we order the subsets of X' by the following: B_1 *precedes* B_2 means B_2 is the image of B_1 under some state transformation of A'. We call B_1 and B_2 *similar* if each precedes the other; we call B_1 *initial in* C_1 if every block of C_1 which precedes B_1 is similar to it and no block of C_1 contains more elements than B_1. Now construct C_2 from C_1 by replacing each block B in an initial similarity class with the cover on B got by

(1) taking every proper subset of B which is a singleton or an image of a block of C_1, and

(2) discarding blocks that are subsets of other blocks that are subsets of B.

Note that all discarded blocks of C_1 are retracts of each other; also, each block of C_2 which is not a block of C_1 is a proper subset of a discarded block; if a block A of C_2 is a subset of a discarded block P of C_1 and R is any other discarded block, then there is a block B of C_2 which is a subset of R for which the transformations that make P and R retracts of each other make A and B retracts of each other.

Next select one of the discarded blocks, B_1, and let C be the set of blocks with which B_1 was replaced; this C is to be the state set of A_2; then X is $C_1 \times C$. As in the retract lemma, for each discarded block B_i, select state transformations $B_1 \xrightarrow{v_i} B_i$ and $B_i \xrightarrow{w_i} B_1$ for which $B_i \xrightarrow{w_i} B_1 \xrightarrow{v_i} B_i$ is an identity; let A tell where A' is in C_2 by the operation $C_1 \times C \to C_2$ that takes each (B_i, E) in $C_1 \times C$ (1) into B_i if B_i is in C_2, or (2) into the image of E under $X \xrightarrow{v_i} X$ otherwise. Note (with the help of remarks made one paragraph ago) that $C_1 \times C \to C_2$ is *onto*.

The stimulus set of A_2 is $C_1 \times U^*$ (where U^* is the stimulus set of A'); to each stimulus (B_j, u) in this set we must assign either a permutation or a reset state transformation. Let B_k be the successor of B_j under u in machine A_1, and F be the successor of E under (B_j, u) in machine A_2.

CASE 1. B_j and B_k are each discarded blocks; then the retract lemma gives a unique completion for

$$\begin{array}{ccc} B_1 & \dashrightarrow & B_1 \\ {\scriptstyle v_j}\downarrow & & \downarrow{\scriptstyle v_k} \\ B_j & \xrightarrow{\quad u \quad} & B_k \end{array}$$

To this completion corresponds, by the uniqueness lemma, a unique permutation of C or a reset. This state transformation of A_2 lets A tell where A' is in C_2.

CASE 2. B_j is in C_2, and B_k is a discarded block; let F contain the image of B_j under $X' \xrightarrow{u} X' \xrightarrow{w_k} X'$. This reset of A_2 lets A tell where A' is in C_2.

CASE 3. B_k is in C_2; let F be E. Since B_k alone tells where A' is in C_2, the assignment of F does not matter.

This completes the proof of the induction step; starting the induction on the trivial cover $\{X'\}$ gives a sequence of covers and a sequence of permutation-reset machines which continues until the cover consisting entirely of singletons is reached; we have built A' as a cascade of permutation-reset machines. Reviewing Case 1 and the retract and uniqueness lemmas, we see that each permutation group that arises is a homomorphic image of the group of all permutations of some state subset D produced by elements of U^*. This completes the proof of the main theorem. ∎

The construction given here is inefficient in that the cascade of components is very long. The reader who wishes to improve the efficiency should rework the induction step, replacing the requirement that all nonreset state transformations of A_2 be uniquely determined. (Hint: instead of throwing out all blocks similar to an initial D when going C_1 to C_2, try throwing out all retracts of D.) The resulting construction permits more rapid completion of a cascade whose first few components are given; the resulting components, no longer permutation reset, are still free of all unnecessary subgroups.

5. Permutation Automata

Having built any automaton as a cascade of permutation-reset components, we next investigate the possibility of building each permutation-reset automaton as a cascade of simpler components. Our plan is to study, first, cascade decomposition of permutation automata, and to show, second, that the results got can easily be carried over to permutation-reset automata. We shall use without further comment the terms group, normal subgroup, coset, factor group, and group homomorphism (see, for example, Hall [3]).

If A' is a permutation automaton whose state transformations generate the group G, and if G has a normal subgroup H with factor group G/H, then there is a homomorphism onto A' from a two-stage cascade automaton A for which the state transformations of A_1, the first component, generate G/H, and the state transformations of A_2, the second component, generate H.

PROOF. To prove this, we shall give A_2 the same state set as A', but allow A_2 only state transformations from H; whenever A_2 is unable to imitate A', because of a state transformation outside H, A_1 will come to the rescue by storing, as its state, a permutation from G which transforms the "mistaken" state of A_2 into the correct state of A'. A_1 will need as states a set of representatives of the cosets in G/H; the state transformations of A_1 will generate G/H.

Let A_1, the first component of A, have, for its stimulus set U^*, the stimulus set of A', and for its state set, a set X_1 of representatives in a left coset decomposition of G by H, and for its operation, $X_1 \times U^* \to X_1$, the one that transforms each $(X' \xrightarrow{g} X', u)$ into the representative of the coset containing $X' \xrightarrow{g} X' \xrightarrow{u} X'$. Let A_2, the second component of A, have for its state set the state set X' of A'. Let the homomorphism from A to A' consist of the identity operation on U^* plus the operation $X_1 \times X' \to X'$ that transforms each $(X' \xrightarrow{g} X', s)$ into $g(s)$. Now we must complete, for each u in U^*, the diagram

$$\begin{array}{ccc} X_1 \times X' & \dashrightarrow & X_1 \times X' \\ \downarrow & & \downarrow \\ X' & \xrightarrow{\quad u \quad} & X' \end{array}$$

so that it commutes.

We consider, as in the proof of the retract lemma, the action on second coordinates (one first coordinate g_1 at a time) via the restricted diagram

$$\begin{array}{ccc} \{g_1\} \times X' & \dashrightarrow & \{g_2\} \times X' \\ \downarrow & & \downarrow \\ X' & \xrightarrow{\quad u \quad} & X' \end{array}$$

By definition of $X_1 \times X' \to X'$, when we further restrict the diagram to second coordinates, we get

$$\begin{array}{ccc} X & \dashrightarrow & X' \\ {\scriptstyle g_1}\downarrow & & \downarrow{\scriptstyle g_2} \\ X' & \xrightarrow{\quad u \quad} & X' \end{array}$$

whose completion is $X' \xrightarrow{g_1} X' \xrightarrow{u} X' \xrightarrow{g_2^{-1}} X'$. Since, by definition of the operation of A_1, g_2 represents the coset containing $X' \xrightarrow{g_1} X' \xrightarrow{u} X'$, the foregoing completion is in H. We have thus proved the desired theorem. ▌

For group representations, the preceding construction was invented by Frobenius before 1900; for automata, it was rediscovered by Krohn in 1962.

Observe that the cascade automaton A can be reset to a state corresponding to any state s of A' by (1) leaving the first coordinate alone, and (2) resetting A_2 to the state whose image under the transformation stored in A_1 is s. In particular, if we let H be the group consisting of the identity transformation alone, we see that each permutation-reset automaton can be built as a group automaton followed by an automaton whose only state transformations are resets or the identity transformation. The group automaton can be built, by exhaustive application of the Frobenius construction, out of group automata whose groups have no proper homomorphisms; the identity-reset automaton can be built, by *any* assignments of rows of 0's and 1's to its states, as a parallel connection of two-state identity-reset automata. We thus arrive at a theorem of Rhodes and Krohn:

Each finite-state automaton can be built as a cascade of two-state automata and simple-group automata.

We next show that no smaller set of components will suffice. After observing that any cascade connection of permutation automata is again a permutation automaton, we see that at least one nonpermutation component is needed in the construction of a nonpermutation automaton; it remains to determine which permutation components are needed in the construction of any given automaton. A preliminary definition is needed. If $G = A_0 \supset A_1 \supset A_2 \supset \cdots \supset A_n$ is a chain of groups in which each A_i is a maximal normal subgroup of A_{i-1}, the chain is called a *composition series* for G, and the factor groups A_{i-1}/A_i are called *composition factors* of G. (The Jordan-Hölder theorem assures us that the list of composition factors is the same regardless of which composition series we choose.)

If A is any cascade decomposition of A' and K is any composition factor of the group of a permutation subautomaton of A', then K is a composition factor of the group of a permutation subautomaton of some component of A.

We shall sketch a proof of this important result, numbering each sticky point, and then discuss the numbered points. Let the automaton A' be a homomorphic image of the cascade automaton A; pick any permutation subautomaton B' of A' and find (1) a permutation subautomaton B of A of which B' is a homomorphic image; then observe that B is a cascade, each of whose components is a subautomaton of the corresponding component of A. Let B^- be B with the last component cut off, and consider the resulting homomorphism from the group of B to the group of B^-; observe (2) that the semigroup of the last component of B must include the kernel of this homomorphism as a subgroup. Proceed inductively to get a sequence of groups $B = A_0 \supset A_1 \supset \cdots \supset A_n$ for which the semigroup of the ith component includes A_{i-1}/A_i as a subgroup. By refining this sequence to a composition series, we find that each composition factor of the group of B is a composition factor of a permutation submachine of some component of B. But each component of B is a submachine of the corresponding component of A, and each composition factor of the group of B' is also a composition factor of the group of B (3); thus, each composition factor of the group of B' is also a composition factor of the group of a permutation subautomaton of some component of A, which is what was to be proved. (1) Let C be the inverse image under $A \to A'$ of B'. We seek a permutation subautomaton B of C for which the image under $A \to A'$ of B is still B'. For each state transformation $X \xrightarrow{u} X$ of A, define the *range* of $X \xrightarrow{u} X$ as the image of X under $X \xrightarrow{u} X$, the *partition* of $X \xrightarrow{u} X$ as the set of all inverse images under $X \xrightarrow{u} X$ of singleton subsets of X, and the *rank* of $X \xrightarrow{u} X$ as the number of states in the range (= number of blocks in the partition). Let C' be the subautomaton of C having the same state set as C and having as stimuli all u's for which rank of $X \xrightarrow{u} X$ is minimum. Among the state transformations of C there is one, call it e, that when composed with itself equals itself ($e \cdot e = e$), for, if t is any state transformation of C, and we keep raising t to powers, eventually $t^p = t^{p+k}$, so that, for all positive integers m and for all $r > p$, $t^r = t^{r+mk}$; if we choose $r = mk =$ smallest multiple of k which exceeds p, then $t^r = t^r \cdot t^r$. $A \to A'$ must map e into the identity in the group of B', for no other permutation equals its own square; thus, for each state transformation t of C, $A \to A'$ must map t and $e \cdot t \cdot e$ into the same state transformation of B'; if we let C'' be the subautomaton of C having as stimuli all u's for which $X \xrightarrow{u} X$ is of the form $e \cdot t \cdot e$, then $A \to A'$ still maps C'' onto B'. All state transformations of C'' have the same partition (that of e) and the same range (that of e), and so we can restrict the state set of C'' to this range to get the permutation subautomaton B that $A \to A'$ maps onto B'. (2) Let B be driven by all stimuli u for which $X \xrightarrow{u} X$ is in the kernel of (group of $B \to$ group of B^-). Although the state transformations of B sweep out H, the states of all components but the last remain unchanged; hence, the last component alone must have enough state transformations to sweep out H. (3) Simply run a composition series for G through the kernel of $G \to G'$.

6. Discussion

Some of the topics mentioned here have a long mathematical history: preserved partitions, when the transformations acting are permutations, are the *systems of imprimitivity* studied by Evariste Galois about 1830; the main construction of Sect. 5, in matrix form, has been known since about 1900 as the *Frobenius Monomial Representation*; for a linear dynamical system, coordinates yielding a parallel canonical form are called *normal modes*; they were studied by Camille Jordan about 1880. These normal coordinates are, at present, a source of some embarrassment, since they should arise as a special case in any adequate theory of cascade coordinatization; it is not yet clear how to get them from the theory described here; the trouble appears to be that we need more powerful tools for specific application to *parallel* decomposition.

A related question is that of *efficient* cascade decomposition. Given a cascade form in permutation-reset components, define the *complexity* of the form as the length of the longest string of coordinates for which, for each coordinate in the string, the corresponding component has a nontrivial permutation group whose motions depend on the previous coordinate in the string. Define the complexity of an automaton as the minimum over all cascade forms of the complexity of the form. It is easy to show that the complexity of an automaton depends only on its semigroup. In Chapter 9 complexity is characterized in several apparently distinct ways and the characterizations are shown to be equivalent. What we would like now is an aesthetically pleasing canonical construction that gives a cascade form of minimum complexity for each automaton.

Acknowledgment

I would like to thank Abraham Ginzburg of Carnegie Institute of Technology, and Elihu Shamir and Y. Perry of Hebrew University of Jerusalem, for pointing out errors in the proof of the main construction, and for suggesting various ingenious corrections, some of which have been incorporated here.

REFERENCES

1. J. Hartmanis and R. E. Stearns, "Algebraic Structure Theory of Sequential Machines." Prentice-Hall, Englewood Cliffs, New Jersey, 1966.
2. C. L. Liu, Tech. Rept. 411, Research Lab. of Electronics, MIT, 1963.
3. M. Hall, "The Theory of Groups." Macmillan, New York, 1959.

CHAPTER 5

The Prime Decomposition Theorem of the Algebraic Theory of Machines[†]

KENNETH KROHN
Krohn-Rhodes Research Institute, Washington, D.C.

JOHN L. RHODES[‡]
University of California, Berkeley, California
Krohn-Rhodes Research Institute, Berkeley, California

BRET R. TILSON
University of California, Berkeley, California

In this chapter, we present machine theory from a purely algebraic view point. The only background required is thus the basic semigroup theory of Chapter 1, although some readers may find our definitions more natural after they have read the more machine-oriented accounts of Chapters 2–4.

1. Basic Definitions

1.1 Definition. Let A and B be sets. Then a *machine* is any function $f : \Sigma A \to B$. The *semigroup of the machine* f is $f^S = \Sigma A/\equiv_f$,[§]

[†] This work was sponsored by the United States Air Force, Office of Scientific Research, Grant Numbers AF-AFOSR-848-66 and AF 49(638)-1550; and the Office of Naval Research, Information Systems Branch, Contract Number Nonr 4705(00).

[‡] Alfred P. Sloan Research Fellow, 1967–1968.

[§] Recall 1.1.4e, i.e., item 1.4e of Chapter 1.

where, for $t_1, t_2 \in \Sigma A$, $t_1 \equiv_f t_2$ iff for all $\alpha, \beta \in (\Sigma A)^1, f(\alpha t_1 \beta) = f(\alpha t_2 \beta)$. Clearly, $\equiv_f$ is a congruence.

If S is a semigroup, then the *machine of the semigroup* S is $S^f : \Sigma S \to S$ given by $S^f(s_1, \ldots, s_n) = s_1 \cdots s_n$.

The semigroup of the machine of the semigroup S is written S^{fS}, and clearly $S^{fS} \cong S$. The machine of the semigroup of the machine f is written f^{Sf}. There exist functions $h_1 : A \to f^S$ and $h_2 : f^S \to B$ such that $f = h_2 f^{Sf} h_1^{\Gamma}$, where $h_1^{\Gamma} : \Sigma A \to \Sigma f^S$, with $h_1^{\Gamma}(a_1, \ldots, a_n) = [h(a_1), \ldots, h(a_n)]$. This is easily proved by letting $h_1(a) = [a]_{\equiv_f}$ and $h_2([a_1, \ldots, a_n]_{\equiv_f}) = f(a_1, \ldots, a_n)$.

Let $\mathscr{F}$ be a collection of machines. Define $\mathscr{F}^S = \{f^S : f \in \mathscr{F}\}$. Similarly, let $\mathscr{S}$ be a collection of semigroups. Define $\mathscr{S}^f = \{S^f : S \in \mathscr{S}\}$.

1.2 Definition. Let S be a semigroup. An *endomorphism* of S is a homomorphism $\varphi : S \to S$. Let $\text{Endo}_L(S)$ be the collection of all endomorphisms of S considered as a subsemigroup of $F_L(S)$ (see I.1.4i).

Let $\varphi : S_1 \to \text{Endo}_L(S_2)$ be a homomorphism. Then $S_2 \times_\varphi S_1$, the *semidirect product of* S_2 *by* S_1 *with connecting homomorphism* φ, is the semigroup $(S_2 \times S_1, \cdot)$, where

$$(s_2, s_1) \cdot (s_2', s_1') = [s_2 \varphi(s_1)(s_2'), s_1 s_1'].$$

The reader can easily verify associativity. If we write ${}^{s_1}(s_2')$ for $\varphi(s_1)(s_2')$, then, since φ is a homomorphism,

$${}^{(s_1 s_1')}(s_2') = {}^{s_1}[{}^{s_1'}(s_2)].$$

Since $\varphi(s)$ is an endomorphism for all $s \in S_1$, we also have

$${}^{s_1}(s_2 s_2') = {}^{s_1}(s_2) {}^{s_1}(s_2').$$

In this notation, the multiplication is given by

$$(s_2, s_1) \cdot (s_2', s_1') = [s_2 \, {}^{s_1}(s_2'), s_1 s_1'].$$

Thus multiplication in S_1 is carried out normally, whereas in S_2 the multiplication is carried out with a "twist" depending on the S_1 coordinate.

Direct products are a special case of semidirect products, since $S_2 \times S_1 = S_2 \times_\varphi S_1$, where $\varphi(s)$ is the identity endomorphism for all $s \in S_1$, i.e., ${}^{s_1}(s_2) = s_2$ for all $s_1 \in S_1$, $s_2 \in S_2$.

1.3 Definition. A *right mapping semigroup* or *right transformation semigroup* is a pair (X, S), where X is a nonempty set, and S is a subsemigroup of $F_R(X)$. For each $x \in X$, $s \in S$, let $xs = (x)s$. Then the following conditions are satisfied:

(1) $x(s_1 s_2) = (xs_1)s_2$.

(2) $s_1, s_2 \in S$ and $s_1 \neq s_2$ imply $xs_1 \neq xs_2$ for some $x \in X$.

For each semigroup T, we can construct the right mapping semigroup $[T^1, R(T)]$ (see I.1.4i), with $R(T) \cong T$. Here $tR(t') = tt'$ for $t \in T^1$, $t' \in T$.

Alternatively, if X is a set, S a semigroup, and $\theta : X \times S \to X$, with $\theta(x, s)$ written xs, then (X, S, θ) is called a *right action* of S on X iff condition 1 is satisfied. The action is *faithful* iff condition 2 is also satisfied. Now, if (X, S, θ) is an action, let $\hat{\theta}(s) : X \to X$ be given by $(x)\hat{\theta}(s) = xs$. Then the *right mapping semigroup associated with* (X, S, θ) is $[X, \hat{\theta}(S)]$. The function $s \to \hat{\theta}(s)$ is a homomorphism of S onto $\hat{\theta}(S) \subseteq F_R(X)$ by condition 1. It is 1 : 1 iff the action is faithful. We will make no distinction between a faithful action and its associated mapping semigroup.

Two mapping semigroups (X_1, S_1) and (X_2, S_2) are *isomorphic*, denoted $(X_1, S_1) \cong (X_2, S_2)$, iff there exists a 1 : 1 function $j : X_1 \twoheadrightarrow X_2$ (so in particular $|X_1| = |X_2|$) and an isomorphism $\varphi : S_1 \twoheadrightarrow S_2$ such that

$$j(xs) = j(x)\,\varphi(s) \qquad \text{for all} \quad x \in X_1,\ s \in S_1.$$

Clearly, $\cong$ is an equivalence relation on the collection of all right mapping semigroups. $S_1 \cong S_2$ does not, in general, imply that $(X_1, S_1) \cong (X_2, S_2)$.

The *abstract semigroup determined by* (X, S) is any semigroup T isomorphic with S.

1.4 Definition. Let (X_j, S_j) be right mapping semigroups for $j = 1, \ldots, n$. Let $X = X_n \times \cdots \times X_1$. Let S be the subsemigroup of $F_R(X)$ consisting of all functions $\psi : X \to X$ satisfying the two following conditions:

(1) (Triangular action). If $p_k : X \to X_k$ denotes the kth projection map, then for each $k = 1,\ldots, n$ there exists $f_k : X_k \times \cdots \times X_1 \to X_k$ such that

$$p_k\psi(t_n ,\ldots, t_{k+1} , t_k ,\ldots, t_1) = f_k(t_k ,\ldots, t_1) \qquad \text{for all} \quad t_i \in X_i , \; i = 1,\ldots, n.$$

That is, the new kth coordinate resulting from the action of ψ depends only on the values of the old first k coordinates and on ψ. We write $\psi = w(f_n ,\ldots, f_1)$.

(2) (kth component action lies in S_k). We require $f_1 \in S_1$, and, for all $k = 2,\ldots, n$ and all $\alpha = (t_{k-1} ,\ldots, t_1) \in X_{k-1} \times \cdots \times X_1$, the function $g_\alpha \in F_R(X_k)$ given by $g_\alpha(y_k) = f_k(y_k , t_{k-1} ,\ldots, t_1)$ is an element of S_k.

Then $(X_n , S_n) \wr \cdots \wr (X_1 , S_1) = (X, S)$ is the *wreath product* of $(X_n , S_n),\ldots, (X_1 , S_1)$, and $(X_n , S_n) \mathrm{w} \cdots \mathrm{w} (X_1 , S_1)$ is the abstract semigroup determined by (X, S).

It can be verified that

$$(X_3 , S_3) \wr [(X_2 , S_2) \wr (X_1 , S_1)] \cong (X_3 , S_3) \wr (X_2 , S_2) \wr (X_1 , S_1)$$

and

$$[(X_3 , S_3) \wr (X_2 , S_2)] \wr (X_1 , S_1) \cong (X_3 , S_3) \wr (X_2 , S_2) \wr (X_1 , S_1)$$

That is, wreath product is an associative operation on right mapping semigroups.

Wreath products and semidirect products are closely related. In fact,

$$(X_2 , S_2) \wr (X_1 , S_1) \cong [X_2 \times X_1 , F(X_1 , S_2) \times_Y S_1],$$

where $Y(s_1)(f)(x_1) = f(x_1 s_1)$ for $s_1 \in S_1$, $f : X_1 \to S_2$, $x_1 \in X_1$, and the action on $X_2 \times X_1$ is given by $(x_2 , x_1)(f, s) = [x_2 f(x_1), x_1 s]$. This equivalence is given by mapping (f_2 , f_1) to (f, s), where $f_1(x) = xs$ and $f_2(x_2 , x_1) = x_2 f(x_1)$. Thus, $(X_2 , S_2) \mathrm{w} (X_1 , S_1)$ is isomorphic to a semidirect product of $F(X_1 , S_2)$ by S_1. Notice that $F(X_1 , S_2) \cong S_2 \times \cdots \times S_2$ ($|X_1|$ times).

Exercises and Extensions

X1.1. Let S be a semigroup. Show that $S^{fS} \cong S$. If $f : \Sigma A \to B$ is a machine, prove that, for suitable functions $h_1 : A \to f^S$ and $h_2 : f^S \to B$, $f = h_2 f^{S_f} h_1^{\Gamma}$, where $h_1^{\Gamma} : \Sigma A \to \Sigma f^S$ is given by $h_1^{\Gamma}(a_1 ,\ldots, a_n) = h(a_1),\ldots, h(a_n)$. (Hint: see Def. 1.1.)

X1.2. Determine $U_3 \times_\varphi \mathbf{Z}_2$, where $\mathbf{Z}_2 = \{0, 1\}$, $U_3 = \{a, b\}^{r1}$,† $\varphi(0)$ is the identity map, and

$$\varphi(1)(x) = \begin{cases} a & x = b \\ b & x = a \,. \\ 1 & x = 1 \end{cases}$$

X1.3. Let (X, S) be a right mapping semigroup with X a finite set. Assume that X contains a *cyclic point* x_0, i.e., $x_0 S^I = X$, where I acts on X by $xI = x$, all $x \in X$:

(a) Let $s_1 \equiv s_2$, for $s_1, s_2 \in S^I$ iff $x_0 s_1 = x_0 s_2$. Show that $\equiv$ is a right congruence on S^I. If $S^I/\equiv$ denotes the set of equivalence classes under $\equiv$ ($S^I/\equiv$ need not have a natural semigroup structure related to that of S^I), then $[s] \to x_0 s$ is a $1:1$ map of $S^I/\equiv$ onto X.

(b) Let $\equiv$ be a right congruence on S^I. Show that $[s]t = [st]$ is a right action of S^I on $S^I/\equiv$. Prove that this action is faithful iff $ss_1 \equiv ss_2$ for all $s \in S^I$ implies $s_1 = s_2$. When S is abelian, this condition reduces to the requirement that $\equiv$ be the identity relation.

(c) Let $\equiv$ be as in (a), and let S^I act on $S^I/\equiv$ by $[s]t = [st]$. Prove that $(X, S) \cong (S^I/\equiv, S)$.

(d) Let S be a commutative semigroup. Then there are at most two nonisomorphic right mapping semigroups (X, S) with cyclic points. Determine these for each abelian semigroup.

X1.4. Show that $S_2 \times_\varphi S_1$, for any φ, is isomorphic with a subsemigroup of $[S_2{}^I, R(S_2{}^I)] \,\mathrm{w}\, [S_1{}^I, R(S_1{}^I)]$. {Hint: map $(s_2, s_1) \to [s_2' \to \varphi(s_1)(s_2'),\ s_1' \to s_1' s_1]$, where $\varphi(I)(s_2') = s_2'$ for $s_2' \in S_2{}^I$.}

X1.5. Let $Y_n = \{0, \ldots, n\}$, and let $S = \{f \in F_R(Y_n) : f(0) = 0\}$. Show that $\mathscr{RM}(n, G)$ is isomorphic with a subsemigroup of $(G^0, R(G^0)) \,\mathrm{w}\, (Y_n, S)$. {Hint: map the matrix M into the function $\pi(M) \in F_R(G^0 \times Y_n)$ given by $(g, i)\,\pi(M) = (gM(i, i^*), i^*)$, where

$$i^* = \begin{cases} 0 & \text{if } i = 0 \\ j & \text{if } M(i, j) \neq 0 \\ 0 & \text{if } M(i, j) = 0, \qquad \text{all } j, \end{cases}$$

and with the convention that $M(i, 0) = 0$, and otherwise $M(i, j)$ denotes the (i, j) entry of M.} See 7.2.16.

X1.6. Let $n \geqslant 2$, and let I_n be the semigroup $\mathscr{M}^0(\{1\}; X_n, X_n; I)$, where $X_n = \{1, \ldots, n\}$, and I is the $n \times n$ identity matrix. Show that $F_R(X_n)$ is a subsemigroup of $2^{X_n \times X_n}$, the semigroup of all relations on X_n, which in turn is a subsemigroup of $(2^{I_n}, \cdot)$, the semigroup of all subsets of I_n under the multiplication of 1.1.4c. Thus, every finite semigroup is isomorphic with a subsemigroup of $(2^{I_n}, \cdot)$ for some n.

X1.7. Let e be an idempotent of S. Prove eSe is the subsemigroup of S consisting of all elements for which e acts as an identity.

† The reader will meet U_3 many times in what follows. $U_3 = \{1, a, b\}$, where 1 is the identity, and a and b are right zeroes.

2. Elementary Properties of Machines; Relations between Machines and Semigroups

2.1 Definition. Let $f : \Sigma A \to B$ be a machine. Then define the *natural extension* $f^\sigma : \Sigma A \to \Sigma B$ of f by $f^\sigma(a_1, a_2, \ldots, a_n) = [f(a_1), f(a_1, a_2), \ldots, f(a_1, \ldots, a_n)]$.

Let $h : A \to B$ be a function. Then define the *unique extension* $h^\Gamma : \Sigma A \to \Sigma B$ of h by $h^\Gamma(a_1, \ldots, a_n) = [h(a_1), \ldots, h(a_n)]$. h^Γ is a homomorphism of ΣA into ΣB.

A homomorphism $H : \Sigma A \to \Sigma B$ is *length-preserving* iff $H(a_1, \ldots, a_n)$ is a sequence of length n in ΣB for all $(a_1, \ldots, a_n) \in \Sigma A$ and all $n = 1, 2, \ldots$. Notice h^Γ is a length-preserving homomorphism. Furthermore, every length-preserving homomorphism H can be uniquely written h^Γ, where $h : A \to B$ is given by $h(a) = H(a)$ for all $a \in A$.

2.2 Notation. We extend the notation of Def. 1.1 in the obvious way. Thus, f^{SfSf} is the machine of the semigroup f^{SfS}; the last letter on the right determines whether the object is a semigroup or a machine. However, since $S \cong S^{fS}$, the length of the superscripts will not get too long, for we have $f^{SfS} = f^S$ and $f^{SfSf} = f^{Sf}$ (after identifying f^{SfS} with f^S).

Along the same vein, we write f^{S1} to mean the semigroup $(f^S)^1$ and f^{SI} to mean $(f^S)^I$ (cf. 1.1.4h). Then, of course, f^{S1f} means $(f^{S1})^f$, and so on. The general rule, then, is to start at the left of the superscript and read to the right to determine the nature of the object the notation represents.

2.3. Remark. Let $f : \Sigma A \to B$ be a machine. Recall that f^S is the semigroup determined by the congruence $\equiv_f$ on ΣA, where, for $\gamma, \delta \in \Sigma A$, $\gamma \equiv_f \delta$ iff $f(\alpha\gamma\beta) = f(\alpha\delta\beta)$ for all $\alpha, \beta \in (\Sigma A)^1$.

We denote the equivalence class (relative to $\equiv_f$) containing $\alpha \in \Sigma A$ by $[\alpha]_f$. Let $h_f : A \to f^S$ be defined by $h_f(a) = [a]_f$. Then $f^{Sf} h_f^\Gamma : \Sigma A \twoheadrightarrow f^S$ is the canonical homomorphism associated with $\equiv_f$. Let $j_f : f^S \to B$ be defined by $j_f[\alpha]_f = f(\alpha)$. Then f can be written $f = j_f \cdot f^{Sf} h_f^\Gamma$, and this is called the *fundamental expansion* of f.

In the following, by assumption all machines will be such that their semigroups have finite order.

2.4 Definition. (a) Let $f : \Sigma A \to B$ and $g : \Sigma C \to D$ be machines. We say f *divides* g (write $f \mid g$) iff there exists a homomorphism $H : \Sigma A \to \Sigma C$ and a function $h : D \to B$ such that $f = hgH$. We say f *divides* g (*length-preserving*) [write $f \mid g$ (lp)] iff H is a length-preserving homomorphism. Notice that machine division and (lp) machine division are reflexive, transitive relations.

(b) Let S and T be semigroups. We say S *divides* T (write $S \mid T$) iff S is a homomorphic image of a subsemigroup of T [i.e., there exists a subsemigroup $T' \subseteq T$ and a homomorphism φ such that $\varphi(T') = S$].

Notice semigroup division is a reflexive, antisymmetric, transitive relation (antisymmetric in the sense $S \mid T$ and $T \mid S$ implies $S \cong T$).

2.5 Remark. (a) There exist machines f, g such that $f \mid g$ but f does not divide g (lp). Let g be $\mathbf{Z}_4{}^f$ restricted to $\Sigma\{1\}$. Then $\mathbf{Z}_2{}^f \mid g$, but the equation $h_2 g h_1{}^\Gamma = \mathbf{Z}_2{}^f$ has no solution for any h_1, h_2.

(b) Let P be a partition on a semigroup S, and let Q be the congruence generated by P, i.e., $s_1 \equiv s_2 \pmod Q$ iff $\alpha s_1 \beta \equiv \alpha s_2 \beta \pmod P$ for all $\alpha, \beta \in S^1$. Thus, in the ordering of relations, $(\bmod\, Q) \subseteq (\bmod\, P)$. If $(\equiv)$ is any other congruence on S such that $(\equiv) \subseteq (\bmod\, P)$, then $(\equiv) \subseteq (\bmod\, Q)$; this is easy to prove. Then in terms of homomorphisms, we have the following: We say an epimorphism $\varphi : S \twoheadrightarrow T$ is a P *homomorphism* and write $\varphi : S \underset{P}{\twoheadrightarrow} T$ if $\varphi(s_1) = \varphi(s_2)$ implies $s_1 \equiv s_2 \pmod P$. Then there exists a *unique minimal P homomorphic image* of S, namely $\eta : S \twoheadrightarrow S/Q$. This means that if $\varphi : S \underset{P}{\twoheadrightarrow} T$ is a P homomorphism, then there exists an epimorphism $\psi : T \twoheadrightarrow S/Q$ such that $\psi\varphi = \eta : S \twoheadrightarrow S/Q$ (cf. Chapter 8, Sect. 1).

It is clear, then, that if $f : \Sigma A \to B$ is a machine, then $f^{Sf} h_f{}^\Gamma : \Sigma A \twoheadrightarrow f^S$ is the unique minimal $(\bmod\, f)$ homomorphic image of ΣA, where $\alpha (\bmod\, f) \beta$ iff $f(\alpha) = f(\beta)$.

Let $\theta : \Sigma A \to S$ be any $(\bmod\, f)$ homomorphism on ΣA. Then there exists an epimorphism $\varphi : \theta(\Sigma A) \twoheadrightarrow f^S$. Then $f^S \overset{\varphi}{\twoheadleftarrow} \theta(\Sigma A) \subseteq S$, so $f^S \mid S$. These remarks will be useful in the proofs that follow.

2.6 Proposition. (a) Let f be a machine. Then $f \mid f^{Sf}(lp)$.

(b) Let S, T be semigroups. Then $S \mid T$ implies $S^f \mid T^f$ (lp).

(c) Let f, g be machines. Then $f \mid g$ implies $f^S \mid g^S$.

PROOF. (a) follows from the fundamental expansion of f.

(b) Suppose $S \mid T$. Let $T' \subseteq T$ be the subsemigroup of T, and let φ be the homomorphism such that $\varphi(T') = S$. For each $s \in S$, pick a representative $\bar{s}$ in $\varphi^{-1}(s) \subseteq T'$. Define $h_1 : S \to T$ by $h_1(s) = \bar{s}$.

Define $h_2 : T \to S$ by $h_2(t) = \varphi(t)$ if $t \in T'$ and arbitrarily if $t \notin T'$. Then $S^f = h_2 T^f h_1^r$, and so $S^f \mid T^f$ (lp).

(c) Suppose $f \mid g$. Then by (a), $f \mid g^{S f}$, and so $f = h g^{S f} H$, where H is a homomorphism. Then $g^{S f} H : \Sigma A \to g^S$ is a (mod f) homomorphism, and so by Remark 2.5 (b) we have $f^S \mid g^S$. ∎

2.7 Remark. Let f be a machine, and suppose S is a semigroup satisfying $f = h S^f H$ for appropriate h and homomorphism H. We know there is at least one solution $S = f^S$ to the equation. In general, we have $f \mid S^f$ so that $f^S \mid S^{fS} = S$. It follows that $S = f^S$ is the unique (up to isomorphism) minimal solution to the equation, and when $S = f^S$ the expression becomes the fundamental expansion.

Exercises and Extensions

X2.1. Let f and g be machines. Prove $f \mid g$ implies $f^{Sf} \mid g^{Sf}$ (lp).

X2.2. Let f be a machine. Prove $j_f f^{Sf} \mid f$.

X2.3. Let f be a machine, and define the *normal form* of f, $NF(f)$, to be the pair (f^S, P_f), where P_f is the partition induced on f^S by $j_f : f^S \to B$ sending $[t]_f$ to $f(t)$, where the partition induced by a function places in a block all those elements that have the same image. Let (S, P) be a semigroup with a partition. Write $(S_1, P_1) \equiv (S_2, P_2)$ iff there exists an isomorphism $\varphi : S_1 \twoheadrightarrow S_2$ such that $s_1 \equiv t_1 (\text{mod } P_1)$ iff $\varphi(s_1) \equiv \varphi(t_1) (\text{mod } P_2)$. Prove that, if f and g are machines such that $f \mid g$ and $g \mid f$, then $NF(f) \equiv NF(g)$.

X2.4. Let (S_1, P_1) and (S_2, P_2) be two semigroups with partitions. Then (S_1, P_1) *divides* (S_2, P_2) [write $(S_1, P_1) | (S_2, P_2)$] iff $S_1 | S_2$ and the homomorphism involved preserves the partition, i.e., if $S \subseteq S_2$ is the subsemigroup of S_2, and $\varphi : S \twoheadrightarrow S_1$ is the epimorphism, then $s \equiv t (\text{mod } P_2)$ implies $\varphi(s) \equiv \varphi(t) (\text{mod } P_1)$, where $s, t \in S$.
Prove that, if f and g are machines, $f \mid g$ iff $NF(f) \mid NF(g)$. [Hint: To show $NF(f) \mid NF(g)$ implies $f \mid g$, it is sufficient to show that $j_f f^{Sf} \mid j_g f^{Sf}$ by X2.2.]

We have seen that, given any machine $f : \Sigma A \to B$, there is a canonical semigroup f^S associated with f, f^S being the unique minimal homomorphic image of ΣA with respect to (mod f) homomorphisms. It is natural to ask the following question. Suppose we take two machines f and g and combine them to make new machines. Then how are the semigroups of the new machines related to f^S and g^S?†

First, if we take a machine $g : \Sigma C \to D$ and code its input and output sets (i.e., define a homomorphism H from a free semigroup

† For an alternate approach to what follows, see Sect. 2 of Chapter 3. However, note that cascades are not quite equivalent to series-parallel compositions.

ΣA generated by a set A to ΣC and a function $h : D \to B$, another set), we obtain the machine $f : \Sigma A \to B$, where $f = hgH$. We have seen that in this case $f^S \mid g^S$, since $f \mid g$.

The two obvious ways to hook machines together are series and parallel composition. (Recall Def. 2.1. for f^σ.)

2.8 Definition. Let $f : \Sigma A \to B$ and $g : \Sigma C \to D$ be machines.

(a) Define the *series composition of f then g with connecting homomorphism* $H : \Sigma B \to \Sigma C$ to be the machine $gHf^\sigma : \Sigma A \to D$.

(b) Define the *parallel composition of f and g* to be the machine $f \times g : \Sigma(A \times C) \to B \times D$ given by

$$(f \times g)[(a_1, c_1), \ldots, (a_n, c_n)] = [f(a_1, \ldots, a_n), g(c_1, \ldots, c_n)].$$

The series and parallel compositions of any finite number of machines are defined similarly.

2.9 Fact. Let $f_1, \ldots, f_n$ be machines, where $f_i : \Sigma A_i \to B_i$, $i = 1, \ldots, n$. Then $(f_n \times \cdots \times f_1)^S \mid f_n{}^S \times \cdots \times f_1{}^S$. In general, $(f_n \times \cdots \times f_1)^S \not\cong f_n{}^S \times \cdots \times f_1{}^S$.

PROOF. Using the fundamental expansion for each machine, we can write

$$f_n \times \cdots \times f_1 = (j_{f_n} \times \cdots \times j_{f_1}) \cdot (f_n^{Sf} h_{f_n}^{\Gamma} \times \cdots \times f_1^{Sf} h_{f_1}^{\Gamma}),$$

where the product is defined in the obvious way.

$$\theta = f_n^{Sf} h_{f_n}^{\Gamma} \times \cdots \times f_1^{Sf} h_{f_1}^{\Gamma} : \Sigma(A_n \times \cdots \times A_1) \to f_n{}^S \times \cdots \times f_1{}^S$$

is a (mod $f_n \times \cdots \times f_1$) homomorphism. Thus, by Remark 2.5 (b), we have the assertion.

A counterexample to the conjecture $(f_n \times \cdots \times f_1)^S \cong f_n{}^S \times \cdots \times f_1{}^S$ is the machine $\mathbf{Z}_2{}^f \times \mathbf{Z}_2{}^f$ restricted to $\Sigma(\{1\} \times \{1\})$. The semigroup of $\mathbf{Z}_2{}^f$ restricted to $\Sigma\{1\}$ is $\mathbf{Z}_2$, and the semigroup of $\mathbf{Z}_2{}^f \times \mathbf{Z}_2{}^f$ restricted to $\Sigma(\{1\} \times \{1\})$ is also $\mathbf{Z}_2$, not $\mathbf{Z}_2 \times \mathbf{Z}_2$. ∎

The series case is not as easy. Recall the definition of the *wreath product* of right mapping semigroups and the relation between wreath products and semidirect products

$$(X_2, S_2) \text{ w } (X_1, S_1) \cong F(X_1, S_2) \times_Y S_1,$$

where the connecting homomorphism Y is given following Def. 1.4.

There is a mapping semigroup that plays a particularly important role in what is to follow. Let S be a semigroup, and let $R(S)$ be the right regular representation of S (I.1.4i). Then $[S^1, R(S)]$ is a right mapping semigroup; for brevity, we write (S^1, S) when we mean $[S^1, R(S)]$, since $S \cong R(S)$.

2.10 Definition. Let (X, S) and (Y, T) be right mapping semigroups. We say (X, S) *divides* (Y, T) [write $(X, S)|(Y, T)$] iff (1) there exists a subset Y' of Y and a subsemigroup T' of T such that Y' is invariant under the action of T', that is, $Y'T' \subseteq Y'$; and (2) there exists a map $\theta : Y' \twoheadrightarrow X$ and an epimorphism $\varphi : T' \twoheadrightarrow S$ such that $\theta(yt) = \theta(y)\,\varphi(t)$ for all $y \in Y'$, $t \in T'$.

Notice that T' is not required to act faithfully on Y'. We write $(Y', T') \subseteq (Y, T)$ and $(Y', T') \overset{(\theta,\varphi)}{\twoheadrightarrow} (X, S)$.

We now define the direct product of mapping semigroups and prove some useful facts about the relations between wreath products, direct products, and division of mapping semigroups.

2.11 Definition. Define the *direct product* $(X, S) \times (Y, T)$ to be the mapping semigroup $(X \times Y, S \times T)$, where $(x, y)(s, t) = (xs, yt)$. The direct product of a finite number of mapping semigroups is defined similarly.

2.12 Remark. The following are easily verified:

(a) Mapping semigroup division is reflexive, antisymmetric, and transitive.

(b) If $(X, S)|(Y, T)$, then $S \mid T$.

(c) $S \mid T$ iff $(S^1, S)|(T^1, T)$.

(d) $(X_i, S_i)|(X_2, S_2) \times (X_1, S_1)$, $i = 1, 2$.

(e) Let $(X_i, S_i)|(Y_i, T_i)$, $i = 1, 2$. Then

$$(X_2, S_2) \times (X_1, S_1)|(Y_2, T_2) \times (Y_1, T_1).$$

2.13 Remark. Suppose $(X, S)|(Y, T)$ and (Y', T') is as defined in Definition 2.10. Define an equivalence relation $\equiv$ on T' by $t_1 \equiv t_2$ iff $yt_1 = yt_2$ for all $y \in Y'$. It is easy to show that $\equiv$ is a congruence and $T'/\equiv$ is the unique maximal homomorphic image $\bar{T}$ of T' such that $(Y', \bar{T})$ is a mapping semigroup, i.e., such that $\bar{T}$ acts faithfully on Y'. Then it is easy to see that $(Y', T'/\equiv) \twoheadrightarrow (X, S)$.

2.14 Fact. (a) $(X_2, S_2) \times (X_1, S_1) | (X_2, S_2) \wr (X_1, S_1)$.

(b) $(X_i, S_i) | (X_2, S_2) \wr (X_1, S_1)$, $i = 1, 2$.

(c) Let X be any set such that (X, S) is a mapping semigroup. Then $(S^1, S) | (X, S) \times \cdots \times (X, S)$ ($|X|$ times).

(d) Let $(X_i, S_i) | (Y_i, T_i)$, $i = 1, 2$. Then

$$(X_2, S_2) \wr (X_1, S_1) | (Y_2, T_2) \wr (Y_1, T_1).$$

PROOF. (a) It is only necessary to prove that

$$S_2 \times S_1 \subseteq F(X_1, S_2) \times_Y S_1,$$

as evidenced by the monomorphism $\varphi(s_2, s_1) = (f_{s_2}, s_1)$, where $f_{s_2}(x) = s_2$ for all $x \in X_1$.

(b) This follows from (a) and Remark 2.12 (d) by the transitivity of mapping semigroup division.

(c) Since (X, S) is a mapping semigroup, S is a subsemigroup of $F_R(X)$. Furthermore, S^1 is a subsemigroup of $F_R(X)$, since if $1 \notin S$ we can adjoin to S the identity function of $F_R(X)$. Since X is finite, label its elements $1, \ldots, n$. Then, for each $f \in F_R(X)$, f can be written as $(i_1, \ldots, i_n)$, where $(k)f = i_k$. If $g = (j_1, \ldots, j_n)$, then $(i_1, \ldots, i_n) * (j_1, \ldots, j_n)$ is defined to be $(j_{i_1}, \ldots, j_{i_n})$. Then $F_R(X)$ can be identified with the semigroup $(X \times \cdots \times X, *)$.

Let $\hat{S}$ be the image of S^1 in $X \times \cdots \times X$. Then

$$[\hat{S}, \{(s, \ldots, s) : s \in S\}] \subseteq (X \times \cdots \times X, S \times \cdots \times S).$$

Furthermore, it can easily be verified that

$$[\hat{S}, \{(s, \ldots, s) : s \in S\}] \cong (S^1, S).$$

Hence, $(S^1, S) | (X \times \cdots \times X, S \times \cdots \times S) = (X, S) \times \cdots \times (X, S)$.

(d) This proof is in four parts.

(1) Let $(Z_1, W_1) \subseteq (Y_1, T_1)$, and let (X, S) be any mapping semigroup. Then $(X, S) \wr (Z_1, W_1/\equiv) | (X, S) \wr (Y_1, T_1)$.

Proof. $V = F(Y_1, S) \times_Y W_1$ is a subsemigroup of $F(Y_1, S) \times_Y T_1$, and so $(X \times Z_1, V) \subseteq [X \times Y_1, F(Y_1, S) \times_Y T_1]$. Define the epimorphism $\theta : V \twoheadrightarrow F(Z_1, S) \times_Y W_1/\equiv$ by $\theta(f, w) = (\hat{f}, [w])$, where $\hat{f} = f$ restricted to Z_1 and $[w]$ is the image of w under the epimorphism associated with $\equiv$ (see Remark 2.13). Hence,

$$[X \times Z_1, F(Z_1, S) \times_Y W_1/\equiv] \twoheadleftarrow (X \times Z_1, V).$$

This proves part 1.

(2) Let $(Z_2, W_2) \subseteq (Y_2, T_2)$. Then

$$(Z_2, W_2/\equiv) \wr (X, S) | (Y_2, T_2) \wr (X, S).$$

Proof. $[Z_2 \times X, F(X, W_2) \times_Y S] \subseteq [Y_2 \times X, F(X, T_2) \times_Y S]$. Define $\theta : F(X, W_2) \times_Y S \twoheadrightarrow F(X, W_2/\equiv) \times_Y S$ by $\theta(f, s) = \{[f(\cdot)], s\}$. θ is an epimorphism. This proves part 2.

(3) Let (Y_1, T_1) be a mapping semigroup, and suppose $(X_1, S_1) \twoheadleftarrow (Y_1, T_1)$. Then $(X, S) \wr (X_1, S_1) | (X, S) \wr (Y_1, T_1)$.

Proof. Let $\theta : Y_1 \twoheadrightarrow X_1$ and $\varphi : T_1 \twoheadrightarrow S_1$ be the maps involved. Define the subsemigroup $V = \{(f, t) \in F(Y_1, S) \times_Y T_1 : f(y_1) = f(y_2)\}$ whenever $\theta(y_1) = \theta(y_2)$. Then

$$(X \times Y_1, V) \subseteq [X \times Y_1, F(Y_1, S) \times_Y T_1].$$

Define $\psi : V \twoheadrightarrow F(X_1, S) \times_Y S_1$ by $\psi(f, t) = [\hat{f}, \varphi(t)]$, where $\hat{f}(x) = f(\bar{x})$, $\bar{x} \in \theta^{-1}(x)$. $\hat{f}$ is well defined by the definition of V. ψ is an epimorphism, and it is easy to verify that

$$[X \times X_1, F(X_1, S) \times_Y S_1] \twoheadleftarrow (X \times Y_1, V),$$

when $\hat{\theta} : X \times Y_1 \twoheadrightarrow X \times X_1$ is given by $\hat{\theta}(x, y_1) = [x, \theta(y_1)]$. This proves part 3.

(4) Let (Y_2, T_2) be a mapping semigroup, and suppose $(X_2, S_2) \twoheadleftarrow (Y_2, T_2)$. Then $(X_2, S_2) \wr (X, S) | (Y_2, T_2) \wr (X, S)$.

Proof. Let θ, φ be as in part 3. Define $\hat{\theta} : Y_2 \times X \twoheadrightarrow X_2 \times X$ by $\hat{\theta}(y_2, x) = [\theta(y_2), x]$. Define $\psi : F(X, T_2) \times_Y S \twoheadrightarrow F(X, S_2) \times_Y S$ by $\psi(f, s) = (\varphi \cdot f, s)$. ψ is an epimorphism, and it is easy to verify that

$$[X_2 \times X, F(X, S_2) \times_Y S] \twoheadleftarrow [Y_2 \times X, F(X, T_2) \times_Y S].$$

This proves part 4.

Now, by (1)–(4), Remark 2.13, and transitivity of division, we have $(X_2, S_2) \wr (X_1, S_1) | (Y_2, T_2) \wr (Y_1, T_1)$ whenever $(X_i, S_i) | (Y_i, T_i)$, $i = 1, 2$. This proves Fact 2.14. ∎

We now proceed with the series case. Let $f : \Sigma A \to B$ be a machine. Then for all $\alpha, \beta \in (\Sigma A)^1$, define the right congruence $\equiv_{Q_f}$ by $\alpha \equiv_{Q_f} \beta$ iff $f(\alpha\gamma) = f(\beta\gamma)$ for all $\gamma \in (\Sigma A)^1$, with the convention that $f(1) \notin B$. Let Q_f be the set of equivalence classes of $\equiv_{Q_f}$, and let $[\alpha]_{Q_f}$ denote the class containing $\alpha \in (\Sigma A)^1$.

As before, let $[\alpha]_f$ denote the element of f^S that $\alpha \in \Sigma A$ is mapped into under $f^{Sf} h_f^{\Gamma}$ (see Remark 2.3).

Then (Q_f, f^S) is a right mapping semigroup under the action $[\alpha]_{Q_f} \cdot [\beta]_f = [\alpha\beta]_{Q_f} \in Q_f$. The action is easily seen to be well-defined and faithful.

The following result gave birth to the entire approach.

2.15 Proposition. Let $F = f_n H_{n-1} f_{n-1}^{\sigma} \cdots f_2^{\sigma} H_1 f_1^{\sigma}$, $n \geqslant 2$, where the f_i are machines and the H_i are connecting homomorphisms. Then

(a) $(Q_F, F^S) | (Q_{f_n}, f_n^S) \wr \cdots \wr (Q_{f_1}, f_1^S)$

(b) $F^S \mid (f_n^{S1}, f_n^S) \text{ w } \cdots \text{ w } (f_1^{S1}, f_1^S)$.

PROOF. (a) It is necessary only to prove (a) for $n = 2$, for then induction can be applied using the transitivity of mapping semigroup division and Fact 2.14d. Let $F = gHf^{\sigma} : \Sigma A \to D$, where $f : \Sigma A \to B$, $g : \Sigma C \to D$, and $H : \Sigma B \to \Sigma C$. We need to show that $(Q_F, F^S) | (Q_g, g^S) \wr (Q_f, f^S)$.

For each $a \in A$, define $\hat{a} \in (Q_g, g^S) \text{ w } (Q_f, f^S)$ by $([\beta]_{Q_g}, [\alpha]_{Q_f})\hat{a} = ([\beta]_{Q_g} \cdot [Hf(\alpha \cdot a)]_g, [\alpha]_{Q_f} \cdot [a]_f)$, where $\alpha \in (\Sigma A)^1$, $\beta \in (\Sigma C)^1$. Then $\alpha \cdot a \in \Sigma A$ and $Hf(\alpha \cdot a) \in \Sigma C$. Let $\hat{A}$ be the subsemigroup of $(Q_g, g^S) \text{ w } (Q_f, f^S)$ generated by the set $\{\hat{a} : a \in A\}$, and let φ be the unique extension of the map $a \to \hat{a}$ to an epimorphism of ΣA onto $\hat{A}$ (1.1.4f). We shall show that φ is a (mod F) homomorphism, thus establishing $F^S \overset{\psi}{\twoheadleftarrow} A \subseteq (Q_g, g^S) \text{ w } (Q_f, f^S)$ via Remark 2.5b; ψ is an epimorphism, and $\psi(a_1 \cdots a_n) = [a_1, \ldots, a_n]_F$.

Let $\alpha = (a_1, \ldots, a_n) \in \Sigma A$. Then $\varphi(\alpha) = \hat{a}_1 \cdots \hat{a}_n$. Let $\varphi(\alpha)$ act on $([1]_{Q_g}, [1]_{Q_f})$.

$$
\begin{aligned}
([1]_{Q_g}, [1]_{Q_f})\,\varphi(\alpha) &= ([1]_{Q_g}, [1]_{Q_f})\,\hat{a}_1 \cdots \hat{a}_n \\
&= ([1]_{Q_g} \cdot [Hf(a_1)]_g \cdot [Hf(a_1, a_2)]_g \cdots [Hf(a_1, \ldots, a_n)]_g, [1]_{Q_f} \cdot [(a_1, \ldots, a_n)]_f) \\
&= ([Hf(a_1) \cdot Hf(a_1, a_2) \cdots Hf(a_1, \ldots, a_n)]_{Q_g}, [(a_1, \ldots, a_n)]_{Q_f}) \\
&= ([Hf^{\sigma}(\alpha)]_{Q_g}, [\alpha]_{Q_f}). \qquad (2.1)
\end{aligned}
$$

Now suppose $\varphi(\alpha) = \varphi(\beta)$, $\alpha, \beta \in \Sigma A$. Then by (2.1),

$$[Hf^{\sigma}(\alpha)]_{Q_g} = [Hf^{\sigma}(\beta)]_{Q_g}$$

which implies $g(Hf^{\sigma}(\alpha)) = g(Hf^{\sigma}(\beta))$. Since $F = gHf^{\sigma}$, we have $F(\alpha) = F(\beta)$, and so φ is a (mod F) homomorphism.

Now, to establish mapping semigroup division, define a subset X of $Q_g \times Q_f$ by $X = 1 \cdot \hat{A} \cup \{1\}$, where $1 = ([1]_{Q_g}, [1]_{Q_f}) \in Q_g \times Q_f$. Then $\hat{A}$ leaves X invariant. Suppose $1 \cdot (\hat{a}_1 \cdots \hat{a}_n) = 1 \cdot (\hat{b}_1 \cdots \hat{b}_m)$. Then by Equation (2.1), we have

$$[(a_1, \ldots, a_n)]_{Q_f} = [(b_1, \ldots, b_m)]_{Q_f}$$

which implies

$$[(a_1, \ldots, a_n)]_{Q_F} = [(b_1, \ldots, b_m)]_{Q_F}.$$

Thus we can define a map $\theta : X \twoheadrightarrow Q_F$ by

$$\theta(x) = \begin{cases} [(a_1, \ldots, a_n)]_{Q_F} & \text{if } x = 1 \cdot (\hat{a}_1 \cdots \hat{a}_n) \\ [1]_{Q_F} & \text{if } x = 1 \end{cases}.$$

Now we have

$$(Q_F, F^S) \xleftarrow{(\theta,\psi)} (X, \hat{A}) \subseteq (Q_g, g^S) \wr (Q_f, f^S)$$

where θ and ψ satisfy the definition of mapping semigroup division. This proves (a).†

(b) This follows from (a) and the fact that $(Q_f, f^S) | (f^{S1}, f^S)$ for any machine f. In fact, $(Q_f, f^S) \xleftarrow{(\theta,\varphi)} (f^{S1}, f^S)$, where φ is the identity isomorphism and $\theta : f^{S1} \twoheadrightarrow Q_f$ is given by $\theta([\alpha]_f) = [\alpha]_{Q_f}$ for $\alpha \in \Sigma A$ and $\theta(1) = [1]_{Q_f}$. It is easy to see that θ is well defined by noticing that (in the ordering of relations on semigroups [cf. 1.1.4d]) $(\equiv_f) \subseteq (\equiv_{Q_f})$. Thus $(Q_f, f^S) | (f^{S1}, f^S)$.

Then by the transitivity of mapping semigroup division and Fact 2.14d, the assertion follows. ∎

We now wish to combine machines in a "loop-free" manner by series and parallel composition. Let $\mathscr{F}$ be a collection of machines. We shall define a family of machines containing $\mathscr{F}$ which is closed under the operations of series and parallel composition and division, however, restricting all homomorphism involved to be length-preserving. (This restriction is desirable from an engineering point of view, since length-preserving connecting homomorphisms correspond to simply running wires between machines.) This family will be defined in a manner that is convenient for inductive proofs.

† See Exercise X2.10 for a useful variation of the method of proof employed here.

2.16 Definition. Let $\mathscr{F}$ be a collection of machines. Define $SP(\mathscr{F})$, the *series parallel closure* of $\mathscr{F}$, by $SP(\mathscr{F}) = \cup \{SP_i(\mathscr{F}) : i = 1, 2, \ldots\}$, where $SP_1(\mathscr{F}) = \mathscr{F}$ and $SP_i(\mathscr{F}) = \{f_2 \times f_1, f_2 h^r f_1^\sigma, h_2 f h_1^r : f_1, f_2 \in SP_{i-1}(\mathscr{F})$ and h, h_1, h_2 are functions$\}$.

What can be said about the semigroups of the machines in $SP(\mathscr{F})$, that is, $SP(\mathscr{F})^S$? From the earlier discussion, we see that $SP(\mathscr{F})^S$ must be closed under direct products, wreath products, and some division. This leads to the following definitions.

2.17 Definition. Let $\mathscr{S}$ be a collection of semigroups. Define a family of mapping semigroups $\overline{W}(\mathscr{S})$, the *wreath divisor closure* of $\mathscr{S}$ by $\overline{W}(\mathscr{S}) = \cup \{\overline{W}_i(\mathscr{S}) : i = 1, 2, \ldots\}$, where $\overline{W}_1(\mathscr{S}) = \{(S^1, S) : S \in \mathscr{S}\}$, and $\overline{W}_i(\mathscr{S}) = \{(X, S) : (X, S) | (X', S')$ for some $(X', S') \in \{\overline{W}_{i-1}(\mathscr{S}) \cup \{[(X_2, S_2) \wr (X_1, S_1) : (X_j, S_j) \in \overline{W}_{i-1}(\mathscr{S})\}\}\}$.
Let $W(\mathscr{S})$ be the abstract semigroups associated with the family $\overline{W}(\mathscr{S})$.

2.18 Fact. Let $\mathscr{S}$ be a family of semigroups. If $(X, S) \in \overline{W}(\mathscr{S})$, then $(X, S) | (S_n{}^1, S_n) \wr \cdots \wr (S_1{}^1, S_1)$, for some $S_i \in \mathscr{S}$, $i = 1, \ldots, n$ and $1 \leqslant n$. In particular, if $S \in W(\mathscr{S})$, then $S \mid (S_n{}^1, S_n) \mathrm{w} \cdots \mathrm{w} (S_1{}^1, S_1)$, each $S_i \in \mathscr{S}$, or $S \mid T \in \mathscr{S}$.

PROOF. The second statement follows from the first. We prove the first assertion by induction on the i for $\overline{W}_i(\mathscr{S})$. For $i = 1$, the assertion is trivially true. Assume true for $i = n$, and let $(X, S) \in \overline{W}_{n+1}(\mathscr{S})$. Then either

(1) $(X, S) | (Y, T) \in \overline{W}_n(\mathscr{S})$; or

(2) $(X, S) | (Y_2, T_2) \wr (Y_1, T_1)$, $(Y_i, T_i) \in \overline{W}_n(\mathscr{S})$, $i = 1, 2$.

For case 1, the assertion follows by induction and transitivity of division. For case 2, the assertion follows by induction, transitivity, and Fact 2.14d. ∎

2.19 Remark. It is in the interest of notational convenience that we now introduce the shorthand symbol $S_2 \mathrm{w} S_1$ for the semigroup $(S_2{}^1, S_2) \mathrm{w} (S_1{}^1, S_1)$. However, this notation must be used with care, since the operation "w" on *semigroups* is *not associative*, although the operations "$\wr$" and "w" on mapping semigroups are associative.

The difficulty arises because "w" requires the use of S_2^1 and S_1^1 as the sets that S_2 and S_1, respectively, act upon. Thus,

$$(S_3 \text{ w } S_2) \text{ w } S_1 = F[S_1^1, F(S_2^1, S_3) \times_Y S_2] \times_Y S_1,$$

whereas

$$S_3 \text{ w } (S_2 \text{ w } S_1) = F([F(S_1^1, S_2) \times_Y S_1]^1, S_3) \times_Y [F(S_1^1, S_2) \times_Y S_1].$$

Since, in general, the cardinality of the two are not equal, it follows that "w" is not associative.

However, the semigroup $(X_2, S_2) \text{ w } (X_1, S_1)$ depends on S_1, S_2, and X_1, but not X_2. Because of this, it is easy to show that

$$(S_3 \text{ w } S_2) \text{ w } S_1 = (S_3^1, S_3) \text{ w } (S_2^1, S_2) \text{ w } (S_1^1, S_1),$$

which is what we want. This leads to the following convention.

2.20 Definition. Let $S_1, \ldots, S_n$ be semigroups. We define $S_1 \text{ w } \cdots \text{ w } S_n = R_n$ inductively by $R_1 = S_1$ and $R_n = R_{n-1} \text{ w } S_n$. (The indices have been reversed for the convenience of the definition.) Then $S_n \text{ w } \cdots \text{ w } S_1 = (S_n^1, S_n) \text{ w } \cdots \text{ w } (S_1^1, S_1)$.

2.21 Fact. (a) If $T \in W(\mathscr{S})$, then $(T^1, T) \in \overline{W}(\mathscr{S})$.

(b) If $S \mid T$ and $T \in W(\mathscr{S})$, then $S \in W(\mathscr{S})$.

(c) If $S_1, S_2 \in W(\mathscr{S})$, then $S_2 \text{ w } S_1 \in W(\mathscr{S})$.

PROOF. (a) $T \in W(\mathscr{S})$ means there exists a set X such that $(X, T) \in \overline{W}(\mathscr{S})$. By Fact 2.14(c), $(T^1, T) | (X, T) \times \cdots \times (X, T)$ ($|X|$ times). But, by Fact 2.14(a), $\overline{W}(\mathscr{S})$ is closed under direct product, and so $(T^1, T) \in \overline{W}(\mathscr{S})$.

(b) $S \mid T$ implies $(S^1, S) | (T^1, T)$, and so, by (a), $(S^1, S) \in \overline{W}(\mathscr{S})$ and $S \in W(\mathscr{S})$.

(c) This follows immediately from (a). ▮

We now give an alternate definition of $W(\mathscr{S})$ which is more useful for what is to follow.

2.22 Definition. Let $\mathscr{S}$ be a family of semigroups. Define the family of semigroups $\hat{W}(\mathscr{S})$ by $\hat{W}(\mathscr{S}) = \cup \{\hat{W}_i(\mathscr{S}) : i = 1, 2, \ldots\}$, where $\hat{W}_1(\mathscr{S}) = \mathscr{S}$ and
$\hat{W}_i(\mathscr{S}) = \{S : S \mid T \text{ for some } T \in \hat{W}_{i-1}(\mathscr{S}) \cup [S_2 \text{ w } S_1 : S_1, S_2 \in \hat{W}_{i-1}(\mathscr{S})]\}$.

2.23 Fact. $\hat{W}(\mathscr{S}) = W(\mathscr{S})$.

PROOF. Clearly $W(\mathscr{S}) \subseteq \hat{W}(\mathscr{S})$ by Fact 2.18. Conversely, suppose $\hat{W}_n(\mathscr{S}) \subseteq W(\mathscr{S})$, and let $S \in \hat{W}_{n+1}(\mathscr{S})$. Then either (1) $S \mid T \in \hat{W}_n(\mathscr{S})$, or (2) $S \mid T_2 \text{ w } T_1$, where $T_1, T_2 \in \hat{W}_n(\mathscr{S})$. In case 1, since $T \in W(\mathscr{S})$ by induction, $S \in W(\mathscr{S})$ by Fact 2.21(b). In case 2, both $T_1, T_2 \in W(\mathscr{S})$, and so, by Fact 2.21(c), $T_2 \text{ w } T_1 \in W(\mathscr{S})$. Thus, $S \in W(\mathscr{S})$ and $\hat{W}_{n+1}(\mathscr{S}) \subseteq W(\mathscr{S})$. So $\hat{W}(\mathscr{S}) \subseteq W(\mathscr{S})$. ∎

A note of warning: Although $\hat{W}(\mathscr{S}) = W(\mathscr{S})$, it is *not true* that $\hat{W}_i(\mathscr{S}) = W_i(\mathscr{S})$ for each i. Thus, when doing a proof by induction on i, take care to stick to one definition of $W(\mathscr{S})$.

Usually, the characterization of $W(\mathscr{S})$ as given by Definition 2.22 will be used. [The notation $\hat{W}(\mathscr{S})$ will be dropped.] We now repeat the results of Fact 2.14, *et al.* in terms of "w" for convenience.

2.24 Fact. (a) $S_2 \times S_1 \mid S_2 \text{ w } S_1$.

(b) $S_i \mid S_2 \text{ w } S_1$, $i = 1, 2$.

(c) If $S_i \mid T_i$, $i = 1, 2$, then $S_2 \text{ w } S_1 \mid T_2 \text{ w } T_1$.

(d) If $S \in W(\mathscr{S})$, then $S \mid S_n \text{ w} \cdots \text{w } S_1$, where each $S_i \in \mathscr{S}$, $i = 1, \ldots, n$ and $1 \leqslant n$.

2.25 Fact. Let $\mathscr{F}$ be a collection of machines. Then

$$SP(\mathscr{F})^S \subseteq W(\mathscr{F}^S).$$

PROOF. The proof is by induction on i of SP_i. Certainly, for $i = 1$, $SP_i(\mathscr{F})^S \subseteq W(\mathscr{F}^S)$, since $SP_1(\mathscr{F}) = \mathscr{F}$. Suppose $SP_n(\mathscr{F})^S \subseteq W(\mathscr{F}^S)$. Let $f \in SP_{n+1}(\mathscr{F})$. Then either (1) $f = h_2 g h_1{}^\Gamma$, where $g \in SP_n(\mathscr{F})$; (2) $f = f_2 \times f_1$, where $f_2, f_1 \in SP_n(\mathscr{F})$; or (3) $f = f_2 h^\Gamma f_1{}^\sigma$, where $f_2, f_1 \in SP_n(\mathscr{F})$.

In case 1, $f^S \mid g^S$, and by induction $g^S \in W(\mathscr{F}^S)$, so that $f^S \in W(\mathscr{F}^S)$. In case 2, $f^S \mid f_2{}^S \times f_1{}^S$, and, by Fact 2.24(a), $f_2{}^S \times f_1{}^S \mid f_2{}^S \text{ w } f_1{}^S \in W(\mathscr{F}^S)$ by induction, and so $f^S \in W(\mathscr{F}^S)$. In case 3, $f^S \mid f_2{}^S \text{ w } f_1{}^S$ by Proposition 2.15, and so $f^S \in W(\mathscr{F}^S)$. Hence, $SP_{n+1}(\mathscr{F})^S \subseteq W(\mathscr{F}^S)$. ∎

What about the converse idea? That is, given a family of semigroups $\mathscr{S}$, is $W(\mathscr{S})^f \subseteq SP(\mathscr{S}^f)$? The answer is no, in general, but, with the inclusion of certain basic machines in SP and a basic semigroup in W, the statement is true.

To develop this idea, we need to define certain semigroups and machines that play a special and important role in this theory.

2.26 Definition. (a) Let A be a nonempty set. Recall the definitions of A^l, A^r (1.1.4a).

(b) Define the semigroups $U_3 = \{r_0, r_1\}^{r1}$, $U_2 = \{r_0\}^1$, $U_1 = \{r_0, r_1\}^r$, and $U_0 = \{1\}$. U_0, U_1, and U_2 are all the proper subsemigroups of U_3 (up to isomorphism). If $S \mid U_3$, then $S \cong U_i$ for some $i = 0, 1, 2, 3$.

(c) The *delay machine* $D_A : \Sigma A \to A \cup \{*\}$ is defined by $D_A(a_1) = *$ (an arbitrary symbol) and $D_A(a_1, ..., a_n) = a_{n-1}$.

(d) The *delay machine* D_1 is D_A, with $A = \{r_0, r_1\}$ and $* = 1$.

(e) The *machine* $2_A : \Sigma A \to (A \cup \{*\}) \times A$ is defined by $2_A(a_1) = (*, a_1)$ and $2_A(a_1, ..., a_n) = (a_{n-1}, a_n)$.

2.27 Remark. Let A be a nonempty set. The natural extension of the machine A^{rf} is the identity map on ΣA. The semigroup A^r can be written as a subsemigroup of a direct product of a suitable number of semigroups U_1. Hence, $A^{rf} \mid U_1^f \times \cdots \times U_1^f (lp)$, and so $A^{rf} \in SP(U_1^f)$.

2.28 Fact. Let $U_1^f \in \mathscr{F}$. Then $SP(\mathscr{F})$ is the set of all machines f written

$$f = h_{n+1} f_n h_n^{\Gamma} f_{n-1}^{\Gamma\sigma} \cdots h_2^{\Gamma} f_1^{\sigma} h_1^{\Gamma},$$

where each f_i is a finite parallel composition of members of $\mathscr{F}$, and the h_i are functions.

PROOF. Once again, the proof goes by induction on i of SP_i. The critical step is as follows. Suppose the statement is true for $SP_n(\mathscr{F})$, and suppose $f \in SP_{n+1}(\mathscr{F})$ is written $f = f_2 \times f_1$; $f_1, f_2 \in SP_n(\mathscr{F})$. Let $f_1 : \Sigma A \to B$, $f_2 : \Sigma C \to D$. Then $f = (f_2 \times B^{rf})\, i^{\Gamma}(C^{rf} \times f_1)^{\sigma}$, where i is the identity function on $C \times B$. Since $f_1 \in SP_n(\mathscr{F})$, write

$$f_1 = h_{n+1} g_n h_n^{\Gamma} \cdots h_2^{\Gamma} g_1 h_1^{\Gamma}.$$

Then it is not difficult to see that $C^{rf} \times f_1$ can be written $\bar{h}_{n+1}(C^{rf} \times g_n)\, \bar{h}_n^{\Gamma} \cdots \bar{h}_2^{\Gamma}(C^{rf} \times g_1)^{\sigma}\, \bar{h}_1^{\Gamma}$. Now $C^{rf} \times g_i$ is a finite parallel composition of members of $\mathscr{F}$, since $U_1^f \in \mathscr{F}$. Doing the same for $f_2 \times B^{rf}$, it follows that f satisfies the condition of the statement. The other parts of the proof are trivial. ∎

2.29 Fact. Let A be a nonempty set.

(a) $A^{rf} \in SP(U_1{}^f)$.

(b) $D_A \in SP(D_1)$.

(c) $2_A \in SP(D_1, U_1{}^f)$.

PROOF. (a) This was shown in the Remark 2.27.

(b) As in the previous Remark, write A as a subset of the direct product of a suitable number of sets $\{r_0, r_1\}$. Then it is easy to see that D_A is the parallel composition of that same number of D_1 machines. Hence, $D_A \in SP(D_1)$.

(c) Verify that $2_A = (D_A \times A^{rf})\, h^{\Gamma}$, where $h : A \to A \times A$, with $h(a) = (a, a)$. Hence, by (a) and (b), $2_A \in SP(D_1, U_1{}^f)$. ∎

We are now ready to prove a converse to Proposition 2.15 and an important corollary.

2.30 Proposition.† Let S_1, S_2 be semigroups, and let $S_2 \times_Y S_1$ be any semidirect product of S_1 by S_2. Then

$$(S_2 \times_Y S_1)^f \in SP(S_1{}^f, S_2{}^f, D_1, U_1{}^f).$$

PROOF. Verify that

$$(S_2 \times_Y S_1)^f = (S_2{}^f \times S_1^{rf})\, h^{\Gamma} 2^{\sigma}_{S_2 \times S_1} (S_2^{rf} \times S_1{}^f)^{\sigma},$$

where $h : [(S_2 \times S_1) \cup \{*\}] \times (S_2 \times S_1) \to S_2 \times S_1$, with

$$h[*, (s_2, s_1)] = (s_2, s_1)$$

and

$$h[(s_2, s_1), (t_2, t_1)] = [Y(s_1)\, t_2, t_1].$$

Hence, by the previous Facts and Remarks, Proposition 2.30 is proved. ∎

2.31 Corollary. Let (X_1, S_1) and (X_2, S_2) be right mapping semigroups. Then

$$[(X_2, S_2) \le (X_1, S_1)]^f \in SP(S_1{}^f, S_2{}^f, D_1, U_1{}^f).$$

† Compare Sect. 2 of Chapter 3. 2.30–2.33 here point up the distinction between cascades and series-parallel closure.

PROOF. The proof follows, since $(X_2, S_2) \le w (X_1, S_1) \cong F(X_1, S_2) \times_Y S_1$ and $F(X_1, S_2) \cong S_2 \times \cdots \times S_2$ ($|X_1|$ times). ▮

2.32 Fact. $D_1^S, U_1 \in W(U_3)$.

PROOF. Clearly, $U_1 \in W(U_3)$, since $U_1 \mid U_3$. Verify that $D_1 = U_3^f h^\Gamma(U_3^f \times U_1^f)^\sigma H$, where

(1) $H : \Sigma U_1 \to \Sigma(U_3 \times U_1)$ is a homomorphism given by $H(x) = [(1, r_0), (x, r_1)]$ for all $x \in U_1$;

(2) $h : U_3 \times U_1 \to U_3$, where $h(x, r_0) = x$ and $h(x, r_1) = 1$ for all $x \in U_3$.

Hence, by Proposition 2.15 we have

$$D_1^S \mid U_3 \text{ w } (U_3^f \times U_1^f)^S \mid U_3 \text{ w } (U_3 \times U_1).$$

Therefore, $D_1^S \in W(U_3)$. ▮

2.33 Remark. Notice that the machine equation

$$D_1 = U_3^f h^\Gamma(U_3^f \times U_1^f)^\sigma H$$

does not imply $D_1 \in SP(U_3^f)$, since the homomorphism H is not length-preserving. In fact, it is true that $D_1 \notin SP(U_3^f)$. In Exercises X2.6–X2.9 at the end of this section, the reader is led through the proof of this fact. This will show the necessity of D_1 in Eq. (2.2) below.

2.34 Proposition. Let $\mathscr{S}$ be a collection of semigroups. Then

$$W(\mathscr{S} \cup \{U_3\}) = SP(\mathscr{S}^f \cup \{D_1, U_3^f\})^S. \tag{2.2}$$

PROOF. By the obvious induction argument, show that $W(\mathscr{S})^f \subseteq SP(\mathscr{S}^f \cup \{D_1, U_1^f\})$, using corollary 2.31. Using Fact 2.25 and the fact that $W(\mathscr{S})^{fS} = W(\mathscr{S})$, we find that

$$W(\mathscr{S}) \subseteq SP(\mathscr{S}^f \cup \{D_1, U_1^f\})^S \subseteq W(\mathscr{S} \cup \{D_1^S, U_1\}).$$

But, by Fact 2.32, $W(\mathscr{S} \cup \{D_1^S, U_1\}) \subseteq W(\mathscr{S} \cup \{U_3\})$. So, by adding a U_3 to $W(\mathscr{S})$ on the left and changing the U_1^f to U_3^f in the SP, we obtain

$$W(\mathscr{S} \cup \{U_3\}) = SP(\mathscr{S}^f \cup \{D_1, U_3^f\}). \quad ▮$$

EXERCISES AND EXTENSIONS

X2.5. Let $\mathscr{S}$ be a collection of semigroups. Define $K(\mathscr{S})$, the *semidirect divisor closure* of $\mathscr{S}$, by $K(\mathscr{S}) = \cup\{K_i(\mathscr{S}) : i = 1, 2, \ldots\}$, where $K_1(\mathscr{S}) = \mathscr{S}$ and $K_i(\mathscr{S}) = \{S' : S' \mid S \text{ for some } S \in K_{i-1}(\mathscr{S}) \cup \{S_2 \times_Y S_1 : S_1, S_2 \in K_{i-1}(\mathscr{S}),\ Y \text{ any connecting homomorphism}\}\}$.

(a) Prove $W(\mathscr{S}) \subseteq K(\mathscr{S})$.
(b) Prove $K(\mathscr{S})^f \subseteq SP(S^f \cup \{D_1, U_1^f\})$.
(c) Conclude that $K(\mathscr{S} \cup \{U_3\}) = W(\mathscr{S} \cup \{U_3\})$.

X2.6. [The next four exercises lead to the proof that $D_1 \notin SP(U_3^f)$.] Let $\alpha \in (\Sigma A)^1$. Define the *left translation* $L_\alpha : \Sigma A \to \Sigma A$ by $L_\alpha(\beta) = \alpha\beta$ for all $\beta \in \Sigma A$. Let $\mathscr{F}$ be a collection of machines containing U_1^f, and let $f : \Sigma A \to B$ belong to $SP(\mathscr{F})$. Then by Fact 2.28, f can be written as $f = h_{n+1} f_n h_n^\Gamma \cdots f_1^\sigma h_1^\Gamma$, where the $f_i : \Sigma A_{i1} \to A_{i2}$ are finite parallel compositions of machines in $\mathscr{F}$, and $h_i : A_{(i-1)2} \to A_{i1}$ are functions, $A_{02} = A$, $A_{(n+1)1} = B$. Let $a \in A$, and define $a_1 = h_1(a)$, $a_k = h_k f_{k-1}(a_{k-1})$. Then prove

$$fL_a = h_{n+1}(f_n L_n)\, h_n^\Gamma \cdots h_2^\Gamma (f_1 L_1)^\sigma h_1^\Gamma,$$

where $L_i = L_{a_i} : \Sigma A_{i1} \to \Sigma A_{i1}$.

X2.7. Let S be a semigroup, and for $s \in S$ define $l_s : S \to S$ by $l_s(t) = st$ for all $t \in S$. (a) Prove $(S^f L_s)^\sigma = (l_s S^f)^\sigma$. (b) Let $\mathscr{S}$ be a collection of semigroups. Using (a), prove $f \in SP(\mathscr{S}^f \cup \{U_1^f\})$ implies $fL_a \in SP(\mathscr{S}^f \cup \{U_1^f\})$.

X2.8. Suppose $f = U_3^f \times \cdots \times U_3^f$, $h : \{r_0, r_1\} \to U_3 \times \cdots \times U_3$ is a function, and $\alpha = [h(r_0), h(r_1)] \in \Sigma(U_3 \times \cdots \times U_3)$. Prove that, if $g = (fL_\alpha)h^\Gamma$, then there exists a function $K : \{r_0, r_1\} \to U_3 \times \cdots \times U_3$ such that $K^\Gamma = g^\sigma$.

X2.9. Prove $D_1 \notin SP(U_3^f)$ by assuming the opposite and deriving a contradiction. [Hint: If $D_1 \in SP(U_3^f)$, then $D_1 L_{(r_0, r_1)} \in SP(U_3^f)$. Expand $D_1 L_{(r_0, r_1)}$ in a minimal way via X2.6, and use X2.8 to get a contradiction.]

X2.10. (a) Let (X, S) and (Y, T) be mapping semigroups with $(Y', T') \subseteq (Y, T)$. Let $\theta : Y' \twoheadrightarrow X$ be an onto mapping, and for each $s \in S$ let $\hat{s} \in T'$ so that $\theta(y'\hat{s}) = \theta(y')s$ for all $y' \in Y'$. Then prove that $(X, S) \mid (Y, T)$. [Hint: Show that $\hat{s}_1 \cdots \hat{s}_n \to s_1 \cdots s_n$ is a well-defined homomorphism of the subsemigroup of T' generated by $\{\hat{s} : s \in S\}$. This follows since $\hat{s}_1 \cdots \hat{s}_n = \hat{r}_1 \cdots \hat{r}_m$ implies $\theta(y'\hat{s}_1 \cdots \hat{s}_n) = \theta(y'\hat{r}_1 \cdots \hat{r}_m)$ for all $y' \in Y'$. But $\theta(y'\hat{s}_1 \cdots \hat{s}_n) = \theta(y'\hat{s}_1 \cdots \hat{s}_{n-1})s_n = \cdots = \theta(y')s_1 \cdots s_n$, etc.]
(b) Re-prove Proposition 2.15 using (a) above.

The results of this section are due to Krohn and Rhodes [1]. For further reading, see Krohn, Mateosian, and Rhodes [2], Krohn and Rhodes [3], and Chapters 2, 3 and 4 of this volume.

3. A Proof of the Prime Decomposition Theorem (Krohn-Rhodes) for Finite Semigroups and Machines

Let f be a machine and $f^S = S$ its semigroup. A natural question to ask is, "What are the basic semigroups that would have to be in a collection $\mathscr{S}$ in order for S to belong to $W(\mathscr{S})$, i.e., what are the smallest necessary ingredients (semigroups) that must be in $\mathscr{S}$ so that $S \in W(\mathscr{S})$?" Or analogously, what are the "basic" machines $\mathscr{F}$ such that $f \in SP(\mathscr{F})$?

Certainly $S \in W(S)$. Suppose there exists S_1, S_2 such that $S \mid S_2 \text{ w } S_1$ but S does not divide either S_1 or S_2. Then $S \in W(S_1, S_2)$. Suppose, in turn, that $S_i \mid T_i \text{ w } W_i$ but S_i does not divide T_i or W_i, $i = 1, 2$. Then, since $S \mid S_2 \text{ w } S_1 \mid (T_2 \text{ w } W_2) \text{ w } (T_1 \text{ w } W_1)$, we have $S \in W(T_1, T_2, W_1, W_2)$.

3.1 Definition. S is an *irreducible* semigroup if $S \mid S_2 \text{ w } S_1$ implies either $S \mid S_1$ or $S \mid S_2$ for all semigroups S_1, S_2. IRR denotes the set of all irreducible semigroups.

We shall see that, given a semigroup S, there exists a collection of semigroups $\mathscr{S} \subseteq \text{IRR}$ such that $S \in W(\mathscr{S})$. So the questions now are

(1) which semigroups are irreducible?

(2) given S, what are the necessary and sufficient conditions for a collection of irreducible semigroups $\mathscr{S}$ to be such that $S \in W(\mathscr{S})$?

3.2 Definition. (a) PRIMES denotes the collection of finite nontrivial simple groups.†

(b) UNITS denotes all divisors of U_3, i.e.,

$$\text{UNITS} = \{U_0, U_1, U_2, U_3\}.$$

(c) Let S be a semigroup. $\text{PRIMES}(S) = \{P \in \text{PRIMES} : P \mid S\}$.‡ If $\mathscr{S}$ is a collection of semigroups, define

$$\text{PRIMES}(\mathscr{S}) = \cup \{\text{PRIMES}(S) : S \in \mathscr{S}\}.$$

(d) $\text{IRR}(S) = \{S' \in \text{IRR} : S' \mid S\}$.

Our aim in the rest of this section is to prove the Prime Decomposition Theorem:

† We assume the reader acquainted with basic facts about group theory, including the basic theory of normal subgroups, up to and including the Jordan-Hölder theorem.

‡ Editor's note: The reader's appreciation of this may be helped by the observation that G being a simple group does not preclude its being divisible by other simple groups. If A_n is the alternating group on n letters, $A_m \mid A_n$ for $m \leqslant n$, but A_n is simple for $n \neq 4$. See X3.5.

3.3 Theorem (Krohn-Rhodes). (a) Let f be a machine with f^S of finite order. Then $f \in SP(\mathscr{S}^f \cup \{D_1, U_3^f\})$ iff

$$\text{PRIMES}(f^S) \subseteq \text{PRIMES}(\mathscr{S}).$$

In particular,

$$f \in SP[\text{PRIMES}(f^S)^f \cup \{D_1, U_3^f\}]. \tag{3.1}$$

(b) Let S be a finite semigroup. Then $S \in W(\mathscr{S} \cup \{U_3\})$ iff $\text{PRIMES}(S) \subseteq \text{PRIMES}(\mathscr{S})$. In particular,

$$S \in W[\text{PRIMES}(S) \cup \{U_3\}]. \tag{3.2}$$

(c) IRR = PRIMES ∪ UNITS.

(d) In general, $S \notin W[\text{IRR}(S)]$.

3.4 Remark. Part (d) of the theorem justifies both the distinction between primes and units and the inclusion of U_3 in the foregoing equations.

3.5 Corollary. Let S be a finite semigroup. Then $S \mid S_n \text{ w} \cdots \text{w } S_1$ for some sequence $S_1, \ldots, S_n$, where $S_i \in \text{PRIMES}(S) \cup \text{UNITS}$, $i = 1, \ldots, n$.

PROOF. This follows from Eq. (3.2) and Fact 2.24. ▮

The proof of the theorem proceeds via several lemmas. The first lemma shows that PRIMES and UNITS are irreducible.

3.6 Lemma. PRIMES ∪ UNITS ⊆ IRR.

PROOF. Define IRR_{SD} to be the set of semigroups S having the property that $S \mid S_2 \times_Y S_1$ implies $S \mid S_1$ or $S \mid S_2$ for all semigroups S_1, S_2 and for all Y. It is easy to see that $\text{IRR}_{SD} \subseteq \text{IRR}$. We shall show $\text{PRIMES} \cup \text{UNITS} \subseteq \text{IRR}_{SD}$.

First we show $\text{PRIMES} \subseteq \text{IRR}_{SD}$. Let G be a nontrivial group, and suppose $G \mid S_2 \times_Y S_1$ for some semigroups S_1, S_2. Then Fact 1.1.9(c) guarantees the existence of a nontrivial subgroup G' of $S_2 \times_Y S_1$, where G is a homomorphic image of G'. Let p_1 be the restriction to G' of the projection mapping of the first coordinate, i.e., $(s_2, s_1) \to s_1$. Since p_1 is a homomorphism, $p_1(G') = G_1$ is a subgroup of S_1. Let (e_2, e_1) be the identity of G'. Then $\ker p_1$ is a normal subgroup of G' that consists of all elements of G' having e_1

as the first coordinate. Let $\varphi : \ker p_1 \to S_2$ be given by $\varphi(s_2, e_1) = Y(e_1)\, s_2$. φ is a monomorphism; to show φ is $1:1$, let $\varphi(s_2, e_1) = \varphi(t_2, e_1)$. Then

$$\begin{aligned}(s_2, e_1) &= (e_2, e_1)(s_2, e_1) = [e_2 Y(e_1)\, s_2, e_1] = [e_2 Y(e_1)\, t_2, e_1] \\ &= (e_2, e_1)(t_2, e_1) = (t_2, e_1).\end{aligned}$$

Let $G_2 = \varphi(\ker p_1)$. Then we have that G' is an extension of the subgroup G_2 of S_2 by the subgroup G_1 of S_1.

Now suppose $G \in \text{PRIMES}$ and θ is the homomorphism such that $\theta(G') = G$. Then $K = \ker \theta$ is a maximal normal subsemigroup of G', and $K \cdot \ker p_1$ is either K or G'. If $K \cdot \ker p_1 = K$, then $G \mid G_1 \subseteq S_1$; if $K \cdot \ker p_1 = G'$, then $G \mid G_2 \subseteq S_2$. This proves $\text{PRIMES} \subseteq \text{IRR}$.

We now prove $U_3 \in \text{IRR}_{SD}$. The proofs for the remaining units are analogous and easier. We first show $U_3 \mid S$ implies U_3 is a subsemigroup of S. Let $S' \subseteq S$, and let φ be a homomorphism of S' onto U_3. Let $s \in S'$ be such that $\varphi(s) = 1$. Then some power e of s is an idempotent, and $\varphi(e) = 1$. Then $\varphi(eS'e) = U_3$, and e is the identity for $eS'e$. Let S_1 be a subsemigroup of $eS'e$ of smallest order so that $\varphi(S_1) = U_1$. Then S_1 is right simple by Fact 1.1.9(c), and so by† Fact 7.1.25 S_1 is isomorphic with $G \times B^r$, where G is a group and B is a nonempty set. B must contain at least two distinct elements b_1 and b_2, since U_1 is not a group. Then $U_3 \cong \{e, (1, b_1), (1, b_2)\} \subseteq S$.

Suppose now that $U_3 \mid (S_2 \times_Y S_1)$. By the foregoing,

$$U_3 = \{(b_I, a_I), (b_0, a_0), (b_1, a_1)\} \subseteq S_2 \times_Y S_1.$$

As before, let p_1 be the homomorphism $p_1(b, a) = a$. $p_1(U_3) = \{a_I, a_0, a_1\} \subseteq S_1$. If $a_0 \neq a_1$, then $p_1(U_3)$ is isomorphic with U_3 and $U_3 \mid S_1$. This is so because, for $i = 0$ or $i = 1$, $a_I = a_i$ implies $za_I = za_i$, which implies $z = a_i$ for all $z \in \{a_I, a_0, a_1\}$.

Now suppose that $a_0 = a_1$. Necessarily, $b_0 \neq b_1$. Let $p_2 : U_3 \to S_2$ be defined by $p_2(b, a) = Y(a_0)(b) \equiv {}^{a_0}b$. By noting that $Y(a_0)\, Y(a_I) = Y(a_0)$, one sees that p_2 is a homomorphism. Also, p_2 is $1:1$, for $(b_1, a_0) = (b_0, a_0)(b_1, a_0)$ implies $b_1 = b_0\, {}^{a_0}b_1$, and $(b_0, a_0) =$

† We assure the reader that 7.1.25 does not rest on the present material and that our present lapse from sequential order is intended to make the present material accessible without a lengthy detour.

$(b_0, a_0)(b_0, a_0)$ implies $b_0 = b_0\,{}^{a_0}b_0$, and so $b_0 \neq b_1$ implies ${}^{a_0}b_0 \neq {}^{a_0}b_1$. Furthermore, $(b_0, a_0) = (b_0, a_0)(b_I, a_I)$ implies $b_0 = b_0\,{}^{a_0}b_I$, and so ${}^{a_0}b_1 \neq {}^{a_0}b_I$. Similarly, ${}^{a_0}b_0 \neq {}^{a_0}b_I$. Hence, $U_3 \cong p_2(U_3)$ and $U_3 \mid S_2$. This proves UNITS $\subseteq$ IRR. ∎

We next prove that Eq. (3.1) is valid.† This is done by induction on the order of f^S. The critical induction step separates into three cases as follows.

3.7 Lemma. Let S be a finite semigroup. Then either

(a) S is left simple,

(b) S is cyclic, or

(c) there exists a proper left ideal $V \subset S$ and a proper subsemigroup $T \subset S$ such that $S = V \cup T$.

PROOF. If S is left simple, we are in case (a); hence we can assume that S is not left simple. Since S is finite, it contains a maximal left ideal $L \neq S$. Let $a \in S - L$. Then $S = L \cup S^1a$.

If $S^1a \neq S$, we are in case (c) with $T = S^1a$ and $V = L$. Thus we may assume that $S^1a = S$. If $a \notin Sa$, then $S = Sa \cup \{a, a^2, \ldots\}$. If $S = \{a, a^2, \ldots\}$, we are in case (b); otherwise we are in case (c) with $V = Sa$ and $T = \{a, a^2, \ldots\}$. Hence, we may assume $a \in Sa$. Thus, $a = ua$ for some $u \in S$.

Let $K = \{k \in S : ka \in L\}$. Since $L \subseteq Sa (= S)$, $K \neq \phi$. Clearly, K is a left ideal of S and $K \neq S$ since $u \notin K$. Since L is maximal, either $K \cup L = L$ or $K \cup L = S$. In the latter case, we are in case (c), and hence we may assume that $K \subseteq L$. Thus, $xa \in L$ implies $x \in L$. Since this holds for every $a \in S - L$, it follows that $S - L$ is a subsemigroup of S and that we are in case (c) again. See Lemma 4.1 for the original proof. This proof is due to A. H. Clifford. ∎

3.8 Lemma. Let f^S be left simple. Then Eq. (3.1) is valid for f.

PROOF. Since f^S is left simple, $f^S = G \times A^l$, for some group G and nonempty set A (Fact 7.1.25). PRIMES(f^S) = PRIMES(G), for, if $P \in$ PRIMES(f^S), then $P \mid f^S = G \times A^l$, and so either $P \mid G$ or $P \mid A^l$, since P is irreducible. But A^l contains no nontrivial groups, and so $P \mid G$ and $P \in$ PRIMES(G). Conversely, let $P \in$ PRIMES(G).

† An alternative proof is given in the next section.

It is clear that $P \mid G$ implies $P \mid G \times A^l$, and so $P \in \text{PRIMES}(f^S)$. Thus, $\text{PRIMES}(G) = \text{PRIMES}(f^S)$.

Let $L = \{r_0, r_1\}^l$. Then verify that $L^f = h_3 U_3^f h_2^r (D_1 \times U_1^f)^\sigma h_1^r$, where

(1) $h_1 : L \to U_1 \times U_1$ with $h_1(r_i) = (r_i, r_i)$, $i = 1, 2$.

(2) $h_2 : U_3 \times U_1 \to U_3$ with $h_2(1, x) = x$ and $h_2(r_i, x) = 1$, $i = 1, 2$.

(3) $h_3 : U_3 \to L$ with $h_3(r_i) = r_i$, $i = 1, 2$. $h_3(1)$ does not occur. So $L^f \in SP(D_1, U_3^f)$. Now A^l is a subsemigroup of the direct product of a suitable number of semigroups L, and so it follows that $A^{lf} \in SP(D_1, U_3^f)$.

Hence we need only verify that Eq. (3.1) is valid for G^f. For if it is, we have

$$f^{Sf} = G^f \times A^{lf} \in SP[\text{PRIMES}(G)^f \cup \{D_1, U_3^f\}],$$

and, since $f \mid f^{Sf}(lp)$ and $\text{PRIMES}(G) = \text{PRIMES}(f^S)$, this proves the assertion.

Claim $G \in W[\text{PRIMES}(G)]$. This is certainly true if G is simple. Suppose G is not simple, and let G_1 be a normal subgroup of G. Let $H = G/G_1$, and let $N : G \twoheadrightarrow H$ be the natural epimorphism. Let $\{\bar{h} \in N^{-1}(h) : h \in H\}$ be a set of representatives of the cosets of G_1 with the condition that $\bar{1} = 1$. Let $(g_1, h) \in G_1 \times H$. For each $g \in G$, define $\hat{g} \in F_R(G_1 \times H)$ by

$$(g_1, h)\,\hat{g} = [g_1 \bar{h} g (\overline{hN(g)})^{-1}, hN(g)].$$

It is easy to verify that $\hat{g} \in G_1 \text{ w } H$ and that the map $g \to \hat{g}$ is an isomorphism. Therefore, $G \mid G_1 \text{ w } H$. The map defined here is the monomial map of group theory introduced by Burnside.

Let $G = G_0 \rhd G_1 \rhd \cdots \rhd G_n = \{1\}$ be a composition series for G with factors $H_i = G_{i-1}/G_i$, $i = 1, \ldots, n$. Then $G \mid G_1 \text{ w } H_1$ and $G_1 \mid G_2 \text{ w } H_2$, etc. Hence, $G \mid H_n \text{ w} \cdots \text{w } H_1$, and $G \in W(H_1, \ldots, H_n)$. Now H_i, being a composition factor, is a PRIME, so

$$H_i \in W[\text{PRIMES}(H_i)] \qquad \text{for each} \quad i = 1, \ldots, n,$$

and so

$$G \in W(\text{PRIMES}\{H_1, \ldots, H_n\}).$$

However,

$$\text{PRIMES}(G) = \text{PRIMES}\{H_1, \ldots, H_n\},$$

for, if $P \in \mathrm{PRIMES}(G)$, then $P \mid G \mid H_n \text{ w} \cdots \text{w } H_1$, which implies $P \mid H_i$ for some i. Hence, $P \in \mathrm{PRIMES}\{H_1, ..., H_n\}$.† Conversely, let $P \in \mathrm{PRIMES}\{H_1, ..., H_n\}$, so that $P \mid H_i$ for some i. But $H_i = G_{i-1}/G_i$ is a homomorphic image of the subsemigroup G_{i-1} of G, and so $P \mid H_i \mid G$. Hence, $P \in \mathrm{PRIMES}(G)$. Hence, $G \in W[\mathrm{PRIMES}(G)]$, and $G^f \in SP(\mathrm{PRIMES}(G)^f \cup \{D_1, U_3^f\})$. ∎

3.9 Lemma. Let f^S be a cyclic semigroup. Then Eq. (3.1) is valid for f.

PROOF. Let $C_{(n,m)}$ denote the cyclic semigroup of index n and period m. All finite cyclic semigroups are of this form (see Fact 1.1.10). Let $\mathbf{Z}_m$ be the cyclic group of order m. Then $C_{(n,m)} \subseteq \mathbf{Z}_m \times C_{(n,1)}$ and is generated by (a, b), where a generates $\mathbf{Z}_m$ and b generates $C_{(n,1)}$. Furthermore, $C_{(n,1)} \subseteq T_n = U_2 \text{ w} \cdots \text{w } U_2$ (n times). This is established by induction on n and the fact that the wreath product of monoids is a monoid. Let q_k generate $C_{(k,1)}$; let 1_k be the unit of T_k. For $n = 1$, let $C_{(1,1)} = \{r_0\} \subseteq U_2$. Now suppose $C_{(n-1,1)} \subseteq T_{n-1}$. Let $q_n = (f, r_0) \in T_{n-1} \text{ w } U_2 = T_n$, where $f : U_2 \to T_{n-1}$ with $f(r_0) = q_{n-1}$ and $f(1) = 1_{n-1}$. It follows that q_n generates $C_{(n,1)} \subseteq T_n$.

Thus we have $C_{(n,m)} \mid \mathbf{Z}_m \times T_n \in W[\mathrm{PRIMES}(\mathbf{Z}_m), U_2]$, since $T_n \in W(U_2)$ and $\mathbf{Z}_m$ is a group. But $\mathrm{PRIMES}(\mathbf{Z}_m) = \mathrm{PRIMES}(C_{(n,m)})$. Thus, $f^{Sf} = C^f_{(n,m)} \in SP[\mathrm{PRIMES}(f^S)^f \cup \{D_1, U_3^f\}]$ and since $f \mid f^{Sf}(lp)$, this proves the assertion. ∎

In considering case (c) of Lemma 3.7, we require the following definitions.

3.10 Definition. Let $f : \Sigma A \to B$ be a machine, and let c be a symbol not belonging to A or B. Define the machine *partial product f*, written $PPf : \Sigma(A \cup \{c\}) \to B \cup \{c\}$, by $PPf(\alpha) = f(\alpha_c)$, where α_c is the element of $(\Sigma A)^1$ obtained by striking out all members of the sequence α occuring before the last c and that last c itself. Set $f(1) = c$.

3.11 Definition. Let $f : \Sigma A \to B$ be a machine, and let e be a symbol not belonging to A or B. Define the machine $ef : \Sigma(A \cup \{e\}) \to B \cup \{e\}$ by $ef(\alpha) = f(\alpha_e)$, where α_e is the element of $(\Sigma A)^1$ obtained by striking out all occurences of e in α. Set $f(1) = e$.

† But note that P need not *be* any H_i.

3.12 Lemma. Let S be a semigroup with a proper left ideal V and a proper subsemigroup T such that $S = V \cup T$. Then

$$S^f \in SP(eV^f, PPT^f, D_1, U_1^f),$$

PROOF. Verify that

$$S^f = h_3(eV^f \times T'^{rf})\, h_2{}^\Gamma 2^\sigma_{V' \times T'}(V'^{rf} \times PPT^f)^\sigma h_1{}^\Gamma,$$

where $T' = T \cup \{c\}$, $V' = V \cup \{e\}$, and where

(1) $h_1 : S \to V' \times T'$ with $h_1(s) = \begin{cases} (s, c) & \text{if } s \in V \\ (e, s) & \text{if } s \in S - V \subseteq T. \end{cases}$

(2) $h_2 : [(V' \times T') \cup \{*\}] \times (V' \times T') \to V' \times T'$ with $h_2[*, (v, t)] = (v, t)$ and

$$h_2[(v_1, t_1), (v_2, t_2)] = \begin{cases} (t_1 v_2, t_2) & \text{if } t_2 = c \text{ and } t_1 \neq c \\ (v_2, t_2) & \text{otherwise.} \end{cases}$$

(3) $h_3 : V' \times T' \to S$ with $h_3(v, t) = vt$, where e and c act like identities. The element (e, c) will never occur. ∎

3.13 Lemma. If Eq. (3.1) is valid for a machine f, then it is valid for ef.

PROOF. We first show that, if $U_1^f \in \mathscr{F}$, then $\{ef : f \in \mathscr{F}\} \subseteq SP(\mathscr{F})$ implies $\{ef : f \in SP(\mathscr{F})\} \subseteq SP(\mathscr{F})$ by using the usual induction argument. Let $f \in SP_n(\mathscr{F})$. Either (1) $f = f_2 h^\Gamma f_1{}^\sigma$, (2) $f = f_2 \times f_1$, or (3) $f = h_2 f_1 h_1{}^\Gamma$, where $f_1, f_2 \in SP_{n-1}(\mathscr{F})$. By induction, $ef_1, ef_2 \in SP(\mathscr{F})$.

In case 1, suppose $f_1 : \Sigma A \to B$ and $f_2 : \Sigma C \to D$. Then verify that

$$ef = (ef_2)\, h_2{}^\Gamma(ef_1 \times A'^{rf})^\sigma h_1{}^\Gamma,$$

where $A' = A \cup \{e\}$, $B' = B \cup \{e\}$, $C' = C \cup \{e\}$, and

$$h_1 : A' \to A' \times A' \quad \text{with} \quad h_1(a) = (a, a) \quad \text{for all} \quad a \in A', \quad \text{and}$$

$$h_2 : B' \times A' \to C' \quad \text{with} \quad h_2(b, a) = \begin{cases} e & \text{if } a = e \\ h(b) & \text{otherwise.} \end{cases}$$

Hence, $ef \in SP(\mathscr{F})$ in this case.

Cases 2 and 3 are handled in the obvious manner.

Now, if (3.1) is valid for f, by the foregoing we need only show that

$$\{eD_1, eU_3^f, eG^f : G \in \text{PRIMES}(f^S)\} \subseteq SP[\text{PRIMES}(f^S)^f \cup \{D_1, U_3^f\}].$$

(a) First, let S be a monoid. Then $eS^f \in SP(S^f, U_3^f)$. Verify that

$$eS^f = h_2(S^f \times U_3^f)\, h_1^{\Gamma},$$

where $h_1 : S \cup \{e\} \to S \times U_3$ with $h_1(e) = (1, 1)$ and $h_1(s) = (s, r_0)$ and $h_2 : S \times U_3 \to S \cup \{e\}$ with $h_2(s, 1) = e$ and $h_2(s, r_0) = s$.

(b) $eD_1 \in SP(D_1, U_3^f)$. Verify that

$$eD_1 = h_4(U_3^f \times U_3^{rf} \times U_3^{rf})\, h_3^{\Gamma} 2_A^{\sigma}(U_3^f \times U_3^f \times U_3^{rf})^{\sigma} h_2^{\Gamma} 2_A^{\sigma} h_1^{\Gamma},$$

where $A = U_3 \times U_3 \times U_3$ and

(1) $h_1 : U_1 \cup \{e\} \to A$ with $h_1(e) = (1, 1, 1)$,
$h_1(r_i) = (1, 1, r_i)$, $i = 0, 1$,

(2) $h_2 : A \cup \{*\} \times A \to A$ with $h_2[*, (1, 1, x)] = (1, 1, x)$,
$h_2[(1, 1, x), (1, 1, y)] = (1, x, y)$ for all $x, y \in U_3$,

(3) $h_3 : A \cup \{*\} \times A \to A$ with

$$h_3[*, (1, x_1, y_1)] = (1, x_1, y_1),$$

$$h_3[(1, x_1, y_1), (1, x_2, y_2)] = \begin{cases} (1, x_2, y_2) & \text{if } y_1 = 1 \\ (x_1, x_2, y_2) & \text{if } y_1 \neq 1, \end{cases}$$

$$x_i, y_i \in U_3,$$

(4) $h_4 : A \to U_3 \cup \{e\}$ with

$$h_4(1, 1, 1) = e,$$

$$h_4(1, 1, r_i) = h_4(1, r_i, 1) = 1,$$

$$h_4(r_k, r_j, r_i) = h_4(1, r_j, r_i) = h_4(r_j, r_i, 1) = r_j, \qquad i, j, k = 0, 1.$$

Since U_3 and groups are monoids, by (a) and (b) we have proved the lemma. ▮

3.14 Lemma. If Eq. (3.1) is valid for f, it is valid for PPf.

PROOF. We first show that $\{PPf : f \in \mathscr{F}\} \subseteq SP(\mathscr{F})$ implies $\{PPf : f \in SP(\mathscr{F})\} \subseteq SP(\mathscr{F})$ using the usual induction. Let $f \in SP_n(\mathscr{F})$. Then either (1) $f = f_2 h^{\Gamma} f_1^{\sigma}$, (2) $f = f_2 \times f_1$, or (3) $f = h_2 f_1 h_1^{\Gamma}$, where $f_1, f_2 \in SP_{n-1}(\mathscr{F})$. By induction, $PPf_1, PPf_2 \in SP(\mathscr{F})$. In case 1, $PPf = PPf_2 h_c^{\Gamma}(PPf_1)^{\sigma}$, where h is extended to h_c by $h_c(c) = c$. Cases 2 and 3 are handled in a similar manner.

Now, if Eq. (3.1) is valid for f, by the foregoing, we need only show that

$$\{PPD_1, PPU_3^f, PPG^f: G \in \text{PRIMES}(f^S)\} \subseteq SP[\text{PRIMES}(f^S)^f \cup \{D_1, U_3^f\}].$$

(a) Let G be a group. Then $PPG^f \in SP(G^f, U_3^f)$. Verify that

$$PPG^f = h_3(G^{rf} \times G^{r1f} \times \{c, *\}^{rf})\, h_2^{\Gamma}[G^f \times (G \cup \{c\})^{rf}]^{\sigma} h_1^{\Gamma}$$

where

(1) $h_1 : G \cup \{c\} \to G \times (G \cup \{c\})$ with $h_1(g) = (g, g)$,
$h_1(c) = (1, c)$,

(2) $h_2 : G \times (G \cup \{c\}) \to G \times (G \cup \{1\}) \times \{c, *\}$ with 1 the identity of G^{r1} and $h_2(g, c) = (g, g, c)$, $h_2(g, g') = (g, 1, *)$,

(3) $h_3 : G \times (G \cup \{1\}) \times \{c, *\} \to G \cup \{c\}$ with

$$h_3(x, y, c) = c \quad \text{for all } x, y,$$

$$h_3(x, y, *) = \begin{cases} x & \text{if } y = 1 \\ y^{-1}x & \text{if } y \neq 1. \end{cases}$$

Now G^{r1} is a subsemigroup of a suitably large finite direct product of U_3^f with itself. Hence, $G^{r1f} \in SP(U_3^f)$, and $PPG^f \in SP(G^f, U_3^f)$.

(b) $PPU_3^f \in SP(U_3^f)$. Verify that $PPU_3^f = h_2(A^{r1f} \times U_1^f)\, h_1^{\Gamma}$, where $A = \{r_0, r_1, c\}$ and

(1) $h_1 : U_3 \cup \{c\} \to A \cup \{1\} \times U_1$ with
$h_1(c) = (c, r_1)$,
$h_1(u) = (u, r_0)$ for all $u \in U_3$,

(2) $h_2 : A \cup \{1\} \times U_1 \to U_3 \cup \{c\}$ with $h_2(c, r_1) = c$,
$h_2(c, r_0) = h_2(1, r_0) = 1$ $h_2(r_i, r_0) = r_i$, $i = 1, 2$.

(c) $PPD_1 \in SP(D_1, U_1^f)$. Verify that

$$PPD_1 = h_2(D_1 \times D_1 \times U_1^f)\, h_1^{\Gamma},$$

where

(1) $h_1 : (U_1 \cup \{c\}) \rightarrow U_1 \times U_1 \times U_1$ with
$h_1(c) = (r_0, r_1, r_1)$,
$h_1(r_i) = (r_i, r_0, r_0)$,

(2) $h_2 : U_3 \times U_3 \times U_1 \rightarrow U_3 \cup \{c\}$ with $h_2(x, y, r_1) = c$ for all $x, y, \in U_3$, $h_2(r_0, r_1, r_0) = h_2(1, 1, r_0) = 1$, $h_2(r_i, r_0, r_0) = r_i$, $i = 1, 2$. Other inputs to h_2 do not occur.

Thus, with the proofs of (a)–(c) we have proved the lemma. ∎

3.15 Lemma. Equation (3.1) is valid.

PROOF. It is sufficient to prove (3.1) valid for f^{S^f}, since $f \mid f^{S^f}(lp)$. Hence, it is sufficient to prove (3.1) for S^f, where S is a finite semigroup.

We proceed by induction on the order of S. The case $|S| = 1$ is trivial. Suppose (3.1) is valid for all semigroups with order less than n. Let $|S| = n$. Then apply Lemma 3.7 to S. In cases (a) and (b), Lemmas 3.8 and 3.9, respectively, apply, and we are done. In case (c), apply Lemmas 3.12–3.14 using induction. Hence,

$$f \in SP[\text{PRIMES}(f^S)^f \cup \{D_1, U_3^f\}]. \quad ∎$$

3.16 Fact. If $S \in \text{IRR}$ and $S \in W(\mathscr{S})$, then $S \mid S'$ for some $S' \in \mathscr{S}$.

PROOF. The proof follows immediately by induction and the definition of IRR. ∎

3.17 Proof of the Theorem. Equation (3.1) applied to S^f gives Eq. (3.2). Equations (3.1) and (3.2) prove that $\text{PRIMES}(f^S) \subseteq \text{PRIMES}(\mathscr{S})$ implies $f \in SP(\mathscr{S}^f \cup \{D_1, U_3^f\})$ and $\text{PRIMES}(S) \subseteq \text{PRIMES}(\mathscr{S})$ implies $S \in W(\mathscr{S} \cup \{U_3\})$, respectively.

To finish (a) and (b), assume $f \in SP(\mathscr{S}^f \cup \{D_1, U_3^f\})$. Then $f^S \in W(\mathscr{S} \cup \{U_3\})$. Let $P \in \text{PRIMES}(f^S)$. Then $P \mid f^S$, so that $P \in W(\mathscr{S} \cup \{U_3\})$, which by Fact 3.16 implies $P \mid S$ for some $S \in \mathscr{S}$ (P cannot divide U_3). Hence, $P \in \text{PRIMES}(\mathscr{S})$. This proves (a) and (b) of the theorem.

To prove (c), we must show $\text{IRR} \subseteq \text{PRIMES} \cup \text{UNITS}$. Let $S \in \text{IRR}$. Then, by (b), $S \in W[\text{PRIMES}(S) \cup \{U_3\}]$, so that either $S \mid G$, a group, or $S \mid U_3$. If $S \mid G$, then S is a group. We know from the proof of Lemma 3.8 that the only groups that are irreducible are simple groups. Hence, $S \in$ PRIMES or $S = \{1\}$, a UNIT. If $S \mid U_3$, S is a UNIT. This proves (c).

For (d), consider the semigroup $L = \{r_0, r_1\}^l$. Then IRR$(L) = \{U_0\}$, and, since U_0 is the trivial one-point semigroup, clearly $L \notin W(U_0)$. The proof of Lemma 3.8, however, shows that $L \in W(U_3)$. This proves the prime decomposition theorem 3.3. ∎

Exercises and Extensions

X3.1. Let S be a semigroup. Prove that PRIMES(S) are the PRIMES of the Jordan Hölder factors of the maximal subgroups of S.

X3.2. Prove S_1, S_2 are monoids implies $S_2 \le S_1$ is a monoid.

X3.3. (Refer to Lemma 3.9.) Prove PRIMES $(\mathbf{Z}_m)$ = PRIMES $(C_{(n,m)})$.

X3.4. Let S be a semigroup. Prove (a) $S \in K(\mathscr{S} \cup \{U_3\})$ iff PRIMES $(S) \subseteq$ PRIMES $(\mathscr{S})$. (b) In particular, $S \in K[\text{PRIMES}(S) \cup \{U_3\}]$. (c) IRR_{SD} = IRR = PRIMES $\cup$ UNITS. (See X2.5).

X3.5. Prove that every finite group is isomorphic to a subgroup of a finite simple group. (Hint: Let G act on $G \cup G'$ by $g_1 \cdot g = g_1 g$ and $g_1' \cdot g = (g_1 g)'$. Thus G is a subgroup of A_{2n}, $n = |G|$.)

3.18 Remark. The method of taking an algebraic object and "putting it up into" a larger algebraic object that is easier to work with has been employed here and is expressed by the notation of semigroup division. $S \mid T$ means S is a homomorphic image of a subsemigroup of T. It is reasonable to ask what could be done along similar lines if division had been defined by $S \mid T$ iff S is a subsemigroup of T.

The answer is "not much." Given this definition of division, the semigroup $F_R(X_n)$, all functions on n letters, is irreducible with respect to semidirect and hence wreath products. Since every semigroup is a subsemigroup of $F_R(X_n)$ for some n, we are in the not very interesting position of having every semigroup dividing an irreducible semigroup. Hence, this definition of division is not useful.

The following facts prove that $F_R(X_n)$ is irreducible given the foregoing definition of division.

3.19 Fact. Let K be the kernel of $F_R(X_n)$, and let $\varphi : F_R(X_n) \to S$ be a homomorphism. Then

(a) if φ is $1:1$ on K, then φ is $1:1$ on $F_R(X_n)$; and
(b) if φ is not $1:1$ on $F_R(X_n)$, then $\varphi(K)$ is one point.

PROOF. (a) The kernel of $F_R(X_n)$ consists of $f_i = (i,..., i)$ (using the obvious notation), the constant functions sending everything to i, $i = 1,..., n$. Each f_i is a right zero of $F_R(X_n)$. Let $f, g \in F_R(X_n) - K$, $f = (i_1, ..., i_n)$, $g = (j_1, ..., j_n)$, such that $\varphi(f) = \varphi(g)$. Then $f_k f = f_{i_k}$ and $f_k g = f_{j_k}$ for each k. Thus, $\varphi(f_{j_k}) = \varphi(f_k g) = \varphi(f_k f) = \varphi(f_{i_k})$ for all k. Since φ is $1:1$ on k, $i_k = j_k$ for all k, so that $f = g$.

(b) If φ is not $1:1$ on $F_R(X_n)$, then by (a) φ is not $1:1$ on K. Suppose $\varphi(f_1) = \varphi(f_2)$. Let f^k be the function $(1, k, ...) \in F_R(X_n)$, $k = 1,..., n$. Then $f_1 f^k = f_1$ and $f_2 f^k = f_k$ for all k. Hence, $\varphi(f_1) = \varphi(f_1 f^k) = \varphi(f_2 f^k) = \varphi(f_k)$ for all k. ▮

3.20 Fact. Suppose $F_R(X_n) \subseteq S_2 \times_Y S_1$. Then either $F_R(X_n) \subseteq S_1$ or $F_R(X_n) \subseteq S_2$.

PROOF. Consider the homomorphism $\pi_1 : S_2 \times_Y S_1 \twoheadrightarrow S_1$, where $\pi_1(s_2, s_1) = s_1$. If π_1 restricted to K, the kernel of $F_R(X_n)$, is $1:1$, then $F_R(X_n) \subseteq S_1$. Hence, K in $S_2 \times_Y S_1$ is of the form $\{(s, 0) :$ for some elements $s \in S_2$ and 0 the zero of $\pi_1(F_R(X_n))\}$. Let $\varphi : S_2 \times_Y S_1 \to S_2$ be defined by $\varphi(s_2, s_1) = {}^0 s_2$. φ is a homomorphism. Furthermore, φ is $1:1$ on $F_R(X_n)$, for let $(s, 0)$ and $(t, 0) \in K$, and suppose ${}^0 s = {}^0 t$. Then $(s, 0) = (s, 0)^2 = (s\,{}^0 s, 0) = (s\,{}^0 t, 0) = (s, 0)(t, 0) = (t, 0)$. Hence, $s = t$ and φ is $1:1$ on K; hence on $F_R(X_n)$. Thus, in this case $F_R(X_n) \subseteq S_2$. ▮

The main decomposition theorem was first proved by Krohn and Rhodes in [1, 3]. For machine corollaries, see Sect. 4 of the forementioned article [1].

The proof here follows Krohn and Rhodes [1]. For other proofs, see especially Zeiger [5] and Chapter 4 of the present volume, and the next section of this chapter.

4. The Prime Decomposition Theorem: A More Algebraic Proof

In this section, we give another proof of the prime decomposition theorem for finite semigroups. This proof does not employ the machine methods used in Sect. 3 but proceeds by algebraic methods alone.

The machine methods, although they may not be pleasant to contemplate, do give a great amount of insight into what is true and provide a strong tool for proving things. The prime decomposition theorem was originally proved via machines; only after the theorem was known to be true was this algebraic proof devised.

First we provide, as a point of information, another proof of Lemma 3.6 which relies on a knowledge of Rees' theorem as presented in Chapter 7. We repeat the statement.

4.1 Lemma (3.7). Let S be a finite semigroup. Then either

(a) S is left simple,

(b) S is cyclic, or

(c) there exists a proper left ideal $V \subset S$ and a proper subsemigroup $T \subset S$ such that $S = V \cup T$.

PROOF. Throughout this proof, we utilize the "picture" of a $\mathcal{J}$ class as provided by Green's and Rees' theorems (Chapter 7). Let J be a maximal $\mathcal{J}$ class of S. Either J is regular or is a one-point null $\mathcal{J}$ class. Suppose J is regular and has only one $\mathcal{L}$ class. Then J is a subsemigroup of S. Let $F(J)$ be the ideal $S - J$. If $F(J) = \phi$, $J = S$ is left simple, case (a). If $F(J) \neq \phi$, let $V = F(J)$ and $T = J$, case (c).

Suppose J is regular and has more than one $\mathcal{L}$ class. Let L be one. If $F(J) = \phi$, let $V = L$ and $T = J - L = S - L$, case (c). If $F(J) \neq \phi$, let $V = L \cup F(J)$ and $T = (J - L) \cup F(J)$, case (c).

Suppose J is a one-point null $\mathcal{J}$ class. Let $J = \{q\}$, and let Q be the semigroup generated by q. Either $Q = S$, case (b), or let $V = F(J)$ and $T = Q$, case (c). This exhausts the possibilities. ▮

4.2 Definition. Let S be a finite semigroup. Then a *system* for S is an ordered finite sequence $(S_1, \ldots, S_n)$ of subsemigroups of S satisfying

(a) $S_n^I \cdot S_{n-1}^I \cdots S_1^I = S^I$, and

(b) for each $(s_n, \ldots, s_1) \in S_n^I \times \cdots \times S_1^I$ and for each $s_0 \in S$, there exists an integer k, $1 \leqslant k \leqslant n$, such that $s_{k-1} \cdots s_1 s_0 \in S_k$.

4.3 Lemma. Let S be a finite semigroup. Then S has a system $(S_1, \ldots, S_n)$ such that each S_i, $i = 1, \ldots, n$, is either left simple or cyclic.

PROOF. We proceed by induction on $|S|$. $S = \{1\}$ clearly satisfies the assertion. Suppose the lemma is true for all semigroups with order less than n, and let S have order n. Since every semigroup S has a trivial system ($S = S_1$), if S is either left simple or cyclic the assertion is proved. So suppose S satisfies case (c) of Lemma 4.1.

By induction, both V and T have systems satisfying the assertion. Let $(V_1, ..., V_m)$ and $(T_1, ..., T_p)$ be the said systems for V and T, respectively. Now let $S_1 = T_1, ..., S_p = T_p, S_{p+1} = V_1, ..., S_{p+m} = V_m$. Claim $(S_1, ..., S_{p+m})$ is a system for S satisfying the assertion.

Condition (a) of the definition of systems is satisfied by $(S_1, ..., S_{p+m})$, since $S^I = V^I T^I$. To prove (b) is satisfied, let $(v_m, ..., v_1, t_p, ..., t_1) \in V_m^I \times \cdots \times V_1^I \times T_p^I \times \cdots \times T_1^I$, and let $s_0 \in S$. If $s_0 \in T$, then there exists k_1, $1 \leqslant k_1 \leqslant p$ such that $t_{k_1-1} \cdots t_1 s_0 \in T_{k_1}$, since $(T_1, ..., T_p)$ satisfies the assertion. If $s_0 \notin T$, then $t_p \cdots t_1 s_0 \in V$, since $s_0 \in V$ and V is a left ideal. Then there exists k_2, $1 \leqslant k_2 \leqslant m$, such that $v_{k_2-1} \cdots v_1(t_p \cdots t_1 s_0) \in V_{k_2}$. Thus, it follows that $(S_1, ..., S_{p+m})$ satisfies (b). ∎

4.4 Lemma. Let $(S_1, ..., S_n)$ be a nontrivial system for a semigroup S. Then

$$(S^1, S) \mid (S_n^I, \tilde{S}_n^I) \text{ w } \cdots \text{ w } (S_1^I, \tilde{S}_1^I),$$

where, if (X, S) is a mapping semigroup, then $(X, \tilde{S})$ means that $\tilde{S}$ is the subsemigroup of $F_R(X)$ consisting of S and the constant maps on X.†

PROOF. Let $s \in S$, and define $\hat{s} \in F_R(S_n^I \times \cdots \times S_1^I)$ by $(s_n, ..., s_1)\,\hat{s} = (s_n, ..., s_{k+1}, s_k \cdots s_1 s, I, ..., I)$, where k is the *smallest* integer satisfying (b) of the systems definition. Then

$$\hat{s} \in (S_n^I, \tilde{S}_n^I) \text{ w } \cdots \text{ w } (S_1^I, \tilde{S}_1^I).$$

For, if we write $(s_n, ..., s_1)\,\hat{s} = [f_n(s_n), ..., f_1(s_1)]$, then, for $j = 1, ..., n$,

$$f_j(s_j) = \begin{cases} s_j & \text{if } s \in S_1 \text{ or } s_1 s \in S_2 \text{ or } \cdots \text{ or } s_{j-2} \cdots s_1 s \in S_{j-1} \\ s_j \cdots s_1 s & \text{if none of the preceding are true and } s_{j-1} \cdots s_1 s \in S_j \\ I & \text{otherwise.} \end{cases}$$

Then f_j depends on s and $s_{j-1}, ..., s_1$ and belongs to $\tilde{S}_j^I$. Notice that, if k is not the smallest integer satisfying (b), $\hat{s}$ will not be in the wreath product.

† Zeiger emphasizes the usefulness of the augmented semigroup. Compare Chapter 4.

Let $\hat{S}$ be the subsemigroup of $(S_n{}^I, \tilde{S}_n{}^I) \text{ w } \cdots \text{ w } (S_1{}^I, \tilde{S}_1{}^I)$ generated by $\{\hat{s} : s \in S\}$. Let $\theta : S_n{}^I \times \cdots \times S_1{}^I \twoheadrightarrow S^1$ be defined by $\theta(s_n, \ldots, s_1) = s_n \cdots s_1$ and $\theta(I, \ldots, I) = 1$. Then clearly $\theta(x\hat{s}) = \theta(x)s$ for all $x \in S_n{}^I \times \cdots \times S_1{}^I$ and $s \in S$. Thus by X2.10,

$$(S^1, S) \mid (S_n{}^I, \widetilde{S_n{}^I}) \wr \cdots \wr (S_1{}^I, \widetilde{S_1{}^I}). \quad \blacksquare$$

4.5 Lemma. Let $\mathscr{S}$ be a family of semigroups, and suppose $(S^1, \tilde{S}) \in \overline{W}(\mathscr{S})$ for all $S \in \mathscr{S}$. Then, for all $(Y, T) \in \overline{W}(\mathscr{S})$, we have $(Y, \tilde{T}) \in \overline{W}(\mathscr{S})$.

PROOF. Induct on n of $\overline{W}_n(\mathscr{S})$. $\overline{W}_1(\mathscr{S})$ consists of (S^1, S), and so by the hypothesis $(S^1, \tilde{S}) \in \overline{W}(\mathscr{S})$. Assume true for $n - 1$ and let $(Y, T) \in \overline{W}_n(\mathscr{S})$. Then either

(1) $(Y, T) | (X, S)$ for some $(X, S) \in \overline{W}_{n-1}(\mathscr{S})$, or
(2) $(Y, T) | (Y_2, T_2) \wr (Y_1, T_1)$, $(Y_i, T_i) \in \overline{W}_{n-1}(\mathscr{S})$, $i = 1, 2$.

In case 1, let (X', S') be such that $(Y, T) \overset{(\theta, \varphi)}{\twoheadleftarrow} (X', S') \subseteq (X, S)$. We shall show that $(Y, \tilde{T}) | (X, \tilde{S})$. Let $V = S' \cup \{\text{constant maps on } X'\}$. V is a subsemigroup of $\tilde{S}$ and leaves the set X' invariant. Thus, $(X', V) \subseteq (X, \tilde{S})$. Denote $\{\text{constant maps on } X'\}$ by $C_{X'}$, and let c_x be the map that sends everything to x. Multiplication in V is $s_1 \cdot s_2 = s_1 s_2$, $c_x \cdot s = c_{xs}$, $c_{x_1} \cdot c_{x_2} = s_1 \cdot c_{x_2} = c_{x_2}$. Let $\theta : X' \twoheadrightarrow Y$ and $\varphi : S' \twoheadrightarrow T$ be the map and epimorphism associated with the division $(Y, T) | (X, S)$. Define $\psi : V \twoheadrightarrow \tilde{T}$ by $\psi(s) = \varphi(s)$, $\psi(c_x) = c_{\theta(x)} \in C_Y$. Let $s \in S'$, and suppose s is a constant map on X', say c_x. $\psi(s) = \varphi(s)$, and $\psi(c_x) = c_{\theta(x)}$. But $\theta(x_1 s) = \theta(x_1)\, \varphi(s)$, and $x_1 s = x$, so that $\theta(x_1 s) = \theta(x)$ for all $x_1 \in X'$. Therefore, $\varphi(s) = c_{\theta(x)}$, so that ψ is well defined. Again relying on the fact that $\theta(xs) = \theta(x)\, \varphi(s)$, it is easy to show that ψ is an epimorphism and $(X', V) \twoheadrightarrow (Y, \tilde{T})$. Thus, $(Y, \tilde{T}) | (X, \tilde{S})$, so that $(Y, \tilde{T}) \in \overline{W}(\mathscr{S})$.

In case 2, we have $(Y, \tilde{T}) | [(Y_2 \times Y_1), (Y_2, T_2) \text{ w } (Y_1, T_1)^{\sim}]$† by the preceding result. Now the constant maps on $Y_2 \times Y_1$ are clearly in $(Y_2, \tilde{T}_2) \text{ w } (Y_1, \tilde{T}_1)$, and so

$$[Y_2 \times Y_1, (Y_2, T_2) \text{ w } (Y_1, T_1)^{\sim}] \mid (Y_2, \tilde{T}_2) \wr (Y_1, \tilde{T}_1) \in \overline{W}(\mathscr{S}).$$

Thus, $(Y, \tilde{T}) \in \overline{W}(\mathscr{S})$. $\blacksquare$

† Where, for a complicated expression E, we write $E^{\sim}$ for $\tilde{E}$.

4.6 Lemma. (a) $(U_3, \tilde{U}_3) \in \overline{W}(U_3)$.

(b) Let G be a group. Then $(G, \tilde{G}) \in \overline{W}(G \cup U_3)$.

PROOF. (a) Since right multiplication by r_0 and r_1 on U_3 is precisely the same as c_{r_0} and c_{r_1}, respectively, acting on U_3, we see that $\tilde{U}_3 = \{c_{r_0}, c_{r_1}, c_1, \text{identity map}\}$, i.e., the constant maps on U_3 and the identity map. Let X be a set, and let $S \subseteq F_R(X)$ consist of the constant maps on X and the identity map. We shall show that $(X, S) \in \overline{W}(U_3)$. Thus, in particular, $(U_3, \tilde{U}_3) \in \overline{W}(U_3)$.

Code X into (a sufficiently large) $U_1 \times \cdots \times U_1$ in a 1 : 1 manner. Let $\bar{X}$ denote the image of X in $U_1 \times \cdots \times U_1$. Let $x \in X$. If $\bar{x} = (r_{i_1}, \ldots, r_{i_n})$, $i_j \in \{0, 1\}$, then define $\varphi : S \to U_3 \times \cdots \times U_3$ by $\varphi(c_x) = (r_{i_1}, \ldots, r_{i_n})$ and $\varphi(Id) = (1, \ldots, 1)$. φ is a monomorphism. Let $\bar{S} = \varphi(S)$. It is easy to see that $(\bar{X}, \bar{S})$ is a mapping semigroup isomorphic to (X, S), and that $(\bar{X}, \bar{S}) \subseteq (U_3, U_3) \times \cdots \times (U_3, U_3) \in \overline{W}(U_3)$. Hence, $(X, S) \in \overline{W}(U_3)$.

(b) Let G be a group. Then $\tilde{G}$ is the disjoint union of G and C_G with multiplication as defined in the proof of Lemma 4.5. If $g \in G$, define $\hat{g} \in F_R(G \times G)$ by $(g_2, g_1)\hat{g} = (g_2, g_1 g)$. If $c_g \in C_G$, define $\hat{c}_g \in F_R(G \times G)$ by $(g_2, g_1)\hat{c}_g = (g_1^{-1}, g_1 g)$. Note that $\hat{g}$ and $\hat{c}_g$ belong to $(G, S) \text{ w } (G, G)$, where $S = \{\text{constant maps on } G \cup \text{identity map}\}$. Let $\hat{G}$ be the subsemigroup of $(G, S) \text{ w } (G, G)$ generated by $\{\hat{g}, \hat{c}_g : g, c_g \in \tilde{G}\}$. Let $\theta : G \times G \twoheadrightarrow G$ be defined by $\theta(g_2, g_1) = g_2 g_1$. Then clearly $\theta(x\hat{s}) = \theta(x)s$ for all $x \in G \times G$ and $s \in \tilde{G}$. Thus by X2.10, $(G, \tilde{G}) | (G, S) \wr (G, G)$. But by (a), we have $(G, S) \in \overline{W}(U_3)$. Thus, $(G, S) \wr (G, G)$ and hence $(G, \tilde{G})$ belong to $\overline{W}(G \cup U_3)$. ∎

4.7 Lemma. Let $\mathscr{S}$ be a family of monoids. Then, if $S \in W(\mathscr{S})$, we have $S^I \in W(\mathscr{S} \cup \{U_3\})$.

PROOF. Let $S \in W_1(\mathscr{S}) = \mathscr{S}$. S is a monoid. Define the monomorphism $\varphi : S^I \to S \times U_3$ by $\varphi(s) = (s, r_0)$ and $\varphi(I) = (1, 1)$. Therefore, $S^I | S \times U_3 | S \text{ w } U_3 \in W(\mathscr{S} \cup \{U_3\})$.

Assume assertion true for $W_{n-1}(\mathscr{S})$, and let $S \in W_n(\mathscr{S})$. Then either (1) $S | T \in W_{n-1}(\mathscr{S})$, which implies $S^I | T^I$, or (2) $S | T_2 \text{ w } T_1$, $T_i \in W_{n-1}(\mathscr{S})$, $i = 1, 2$. Then

$$S^I | (T_2 \text{ w } T_1)^I | T_2{}^I \text{ w } T_1{}^I \in W(\mathscr{S} \cup \{U_3\}). \quad ∎$$

4.8 Lemma. Suppose Eq. (3.2) is valid for S, i.e.,

$$S \in W[\text{PRIMES}(S) \cup \{U_3\}].$$

Then

$$(S^I, \tilde{S}^I) \in \overline{W}[\text{PRIMES}(S) \cup \{U_3\}].$$

PROOF. Since PRIMES(S) and U_3 are monoids, Lemma 4.7 says $S^I \in W[\text{PRIMES}(S) \cup \{U_3\}]$. Then, by Fact 2.21,

$$(S^I, S^I) \in \overline{W}[\text{PRIMES}(S) \cup \{U_3\}].$$

But, by Lemma 4.6, $\overline{W}[\text{PRIMES}(S) \cup \{U_3\}]$ satisfies the hypothesis of Lemma 4.5, so that

$$(S^I, \tilde{S}^I) \in \overline{W}[\text{PRIMES}(S) \cup \{U_3\}]. \quad ▮$$

We now restate for convenience results in Sect. 3 which were proved by algebraic arguments.

4.9 Lemma. (a) PRIMES ∪ UNITS ⊆ IRR (Definitions 3.1 and 3.2).

(b) If S is a cyclic semigroup, Eq. (3.2) is valid for S.

(c) If G is a group, Eq. (3.2) is valid for G.

PROOF. (a) See Lemma 3.6.

(b) See Lemma 3.9.

(c) See proof of Lemma 3.8. ▮

4.10 Lemma. If S is left simple, Eq. (3.2) is valid for S.

PROOF. If S is left simple, $S \cong G \times A^l$, where G is a group and A is a nonempty set. PRIMES(S) = PRIMES(G) (see proof of Lemma 3.8). Hence, $S \in W[\text{PRIMES}(S) \cup \{U_3, A^l\}]$ by Lemma 4.9(c). We need only show that $A^l \in W(U_3)$. (This was done by a machine proof in Lemma 3.8.) Then the assertion will be proved.

Let $L = \{a, b\}^l$. Then $L \subseteq U_3 \text{ w } U_1 \cong F(U_1, U_3) \times_Y U_1$, for the subsemigroup $\{[(r_0, 1), r_1], [(r_1, 1), r_1]\}$ is isomorphic to L. [The notation $(r_0, 1)$ means the function $f \in F(U_1, U_3)$, defined by $f(r_0) = r_0$ and $f(r_1) = 1$.] Now, since A^l is a subsemigroup of a suitable number of direct products of L, we have $A^l \in W(U_3)$. ▮

4.11 Theorem (3.3) Let S be a finite semigroup.

(a) $S \in W(\mathscr{S} \cup \{U_3\})$ iff PRIMES(S) ⊆ PRIMES($\mathscr{S}$). In particular, recall Eq. 3.2:

$$S \in W(\text{PRIMES}(S) \cup \{U_3\}). \tag{4.1}$$

(b) PRIMES $\cup$ UNITS $=$ IRR.

(c) In general, $S \notin W[\text{IRR}(S)]$.

PROOF. We first prove the validity of (4.1). If S is left simple or cyclic, we are done. If not, then S has a nontrivial system $(S_1, \ldots, S_n)$, where each S_i is left simple or cyclic. Apply Lemmas 4.4 and 4.8 to get

$$S \in W(\text{PRIMES}\{S_1, \ldots, S_n\} \cup \{U_3\}).$$

But clearly $\text{PRIMES}\{S_1, \ldots, S_n\} \subseteq \text{PRIMES}(S)$, and so Eq. (4.1) is valid.

Now (4.1) implies that, if $\text{PRIMES}(S) \subseteq \text{PRIMES}(\mathscr{S})$, then $S \in W(\mathscr{S} \cup \{U_3\})$. To prove the converse, let $S \in W(\mathscr{S} \cup \{U_3\})$ and let $P \in \text{PRIMES}(S)$. Then $P \in W(\mathscr{S} \cup \{U_3\})$, and, by Fact 3.16, $P \mid S$ for some $S \in \mathscr{S}$, since a group cannot divide U_3. Hence $P \in \text{PRIMES}(\mathscr{S})$. This proves (a). Refer to the proof of Theorem 3.3 for the proof of (b) and (c). ▮

4.12 Remark. Part (c) of the theorem justifies both the distinction between PRIMES and UNITS and the inclusion of U_3 in the foregoing equations.

4.13 Corollary (3.5). Let S be a finite semigroup. Then $S \mid S_n \text{ w} \cdots \text{w } S_1$ for some sequence $S_1, \ldots, S_n$, where

$$S_i \in \text{PRIMES}(S) \cup \text{UNITS}, \qquad i = 1, \ldots, n.$$

PROOF. Refer to Corollary 3.5. ▮

4.14 Remark. (For readers *au fait* with Chapter 7.) If S is a union of groups semigroup, then each $\mathscr{J}$ class is a simple semigroup. The sequence $(J_1, \ldots, J_n)$ of all $\mathscr{J}$ classes of S where $i < j$ implies $J \nleq_i J_j$ is a system for S which plays an important role in the work on complexity (to be defined in Chapter 6) of semigroups that are unions of groups. See Chapter 9.

By the preceding ordering condition, J_1 must be a maximal $\mathscr{J}$ class of S, and J_n is the kernel of S. To prove that $(J_1, \ldots, J_n)$ is a system, induct on the number of $\mathscr{J}$ classes in S. Assume true for semigroups with $n - 1$ $\mathscr{J}$ classes, and let S have n $\mathscr{J}$ classes. Choose a maximal $\mathscr{J}$ class, and call it J_1. $S - J_1$ is an ideal of S which is a union of groups with $n - 1$ $\mathcal{J}$ classes (which are, of course, the remaining $\mathcal{J}$ classes of S). Proceed as in the proof of Lemma 4.3 to prove $(J_1, ..., J_n)$ a system for S.

The proof of the theorem given here is due to Krohn and Rhodes (previously unpublished). See also Zeiger [5] and Hartmanis and Stearns [6]. For a generalization, see Krohn, Mateosian, and Rhodes [2].

5. Some Results on Combinatorial Semigroups; An Application of the Prime Decomposition Theorem

We first give the definition and some facts about combinatorial semigroups.

5.1 Definition. A semigroup S is *combinatorial* iff each subgroup of S is of order 1.

5.2 Fact. Homomorphic images, subsemigroups, and finite direct products of combinatorial semigroups are combinatorial.

PROOF. Use Fact I.1.7. ∎

5.3 Fact. (a) There exists a positive integer $p = p(S)$ such that $s^p = s^{p+1}$ for all $s \in S$ iff S is combinatorial.

(b) PRIMES$(S) = \phi$ iff S is combinatorial.

(c) Combinatorial semigroups are closed under wreath and semidirect products. That is, if S_1, S_2 are combinatorial, then $S_2 \text{ w } S_1$ and $S_2 \times_Y S_1$ are combinatorial. Furthermore, if $S_2 \text{ w } S_1$ is combinatorial, then both S_1 and S_2 are.

PROOF. (a) and (b) are left as exercises. To prove (c), notice that, if $P \in$ PRIMES$(S_2 \text{ w } S_1)$ or PRIMES$(S_2 \times_Y S_1)$, then $P \in$ PRIMES(S_1) or PRIMES(S_2). If the latter are empty, the former are. This proves the first assertion. Since $S_i \mid S_2 \text{ w } S_1$, $i = 1, 2$, we have PRIMES$(S_i) \subseteq$ PRIMES$(S_2 \text{ w } S_1)$, so that, if $S_2 \text{ w } S_1$ is combinatorial, S_1 and S_2 must be. ∎

5.4 Principle of Induction for Combinatorial Semigroups. Let $\mathcal{P}$ be any property of finite semigroups such that

(1) $\mathscr{P}$ is closed under division, and

(2) $U_3^{(n)} \equiv U_3 \le \cdots \le U_3$ (n times) satisfies $\mathscr{P}$.

Then every combinatorial semigroup satisfies $\mathscr{P}$.

PROOF. Let $\mathscr{P}$ be a property of finite semigroups satisfying (1) and (2), and let S be combinatorial. Then PRIMES(S) $= \phi$, and so $S \in W(U_3)$ and $S \mid U_3^{(n)}$ for some n, by the prime decomposition theorem. Hence, S satisfies $\mathscr{P}$. ▮

5.5 Notation. (a) Let A be a nonempty set. Let $\Pi(A)$ denote the set of all infinite sequences of elements of A.

(b) Let S be a semigroup. Define the nth *iteration of the machine* S^f by $(S^{f\sigma})^n : \Sigma S \to \Sigma S$, where $(S^{f\sigma})^2 = S^{f\sigma}S^{f\sigma}$ and $(S^{f\sigma})^n = S^{f\sigma}(S^{f\sigma})^{n-1}$.

(c) Let S be a semigroup, and let $X \in \Pi(S^1)$, $X = (x_1, x_2, \ldots)$. Then $P_X : \Sigma S \to \Sigma S$ is defined by $P_X(s_1, \ldots, s_n) = (x_1 s_1, \ldots, x_n s_n)$.

Next we give the main result of this section, which says that, if the machine of a combinatorial semigroup is iterated long enough, the $n + 1$th iterated machine is the same as the nth iterated machine. Furthermore, if the output of the combinatorial machine is altered as a function of time by left multiplication, the same thing happens.

5.6 Proposition. The following statements are equivalent:

(a) S is a combinatorial semigroup.

(b) There exists a positive integer $m = m(S)$ such that

$$(S^{f\sigma})^m = (S^{f\sigma})^{m+1}. \tag{5.1}$$

(c) There exists a positive integer $q = q(S)$ such that, for all $X \in \Pi(S^1)$,

$$(P_X S^{f\sigma})^q = (P_X S^{f\sigma})^{q+1}, \tag{5.2}$$

$$(S^{f\sigma} P_X)^q = (S^{f\sigma} P_X)^{q+1} \tag{5.3}$$

PROOF. (*c*) *implies* (*b*) by taking $X = (1, 1, \ldots)$.

(*b*) *implies* (*a*): Suppose S is a semigroup with a nontrivial subgroup G (i.e., S is noncombinatorial). Let $g \in G$, $g \neq 1$, the identity of G. Then $(S^{f\sigma})^n (g, 1) = (g, g^n)$ for all $n = 1, 2, \ldots$. Since $g \neq 1$, there exists no positive integer m such that $(S^{f\sigma})^m = (S^{f\sigma})^{m+1}$.

(*a*) *implies* (*c*): First we note that (5.2) and (5.3) are equivalent. Assume (5.2) is true. Then

$$(S^{f\sigma}P_X)^{q+1} = S^{f\sigma}(P_X S^{f\sigma})^q P_X = S^{f\sigma}(P_X S^{f\sigma})^{q+1} P_X = (S^{f\sigma}P_X)^{q+2}.$$

Similarly, (5.3) implies (5.2).

Let $\mathscr{P}$ be the collection of all semigroups satisfying Eq. (5.2). We shall show that $\mathscr{P}$ is closed under division and $U_3^{(n)} \in \mathscr{P}$ for all n, thus applying the principle of induction for combinatorial semigroups (5.4) to prove the proposition.

(1) *$\mathscr{P}$ is closed under division.* Let $S \mid T$ and $T \in \mathscr{P}$. Write $S \overset{\varphi}{\twoheadleftarrow} T' \subseteq T$. Then $S^f \mid T^f$ and $S^{f\sigma} = h_2{}^\Gamma T^{f\sigma} h_1{}^\Gamma$, where $h_1 : S \to T'$, $h_1(s) = \bar{s}$, where $\bar{s}$ is a fixed representative of $\varphi^{-1}(s)$, and $h_2 : T' \twoheadrightarrow S$, $h_2(t) = \varphi(t)$. [Refer to the proof of Proposition 2.6(b) for this notation.] Let $X \in \Pi(S^1)$, $X = (x_1, x_2, \ldots)$, and let $q = q(T)$. Then

$$(P_X S^{f\sigma})^{q+1} = (P_X h_2{}^\Gamma T^{f\sigma} h_1{}^\Gamma)^{q+1} = P_X h_2{}^\Gamma (T^{f\sigma} h_1{}^\Gamma P_X h_2{}^\Gamma)^q T^{f\sigma} h_1{}^\Gamma. \quad (5.4)$$

Now we claim

$$h_2{}^\Gamma (T^{f\sigma} h_1{}^\Gamma P_X h_2{}^\Gamma)^p = h_2{}^\Gamma (T^{f\sigma} P_Y)^p \qquad \text{for all} \quad p = 1, 2, \ldots, \quad (5.5)$$

where $Y \in \Pi(T^1)$, $Y = (\bar{x}_1, \bar{x}_2, \ldots)$. For $p = 1$, (5.5) is easy to verify. Suppose (5.5) true for $p - 1$. Let

$$\begin{aligned}(t_1, \ldots, t_n) &= h_2{}^\Gamma (T^{f\sigma} h_1{}^\Gamma P_X h_2{}^\Gamma)^{p-1} (t_1', \ldots, t_n') \\ &= h_2{}^\Gamma (T^{f\sigma} P_Y)^{p-1} (t_1', \ldots, t_n').\end{aligned}$$

Then to prove (5.5) it is sufficient to show that

$$h_2{}^\Gamma T^{f\sigma} h_1{}^\Gamma P_X (t_1, \ldots, t_n) = h_2{}^\Gamma T^{f\sigma} P_Y (u_1, \ldots, u_n),$$

where u_i is any element of $\varphi^{-1}(t_i)$, $i = 1, \ldots, n$. This is easily verified.

Now, since $(T^{f\sigma}P_Y)^q = (T^{f\sigma}P_Y)^{q+1}$, it follows easily by (5.4) and (5.5) that $(P_X S^{f\sigma})^{q+1} = (P_X S^{f\sigma})^{q+2}$. Thus, $\mathscr{P}$ is closed under division.

(2) $U_3^{(n)} \in \mathscr{P}$. Verify that $(P_X U_3^{f\sigma})^2 = (P_X U_3^{f\sigma})^3$ for all $X \in \Pi(U_3)$. Also verify that $\mathscr{P}$ is closed under finite direct products. Both are easy. Furthermore, if S_1, S_2 are combinatorial, then $q(S_1 \times S_2) = \max\{q(S_1), q(S_2)\}$.

Now assume there exists q_n such that (5.2) holds for $U_3^{(n)}$. We shall find a q_{n+1} in terms of q_n such that (5.2) holds for $U_3^{(n+1)} = F(U_3, U_3^{(n)}) \times_Y U_3$. Notice that q_n is the integer such that (5.2) holds for $F(U_3, U_3^{(n)})$. Let $X \in \Pi(U_3^{(n+1)})$, with $X = [(g_1, b_1), (g_2, b_2), \ldots]$, $b_i \in U_3$, $g_i \in F(U_3, U_3^{(n)})$. Let $M = P_X U_3^{(n+1)f\sigma}$, and let $Y \in \Sigma U_3^{(n+1)}$, with $Y = [(f_1, a_1), \ldots, (f_k, a_k)]$.

We want to get into a position where we can apply the induction hypothesis. We can do this if we can get the semidirect product acting like the direct product. If all the a_i's and b_i's equal 1, this is the situation. Let r be the largest integer such that $a_1, \ldots, a_{r-1}, b_1, \ldots, b_{r-1}$ all equal 1. Then, on the first $r - 1$ terms of Y, M^p acts exactly like $[P_{X'} F(U_3, U_3^{(n)})^f \times U_3^f]^{\sigma p}$, where $X' \in \Pi F(U_3, U_3^{(n)})$ with $X' = (g_1, g_2, \ldots)$. So, after q_n iterations of M, the first $r - 1$ terms of Y do not change. Write $M^{q_n}(Y) = [(h_1, 1), \ldots, (h_{r-1}, 1), (h_r', c_r), \ldots, (h_k', c_k)]$. Note that each $c_i \in \{r_0, r_1\}$ after the second iteration, and q_n is certainly $\geqslant 2$. Thus $xc_i = c_i$ for all $x \in U_3$.

Now after another $q_n + 1$ iterations the rth term will become stable. To see this, start with $M^{q_n}(Y)$, and iterate p times. The new rth term will be $\{g_r[{}^{b_r}(h_1 \cdots h_{r-1} g_r)]^{p-1} \cdot {}^{b_r}(h_1 \cdots h_r'), c_r\}$. Now, for all $f \in F(U_3, U_3^{(n)})$, we have $f^{q_n} = f^{q_n+1}$. {Consider $[F(U_3, U_3^{(n)})^{f\sigma}]^{q_n}(f, f)$.} Thus, when $p = q_n + 1$, the rth term is stabilized. Write $M^{2q_n+1}(Y) = [(h_1, 1), \ldots, (h_r, c_r), \ldots, (h_k, c_k)]$.

We shall now show that after another $q_n + 1$ iterations all the terms become stable, so that $q_{n+1} \leqslant 3q_n + 2$, proving the assertion. Let c_1 denote the identity of $F(U_3, U_3^{(n)})$. Define the machine $f : \Sigma U_3^{(n+1)} \to U_3^{(n+1)}$ by

$$f[(k_1, d_1), \ldots, (k_n, d_n)] = \begin{cases} ({}^{d_{n-1}}k_n, d_n) & \text{if } n \geqslant 2,\ d_{n-1} \neq 1 \\ (c_1, d_n) & \text{otherwise.} \end{cases}$$

Also define $X_1 \in \Pi F(U_3, U_3^{(n)})$ by

$$X_1 = [j_1, \ldots, j_r, {}^{c_r}g_{r+1}{}^{c_r b_{r+1}}(h_1 \cdots h_r), \ldots,$$
$${}^{c_{k-1}}g_k{}^{c_{k-1} b_k}(h_1 \cdots h_r), j_{k+1}, \ldots],$$

where each $j_i = c_1$. Define $X_2 \in \Pi(U_3^{(n+1)})$ by

$$X_2 = [(h_1, 1), \ldots, (h_r, 1), (g_{r+1}{}^{b_{r+1}}(h_1 \cdots h_r), 1), \ldots,$$
$$(g_k{}^{b_k}(h_1 \cdots h_r), 1), (j_{k+1}, 1), \ldots],$$

where once again each $j_i = c_1$. Note that X_1 and X_2 are functions of X and Y. Let $F = [F(U_3, U_3^{(n)})]^f$. Then, by direct computation, verify that

$$M^{2q_n+2+p}(Y) = P_{X_2} U_3^{(n+1)f\sigma} [P_{X_1} F \times U_3^f]^{\sigma p f \sigma} M^{2q_n+1}(Y)$$

for $p = 1, 2, \ldots$. But by induction $[P_{X_1} F \times U_3^f]^{\sigma q_n} = [P_{X_1} F \times U_3^f]^{\sigma(q_n+1)}$ for all $X_1 \in \Pi F(U_3, U_3^{(n)})$. Thus, $M^{3q_n+2}(Y) = M^{3q_n+3}(Y)$ for all $Y \in \Sigma U_3^{(n+1)}$. ∎

5.7 Remark. A way of visualizing $(S^{1f\sigma})^p$ is by the "Pascal Array" of the multiplication table of S^1. Let $X = (x_1, x_2, \ldots)$ and $Y = (s_1, s_2, \ldots) \in \Pi(S^1)$. Consider Fig. 1. Let $a_{0i} = s_i$, $a_{j0} = x_j$, and

	$s_1 = a_{01}$	$s_2 = a_{02}$	$s_3 = a_{03}$	$\cdots$
$x_1 = a_{10}$	$x_1 s_1 = a_{11}$	$x_1 s_1 s_2 = a_{12}$	$x_1 s_1 s_2 s_3 = a_{13}$	$\cdots$
$x_2 = a_{20}$	$x_2 x_1 s_1 = a_{21}$	$x_2 x_1 s_1 x_1 s_1 s_2 = a_{22}$	$a_{22} \cdot a_{13} = a_{23}$	$\cdots$
$x_3 = a_{30}$	$x_3 x_2 x_1 s_1 = a_{31}$	$a_{31} \cdot a_{22} = a_{32}$	$a_{32} \cdot a_{23} = a_{33}$	$\cdots$
$\vdots$	$\vdots$	$\vdots$	$\vdots$	

FIG. 1. Pascal array of S^1.

compute the entries in the array by the formula $a_{mn} = a_{m(n-1)} \cdot a_{(m-1)n}$. If $x_1 = x_2 = \cdots = 1$, then $(a_{p1}, a_{p2}, \ldots)$ will be the output of $(S^{1f\sigma})^p (s_1, s_2, \ldots)$. Thus, Proposition 5.6(b) says that S is combinatorial iff there exists $m = m(S^1)$ such that for all $Y \in \Pi(S^1)$ the $m, m+1, \ldots$ rows of the array are identical.

Let $f_i = S^{1f} L_{x_i}$, where $L_{x_i}(s_1, \ldots, s_n) = (x_i, s_1, \ldots, s_n)$ (see Exercise X2.6). Then $a_{jk} = f_j f_{j-1}^\sigma \cdots f_1^\sigma(s_1, \ldots, s_k)$.

We have the following "duality." Transposition in Fig. 1 about the diagonal, i.e., the transformation taking a_{jk} to a_{kj}, may be effected by interchanging X and Y and replacing S^1 by $r(S^1)$, the reverse semigroup of S^1. The dual result of Proposition 5.6(b) is the following.

5.8 Proposition. S is combinatorial iff there exists an integer $n = n(S)$ such that, if

$$b_{jk} = f_j f_{j-1}^{\sigma} \cdots f_1(1,\ldots,1) \quad (k \text{ times}),$$

then $b_{jn} = b_{j(n+1)} = \cdots$ for all $j = 1, 2, \ldots$ and for all $(x_1, x_2, \ldots) \in \Pi(S^1)$.

PROOF. Let $\overline{a_{kj}} = f'_k f'^{\sigma}_{k-1} \cdots f'^{\sigma}_1(x_1, \ldots, x_j)$, where $f'_i = r(S^1)^f L_{s_i}$, represent the $k - j$th entry in the "Pascal Array" of $r(S^1)$. Then, since $r(S^1)$ is combinatorial, if $s_1 = s_2 = \cdots = 1$, there exists an integer n such that $\overline{a_{nj}} = \overline{a_{(n+1)j}} = \cdots$ for all $j = 1, 2\ldots$, and for all $(x_1, x_2, \ldots)$. But $\overline{a_{kj}} = a_{jk}$, as defined in the foregoing remark. Writing $b_{jk} = a_{jk}$ when $s_1 = s_2 = \cdots = 1$, we have the assertion. ▮

This section is from Sect. 1 of Rhodes [7]. For other applications of the prime decomposition theorem, see Sect. 4 of Krohn and Rhodes [1].

REFERENCES

1. K. Krohn and J. Rhodes, Algebraic theory of machines. I. Prime decomposition theorem for finite semigroups and machines, *Trans. Amer. Math. Soc.* **116**, 450–464 (1965).
2. K. Krohn, R. Mateosian, and J. Rhodes, Methods of the algebraic theory of machines. I, *J. Computer System Sci.* **1**, 55–85 (1967).
3. K. Krohn and J. Rhodes, Algebraic theory of machines, *in* "Proceedings of the Symposium on the Mathematical Theory of Automata" (J. Fox, ed.), pp. 341–384. Polytechnic Institute of Brooklyn, New York, 1962.
4. K. Krohn and J. Rhodes, Results on finite semigroups derived from the algebraic theory of machines, *Proc. Nat. Acad. Sci. U.S.A.* **3**, 499–501 (1965).
5. H. P. Zeiger, Cascade synthesis of finite-state machines, *Information and Control* **10**, 419–433 (1967).
6. J. Hartmanis and R. E. Stearns, "Algebraic Structure Theory of Sequential Machines." Prentice-Hall, Englewood Cliffs, New Jersey, 1966.
7. J. Rhodes, Some results of finite semigroups, *J. Algebra* **3**, 471–504 (1966).

CHAPTER 6

Complexity and Group Complexity of Finite-State Machines and Finite Semigroups

MICHAEL A. ARBIB[†]
Stanford University, Stanford, California

JOHN L. RHODES[‡§]
University of California, Berkeley, California
Krohn-Rhodes Research Institute, Berkeley, California

BRET R. TILSON[‡]
University of California, Berkeley, California

1. Definitions of Group Complexity

We have become accustomed to viewing finite-state sequential machines at three levels of abstraction:

(i) as machines (X, Y, Q, δ, β) replete with inputs and outputs, as well as internal states;

(ii) as abstract finite semigroups S; and

(iii) as transformation semigroups (Q, S) (where the set of transformations S of Q comprises the motions of Q induced by input sequences).

[†] This research was supported in part by U.S. Air Force Office of Scientific Research, Information Sciences Directorate, under Grant No. AF-AFOSR-1198-67.

[‡] This work was supported by the United States Air Force, Air Force Systems Command, Contract Number AF 33(615)-3893.

[§] Alfred P. Sloan Research Fellow, 1967–1968.

For each representation, we have an appropriate decomposition theorem:

(i) We say that a machine M is a *group* or *permutation* machine if each input to M permutes its states; in this case, M^S is a group. We say that a machine M is a *basic combinatorial* or *identity-reset* machine if each input to M is a reset (i.e., constant map) or the identity map. We say that a machine is *combinatorial* or *group-free* if it can be simulated by a cascade of identity-reset machines; equivalently, M^S is combinatorial, i.e., has no subgroups of order greater than 1.

Then the decomposition theorem says that any reduced finite-state sequential machine has a GC-decomposition X, i.e., it can be simulated by a cascade X of machines $M_1, \ldots, M_n$, where each M_j is a finite-state reduced sequential machine that is a group-machine or else combinatorial, where as usual the input to M_j at time t is determined by the input to the system at time t and the outputs at time t of each $M_1, \ldots, M_{j-1}$, and no feedback occurs.

(ii) Given a semigroup S, there exist semigroups

$$S_1, \ldots, S_n \in \mathrm{PRIMES}(S) \cup \{U_3\}$$

such that

$$(S^1, S) \mid (S_n, S_n) \wr \cdots \wr (S_1, S_1). \tag{1.1}$$

If (X_1, S_1) and (X_2, S_2) are transformation groups (i.e., S_i is a group and the identity of S_i acts as the identity on X_i), then $(X_2, S_2) \wr (X_1, S_1)$ is a transformation group. Furthermore, if (X_1, S_1) and (X_2, S_2) are combinatorial transformation semigroups (i.e., S_1 and S_2 are combinatorial semigroups), then $(X_2, S_2) \wr (X_1, S_1)$ is a combinatorial transformation semigroup. Since PRIMES are groups, (G, G) is a transformation group if G is a group, and U_3 is a combinatorial semigroup, we can collect contiguous terms in (1.1) to get (S^1, S) dividing the wreath product of transformation semigroups that are alternatively transformation groups and combinatorial transformation semigroups.

(iii) Let (X, S) be a transformation semigroup. Then, since S is a subsemigroup of $F_R(X)$, the semigroup of all functions on X, it is easy to show that

$$(X, S) \mid (X, F_R(X)) \mid (F_R(X), F_R(X)),$$

and so by (ii) there exist semigroups $S_1, \ldots, S_m \in \text{PRIMES} \cup \{U_3\}$ such that

$$(X, S) \mid (S_m, S_m) \wr \cdots \wr (S_1, S_1). \tag{1.2}$$

[However, in this case, we have not shown that the simple groups need belong to PRIMES(S). We shall show later, nevertheless, that decompositions for (X, S) can be obtained where the $S_i \in \text{PRIMES}(S) \cup \{U_3\}$.]

As in (ii), then, we can gather contiguous terms to get (X, S) dividing the wreath product of alternating transformation groups and combinatorial transformation semigroups.

The natural question that arises is, then, "What is the smallest number of groups required for decomposing an object in the preceding fashion into group and combinatorial objects?" It turns out that this number is independent of which of the foregoing three representations is chosen, and depends only on the semigroup S. We call this number the *group complexity* of S, $\#_G(S)$, and devote this chapter to exploring some of its basic properties. The subject is further explored in Chapter 9 after the necessary algebraic preliminaries have been elaborated in Chapters 7 and 8.

1.1 Definition. Let X be a GC-decomposition of a finite-state reduced sequential machine M into a cascade of group and combinatorial machines $M_1, \ldots, M_n$, in that order. Let $\#_G(X)$ denote the number of group machines among $M_1, \ldots, M_n$. Then the *group complexity* of M [definition (a)] is

$$\#_G{}^a(M) = \min\{\#_G(X)\colon X \text{ is a } GC\text{–decomposition of } M\}.$$

For a semigroup S with machine S_M we set

$$\#_G{}^a(S) = \#_G{}^a(S^M)$$

1.2 Definition. Let S be a finite semigroup. Then the *group complexity* of S [definition (b)], $\#_G{}^b(S)$, is the smallest nonnegative integer n such that

$$(S^1, S) \mid (Y_n, C_n) \wr (X_n, G_n) \wr (Y_{n-1}, C_{n-1}) \wr \cdots$$
$$\wr (Y_1, C_1) \wr (X_1, G_1) \wr (Y_0, C_0),$$

where (X_i, G_i), $i = 1, ..., n$, are nontrivial transformation groups, and $C_1, ..., C_{n-1}$ are nontrivial combinatorial semigroups. (C_0 and C_n may be trivial.)

1.3 Theorem. $\#_G{}^a(M) = \#_G{}^b(M^S)$, so that, in particular, definitions (a) and (b) of $\#_G(S)$ are equivalent, and two machines with the same semigroup have equal group complexity.

PROOF. This follows from Chapter 3 (Theorem 2.6), which says that S^M can be simulated by a cascade of M_1^{SM} and M_2^{SM} if S divides the wreath product of $M_1{}^S$ and $M_2{}^S$. ∎

1.4 Definition. Let (X, S) be a transformation semigroup. Then the *group complexity* [definition (c)] of (X, S) $\#_G{}^c(X, S)$ is the smallest nonnegative integer n such that

$$\begin{aligned}(X, S) \mid (Y_n, C_n) \wr (X_n, G_n) \wr (Y_{n-1}, C_{n-1}) \wr \cdots \\ \wr (Y_1, C_1) \wr (X_1, G_1) \wr (Y_0, C_0),\end{aligned} \qquad (1.3)^\dagger$$

where (X_i, G_i), $i = 1, ..., n$, are nontrivial transformation groups, and $C_1, ..., C_{n-1}$ are nontrivial combinatorial semigroups. (C_0 and C_n may be trivial.)

Notice that, if $(X, S) \mid (Y, T)$, then $\#_G{}^c(X, S) \leqslant \#_G{}^c(Y, T)$.

1.5 Theorem. (a) If (X, S) is a transformation semigroup, then $(X, S) \in \overline{W}[\text{PRIMES}(S) \cup \{U_3\}]$.

(b) $\#_G{}^c(X, S) = \#_G{}^b(S)$ for all sets X such that (X, S) is a transformation semigroup (i.e., such that S acts faithfully on X).

PROOF. We first consider $(X, \{0\})$, where $\{0\}$ acts like the identity on X. Let S be a nontrivial semigroup with identity 1. Then code X into a direct product of a suitable number of copies of S. Then it is easy to see that

$$(X, \{0\}) \mid [(S \times \cdots \times S), \{1\}] \mid (S, S) \times \cdots \times (S, S).$$

† The reader may consult Krohn, Langer and Rhodes [1] for the claim that relations of this form are intimately related to finite physics. Component actions are considered as analogous to "eigenvectors," so that, heuristically, $\#_G(S)$ is the smallest number of "group or permutation eigenvectors" in a triangularization of S (into permutation or constant component action).

Since wreath product closures are closed under division and direct product, letting $S = U_3$ yields

$$(X, \{0\}) \in \overline{W}[\text{PRIMES}(\{0\}) \cup \{U_3\}] = \overline{W}(U_3).$$

Therefore, $\#_G{}^c(X, \{0\}) = 0$.

Now let (X, S) be any transformation semigroup. Since, in general, for any mapping semigroup (X, S),

$$(S^1, S) \mid (X, S) \times \cdots \times (X, S) \ (|X| \text{ times}),$$

we have $\#_G{}^c(S^1, S) \leqslant \#_G{}^c(X, S)$ [see 5.2.14(c) and Fact 2.2(c)].

Let $x \in X$, and define the cyclic subset of X generated by x to be $xS \cup \{x\}$. (There may be no element of S which leaves x fixed.) X can be written as the (not necessarily disjoint) union of cyclic subsets of X generated by (say) elements $x_1, \ldots, x_n$. Let $I_n = \{1, \ldots, n\}$. Then it is easy to see that

$$(X, S) \mid (S^I \times I_n, S^I \times \{0\}) = (S^I, S^I) \times (I_n, \{0\}),$$

where $\{0\}$ acts as the identity on I_n, and

$$(S^I \times I_n, S^I \times \{0\}) \supseteq (S^I \times I_n, S \times \{0\}) \xrightarrow{(\theta, \varphi)} (X, S$$

by $\theta(s, i) = x_i s$ and $\theta(I, i) = x_i$, and $\varphi(s, 0) = s$.

Thus, since $(S^I, S^I) \mid (S^1, S) \times (\{0\}^I, \{0\}^I)$, we have

$$(X, S) \in \overline{W}[\text{PRIMES}(S) \cup \{U_3\}],$$

and from Fact 2.2(c),

$$\#_G{}^c(S^I, S^I) = \#_G{}^c(S^1, S).$$

Thus, $\#_G{}^c(X, S) = \#_G{}^c(S^1, S) = \#_G{}^b(S)$. ∎

In summary, then, we have proved, modulo a certain amount of effort on the part of the reader, that definitions (a), (b), and (c) are equivalent. Henceforth, we write $\#_G(S)$ for $\#_G{}^a(S) = \#_G{}^b(S) = \#_G{}^c(X, S)$.

It is now hoped that the reader is convinced of the naturalness and importance of $\#_G(S)$, either in the cascade decomposition of finite-state machines or in the structure theory of finite semigroups. It represents a step from the mere description of necessary components to a discussion of the possible order in which they may occur in the composition of a machine or semigroup.

We add some simple facts and examples.

1.6 Fact. (a) If $T \mid S$, then $\#_G(T) \leqslant \#_G(S)$.

(b) If $T \mid (X_2, S_2) \text{ w } (X_1, S_1)$ (or, equivalently, T^M is simulable by a cascade of M_1 and M_2 with $M_1{}^S = S_1$ and $M_2{}^S = S_2$), then $\#_G(T) \leqslant \#_G(S_2) + \#_G(S_1)$.

(c) Cascading a machine with combinatorial machines cannot increase its group complexity.

1.7 Examples (Some without Proof).

(a) If S is simple or 0-simple, then $\#_G(S) \leqslant 1$. From 7.1.21 we know if S is simple or 0-simple, then S^0 is isomorphic to a regular Rees matrix semigroup $\mathscr{M}^0(G; A, B; C)$ in which $(g, a, b)(g', a', b') = (g'', a, b')$, with $g'' = gC(b, a')g$. Then the result is immediate on observing that the cascade of Fig. 1 uses at most one group machine to simulate $\mathscr{M}^0(G; A, B; C)$.

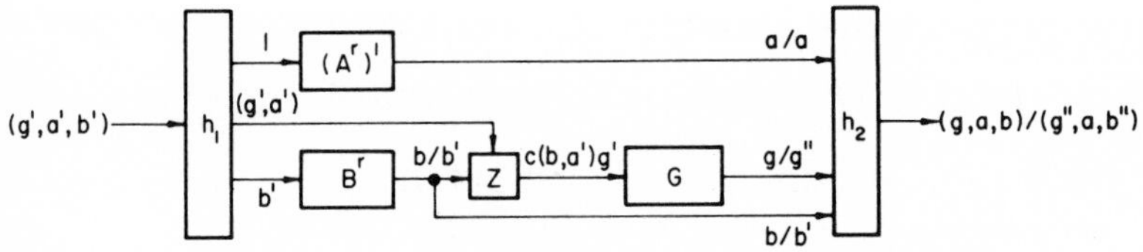

FIG. 1

(b) $\#_G[F_R(X_n)] = n - 1$. See Rhodes [3], Section 5 for a proof. Also $\#_G[F_L(X_n)] = n - 1$, (Dennis P. Allen, Jr., unpublished). Notice that $F_L(X_n) = r[F_R(X_n)]$, the reverse semigroup of $F_R(X_n)$. The reader is cautioned that, in general, $\#_G(S) \neq \#_G[r(S)]$. In fact, Zalcstein has constructed semigroups whose complexity and reverse complexity can differ by an arbitrary amount (unpublished).

(c) Let $G \neq \{1\}$ be a group, and let n be a positive integer. Then there exists a semigroup S such that (1) S is a union of groups, each isomorphic to G, and (2) $\#_G(S) = n$. This can be proved using the methods of Chapter 9. See Krohn and Rhodes [2], Remark 7.1.

(d) Let S be an abelian semigroup. Then $\#_G(S) \leqslant 1$.

(e) Let S be an inverse semigroup (see 7.2.27). Then $\#_G(S) \leqslant 1$. (Tilson, unpublished.)

2. Definition of Complexity: Existence of Semigroups of Arbitrary Complexity

We claimed, but did not prove, in Examples 1.7 that $\#_G[F_R(X_n)] = n - 1$, thus implying that there are semigroups of every group complexity. In this section, we shall actually verify this implication, and, by introducing a more comprehensive definition of complexity, we shall reveal some subtler properties of this quantity.

This new definition of complexity differs from group complexity in that we also count the combinatorials and indicate whether the first coordinate is a group or a combinatorial.

2.1 Definition. Let (X, S) be a transformation semigroup. Then $\#(X, S)$, the *complexity number*† of (X, S), is the smallest positive integer n such that

$$(X, S) \mid (X_n, S_n) \wr \cdots \wr (X_1, S_1),$$

where either (a) $(X_1, S_1), (X_3, S_3), (X_5, S_5),\ldots$ are transformation groups and $S_2, S_4, S_6,\ldots$ are combinatorial semigroups; or (b) $S_1, S_3, S_5,\ldots$ are combinatorial semigroups and (X_2, S_2), $(X_4, S_4), (X_6, S_6),\ldots$ are transformation groups.

The *complexity* of (X, S), $C(X, S)$ equals

$(n, \mathbf{G})$ iff (a) holds with $n = \#(X, S)$ but (b) never holds with $n = \#(X, S)$;

$(n, \mathbf{C})$ iff (b) holds with $n = \#(X, S)$ but (a) never holds with $n = \#(X, S)$;

$(n, \mathbf{C} \vee \mathbf{G})$ iff both (a) and (b) can hold with $n = \#(X, S)$.

2.2 Fact. (a) The set of all complexities is a lattice under the ordering $\leqslant$, where $(n, \alpha) \leqslant (m, \beta)$ iff either $(n, \alpha) = (m, \beta)$, or $n < m$, or $n = m$ and $\alpha = \mathbf{C} \vee \mathbf{G}$. The minimal element of the lattice is $(1, \mathbf{C} \vee \mathbf{G})$.

(b) If $(X, S) | (Y, T)$, then $C(X, S) \leqslant C(Y, T)$.

(c) $C[(X_1, S_1) \times \cdots \times (X_n, S_n)] = \mathrm{LUB}\{C(X_i, S_i) : i = 1,\ldots, n\}$.

PROOF. The reader is invited to supply the details of the proofs of (a) and (b). For (c), since $(X_i, S_i) | (X_1, S_1) \times \cdots \times (X_n, S_n)$, we

† It is *not* the same as the group complexity $\#_G(S)$.

have $C(X_i, S_i) \leqslant C[(X_1, S_1) \times \cdots \times (X_n, S_n)]$, and so we have the inequality one way. The proof in the other direction relies on the fact that

$$[(X_2, S_2) \wr (X_1, S_1)]$$
$$\times [(Y_2, T_2) \wr (Y_1, T_1)] \mid [(X_2, S_2) \times (Y_2, T_2)] \wr [(X_1, S_1) \times (Y_1, T_1)],$$

for then, by lining up the group components of each (X_i, S_i) and applying the foregoing fact, the inequality in the other direction is obtained.

We verify the above equation.

$$[(X_2, S_2) \times (Y_2, T_2)] \wr [(X_1, S_1) \times (Y_1, T_1)]$$
$$\cong [(X_2 \times Y_2 \times X_1 \times Y_1), F(X_1 \times Y_1, S_2 \times T_2) \times_Y (S_1 \times T_1)].$$

Let p_1 and p_2 be the projection maps on $S_2 \times T_2$. Let F be the set of those $f \in F(X_1 \times Y_1, S_2 \times T_2)$ such that $\{p_1 f(x_0, y) : y \in Y_1\}$ is a single point for each $x_0 \in X_1$ and $\{p_2 f(x, y_0) : x \in X\}$ is a single point for each $y_0 \in Y_1$.

F is a subsemigroup of $F(X_1 \times Y_1, S_2 \times T_2)$ and $Y(S_1 \times T_1)F \subseteq F$, so $F \times_Y (S_1 \times T_1)$ is a subsemigroup of

$$F(X_1 \times Y_1, S_2 \times T_2) \times_Y (S_1 \times T_1).$$

If $f \in F$, then there exist $f_1 \in F(X_1, S_2)$ and $f_2 \in F(Y_1, T_2)$ such that $f_1(x_1) = p_1 f(x_1, y)$ for all $y \in Y_1$ and $f_2(y_1) = p_2 f(x, y_1)$ for all $x \in X_1$. Then

$$[(X_2 \times Y_2 \times X_1 \times Y_1), F \times_Y (S_1 \times T_1)] \xrightarrow{(\theta,\varphi)} [(X_2 \times X_1 \times Y_2 \times Y_1),$$
$$(F(X_1, S_2) \times_Y S_1) \times (F(Y_1, T_2) \times_Y T_1)]$$
$$\cong [(X_2, S_2) \wr (X_1, S_1)] \times [(Y_2, T_2) \wr (Y_1, T_1)]$$

where $\theta(x_2, y_2, x_1, y_1) = (x_2, x_1, y_2, y_1)$ and $\varphi[f, (s, t)] = [(f_1, s), (f_2, t)]$. Verify that φ is an epimorphism and that

$$\theta((x_2, y_2, x_1, y_1) \cdot [f, (s, t)]) = \theta(x_2, y_2, x_1, y_1) \cdot \varphi[f, (s, t)].$$

Then the assertion is proved. ▮

2.3 Theorem. Let (X, S) be a transformation semigroup. Then $C(X, S) = C(S^1, S)$ except in the case where S is a group and the identity of S does not act as the identity function on X. In this case, we have

$$C(X, G) = \begin{cases} (1, \mathbf{C}) & \text{if } G = \{1\} \\ (2, \mathbf{C} \vee \mathbf{G}) & \text{if } G \text{ a nontrivial group.} \end{cases}$$

PROOF. The proof is an exact mimic of the proof of Theorem 1.5. First prove that $C(X, \{0\}) = (1, \mathbf{C} \vee \mathbf{G})$ if $\{0\}$ acts as the identity. Then, since $C(S^I, S^I) = C(S^1, S)$ except when S is a group, we easily obtain the general assertion. The special cases are easily handled. ∎

2.4 Notation. We write $C(S)$ to mean $C(S^1, S)$, and, of course, $C(S^1, S) = C(X, S)$ in all but the special cases mentioned previously. However, these special cases never, by definition, arise in the group-combinatorial decompositions that define complexity, and so they will not trouble us. Thus, in the interest of tidiness, we exclude them from our consideration. Then $C(S) = (1, \mathbf{C} \vee \mathbf{G})$ iff $S = \{0\}$, $C(S) = (1, \mathbf{G})$ iff S is a nontrivial group, and $C(S) = (1, \mathbf{C})$ iff S is a nontrivial combinatorial semigroup.

2.5 Definition. We define addition $\oplus$ for complexities in the obvious way:

m even

$\oplus$	$(m, \mathbf{G})$	$(m, \mathbf{C})$	$(m, \mathbf{C} \vee \mathbf{G})$
$(n, \mathbf{G})$	$(n + m, \mathbf{G})$	$(n + m - 1, \mathbf{C})$	$(n + m - 1, \mathbf{C})$
$(n, \mathbf{C})$	$(n + m - 1, \mathbf{G})$	$(n + m, \mathbf{C})$	$(n + m - 1, \mathbf{G})$
$(n, \mathbf{C} \vee \mathbf{G})$	$(n + m - 1, \mathbf{G})$	$(n + m - 1, \mathbf{C})$	$(n + m - 1, \mathbf{C} \vee \mathbf{G})$

m odd

$\oplus$	$(m, \mathbf{G})$	$(m, \mathbf{C})$	$(m, \mathbf{C} \vee \mathbf{G})$
$(n, \mathbf{G})$	$(n + m - 1, \mathbf{G})$	$(n + m, \mathbf{C})$	$(n + m - 1, \mathbf{G})$
$(n, \mathbf{C})$	$(n + m, \mathbf{G})$	$(n + m - 1, \mathbf{C})$	$(n + m - 1, \mathbf{C})$
$(n, \mathbf{C} \vee \mathbf{G})$	$(n + m - 1, \mathbf{G})$	$(n + m - 1, \mathbf{C})$	$(n + m - 1, \mathbf{C} \vee \mathbf{G})$

Then, for example,

(a) $(n, \mathbf{C}) \oplus (1, \mathbf{G}) = (n + 1, \mathbf{G})$;

(b) $(n, \mathbf{G}) \oplus (1, \mathbf{G}) = (n, \mathbf{C} \vee \mathbf{G}) \oplus (1, \mathbf{G}) = (n, \mathbf{G})$;

(c) $(n, \mathbf{G}) \oplus (1, \mathbf{C}) = (n + 1, \mathbf{C})$; and

(d) $(n, \mathbf{C}) \oplus (1, \mathbf{C}) = (n, \mathbf{C} \vee \mathbf{G}) \oplus (1, \mathbf{C}) = (n, \mathbf{C})$.

Notice that $\oplus$ is not commutative.

2.6 Fact. If $S \mid (X_2, S_2) \le w (X_1, S_1)$, then $C(S) \leqslant C(S_2) \oplus C(S_1)$. ▮

The next three lemmas lead to the theorem that is the central result of this section.

2.7 Lemma. If $S \mid (X_2, T) \text{ w } (X_1, G)$, where (X_1, G) is a transformation group, then $C[IG(S)] \leqslant C(T)$. [Recall that $IG(S)$ is the semigroup generated by the idempotents of S, $E(S)$.]

PROOF. $(X_2, T) \text{ w } (X_1, G) \cong F(X_1, T) \times_Y G$, and, if e is the identity of G, then $Y(e)$ is the identity automorphism on $F(X_1, T) \equiv F$. If $(f, g) \in E(F \times_Y G)$, then $(f, g) = (f, g)^2 = [fY(g)f, g^2]$. So $g = e$ and $f^2 = f$. Therefore,

$$E(F \times_Y G) = E(F) \times E(G) = E(F) \times \{e\},$$

and $IG(F \times_Y G) \cong IG(F)$. Then, since $S_1 \mid S_2$ implies $IG(S_1) \mid IG(S_2)$, we have $IG(S) \mid IG(F) \mid F = F(X_1, T)$. But, since $F(X_1, T) \cong T \times \cdots \times T$ ($|X_1|$ times), $C[F(X_1, T)] = C(T)$. Therefore, $C[IG(S)] \leqslant C(T)$. ▮

2.8 Lemma. Let S be a monoid and C be a combinatorial semigroup such that $U_1 \subseteq C$. (Recall $U_1 = \{r_0, r_1\}^r$). Then $S \mid IG[(X_2, S) \text{ w } (X_1, C)]$ and $C(S) \leqslant C\{IG[(X_2, S) \text{ w } (X_1, C)]\}$.

PROOF. There exists an $x \in X_1$ such that $xr_0 \neq xr_1$. Let $x_0 = xr_0$, $x_1 = xr_1$. Then $x_i r_j = x_j$, $i, j = 0, 1$. Let $Y = \{x_0, x_1\}$; then (Y, U_1) is a transformation semigroup, and $(Y, U_1) \mid (X_1, C)$, and so

$$(X_2, S) \text{ w } (Y, U_1) \mid (X_2, S) \text{ w } (X_1, C),$$

and

$$IG[(X_2, S) \text{ w } (Y, U_1)] \mid IG[(X_2, S) \text{ w } (X_1, C)].$$

$(X_2, S) \le (Y, U_1) \cong F(Y, S) \times_Y U_1$. Let F_S be the subsemigroup of $F(Y, S)$ consisting of all the constant maps, i.e.,

$$F_S = \{f_s \in F(Y, S): f_s(x) = s \text{ for all } x \in Y\}.$$

$F_S \times_Y \{r_0\}$ is a subsemigroup of $F(Y, S) \times_Y U_1$, and $F_S \times_Y \{r_0\} \cong S$ under the map $(f_s, r_0) \to s$.

Now let $f \in F(Y, S)$ be the function defined by $f(x_0) = 1$, $f(x_1) = s$. Then $(f_s, r_0) = (f_1, r_1)(f, r_0)$, and both (f_1, r_1) and (f, r_0) are idempotents. Therefore,

$$F_S \times_Y \{r_0\} \subseteq IG[(X_2, S) \mathrm{w} (Y, U_1)]. \quad \blacksquare$$

2.9 Lemma. Suppose

$$(X_2, S_1) \mathrm{w} (X_1, G) \mid (Y_2, S_2) \mathrm{w} (Y_1, C),$$

where S_1 is a monoid, S_2 a semigroup, (X_1, G) a nontrivial transformation group, and C a combinatorial semigroup. Then $C(S_1) \leqslant C(S_2)$.

PROOF. $(X_2, S_1) \mathrm{w} (X_1, G) \cong F(X_1, S_1) \times_Y G$. Let

$$H = \{(f_1, g) : g \in G\},$$

where $f_1(x) = 1$, the identity of S_1, for all $x \in X_1$. H is a subgroup of $F(X_1, S_1) \times_Y G$.

Let e be the identity of G, and let $h \neq e \in G$. Then there exist $x_0 \in X_1$ such that $x_0 h \neq x_0 e = x_0$. Let $T = \{(f, e) : f(x_0) = 1\}$. T is a subsemigroup of $F(X_1, S_1) \times_Y G$.

Let (f, g) be a general element of $F(X_1, S_1) \times_Y G$. Let $f', f'' \in F(X_1, S_1)$ be given by

$$f'(x) = \begin{cases} f(x_0) & \text{if } x = x_0 h \\ 1 & \text{otherwise,} \end{cases}$$

$$f''(x) = \begin{cases} 1 & \text{if } x = x_0 \\ f(x) & \text{otherwise.} \end{cases}$$

Clearly, (f', e) and $(f'', e) \in T$, and

$$(f, g) = (f_1, h)(f', e)(f_1, h^{-1})(f'', e)(f_1, g).$$

(Let $\langle X \rangle$ denote the semigroup generated by the set X.) Therefore, we have shown that

$$\langle H \cup T \rangle = (X_2, S_1) \text{ w } (X_1, G).$$

Let $P_1 = F(X_1, S_1) \times_Y \{e\}$, a subsemigroup of $(X_2, S_1) \text{ w } (X_1, G)$. Clearly, $T \subseteq P_1$. Define the epimorphism $\theta_1 : P_1 \twoheadrightarrow S_1$ by $\theta_1(f, e) = f(x_0)$. Notice that $\theta_1(T) = \{1\}$.

Let $t \in T$. Then tP_1t is a subsemigroup of the semigroup $t[(X_2, S_1) \text{ w } (X_1, G)]t$, and $\theta_1(tP_1t) = S_1$. Thus ,

$$S_1 \mid t[(X_2, S_1) \text{ w } (X_1, G)]\, t$$

for all $t \in T$.

Let $(Y_2, S_2) \text{ w } (Y_1, C) \supseteq M \overset{\varphi}{\twoheadrightarrow} (X_2, S_1) \text{ w } (X_1, G)$. There exists a subgroup H' of M such that $\varphi(H') = H$. Let $R = \varphi^{-1}(T)$, and let $T' = 1'R1'$, where $1'$ is the identity of H'. Then $\varphi(T') = T$. Let $M' = \langle H' \cup T' \rangle$, the semigroup generated by H' and T'; notice $1'$ is the identity of M', and $\varphi(M') = (X_2, S_1) \text{ w } (X_1, G)$. Therefore, $S_1 \mid t'M't'$ for all $t' \in T'$.

Let $p_1 : (Y_2, S_2) \text{ w } (Y_1, C) \twoheadrightarrow C$ be the projection homomorphism. Let t' be an idempotent in $K(T')$. Then $t'T't'$ is a subgroup in $K(T')$. p_1 sends subgroups of $(Y_2, S_2) \text{ w } (Y_1, C)$ to single elements, since C is combinatorial. Thus, $p_1(H') = \{\hat{1}\}$, the identity of $p_1(M')$. Let $p_1(t') = \hat{t}$. Then

$$\begin{aligned} p_1(t'M't') &= \hat{t}p_1\langle H' \cup T' \rangle\, \hat{t} \\ &= \hat{t}\langle \{1\} \cup p_1(T') \rangle\, \hat{t} \\ &= \hat{t}p_1(T')\, \hat{t} \\ &= p_1(t'T't') \\ &= \{p_1(t')\} = \{\hat{t}\}. \end{aligned}$$

Thus, the first coordinate of $t'M't'$ as a subsemigroup of $(Y_2, S_2) \text{ w } (Y_1, C) \cong F(Y_1, S_2) \times_Y C$ consists of a single idempotent element, $\hat{t}$. Define the homomorphism $\psi : t'M't' \to F(Y_1, S_2)$ by $(f, \hat{t}) \to {}^{\hat{t}}f$. [Recall ${}^{\hat{t}}f \equiv Y(\hat{t})\, f$.]

Let $t' = (\bar{f}, \hat{t})$. t' is the identity of $t'M't'$. Suppose $\psi(f, \hat{t}) = \psi(f', \hat{t})$, i.e., ${}^{\hat{t}}f = {}^{\hat{t}}f'$. Then

$$(f, \hat{t}) = (\bar{f}, \hat{t})(f, \hat{t}) = (\bar{f}\,{}^{\hat{t}}f, t) = (\bar{f}\,{}^{\hat{t}}f', \hat{t}) = (\bar{f}, \hat{t})(f', \hat{t}) = (f', \hat{t}).$$

So ψ is $1:1$, and $t'M't' \mid F(Y_1, S_2)$. Thus, $S_1 \mid F(Y_1, S_2)$, and $C(S_1) \leqslant C[F(Y_1, S_2)] = C(S_2)$. ▮

2.10 Theorem. Let S be a monoid.

(a) Let C be a combinatorial semigroup containing U_1. Then

$$C[(X, S) \text{ w } (Y, C)] = C(S) \oplus (1, \mathbf{C}). \tag{2.1}$$

(b) Let (Y, G) be a nontrivial transformation group. Then

$$C[(X, S) \text{ w } (Y, G)] = C(S) \oplus (1, \mathbf{G}) \tag{2.2}$$

PROOF. (a) If $C(S) = (n, \mathbf{C})$, then (2.1) holds. Suppose $C(S) = (n, \mathbf{G})$ or $(n + 1, \mathbf{C} \vee \mathbf{G})$. Then

$$(n, \mathbf{G}) \leqslant C[(X, S) \text{ w } (Y, C)] \leqslant (n + 1, \mathbf{C}).$$

Suppose $C[(X, S) \text{ w } (Y, C)] \neq (n + 1, \mathbf{C})$. Then

$$C[(X, S) \text{ w } (Y, C)] = (n, \mathbf{G}) \quad \text{or} \quad (n + 1, \mathbf{C} \vee \mathbf{G}).$$

In either case, there exists a semigroup T such that

$$(X, S) \text{ w } (Y, C) \mid (X_1, T) \text{ w } (Y_1, G),$$

where $C(T) \leqslant (n, \mathbf{C})$. By Lemmas 2.7 and 2.8, we have

$$C(S) \leqslant C(IG[(X, S) \text{ w } (Y, C)]) \leqslant C(T),$$

so that $C(S) \leqslant (n, \mathbf{C})$, a contradiction. Hence, $C[(X, S) \text{ w } (Y, C)] = (n + 1, \mathbf{C})$, and, since this argument holds for all $n \geqslant 1$,

$$C[(X, S) \text{ w } (Y, C)] = C(S) \oplus (1, \mathbf{C}).$$

(b) If $C(S) = (n, \mathbf{G})$, then (2.2) holds. Suppose $C(S) = (n, \mathbf{C})$ or $(n + 1, \mathbf{C} \vee \mathbf{G})$. Then

$$(n, \mathbf{C}) \leqslant C[(X, S) \text{ w } (Y, G)] \leqslant (n + 1, \mathbf{G}).$$

Suppose $C[(X, S) \text{ w } (Y, G)] \neq (n + 1, \mathbf{G})$. Then

$$C[(X, S) \text{ w } (Y, G)] = (n, \mathbf{C}) \quad \text{or} \quad (n + 1, \mathbf{C} \vee \mathbf{G}).$$

In either case, there exists a semigroup T such that

$$(X, S) \text{ w } (Y, G) \mid (X_1, T) \text{ w } (Y_1, C),$$

where $C(T) \leqslant (n, \mathbf{G})$. But, by Lemma 2.9, $C(S) \leqslant C(T) \leqslant (n, \mathbf{G})$, a contradiction. Hence, $C[(X, S) \text{ w } (Y, G)] = (n + 1, \mathbf{C})$, and, since this argument holds for all $n \geqslant 1$, Eq. (2.2) holds. ∎

2.11 Remark. We offer counterexamples to the conjecture that the restrictions imposed in Theorem 2.10 are not necessary:

(a) $C(A^l \text{ w } G) = (2, \mathbf{C} \vee \mathbf{G})$, not $(2, \mathbf{G})$. This violates 2.10, since A^l is not a monoid.

(b) $C(G \text{ w } A^{l1}) = (2, \mathbf{C} \vee \mathbf{G})$, not $(2, \mathbf{C})$. Notice that $U_1 \not\subseteq A^{l1}$.

The validity of (a) is easy to check; (b) follows from Rhodes [3], Lemma 5.5(b).

2.12 Corollary. There are semigroups of each complexity. In other words, given an arbitrary cascade of group machines and combinatorial machines, it is not, in general, possible to rearrange them so that all the group machines are grouped together.

PROOF. The trivial semigroup has complexity $(1, \mathbf{C} \vee \mathbf{G})$; $C(U_3) = (1, \mathbf{C})$; $C(G) = (1, \mathbf{G})$, G a nontrivial group. $C(U_3 \text{ w } G) = (2, \mathbf{G})$, $C(G \text{ w } U_3) = (2, \mathbf{C})$, etc. If $C(S) = (n, \mathbf{G})$ and $C(T) = (n, \mathbf{C})$, then $C(S \times T) = (n + 1, \mathbf{C} \vee \mathbf{G})$. ∎

3. Complexity and Ideals

3.1 Theorem (Generalized Embedding Theorem). Let S be a semigroup with a subsemigroup V and a subset T such that $VT = S$. Let $t : S \to T$ and $v : S \to V$ be functions so chosen that $v(s)t(s) \equiv s$. Let $f_t : \Sigma S \to T$ be defined inductively by

$$f_t(s_1) = t(s_1),$$

$$f_t(s_1, \ldots, s_n) = t[f_t(s_1, \ldots, s_{n-1})\, s_n].$$

Then S^M can be simulated by a cascade of V^M and f_t^M. In particular,

$$\#_G(S) \leqslant \#_G(V) + \#_G(f_t^S).$$

PROOF. Consider the cascade in Fig. 2, where

$$Z : T \times S \to T : (x, s') \to v(xs')$$

and

$$h : V \times T \to S : (y, x) \to yx.$$

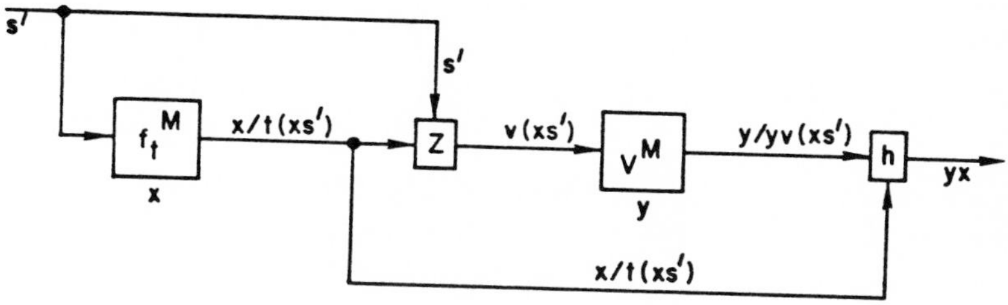

FIG. 2

Then it behaves as S^M, since, if the present state (x, y) encodes $s = yx$ and the input is s', then the next state will be $[t(xs'), yv(xs')]$, which encodes $yv(xs')\, t(xs') = yxs' = ss'$. ▮

Our next definition is immediately motivated by the corollary to the generalized embedding theorem which follows it.

3.2 Definition. Let T be a semigroup. Then define REP(T) to have input set T, state set T^1, next state function

$$(x, s) \to s \qquad \text{if} \quad x = 0,$$
$$(x, s) \to xs \qquad \text{if} \quad x \neq 0$$

and output always equal to its state.

3.3 Corollary. Let S be a semigroup with a subsemigroup T and a left ideal V such that $T \cup V = S$ and $T \cap V$ is an ideal of T. We may introduce the Rees quotient $T_V = T/(T \cap V)$. Then S^M may be simulated by a cascade of REP(T_V) with state 0 decoded as 1, and $(V^1)^M$.

PROOF. We note that $S^1 = V^1 T_V{}^1$. Define $t : S \to T_V{}^1$ and $v : S \to V^1$ by

$$t(s) = s, \qquad v(s) = 1 \qquad \text{if} \quad s \in T - V,$$
$$t(s) = 1, \qquad v(s) = s \qquad \text{if} \quad s \notin T - V.$$

Then certainly $v(s)\, t(s) = s$ for all $s \in S$.

If the f_t machine is in state x and receives input s, its next state is xs if $xs \in T - V$, and 1 if $xs \in V \cap T$, so that it is REP(T_V), with state 0 decoded as 1. ▮

3.4 Lemma. (a) If S is a null semigroup (i.e. the product of any two elements is 0) and $T \mid S$, then $\#_G[\mathrm{REP}(T)] \leqslant 1$.

(b) If S is a 0-simple semigroup and $T \mid S$, then $\#_G[\mathrm{REP}(T)] \leqslant 1$.

PROOF. (a) If S is null, odd-numbered inputs t_n yield output t_n, and even-numbered outputs yield output 0. Thus, REP(S) may be constructed as a parallel cascade using only one group machine, namely, that of $\mathbf{Z}_2 = (\{0, 1\}, +)$, and S^r, with input coding

$$h_1 : S \to S^r \times \mathbf{Z}_2 : s \to (s, 1)$$

and output coding

$$h_2 : S^r \times \mathbf{Z}_2 \to S^1 : \begin{cases} (s, 0) \to 0 \\ (s, 1) \to s. \end{cases}$$

(b) Let $S \cong \mathscr{M}^0(G; A, B; C)$. That $\#_G(S) \leqslant 1$ is proved by inspection of Fig. 3, since at most one group machine is used in

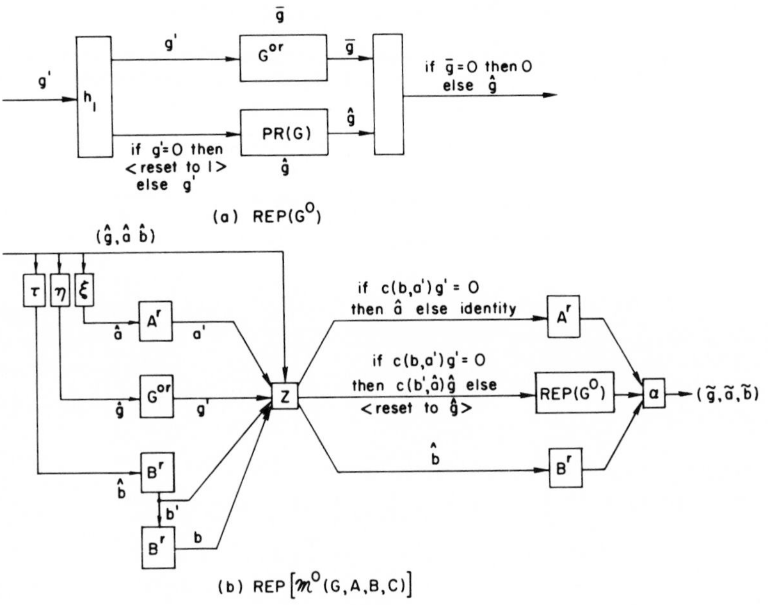

FIG. 3

REP(S), namely, that in REP(G^0). Finally, we note that, if $T \mid S$ and the zero's of S and T (if they exist) coincide, then REP(T) | REP(S).† ∎

3.5 Definition. We say of ideals I_1 and I_2 of a semigroup S that I_1 is *nearly maximal* in I_2 if $I_1 \subseteq I_2$ and the Rees quotient I_2/I_1 divides a null or 0-simple semigroup.

3.6 Lemma. Let I_1 and I_2 be ideals of a semigroup with I_1 nearly maximal in I_2. Then

$$\#_G(I_1) \leqslant \#_G(I_2) \leqslant \#_G(I_1) + 1.$$

PROOF. By Corollary 3.3, it follows that

$$\#_G(I_2) \leqslant \#_G(I_1) + \#_G[\text{REP}(I_2/I_1)],$$

and the result is then immediate from Lemma 3.4. ∎

The reader may verify that, if I_1 is *maximal* in I_2 (i.e. the only ideal of I_2 exceeding I_1 is I_2 itself) then I_1 is *nearly maximal* in I_2. Thus, we may immediately deduce the following theorem.

3.7 Theorem. (a) Let I_1 and I_2 be ideals of a semigroup S, with I_1 maximal in I_2. Then

$$\#_G(I_1) \leqslant \#_G(I_2) \leqslant \#_G(I_1) + 1.$$

(b) Let V be an ideal of S, with $\#_G(S) = n \geqslant k = \#_G(V)$. Then there are ideals $V_n, \ldots, V_k$ of S with

$$V = V_k \subset V_{k+1} \subset \cdots \subset V_n = S,$$

and $\#_G(V_j) = j$, $k \leqslant j \leqslant n$.

(c) Let T be a subideal of S, i.e., there exist subsemigroups $S_0, \ldots, S_k$ such that

$$T = S_k \subseteq S_{k-1} \subseteq \cdots \subseteq S_0 = S,$$

with S_j an ideal of S_{j-1} for $j = 1, \ldots, k$. Assume that

$$\#_G(S) = n \leqslant k = \#_G(T).$$

† For a proof of 3.4 using the machine methods of Chapter 5 see Krohn, Mateosian, and Rhodes [6].

Then there exist subideals $V_n, \ldots, V_k$ with

$$T = V_k \subset V_{k+1} \subset \cdots \subset V_n = S$$

and V_i a subideal of V_{i+1} for $i = k, \ldots, n-1$ and $\#_G(V_i) = i$, $i = k, \ldots, n$. ∎

The fact that each ideal I of S is contained in a chain of ideals

$$I \subset I_1 \subset I_2 \subset \cdots \subset S$$

through which $\#_G$ increases in steps of 1, is called "*continuity of complexity with respect to ideals.*"

(c) cannot be strengthened in the last line to read "V_i is an ideal of V_{i+1}." The following counterexample is due to Bill Rounds (personal communication).

Let $N = \{0, n_0, n_1\}$ be a null semigroup, and let $\mathbf{Z}_2 = \{z_0, z_1\}$ be the two-element group.

$S = N \cup \mathbf{Z}_2$ becomes a semigroup with the multiplication

$$\left.\begin{aligned} zn &= n_0 = nz \\ 0z &= z0 = 0 \end{aligned}\right\} \qquad \text{for } \; 0 \neq n \in N, \; z \in \mathbf{Z}_2 .$$

Then $T = \{0, n_1\}$ is an ideal of N, and N is an ideal of S, but T is not an ideal of S, and $\#_G(S) = 1$, whereas $\#_G(N) = \#_G(T) = 0$.

Now we can elevate this from complexity 1 to complexity n by using Theorem 2.10.

Take R with $\#_G(R) = n - 1$. Then

$$\begin{aligned} S' &= (R \,\mathrm{w}\, U_3) \,\mathrm{w}\, S & &\text{has} & \#_G(S') &= n; \\ N' &= (R \,\mathrm{w}\, U_3) \,\mathrm{w}\, N & &\text{has} & \#_G(N') &= n - 1; \\ T' &= (R \,\mathrm{w}\, U_3) \,\mathrm{w}\, T & &\text{has} & \#_G(T') &= n - 1; \end{aligned}$$

and T' is an ideal of N', and N' is an ideal of S', but T' is not an ideal of S'.

Note that we had to use null semigroups somewhere in the construction, since we know that, if I_2/I_1 is null for no ideals I_2 and I_1 of S, then S is regular and every subideal of S is an ideal of S (7.2.22(f)).

3.8 Theorem. Let M be a reduced finite-state sequential machine with semigroup S and state-space Q.

(a) Let $r_k = \{f \in S : |f(Q)| \leqslant k\}$.

Then r_k is an ideal of S, and $\#_G(r_k) \leqslant \#_G(r_{k+1}) \leqslant \#_G(r_k) + 1$ for $1 \leqslant k \leqslant |Q|$.

(b) Let $\text{spec}(M) = \{k > 1 : r_k - r_{k-1} \neq \phi\}$ (the *spectrum* of M). Then $\#_G(M) \leqslant |\text{spec}(M)|$.

(c) When $S = F_R(Q)$, then $\#_G(M) = |\text{spec}(M)| = |Q| - 1$.

PROOF. To prove (a) and (b), we need only show that, if k and $k + j$ are in spec(M) but $r_{k+i} \notin \text{spec}(M)$ for $i = 1,..., j - 1$, then r_k is nearly maximal in r_{k+j}, for we may then apply Lemma 3.6. This is left as an exercise for the reader.

(b) implies half of (c), namely, that $\#_G[F_R(Q)] \leqslant |Q| - 1$. The converse result, that $\#_G[F_R(Q)] \geqslant |Q| - 1$, is much harder, and for it we refer the reader to Sect. 5 of Rhodes [3]. ∎

(b) may also be proved by applying Zeiger's [5] cover construction (Chapter 4) to the nested sequence of covers $\{C_j : j \in \text{spec}(M)\}$, on taking C_j to be the cover composed of j-element subsets of Q.

NOTES AND REFERENCES

The notions of complexity discussed here were first introduced by Krohn and Rhodes [2, 3, 6, 7]. Some of the material of Sect. 1 occurs in each of these four references.

Section 2 covers essentially the same ground as an old Sect. 2 of Krohn and Rhodes [2]. However, Arbib and Tilson have modified the proofs therein to obtain much more general results.

Section 3 presents the main theorems of Krohn, Mateosian, and Rhodes [6]. The generalized embedding theorem first appeared in two works [2, 6], but in a more cumbersome form.

1. K. Krohn, R. Langer, and J. Rhodes, Algebraic principles for the analysis of a biochemical system, *J. Computer Systems Sci.* **1**, 119–136 (1967).
2. K. Krohn and J. Rhodes, Complexity of finite semigroups, *Ann. of Math.* (in press).
3. J. Rhodes, Some results on finite semigroups, *J. Algebra* **4**, 471–504 (1966).
4. A. H. Clifford and G. B. Preston, "The Algebraic Theory of Semigroups," Vol. 1, Math Surveys No. 7. Am. Math. Soc., Providence, Rhode Island, 1962.
5. H. P. Zeiger, Cascade synthesis of finite-state machines, *Information and Control* **10**, 419–433 (1967).
6. K. Krohn, R. Mateosian, and J. Rhodes, Complexity of ideals in finite semigroups and finite-state machines, *Math. System Theory* **1**, 59–66 (1967), and Erratum **1**, 373 (1967).
7. K. Krohn and J. Rhodes, Results on finite semigroups derived from the algebraic theory of machines, *Proc. Nat. Acad. Sci. U.S.A.* **3**, 499–501 (1965).

CHAPTER 7

Local Structure Theorems for Finite Semigroups[†]

John L. Rhodes[‡]

University of California, Berkeley, California
Krohn-Rhodes Research Institute, Berkeley, California

Bret R. Tilson

University of California, Berkeley, California

1. Local Coordinates: Rees Theorem

In this section we develop two important tools for the study of finite semigroups. The first is that of the Green's relations, and the second is the Rees theorem, which together determine the local structure of finite semigroups.

All semigroups considered in this chapter are assumed to be of finite order unless the contrary is explicitly stated.

At this stage, the reader may wish to review the basic material on ideals contained in Chapter 1, 1.5–1.9.

1.1 Definition. If $I \subseteq S$ is an ideal, the *quotient semigroup*, S/I, is defined to be $((S - I) \cup \{0\}, \cdot)$, where $0 \notin S - I$ and

$$s_1 \cdot s_2 = \begin{cases} s_1 s_2 & \text{if } s_1 s_2 \in S - I \\ 0 & \text{otherwise.} \end{cases}$$

[†] This work was sponsored by the Office of Naval Research, Information Systems Branch, Contract Number Nonr 4705(00).

[‡] Alfred P. Sloan Research Fellow, 1967–1968.

Associativity of the multiplication follows from the fact that I is an ideal.

The *natural epimorphism* $\eta_I : S \twoheadrightarrow S/I$ is given by

$$\eta_I(s) = \begin{cases} s & \text{if } s \in S - I \\ 0 & \text{if } s \in I. \end{cases}$$

Thus, $S/S = \{0\}$. By convention, $S/\phi = S^0$.

1.2 Fact. (a) Let S_1 be a semigroup, I an ideal of S_1, and let $S_2 = S_1/I$. If $\varphi = \eta_I$ is the natural epimorphism, then $T \to \varphi^{-1}(T)$ is a $1:1$ inclusion-preserving mapping of the sets of left, right, and two-sided ideals of S_2 *onto* the corresponding set of ideals of S_1 containing I. The inverse of $T \to \varphi^{-1}(T)$ is $J \to \varphi(J)$.

(b) If A and B are subsemigroups of a semigroup S, then $A \cup B$ is a subsemigroup of S iff $AB \cup BA \subseteq A \cup B$. In particular, this inclusion holds if A and B are both left ideals or both right ideals, or if either A or B is an ideal.

(c) Let J be an ideal and T a subsemigroup of S. Then $J \cap T = \phi$, or $J \cap T$ is an ideal of T and $J \cup T$ is a subsemigroup of S containing J as an ideal. Hence, $(J \cup T)/J = T/(J \cap T)$.

(d) Let $I_1 \subseteq I_2 \subseteq S$, with I_1 and I_2 ideals of S. Then I_2/I_1 is an ideal of S/I_1, and $(S/I_1)/(I_2/I_1) = S/I_2$.

(e) Let $I_1 \subseteq I_2 \subseteq S$, with I_2 an ideal of S and I_1 an ideal of I_2. If $I_1^2 = I_1$, then I_1 is an ideal of S. (In Remark 1.4, we show that I_1 need not be an ideal of S if $I_1^2 \neq I_1$.)

PROOF. Assertions (a)–(d) are left as exercises for the reader. For (e), since $I_1^2 = I_1$, we have $I_1^3 = I_1$. Hence,

$$SI_1S = SI_1^3S = (SI_1)I_1(I_1S) \subseteq I_2I_1I_2 \subseteq I_1.$$

So I_1 is an ideal of S. ∎

1.3 Definition. Let $n > 1$, and let N_n be the semigroup $(\{0, 1,\dots, n-1\}, \cdot)$, where $\alpha \cdot \beta = 0$ for $\alpha, \beta \in \{0, 1,\dots, n-1\}$. N_n is the *standard null semigroup* of order n.

1.4 Remark. Let $n > 1$, and let S_{n+1} be the semigroup $(N_n \cup \{e\}, *)$, with N_n and $\{e\}$ as subsemigroups, $e * 0 = 0 = 0 * e$, and $e * \alpha = 1 = \alpha * e$ for $\alpha \in N_n - \{0\}$; let $I = N_n - \{1\}$. Then I is an ideal of N_n, and N_n is an ideal of S_{n+1}, but I is not an ideal of

S_{n+1}. Note that $I^2 = \{0\} \neq I$, thus providing the example required by Fact 1.2(e).

Recall (Chapter 1, Remark 1.6) that the kernel of S, $K(S)$, is the minimal ideal of S.

1.5 Definition. Let S be a semigroup, and define a *principal ideal series of* S to be a sequence $S = I_0 \supset I_1 \supset \cdots \supset I_n = K(S)$ such that, for $j = 1,\ldots, n$, I_j is an ideal S, and no ideal of S properly containing I_j is properly contained in I_{j-1}. Notice S is the disjoint union of $(I_0 - I_1)$, $(I_1 - I_2),\ldots, (I_{n-1} - I_n)$, I_n. The *principal ideal factors* are the semigroups $F_j = I_{j-1}/I_j$ for $j = 1,\ldots, n$ and $F_{n+1} = I_n/\phi = K(S)^0$.

1.6 Remark. We want to decompose a semigroup into smaller pieces or "building blocks" and investigate these pieces to determine a "local" structure. As a start, then, it seems reasonable to investigate the principal ideal factors of a principal ideal series. The next fact shows these factors to be either 0-simple or null semigroups. Later we show that the factors of every principal ideal series are the same. Since the structure (i.e., multiplication) of null semigroups is known ($ab = 0$ for all $a, b \in S$), we need only determine the structure of 0-simple semigroups to know the "local" structure of a semigroup. The Rees theorem, via the Green relations, gives the structure of 0-simple semigroups, and it is toward this theorem that we are now working.

1.7 Fact. The factors of a principal ideal series are either 0-simple or null semigroups.

PROOF. Since by 1.1.7(c) $K(S)$ is always simple, $F_{n+1} = K(S)^0$ is 0-simple. For $j = 1,\ldots, n$, let K be a nonzero ideal of S/I_j contained in $F_j = I_{j-1}/I_j$, and let $\eta : S \twoheadrightarrow S/I_j$ be the natural epimorphism. Then $\eta^{-1}(K)$ is an ideal of S contained in I_{j-1} and properly containing I_j. Hence, $\eta^{-1}(K) = I_{j-1}$, and $K = F_j$. Thus, F_j contains no proper ideals of S/I_j other than $\{0\}$, and hence is 0-minimal in S/I_j, which implies F_j is either 0-simple or null by 1.1.7(d). ▌

Exercises and Extensions

X1.1. Show that the intersection of left, right, or two-sided ideals, when non-empty, yields a left, right, or two-sided ideal, respectively. Thus, show that S^1s is the intersection of all left ideals containing s and is therefore the unique smallest (under inclusion) left ideal containing s. Do the same for right ideals (sS^1) and ideals (S^1sS^1).

X1.2. Verify the unproved assertions of Fact 1.2.

X1.3. Show that a Rees matrix semigroup is 0-simple iff it is regular (i.e., its structure matrix is nonzero at least once in each row and column). See Example 1.1.4m. Under what condition on the structure matrix does $\{0\}$ break off (see 1.1.8) from a Rees matrix semigroup S? Show that $S - \{0\}$ is simple in this case.

X1.4. Compute the left, right, and two-sided ideals and the kernels of (a) $F_R(X_n)$, where $X_n = \{1,..., n\}$; (b) $(2^{X_n}, \cap)$; and (c) the semidirect product $U_3 \times_\varphi \mathbf{Z}_2$ of Exercise 5.1.2.

X1.5. Show that a finite semigroup S is right simple iff it is of the form $G \times B^r$ for some group G and finite set B. Also, prove the dual assertion.

X1.6. Show that a (possibly infinite) semigroup G is a group iff G is left simple and right simple.

X1.7. What statements of Fact 1.1.9 are false for infinite semigroups? Construct counterexamples.

X1.8. Define "left 0-simple." Prove that $T \neq \{0\}$ is left 0-simple iff T is left simple or $T = L^0$, where L is left simple.

1.8 Definition (Green). Let S be a semigroup. For $s \in S$, $L(s) = S^1s$, $R(s) = sS^1$, and $J(s) = S^1sS^1$ are, respectively, the *principal left ideal*, *principal right ideal*, and *principal ideal* generated by s.

Define binary relations $\mathcal{J}$, $\mathcal{L}$, $\mathcal{R}$, $\mathcal{H}$, and $\mathcal{D}$ on S as follows:

(1) $s_1 \mathcal{J} s_2$ iff $J(s_1) = J(s_2)$.
(2) $s_1 \mathcal{L} s_2$ iff $L(s_1) = L(s_2)$.
(3) $s_1 \mathcal{R} s_2$ iff $R(s_1) = R(s_2)$.
(4) $s_1 \mathcal{H} s_2$ iff $s_1 \mathcal{L} s_2$ and $s_1 \mathcal{R} s_2$.
(5) $s_1 \mathcal{D} s_2$ iff there exists $s \in S$ such that $s_1 \mathcal{L} s$ and $s \mathcal{R} s_2$ or, equivalently [Fact 1.9(h)], iff there exists $t \in S$ such that $s_1 \mathcal{R} t$ and $t \mathcal{L} s_2$.

1.9 Fact. (a) $\mathcal{L}$, $\mathcal{R}$, $\mathcal{J}$, and $\mathcal{H}$ are equivalence relations on S. We denote by L_s, R_s, J_s, and H_s the $\mathcal{L}$, $\mathcal{R}$, $\mathcal{J}$, and $\mathcal{H}$ equivalence classes, respectively, containing s.

(b) $\mathcal{L}$ is a right congruence.

(c) $\mathcal{R}$ is a left congruence.

(d) $s_1 \mathscr{J} s_2$ iff there exist $x, y, z, w \in S^1$ such that $xs_1y = s_2$ and $zs_2w = s_1$.

(e) $s_1 \mathscr{L} s_2$ iff there exist $x, y \in S^1$ such that $xs_1 = s_2$ and $ys_2 = s_1$.

(f) $s_1 \mathscr{R} s_2$ iff there exist $x, y \in S^1$ such that $s_1x = s_2$ and $s_2y = s_1$.

(g) $s_1 \mathscr{D} s_2$ iff there exist $s \in S$ and $x, y, z, w \in S^1$ such that $xs_1 = s$, $ys = s_1$, $sz = s_2$, $s_2w = s$.

(h) $\mathscr{D} = \mathscr{L} \cdot \mathscr{R} = \mathscr{R} \cdot \mathscr{L}$, and so $\mathscr{D} = \text{LUB}(\mathscr{L}, \mathscr{R})$ (see Example 1.1.4d).

PROOF. The assertions of (a)–(g) are easy to verify. For (h), it is sufficient to show that $\mathscr{L} \cdot \mathscr{R} \subseteq \mathscr{R} \cdot \mathscr{L}$, for then $\mathscr{R} \cdot \mathscr{L} = \mathscr{R}^{-1} \cdot \mathscr{L}^{-1} = (\mathscr{L} \cdot \mathscr{R})^{-1} \subseteq (\mathscr{R} \cdot \mathscr{L})^{-1} = \mathscr{L}^{-1} \cdot \mathscr{R}^{-1} = \mathscr{L} \cdot \mathscr{R}$, so that $\mathscr{L} \cdot \mathscr{R} = \mathscr{R} \cdot \mathscr{L}$. To show $\mathscr{L} \cdot \mathscr{R} \subseteq \mathscr{R} \cdot \mathscr{L}$, let $s_1, s_2 \in S$ be such that $s_1(\mathscr{L} \cdot \mathscr{R})s_2$. Then, for some $s \in S$, $s_1 \mathscr{L} s$ and $s \mathscr{R} s_2$, and so there exist $w, x, y, z \in S^1$ such that $ws_1 = s$, $xs = s_1$, $sy = s_2$, and $s_2z = s$. Let $a = s_1y = xsy = xs_2$. Then, since $\mathscr{L}$ is a right congruence and $\mathscr{R}$ a left congruence, $s_1 \mathscr{L} s$ implies $a = s_1y \mathscr{L} sy = s_2$, and $s \mathscr{R} s_2$ implies $s_1 = xs \mathscr{R} xs_2 = a$, so that $s_1(\mathscr{R} \cdot \mathscr{L})s_2$. ∎

1.10 Definition. Let S be a semigroup, and define the following orderings on the $\mathscr{J}$, $\mathscr{R}$, and $\mathscr{L}$ classes of S:

(a) $J_a \leqslant J_b$ iff $J(a) \subseteq J(b)$.

(b) $R_a \leqslant R_b$ iff $R(a) \subseteq R(b)$.

(c) $L_a \leqslant L_b$ iff $L(a) \subseteq L(b)$.

These orderings are reflexive, antisymmetric, and transitive.

1.11 Remark. Notice an ideal I is a union of principal ideals and is a disjoint union of $\mathscr{J}$ classes J, for, if $a \in J \cap I$ and $b \in J$, then there exist $x, y \in S^1$ such that $b = xay \in S^1IS^1 = I$. Hence, $J \subseteq I$. If $J \subseteq I$, then the ideal generated by J is contained in I. Thus, a $\mathscr{J}$ class J generates an ideal I iff $J \geqslant J'$ for all $\mathscr{J}$ classes $J' \subseteq I$.

Naturally associated with every $\mathscr{J}$ class J of a semigroup S is a semigroup J^0 realized as follows. Define $B(J)$ to be the union of all $\mathscr{J}$ classes strictly less than J. Either $B(J) = \phi$ or $B(J)$ is an ideal of S. In either case, $S^1JS^1 - B(J) = J$, and so define $J^0 = S^1JS^1/B(J)$ [In the case $B(J) = \phi$, we have $J = K(S)$, and so $J^0 = K(S)^0$ is a semigroup.] Thus, $J^0 = (J \cup \{0\}, \circ)$ where

$$x \circ y = \begin{cases} xy & \text{if } xy \in J \\ 0 & \text{otherwise.} \end{cases}$$

1.12 Fact. (a) If I_1 and I_2 are ideals of S, and I_2 is maximally contained in I_1, then $I_1 - I_2$ is exactly one $\mathscr{J}$ class J of S. Hence, $I_1/I_2 = J^0$.

(b) The factors of every principal ideal series of S are exactly the semigroups $\{J^0 : J \text{ a } \mathscr{J} \text{ class of } S\}$.

(c) If J is a $\mathscr{J}$ class of S, then J^0 is either 0-simple or null.

PROOF. (a) Clearly, $I_1 - I_2$ is a union of $\mathscr{J}$ classes. Let J be minimal in $I_1 - I_2$. Claim $J \cup I_2$ is an ideal of S. For $S^1JS^1 = J \cup B(J)$, and $B(J) \subseteq I_2$, since J is minimal in $I_1 - I_2$. Hence, $S^1JS^1 = J \cup B(J) \subseteq J \cup I_2$, so that $J \cup I_2$ is an ideal of S contained in I_1 and properly containing I_2. Thus, $I_1 = I_2 \cup J$, and the assertion is proved.

(b) The assertion follows from (a), since every principal ideal series is obtained as follows. Choose any maximal $\mathscr{J}$ class J_1 in S, and let $I_1 = S - J_1$. Choose any maximal $\mathscr{J}$ class J_2 of S in I_1, and let $I_2 = I_1 - J_2$, etc. In this way, every $\mathscr{J}$ class of S will eventually be chosen in the preceding manner. This proves the assertion.

(c) This follows from (b) and Fact 1.7. ▮

1.13 Definition. Let J be a $\mathscr{J}$ class of a semigroup S. Call J a *regular* $\mathscr{J}$ *class* iff J^0 is 0-simple. Call J a *null* $\mathscr{J}$ *class* iff J^0 is null.

1.14 Remark. Since the factors of a principal ideal series of S are exactly the semigroups J^0 arising from the $\mathscr{J}$ classes of S, it would be useful to investigate the structure of $\mathscr{J}$ classes of S.

From the definition of $\mathscr{H}$, $\mathscr{L}$, $\mathscr{R}$, and $\mathscr{J}$, it is easily seen that

(1) $\mathscr{R}$ and $\mathscr{L}$ classes are disjoint unions of $\mathscr{H}$ classes;

(2) $\mathscr{J}$ classes are disjoint unions of $\mathscr{L}$ classes;

(3) $\mathscr{J}$ classes are disjoint unions of $\mathscr{R}$ classes;

(4) Hence, $\mathscr{J}$ classes are disjoint unions of $\mathscr{H}$ classes;

(5) Every $\mathscr{H}$ class is the intersection of an $\mathscr{L}$ and $\mathscr{R}$ class; and

(6) The intersection of an $\mathscr{L}$ and $\mathscr{R}$ class is either empty or is an $\mathscr{H}$ class.

The following fact establishes (for finite semigroups) that within a $\mathscr{J}$ class the intersection of an $\mathscr{R}$ and an $\mathscr{L}$ class is never empty, and that all the $\mathscr{H}$ classes in a $\mathscr{J}$ class are in a natural $1:1$ correspondence.

1.15 Fact (Green). Let S be a semigroup. Then we have the following:

(a) $\mathscr{J} = \mathscr{D}$.†

(b) Let J be a $\mathscr{J}$ class of S. Then $L \cap R \neq \phi$ for all $\mathscr{L}$ classes L in J and $\mathscr{R}$ classes R in J.

(c) $h \mathscr{J} hx$ iff $h \mathscr{R} hx$, all $x, h \in S$.

(d) $h \mathscr{J} xh$ iff $h \mathscr{L} xh$, all $x, h \in S$.

(e) Let $s_1, s_2 \in S$ with $s_1 \mathscr{L} s_2$. Let $x, y \in S^1$ be such that $xs_1 = s_2$ and $ys_2 = s_1$. Let $\varphi : R_{s_1} \to R_{s_2}$ and $\theta : R_{s_2} \to R_{s_1}$ be maps given by $\varphi(s) = xs$ and $\theta(t) = yt$. Then φ and θ are both $1:1$ and onto, and $\varphi^{-1} = \theta$. For $a, b \in R_{s_1}$, $a \mathscr{L} b$ implies $\varphi(a) \mathscr{L} \varphi(b)$. Hence, $a \mathscr{H} b$ iff $\varphi(a) \mathscr{H} \varphi(b)$, i.e., the maps φ and θ take $\mathscr{H}$ classes onto $\mathscr{H}$ classes. The dual proposition is also valid.

(f) Let $s_1, s_2 \in S$ with $s_1 \mathscr{J} s_2$. Let $s \in S$, $w, x, y, z \in S^1$ be such that $ws_1 = s$, $xs = s_1$, $sy = s_2$, and $s_2z = s$. Let $\alpha : H_{s_1} \to H_{s_2}$ and $\beta : H_{s_2} \to H_{s_1}$ be maps given by $\alpha(t) = wty$ and $\beta(u) = xuz$. Then α and β are both $1:1$ and onto, and $\alpha^{-1} = \beta$. Thus, any two $\mathscr{H}$ classes of S which are contained in the same $\mathscr{J}$ class are in $1:1$ correspondence.

PROOF. (a) If $s_1 \mathscr{D} s_2$, then there exists $s \in S$ such that $s_1 \mathscr{L} s$ and $s \mathscr{R} s_2$. Hence, $s_1 \mathscr{J} s \mathscr{J} s_2$, so that $s_1 \mathscr{D} s_2$ implies $s_1 \mathscr{J} s_2$.

Conversely, suppose that $s_1 \mathscr{J} s_2$. Then there exist $w, x, y, z \in S^1$ such that $ws_1x = s_2$ and $ys_2z = s_1$. Thus, $yws_1xz = s_1$, and so $(yw)^n s_1 (xz)^n = s_1$ for $n \geqslant 1$. For some $N > 2$ $(yw)^N = e_1$ and $(xz)^N = e_2$ are idempotents (Fact 1.1.11). Thus, $e_1s_1 = e_1(e_1s_1e_2) = e_1s_1e_2 = s_1$, so that $[(yw)^{N-1}y]\, ws_1 = s_1$, and so $ws_1 \mathscr{L} s_1$. Similarly, $s_1x \mathscr{R} s_1$. Hence, $s_2 = ws_1x \mathscr{R} ws_1 \mathscr{L} s_1$, so that $s_1 \mathscr{D} s_2$ by the fact that $\mathscr{R}$ is a left congruence. Thus, $\mathscr{J} = \mathscr{D}$.

(b) Let L and R be an $\mathscr{L}$ and $\mathscr{R}$ class, respectively, in J. Let $a \in L$, $b \in R$. Then $a \mathscr{J} b$, so that $a \mathscr{D} b$, i.e., there exists $c \in S$ such that $a \mathscr{L} c \mathscr{R} b$. Then $c \in L \cap R$, proving the assertion.

(c), (d) Let $x, h \in S$. If $h \mathscr{R} hx$, then $h \mathscr{J} hx$. Conversely, if $h \mathscr{J} hx$, then there exist $a, b \in S^1$ such that $h = ahxb = a^n h (xb)^n$ for all

† Recall that we only talk of finite semigroups unless explicit mention is made to the contrary. There are infinite semigroups for which $\mathscr{J} \neq \mathscr{D}$. Actually, $\mathscr{J} = \mathscr{D}$ if every element of S has a power that is an idempotent.

$n > 0$, and so, by the same argument as in (a), $h \mathscr{R} hx$. The proof of (d) is the dual of that of (c).

(e) φ and θ have the stated ranges because $\mathscr{R}$ is a left congruence. If $s \in R_{s_2}$, let $s = s_2 z$ for some $z \in S^1$. Then $\varphi\theta(s) = xys_2 z = s_2 z = s$, and a similar argument shows that $\theta\varphi(t) = t$ for $t \in R_{s_1}$. Thus, θ and φ are 1 : 1 and onto, and $\theta^{-1} = \varphi$. Since, for $s \in R_{s_1}$, $\varphi(s) = xs$ and $y\varphi(s) = s$, it follows that $s \mathscr{L} \varphi(s)$ for all $s \in R_{s_1}$, so that, in particular, $s_1 \mathscr{L} s_2$ implies $\varphi(s_1) \mathscr{L} \varphi(s_2)$.

(f) Compose the maps $a \to wa$ and $c \to cy$ and apply (e) and its dual. ▮

1.16 Remark. From Fact 1.15(f), we observe immediately that, if φ is a homomorphism on a semigroup S that is 1 : 1 when restricted to an $\mathscr{H}$ class H, then φ is 1 : 1 on every $\mathscr{H}$ class that is $\mathscr{J}$ equivalent to H. For, let $H_1 \mathscr{J} H$, and let $h_1, h_2 \in H_1$ be such that $\varphi(h_1) = \varphi(h_2)$. Then we know there exist $x, y \in S^1$ such that $xH_1y = H$. Now $xh_1y, xh_2y \in H$ and $\varphi(xh_1y) = \varphi(xh_2y)$, so that $xh_1y = xh_2y$. But, since the map $h \to xhy$ is 1 : 1, this implies $h_1 = h_2$.

Exercises and Extensions

X1.9. Verify that Fact 1.9 and parts (e) and (f) of Fact 1.15 hold for all semigroups, and that parts (a)–(d) of Fact 1.15 hold for all torsion semigroups (1.1.2).

X1.10. Compute the $\mathscr{L}$, $\mathscr{R}$, $\mathscr{H}$, and $\mathscr{J} = \mathscr{D}$ classes of (a) $F_R(X_n)$, where $X_n = \{1, \ldots, n\}$; (b) $\mathscr{M}^0(G; A, B; C)$ when C is regular; (c) $(2^{X_n}, \cap)$; (d) $U_3 \times_\varphi \mathbf{Z}_2$ of Exercise 5.1.2; and (e) a finite cyclic semigroup.

X1.11. Let S be a finite abelian semigroup. Then $\mathscr{H} = \mathscr{L} = \mathscr{R} = \mathscr{J}$. Is the converse true?

X1.12. Let $\mathscr{T}$ be any one of $\mathscr{H}$, $\mathscr{R}$, $\mathscr{L}$, or $\mathscr{J}$. If T is a subsemigroup of S and $t_1, t_2 \in T$, then $t_1 \mathscr{T} t_2$ in T implies $t_1 \mathscr{T} t_2$ in S. Construct a finite semigroup S and a subsemigroup T with $t_1, t_2 \in T$, for which $t_1 \mathscr{T} t_2$ in S but not in T. Show that $t_1 \mathscr{T} t_2$ in S implies that $t_1 \mathscr{T} t_2$ in T if t_1 and t_2 are $\mathscr{T}$-related in T to idempotents and $\mathscr{T}$ is not $\mathscr{J}$.

X1.13. Let S be a 0-simple semigroup, and let $0 \neq a \in S$. Show that there are idempotents $e_1, e_2 \in S - \{0\}$ such that $e_1 \mathscr{L} a$ and $a \mathscr{R} e_2$.

1.17 Remark. We next show that we can coordinatize each $\mathscr{J}$ class, J, of S and that the multiplication in J^0 has a natural form with respect to this coordinate system.

Let J be a $\mathscr{J}$ class of a semigroup S. Let $R_1, \ldots, R_m$ be the $\mathscr{R}$ classes in J, and let $L_1, \ldots, L_n$ be the $\mathscr{L}$ classes in J. Then, by Fact 1.15, the $\mathscr{H}$ classes in J are exactly $\{H_{ij} = R_i \cap L_j : i = 1, \ldots, m; j = 1, \ldots, n\}$. Thus, we have a "picture" of J as an "eggbox"; each row an $\mathscr{R}$ class, each column an $\mathscr{L}$ class, and the intersection of each row and column (i.e., each compartment) an $\mathscr{H}$ class (see Fig. 1). Fact 1.15(f) tells

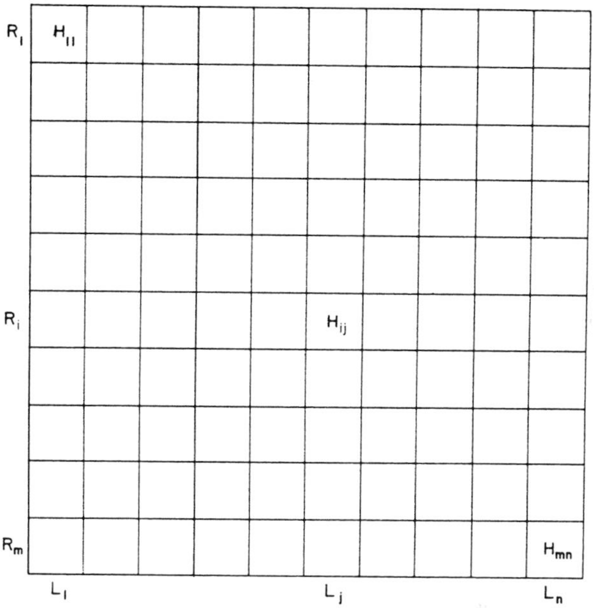

FIG. 1. The "coordinatized picture" of a $\mathscr{J}$ class J. The rows are the $\mathscr{R}$ classes of S contained in J. The columns are the $\mathscr{L}$ classes of S contained in J. Their intersections are the $\mathscr{H}$ classes of S contained in J. J is either null or regular. If J is regular, these classes coincide with the nonzero classes of J^0, and the multiplication is given by the Rees theorem.

us that each of the $\mathscr{H}$ classes is in a 1 : 1 correspondence and describes the maps that take one $\mathscr{H}$ class onto another.

1.18 Fact (Green). Let S be a semigroup.

(a) Every subgroup of S is contained in some $\mathscr{H}$ class of S. An $\mathscr{H}$ class H is a subgroup of S iff there exists $s_1, s_2 \in H$ such that $s_1 s_2 \in H$. Thus, H is a subgroup of S iff H contains an idempotent. Hence, the maximal subgroups of S are exactly those $\mathscr{H}$ classes of S containing idempotents.

(b) Let S be 0-simple. Then every $\mathscr{R}$ and $\mathscr{L}$ class of S contains an idempotent.

PROOF. Clearly, every subgroup of S is contained in an $\mathscr{H}$ class. For the second statement, if $s_1, s_2, s_1s_2 \in H$, then $s \to ss_2$ and $s \to s_1s$ are $1:1$ maps of H onto itself (by Fact 1.15). Thus, $s_1H = H = Hs_2$, so that, if $x_1, x_2 \in H$, then $x_1s_2 \in Hs_2 = H$ and $s_1x_2 \in s_1H = H$, and so, by the foregoing reasoning, $x_1H = H = Hx_2$. Since this holds for all $x_1, x_2 \in H$, it follows that H is a subsemigroup of S which is left simple and right simple. Thus, H is a group (X1.6). The remaining assertions of (a) now follow easily.

(b) Let S be 0-simple. Then $S - \{0\}$ is a $\mathscr{J}$ class of S. From Fact 1.15, it can be seen that for all nonzero $a \in S$, $R(a) = R_a \cup \{0\}$ and $L(a) = L_a \cup \{0\}$, that is, the right ideal generated by a is merely the $\mathscr{R}$ class containing a along with zero, etc.

Now let $a \in S - \{0\}$. Then $SaS = S$, and so there exists $x, y \in S$ such that $xay = a$. Thus, $x^nay^n = a$ for all $n \geqslant 1$, and so there are nonzero idempotents e_1, e_2 such that $e_1ae_2 = a$. Then $e_1a = a$ and $ae_2 = a$. $e_1a = a$ implies that $a \in R(e_1)$. Since $a \neq 0$, we have $a \in R_{e_1}$, and so $R_a = R_{e_1}$ and $e_1 \in R_a$. Similarly, $e_2 \in L_a$. ▌

1.19 Fact. If J is a regular $\mathscr{J}$ class of a semigroup S, then the $\mathscr{R}$, $\mathscr{L}$, and $\mathscr{H}$ classes of S in J are exactly the nonzero $\mathscr{R}$, $\mathscr{L}$, and $\mathscr{H}$ classes, respectively, of the 0-simple semigroup J^0.

PROOF. We shall prove the assertion for $\mathscr{L}$ classes; the proof is similar for $\mathscr{R}$ classes. Then, since $\mathscr{H}$ classes are intersections of $\mathscr{L}$ and $\mathscr{R}$ classes, the assertion is true for $\mathscr{H}$ classes.

Let $\mathscr{L}(S)$ and $\mathscr{L}(J)$ be the $\mathscr{L}$ equivalence relations for the semigroup S and J^0, respectively. Clearly, if L' is a nonzero $\mathscr{L}$ class of J^0, then L' is contained in an $\mathscr{L}$ class of S in J.

Conversely, let $a, b \in J$, and suppose $a\ \mathscr{L}(S)\ b$. By Fact 1.18, there exist idempotents $e_a, e_b \in J^0$ such that $e_a\ \mathscr{L}(J)\ a$ and $e_b\ \mathscr{L}(J)\ b$. Since $\mathscr{L}(J)$-equivalent implies $\mathscr{L}(S)$-equivalent, we have $e_a\ \mathscr{L}(S)\ a\ \mathscr{L}(S)\ b\ \mathscr{L}(S)\ e_b$, i.e., $e_a\ \mathscr{L}(S)\ e_b$. Therefore, there exists $x, y \in S^1$ such that $xe_a = e_b$ and $ye_b = e_a$. Then $e_ae_b = ye_be_b = ye_b = e_a$, and similarly $e_be_a = e_b$. Hence, $e_a\ \mathscr{L}(J)\ e_b$, and so $a\ \mathscr{L}(J)\ e_a\ \mathscr{L}(J)\ e_b\ \mathscr{L}(J)\ b$. ▌

1.20 Remark. We now know that, if J is a regular $\mathscr{J}$ class, the picture we have of J (Fig. 1) coincides exactly with the picture of the nonzero $\mathscr{J}$ class of J^0. We now state and prove Rees theorem, which completely determines the structure of 0-simple semigroups in terms of this "eggbox picture." Then by Fact 1.19 we shall know the structure of regular $\mathscr{J}$ classes.

1.21 Theorem (Rees). If S is a 0-simple semigroup, then S^0 is isomorphic to a *regular* Rees matrix semigroup. Conversely, a regular Rees matrix semigroup is 0-simple.

PROOF. Let S be 0-simple, and let J be its (only) nonzero $\mathscr{J}$ class. As in the Remark preceding Fact 1.18, let $R_1, \ldots, R_m$ and $L_1, \ldots, L_n$ be the $\mathscr{R}$ and $\mathscr{L}$ classes of S in J. Then $H_{ij} = R_i \cap L_j$ are the $\mathscr{H}$ classes of S in J. By Fact 1.18, at least one $\mathscr{H}$ class in J is a subgroup of S. By convention, number the $\mathscr{R}$ and $\mathscr{L}$ classes so that $H_{11} = R_1 \cap L_1$ is that subgroup. Let e be the identity of H_{11}. For $i = 1, \ldots, m$ and $j = 1, \ldots, n$, choose elements $l_i \in H_{i1}$ and $r_j \in H_{1j}$. Now $e \mathscr{L} l_i$, so that there exists $x \in S^1$ such that $xe = l_i$. Then $l_i e = xee = xe = l_i$. Similarly, $er_j = r_j$. Then, by Fact 1.15, $g \to l_i g r_j$ is a $1:1$ map of H_{11} onto H_{ij} for all $i = 1, \ldots, m$ and $j = 1, \ldots, n$. Hence, given the l_i's and r_j's, each element $s \in J$ has a unique representation $s = l_i g r_j$, where $g \in H_{11}$.

Now let $A = \{1, \ldots, m\}$, $B = \{1, \ldots, n\}$, and $G = H_{11}$. Let $\psi : S^0 \to \mathscr{M}^0(G; A, B; C)$ be given by $\psi(l_i g r_j) = (g, i, j)$ and $\psi(0) = 0$. By the preceding discussion, ψ is $1:1$ and onto. Define $C : B \times A \to G^0$ to be $C(j, i) = r_j l_i$. Now $r_j \in R_1 \cup \{0\}$, a right ideal of S, and $l_i \in L_1 \cup \{0\}$, a left ideal of S. Hence, $r_j l_i \in (R_1 \cap L_1) \cup \{0\} = G^0$. It is easy to see that ψ is an isomorphism.

To complete the proof, it is necessary to prove that a Rees matrix semigroup is 0-simple iff it is regular. This was left as an exercise (X1.3). ∎

SUMMARY. We are now in a position to know the "local multiplication" of a semigroup S, that is, multiplication within the $\mathscr{J}$ classes in the following sense. If the product of two elements in a $\mathscr{J}$ class, J, is again in J, we know what the product is. If the product is not in J, it "falls out" or "drops" to a lower $\mathscr{J}$ class, i.e., a $\mathscr{J}$ class less than J (in the $\mathscr{J}$ class ordering). We are told this fact, but not what the product is or what $\mathscr{J}$ class it is in.

We know the "local multiplication" because a $\mathscr{J}$ class, J, is either regular or else it is null. If J is null, the product of two elements always drops to a lower $\mathscr{J}$ class. If J is regular, the

Rees matrix semigroup isomorphic to J^0 tells us whether or not a product drops, and, if it does not drop, we know what the product is.

This characterization of regular $\mathscr{J}$ classes in terms of regular Rees matrix semigroups is extremely useful, and it is recommended that the reader become very familiar with this special class of semigroups. *From this point forth, most proofs will be stated in terms of the Rees theorem and regular Rees matrix semigroups.*

1.22 Remark. The isomorphism $\psi : S^0 \twoheadrightarrow \mathscr{M}^0(G; A, B; C)$ defined in the proof of the Rees theorem was determined entirely by the choice of elements $l_i \in H_{i1}$ and $r_j \in H_{1j}$. Since the choices l_i and r_j were arbitrary (within the proper $\mathscr{H}$ class), there are many such isomorphisms of S^0. Any isomorphism of S^0 defined in this manner is called a *coordinate map for the* (0-*simple*) *semigroup* S. The next fact gives a useful characterization of all coordinate maps for S.

1.23 Fact. Let S be a 0-simple semigroup, and let

$$\psi : S^0 \twoheadrightarrow \mathscr{M}^0(G; A, B; C)$$

and

$$\psi' : S^0 \twoheadrightarrow \mathscr{M}^0(G; A, B; P)$$

be two coordinate maps for S. Let $l_i \in H_{i1}$, $r_j \in H_{1j}$ and $l_{i'} \in H_{i1}$, $r_{j'} \in H_{1j}$, $i = 1,\ldots, n$, $j = 1,\ldots, m$, be the choices of elements that defined ψ and ψ', respectively. Then there exist maps $\lambda : A \to G$ and $\delta : B \to G$ such that $P(j, i) = \delta(j)\, C(j, i)\, \lambda(i)$, and the map $\theta : \mathscr{M}^0(G; A, B; C) \twoheadrightarrow \mathscr{M}^0(G; A, B; P)$ defined by $\theta(g, i, j) = (\lambda(i)^{-1} g \delta(j)^{-1}, i, j)$ is an isomorphism such that $\psi' = \theta\psi$.

Conversely, given any maps $\lambda : A \to G$ and $\delta : B \to G$, if a structure matrix $P : B \times A \to G^0$ is defined by $P(j, i) = \delta(j)\, C(j, i)\, \lambda(i)$, then the map θ just defined is an isomorphism from $\mathscr{M}^0(G; A, B; C)$ onto $\mathscr{M}^0(G; A, B; P)$, and the isomorphism $\psi' = \theta\psi$ is a coordinate map for S.

PROOF. Let ψ and ψ' be two coordinate maps for S as defined previously. Since left multiplication by l_i is a $1:1$ onto map from $H_{11} = G$ to H_{i1}, there exists a unique element $g_i \in G$ such that $l_i g_i = l_{i'}$. Similarly, there exists a unique $g_j \in G$ such that $g_j r_j = r_{j'}$. Define λ and δ by $\lambda(i) = g_i$ and $\delta(j) = g_j$. Then $P(j, i) = r_{j'} l_{i'} = \delta(j)\, C(j, i)\, \lambda(i)$, and θ is an isomorphism such that $\psi' = \theta\psi$.

Conversely, θ is clearly an isomorphism. Define $l_{i'} = l_i \lambda(i) \in H_{i1}$

and $r_{j'} = \delta(j)\, r_j \in H_{1j}$. It is easy to see that the elements $l_{i'}$ and $r_{j'}$ define the map $\psi' = \theta\psi$, so that ψ' is a coordinate map for S. ∎

1.24 Remark. It follows from the foregoing that there may be two different coordinate maps for S taking S^0 onto the same regular Rees matrix semigroup, $\mathcal{M}^0(G; A, B; C)$. For example, suppose G is a nonabelian group and $C(B \times A)$ is contained in the center of G. Let $g_0 \in G$ be any element not in the center, and define $\lambda(i) = g_0$, $\delta(j) = g_0^{-1}$ for all i, j. Then $P(j, i) = C(j, i)$, but the map $(g, i, j) \to [\lambda(i)^{-1} g\delta(j)^{-1}, i, j]$ is not the identity.

1.25 Fact. Let S be a 0-simple semigroup. Then there exists a coordinate map for S such that all entries in any one selected row and column of the resulting structure matrix are zeros and ones (the identity of G).

PROOF. This follows from Fact 1.23 by making appropriate choice for $\lambda : A \to G$ and $\delta : B \to G$. ∎

1.26 Fact. Let S be a semigroup.

(a) If S is left simple, then $S \cong G \times A^l$, where G is a group and A is a finite set.

(b) If S is right simple, then $S \cong G \times B^r$, where G is a group and B is a finite set.

PROOF. The proof is left as an exercise in the application of Rees theorem. (Hint: Consider Fact 1.25.) ∎

Exercises and Extensions

X1.14. Let S be a finite semigroup. The sequence $K(S) = I_n \subset I_{n-1} \subset \cdots \subset I_0 = S$ is a *composition ideal series* for S if, for $j = 1,..., n$, I_j is a maximal ideal of I_{j-1}. For $j = 1,..., n$, $F_j = I_{j-1}/I_j$, and $F_{n+1} = I_n{}^0 = K(S)^0$. $F_1, ..., F_{n+1}$ are the *factors* of the composition series. Show that the factors of every composition ideal series are the semigroups $\{J^0 : J$ is a regular $\mathcal{J}$ class of $S\}$ and a collection of two-point null semigroups (N_2; see Definition 1.3) arising as composition ideal factors from the null $\mathcal{J}$ classes of S. What can be said in the case in which S is infinite?

X1.15. For each $\mathcal{J}$ class J of $F_R(X_n)$, where $X_n = \{1,..., n\}$, find an isomorphism of J^0 with a regular Rees matrix semigroup.

X1.16. (a) Determine up to isomorphism all simple semigroups of prime order p. (b) Determine up to isomorphism all semigroups of order 3.

X1.17. Let $S = \mathscr{M}(G; A, B; C)$ be a simple semigroup, i.e., for all $a \in A$, $b \in B$; $C(b, a) \neq 0$. Let T be a subsemigroup of S, and let (g_1, a_1, b_1), $(g_2, a_2, b_2) \in T$. Let G_1 be the subgroup of G generated by g_1, g_2 and $C(\{b_1, b_2\} \times \{a_1, a_2\})$. Show that $G_1 \times \{a_1, a_2\} \times \{b_1, b_2\}$ is a subsemigroup of T.

X1.18. Prove that any subsemigroup of a simple semigroup is simple.

X1.19. If $\phi \neq A' \subset A$ and $\phi \neq B' \subset B$, give necessary and sufficient conditions for $\mathscr{M}^0(G; A, B; C) - G \times A' \times B'$ to be a subsemigroup of $\mathscr{M}^0(G; A, B; C)$. (Hint: What can be said about C?)

The theorems of Sect. 1 were first proved by Green [1] and Rees [2]. The presentation here follows the outline of Green and the book of Clifford and Preston [3].

2. Applications of Rees Theorem and the Schützenberger Group; Local Homomorphisms and Translations; Local Properties of Semigroups

In this section, an important tool, the Schützenberger group, is introduced for finite semigroups. It, along with the Rees theorem, is used to determine the form and structure of local homomorphisms and translations of semigroups and to describe various local properties of semigroups.

By "local homomorphism" we mean the restriction of an epimorphism $\varphi : S_1 \twoheadrightarrow S_2$ to a $\mathscr{J}$ class of S_1. We shall determine the form of all such restrictions in terms of the Green-Rees coordinate picture for $\mathscr{J}$ classes.

2.1 Fact. Let $\varphi : S_1 \twoheadrightarrow S_2$ be an epimorphism. Let $\alpha(S_i)$ be any of the relations $\mathscr{J}$, $\mathscr{L}$, $\mathscr{R}$, or $\mathscr{H}$ on S_i, $i = 1, 2$.

(a) If $s\ \alpha(S_1)\ t$, then $\varphi(s)\ \alpha(S_2)\ \varphi(t)$. Thus, φ sends α classes of S_1 into α classes of S_2.

(b) Let A_2 be an α class of S_2. Then $\varphi^{-1}(A_2)$ is a union of α classes of S_1.

(c) Let J_2 be a $\mathscr{J}$ class of S_2, and let J_1 be a minimal $\mathscr{J}$ class (see Definition 1.10) of S_1 contained in $\varphi^{-1}(J_2)$. Then $\varphi(J_1) = J_2$, and φ induces an epimorphism $\varphi' : J_1^0 \twoheadrightarrow J_2^0$.

(d) Each $\mathscr{R}$ and $\mathscr{L}$ class of S_1 contained in J_1 maps under φ onto an $\mathscr{R}$ and $\mathscr{L}$ class, respectively, of S_2 contained in J_2. (The statement is not, in general, true for $\mathscr{H}$ classes unless J_2 is regular. See Proposition 2.5 and the Remark 2.11 for proof and counterexample, respectively.)

(e) J_1 is regular iff J_2 is regular. If J_2 is null, then every $\mathscr{J}$ class in $\varphi^{-1}(J_2)$ is null. When J_2 is regular J_1 is the unique minimal $\mathscr{J}$ class of $\varphi^{-1}(J_2)$.

PROOF. The proof of (a) is trivial, and (b) follows immediately from (a).

(c) Let J_1 be as in (c). Then $\varphi(S_1{}^1 J_1 S_1{}^1)$ is an ideal of S_2 which meets, and hence contains, J_2. Furthermore, $B(J_1) = S^1 J_1 S^1 - J_1$ is an ideal of S_1, and $B(J_1) \cap \varphi^{-1}(J_2) = \phi$ by the minimality of J_1. Hence, $\varphi[B(J_1)] \cap J_2 = \phi$, and $\varphi(J_1) = J_2$. $\varphi'\colon J_1{}^0 \twoheadrightarrow J_2{}^0$ is well defined, since J_1 is minimal in $\varphi^{-1}(J_2)$.

(d) Since J_1 is minimal, each $\mathscr{R}$ and $\mathscr{L}$ class of S_1 contained in J_1 is minimal in the $\mathscr{R}$ and $\mathscr{L}$ class ordering, respectively. Let L_1 be an $\mathscr{L}$ class of S_1 contained in J_1, and suppose $\varphi(L_1) \subseteq L_2$, an $\mathscr{L}$ class of S_2 contained in J_2. Then L_1 is minimal in $\varphi^{-1}(L_2)$, a union of $\mathscr{L}$ classes. Now the assertion of (d) is proved by an argument similar to (c).

(e) If J_2 is regular, it contains an idempotent e. Let $s \in J_1$ such that $\varphi(s) = e$. For some n, s^n is an idempotent, and $\varphi(s^n) = e^n = e$. Therefore, $s^n \in J_1$, and J_1 is regular. If J_2 is null, then J_2 has no idempotents. Let e be an idempotent of some $\mathscr{J}$ class in $\varphi^{-1}(J_2)$. Then $\varphi(e) \in J_2$ is an idempotent. Thus, each $\mathscr{J}$ class in $\varphi^{-1}(J_2)$ is null if J_2 is null.

For the last statement, let J_2 be regular, and let J_1 and J_1' be two minimal $\mathscr{J}$ classes in $\varphi^{-1}(J_1)$. Then $\varphi(J_1) = \varphi(J_1') = J_2$. Since J_2 is regular, we have $J_2 \subseteq J_2{}^2$ by the Rees theorem. Then

$$J_2 \subseteq J_2 J_2 = \varphi(J_1)\,\varphi(J_1') = \varphi(J_1 J_1').$$

If J_1 and J_1' are distinct $\mathscr{J}$ classes, then $J_1 J_1'$, which belongs to $S_1{}^1 J_1 S_1{}^1 \cap S_1{}^1 J_1' S_1{}^1$, does not meet $\varphi^{-1}(J_2)$. Therefore, $J_1 = J_1'$. ∎

2.2 Definition. Let S' be a subset of a semigroup S. Let φ be a map from S' into a semigroup T. Then φ is a *partial homomorphism* iff for all $s_1, s_2 \in S'$ such that $s_1 s_2 \in S'$ we have $\varphi(s_1)\,\varphi(s_2) = \varphi(s_1 s_2)$. If $s_1 s_2 \notin S'$, there is no condition on $\varphi(s_1)\,\varphi(s_2)$.

2.3 Remark. Let $\varphi : S_1 \twoheadrightarrow S_2$ be an epimorphism. The restriction of φ to any $\mathcal{J}$ class of S_1 is a partial homomorphism. Notice that any function defined on a null $\mathcal{J}$ class is a partial homomorphism. The next proposition gives a simple description of all partial homomorphisms of regular $\mathcal{J}$ classes in terms of the Green-Rees picture for $\mathcal{J}$ classes.

2.4 Definition. The concept of a coordinate map for a 0-simple semigroup can be pulled back to regular $\mathcal{J}$ classes in the obvious way. The *coordinate maps for a regular $\mathcal{J}$ class J* are the restrictions of coordinate maps $C : J^0 \twoheadrightarrow \mathcal{M}^0(G; A, B; P)$ to J, sending J onto $\mathcal{M}^0(G; A, B; P) - \{0\}$. Thus, a coordinate map for J gives a description of J as the nonzero part of a regular Rees matrix semigroup.

2.5 Proposition. Let J_1 be a regular $\mathcal{J}$ class of S_1, and let $\varphi : J_1 \to S_2$ be a partial homomorphism. Then we have the following:

(a) $\varphi(J_1)$ is contained in a regular $\mathcal{J}$ class (say J_2) of S_2, and the $\mathcal{R}$, $\mathcal{L}$, and $\mathcal{H}$ classes of S_1 in J_1 are carried into $\mathcal{R}$, $\mathcal{L}$, and $\mathcal{H}$ classes of S_2 in J_2 by φ.

(b) (For convenience, number the $\mathcal{R}$ and $\mathcal{L}$ classes of J_2 so that the group H_{11} of J_1 goes into the group $\overline{H_{11}}$ of J_2.) Now let

$$C_1' : J_1 \twoheadrightarrow \mathcal{M}^0(G; A, B; P') - \{0\}$$

and

$$C_2' : J_2 \twoheadrightarrow \mathcal{M}^0(H; C, D; Q') - \{0\}$$

be any coordinate maps for J_1 and J_2. Then there exists a homomorphism $\omega : G \to H$ and maps $\psi_L : A \to C$, $\psi_R : B \to D$, $\lambda : A \to H$, and $\delta : B \to H$ such that the partial homomorphism

$$\theta = C_2' \varphi C_1'^{-1} : \mathcal{M}^0(G; A, B; P') - \{0\} \to \mathcal{M}^0(H; C, D; Q') - \{0\}$$

is given by

$$\theta(g, a, b) = (\lambda(a)^{-1}\, \omega(g)\, \delta(b)^{-1}, \psi_L(a), \psi_R(b)). \tag{2.1}$$

Furthermore, if $P'(b, a) \neq 0$, then

$$Q'[\psi_R(b), \psi_L(a)] = \delta(b)\, \omega[P'(b, a)]\, \lambda(a). \tag{2.2}$$

Conversely, any such functions satisfying (2.1) and (2.2) define a partial homomorphism of a regular $\mathcal{J}$ class.

(c) Let J_1 be the minimal $\mathscr{J}$ class in $\varphi^{-1}(J_2)$. Then $\varphi(J_1) = J_2$, and $\varphi' : J_1{}^0 \twoheadrightarrow J_2{}^0$ is an epimorphism (see Fact 2.1). In this case, there exist coordinate maps $C_1 : J_1{}^0 \twoheadrightarrow \mathscr{M}^0(G; A, B; P)$ and $C_2 : J_2{}^0 \twoheadrightarrow \mathscr{M}^0(H; C, D; Q)$ for $J_1{}^0$ and $J_2{}^0$ such that the epimorphism $\theta' = C_2\varphi' C_1^{-1}$ is given by

$$\begin{aligned} \theta'(g, a, b) &= (\omega(g), \psi_L(a), \psi_R(b)), \\ \theta'(0) &= 0, \end{aligned} \tag{2.3}$$

where ω, ψ_L, ψ_R are as defined in (b) and are onto maps. Furthermore,

$$Q[\psi_R(b), \psi_L(a)] = \begin{cases} \omega[P(b, a)] & \text{if } P(b, a) \neq 0 \\ 0 & \text{if } P(b, a) = 0. \end{cases} \tag{2.4}$$

Conversely, any such functions satisfying (2.3) and (2.4) define an epimorphism of a regular Rees matrix semigroup.

PROOF. (a) Let $s_1, s_2 \in J_1$. Since J_1 is regular, by Rees theorem we can find $x, y, z, w \in J_1$ such that $xs_1y = s_2$ and $zs_2w = s_1$. Since φ is a partial homomorphism, we have $\varphi(x)\,\varphi(s_1)\,\varphi(y) = \varphi(s_2)$ and $\varphi(z)\,\varphi(s_2)\,\varphi(w) = \varphi(s_1)$, and so $\varphi(s_1)\ \mathscr{J}\ \varphi(s_2)$, and all elements of $\varphi(J_1)$ are $\mathscr{J}$ equivalent.

By the same argument, the remaining assertions are proved.

(b) Let θ be the partial homomorphism. Define ψ_L and ψ_R by $\varphi(H_{ab}) \subseteq \bar{H}_{\psi_L(a)\psi_R(b)}$. They are well defined by (a). Define the map $\gamma : \mathscr{M}^0(G; A, B; P') - \{0\} \to H$ by

$$\theta(g, a, b) = (\gamma(g, a, b), \psi_L(a), \psi_R(b)).$$

An $\mathscr{H}$ class H_{ab} of a Rees matrix semigroup has an idempotent iff $P'(b, a) \neq 0$, and, since an $\mathscr{H}$ class has at most one idempotent, all nonzero idempotents of Rees matrix semigroups are of the form $(P'(b, a)^{-1}, a, b)$.

Now let $(g_0, a_0, b_0) \in \mathscr{M}^0(G; A, B; P') - \{0\}$ be an idempotent [which exists since $\mathscr{M}^0(G; A, B; P')$ is regular]. Therefore, $g_0 = P'(b_0, a_0)^{-1}$. Let $(g, a, b) \in \mathscr{M}^0(G; A, B; P') - \{0\}$. Then (g, a, b) can be written $(g, a, b) = (g_0, a, b_0)(gg_0, a_0, b_0)(1, a_0, b)$. Then, since φ is a homomorphism,

$$\gamma(g, a, b) = \gamma(g_0, a, b_0)\, h_0 \gamma(gg_0, a_0, b_0)\, h_0 \gamma(1, a_0, b),$$

where $h_0 = Q'[\psi_R(b_0), \psi_L(a_0)]$ is nonzero, since θ is a partial homomorphism.

Define $\omega(g) = h_0\gamma(gg_0, a_0, b_0)$, $\lambda(a)^{-1} = \gamma(g_0, a, b_0)$, and $\delta(b)^{-1} = h_0\gamma(1, a_0, b)$. It is easy to verify that ω is a homomorphism. Thus (2.1) is satisfied.

To verify (2.2), let $P'(b, a) \neq 0$, and consider the idempotent $\theta(P'(b, a)^{-1}, a, b)$:

$$\begin{aligned}\theta(P'(b, a)^{-1}, a, b) &= (\gamma(P'(b, a)^{-1}, a, b), \psi_L(a), \psi_R(b)) \\ &= (\lambda(a)^{-1}\omega[P'(b, a)^{-1}]\, \delta(b)^{-1}, \psi_L(a), \psi_R(b)).\end{aligned}$$

But, since the (partial) homomorphic image of an idempotent is an idempotent, we have

$$\gamma(P'(b, a)^{-1}, a, b) = Q'[\psi_R(b), \psi_L(a)]^{-1}.$$

Thus, (2.2) is satisfied.

The converse is clear, and so this proves (b).

(c) Let J_1 be as described, and let all the maps be as defined in (b). Then $\theta = C_2'\varphi' C_1'^{-1} : \mathcal{M}^0(G; A, B; P) \twoheadrightarrow \mathcal{M}^0(H; C, D; Q')$ is a homomorphism that satisfies (2.1) and also satisfies (2.2) even when $P'(b, a) = 0$. That is,

$$Q'(\psi_R(b), \psi_L(a)) = \begin{cases} \delta(b)\, \omega[P'(b, a)]\, \lambda(a) & \text{if } P'(b, a) \neq 0 \\ 0 & \text{if } P'(b, a) = 0 \end{cases}.$$

To see this, compute both sides of the equation

$$\theta[(1, 1, b) \cdot (1, a, 1)] = [\theta(1, 1, b)] \cdot [\theta(1, a, 1)]$$

using (2.1).

For each $c \in \psi_L(A)$ and $d \in \psi_R(B)$, choose representatives $\bar{c} \in \psi_L^{-1}(c) \subseteq A$ and $\bar{d} \in \psi_R^{-1}(d) \subseteq B$, respectively. Furthermore, for $a \in A$, $b \in B$, let $\bar{a} = \overline{\psi_L(a)}$ and $\bar{b} = \overline{\psi_R(b)}$, respectively.

Now we claim that, for each $a \in A$, there exists $g_a \in G$ such that $\lambda(a) = \omega(g_a)\, \lambda(\bar{a})$. For each $a \in A$, there exists $b \in B$ such that $P'(b, a) \neq 0$, by regularity. Now $\psi_L(a) = \psi_L(\bar{a})$, so that

$$\begin{aligned}\omega[P'(b, a)]\, \lambda(a) &= \delta(b)^{-1}Q'[\psi_R(b), \psi_L(a)] \\ &= \delta(b)^{-1}Q'[\psi_R(b), \psi_L(\bar{a})] \\ &= \omega[P'(b, \bar{a})]\, \lambda(\bar{a}). \qquad (2.5)\end{aligned}$$

Thus,

$$\lambda(a) = \omega[P'(b, a)^{-1}P'(b, \bar{a})]\, \lambda(\bar{a})$$

and so let

$$g_a = P'(b, a)^{-1}P'(b, \bar{a}).$$

In a similar manner, for each $b \in B$ there exists $g_b \in G$ such that $\delta(b) = \delta(\bar{b})\,\omega(g_b)$.

Now define the isomorphism $i : \mathscr{M}^0(G; A, B; P') \twoheadrightarrow \mathscr{M}^0(G; A, B; P)$ by $i(0) = 0$, $i(g, a, b) = (g_a^{-1} g g_b^{-1}, a, b)$ and by letting $P(b, a) = g_b P'(b, a)\, g_a$ (see Fact 1.23). Then $C_1 \equiv iC_1'$ is a coordinate map for S.

Define the isomorphism $j : \mathscr{M}^0(H; C, D; Q') \twoheadrightarrow \mathscr{M}^0(H; C, D; Q)$ by $j(0) = 0$, $j(h, c, d) = (\lambda(\bar{c})\, h\delta(\bar{d}), c, d)$ and by letting $Q(d, c) = \delta(\bar{d})^{-1}\, Q'(d, c)\, \lambda(\bar{c})^{-1}$. Then $C_2 \equiv jC_2'$ is a coordinate map for T.

It is easy to check that $\theta' = C_2 \varphi' C_1^{-1}$ satisfies (2.3) and (2.4). Once again, the converse is clear. ∎

2.6 Remark. From the simplification obtained in part (c) of the previous proposition, it follows that $\mathscr{H}$ classes in J_1 must map *onto* $\mathscr{H}$ classes in J_2 whenever J_2 is regular and J_1 is the unique minimal member of $\varphi^{-1}(J_2)$, thus proving part of the assertion of Fact 2.1(d).

One might wonder if the same simplification could be performed on partial homomorphisms of regular $\mathscr{J}$ classes. The proof of (c) does not carry over to partial homomorphisms, because it fails at Eq. (2.5). If the simplification were possible, it would imply that two different $\mathscr{H}$ classes in J_1 which are mapped into the same $\mathscr{H}$ class in J_2 must have identical images. The following example shows this not to be the case.

Let $\mathbf{Z}_2 = \{1, -1\}$ be the multiplicative group of order 2. Let $J_1 = \mathscr{M}^0(\mathbf{Z}_2\,; \{1, 2\}, \{1, 2\}; \left(\begin{smallmatrix}1 & 0\\ 0 & 1\end{smallmatrix}\right)) - \{0\}$. Define $\omega : \mathbf{Z}_2 \to \mathbf{Z}_2$ by $\omega(z) = 1$ for all $z \in \mathbf{Z}_2$. Define $\psi_L, \psi_R, \lambda, \delta$ as follows: $\psi_L(1) = 1$, $\psi_L(2) = 2$; $\psi_R(1) = \psi_R(2) = 1$; $\lambda(1) = -1$, $\lambda(2) = -1$; and $\delta(1) = 1$, $\delta(2) = -1$.

Now $P(1, 1) = P(2, 2) = 1$, and $P(1, 2) = P(2, 1) = 0$. Define

$$Q(1, 1) = \delta(1)\,\omega[P(1, 1)]\,\lambda(1) = -1$$

and

$$Q(1, 2) = \delta(2)\,\omega[P(2, 2)]\,\lambda(2) = 1.$$

Then Proposition 2.5(b) tells us that

$$\varphi(z, i, j) = (\lambda(i)^{-1}\omega(z)\,\delta(j)^{-1}, \psi_L(i), \psi_R(j))$$

defines a partial homomorphism of J_1 onto $\mathscr{M}^0(\mathbf{Z}_2\,; \{1, 2\}, \{1\}; Q) - \{0\}$. Now $\varphi(H_{11}) \subseteq \bar{H}_{11}$ and $\varphi(H_{12}) \subseteq \bar{H}_{11}$, but $\varphi(H_{11}) = \{(-1, 1, 1)\}$ and

$\varphi(H_{12}) = \{(1, 1, 1)\}$. Hence, $\varphi(H_{11}) \neq \varphi(H_{12})$. Thus, partial homomorphisms cannot, in general, be reduced to the form of Eq. (2.3).

We next introduce an important tool, the Schützenberger group, which allows us (among other things) to extend the idea of a coordinate map to null $\mathscr{J}$ classes, and hence all $\mathscr{J}$ classes. Then we obtain a description of homomorphic images of null $\mathscr{J}$ classes similar in form to those of Proposition 2.5.

Let H be any $\mathscr{H}$ class of a semigroup S. We now show the following:

(1) Associated with H is a group, $\mathscr{G}(H)$, called the Schützenberger group of H.

(2) $\mathscr{G}(H)$ actually depends only on the $\mathscr{J}$ class that H is in.

(3) If H is a group, then $H \cong \mathscr{G}(H)$.

2.7 Definition. Let S be a semigroup, and let X and T be nonempty subsets of S^1. Then the *right idealizer*, the *left idealizer*, and the *idealizer* of X in T are defined, respectively, by

$$RI_T(X) = \{t \in T^1 : Xt \subseteq X\},$$
$$LI_T(X) = \{t \in T^1 : tX \subseteq X\},$$
$$I_T(X) = RI_T(X) \cap LI_T(X).$$

We write $RI(X)$, $LI(X)$, and $I(X)$ if $T = S$. $RI(X)$, $LI(X)$, and $I(X)$ are subsemigroups of S.

Define $M_X^R : RI(X) \to F_R(X)$ and $M_X^L : LI(X) \to F_L(X)$ to be the homomorphisms sending t to $(x \to xt)$ and $(x \to tx)$, respectively.

2.8 Proposition (Schützenberger). Let H be an $\mathscr{H}$ class of S.

(a) $M_H^R[RI(H)] = P$ is a regular transitive group of permutations of H [i.e., for all $h, h' \in H$, there exists a *unique* $\pi \in P$ such that $(h)\pi = h'$]. Dually, $M_H^L[LI(H)] = P'$ is a regular transitive group of permutations of H. Elements of P and P' commute, i.e., if $\pi \in P$, $\pi' \in P'$, $h \in H$, then $(\pi' h)\,\pi = \pi'(h\pi)$. Furthermore, if h_0 is a fixed element of H, then an isomorphism of P with P' is given by $\pi \to \pi'$, where, for $\pi \in P$, π' is the unique element of P' such that $(h_0)\pi = \pi'(h_0)$.

(b) We can define a group structure on H as follows. Choose a fixed basepoint $h_0 \in H$, and, for $h_1, h_2 \in H$, let π_1, π_2 be the unique elements of P such that $(h_0)\,\pi_1 = h_1$ and $(h_0)\,\pi_2 = h_2$. Set $h_1 * h_2 = (h_0)\,\pi_1\pi_2$. Then $(H, *)$ is a group, independent (up to isomorphism) of the choice of h_0. P, as a subgroup of $F_R(H)$, is isomorphic to the right regular representation of $(H, *)$.

(c) We can define a group structure $(H, \circ)$ on H in a dual manner using P'. Then P', as a subgroup of $F_L(H)$, is isomorphic to the left regular representation of $(H, \circ)$.

(d) If H is a group (in the semigroup), then $H \cong (H, *) \cong (H, \circ)$, where the basepoints are taken to be the identity of H.

(e) We denote the abstract group $(H, *) \cong P \cong P' \cong (H, \circ)$ by $\mathscr{G}(H)$ and call it the *Schützenberger group of H*. If H, H' are $\mathscr{H}$ classes belonging to the same $\mathscr{J}$ class J, then $\mathscr{G}(H) \cong \mathscr{G}(H')$. Hence, we also denote this group by $\mathscr{G}(J)$.

PROOF. (a) P is a subsemigroup of $F_R(H)$, since it is a homomorphic image of the semigroup $RI(H)$. By Fact 1.15(e), it can be seen that each element of P is a permutation of H, so that $P \subseteq \mathrm{SYM}_R(H)$ and hence is a subgroup, by Fact 1.1.11(b). That P is transitive follows from the definition of $\mathscr{H}$. To prove the uniqueness, suppose, for some $h \in H$, $h\pi_1 = h\pi_2$. Let h' be any element in H. Then there exists $s \in S^1$ such that $h' = sh$. Thus, $h'\pi_1 = sh\pi_1 = sh\pi_2 = h'\pi_2$, so that $\pi_1 = \pi_2$.

The dual arguments apply to $M_H^L[LI(H)] = P'$. To show that P and P' commute, let $\pi \in P$, $\pi' \in P'$, and let $s \in RI(H)$, $s' \in LI(H)$ such that $M_H^R(s) = \pi$ and $M_H^L(s') = \pi'$, respectively. Then, by associativity of semigroup multiplication, we have $(\pi'h)\,\pi = (s'h)\,s = s'(hs) = \pi'(h\pi)$.

Finally, the map $\pi \to \pi'$ is clearly $1:1$ and onto. Let $\pi_1, \pi_2 \in P$. Then $(\pi_1\pi_2)'\,h_0 = h_0(\pi_1\pi_2) = (h_0\pi_1)\pi_2 = (\pi_1'h_0)\,\pi_2 = \pi_1'(h_0\pi_2) = (\pi_1'\pi_2')\,h_0$. Hence, the map is an isomorphism.

Parts (b)–(d) are left as exercises.

(e) Suppose $a \mathscr{L} b$. Then $RI(H_a) = RI(H_b)$. Define $\psi : \mathscr{G}(H_a) \twoheadrightarrow \mathscr{G}(H_b)$ by $\psi(\pi) = M_{H_b}^R(\bar{\pi})$, where $\bar{\pi}$ is a representative of $M_{H_a}^{R^{-1}}(\pi) \subseteq RI(H_a)$. It is easy to verify that ψ is an isomorphism, so $\mathscr{G}(H_a) \cong \mathscr{G}(H_b)$. Dually, if $b \mathscr{R} c$, then $\mathscr{G}(H_b) \cong \mathscr{G}(H_c)$. Hence, if $a \mathscr{J} c$, then $\mathscr{G}(H_a) \cong \mathscr{G}(H_c)$. ∎

2.9 Definition. Let J be a $\mathscr{J}$ class of a semigroup S. As before, let $R_1, \ldots, R_m$ and $L_1, \ldots, L_n$ be the $\mathscr{R}$ and $\mathscr{L}$ classes of S in J, respectively, and let $\{H_{ij} = R_i \cap L_j\}$, $i = 1, \ldots, m$; $j = 1, \ldots, n$, be the $\mathscr{H}$ classes of S in J. Let h_0 be a fixed element of H_{11}. For $i = 1, \ldots, m$; $j = 1, \ldots, n$, choose $l_i, r_j \in S^1$ such that $h_0 r_j \in H_{1j}$ and $l_i h_0 \in H_{i1}$.

(The l_i, r_j may not belong to J.) By convention, choose $l_1 = r_1 = 1$. Then, by Fact 1.15, $h \to l_i h r_j$ is a $1:1$ map of H_{11} onto H_{ij}. Now, for each $h \in H_{11}$, there exists a unique element $\pi \in P \cong \mathscr{G}(J)$ such that $h = h_0\pi$. Hence, given the l_i's and r_j's, each element $s \in J$ has a unique representation $s = l_i(h_0\pi)\, r_j \in H_{ij}$. The $1:1$, onto map $C: J \twoheadrightarrow \mathscr{G}(J) \times \{1,\ldots, m\} \times \{1,\ldots, n\}$ given by $C[l_i(h_0\pi)r_j] = (\pi, i, j)$ is a *coordinate map for* J. Each choice of l_i's and r_j's determines a coordinate map for J.

If J is regular and H_{11} is chosen to be a group and h_0 is chosen to be the identity of H_{11}, then the definition of coordinate maps just given coincides with the earlier definitions.

The coordinate maps for J are extended to J^0 by sending zero into a zero added to the range. If J is regular, these extensions are, of course, the coordinate maps for the 0-simple semigroup J^0. If J is null, the images of the extensions can be considered the (nonregular) Rees matrix semigroup $\mathscr{M}^0(\mathscr{G}(J)\,; \{1,\ldots, m\}, \{1,\ldots, n\}; P)$, where $P(j, i) = 0$ for all i, j.

We now return to the situation described in Fact 2.1.

2.10 Fact. (a) Let J_1 be a (null) $\mathscr{J}$ class of S_1 contained in $\varphi^{-1}(J_2)$. Then there exist coordinate maps $C_1: J_1 \twoheadrightarrow \mathscr{G}(J_1) \times A \times B$ and $C_2: J_2 \twoheadrightarrow \mathscr{G}(J_2) \times C \times D$ such that $\theta = C_2\varphi C_1^{-1}$ is given by

$$\theta(g, a, b) = (\lambda(a)\, \omega(g)\, \delta(b), \psi_L(a), \psi_R(b)), \tag{2.6}$$

where $\omega: \mathscr{G}(J_1) \to \mathscr{G}(J_2)$ is a homomorphism, and $\psi_L: A \to C$, $\psi_R: B \to D$, $\lambda: A \to \mathscr{G}(J_2)$, and $\delta: B \to \mathscr{G}(J_2)$ are maps.

(b) Let J_1 be minimal in $\varphi^{-1}(J_2)$. Then $\varphi(J_1) = J_2$, and each $\mathscr{L}$ and $\mathscr{R}$ class in J_1 is mapped *onto* an $\mathscr{L}$ and $\mathscr{R}$ class, respectively, in J_2 (Fact 2.1). Hence, for each $c \in C$, we have

$$\mathscr{G}(J_2) = \lambda[\psi_L^{-1}(c)]\, \omega[\mathscr{G}(J_1)],$$

and, for each $d \in D$,

$$\mathscr{G}(J_2) = \omega[\mathscr{G}(J_1)]\, \delta[\psi_R^{-1}(d)].$$

PROOF. (a) As in Proposition 2.5, renumber the $\mathscr{R}$ and $\mathscr{L}$ classes in J_2 so that $\varphi(H_{11}) \subseteq \bar{H}_{11}$. Choose a basepoint $h_0 \in H_{11}$, and let C_1 be any coordinate map for J_1 defined by $C_1[l_a(h_0\pi)\, r_b] = (\pi, a, b)$, where $\pi \in P \cong \mathscr{G}(J_1)$. Let C_2 be any coordinate map for J_2 defined by $C_2(x_c[\varphi(h_0)\, q]\, y_d) = (q, c, d)$, where $q \in Q \cong \mathscr{G}(J_2)$.

Notation: Let $\pi' \in P' \subseteq F_L(H_{11})$ be the unique element such that $\pi'(h_0) = (h_0)\,\pi$, $\pi \in P \subseteq F_R(H_{11})$ [see Prop. 2.8(a)]. Similarly, let q' be the unique element in Q' such that $q'\varphi(h_0) = \varphi(h_0)\, q$. Let $\bar{\pi}$ be any element of $RI(H_{11})$ such that $M^R_{H_{11}}(\bar{\pi}) = \pi$, i.e., $(h_0)\,\pi = h_0\bar{\pi}$. Use similar notation for π', q, q'.

Define $\omega : P \to Q$ as follows. Let $\pi \in P$, and define $\omega(\pi)$ to be the unique element of Q such that $\varphi(h_0\bar{\pi}) = \varphi(h_0)\, \omega(\pi)$. To show ω is a homomorphism, let $\pi_1, \pi_2 \in P$. Then

$$\begin{aligned}\varphi(h_0)\, \omega(\pi_1\pi_2) &= \varphi[h_0(\overline{\pi_1\pi_2})] = \varphi[(h_0\bar{\pi}_1)\, \bar{\pi}_2] = \varphi[\bar{\pi}_1'(h_0\bar{\pi}_2)] \\ &= \varphi(\bar{\pi}_1')\, \varphi(h_0\bar{\pi}_2) = \varphi(\bar{\pi}_1')\, \varphi(h_0)\, \omega(\pi_2) = \varphi(\bar{\pi}_1' h_0)\, \omega(\pi_2) \\ &= \varphi(h_0\bar{\pi}_1)\, \omega(\pi_2) = \varphi(h_0)[\omega(\pi_1)\, \omega(\pi_2)].\end{aligned}$$

Utilizing the uniqueness of the representation, we have ω a homomorphism.

Define ψ_L and ψ_R by $\varphi(H_{ab}) \subseteq \bar{H}_{\psi_L(a)\psi_R(b)}$, as in Proposition 2.5. Define $\lambda : A \to Q$ by letting it describe $\varphi(l_a h_0)$ for each $a \in A$. That is, $\varphi(l_a h_0) \in \bar{H}_{\psi_L(a)1}$, and so let $\lambda(a) \in Q$ be the unique element such that $\varphi(l_a h_0) = x_{\psi_L(a)}[\varphi(h_0)\, \lambda(a)]$. (Recall that $l_1, r_1, x_1, y_1 = 1$ by convention.) Similarly, define $\delta : B \to Q$ by $\varphi(h_0 r_b) = [\varphi(h_0)\, \delta(b)]\, y_{\varphi_R(b)}$.

Let $s = l_a(h_0\bar{\pi})\, r_b \in J_1$. Then

$$\begin{aligned}\varphi(s) &= \varphi(l_a)\, \varphi(h_0\bar{\pi})\, \varphi(r_b) = \varphi(l_a)[\varphi(h_0)\, \omega(\pi)]\, \varphi(r_b) \\ &= \varphi(l_a h_0)\, \overline{\omega(\pi)}\, \varphi(r_b) = x_{\psi_L(a)}[\varphi(h_0)\, \lambda(a)]\, \overline{\omega(\pi)}\, \varphi(r_b) \\ &= x_{\psi_L(a)}(\varphi(h_0)[\lambda(a)\, \omega(\pi)])\, \varphi(r_b) = x_{\psi_L(a)}([\overline{\lambda(a)\, \omega(\pi)}]'\, \varphi(h_0))\, \varphi(r_b) \\ &= x_{\psi_L(a)}[\overline{\lambda(a)\, \omega(\pi)}]'\, [\varphi(h_0)\, \delta(b)]\, y_{\psi_R(b)} \\ &= x_{\psi_L(a)}(\varphi(h_0)[\lambda(a)\, \omega(\pi)\, \delta(b)])\, y_{\psi_R(b)}.\end{aligned}$$

Thus, $\theta = C_2\varphi C_1^{-1}$ has the required form.

(b) Since each $\mathscr{R}$ class of J_1 maps onto an $\mathscr{R}$ class of J_2, we have $\varphi(R_1) = \bar{R}_1$. Consider the inverse image in R_1 of an arbitrary $\mathscr{H}$ class in $\bar{R}_1$, say $\bar{H}_{1d}$. This inverse image is a union of $\mathscr{H}$ classes in R_1, say $\bigcup \{H_{1b} : b \in \psi_R^{-1}(d)\}$. The image of each $\mathscr{H}$ class in this set is

$$\begin{aligned}\varphi(H_{1b}) &= \varphi[\mathscr{G}(J_1), 1, b] \\ &= (\lambda(1)\, \omega[\mathscr{G}(J_1)]\, \delta(b), 1, d) \quad \text{for all} \quad b \in \psi_R^{-1}(d).\end{aligned}$$

But by assumption, $\lambda(1) = 1$, the identity of $\mathscr{G}(J_2)$. Then since $\bigcup \{H_{1b} : b \in \psi_R^{-1}(d)\}$ maps onto $\bar{H}_{1d}$, we have

$$\bigcup \{\omega[\mathscr{G}(J_1)]\ \delta(b) : b \in \psi_R^{-1}(d)\} = \mathscr{G}(J_2).$$

But, since $\mathscr{G}(J_2)$ is a group, this is clearly equivalent to the assertion

$$\mathscr{G}(J_2) = \omega[\mathscr{G}(J_1)]\ \delta[\psi_R^{-1}(d)].$$

The dual argument proves the remaining assertion. ∎

2.11 Remark. The following example shows that, in general, if J_1 is minimal in $\varphi^{-1}(J_2)$ (in the situation described in Fact 2.1), $\mathscr{H}$ classes of S_1 in J_1 need not map onto $\mathscr{H}$ classes of S_2 in J_2.

Let G be a group, H a subgroup, $\bar{x}_1, \ldots, \bar{x}_n$ a set of representatives for the cosets $\{gH : g \in G\}$, and $\bar{y}_1, \ldots, \bar{y}_n$ a set of representatives for $\{Hg : g \in G\}$. Let A and B be finite sets. Let R denote the set $\{0\} \cup (A \times \{\bar{x}_1, \ldots, \bar{x}_n\} \times H \times \{\bar{y}_1, \ldots, \bar{y}_n\} \times B)$, and let V denote the set $(A \times G \times B) \cup \{0\}$. Let T denote the group $\mathrm{SYM}_L(A) \times G \times \mathrm{SYM}_R(B)$. Let S_1 be the semigroup with elements $T \cup R$ (disjoint union), where T is a subgroup, R is a null subsemigroup, 0 is the zero of S_1, and, for $(f_1, g, f_2) \in T$, $(a, \bar{x}_k, h, \bar{y}_j, b) \in R - \{0\}$, we have

$$(f_1, g, f_2) \cdot (a, \bar{x}_k, h, \bar{y}_j, b) = (f_1(a), \bar{x}_{k'}, h'h, \bar{y}_j, b)$$

and

$$(a, \bar{x}_k, h, \bar{y}_j, b) \cdot (f_1, g, f_2) = (a, \bar{x}_k, hh^*, \bar{y}_{j'}, f_2(b)),$$

where h', h^*, $\bar{x}_{k'}$, $\bar{y}_{j'}$ are defined by $g\bar{x}_k = \bar{x}_{k'}h'$ and $\bar{y}_j g = h^*\bar{y}_{j'}$. Let S_2 be the semigroup with elements $T \cup V$ (disjoint union), where T is a subgroup, V is a null subsemigroup, 0 is the zero of S_2, and, if $(f_1, g, f_2) \in T$ and $(a, g', b) \in V - \{0\}$, then

$$(f_1, g, f_2) \cdot (a, g', b) = (f_1(a), gg', b)$$

and

$$(a, g', b) \cdot (f_1, g, f_2) = (a, g'g, f_2(b)).$$

Two elements of R (respectively V) are $\mathscr{H}$ equivalent in S_1 (respectively S_2) iff all but their center, i.e., H (respectively G), coordinates agree. Let $\varphi : S_1 \twoheadrightarrow S_2$ be defined as follows: φ is the identity on T, whereas $\varphi(0) = 0$ and $\varphi(a, \bar{x}_k, h, \bar{y}_j, b) = (a, \bar{x}_k h \bar{y}_j, b)$.

Then φ is an epimorphism, but φ carries each $\mathscr{H}$ class of S_1 onto an $\mathscr{H}$ class of S_2 iff $H = G$.

Note that the multiplication just defined for S_1 and S_2 must be checked for associativity. See the Remark 2.17 below for comments on the general method of constructing new semigroups out of other semigroups in the manner in which S_1 and S_2 were constructed.

We next introduce a particularly important set of transformations of a semigroup, the translations.

2.12 Definition. Let S be a semigroup. Then $\alpha \in F_R(S)$ is a *right translation* of S iff, for all $s_1, s_2 \in S$, $(s_1 s_2)\,\alpha = s_1[(s_2)\,\alpha]$. Similarly, $\beta \in F_L(S)$ is a *left translation* of S iff, for all $s_1, s_2 \in S$, $\beta(s_1 s_2) = [\beta(s_1)]\,s_2$.

A right translation α and a left translation β are *linked* iff for all $s_1, s_2 \in S$ we have $(s_1\alpha)\,s_2 = s_1(\beta s_2)$.

It is easy to verify that the set of right translations of S is a subsemigroup of $F_R(S)$; denote the semigroup of right translations by $RT(S)$. Similarly, denote the semigroup of left translations by $LT(S)$.

2.13 Remark. Let $s \in S$. Then right multiplication by s on S is a right translation of S. In fact, the right regular representation of S, $R(S)$ is a subsemigroup of $RT(S^1)$. Similarly, $L(S) \subseteq LT(S^1)$.

If $s \in S$, then notice that $R(s) \in RT(S)$ and $L(s) \in LT(S)$ are linked.

Similar to our study of the form of local homomorphisms, we now determine the form of all right and left translations of a regular Rees matrix semigroup in terms of the Green-Rees picture. For convenience, we denote the set underlying the Rees matrix semigroup $\mathscr{M}^0(G; A, B; C)$ by $G^0 \times A^0 \times B^0$ [instead of $(G \times A \times B) \cup \{0\}$] and identify triples with one or more zeros with the zero of $(G \times A \times B) \cup \{0\}$. Multiplication remains consistent by extending $C : B \times A \to G^0$ to $C : B^0 \times A^0 \to G^0$, where

$$C(0, 0) = C(b, 0) = C(0, a) = 0.$$

2.14 Fact. Let $M = \mathscr{M}^0(G; A, B; C)$ be a regular Rees matrix semigroup.

(a) Let $\alpha \in RT(M)$. Then there exist functions $\psi_R(\alpha) : B^0 \to B^0$ and $\delta(\alpha) : B^0 \to G^0$ such that, for all $(g, a, b) \in M$,

$$(g, a, b)\,\alpha = (g\delta(\alpha)(b), a, \psi_R(\alpha)(b)). \tag{2.7}$$

Furthermore, $\psi_R(\alpha)(b) = 0$ iff $\delta(\alpha)(b) = 0$, and $\psi_R(\alpha)(0) = 0$. Conversely, any such functions define a right translation by (2.7).

(b) Let $\beta \in LT(M)$. Then there exist functions $\psi_L(\beta) : A^0 \to A^0$ and $\lambda(\beta) : A^0 \to G^0$ such that, for all $(g, a, b) \in M$,

$$\beta(g, a, b) = (\lambda(\beta)(a)g, \psi_L(\beta)(a), b). \tag{2.8}$$

Furthermore, $\psi_L(\beta)(\mathrm{a}) = 0$ iff $\lambda(\beta)(\mathrm{a}) = 0$, and $\psi_L(\beta)(0) = 0$. Conversely, any such functions define a right translation by (2.8).

(c) $RT(M)$ and $LT(M)$ commute. That is, for all $m \in M$, $\alpha \in RT(M)$, and $\beta \in LT(M)$, $(\beta m)\alpha = \beta(m\alpha)$.

(d) Let $\alpha \in RT(M)$ and $\beta \in LT(M)$. Then α and β are linked iff for all $a \in A$, $b \in B$ the following relationship holds:

$$\delta(\alpha)(b)\, C[\psi_R(\alpha)(b), a] = C[b, \psi_L(\beta)(a)]\, \lambda(\beta)(a). \tag{2.9}$$

PROOF. (a) Let $\alpha \in RT(M)$, and let $(g, a, b) \in M$ be nonzero. Since M is regular, there exists an idempotent $(g_0, a_0, b) \in M$ such that $(g, a, b)(g_0, a_0, b) = (g, a, b)$. First consider α acting on the idempotent. Either $(g_0, a_0, b)\,\alpha = 0$ or

$$(g_0', a_0', b') \equiv (g_0, a_0, b)\,\alpha = (g_0, a_0, b)[(g_0, a_0, b)\,\alpha].$$

Therefore, $a_0' = a_0$. Now

$$(g, a, b)\,\alpha = (g, a, b)[(g_0, a_0, b)\,\alpha] = \begin{cases} 0 \\ (gg_0^{-1}g_0', a, b'). \end{cases}$$

Now define $\psi_R(\alpha) : B^0 \to B^0$ by

$$\psi_R(\alpha)(b) = \begin{cases} 0 & \text{if } (g, a, b)\,\alpha = 0 \\ b' & \text{otherwise,} \end{cases}$$

and define $\delta(\alpha) : B^0 \to G^0$ by

$$\delta(\alpha)(b) = \begin{cases} 0 & \text{if } \psi_R(\alpha)(b) = 0 \\ g_0^{-1}g_0' & \text{otherwise.} \end{cases}$$

It is easy to verify that these maps are well defined functions and they satisfy (2.7). The converse is clear.

(b) The dual argument applies to (b).

(c) This follows from the form of Eq. (2.7) and (2.8).

(d) Let α and β be linked. Consider $[(g, c, b)\,\alpha](h, a, d) = (g, c, b)[\beta(h, a, d)]$. The left-hand side yields $[(g, c, b)\,\alpha](h, a, d) = (g\delta(\alpha)(b)\,C[\psi_R(\alpha)(b), a]\,h, c, d)$, whereas the right-hand side equals $(gC[b, \psi_L(\beta)(a)]\,\lambda(\beta)(a)\,h, c, d)$. Therefore, α and β are linked iff

$$\delta(\alpha)(b)\,C[\psi_R(\alpha)(b), a] = C[b, \psi_L(\beta)(a)]\,\lambda(\beta)(a). \quad \blacksquare$$

$RT(M)$ and $LT(M)$ can be represented in two interesting ways. The first of these represents $RT(M)$ and $LT(M)$ as row-monomial and column-monomial matrices (see Example 1.1.4(o)).

2.15 Fact. Let $M = \mathscr{M}^0(G; A, B; C)$ be a regular Rees matrix semigroup, and let $|A| = m$ and $|B| = n$. Then

(a) $RT(M) \cong \mathscr{RM}(n, G)$, the $n \times n$ row-monomial matrices over G^0;

(b) $LT(M) \cong \mathscr{CM}(m, G)$, the $m \times m$ column-monomial matrices over G^0.

PROOF. (a) Viewing each nonzero element $(g, a, b) \in M$ as an $m \times n$ matrix with the entry g in the (a, b) spot and zeros everywhere else, and viewing $0 \in M$ as the $m \times n$ matrix with all zeros as entries (see Example 1.1.4(m)), it is easy to write down each element of $RT(M)$ as a row-monomial matrix. Precisely, let $\alpha \in RT(M)$, and let $\psi_R(\alpha)$ and $\delta(\alpha)$ be defined as in Fact 2.14. Define the $n \times n$ row-monomial matrix $\alpha^* : B \times B \to G^0$ by

$$\alpha^*(b, b') = \begin{cases} \delta(\alpha)(b) & \text{if } b' = \psi_R(\alpha)(b) \\ 0 & \text{otherwise.} \end{cases}$$

The map $\alpha \to \alpha^*$ is clearly an isomorphism. (b) is proved by the dual argument. $\blacksquare$

Let $\alpha \in RT(M)$. By Eq. (2.7), we see that the action of α on $G^0 \times A^0 \times B^0$ is in triangular form. This suggets that $RT(M)$ can be represented in wreath product form (see Def. 5.1.4). The following fact will be of great use in the next two chapters.

2.16 Fact. Define

$$S = \{f \in F_R(B^0) : f(0) = 0\}$$

and

$$S' = \{f \in F_L(A^0) : f(0) = 0\}.$$

S and S' are subsemigroups.

(a) $RT(M)$ is isomorphic to a subsemigroup of $(G^0, R(G^0))$ w (B^0, S).

(b) $LT(M)$ is isomorphic to a subsemigroup of (S', A^0) w* $(L(G^0), G^0)$, where w* is the wreath product for *left* transformation semigroups (the dual of the concept defined in Def. 5.1.4). Notice the action is triangular from the left for w*.

PROOF. (a) $(G^0, R(G^0))$ w $(B^0, S) \cong F(B^0, G^0) \times_Y S$, where $Y : S \to \text{Endo}_L[F(B^0, G^0)]$ is a homomorphism defined as follows: Let $f \in F(B^0, G^0)$, $s \in S$, and $b \in B^0$. Then $[Y(s)f](b) = f(bs)$.

Let $\alpha \in RT(M)$. Then the map $\alpha \to (\delta(\alpha), \psi_R(\alpha)) \in F(B^0, G^0) \times_Y S$ is a $1:1$ homomorphism. To check this, let $\alpha, \beta \in RT(M)$. Then

$$\begin{aligned}(g, a, b)\,\alpha\beta &= (g\delta(\alpha)(b), a, (b)\,\psi_R(\alpha))\,\beta\\ &= (g\delta(\alpha)(b)\,\delta(\beta)((b)\,\psi_R(\alpha)), a, (b)\,\psi_R(\alpha)\,\psi_R(\beta)).\end{aligned}$$

Therefore $\alpha\beta \to (\delta(\alpha)\,Y(\psi_R(\alpha))\,\delta(\beta), \psi_R(\alpha)\,\psi_R(\beta))$, and the map is a homomorphism. Since specification of δ and ψ_R completely determines a right translation, the map is $1:1$. (b) is proved by the dual argument. ∎

2.17 Remark. In Remark 2.11, semigroups were constructed from other semigroups. The method used is a convenient way to construct examples. Let T (top) and B (bottom) be two semigroups, and suppose we wished to form a new semigroup $(T \cup B, \cdot) = S$ (disjoint union), where $t \cdot b \in B$ and $b \cdot t \in B$ for all $t \in T, b \in B$ (hence the descriptive labels), and T and B are subsemigroups of S. The multiplication dot must be associative, and so the following eight associativity patterns must be satisfied: (1) TTT, (2) BBB, (3) TTB, (4) BTT, (5) BBT, (6) TBB, (7) BTB, and (8) TBT.

Since we have required T and B to be subsemigroups of S, (1) and (2) are satisfied. Since $t \cdot b \in B$ and $b \cdot t \in B$, we can define functions $\varphi_L : T \to F_L(B)$ and $\varphi_R : T \to F_R(B)$. Then define $t \cdot b = \varphi_L(t)b$ and $b \cdot t = b\varphi_R(t)$. To satisfy (3) and (4), φ_L and φ_R must be homomorphisms. To satisfy (5) and (6), we must require $\varphi_L(T) \subseteq LT(B)$ and $\varphi_R(T) \subseteq RT(B)$. To satisfy (7), $\varphi_L(t)$ and $\varphi_R(t)$ must be linked for all $t \in T$, and, to satisfy (8), $\varphi_L(T)$ and $\varphi_R(T)$ must commute.

If B is a null semigroup, as in Remark 2.11, then (5)–(7) are automatically satisfied. One way to satisfy (8) is that for all $b \in B$ we have $\varphi_L(t)b = b\varphi_R(t)$ for all $t \in T$. Note that this implies that $\varphi_L(T)$ and $\varphi_R(T)$ are commutative semigroups.

2.18 Definition. A collection $\mathscr{P}$ of finite semigroups is a *property* of finite semigroups iff, whenever $S \in \mathscr{P}$ and $T \cong S$, then $T \in \mathscr{P}$. We say that S has property $\mathscr{P}$ iff $S \in \mathscr{P}$.

$\mathscr{P}$ is a *local* property of finite semigroups iff, whenever T is a finite semigroup each of whose principal ideal factors J^0 is isomorphic to some $S \in \mathscr{P}$, then $T \in \mathscr{P}$. For example, by Definition 2.21, S is regular iff each $\mathscr{J}$ class of S is regular. Thus, regular is a local property.

The remainder of this section will be devoted to the definition and characterization of several important local properties of finite semigroups.

2.19 Definition. An element a of a semigroup S is *regular* iff $a \in aSa$, i.e., iff there exists $b \in S$ such that $a = aba$.

2.20 Fact. Let $a, b \in S$ be regular elements.

(a) $L_a \leqslant L_b$ iff there exist (idempotents) $a_1 \in L_a$ and $b_1 \in L_b$ such that $a_1 b_1 = a_1$.

(b) $R_a \leqslant R_b$ iff there exist (idempotents) $a_1 \in R_a$ and $b_1 \in R_b$ such that $b_1 a_1 = a_1$.

(c) $J_a \leqslant J_b$ iff there exist (idempotents) $a_1 \in J_a$ and $b_1 \in J_b$ such that $a_1 b_1 = a_1 = b_1 a_1$ (so that $a_1 \leqslant b_1$ if a_1 and b_1 are idempotents).

PROOF. (a) Suppose $L_a \leqslant L_b$. Since a, b are regular, there exists $x, y \in S^1$ such that $a = axa$ and $b = byb$. Notice that $xa \mathrel{\mathscr{L}} a$ and $yb \mathrel{\mathscr{L}} b$. Then, since $xa \in L_a \leqslant L_b$, we have $xa \in S^1 b$. Write $xa = sb$. Then $(xa)(yb) = sbyb = sb = xa$. (Notice xa and yb are idempotents.)

Conversely, if there exist $a_1 \in L_a$ and $b_1 \in L_b$ such that $a_1 b_1 = a_1$, then $S^1 a = S^1 a_1 = S^1 a_1 b_1 \subseteq S^1 b_1 = S^1 b$, so that $L_a \leqslant L_b$. The dual proof applies to (b).

(c) Suppose there exist $a_1 \in J_a$, $b_1 \in J_b$ such that $a_1 b_1 = a_1 = b_1 a_1$. Then $S^1 a_1 S^1 = S^1 a_1 b_1 S^1 \subseteq S^1 b_1 S^1$, so that $J_a \leqslant J_b$. Conversely, if $J_a \leqslant J_b$, let $x \in J_a$, $y \in J_b$ be such that $a = axa$ and $b = byb$. Let $b_1 = yb$, and let $a_2 = xa$. Then b_1 and a_2 are idempotents. Also, $b_1 \in J_b$ and $a_2 \in J_a$, so that, in particular, $a_2 \in J(a) \subseteq J(b) = J(b_1) = S^1 b_1 S^1$. Let $s_1, s_2 \in S^1$ be such that $s_1 b_1 s_2 = a_2$. Let $a_1 = b_1 s_2 a_2 s_1 b_1$. Then a_1 is idempotent, and $a_2 = s_1 a_1 s_2$, so that $J_a = J_{a_1}$. Finally, $a_1 b_1 = a_1 = b_1 a_1$. ∎

2.21 Definition. A semigroup S is *regular* iff each $\mathscr{J}$ class J of S is regular.

2.22 Fact. (a) A semigroup S is regular iff each element of S is regular.

(b) S is regular iff, for all $a \in S$, L_a (or R_a) contains an idempotent.

(c) S is regular iff $J \subseteq J^2$ for each $\mathcal{J}$ class J of S.

(d) S is regular iff, for every right ideal A and left ideal B, $AB = A \cap B$.

(e) If S, T are regular, then $S \times T$ and homomorphic images of S are regular. Ideals of S are regular semigroups, but right or left ideals (hence subsemigroups) need not be regular.

(f) If S is regular, then every composition ideal series is a principal ideal series.

(g) Every semigroup is a subsemigroup of a regular semigroup.

PROOF. (a), (b) Let S be regular. Then, by the Rees theorem, every element of S is regular, for let $a \in S$. Then $J_a{}^0$ is isomorphic to a regular Rees matrix semigroup $\mathcal{M}^0(G; A, B; C)$. Let $a = (g)_{ij}$, $i \in A$, $j \in B$, $g \in G$. There exist $k \in B$ and $l \in A$ such that $C(j, k) \neq 0$ and $C(l, i) \neq 0$. Then $b = (C(j, k)^{-1} g^{-1} C(l, i)^{-1})_{kl}$ is an element of S such that $a = aba$ (and $b = bab$).

If a is regular, i.e., if $a = aba$ for some b, then $ba \in L_a$ and $ab \in R_a$ are idempotents.

If every $\mathcal{L}$ class, and hence every $\mathcal{J}$ class, contains an idempotent, then there are no null $\mathcal{J}$ classes in S. Hence, S is regular. This proves (a) and (b).

(c) Let S be regular and let $a \in S$. Then $a = aba$ for some b. Since $a \mathcal{J} ba$, we have $a = aba \in J_a{}^2$. Thus, $J \subseteq J^2$ for all J in S. Conversely, $J \subseteq J^2$ implies $(J^0)^2 \neq \{0\}$. So each J is regular.

(d) Let S be regular and $x \in A \cap B$. There exists $y \in S$ such that $xyx = x$. But $x \in B$ implies that $yx \in B$, so that $x = xyx \in AB$, and $AB = A \cap B$. Conversely, if $AB = A \cap B$ for every right ideal A and left ideal B, then, for any $x \in S$, $x \in xS^1 \cap S^1x = xS^1x$, so that $x \in xSx$ or $x = x1x = x^2 = x^3 \in xSx$. This proves (d).

(e) The property $a \in aSa$ is preserved under homomorphic images and finite direct products. Let I be an ideal of S, and let $a \in I$. Since S is regular, there exists $b \in S$ such that $a = aba$ and $b = bab$. But then $b \in I$, so I is regular.

To complete the proof of (e), note that $B = \{(1, 1, 1), (1, 1, 2), 0\}$ is a right ideal of $S = S_{22}(\{1\}, (\begin{smallmatrix}1&0\\0&1\end{smallmatrix}))$, but that $B \supseteq \{(1, 1, 2), 0\} \supseteq \{0\}$ is a principal ideal series for B with second factor null, whereas S is, of course, regular.

(f) Let I_2 be an ideal of I_1, an ideal of S. Then I_2 is a union of $\mathscr{J}$ classes of I_1, all of which are regular by (e). Then, by (c), $I_2{}^2 = I_2$, so that I_2 is an ideal of S by Fact 1.2(e).

(g) S is isomorphic to its right regular representation, $R(S)$, which is a subsemigroup of the regular semigroup $F_R(S^1)$ (Example 1.1.4i). ∎

We now consider semigroups that are unions of groups.

2.23 Definition. A semigroup S is a *union of groups* iff each element of S belongs to a subgroup of S.

2.24 Proposition (Clifford). Let S be a semigroup.

(a) S is a union of groups iff each $\mathscr{H}$ class is a group. Hence, S is the disjoint union of its maximal subgroups.

(b) S is a union of groups iff, for each $\mathscr{J}$ class J of S, J^0 has the form $\mathscr{M}^0(G; A, B; C)$, where C has no zero entries. This is equivalent to the property that every $\mathscr{J}$ class of S is a (simple) subsemigroup.

(c) S is a union of groups iff, for each $a, b \in S$, $J(ab) = J(a) \cap J(b) = J(ba)$. Thus, S is a union of groups iff $s \to J(s)$ is a homomorphism of S onto the commutative band (cf. 1.1.4n) $\{J(s) : s \in S\} = B \subseteq (2^S, \cap)$. The inverse image of any $J(s) \in B$ is the simple semigroup J_s.

(d) S is a union of groups iff $\mathscr{J}$ is a congruence and S is regular.

(e) Homomorphic images, subsemigroups, and finite direct products of semigroups that are unions of groups are again unions of groups.

PROOF. (a) Since every element $a \in S$ is an element of a subgroup, this forces H_a to be a subgroup.

(b) The proof follows from the Rees theorem.

(c) Assume S is a union of groups and $a, b \in S$. Then $ab\mathscr{H}(ab)^2 \in SbaS \subseteq J(ba)$, so that $ab \in J(ba)$. Thus, $J(ab) = J(ba)$. Now clearly $J(ab) \subseteq J(a) \cap J(b)$. Let $c \in J(a) \cap J(b)$, so that, for some $u, v, x, y \in S^1$, $c = uav = xby$. Then $c \mathscr{H} c^2 = xbyuav \in J(byua) = J(uaby) \subseteq J(ab)$, so that $c \in J(ab)$, and $J(ab) = J(a) \cap J(b)$.

Conversely, if S satisfies $J(ab) = J(a) \cap J(b)$ for all $a, b \in S$, then, for all $a, b \in S$, $a \mathscr{J} b$ implies $J(ab) = J(a) \cap J(b) = J(a) = J(b)$, so that the $\mathscr{J}$ classes of S are simple semigroups, and so S is a union of groups.

(d) Suppose S is a union of groups. Then S is regular. Let $a, b, x \in S$ with $a \mathcal{J} b$. Then $J(a) = J(b)$, and so $J(xa) = J(ax) = J(a) \cap J(x) = J(b) \cap J(x) = J(bx) = J(xb)$, so that $ax \mathcal{J} bx$ and $xa \mathcal{J} xb$, proving that $\mathcal{J}$ is a congruence.

Conversely, assume that S is a regular semigroup for which $\mathcal{J}$ is a congruence. Let $a \in S$, and let $e \in J_a$ be an idempotent such that $ae = a$. Now let $b \in S$ such that $b \mathcal{J} a$. Then $b \mathcal{J} e$ implies $ab \mathcal{J} a$, since $\mathcal{J}$ is a congruence. Thus, the $\mathcal{J}$ classes of S are subsemigroups, and so S is a union of groups.

(e) Clearly, the homomorphic image of a union of groups is a union of groups. For subsemigroups, let $T \subseteq S$ be a subsemigroup of S. Let $t \in T$. t belongs to a subgroup of S, and so the cyclic group generated by t is contained in T. Thus, T is a union of groups.

Let S, T be unions of groups. Let $(a, b) \in S \times T$. Since a and b belong to subgroups G_a and G_b, respectively, of S, we have $(a, b) \in G_a \times G_b$ a subgroup of $S \times T$. See also Exercise X1.18. ▌

2.25 Definition. An element $b \in S$ is a *semigroup inverse* for $a \in S$ iff $a = aba$ and $b = bab$. Note that $a \mathcal{J} b$.

2.26 Fact. (a) $a = aba$ and $a \mathcal{J} b$ imply $b = bab$.

(b) S is a regular semigroup iff every element has a semigroup inverse.

PROOF. (a) Since $aba = a$, the element ba is an idempotent, and $ba \mathcal{J} a$. But $a \mathcal{J} b$ by assumption, so $ba \mathcal{J} b$. But by Fact 1.15(c) then, $ba \mathcal{R} b$. Now, if $e \mathcal{R} x$, where e is an idempotent, then $ex = x$. Thus $(ba)b = b$.

(b) Clear by Rees theorem. ▌

2.27 Definition. A semigroup S is an *inverse semigroup* iff each element $s \in S$ has a unique semigroup inverse, denoted s^{-1}. T is an *inverse subsemigroup* of S iff $x \in T$ implies $x^{-1} \in T$.

2.28 Fact. (a) S is an inverse semigroup iff S is regular and the set of its idempotents, $E(S)$, is a commutative semigroup.

(b) S is an inverse semigroup iff its kernel $K(S)$ is a group and, for every other $\mathcal{J}$ class J of S, J^0 is of the form $\mathcal{M}^0(G; A, A; \Delta)$, where Δ is the $|A| \times |A|$ identity matrix.

(*c*) Homomorphic images, inverse subsemigroups, ideals, and finite direct products of inverse semigroups are inverse semigroups. Left or right ideals (hence subsemigroups) of inverse semigroups need not be inverse semigroups.

PROOF. (a) Let S be an inverse semigroup. Then S is regular. Let $e_1, e_2 \in E(S)$, and let a be the inverse of e_1e_2. Then ae_1 and e_2a are also inverses of e_1e_2, so that $a = ae_1 = e_2a$. Then $a^2 = (ae_1)(e_2a) = a$, so that $a \in E(S)$. Thus $a^{-1} = e_1e_2 \in E(S)$. Then e_2e_1 is also an inverse of e_1e_2, and so $e_1e_2 = e_2e_1$.

Conversely, let $x \in S$, a regular semigroup. Let y, z be inverses of x. Then, since $E(S)$ commutes and $xz, xy, zx, yx \in E(S)$,

$$\begin{aligned} y &= yxy = y(xzxzx)y = yxz(xz)(xy) = yxz(xy)(xz) = (yx)(zx)yxz \\ &= (zx)(yx)yxz = zxz = z. \end{aligned}$$

Therefore, inverses are unique.

(b) Clearly, a semigroup whose local structure is as in (b) is an inverse semigroup. Conversely, if J is a $\mathscr{J}$ class of an inverse semigroup and $J^0 = \mathscr{M}^0(G; A, B; C)$, then C has exactly one nonzero entry in each row and column, since the element (g, a, b) has exactly one inverse of the form (g_1, a_1, b_1) for each pair of nonzero matrix elements $C(b, a_1)$ and $C(b_1, a)$. Since $K(S)$ is simple, this condition forces $K(S)$ to have just one $\mathscr{H}$ class, and hence $K(S)$ is a group. Now (b) follows from Fact 1.23.

(c) The proof is left as an exercise for the reader. ▮

2.29 Definition. Let S be a semigroup. S is *nilpotent* iff S has a zero and $S^n = \{0\}$ for some integer n. The smallest such integer, $cl(S)$, is the *nilpotent class* of S.

2.30 Fact. (a) The following statements are equivalent:

(i) S is a nilpotent semigroup.

(ii) S has a zero, and each nonzero $\mathscr{J}$ class of S is null.

(iii) $E(S) = \{0\}$.

(iv) For each $x \in S$, there exists an integer $n(x)$ such that $x^{n(x)} = 0$.

(v) For each ideal I of S, I and S/I are nilpotent.

(b) Homomorphic images, subsemigroups, and finite direct products of nilpotent semigroups are nilpotent.

(c) Let S be a semigroup, and let n be the smallest positive integer such that $S^n = S^{n+1}$. Then $S \twoheadrightarrow S/S^n$ is the maximal nilpotent homomorphic image of S, and $cl(S/S^n) = n$. (Refer to Definition 7.1.2 for the definition of maximal homomorphic image with respect to a property.)

PROOF. (b) is easy to verify.

(a) It is easy to see that (i) implies (iii), (iii) implies (iv), and (iv) implies (iii). To prove (iii) implies (ii), let $E(S) = \{0\}$, and let J be a nonzero $\mathscr{J}$ class. Then J contains no idempotents, and so J^0 contains no nonzero idempotents. Thus, J^0 is not 0-simple, i.e., J is null.

To prove (ii) implies (i), let every nonzero $\mathscr{J}$ class of S be null, and let $0 \in S$. Furthermore, let $S = I_0 \supseteq I_1 \supseteq \cdots \supseteq I_n = \{0\}$ be a principal ideal series for S. Then S/I_1 is a null semigroup, and so $S^2 \subseteq I_1$. I_1/I_2 is a null semigroup, and so $S^4 \subseteq I_1{}^2 \subseteq I_2$. Continuing, we have that $S^{2^n} \subseteq I_n = \{0\}$, and so S is nilpotent.

(i) implies (v) follows from (b). To prove (v) implies (i), let I and S/I be nilpotent, with $n_1 = cl(S/I)$ and $n_2 = cl(I)$. Then $S^{n_1} \subseteq I$, so that $S^{n_1 n_2} \subseteq \{0\}$, and so S is nilpotent.

(c) To show that $\eta : S \twoheadrightarrow S/S^n$ is the maximal nilpotent image of S, let $\varphi : S \twoheadrightarrow N$, with $N^k = \{0\}$. Let $m = \max(n, k)$, and so $\varphi(S^n) = \varphi(S^m) = N^m = \{0\}$. Let $\varphi^* : S/S^n \twoheadrightarrow N$ be given by $\varphi^*(0) = 0$ and $\varphi^*(s) = \varphi(s)$ for $s \in S - S^n$. Then $\varphi^*\eta = \varphi$, proving maximality. $cl(S/S^n) = n$ by definition of n and cl. ∎

We may recall (compare Sect. 5 of Chapter 5) the following.

2.31 Definition. A semigroup S is *combinatorial* iff each subgroup of S is of order 1.

2.32 Fact. (a) S is combinatorial iff each $\mathscr{H}$ class of S contains exactly one element.

(b) Homomorphic images, subsemigroups, finite direct products, and wreath products of combinatorial semigroups are combinatorial.

PROOF. (a) Since any subgroup of S is contained in an $\mathscr{H}$ class, the condition on $\mathscr{H}$ classes implies that S is combinatorial. Conversely, if H is an $\mathscr{H}$ class of S with $|H| \geqslant 2$, then the Schützenberger group, $\mathscr{G}(H)$, has order $\geqslant 2$. But $\mathscr{G}(H)$ is a homomorphic image of $RI(H) \subseteq S^1$, and by Fact 1.1.9(c), there exists a group $G \subseteq RI(H)$

such that $G \twoheadrightarrow \mathcal{G}(H)$. Thus $|G| \geqslant 2$, and $G \subseteq S^1$. However, if $S^1 \neq S$, then the subgroup containing 1 has only one element, and so, in any case, S contains a nontrivial subgroup, a contradiction.

(b) This is left as an exercise. ∎

Exercises and Extensions

X2.1. If S is a semigroup and $X \subseteq S$, then $\mathrm{Perm}_R(X)$, the *right permuter* of X, is $\{s \in S^1 : Xs = X\}$. $\mathrm{Perm}_R(X) \subseteq RI(X)$. $\mathrm{Perm}_L(X)$ is defined dually, and $\mathrm{Perm}(X) = \mathrm{Perm}_R(X) \cap \mathrm{Perm}_L(X)$.

A subsemigroup U of S is *right unitary* iff, for all $x \in S - U$, we have $Ux \cap U = \phi$. U is *left unitary* if for all $x \in S - U$ we have $xU \cap U = \phi$.

If $1 \in S$ and U is a unitary subsemigroup of S, then $1 \in U$.

A subsemigroup U of S is right unitary iff, for some action of S on some set X and for some $x \in X$, $U = \{s \in S : xs = x\}$. It is easy to see that a subsemigroup U satisfying this condition is right unitary. For the converse, let S act on the collection of equivalence classes of elements of S^1 under the relation $s_1 \equiv s_2$ iff, for all $x \in S^1$, s_1x and s_2x are either both in U or both not in U. U is a $(\equiv)$ class, and U is the set of elements of S fixing U.

If H is an $\mathcal{H}$ class of S, then $\mathrm{Perm}_R(H) = RI(H)$, and $\mathrm{Perm}_R(H)$ is right unitary. (Hint: Let S act on the right of 2^S, and use the foregoing.) If H is a group, then there is a homomorphism from $\mathrm{Perm}_R(H)$ onto H fixing H. Thus, for any maximal subgroup H of S, there is a unitary subsemigroup U of S of which H is a retract, i. e., $H \subseteq U \subseteq S$, U is unitary, and there is a homomorphism $\varphi : U \twoheadrightarrow H$ which is the identity when restricted to H.

X2.2. Let A be a set. For $a, b \in A$, let $T(a, b) \in F_R(A)$ be the function sending a to b and fixing every other element of A. If $|A| \geqslant 2$, then the subsemigroup of $F_R(A)$ generated by $\{T(a, b) : a, b \in A\}$ is $(F_R(A) - \mathrm{SYM}_R(A)) \cup \{1\}$.

Thus, $F_R(A)$ is generated by three elements, and no smaller number of generators will suffice if $|A| \geqslant 3$. [Hint: Show that $\mathrm{SYM}_R(A)$ is generated by two elements, and that $\mathrm{SYM}_R(A)$ and any element whose range contains $|A| - 1$ elements are sufficient to generate any $T(a, b)$.]

X2.3. Let J be a simple $\mathcal{J}$ class of a semigroup S. Let $x \in S$. Prove that if $j \in J$ and $jx \in J$, then $xJ \subseteq J$. Then, be applying the dual result, prove $Jx \subseteq J$.

X2.4. Let I be a nonempty subset of a semigroup S. Then I is an ideal iff I is a union of $\mathcal{J}$ classes of S such that, whenever J_1 and J_2 are $\mathcal{J}$ classes of S with $J_1 \leqslant J_2$ and $J_2 \subseteq I$, then $J_1 \subseteq I$. I is a left (respectively right) ideal iff I is a union of $\mathcal{L}$ classes (respectively $\mathcal{R}$ classes) satisfying the above condition on ordering. If I is a maximal ideal, then $S - I$ is a single $\mathcal{J}$ class. The corresponding fact is true for maximal left or right ideals. If I is a maximal left ideal, need the $\mathcal{J}$ class containing $S - I$ be maximal?

X2.5. (a) For $x, y \in S$, prove $L_xR_y \subseteq J_{xy}$. (b) Let h_1, h_2, h_1', h_2' be elements of a semigroup S with $h_i \mathcal{H} h_i'$ for $i = 1, 2$. Then $h_1h_2 \mathcal{J} h_1'h_2'$, and, if $h_1 \mathcal{J} h_2$ and $h_1 \mathcal{J} h_1h_2$, then $h_1h_2 \mathcal{H} h_1'h_2'$.

X2.6. Let S be a nilpotent finite semigroup. Then the $\mathscr{J}$, $\mathscr{L}$, $\mathscr{R}$, and $\mathscr{H}$ classes of S each consist of a single element. [Hint: If $s_1 \neq 0 \neq s_2$ and $xs_1 = s_2$, $ys_2 = s_1$, then $(yx)^n s_1 = s_1$ for all n, and so some power of (yx) is a nonzero idempotent.]

X2.7. Let T be a subsemigroup of S, and let $\alpha(T)$ and $\alpha(S)$ denote any of $\mathscr{H}$, $\mathscr{L}$, $\mathscr{R}$, or $\mathscr{J}$ on T or S, respectively. Then $s_1 \alpha(S) s_2$ implies $s_1 \alpha(T) s_2$ if we have one of the following:

(a) T is a cyclic semigroup.

(b) T is regular and $\alpha \neq \mathscr{J}$.

(c) S is a nilpotent extension of a union of groups (i.e., M is a union of groups and an ideal of S, and S/M is nilpotent). In particular, if S is cyclic, nilpotent, or a union of groups, the result holds.

(d) $T = eSe$ for some idempotent $e \in S$ (see Exercise 5.1.7).

X2.8. Find all subsemigroups of an inverse 0-simple semigroup.

X2.9. Characterize semigroups that are inverse combinatorial unions of groups.

X2.10. Let C_1 and C_2 be combinatorial semigroups, and let $\varphi : C_1 \to \text{Endo}(C_2)$ be a homomorphism. Show that $C_2 \times_\varphi C_1$ is combinatorial.

X2.11. (a) A semigroup S is regular iff, for each $x \in S$, there exist $e_1, e_2 \in E(S)$ such that $e_1 \mathscr{L} x$ and $e_2 \mathscr{R} x$.

(b) S is regular iff each element of S has at least one semigroup inverse.

(c) $x, y \in S$ are inverses in the group sense iff x is a semigroup inverse for y, y is a semigroup inverse for x, and $xy = yx$.

(d) If $X_n = \{1,..., n\}$, then $F_R(X_n)$ is regular.

(e) If A and B are finite nonempty sets, any two elements of $A^l \times B^r$ are inverses.

(f) S is regular iff $r(S)$ is regular.

X2.12. (a) S is an inverse semigroup iff, for each $x \in S$, there exist unique $e_1, e_2 \in E(S)$ such that $S^1 x = Se_1$ and $xS^1 = e_2 S$.

(b) If S is an inverse semigroup, then $(a^{-1})^{-1} = a$, and $(ab)^{-1} = b^{-1}a^{-1}$ for all $a, b \in S$. Thus, $a \to a^{-1}$ is an isomorphism of S with $r(S)$.

(c) Let G be a finite group, and let $S = (2^G, \cdot)$, where $H_1 \cdot H_2 = \{h_1 h_2 : h_1 \in H_1, h_2 \in H_2\}$. Then $E(S)$ is the collection of subgroups of G. In general, $E(S)$ is noncommutative, even though each regular principal factor of S is an inverse semigroup.

X2.13. Let $A = \{a_1, ..., a_n\}$, and let I be the ideal of ΣA consisting of all $(x_1, ..., x_k)$ such that $k \geqslant c$, for some fixed integer c. Then $FN(n, c)$, the *free nilpotent semigroup of class c on n generators*, is $(\Sigma A)/I$. S is a nilpotent semigroup with at most n generators and with $cl(S) \leqslant c$ iff there is a homomorphism $\varphi : FN(n, c) \twoheadrightarrow S$.

X2.14. Let J be a $\mathscr{J}$ class of a semigroup S. Define $F(J) = \cup \{J' : J' \text{ a } \mathscr{J} \text{ class of } S \text{ and } J \nleqslant J'\}$.

(a) $F(J) = \phi$, or $F(J)$ is an ideal of S.

(b) $F(J) = \phi$ iff $J = K(S)$.

(c) If $F(J) \neq \phi$, then J^0 is the unique 0-minimal ideal of $S/F(J)$.

X2.15. Let $M = \mathscr{M}^0(G; A, B; C)$ be a regular Rees matrix semigroup. Let $\alpha \in RT(M)$ and $\beta \in LT(M)$ be linked. Then, viewing α, β, and C as matrices, prove $\alpha C = C\beta$. This is the matrix form of (2.9).

The group associated with each $\mathscr{H}$ class was first defined by Schützenberger [4]. Munn [5] determined the homomorphisms on regular Rees matrix semigroups. For the form of the left and right translations, see Schützenberger [4]. The presentation here follows Clifford and Preston [3] and Rhodes [6], Sect. 3.

The results on semigroups that are unions of groups are due to Clifford [7]. See Clifford and Preston [3] for history and for further results on regular and inverse semigroups.

3. Subsemigroups

In this section, we apply the tools developed in Sects. 1 and 2 to prove some facts about subsemigroups of finite semigroups. All semigroups considered are finite.

3.1 Definition. M is a *maximal proper subsemigroup* of a semigroup S iff M is a proper subsemigroup of S such that, whenever $M \subseteq T \subseteq S$ for some subsemigroup T of S, either $M = T$ or $T = S$.

M is a *maximal combinatorial* subsemigroup of S iff M is a combinatorial subsemigroup such that, if T is a combinatorial subsemigroup of S containing M, then $T = M$.

3.2 Fact. Let C be a maximal combinatorial subsemigroup of a semigroup S. Then $I(C) = LI(C) = RI(C) = C$ (see Definition 2.7).

PROOF. It suffices by duality to prove that $LI(C) = C$. Suppose not. Then there exists a subsemigroup T of S which is minimal with respect to the property $C \subset T \subseteq LI(C)$. Then T is not combinatorial, and C is a maximal left ideal of T.

Let $L = T - C$. L is an $\mathscr{L}$ class of T (Exercise 2.4) and L contains a nontrivial group since T is not combinatorial. Thus the $\mathscr{J}$ class of T that L belongs to is regular. Then L must be that $\mathscr{J}$ class, for otherwise C would contain a nontrivial group. Thus L is a regular $\mathscr{J}$ class with one $\mathscr{L}$ class. By Rees theorem, L is a left simple semigroup and $L^2 = L$.

Let $e \in L$ be an idempotent. We will now show that $C \cup \{e\}$ is a combinatorial subsemigroup of T, contradicting the maximality of C.

To prove that $C \cup \{e\}$ is a subsemigroup, it is sufficient, since C is a left ideal, to show that $Ce \subseteq C$. Let $l \in L$, $c \in C$, and suppose $ce \in L$. Then $lce \in L^2 = L$, and we have

$$S^1LS^1 = S^1lceS^1 \subseteq S^1lcS^1 \subseteq S^1lS^1 = S^1LS^1.$$

Thus, $lc \in L$, a contradiction, since C is a left ideal. So $Ce \subseteq C$. ∎

The next proposition gives a complete classification of maximal subsemigroups. Every maximal subsemigroup of a semigroup S has a natural presentation with respect to the Green-Rees coordinates.

3.3 Proposition. Let M be a maximal subsemigroup of the finite semigroup S. Then we have the following:

(a) For some $\mathscr{J}$ class $J(M)$ of S, $S - M \subseteq J(M)$.

(b) M meets (intersects nontrivially) each $\mathscr{H}$ class of S, or M is a union of $\mathscr{H}$ classes of S.

(c) If $J(M)$ is null, then $J(M) \cap M = \phi$, and so $M = S - J(M)$.

(d) If $M \cap J(M) \neq \phi$ [so $J(M)$ is regular by (c) and $J(M)^0$ is isomorphic to a regular Rees matrix semigroup], two cases arise from the two possibilities in (b).

Case 1. If M meets each $\mathscr{H}$ class of S, then an isomorphism $j : J(M)^0 \to \mathscr{M}^0(G; A, B; C)$ can be so chosen that $j[M \cap J(M)] = G_1 \times A \times B$, where G_1 is a maximal subgroup of G. In this case, $[M \cap J(M)]^0$ is a maximal subsemigroup of J^0.

Case 2. If M is a union of $\mathscr{H}$ classes of S, then an isomorphism $j : J(M)^0 \to \mathscr{M}^0(G; A, B; C)$ can be so chosen that $j[M \cap J(M)]$ is the complement of a "rectangle" of $\mathscr{H}$ classes of $\mathscr{M}^0(G; A, B; C)$. Precisely, $j[M \cap J(M)]$ has one of the following three forms:

(i) $G \times (A - A') \times B$, A' a proper nonempty subset of A.

(ii) $G \times A \times (B - B')$, B' a proper nonempty subset of B.

(iii) $(G \times A \times B) - (G \times A' \times B')$, A', B' proper nonempty subsets of A and B, respectively.

In Case 2, $[M \cap J(M)]^0$ is a maximal subsemigroup of $J(M)^0$ if $j[M \cap J(M)]$ has form (iii) but need not be in the other two cases.

PROOF. For (a), let J be minimal (in the usual ordering $J_1 \leqslant J_2$ iff $S^1J_1S^1 \subseteq S^1J_2S^1$) among the $\mathscr{J}$ classes of S not contained in M. Then $M \cup J$ is a subsemigroup of S properly containing M, so that $M \cup J = S$. Thus, $S - M \subseteq J \equiv J(M)$.

For (b), let $J = J(M)$. Define M' to be the union of all $\mathscr{H}$ classes that M meets. We shall show M' to be a subsemigroup of S containing M, and so, by the maximality of M, either $M' = M$ or $M' = S$. The former implies M is a union of $\mathscr{H}$ classes; the latter shows that M meets every $\mathscr{H}$ class of S.

To show M' a subsemigroup, let $h_1, h_2 \in M'$. If $h_1h_2 \in M \subseteq M'$, done, so suppose not. Then $h_1h_2 \in J$, and at least one of $h_1, h_2 \in J$. By the definition of M', there exist $m_1, m_2 \in M$ such that $h_i \mathscr{H} m_i$, $i = 1, 2$. There are two cases.

Case A. Suppose $h_1 \in M$, $h_2 \in J$. Since (by assumption) $h_1h_2 \in J$, left multiplication by h_1 moves the $\mathscr{H}$ class containing h_2 onto the $\mathscr{H}$ class containing h_1h_2. Thus, $h_2 \mathscr{H} m_2$ implies $h_1h_2 \mathscr{H} h_1m_2 \in M$, and so $h_1h_2 \in M'$. (The case $h_1 \in J$, $h_2 \in M$ is handled dually.)

Case B. Suppose $h_1, h_2 \in J$. Then, using the Rees theorem, $h_i \mathscr{H} m_i$, $i = 1, 2$, implies $h_1h_2 \mathscr{H} m_1m_2 \in M$, and so $h_1h_2 \in M'$. This exhausts the possibilities, and so M' is a semigroup and (b) is proved.

For (c), let $J = J(M)$. Let J be null, and let $n_1, n_2 \in J$. Then $n_1 = s_1n_2s_2$ for some $s_1, s_2 \in S^1$ by the definition of $\mathscr{J}$, and $s_1, s_2 \notin J$, since, by the definition of null, the product of two or more elements of J is in $S^1JS^1 - J$. Thus, $s_1, s_2 \in M^1$, so that $n_2 \in M$ implies $n_1 \in M$. Hence, $J \cap M = \phi$.

For Case 1 of (d), assume that M meets every $\mathscr{H}$ class of S. Let j' be an isomorphism of J^0 onto $T = \mathscr{M}^0(G; A, B; C')$. Then $T_1 = j'(M \cap J)^0$ is a subsemigroup of T meeting each $\mathscr{H}$ class $H(a, b) = (G, a, b) = \{(g, a, b) : g \in G\}$. Let

$$T_1 \cap H(a, b) = M(a, b) = (X(a, b), a, b) = \{(x, a, b) : x \in X(a, b) \subseteq G\}.$$

Now let $H(a_0, b_0)$ be a fixed nonzero $\mathscr{H}$ class of T for which $g_0 = C(b_0, a_0) \neq 0$, i.e., $H(a_0, b_0)$ is a subgroup of T isomorphic to G under the isomorphism $(g, a_0, b_0) \to g_0g$. Then $X(a_0, b_0) = \{g_0^{-1}g : g \in G_1\} = g_0^{-1}G_1$ for some subgroup G_1 of G, since $M(a_0, b_0)$ is a subgroup of T contained in $H(a_0, b_0)$. For each $a \in A$, let g_a be a fixed element of $X(a, b_0)$, and, for each $b \in B$, let y_b be a fixed element of $X(a_0, b)$. Then

$$(g_a, a, b_0)\, M(a_0, b_0)(y_b, a_0, b)$$
$$= (g_a G_1 g_0 y_b, a, b) \subseteq M(a, b) = (X(a, b), a, b).$$

But, by a similar argument, there exist elements $t_1, t_2 \in T_1$ such that

$$t_1 M(a, b)\, t_2 \subseteq M(a_0, b_0) = (X(a_0, b_0), a_0, b_0),$$

so that $|X(a, b)| = |X(a_0, b_0)| = |G_1| = |g_a G_1 g_0 y_b|$. For each $b \in B$, let $h_b = g_0 y_b$. Then $X(a, b) = g_a G_1 h_b$. Let $C : B \times A \to G^0$ be the matrix given by

$$C(b, a) = h_b C'(b, a)\, g_a .$$

Then $\mathscr{M}^0(G; A, B; C')$ is isomorphic to $\mathscr{M}^0(G; A, B; C)$ by the isomorphism $j_1 : \mathscr{M}^0(G; A, B; C') \to \mathscr{M}^0(G; A, B; C)$ given by

$$j_1(g, a, b) = (g_a^{-1} g h_b^{-1}, a, b), \qquad j_1(0) = 0.$$

Thus, $j_1(T_1 - \{0\}) = G_1 \times A \times B$ in $\mathscr{M}^0(G; A, B; C)$, and so, letting $j = j_1 j'$, we have $j(M \cap J) = G_1 \times A \times B$.

Finally, we shall show that G_1 is a maximal subgroup of G, so that $(M \cap J)^0$ is a maximal subsemigroup of J^0. Let G_1' be a subgroup of G such that $G_1 \subseteq G_1' \subseteq G$, and let $T = j^{-1}(G_1' \times A \times B)$. Define $M' = M \cup T$. We shall show M' to be a semigroup, and so by the maximality of M the assertion is proved.

Since $C(b, a) \in G_1{}^0$, $\mathscr{M}^0(G_1'; A, B; C)$ is a semigroup, and so $T \cup \{0\} = j^{-1}[(G_1' \times A \times B) \cup \{0\}]$ is a subsemigroup of J^0.

Since T^0 is a subsemigroup of J^0, we need only show that for $m \in M$ and $x \in T$ we have $mx \in M'$ and $xm \in M'$. If $mx, xm \in M \subset M'$, done, and so assume $mx, xm \in J$. Since J is regular, there exist idempotents $e_1, e_2 \in J$ such that $e_1 x = x$, $xe_2 = x$. Also, $e_1, e_2 \in M$, since M meets each H class of S, and so $me_1, e_2 m \in M$. Furthermore, $me_1, e_2 m \in J$, since $mx = (me_1)\, x \in J$ and $xm = x(e_2 m) \in J$. Thus, $me_1, e_2 m \in J \cap M \subset T$, which implies $(me_1)\, x = mx \in M'$ and $x(e_2 m) = xm \in M'$. Thus, M' is a subsemigroup of S, which proves the assertions.

In Case 2 of (d), M is a union of $\mathscr{H}$ classes, and $M \cap J \neq 0$. Let $J = J(M)$, and let $\{R(a) : a \in A\}$, $\{L(b) : b \in B\}$, and $\{H(a, b) = R(a) \cap L(b)\}$ be the $\mathscr{R}$, $\mathscr{L}$, and $\mathscr{H}$ classes, respectively, of S contained in J. Let $A' = \{a \in A : R(a) \not\subseteq M\}$ and $B' = \{b \in B : L(b) \not\subseteq M\}$. Clearly, A' and B' are not empty for then $J \subseteq M$, a contradiction.

Let $a_1 \in A'$. Then $T = M^1R(a_1) \cup M$ is a subsemigroup of S properly containing M. To prove this, utilize the fact that $R(a_1)\, M \subseteq R(a_1) \cup M \subseteq T$. [For let $r \in R(a_1)$, $m \in M$, and suppose $rm \notin M$. Then $rm \in J$, so that $rm \mathscr{J} r$, which implies $rm \mathscr{R} r$, i.e., $rm \in R(a_1)$]. Hence, $T = S$. Let $a_2 \in A'$, so that $R(a_2) \not\subseteq M$. Then $M^1\, R(a_1) \cap R(a_2) \neq \phi$, i.e., there exists $m \in M^1$ such that $mR(a_1) \cap R(a_2) \neq \phi$. But, by Fact 1.15, $mR(a_1) = R(a_2)$, and, in particular, $mH(a_1, b) = H(a_2, b)$ for all $b \in B$. Similarly (using $\mathscr{L}$ classes), there exists $m \in M^1$ such that, for $b_1, b_2 \in B'$, $H(a, b_1)\, m = H(a, b_2)$ for all $a \in A$.

Now, to see what $\mathscr{H}$ classes of J are not in M, we prove the lemma: $a \in A'$, $b \in B'$ iff $H(a, b) \cap M = \phi$.

Let $a \in A'$, $b \in B'$, and suppose $H(a, b) \subseteq M$. Then, for each $a_i \in A'$, there exists $m_i \in M^1$ such that $m_i H(a, b) = H(a_i, b)$. Thus, for all $a_i \in A$, $H(a_i, b) \subseteq M$, which implies $L(b) \subseteq M$, a contradiction. The converse is clear.

Thus, if $B' = B$, it is easy to see that $j(M \cap J)$ has form (i). Similarly, if $A' = A$, $j(M \cap J)$ has form (ii). If both A' and B' are proper subsets of A and B, then $j(M \cap J)$ has form (iii).

Since it is easy to construct examples in which $j(M \cap J)$ has the form (i) or (ii) but in which $(M \cap J)^0$ is not maximal in J^0 (see the second Remark following this proof), we shall complete the proof by showing that $(M \cap J)^0$ is maximal in J^0 if $j(M \cap J)$ has the form (iii). By the foregoing argument, it suffices to show that, for each $a_1, a_2 \in A'$, there exists $m \in M \cap J$ (rather than merely $m \in M^1$ as in the foregoing) such that $mR(a_1) = R(a_2)$ and that, for each $b_1, b_2 \in B'$, there exists $m' \in M \cap J$ such that $L(b_1)\, m' = L(b_2)$. Furthermore, by the definition of the orderings on the $\mathscr{J}$ classes, it is equivalent to show that such m, m' can be chosen in $M \cap J^*$, where $J^* = \cup \{J' : J'$ is a $\mathscr{J}$ class of S and $J' \leqslant J\}$, since $J^* - J$ is an ideal of S.

Let $R(A') = \cup \{R(a) : a \in A'\}$. Now, for all $a \in A'$, we have just shown that $R(A') \subseteq M^1R(a)$. Also, by the definition of J^*, we have $(M \cap J^*)\, M^1 = M \cap J^* = M^1(M \cap J^*)$. Now, for any $a \in A'$, $R(A') \subseteq (M \cap J^*)\, R(a)$, or $R(A') \cap (M \cap J^*)\, R(a) = \phi$, since, if $mR(a) \cap R(a') \neq \phi$ for some $a' \in A'$ and $m \in M$, then $mR(a) = R(a')$, and so

$$R(a') \subseteq (M \cap J^*)\, R(a)$$

and

$$R(A') \subseteq M^1R(a') \subseteq M^1(M \cap J^*)\, R(a) = (M \cap J^*)\, R(a).$$

If $R(A') \cap (M \cap J^*)\, R(a) = \phi$, then

$$(M \cap J^*)\, R(A') \cap R(A') \subseteq (M \cap J^*)\, M^1R(a) \cap R(A')$$
$$= (M \cap J^*)\, R(a) \cap R(A') = \phi.$$

Now $j(J^0) = \mathscr{M}^0(G; A, B; C)$, and

$$j(M \cap J)^0 = [(G \times A \times B) - (G \times A' \times B')] \cup \{0\}$$

is a subsemigroup, and so

$$C(b, a) = 0 \qquad \text{for all} \quad (a, b) \in (A - A') \times (B - B').$$

If, for $a \in A'$, we have $R(A') \cap (M \cap J^*)\, R(a) = \phi$, then, by the foregoing, $R(A') \cap (M \cap J^*)\, R(A') = \phi$, so that in particular, $[G \times A' \times (B - B')](G \times A' \times B) = \{0\}$, showing that $C(b, a) = 0$ for all $(a, b) \in A \times (B - B')$, contradicting the regularity of J. It follows that $R(A') \subseteq (M \cap J^*)\, R(a)$ for any $a \in A'$, i.e., for all $a_1, a_2 \in A'$, there exists $m \in M \cap J$ (we replace J^* by J, since no element of $J^* - J$ could satisfy the condition) such that $mR(a_1) = R(a_2)$. The proof for $\mathscr{L}$ classes is analogous. ∎

3.4 Remark. Let $S = \mathscr{M}^0(G; A, B; C)$ be a regular Rees matrix semigroup. If M is a maximal subsemigroup of S, then $J(M) = \{0\}$ or $J(M) = S - \{0\}$. In the first case, $S - \{0\}$ is a subsemigroup, and $M = S - \{0\}$. In the second case, $M \cap J(M) = \phi$ iff $S - \{0\}$ is a simple abelian group [i.e., $(\mathbf{Z}_p, +)$ for some prime p]. Otherwise, $M \cap J(M)$ has one of the following forms in some coordinate system:

(1) $(G' \times A \times B)$, G' a maximal subgroup of G.

(2) $(G \times A \times B')$, where $B' = B - \{b\}$ for some $b \in B$, and C restricted to $B' \times A$ is regular (i.e., nonzero at least once in each row and column).

(3) $(G \times A' \times B)$, where $A' = A - \{a\}$ for some $a \in A$, and C restricted to $B \times A'$ is regular.

(4) $(G \times A \times B) - (G \times A' \times B')$, where $A' = A - Y$, $B' = B - X$, and $X \times Y$ is a *maximal* "rectangle" on which C is identically zero.

Furthermore, each subsemigroup M of S containing all but one $\mathscr{J}$ class $J(M)$ and such that $M \cap J(M)$ has one of the preceding forms is a maximal subsemigroup of S.

3.5 Remark. A counterexample to show that $(M \cap J)^0$ need not be a maximal subsemigroup of J^0 when $j(M \cap J)$ has form (i) of (d), Case 2, can be constructed as follows.

Let $F(X_n)$, $n \geqslant 2$, be the semigroup of all functions on n letters $x_1, \ldots, x_n$ under ordinary composition. Let $\{x_1, \ldots, x_n, z\}^l$ be the semigroup defined by $xy = x$ for all $x, y \in \{x_1, \ldots, x_n, z\}$. Form the semigroup, $S = F(X_n) \cup \{x_1, \ldots, x_n, z\}$ by defining the multiplication as follows. Let $F(X_n)$ and $\{x_1, \ldots, x_n, z\}$ be subsemigroups, and, for all $f \in F(X_n)$,

$$f \circ x_i = f(x_i) \qquad \text{for all} \quad x_i \in X_n,$$

$$x_i \circ f = x_i \qquad \text{for all} \quad x_i \in X_n,$$

$$f \circ z = z \circ f = z.$$

Then $M = F(X_n) \cup \{z\}$ is a maximal subsemigroup of S, and $J(M) = \{x_1, \ldots, x_n, z\}$. Since each element of $J(M)$ is an $\mathscr{R}$ class, $j[M \cap J(M)]$ is of form (i). But, by Remark 3.4, $j[M \cap J(M)]^0$ is not a maximal subsemigroup of $j[J(M)^0]$.

A counterexample for form (ii) is constructed dually.

The classification of maximal subsemigroups is from Graham, Graham, and Rhodes [8]. For an analysis of subsemigroups of 0-simple semigroups, see Graham [9].

REFERENCES

1. J. A. Green, On the structure of semigroups, *Ann. of Math.* **54**, 163–172 (1951).
2. D. Rees, On semigroups, *Proc. Cambridge Philos. Soc.* **36**, 387–400 (1940).
3. A. H. Clifford and G. B. Preston, "The Algebraic Theory of Semigroups," Vol. 1, Math. Surveys 7. Am. Math. Soc., Providence, Rhode Island, 1962.
4. M. P. Schützenberger, $\bar{\mathscr{D}}$ Représentation des demi-groupes, *Compt. Rend. Acad. Sci. Paris* **224**, 1994–1996 (1957).
5. W. D. Munn, "Semigroups and Their Algebras," Dissertation, Cambridge Univ. (1955).
6. J. Rhodes, Some results on finite semigroups, *J. Algebra* **3**, 471–504 (1966).
7. A. H. Clifford, Semigroups admitting relative inverses, *Ann. of Math.* **42**, 1037–1049 (1941).
8. N. Graham, R. Graham, and J. Rhodes, Maximal subsemigroups of finite semi-groups, *J. Combinatorial Theory* (to be published).
9. R. Graham, Subsemigroups of finite 0-simple semigroups, *Math. System Theory* (to be published).

CHAPTER 8

Homomorphisms and Semilocal Theory[†]

KENNETH KROHN
Krohn-Rhodes Research Institute, Washington, D.C.

JOHN L. RHODES[‡]
University of California, Berkeley, California
Krohn-Rhodes Research Institute, Berkeley, California

BRET R. TILSON
University of California, Berkeley, California

1. Homomorphisms

In this section, it is shown that, if $\theta : S \twoheadrightarrow T$ is a maximal proper epimorphism (MPE, Definition 1.12), then θ is either 1 : 1 when restricted to $\mathscr{H}$ classes [$\gamma(\mathscr{H})$ epimorphism], or θ separates $\mathscr{H}$ classes ($\mathscr{H}$ epimorphism). It then follows that every epimorphism between two finite semigroups can be decomposed into $\gamma(\mathscr{H})$ and $\mathscr{H}$ epimorphisms.

Furthermore, if θ is an MPE, it is proved that there exists a $\mathscr{J}$ class J such that θ is 1 : 1 on $S - J$. Thus, a further analysis of θ via the Green-Rees theorems applied to J can be undertaken.

1.1 Definition. Let S be a fixed semigroup. A *property of homomorphisms of* S is a collection $\mathscr{P}$ of pairs (φ, T), where $\varphi : S \twoheadrightarrow T$,

[†] This work was sponsored by the United States Air Force, Office of Scientific Research, Grant Numbers AF-AFOSR-848-66 and AF 49(638)-1550.

[‡] Alfred P. Sloan Research Fellow, 1967–1968.

such that, whenever $(\varphi_1, T_1) \in \mathscr{P}$ and $j : T_1 \twoheadrightarrow T_2$ is an isomorphism, then $(j\varphi_1, T_2) \in \mathscr{P}$.

We write $(\varphi_1, T_1) \leqslant (\varphi_2, T_2)$ iff there exists an epimorphism $j : T_2 \twoheadrightarrow T_1$ such that $\varphi_1 = j\varphi_2$. If $(\varphi_1, T_1) \leqslant (\varphi_2, T_2)$ and $(\varphi_2, T_2) \leqslant (\varphi_1, T_1)$, then T_1 and T_2 are isomorphic. We then say (φ_1, T_1) and (φ_2, T_2) are *isomorphic.*

1.2 Definition. Let $\mathscr{P}$ be a property of homomorphisms of a semigroup S. We say $(\varphi, T) \in \mathscr{P}$ is a *minimal* (respectively *maximal*) *homomorphic image of S with respect to* $\mathscr{P}$ iff (φ, T) is the unique (up to isomorphism) minimal (respectively maximal) element of $\mathscr{P}$ under $\leqslant$.

Thus, to say that (φ, T) is minimal (respectively maximal) means that, if $(\varphi_1, T_1) \in \mathscr{P}$, then there exists a homomorphism $j_1 : T_1 \twoheadrightarrow T$ (respectively $j_2 : T \twoheadrightarrow T_1$) to make diagram (a) [respectively diagram (b)] below commute:

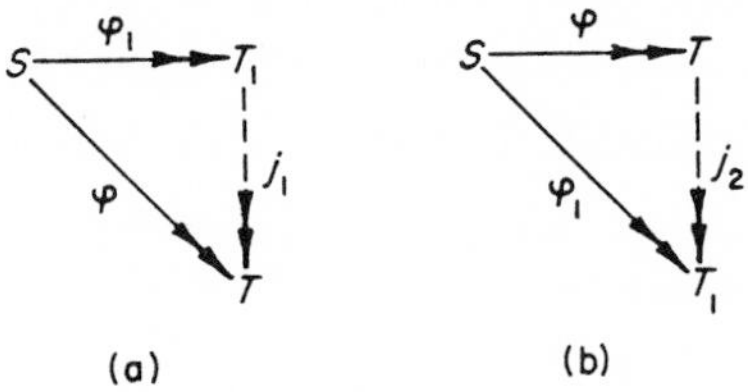

1.3 Remark. $\mathscr{P}$ need not have either a maximal or minimal homomorphic image. For example, if $|A| \geqslant 3$, then A^r has no minimal or maximal homomorphic image with respect to $\mathscr{P}$, where $\mathscr{P}$ is the collection of (φ, T) such that $\varphi : A^r \twoheadrightarrow T$, where $|T| = 2$.

1.4 Fact. Let $\mathscr{P}'$ be a property of *semigroups* that is closed under direct products and subsemigroups (i.e., if $S_1, S_2 \in \mathscr{P}'$, then $S_1 \times S_2 \in \mathscr{P}'$, and if T is a subsemigroup of $S \in \mathscr{P}'$, then $T \in \mathscr{P}'$). Then let S be a semigroup, and let $\mathscr{P}$ be the property of homomorphisms of S defined by $(\varphi, T) \in \mathscr{P}$ iff $T \in \mathscr{P}'$. Then S has a maximal homomorphic image with respect to $\mathscr{P}$.

PROOF. Let $\mathscr{P} = \{(\varphi_i, T_i) : i = 1,..., n\}$, since it is clear that $\mathscr{P}$ can have only finitely many nonisomorphic members. Then $T_1 \times \cdots \times T_n \in \mathscr{P}'$. Consider the homomorphism

$$\varphi = (\varphi_1 \times \cdots \times \varphi_n) \Delta : S \to T_1 \times \cdots \times T_n$$

(into), where $\Delta : S \to S \times \cdots \times S$ (n times) is defined by $\Delta(s) = (s, \ldots, s)$. Then $\varphi(S)$ is a subsemigroup of $T_1 \times \cdots \times T_n$, so that $\varphi(S) \in \mathscr{P}'$ and $(\varphi, \varphi(S)) \in \mathscr{P}$. Clearly, $(\varphi, \varphi(S))$ is the maximal homomorphic image of S with respect to $\mathscr{P}$. ▮

1.5 Remark. Examples of collections of semigroups that are closed under direct products and subsemigroups are (1) groups (finite), (2) combinatorial semigroups, (3) union of groups semigroups, (4) abelian semigroups, (5) bands, etc.

As an example, we construct the maximal group homomorphic image of a finite semigroup. First, we introduce the following lemma.

1.6 Lemma. Let S be a semigroup with ideal I, and let $\varphi : I \twoheadrightarrow T^1$ be an epimorphism. Then there exists a unique extension of φ to S.

PROOF. Let $x \in \varphi^{-1}(1)$. Define $\hat{\varphi} : S \twoheadrightarrow T^1$ by $\hat{\varphi}(s) = \varphi(xsx)$. It is easy to verify that $\hat{\varphi}$ is an epimorphism, using the fact that $\varphi(x) = 1$. Let $s \in I$. Then $\hat{\varphi}(s) = \varphi(xsx) = \varphi(s)$, and so $\hat{\varphi}$ is an extension of φ.

Let $\bar{\varphi}$ be any other extension of φ to S, and let $s \in S$. Then $\hat{\varphi}(s) = \varphi(xsx) = \bar{\varphi}(xsx)$, since $xsx \in I$. But $\bar{\varphi}(xsx) = \bar{\varphi}(x)\bar{\varphi}(s)\bar{\varphi}(x) = \bar{\varphi}(s)$, since $\bar{\varphi}(x) = \varphi(x) = 1$. Therefore, $\bar{\varphi} = \hat{\varphi}$. ▮

1.7 Example. We now construct the maximal group homomorphic image of a finite semigroup S. If $\varphi : S \twoheadrightarrow H$, a group, then $\varphi[K(S)] = H$, since epimorphisms map kernels onto kernels, and a group is its own kernel. Let us investigate the nature of φ on $K(S)$. Since $K(S)$ is a regular $\mathscr{J}$ class, we can apply the results on local homomorphisms from Sect. 7.2.

Let $K(S) \cong \mathscr{M}(G; A, B; C)$, where C has been chosen so that the homomorphism φ can be described in normalized form, i.e.,

$$\varphi(g, a, b) = (\omega(g), \psi_L(a), \psi_R(b)).$$

But the range of φ is a group, and so $\psi_L(a) = 1$ for all $a \in A$, $\psi_R(b) = 1$ for all $b \in B$, and $\omega[C(b, a)] = 1$ for all $a \in A$, $b \in B$. [Remember, $C(b, a) \neq 0$ for all $a \in A$, $b \in B$, since $K(S)$ is a simple semigroup.] Then $C(B \times A)$ must belong to the kernel of ω.

Now construct the following homomorphism on $K(S)$. Let N be the normal subgroup of G generated by $C(B \times A)$. Let $\nu : G \twoheadrightarrow G/N$ be the natural homomorphism. Then let $\psi_L(A) = \{1\}$ and $\psi_R(B) = \{1\}$, and define $\theta : K(S) \twoheadrightarrow \nu(G)$ by

$$\theta(g, a, b) = (\nu(g), 1, 1) = \nu(g).$$

We claim θ extended uniquely to S by Lemma 1.6 is the maximal group homomorphism of S. If φ is a homomorphism such that $\varphi(S)$ is a group, then the homomorphism ω on G associated with φ has N contained in its kernel. Thus, there exists a homomorphism $\mu : \nu(G) \twoheadrightarrow \omega(G)$, i.e., $\omega = \mu\nu$. But $\theta(S) = \nu(G)$ and $\varphi(S) = \omega(G)$, and so $\mu : \theta(S) \twoheadrightarrow \varphi(S)$ and $\varphi = \mu\theta$.

1.8 Definition. Let P be a partition on a semigroup S. Let $\mathscr{P}(S, P)$ be the collection of (φ, T), $\varphi : S \twoheadrightarrow T$, such that $\varphi(s_1) = \varphi(s_2)$ implies $s_1 \equiv s_2 \pmod P$. If $(\varphi, T) \in \mathscr{P}(S, P)$, we write $\varphi : S \underset{P}{\twoheadrightarrow} T$ and call φ a *P homomorphism of S*.

1.9 Fact. Let P be any partition on a semigroup S. Then $\mathscr{P}(S, P)$ has a minimal homomorphic image, denoted S^P.

PROOF. Let Q be the congruence generated by P, i.e., $s_1 \equiv s_2 \pmod Q$ iff $\alpha s_1 \beta \equiv \alpha s_2 \beta \pmod P$ for all $\alpha, \beta \in S^1$. Let $\eta : S \twoheadrightarrow S/Q$ be the natural homomorphism. Then it is easy to prove that $(\eta, S/Q)$ is the minimal homomorphic image of S with respect to $\mathscr{P}(S, P)$. ▮

1.10 Remark. (a) An important example of a minimal homomorphic image with respect to a partition was introduced in Chapter 5. If $f : \Sigma A \to B$ is a machine, then the semigroup of the machine f, f^S, is exactly the minimal homomorphic image of $\mathscr{P}(\Sigma A, (\text{mod}\, f))$, where $(\text{mod}\, f)$ is the partition that f induces on ΣA. In other words, $f^S = \Sigma A^{(\text{mod} f)}$.

(b) Let $\varphi : S \twoheadrightarrow T$ be an epimorphism. Then (φ, T) is the minimal homomorphic image of $\mathscr{P}(S, \text{mod}\, \varphi)$. Thus, if $\theta : S \twoheadrightarrow T_1$ is an epimorphism such that $\theta(s_1) = \theta(s_2)$ implies $s_1 \equiv s_2 \pmod \varphi$ for all $s_1, s_2 \in S$, then $(\theta, T_1) \in \mathscr{P}(S, \text{mod}\, \varphi)$. Hence, there exists an epimorphism $j : T_1 \twoheadrightarrow T$ such that $\varphi = j\theta$.

1.11 Notation. Let α be any of the relations $\mathscr{J}, \mathscr{R}, \mathscr{L}$, or $\mathscr{H}$ on S. Then α is a partition on S, and $\mathscr{P}(S, \alpha)$ has a minimal homomorphic image, S^α. $\theta : S \twoheadrightarrow T$ is an α *homomorphism* (or *epimorphism*) if $(\theta, T) \in \mathscr{P}(S, \alpha)$. For example, θ is an $\mathscr{H}$ epimorphism iff, for all $s_1, s_2 \in S$, $\theta(s_1) = \theta(s_2)$ implies $s_1 \mathscr{H} s_2$.

1.12 Definition. Let $\theta : S \twoheadrightarrow T$. θ is a γ *epimorphism* iff θ is $1:1$ when restricted to each subgroup of S. Let α be one of $\mathscr{H}$, $\mathscr{R}$,

$\mathscr{L}$, or $\mathscr{J}$. Then θ is a $\gamma(\alpha)$ *epimorphism* iff θ is $1:1$ when restricted to each α class of S. In particular, $\gamma(\alpha)$ epimorphisms are γ epimorphisms.

1.13 Fact. Let α be any of $\mathscr{J}$, $\mathscr{R}$, $\mathscr{L}$, or $\mathscr{H}$. Then

(a) the composition of two α epimorphisms is an α epimorphism; and

(b) the composition of two $\gamma(\alpha)$ epimorphisms (respectively γ epimorphisms) is a $\gamma(\alpha)$ epimorphism (respectively γ epimorphism).

PROOF. (a) We shall prove that, if $\varphi : S \twoheadrightarrow T$ is an α epimorphism, then each α class of S is mapped *onto* an α class of T. Thus, the α classes of S and those of T are in $1:1$ correspondence, and the assertion follows easily.

Let $\alpha = \mathscr{J}$, and assume $\varphi(j_1) \mathscr{J} \varphi(j_2)$. Let $s, t, u, v \in S$ be any elements such that $\varphi(s)\varphi(j_1)\varphi(t) = \varphi(j_2)$ and $\varphi(u)\varphi(j_2)\varphi(v) = \varphi(j_1)$. Then, since φ is a $\mathscr{J}$ epimorphism, we have $sj_1t \mathscr{J} j_2$ and $uj_2v \mathscr{J} j_1$. This implies $j_1 \mathscr{J} j_2$, so $j_1 \mathscr{J} j_2$ iff $\varphi(j_1) \mathscr{J} \varphi(j_2)$.

For $\alpha = \mathscr{R}$, $\mathscr{L}$, and $\mathscr{H}$, the proofs are very similar.

(b) is left as an exercise. ∎

We now prove the main result of this section: that every epimorphism between two finite semigroups can be decomposed into $\gamma(\mathscr{H})$ and $\mathscr{H}$ epimorphisms.

1.14 Theorem. Let $\theta : S \twoheadrightarrow T$ be an epimorphism. Then θ can be written as $\theta = \theta_n \cdots \theta_1$, where $\theta_1, \theta_3, \theta_5, \ldots$ are $\gamma(\mathscr{H})$ epimorphisms and $\theta_2, \theta_4, \theta_6, \ldots$ are $\mathscr{H}$ epimorphisms, or vice versa.

To prove Theorem 1.14, we introduce the following definition.

1.15 Definition. Let $\theta : S \twoheadrightarrow T$ be an epimorphism. Then θ is a *maximal proper epimorphism* (MPE) iff $\theta = \theta_2\theta_1$, where θ_1 and θ_2 are epimorphisms, implies exactly one of θ_1, θ_2 is $1:1$.

Clearly, any epimorphism θ is an isomorphism, or can be written as $\theta = \theta_n \cdots \theta_1$ with each θ_k an MPE. Thus, it follows easily by virtue of Fact 1.13 that Theorem 1.14 is equivalent with the following.

1.16 Theorem. Let $\theta : S \twoheadrightarrow T$ be an MPE. Then θ is either a $\gamma(\mathscr{H})$ or an $\mathscr{H}$ epimorphism.

To give proofs of the preceding theorems, we require the following definition and lemma.

1.17 Definition. Let $\theta : S \twoheadrightarrow T$ be an epimorphism. Then a $\mathscr{J}$ class J of S is *θ-singular* iff θ is $1:1$ on $S - J$.

1.18 Lemma. Let $\theta : S \twoheadrightarrow T$ be an MPE. Then there exists a θ-singular $\mathscr{J}$ class of S.

PROOF. Let I_1 be a maximal member (under inclusion) of $\mathscr{I} = \{I : I \text{ is an ideal of } S, \text{ and } \theta \text{ restricted to } I \text{ is } 1:1\}$. $I_1 \neq S$, since θ is not $1:1$ on S. ($\mathscr{I}$ may be empty, but for convenience we shall consider the empty set ϕ an ideal). Let J_1 be a $\leqslant$-minimal element of $\{J : J \text{ is a } \mathscr{J} \text{ class of } S, \text{ and } J \cap I_1 = \phi\}$. Let $I_2 = I_1 \cup J_1$. Then I_2 is an ideal of S properly containing I_1. Thus, from the definition of I_1, θ restricted to I_2 is not $1:1$.

Let (mod θ) be the congruence on S given by $s_1 \equiv s_2 \pmod{\theta}$ iff $\theta(s_1) = \theta(s_2)$.

Define the equivalence relation $\equiv$ on S by $s_1 \equiv s_2$ iff we have $s_1 = s_2$ or $s_1, s_2 \in I_2$ and $\theta(s_1) = \theta(s_2)$. It is easy to verify that $\equiv$ is a congruence. Let $\theta_1 : S \twoheadrightarrow S/\!\equiv$ be the natural epimorphism. Then clearly, $\theta_1(s_1) = \theta_1(s_2)$ implies $s_1 \equiv s_2 \pmod{\theta}$, and so, by Remark 1.10(b), there exists an epimorphism $\theta_2 : S/\!\equiv \twoheadrightarrow T$ such that $\theta = \theta_2\theta_1$. But, since $\theta = \theta_1$ on I_2 and θ is not $1:1$ on I_2, θ_1 is not $1:1$. Hence, θ_2 is $1:1$ since θ is an MPE. Therefore, $\equiv$ equals (mod θ) and J_1 is a θ-singular $\mathscr{J}$ class. ∎

PROOF OF THEOREM 1.16. First note that an epimorphism that is both a $\gamma(\mathscr{H})$ and an $\mathscr{H}$ epimorphism is an isomorphism. Let $\theta : S \twoheadrightarrow T$ be an MPE with J a θ-singular $\mathscr{J}$ class. If θ is a $\gamma(\mathscr{H})$ epimorphism, we are done, and so assume otherwise.

Define the equivalence relation $\equiv$ on S by $s_1 \equiv s_2$ iff $s_1 \mathscr{H} s_2$ and $\theta(s_1) = \theta(s_2)$. Since J is θ-singular, restricted to $S - J$, this relation reduces to $s_1 \equiv s_2$ iff $s_1 = s_2$.

We next verify that $\equiv$ is a congruence on S. Clearly, $\equiv$ is a congruence on $S - J$. Let $s_1 \equiv s_2$, s_1 and $s_2 \in J$. Let $x, y \in S^1$. Since $s_1 \mathscr{H} s_2$, from Green (Fact 7.1.15) we know that either both xs_1y and xs_2y do not belong to J or $xs_1y \mathscr{H} xs_2y$. In either case, $\theta(xs_1y) = \theta(xs_2y)$. Since J is θ-singular, if $xs_1y, xs_2y \in S - J$, then $xs_1y = xs_2y$. Hence $\equiv$ is a congruence. Since θ is not a $\gamma(\mathscr{H})$ epimorphism, $\equiv$ is not the identity congruence.

Now let $\theta_1 : S \twoheadrightarrow S/\equiv$ be the natural epimorphism. θ_1 is an $\mathscr{H}$ epimorphism and is not $1 : 1$. Furthermore, $\theta_1(s_1) = \theta_1(s_2)$ implies $s_1 \equiv s_2 \pmod{\theta}$. So, as in the proof of Lemma 1.18, since θ is an MPE, we have $\equiv$ equal to $(\bmod\ \theta)$. Then θ is an $\mathscr{H}$ epimorphism. This proves Theorem 1.16 and hence Theorem 1.14. ∎

1.19 Remark. The foregoing classification of MPE is extremely useful in proving (and discovering) statements true for all finite semigroups by the method of considering the "minimal counterexample" (i.e., induction). By induction, the statement would be valid for each MPE image, and so it is necessary only to "pull the statement through the MPE" via the classification theorem (thus contradicting the existence of a counterexample).

The results of this section are from Rhodes [1]. This paper, in addition to the material presented here, contains a detailed classification of maximal proper epimorphisms, examples, and the elementary theory of $\mathscr{H}$ homomorphisms.

2. Semilocal Theory

This section decomposes an arbitrary finite semigroup into subdirect products of semigroups possessing special important properties. We give methods for constructing homomorphisms of semigroups by acting on ideals or $\mathscr{J}$ classes by left and right multiplication, giving rise to homomorphic images in terms of left or right translations.

2.1 Definition. Let $S, T_1, \ldots, T_n$ be semigroups. S is a *subdirect product* of $T_1, \ldots, T_n$ (write $S \leqslant\!\leqslant T_1 \times \cdots \times T_n$) iff S is (isomorphic to) a subsemigroup of $T_1 \times \cdots \times T_n$ such that $p_i(S) = T_i$, where p_i is the ith projection map, $i = 1, \ldots, n$.

2.2 Notation. Let $\varphi_i : S_i \twoheadrightarrow T_i$ be epimorphisms for $i = 1, \ldots, n$. Then $\varphi_1 \times \cdots \times \varphi_n : S_1 \times \cdots \times S_n \twoheadrightarrow T_1 \times \cdots \times T_n$ is defined by $\varphi_1 \times \cdots \times \varphi_n(s_1, \ldots, s_n) = (\varphi_1(s_1), \ldots, \varphi_n(s_n))$.

Let $\Delta : S \to S \times \cdots \times S$ (n times) be the monomorphism defined by $\Delta(s) = (s, \ldots, s)$. Let $\varphi_i : S \twoheadrightarrow T_i$ be epimorphisms for $i = 1, \ldots, n$. Then $\Pi\varphi_i : S \to T_1 \times \cdots \times T_n$ is the homomorphism defined by $\Pi\varphi_i = (\varphi_1 \times \cdots \times \varphi_n)\,\Delta$.

Notice that $\Pi\varphi_i(S) \leqslant\leqslant T_1 \times \cdots \times T_n$. Then S is a subdirect product of $T_1, \ldots, T_n$ if $\Pi\varphi_i$ is $1:1$. Thus, we may decompose a semigroup S into a subdirect product by finding a collection of homomorphisms $\{\varphi_i\}$ on S such that $\Pi\varphi_i$ is $1:1$.

The following fact gives criterion for finding such a collection of homormorphisms on S using the $\mathscr{J}$ classes of the semigroup. We recall the definition of the ideal $F(J)$, J a $\mathscr{J}$ class of S (X7.2.14), and of the ideal $B(J)$ (Remark 7.1.11):

$$F(J) = \cup \{J' : J' \text{ a } \mathscr{J} \text{ class of } S \text{ and } J \nleqslant J'\};$$

$$B(J) = \cup \{J' : J' \text{ a } \mathscr{J} \text{ class of } S \text{ and } J' \lneqq J\}.$$

2.3 Fact. Let $J_1, \ldots, J_n$ be the $\mathscr{J}$ classes of a semigroup S. Let $\{\varphi_i : i = 1, \ldots, n\}$ be homomorphisms on S satisfying

(1) φ_i is $1:1$ and nonzero on J_i; and

(2) $\varphi_i[F(J_i)] = 0, i = 1, \ldots, n$.

Then $\Pi\varphi_i$ is $1:1$, and so $S \leqslant\leqslant \varphi_1(S) \times \cdots \times \varphi_n(S)$.

PROOF. We show that $\Pi\varphi_i$ is $1:1$. Let $s_i \in J_i$, $s_j \in J_j$, and suppose $s_i \neq s_j$. If $i = j$, then $\varphi_i(s_i) \neq \varphi_i(s_j)$, since φ_i is $1:1$ on J_i. Hence, $\Pi\varphi_i(s_i) \neq \Pi\varphi_i(s_j)$. If $i \neq j$, then either $J_i \subseteq F(J_j)$ or $J_j \subseteq F(J_i)$ (or both). Without loss of generality, suppose the former. Then $\varphi_j(s_i) = 0$, and $\varphi_j(s_j) \neq 0$, and so again $\Pi\varphi_i(s_i) \neq \Pi\varphi_i(s_j)$. ∎

One obvious application of Fact 2.3 is given below.

2.4 Corollary. $S \leqslant\leqslant S/F(J_1) \times \cdots \times S/F(J_n)$.

PROOF. This follows immediately, since the natural epimorphisms $\{\eta_i : S \twoheadrightarrow S/F(J_i) : i = 1, \ldots, n\}$ satisfy (1) and (2) of Fact 2.3. ∎

We now proceed to find a collection of homomorphisms on S which is "minimal" with respect to conditions (1) and (2) of Fact 2.3.

2.5 Definition. Recall the definitions of the homomorphisms $M_X^R : RI(X) \to F_R(X)$ and $M_X^L : LI(X) \to F_L(X)$ (Definition 7.2.7). M_X^R sends a t such that $Xt \subseteq X$ to the map $(x \to xt)$, whereas M_X^L sends a t such that $tX \subseteq X$ to the map $(x \to tx)$. Let J be a $\mathscr{J}$ class of S, let $\eta_J : S \twoheadrightarrow S/F(J)$ be the natural epimorphism, and notice that J^0 is the unique 0-minimal ideal of $S/F(J)$.

Define

$$RM_J : S \to F_R(J^0) \quad \text{by} \quad RM_J = M_J{}^R \circ \eta_J \,,$$

and define

$$LM_J : S \to F_L(J^0) \quad \text{by} \quad LM_J = M_J{}^L \circ \eta_J \,.$$

Then, for example,

$$LM_J(s)(j) = \begin{cases} sj & \text{if } sj \in J \\ 0 & \text{if } sj \notin J \end{cases} \qquad \text{for all} \quad j \in J,$$

$$LM_J(s)(0) = 0.$$

Let J be a null $\mathscr{J}$ class of S. Define the map $\psi_J : S \twoheadrightarrow J^0$ by

$$\psi_J(s) = \begin{cases} s & \text{if } s \in J \\ 0 & \text{if } s \notin J. \end{cases}$$

Let P_J be the partition induced on S by ψ_J. Then, by Fact 1.7, $\mathscr{P}(S, P_J)$ has a minimal homomorphic image $(N_J, S/Q_J)$, where $N_J(s_1) = N_J(s_2)$ iff $\psi_J(\alpha s_1 \beta) = \psi_J(\alpha s_2 \beta)$ for all $\alpha, \beta \in S^1$.

N_J is the unique minimal homomorphism on S which is $1:1$ on J and which separates J and $S - J$, and $N_J(F(J)) = \{0\}$.

2.6 Proposition. (a) Let J be a regular $\mathscr{J}$ class of a semigroup S. Then $(LM_J \times RM_J)\,\Delta$ is the unique minimal homomorphism of S which is $1:1$ nonzero on J and zero on $F(J)$.

(b) Let $J_1 ,..., J_k$ be the regular $\mathscr{J}$ classes, and let $J_{k+1} ,..., J_n$ be the null $\mathscr{J}$ classes of S. Then

$$S \leqslant\!\leqslant LM_{J_1}(S) \times \cdots \times LM_{J_k}(S) \times RM_{J_1}(S) \times \cdots \times RM_{J_k}(S)$$
$$\times\, N_{J_{k+1}}(S) \times \cdots \times N_{J_n}(S).$$

(c) (**Schützenberger-Preston**). Let S be a regular semigroup. Then S can be represented as a subdirect product of semigroups of row and column mononomial matrices. Specifically (for notation, see 7.2.15 and 7.2.16), let $J_1 ,..., J_n$ be the $\mathscr{J}$ classes of S, and let $J_i^0 \cong \mathscr{M}^0(G_i\,; A_i\,, B_i\,; C_i)$, $i = 1,..., n$. Then

$$S \leqslant\!\leqslant T_1 \times \cdots \times T_n \times T_1' \times \cdots \times T_n'$$

where T_i is a subsemigroup of $\mathscr{RM}(|B_i|, G_i)$ and T_i' is a subsemigroup of $\mathscr{CM}(|A_i|, G_i)$, $i = 1,..., n$. Or equivalently,

$$S \leqslant\leqslant W_1 \times \cdots \times W_n \times W_1' \times \cdots \times W_n'$$

where W_i is a subsemigroup of $(G_i^0, R(G_i^0))$ w (B_i^0, S_i) and W_i' is a subsemigroup of (S_i', A_i^0) w* $(L(G_i^0), G_i^0)$, $i = 1,..., n$.

PROOF. (a) Let $\theta = (LM_J \times RM_J)\Delta$. We first show that θ is $1:1$ nonzero on J, and $\theta[F(J)] = 0$. Let $a, b \in J$, and suppose $\theta(a) = \theta(b)$. This implies (1) $ja = jb$, and (2) $aj = bj$ in $S/F(J)$ for all $j \in J$. Now $a \mathscr{L} b$ by (1), and so, by the regularity of J, a and b have a right identity, say $e \in J$, in common. But $a = ae = be = b$ by (2). Thus, θ is $1:1$ on J, and θ is clearly nonzero on J and zero on $F(J)$.

Now let Q_L and Q_R be the congruences associated with LM_J and RM_J, respectively. Then $Q_L \cap Q_R$ is the congruence associated with θ. Let φ be any homomorphism on S which is $1:1$ nonzero on J, and $\varphi[F(J)] = 0$. We must show $s_1 \not\equiv s_2 \pmod{Q_L \cap Q_R}$ implies $\varphi(s_1) \neq \varphi(s_2)$.

Suppose $s_1 \not\equiv s_2 \pmod{Q_L}$. Then there exist $j \in J$ such that $s_1 j \neq s_2 j$ in $S/F(J)$. But $s_1 j, s_2 j \in J^0$, the 0-minimal ideal of $S/F(J)$, and φ is $1:1$ on J^0. Therefore, $\varphi(s_1 j) \neq \varphi(s_2 j)$, which implies $\varphi(s_1) \neq \varphi(s_2)$. Similarly, $s_1 \not\equiv s_2 \pmod{Q_R}$ implies $\varphi(s_1) \neq \varphi(s_2)$, which implies $s_1 \not\equiv s_2 \pmod{Q_L \cap Q_R}$ implies $\varphi(s_1) \neq \varphi(s_2)$.

(b) This follows immediately from (a) and Fact 2.3.

(c) Notice that $RM_J(S)$ is a subsemigroup of right translations on J^0, $RT(J^0)$, and $LM_J(S) \subseteq LT(J^0)$. Now, by Facts 7.2.15 and 7.2.16 and (b), the result follows. ∎

2.7 Remark. From this point on, assume that J has been given a fixed Rees matrix representation, i.e., $J^0 \cong \mathscr{M}^0(G; A, B; C)$. Notice that two elements $s_1, s_2 \in S$ are equivalent under $Q_L \cap Q_R$ iff they act the same on the right of J and they act the same on the left of J. Using the notation developed for describing left and right translations of regular Rees matrix semigroups (Fact 7.2.14) and considering multiplying by s_1 and s_2 as translations, we find that $s_1 \equiv s_2 \pmod{Q_L \cap Q_R}$ iff $\psi_R(s_1) = \psi_R(s_2)$, $\psi_L(s_1) = \psi_L(s_2)$, $\delta(s_1) = \delta(s_2)$, and $\lambda(s_1) = \lambda(s_2)$.

However, $RM_J(s)$ and $LM_J(s)$ are linked for all $s \in S$. Applying Fact 7.2.14(d), we discover that, if ψ_R, ψ_L, and δ agree for s_1 and s_2, then λ agrees on s_1 and s_2. This suggests that there is some duplication of information in representing $(LM_J \times RM_J)\Delta$ as the homomorphism associated with $Q_L \cap Q_R$. We develop this more explicitly.

2.8 Definition.[†] Let S be a semigroup with J a regular $\mathscr{J}$ class.

(a) Define $LLM_J : S \twoheadrightarrow [S/F(J)]/{\equiv_L}$, where, for all $s_1, s_2 \in S/F(J)$, $s_1 \equiv_L s_2$ iff $s_1 x \mathscr{R} s_2 x$ in $S/F(J)$ for all $x \in J$. Thus, $s_1 \equiv_L s_2$ iff they act the same on the left letters, i.e., iff $\psi_L(s_1) = \psi_L(s_2)$. It is easy to show that $\equiv_L$ is a congruence.

(b) Similarly, define $RLM_J : S \twoheadrightarrow [S/F(J)]/{\equiv_R}$, where, for all $s_1, s_2 \in S/F(J)$, $s_1 \equiv_R s_2$ iff $xs_1 \mathscr{L} xs_2$ in $S/F(J)$ for all $x \in J$. Thus, $s_1 \equiv_R s_2$ iff $\psi_R(s_1) = \psi_R(s_2)$.

2.9 Fact. (a) $(LLM_J \times RM_J)\Delta$ induces $Q_L \cap Q_R$.

(b) $(LM_J \times RLM_J)\Delta$ induces $Q_L \cap Q_R$.

PROOF. (a) Clearly, $s_1 \equiv s_2 \bmod(Q_L \cap Q_R)$ implies

$$[LLM_J(s_1), RM_J(s_1)] = [LLM_J(s_2), RM_J(s_2)].$$

Conversely, suppose $(LLM_J \times RM_J)\Delta(s_1) = (LLM_J \times RM_J)\Delta(s_2)$. Then ψ_L, ψ_R, and δ agree on s_1 and s_2. Suppose $\lambda(s_1)(a) = 0$. This implies $\psi_L(s_1)(a) = 0$, which implies $\psi_L(s_2)(a) = 0$. Hence, $\lambda(s_2)(a) = 0$. Suppose $\lambda(s_1)(a) \neq 0$. Then $\psi_L(s_1)(a) \neq 0$, and, by the linked equation [Fact 7.2.14(d)] and the regularity of J, there exist $b \in B$ such that

$$\begin{aligned}\lambda(s_1)(a) &= C[b, \psi_L(s_1)(a)]^{-1}\,\delta(s_1)(b)\,C[\psi_R(s_1)(b), a]\\ &= C[b, \psi_L(s_2)(a)]^{-1}\,\delta(s_2)(b)\,C[\psi_R(s_2)(b), a]\\ &= \lambda(s_2)(a).\end{aligned}$$

Therefore, $s_1 \equiv s_2 \bmod(Q_L \cap Q_R)$.

(b) This proof is similar to (a). ∎

2.10 Remark. We now have congruences on $S/F(J)$ which identify two elements if they act the same on the left letters and right letters, respectively, and $Q_L \cap Q_R$ is contained in both of them. We would like to find a third homomorphism on S so that it, combined with LLM_J and RLM_J, would give $Q_L \cap Q_R$. This new homomorphism would necessarily have to say something about how two elements act on the group coordinate.

[†] For an alternate and perhaps clarifying definition of LLM_J and RLM_J, the reader should see Exercise X2.2.

2.11 Definition.† Let J be a regular $\mathscr{J}$ class of S. Define $GGM_J : S \twoheadrightarrow [S/F(J)]/\equiv$ by $s_1 \equiv s_2$ iff $x_1s_1x_2 = x_1s_2x_2$ in $S/F(J)$ for all $x_1, x_2 \in J$. Clearly, $\equiv$ is a congruence.

We call a $\mathscr{J}$ class *combinatorial* if and only if it contains no nontrivial groups. A $\mathscr{J}$ class is called *noncombinatorial* if and only if it is not combinatorial, i.e., if and only if it contains a nontrivial group. Therefore, combinatorial $\mathscr{J}$ classes are either null or are regular with one-element $\mathscr{H}$ classes.

Equivalently, a $\mathscr{J}$ class J is combinatorial if and only if J^0 is combinatorial, and J is noncombinatorial if and only if J^0 is not combinatorial.

Define the homomorphism GM_J on S by

$$GM_J(S) = \begin{cases} GGM_J(S) & \text{if } J \text{ is noncombinatorial} \\ \{0\} & \text{if } J \text{ is combinatorial.} \end{cases}$$

2.12 Proposition. (a) $(LLM_J \times GM_J \times RLM_J)\Delta$ induces $\mathscr{Q}_L \cap \mathscr{Q}_R$.

(b) Let $J_1, \ldots, J_k$ be the regular $\mathscr{J}$ classes of S, and let $J_{k+1}, \ldots, J_n$ be the null $\mathscr{J}$ classes of S. Then

$$S \leqslant\leqslant \Pi\{LLM_{J_i}(S) : i = 1,\ldots, k\} \times \Pi\{GM_{J_i}(S) : i = 1,\ldots, k\}$$
$$\times \Pi\{RLM_{J_i}(S) : i = 1,\ldots, k\} \times \Pi\{N_{J_i}(S) : i = k+1,\ldots, n\}.$$

PROOF. (a) First assume the regular $\mathscr{J}$ class J is combinatorial, i.e., the $\mathscr{H}$ classes of J have only one element. Then by definition $GM_J(S) = \{0\}$. Therefore, $(LLM_J \times GM_J \times RLM_J)\,\Delta(s_1) = (LLM_J \times GM_J \times RLM_J)\,\Delta(s_2)$ implies only that $\psi_R(s_1) = \psi_R(s_2)$ and $\psi_L(s_1) = \psi_L(s_2)$. But this is enough. For, suppose $\psi_R(s_1)(b) = 0 = \psi_R(s_2)(b)$. Then $\delta(s_1)(b) = \delta(s_2)(b) = 0$. If $\psi_R(s_1)(b) = \psi_R(s_2)(b) \neq 0$, then $\delta(s_1)(b) = \delta(s_2)(b) = 1$, since J is combinatorial. Similarly, $\psi_L(s_1) = \psi_L(s_2)$ implies $\lambda(s_1) = \lambda(s_2)$. Therefore, if $\mathscr{Q}$ is the congruence induced by $(LLM_J \times GM_J \times RLM_J)\,\Delta$ on S, then $\mathscr{Q} \subseteq \mathscr{Q}_L \cap \mathscr{Q}_R$. Clearly, $\mathscr{Q}_L \cap \mathscr{Q}_R \subseteq \mathscr{Q}$.

Now assume J is noncombinatorial, so that $GM_J(S) = GGM_J(S)$. Let $s_1, s_2 \in S$, and suppose $GM_J(s_1) = GM_J(s_2)$. Let (g, a, b), $(h, c, d) \in J$. Then, since

$$(g, a, b)\, s_1(h, c, d) = (g, a, b)\, s_2(h, c, d),$$

† See Exercise X2.3 for an alternate definition of GGM_J.

we have

$$\delta(s_1)(b)\, C[\psi_R(s_1)(b), c] = \delta(s_2)(b)\, C[\psi_R(s_2)(b), c] \tag{2.1}$$

and

$$C[b, \psi_L(s_1)(c)]\, \lambda(s_1)(c) = C[b, \psi_L(s_2)(c)]\, \lambda(s_2)(c). \tag{2.2}$$

Now, if $RLM_J(s_1) = RLM_J(s_2)$, then $\psi_R(s_1) = \psi_R(s_2)$. If $\psi_R(s_1)(b) = 0$, then both $\delta(s_1)(b)$ and $\delta(s_2)(b)$ are zero. If $\psi_R(s_1)(b) \neq 0$, then there exist $c \in A$ such that $C[\psi_R(s_1)(b), c] \neq 0$, and, by (2.1), $\delta(s_1)(b) = \delta(s_2)(b)$. Similarly, $LLM_J(s_1) = LLM_J(s_2)$ implies $\lambda(s_1) = \lambda(s_2)$. Therefore, $Q \subseteq Q_L \cap Q_R$. On the other hand, it is easy to see that $Q_L \cap Q_R \subseteq Q$, and so (a) is proved.

(b) This follows from Proposition 2.6 and (a), since for J regular, the congruences of $(LLM_J \times GM_J \times RLM_J)\,\Delta$ and $(LM_J \times RM_J)\,\Delta$ are equal. ∎

We now investigate the nature of the semigroups $RM_J(S)$, $LM_J(S)$, $RLM_J(S)$, $LLM_J(S)$, $GGM_J(S)$, and $GM_J(S)$.

2.13 Fact. Let $J \neq \{0\}$ be a regular $\mathscr{J}$ class of a semigroup S.

(a) RM_J is $1:1$ when restricted to subgroups, hence $\mathscr{H}$ classes, of J. $RM_J(S)$ has a unique 0-minimal regular ideal I, which is the image of $J \cup F(J)$, and each element of $RM_J(S)$ is a distinct right translation of I. In other words, the homomorphism M_I^R is $1:1$ on $RM_J(S)$.

(b) LM_J is $1:1$ when restricted to subgroups, hence $\mathscr{H}$ classes, of J. $LM_J(S)$ has a unique 0-minimal regular ideal I, which is the image of $J \cup F(J)$, and M_I^L is $1:1$ on $LM_J(S)$.

(c) $RLM_J(S)$ has a unique 0-minimal regular combinatorial ideal I, which is the image of $J \cup F(J)$, and M_I^R is $1:1$ on $RLM_J(S)$.

(d) $LLM_J(S)$ has a unique 0-minimal regular combinatorial ideal I, which is the image of $J \cup F(J)$, and M_I^L is $1:1$ on $LLM_J(S)$.

(e) GGM_J is $1:1$ when restricted to subgroups, hence $\mathscr{H}$ classes, of J. $GGM_J(S)$ has a unique 0-minimal regular ideal I, the image of $J \cup F(J)$, and both M_I^L and M_I^R are $1:1$ on $GGM_J(S)$.

(f) $GM_J(S)$ is either $\{0\}$ or equals $GGM_J(S)$. If $GM_J(S) = GGM_J(S)$, then I is a *noncombinatorial* ideal.

PROOF. (a) We will prove that M_I^R is $1:1$ on $RM_J(S)$; the other assertions follow clearly from the definition of RM_J.

Let $RM_J(s_1)$, $RM_J(s_2)$ be such that $(i)RM_J(s_1) = (i)RM_J(s_2)$ for all $i \in I - \{0\}$. Since J maps onto $I - \{0\}$, this is equivalent to $RM_J(js_1) = RM_J(js_2)$ for all $j \in J$. Thus for all $j_1 \in J$ we have $j_1(js_1) = j_1(js_2)$ in $S/F(J)$. Since J is regular, each element j has a left identity, say e_j. Then $e_j js_1 = e_j js_2$ in $S/F(J)$ so $js_1 = js_2$ in $S/F(J)$ for all $j \in J$. Thus, $RM_J(s_1) = RM_J(s_2)$, and M_I^R is $1:1$ on $RM_J(S)$.

The proofs of (b)–(f) are straightforward utilizations of the ideas of the proof of (a). ▮

We now give names to semigroups having the preceding properties.

2.14 Definition. (a) S is a *right mapping* (RM) semigroup iff S has a minimal or 0-minimal ideal I for which M_I^R is $1:1$.

(b) S is a *left mapping* (LM) semigroup iff S has a minimal or 0-minimal ideal I for which M_I^L is $1:1$.

(c) S is a *right letter mapping* (RLM) semigroup iff S is an RM semigroup whose ideal I is combinatorial (see Fact 2.15(c), below).

(d) S is a *left letter mapping* (LLM) semigroup iff S is an LM semigroup whose ideal I is combinatorial.

(e) S is a *generalized group mapping* (GGM) semigroup iff S is both an RM and LM semigroup.

(f) S is a *group mapping* (GM) semigroup iff $S = \{0\}$ or S is a GGM semigroup whose ideal is noncombinatorial.

2.15 Fact. (a) Let J be a regular $\mathscr{J}$ class of a semigroup S. Then $RM_J(S)$, $LM_J(S)$, $RLM_J(S)$, $LLM_J(S)$, $GGM_J(S)$, and $GM_J(S)$ are, respectively, RM, LM, RLM, LLM, GGM, and GM semigroups. Furthermore, GM, GGM, and RLM semigroups are RM semigroups, and GM, GGM, and LLM semigroups are LM semigroups. If S is a GGM semigroup that is not a GM semigroup, then S is both RLM and LLM.

(b) If $S \neq \{0\}$, the ideal I alluded to in each part of Def. 2.14 is necessarily regular and nonzero.

(c) Let I be a minimal or 0-minimal ideal of $S \neq \{0\}$ for which either M_I^R or M_I^L is $1:1$. Then I is the unique (except possibly for 0) minimal or 0-minimal ideal of S. Hence, the ideal I in each part of Definition 2.14 is necessarily unique.

PROOF. (a) Clear from Fact 2.13.

(b) Suppose the nonzero $\mathcal{J}$ class in I is null. Then $M_I^R(I) = 0$, and $M_I^L = 0$. In each part of Definition 2.14, one of M_I^R and M_I^L is always $1:1$. Hence, in each case, $I = \{0\}$, a contradiction.

(c) Since $S \neq \{0\}$ and M_I^R is $1:1$ on S, $I \neq \{0\}$. Let J be another 0-minimal ideal of S. Since $J \neq \{0\}$, $M_I^R(J) \neq \{0\}$, and so the ideal $IJ \neq \{0\}$. But $I \supseteq IJ$ and $J \supseteq IJ$, so that $I = IJ = J$ by minimality, and similarly for M_I^L. ∎

2.16 Notation. (a) Let S be a semigroup. Define $S^\# \equiv S^0 - \{0\}$. In other words, $S^\#$ is the nonzero part of S.

The unique regular minimal or 0-minimal ideal I of an RM, LM, RLM, LLM, GM, or GGM semigroup is called the *distinguished ideal*, and $I^\#$ is called the *distinguished $\mathcal{J}$ class.*

(b) Often the J is dropped from the homomorphisms when there is no confusion as to what $\mathcal{J}$ class the homomorphism is being defined on. For example, $RLM[GM_J(S)]$ means take the right letter mapping of $GM_J(S)$ with respect to its distinguished $\mathcal{J}$ class.

2.17 Proposition. (a) Let S be a regular semigroup. Then S can be written as a subdirect product of GM, RLM, and LLM semigroups.

(b) Let T be an RM semigroup with distinguished $\mathcal{J}$ class J. Let G be a maximal subgroup of J and let B be the set of $\mathcal{L}$ classes of J. Then

$$T \subseteq (G^0, R(G^0)) \text{ w } (B^0, RLM_J(T)).$$

(c) Let T be an LM semigroup with distinguished $\mathcal{J}$ class J. Let G be a maximal subgroup of J and let A be the set of $\mathcal{R}$ classes of J. Then

$$T \subseteq (LLM_J(T), A^0) \text{ w}^* (L(G^0), G^0).$$

(d) A semigroup S is an RM semigroup iff $r(S)$ is an LM semigroup. In general, however, $RM_J(T)$ is not anti-isomorphic to $LM_J(T)$.

PROOF. (a) Clear from Fact 2.15 and Proposition 2.12.

(b) Let $I = J \cup \{0\}$. Since M_I^R is $1:1$ on T, each element of T is a distinct right translation of I. Hence, by Fact 7.2.16,

$$T \subseteq (G^0, R(G^0)) \text{ w } (B^0, S)$$

where $S = \{f \in F_R(B^0) : f(0) = 0\}$. Now, viewing each element of T as an element of the wreath product, it is easy to see that two elements have the same first coordinate iff they act the same on the right letters, B^0. But that is the definition of RLM_J. Clearly, $RLM_J(T) \subseteq S$, so it is easy to see that

$$T \subseteq (G^0, R(G^0)) \text{ w } (B^0, RLM_J(T))$$

(c) The argument dual to (b) proves (c).

(d) The first statement is clear. Consider the following counterexample to the conjecture that $RM_J(T)$ is anti-isomorphic to $LM_J(T)$. Let $T = \mathscr{M}^0(\{1\}; A, B; C)$, where $A = \{a_1, a_2, a_3\}$, $B = \{b_1, b_2\}$, and

$$C = \begin{pmatrix} 1 & 1 & 0 \\ 0 & 0 & 1 \end{pmatrix}.$$

Then it is easy to check that $LM(T) = T$ while $RM(T) \cong \mathscr{M}^0(\{1\}; \{1, 2\}, \{1, 2\}; I)$, where I is the 2×2 identity matrix. Thus $|LM(T)| \neq |RM(T)|$.

We give another example, this time where S is a GM union of groups semigroup with distinguished $\mathscr{J}$ class T. We will show that $RLM_T(S)$ is not anti-isomorphic to $LLM_T(S)$.

Let $\mathbf{Z}_2$ be the group $\{1, -1\}$ under multiplication. Let $T = S_{22}(\mathbf{Z}_2, C)$, where

$$C = \begin{pmatrix} 1 & 1 \\ 1 & -1 \end{pmatrix}.$$

Let $S = \mathbf{Z}_2 \cup T$ be a new semigroup with the following multiplication: $\mathbf{Z}_2$ and T are subsemigroups of S; $1 \in \mathbf{Z}_2$ is the identity of S; and

$$RM_T(-1) = \begin{pmatrix} 0 & 1 \\ 1 & 0 \end{pmatrix} \in \mathscr{RM}(2, \mathbf{Z}_2),$$

$$LM_T(-1) = \begin{pmatrix} 1 & 0 \\ 0 & -1 \end{pmatrix} \in \mathscr{CM}(2, \mathbf{Z}_2).$$

Now it can be verified that S is a GM union of groups semigroup with T the distinguished ideal. However, some computation will show that $|RLM_T(S)| = 4$, whereas $|LLM_T(S)| = 3$. Therefore, $RLM_T(S)$ and $LLM_T(S)$ are not anti-isomorphic. ∎

2.18 Definition. (a) Recall the definition of a maximal proper epimorphism (MPE) of a semigroup S (Definition 1.15). We say S has a *unique MPE* (UMPE) $\theta : S \twoheadrightarrow T$ iff for all proper epimorphisms (i.e., not 1 : 1) $\varphi : S \twoheadrightarrow \varphi(S)$ there exists an epimorphism $\alpha : T \twoheadrightarrow \varphi(S)$ such that $\varphi = \alpha\theta$, that is, the following diagram commutes:

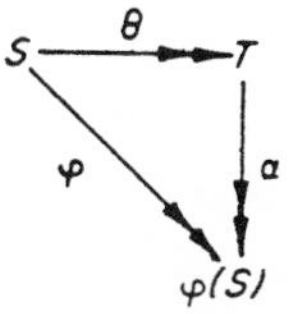

(b) A semigroup S is *subdirectly indecomposable* iff, whenever $S \leqslant\!\!\leqslant S_1 \times \cdots \times S_n$, then $S \cong S_i$ for some $i = 1,\dots, n$.

2.19 Lemma. (a) S has a UMPE iff S is subdirectly indecomposable. Thus, S can be written as a subdirect product of UMPE semigroups.

(b) Let S be subdirectly indecomposable. Either S has a nonzero combinatorial ideal I so that $|S/I| < |S|$, or S is a GM semigroup.

PROOF. (a) Let S have a UMPE, say θ. Let $S \leqslant\!\!\leqslant S_1 \times \cdots \times S_n$, and let p_i be the ith projection homomorphism. Then $p_i(S) = S_i$, and $\Pi p_i = (p_1 \times \cdots \times p_n)\,\Delta$ is 1 : 1 on S. Suppose each p_i is a proper homomorphism. Then there exist q_i's such that $p_i = q_i\theta$ for all $i = 1,\dots, n$. Then

$$\begin{aligned}(p_1 \times \cdots \times p_n)\,\Delta &= (q_1\theta \times \cdots \times q_n\theta)\,\Delta \\ &= (q_1 \times \cdots \times q_n)\,\Delta\theta,\end{aligned}$$

so that Πp_i is not 1 : 1, since θ is not 1 : 1. This is a contradiction. Hence, for some $i = 1,\dots, n$, p_i is an isomorphism and $S \cong S_i$. Conversely, suppose S is subdirectly indecomposable. Let $\{\varphi_i : i = 1,\dots, n\}$ be the set of all proper homomorphisms on S. By the assumption, $\Pi\varphi_i$ is not 1 : 1 on S, for, if it was, then $\varphi_i(S) \cong S$ for some $i = 1,\dots, n$. It is easy to verify that $\Pi\varphi_i = (\varphi_1 \times \cdots \times \varphi_n)\,\Delta$ is the UMPE of S.

(b) By Proposition 2.12 and (a), S is of the form $N_J(S)$ for some null $\mathscr{J}$ class J or S is an RLM, LLM, or GM semigroup. In the first three cases, S has a nonzero combinatorial ideal. ∎

We further describe semigroups with UMPE, as follows.

2.20 Lemma. Let S have a UMPE, say θ.

(a) S has a unique 0-minimal ideal I, and θ is $1:1$ on $S - I^{\#}$. No proper epimorphism of S is $1:1$ on $I^{\#}$.

(b) Let S be regular. Then either $S \cong RLM_{I^{\#}}(S)$, $S \cong LLM_{I^{\#}}(S)$, or $S \cong GM_{I^{\#}}(S)$.

PROOF. (a) Let Q^* be the congruence associated with θ. If Q is any other congruence associated with a proper homomorphism φ on S, then $Q^* \subseteq Q$. Now, since $Q^* = Q^* \cap Q$, we have $(\theta \times \varphi)\Delta = \theta$ for all proper homomorphisms φ on S.

Let $I \neq \{0\}$ be any proper ideal of S, and let $\eta : S \twoheadrightarrow S/I$. Suppose θ is $1:1$ on I. Then $(\theta \times \eta)\Delta$ is $1:1$ on S. But $(\theta \times \eta)\Delta = \theta$, and θ is not $1:1$ on S, a contradiction. Thus, θ is not $1:1$ on any proper ideal of S.

Let I be a 0-minimal ideal. Then since θ is not $1:1$ on I, by Lemma 1.18, θ is $1:1$ on $S - I^{\#}$. Hence, if S had another 0-minimal ideal, θ would be $1:1$ on it, a contradiction. Thus I is unique.

If φ is a proper homomorphism that is $1:1$ on I, then $(\theta \times \varphi)\Delta = \theta$ is $1:1$ on I, a contradiction. This proves (a).

(b) Let S be regular. Then its unique 0-minimal ideal I is regular. Then $(LLM_{I^{\#}} \times GM_{I^{\#}} \times RLM_{I^{\#}})\Delta$ is $1:1$ on I, and hence by (a) it is $1:1$ on S, i.e.,

$$S \leqslant\leqslant LLM_{I^{\#}}(S) \times GM_{I^{\#}}(S) \times RLM_{I^{\#}}(S).$$

Hence, by Lemma 2.19(a), the assertion is proved. ∎

We now take a closer look at RM and LM semigroups.

2.21 Definition. Let $C : B \times A \to G^0$ be a structure matrix for a Rees matrix semigroup. Two *rows* of C are *proportional* (*on the left*) iff there exists a $g \in G$ such that $gC(b_1, a) = C(b_2, a)$ for all $a \in A$. Two *columns* of C are *proportional* (*on the right*) iff there exist $g \in G$ such that $C(b, a_1)g = C(b, a_2)$ for all $b \in B$.

2.22 Fact. (a) Let S be an LM semigroup with distinguished ideal I. Assume $I^0 \cong \mathscr{M}^0(G; A, B; C)$. Then no two rows of the structure matrix C are proportional (on the left).

(b) Let S be a semigroup, and let J be a regular $\mathscr{J}$ class of S with $J^0 \cong \mathscr{M}^0(G; A, B; C)$. Then LM_J identifies $\mathscr{L}$ classes of J if the associated rows of C are proportional.

(c) Let S be an RM semigroup with distinguished ideal I. Assume $I^0 \cong \mathscr{M}^0(G; A, B; C)$. Then no two columns of the structure matrix C are proportional (on the right).

(d) Assuming the situation of (*b*), RM_J identifies $\mathscr{R}$ classes of J if the associated columns of C are proportional.

(e) Let S be a GGM semigroup with distinguished ideal I. Assume $I^0 \cong \mathscr{M}^0(G; A, B; C)$. Then no two columns of C are proportional (on the right) and no two rows of C are proportional (on the left).

(f) Assuming the situation of (*b*), GGM_J identifies $\mathscr{R}$ classes of J if the associated columns of C are proportional and identifies $\mathscr{L}$ classes of J if the associated rows of C are proportional.

PROOF. (a) Suppose two rows of C are proportional. That is, for some $b_1, b_2, b_1 \neq b_2$ there exists $g_1 \in G$ such that $g_1C(b_1, a) = C(b_2, a)$ for all $a \in A$. Then, for all $(g, a, b) \in I$,

$$(g_1, a, b_1)(g, a, b) = (1, a, b_2)(g, a, b).$$

That is, $M_I^L(g_1, a, b_1) = M_I^L(1, a, b_2)$. But M_I^L is $1:1$, a contradiction.

(b) First notice that, if two rows of C are proportional, then the same two rows of any other structure matrix for J^0 are proportional. For, by Fact 7.1.23, all new structure matrices P for J^0 are given by

$$P(b, a) = \delta(b)C(b, a)\,\lambda(a).$$

So, if $C(b_1, a) = gC(b_2, a)$ for all $a \in A$, then

$$\begin{aligned} P(b_1, a) &= \delta(b_1)\, C(b_1, a)\,\lambda(a) \\ &= \delta(b_1)\, gC(b_2, a)\,\lambda(a) \\ &= \delta(b_1)\, g\delta(b_2)^{-1}\,\delta(b_2)\, C(b_2, a)\,\lambda(a) \\ &= \delta(b_1)\, g\delta(b_2)^{-1}P(b_2, a) \\ &= g'P(b_2, a) \qquad \text{for all} \quad a \in A. \end{aligned}$$

Let I be the distinguished ideal of $LM_J(S)$. Then $LM_J(J) = I^\#$. Normalize the structure matrices for J^0 and I so that the homomorphism LM_J on J^0 is described in the normalized form given by Proposition 7.2.5, Eq. (2.3) and (2.4). Then, if $J^0 \cong \mathscr{M}^0(G; A, B; C)$, we have $I \cong \mathscr{M}^0(\omega(G); \psi_L(A), \psi_R(B); Q)$.

Now suppose $C(b_1, a) = gC(b_2, a)$ for all $a \in A$. Then, since $\omega[C(b, a)] = Q[\psi_R(b), \psi_L(a)]$, we have

$$Q[\psi_R(b_1), \psi_L(a)] = \omega(g)\, Q[\psi_R(b_2), \psi_L(a)] \qquad \text{for all} \quad \psi_L(a) \in \psi_L(A).$$

By (a), this implies that $\psi_R(b_1) = \psi_R(b_2)$ (and $g \in \ker\, \omega$), which in turn implies that the $\mathscr{L}$ classes L_{b_1} and L_{b_2} of J are identified under LM_J.

(c) and (d) are proved using the dual arguments of (a) and (b), respectively.

(e) This follows from (a) and (c) since a *GGM* semigroup is both *RM* and *LM*.

(f) The proof is exactly that of (b) and (d), utilizing (e). For an alternate proof, use the fact that $GGM_J(S) \cong RM[LM_J(S)] \cong LM[RM_J(S)]$ (see X2.3). ▮

Let S be *GGM* semigroup with distinguished ideal I. Then, if it is known how an element of S acts on the right of I, this completely determines how it acts on the left, and vice versa. If $0 \in I$ and $I^\#$ is a simple semigroup, then 0 breaks off of S, i.e., $S - \{0\}$ is a subsemigroup of S. These statements are proved below.

2.23 Fact. Let S be a *GM* semigroup with distinguished ideal I. Then we have the following:

(a) Let $s \in S$. Then xs is known for all $x \in I$ iff sx is known for all $x \in I$.

(b) If $0 \in S$ and $I^\#$ is a simple semigroup, then $S - \{0\}$ is a subsemigroup of S.

PROOF. (a) Let $s \in S$, $s \neq 0$, and let $\psi_R(s)$, $\psi_L(s)$, $\delta(s)$, and $\lambda(s)$ be the functions that describe the action of right and left multiplication on $I \cong \mathscr{M}^0(G; A, B; C)$. Since left and right multiplication by s are linked, we have

$$\delta(b)\, C[\psi_R(b), a] = C[b, \psi_L(a)]\, \lambda(a) \qquad \text{for all} \quad a \in A, b \in B, \tag{2.3}$$

where the s has been dropped from the notation for convenience [e.g., $\psi_R(b) \equiv \psi_R(s)(b)$].

Now suppose we know how s acts on the right of I; that is, $\psi_R(b)$ and $\delta(b)$ are known for all $b \in B$. We must show that this completely determines $\psi_L(a)$ and $\lambda(a)$ for all $a \in A$. Suppose ψ_L, λ and ψ'_L, λ' are two possible sets of functions describing the action of s on the left of I that satisfy (2.3). Fixing an $a \in A$, from (2.3) we have

$$f(b) = C[b, \psi_L(a)]\,\lambda(a) = C[b, \psi'_L(a)]\,\lambda'(a) \quad \text{for all} \quad b \in B. \tag{2.4}$$

If $f(b)$ is 0 for all $b \in B$, then $\psi_L(a) = 0$ by the regularity of C. This forces $\psi'_L(a) = 0$, $\lambda(a) = 0$ and $\lambda'(a) = 0$, so $\psi_L(a) = \psi'_L(a) = 0$ and $\lambda(a) = \lambda'(a) = 0$ in this case. If there exists $b \in B$ such that $f(b)$ is not zero, then $\psi_L(a)$, $\psi'_L(a)$, $\lambda(a)$ and $\lambda'(a)$ are not zero. Then

$$C[b, \psi_L(a)] = C[b, \psi'_L(a)]\,\lambda'(a)\,\lambda(a)^{-1}. \tag{2.5}$$

Thus, columns $\psi_L(a)$ and $\psi'_L(a)$ of C are proportional on the right. But S is a GGM semigroup, so by Fact 2.22 $\psi_L(a) = \psi'_L(a)$ and hence $\lambda(a) = \lambda'(a)$. Thus, there is only one solution. To determine the values $\psi_L(a)$ and $\lambda(a)$, consider the known quantity $f(b)$. By (2.4), $f(b)$ is proportional on the right to the column $\psi_L(a)$ of C. Since S is GGM, column $\psi_L(a)$ can be found by inspection of C, and the proportionality constant between $f(b)$ and $C(b, \psi_L(a))$ is $\lambda(a)$. Thus ψ_L and λ are completely determined. The proof of the converse is the dual argument.

(b) We must show that, for all $s_1, s_2 \in S - \{0\}$, $s_1 s_2 \neq 0$. Since $I^\#$ is a simple semigroup, we have $I^\# \cong \mathscr{M}(G; A, B; C)$ where $C(b, a) \neq 0$ for all $a \in A$, $b \in B$. We first show that no element $s \in S - \{0\}$ drives any element of $I^\#$ to zero.

Since $s \neq 0$, and M_I^R is faithful, there exists $b \in B$ such that $\psi_R(b) \neq 0$. This implies $\delta(b) \neq 0$, and, since $C(b, a) \neq 0$ for all $a \in A$, $b \in B$, this also implies $C[\psi_R(b), a] \neq 0$. Hence, by (2.3), $C[b, \psi_L(a)]\,\lambda(a) \neq 0$ for all $a \in A$, which in turn implies that $C[b, \psi_L(a)] \neq 0$, which implies that $\psi_L(a) \neq 0$ for all $a \in A$. Reversing the argument shows that $\psi_R(b) \neq 0$ for all $b \in B$.

We have seen that no element of $S - \{0\}$ drives an element of $I^\#$ to zero. So we only need to check that, if $s_1, s_2 \in S - I$, then $s_1 s_2 \neq 0$. Let $x \in I^\#$. Then $s_2 x \neq 0$ and $s_2 x \in I^\#$, so that $s_1(s_2 x) \neq 0$, which implies $s_1 s_2 \neq 0$. ∎

2.24 Remark. Given the situation of Fact 2.23(b), normalize the structure matrix of I so that one row and one column are all 1's. This we can do by Fact 7.1.25. For example, suppose we make $C(1, a) = 1$ for all $a \in A$, and $C(b, 1) = 1$ for all $b \in B$.

We now show how the action of any element of S on I is tied to the structure matrix of I. For, consider

$$\delta(b)\, C[\psi_R(b), 1] = C[b, \psi_L(1)]\, \lambda(1).$$

Then, since $C[\psi_R(b), 1] = 1$, we have

$$\delta(b) = C[b, \psi_L(1)]\, \lambda(1) \qquad \text{for all} \quad b \in B.$$

So $\delta(b)$ is directly proportional to some column of C. Similarly, $\lambda(a) = \delta(1)\, C[\psi_R(1), a]$, and so λ and some row of C are proportional. This strong dependence between the structure matrix and the action depended heavily on the fact that $C(b, a) \neq 0$ for all $a \in A$ and for all $b \in B$. In the cases where C has some zero entries, the dependence weakens accordingly. Fact 2.23 and Remark 2.24 are due to Dennis Allen, Jr.

Exercises and Extensions

X2.1. Let J be a null $\mathcal{J}$ class of a semigroup S. Prove that $N_J(S)$ has a nontrivial combinatorial ideal.

X2.2. Let J be a regular $\mathcal{J}$ class of S.

(a) Define the equivalence relation $\equiv$ on S as follows:

$$s_1 \equiv s_2 \quad \text{iff} \quad \begin{cases} s_1, s_2 \in F(J), \\ s_1, s_2 \in J \quad \text{and} \quad s_1 \mathcal{H} s_2, \\ s_1, s_2 \in S - (J \cup F(J)) \quad \text{and} \quad s_1 = s_2. \end{cases}$$

Prove $\equiv$ is a congruence.

(b) Let φ be the homomorphism associated with $\equiv$, and let $J' = \varphi(J)$, a $\mathcal{J}$ class of $\varphi(S)$. Prove that $RM_{J'}[\varphi(S)] \cong RLM_J(S)$ and $LM_{J'}[\varphi(S)] \cong LLM_J(S)$.

X2.3. Let J be a regular $\mathcal{J}$ class of S. Prove $GGM_J(S) \cong RM[LM_J(S)] \cong LM[RM_J(S)]$.

The original idea of the homomorphisms developed in this section is due to Schützenberger [2]. The Schützenberger-Preston representation for regular semigroups [Proposition 2.6(c)] follows from Schützenberger [2] and Preston [3].

These ideas were applied by Krohn and Rhodes [4], where they introduce GM, RLM, LLM, and GGM semigroups. Proposition 2.12

is an adaptation by Krohn and Rhodes [4] and Rhodes [5] of the Schützenberger-Preston representation, which is important in the study of the complexity of finite semigroups in the next chapter.

3. Decomposition of Homomorphisms

This section is concerned with various decompositions of homomorphisms on finite semigroups. We prove that a semigroup has a functorially minimal γ homomorphic image as well as minimal homomorphic images with respect to other properties of homomorphisms. We prove that, if G is a group and S a monoid, then the projection homomorphism $G \text{ w } S \twoheadrightarrow S$ is an $\mathscr{L}$ homomorphism; also, if C is a combinatorial semigroup and S is any finite semigroup, then $C \text{ w } S \twoheadrightarrow S$ is a $\gamma(\mathscr{H})$ homomorphism.

This calculus of homomorphisms is somewhat detailed; all the results presented here are needed in the next sections. As an alternative, the reader, instead of reading this section directly, might prefer to go on to Chapter 9 and refer back to this section when necessary.

Let P be a partition on a semigroup S. Recall the definition of a P homomorphism (Definition 1.8), and recall the existence of S^P, the minimal homomorphic image with respect to $\mathscr{P}(S, P)$ (Fact 1.9).

3.1 Remark. (a) Let $\mathscr{P}$ be a property of the homomorphisms of S. If Q is a congruence on S, let $(\eta Q) : S \twoheadrightarrow S/Q$ be the natural homomorphism. Let $Q' = \text{lub}\{Q : Q \text{ is a congruence on } S \text{ and } ((\eta Q), S/Q) \in \mathscr{P}\}$. Then S has a minimal homomorphic image with respect to $\mathscr{P}$ iff $((\eta Q'), S/Q') \in \mathscr{P}$. In this case, $((\eta Q'), S/Q')$ is the minimal homomorphic image. Thus, if $\mathscr{P}$ is nonempty, then S has a minimal homomorphic image with respect to $\mathscr{P}$ if $((\eta Q_1), S/Q_1), ((\eta Q_2), S/Q_2) \in \mathscr{P}$ implies $((\eta Q), S/Q) \in \mathscr{P}$, where $Q = \text{lub}\{Q_1, Q_2\} \equiv Q_1 \vee Q_2$.

(b) Let P be a partition on S. Let φ be a homomorphism of S, and let Q be the congruence induced on S by φ. Then φ is a P homomorphism iff $Q \subseteq P$.

(c) If φ is a P homomorphism, then φ separates the P classes of S [i.e., $\varphi(P_i) \cap \varphi(P_j) = \phi$]. Thus, φ induces a partition P' on $\varphi(S)$ defined by $\varphi(s_1) \equiv \varphi(s_2) \pmod{P'}$ iff $s_1 \equiv s_2 \pmod{P}$. The P classes of S and the P' classes of $\varphi(S)$ are in $1:1$ correspondence under φ.

Hence, if $x \equiv y \pmod{P'}$, then $\varphi^{-1}(x) \cup \varphi^{-1}(y)$ is contained in one P class of S. If P is a congruence, then P' is a congruence.

3.2 Proposition. (a) Let S be a semigroup with a partition P. Let $S \xrightarrow{\varphi_1} T \xrightarrow{\varphi_2} U$ be given. Then $\varphi_2\varphi_1$ is a P homomorphism iff φ_1 is a P homomorphism and φ_2 is a P' homomorphism.

(b) Let α denote any of $\mathscr{J}$, $\mathscr{L}$, $\mathscr{R}$, or $\mathscr{H}$. Let $\varphi : S \twoheadrightarrow T$. Then $S^\alpha \twoheadrightarrow T^\alpha$ for each α, and the diagram

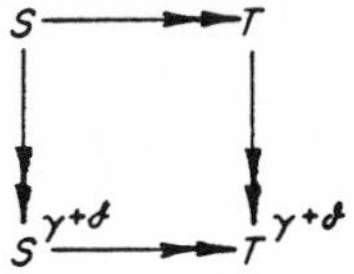

commutes.

PROOF. (a) Let φ_1 be a P homomorphism, and φ_2 be a P' homomorphism. Let $x, y \in S$ be such that $x \not\equiv y \pmod{P}$. Then $\varphi_1(x) \not\equiv \varphi_1(y) \pmod{P'}$. Since φ_2 is a P' homomorphism, $\varphi_2\varphi_1(x) \neq \varphi_2\varphi_1(y)$, so that $\varphi_2\varphi_1$ is a P homomorphism. Conversely, let $\varphi_2\varphi_1$ be a P homorphism, and let $x \not\equiv y \pmod{P}$. Then $\varphi_2\varphi_1(x) \neq \varphi_2\varphi_1(y)$, so that $\varphi_1(x) \neq \varphi_1(y)$, and φ_1 is a P homomorphism. Thus, P' is induced on T. Suppose $\varphi_1(a) \not\equiv \varphi_1(b) \pmod{P'}$. Then $a \not\equiv b \pmod{P}$ and $\varphi_2\varphi_1(a) \neq \varphi_2\varphi_1(b)$, and so φ_2 is a P' homomorphism.

(b) The proof rests upon the fact that homomorphisms take α classes into α classes. Let $\alpha = \mathscr{J}$. Let Q and Q_J be the congruences on S such that $S/Q \cong T$ and $S/Q_J \cong S^{\mathscr{J}}$. Let $J_1, \ldots, J_n$ be the $\mathscr{J}$ classes of T. The sets $\varphi^{-1}(J_i)$, $i = 1, \ldots, n$ are disjoint and partition S. Call this partition P. Then $Q \subseteq P$ and $Q_J \subseteq P$, so that $Q \vee Q_J \subseteq P$. Note that $s_1 \equiv s_2 \pmod{P}$ iff $\varphi(s_1) \mathscr{J} \varphi(s_2)$. Consider the commutative diagram

$$\begin{array}{ccc} S & \xrightarrow{\ \varphi\ } & T = S/Q \\ \downarrow & & \downarrow \theta \\ S/Q_J = S^{\mathscr{J}} & \xrightarrow{\ \eta\ } & S/(Q \vee Q_J) \end{array}$$

Suppose $\theta\varphi(s_1) = \theta\varphi(s_2)$. Then $s_1 \equiv s_2 \bmod (Q \vee Q_J)$, so that $s_1 \equiv s_2 \pmod{P}$. This implies $\varphi(s_1) \mathscr{J} \varphi(s_2)$ in T. Therefore, θ is a $\mathscr{J}$ homomorphism, and there exists a homomorphism $\psi : S/Q \vee Q_J \twoheadrightarrow T^{\mathscr{J}}$. Then $\psi\eta : S^{\mathscr{J}} \twoheadrightarrow T^{\mathscr{J}}$. The proofs for $\mathscr{L}$, $\mathscr{R}$, and $\mathscr{H}$ are similar. ∎

3.3 Fact. Let T be a subsemigroup of S. Let $\alpha(S)$ and $\alpha(T)$ be any of the relations $\mathscr{J}$, $\mathscr{R}$, $\mathscr{L}$, or $\mathscr{H}$ of S and T, respectively.

(a) If $t_1, t_2 \in T$ are regular elements of T and α is any of $\mathscr{R}$, $\mathscr{L}$, or $\mathscr{H}$, then $t_1 \alpha(T)\, t_2$ iff $t_1 \alpha(S)\, t_2$.

(b) If S is a union of groups, then the result of (a) holds for $\alpha = \mathscr{J}$ also.

(c) Let $\varphi : S \underset{\alpha(S)}{\twoheadrightarrow} S'$. Then φ restricted to T is an $\alpha(T)$ homomorphism when (1) S is a union of groups and α is any of $\mathscr{J}$, $\mathscr{L}$, $\mathscr{R}$, or $\mathscr{H}$; or (2) T is regular and α is any of $\mathscr{L}$, $\mathscr{R}$, or $\mathscr{H}$.

PROOF. (a) Refer to the proof of Fact 7.1.19.

(b) Let $t_1 \mathscr{J}(S)\, t_2$, and let J be the $\mathscr{J}$ class of S containing t_1 and t_2. J is a simple semigroup so that $T \cap J$ is simple (see Exercises 7.1.17–7.1.18). Since a simple semigroup has only one $\mathscr{J}$ class, $t_1 \mathscr{J}(T \cap J)\, t_2$, which implies $t_1 \mathscr{J}(T)\, t_2$. Clearly, the converse holds.

(c) This follows from (a) and (b). ∎

3.4 Proposition. Let $\varphi : S \twoheadrightarrow T$, and suppose T is an *RLM*, *LLM*, *GGM*, or *GM* semigroup with distinguished ideal I. Let J be the minimal $\mathscr{J}$ class of S such that $\varphi(J) = I^{\#}$. Then $RLM_J(S) \twoheadrightarrow T$, $LLM_J(S) \twoheadrightarrow T$, $GGM_J(S) \twoheadrightarrow T$, or $GM_J(S) \twoheadrightarrow T$, respectively.

PROOF. Let T be an *RLM* semigroup. Let $s_1, s_2 \in S$, and suppose $RLM_J(s_1) = RLM_J(s_2)$. We must show that $\varphi(s_1) = \varphi(s_2)$.

For each $x \in J$, either $xs_1 \mathscr{L} xs_2$ in J or both xs_1 and $xs_2 \in B(J)$. In the latter case, by the minimality of J we have $\varphi(xs_1) = \varphi(xs_2) = 0$. If $xs_1 \mathscr{L} xs_2$, then $xs_1 \mathscr{H} xs_2$. Thus, $\varphi(xs_1) \mathscr{H} \varphi(xs_2)$, and, since $I^{\#}$ is combinatorial, this implies $\varphi(xs_1) = \varphi(xs_2)$. Hence, for all $i \in I$, we have $i\varphi(s_1) = i\varphi(s_2)$. Hence, $\varphi(s_1) = \varphi(s_2)$, since T is an *RLM* semigroup. The dual argument proves the assertion if T is an *LLM* semigroup.

Let T be a *GGM* semigroup. Let $s_1, s_2 \in S$ such that $GGM_J(s_1) = GGM_J(s_2)$. For all $x_1, x_2 \in J$, either $x_1 s_1 x_2 = x_1 s_2 x_2$ in J or both $x_1 s_1 x_2$ and $x_1 s_2 x_2 \in B(J)$. Thus, $\varphi(x_1 s_1 x_2) = \varphi(x_1 s_2 x_2)$ for all $x_1, x_2 \in J$ or $i_1 \varphi(s_1)\, i_2 = i_1 \varphi(s_2)\, i_2$ for all $i_1, i_2 \in I$. Since T is *GGM*, this implies $i_1 \varphi(s_1) = i_1 \varphi(s_2)$ for all $i_1 \in I$, which in turn implies $\varphi(s_1) = \varphi(s_2)$.

Let T be a *GM* semigroup. If $T = \{0\}$, the assertion is trivially satisfied. Suppose $T \neq \{0\}$. Then $I^{\#}$ is regular noncombinatorial. Now the proof is identical to the GGM case. ▮

3.5 Definition. Let S be a semigroup.

(a) Let $Q(GM) = glb\{Q' : Q'$ is a congruence on S and S/Q' a GM semigroup$\}$. Define $S^{GM} = S/Q(GM)$. Note that S^{GM} is not necessarily a GM semigroup.

(b) Let $Q(GGM) = glb\{Q' : Q'$ a congruence and S/Q' a GGM semigroup$\}$. Define $S^{GGM} = S/Q(GGM)$. Note that S^{GGM} is not necessarily a GGM semigroup.

(c) Let $Q(RLM) = glb\{Q' : Q'$ a congruence and S/Q' an RLM semigroup$\}$. Define $S^{RLM} = S/Q(RLM)$. S^{RLM} is not an RLM semigroup in general.

(d) Define $S^{LLM} = S/Q(LLM)$ dually.

3.6 Fact. Let $J_1, \ldots, J_n$ be the regular $\mathscr{J}$ classes of S.

(a) $S^{GM} \cong (GM_{J_1} \times \cdots \times GM_{J_n})\, \Delta(S)$.

(b) $S^{GGM} \cong (GGM_{J_1} \times \cdots \times GGM_{J_n})\, \Delta(S)$.

(c) $S^{RLM} \cong (RLM_{J_1} \times \cdots \times RLM_{J_n})\, \Delta(S)$.

(d) $S^{LLM} \cong (LLM_{J_1} \times \cdots \times LLM_{J_n})\, \Delta(S)$.

PROOF. (a) Let Q_i be the congruence on S induced by GM_{J_i}, $i = 1, \ldots, n$. Then Proposition 3.4 says that, for each congruence Q, where S/Q is GM, there exists an i such that $Q_i \subseteq Q$. Thus, it is easy to see that $Q(GM) = Q_1 \cap \cdots \cap Q_n$, so that $S^{GM} \cong (GM_{J_1} \times \cdots \times GM_{J_n})\, \Delta(S)$.

The proofs of (b)–(d) are nearly identical. ▮

3.7 Fact. Let α be any of GM, GGM, RLM, or LLM.

(a) $S \overset{\psi}{\twoheadrightarrow} T$ implies $S^{\alpha} \twoheadrightarrow T^{\alpha}$, and the following diagram commutes:

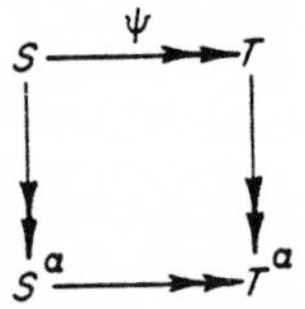

(b) If T is a subsemigroup of S, then $T^{\alpha} \mid S^{\alpha}$.

(c) $T \mid S$ implies $T^{\alpha} \mid S^{\alpha}$.

PROOF. (a) We will prove (a) for $\alpha = GM$. The other proofs are similar. Let $K_1, \ldots, K_m$ be the regular noncombinatorial $\mathcal{J}$ classes of T. Then $T^{GM} = (GM_{K_1} \times \cdots \times GM_{K_m}) \Delta(T)$. By Proposition 3.4, there exists a distinct noncombinatorial regular $\mathcal{J}$ class, J_i, of S such that $GM_{J_i}(S) \overset{\varphi_i}{\twoheadrightarrow} GM_{K_i}(T)$ for each $i = 1, \ldots, m$. So we have $\varphi_i GM_{J_i} = GM_{K_i}\psi$ for each $i = 1, \ldots, m$. Let $J_1, \ldots, J_m, \ldots, J_n$ be all the regular noncombinatorial $\mathcal{J}$ classes of S. Then $S^{GM} = (GM_{J_1} \times \cdots \times GM_{J_n}) \Delta(S)$. Let Π be the direct product of the first m projection maps of $GM_{J_1}(S) \times \cdots \times GM_{J_n}(S)$. Then

$$
\begin{aligned}
(\varphi_1 \times \cdots \times \varphi_m)\Pi : S^{GM} &\twoheadrightarrow (\varphi_1 GM_{J_1} \times \cdots \times \varphi_m GM_{J_m}) \Delta(S) \\
&= (GM_{K_1}\psi \times \cdots \times GM_{K_m}\psi) \Delta(S) \\
&= (GM_{K_1} \times \cdots \times GM_{K_m}) \Delta\psi(S) \\
&= T^{GM} \qquad \text{since} \quad \psi(S) = T.
\end{aligned}
$$

Clearly, the diagram commutes.

(b) We now show that, if T is a subsemigroup of S, then $T^{GM} \mid S^{GM}$. Let $\psi : S \twoheadrightarrow S^{GM}$. We must show that $\psi(T) \twoheadrightarrow T^{GM}$. Let $S^{GM} = S/Q_S(GM)$ and $T^{GM} = T/Q_T(GM)$. Then it is sufficient to show that, for $t_1, t_2 \in T$, if $t_1 \not\equiv t_2 \pmod{Q_T(GM)}$, then $t_1 \not\equiv t_2 \pmod{Q_S(GM)}$. Suppose $t_1 \not\equiv t_2 \pmod{Q_T(GM)}$. Then there exists a $\mathcal{J}$ class J of T and $x_1, x_2 \in J$ such that either (i) $x_1t_1x_2, x_1t_2x_2 \in J$, and $x_1t_1x_2 \neq x_1t_2x_2$; (ii) $x_1t_1x_2 \in J$ and $x_1t_2x_2 \notin J'$, the $\mathcal{J}$ class of S containing J; or (iii) $x_1t_1x_2 \in J$, and $x_1t_2x_2 \in J' - J$. In cases (i) and (iii), $x_1t_1x_2, x_1t_2x_2 \in J'$ and $x_1t_1x_2 \neq x_1t_2x_2$, so that $t_1 \not\equiv t_2 \pmod{Q_S(GM)}$. In case (ii), $x_1t_1x_2 \in J'$, and $x_1t_2x_2 \notin J'$, so that again $t_1 \not\equiv t_2 \pmod{Q_S(GM)}$.

Therefore, if $T \subseteq S$, then $T^{GM} \mid S^{GM}$. The proof for $\alpha = GGM$ is identical, and the proofs for $\alpha = RLM$ and LLM proceed along similar lines and use Fact 3.3(a).

(c) This follows immediately from (a) and (b). ∎

3.8 Definition. Let α be one of the relations $\mathcal{J}$, $\mathcal{L}$, $\mathcal{R}$, or $\mathcal{H}$. We say $\varphi : S \twoheadrightarrow T$ is an α' *homomorphism* (and write $\varphi : S \xrightarrow[\alpha']{} \!\!\!\twoheadrightarrow T$) iff, for all regular elements $s_1, s_2 \in S$, $\varphi(s_1) = \varphi(s_2)$ implies $s_1 \,\alpha\, s_2$.

Let $\mathcal{P}(S, \alpha')$ be the collection of (φ, T) such that φ is an α' homomorphism. Notice that, if S is regular, $\mathcal{P}(S, \alpha') = \mathcal{P}(S, \alpha)$.

3.9 Fact. (a) $\varphi : S \xrightarrow[\alpha]{} T$ implies $\varphi : S \xrightarrow[\alpha']{} T$ for $\alpha = \mathscr{R}$, $\mathscr{H}$, $\mathscr{L}$, or $\mathscr{J}$. $\varphi : S \xrightarrow[\alpha']{} T$ and S_1 a subsemigroup of S implies φ restricted to S_1 is an α' map for $\alpha = \mathscr{L}, \mathscr{R}$, or $\mathscr{H}$.†

(b) Let $\varphi : S \xrightarrow[\alpha']{} T$, and let J be a regular $\mathscr{J}$ class of S. Then $\varphi(J)$ is a $\mathscr{J}$ class of T, and J is the unique regular and unique minimal $\mathscr{J}$ class of S contained in $\varphi^{-1}[\varphi(J)]$.

(c) S has a minimal homomorphic image with respect to $\mathscr{P}(S, \alpha')$, denoted $S \twoheadrightarrow S^{\alpha'}$, for $\alpha = \mathscr{L}$, $\mathscr{R}$, and $\mathscr{H}$.† $(S^{\alpha'})^{\alpha'} = S^{\alpha'}$. In fact (1) $S^{\mathscr{L}'} \cong S^{RLM}$, (2) $S^{\mathscr{R}'} \cong S^{LLM}$, and (3) $S^{\mathscr{H}'}$ is induced by $Q(LLM) \cap Q(RLM)$.

Thus, in particular, S an RLM semigroup implies that $S = S^{\mathscr{L}'}$, and S an LLM semigroup implies that $S = S^{\mathscr{R}'}$.

(d) $\varphi : S \xrightarrow[\alpha']{} T$ iff s_1, s_2 are regular elements of S and $\varphi(s_1) \mathrel{\alpha} \varphi(s_2)$ imply $s_1 \mathrel{\alpha} s_2$, where $\alpha = \mathscr{L}$, $\mathscr{R}$, $\mathscr{H}$, or $\mathscr{J}$. Hence, $\varphi\psi$ is an α' homomorphism iff φ and ψ are α' homomorphisms.

(e) $S \mid T$ implies $S^{\alpha'} \mid T^{\alpha'}$ for $\alpha = \mathscr{L}$ or $\mathscr{R}$.†

PROOF. (a) The first statement of (a) is obvious. For the second, let s_1, s_2 be regular elements of S such that $\varphi(s_1) = \varphi(s_2)$. Since φ is an α' homomorphism, $s_1 \mathrel{\alpha} s_2$ in S. But by Fact 3.3(a), $s_1 \mathrel{\alpha} s_2$ in S_1. Thus, φ restricted to S_1 is an α' homomorphism.

(b) Since φ is a homomorphism, there is a $\mathscr{J}$ class $J_1 \subseteq T$ such that $\varphi(J) \subseteq J_1$, and J_1 is regular, since J is regular. Then by Fact 7.2.1 $\varphi^{-1}(J_1)$ is a union of $\mathscr{J}$ classes of S with a unique minimal class J' and $\varphi(J') = J_1$. J' is regular, since J_1 is regular, and hence there exist $x \in J$, $x' \in J'$, such that $\varphi(x) = \varphi(x')$. Since φ is an α' map, this implies that $x \mathrel{\alpha} x'$, which in turn implies $x \mathrel{\mathscr{J}} x'$. Thus, $J = J'$. If J'' is any regular $\mathscr{J}$ class of S contained in $\varphi^{-1}[\varphi(J)]$, then the same argument shows that $J = J''$. Thus, J is the unique regular $\mathscr{J}$ class in $\varphi^{-1}[\varphi(J)]$.

(c) Let $J_1, \ldots, J_n$ be the regular $\mathscr{J}$ classes of S. We first show that $\Pi RLM_{J_i} : S \twoheadrightarrow S^{RLM}$ is an $\mathscr{L}'$ homomorphism. Let s_1, $s_2 \in S$ be regular, and suppose $\Pi RLM_{J_i}(s_1) = \Pi RLM_{J_i}(s_2)$. Then $RLM_{J_i}(s_1) = RLM_{J_i}(s_2)$ for each $i = 1, \ldots, n$, and this implies $s_1 \mathrel{\mathscr{J}} s_2$, and hence $s_1 \mathrel{\mathscr{L}} s_2$.

We now show that $S^{RLM} \cong S^{\mathscr{L}'}$. Let $\varphi : S \twoheadrightarrow T$ be an $\mathscr{L}'$ homomorphism, and suppose $\varphi(s_1) = \varphi(s_2)$ and that s_1, s_2 are regular.

† These results have recently been shown to be valid for $\alpha = \mathscr{J}$, also.

We must show $RLM_{J_i}(s_1) = RLM_{J_i}(s_2)$ for all $i = 1,..., n$. That is, for each J_i and all $x \in J_i$, either (1) $xs_1, xs_2 \in J_i$ and $xs_1 \mathscr{L} xs_2$, or (2) $xs_1, xs_2 \in B(J_i)$.

Suppose $xs_1 \in J_i$ and $xs_2 \notin J_i$. Then $xs_2 \in B(J_i)$, and, since $\varphi(xs_1) = \varphi(xs_2)$, $\varphi(J_i) \cap \varphi[B(J_i)] \neq \phi$. But this is a contradiction, since J_i is the unique minimal $\mathscr{J}$ class of $\varphi^{-1}[\varphi(J_i)]$ by (b). Thus, for each $i = 1,..., n$, $RLM_{J_i}(s_1) = RLM_{J_i}(s_2)$. The proof for $\mathscr{R}$ is similar, and the proof for $\mathscr{H}$ follows easily.

(d) Let $\varphi : S \xrightarrow[\alpha']{} \!\!\!\!\rightarrow T$, let $s_1, s_2 \in S$ be regular, and suppose $\varphi(s_1) \alpha \varphi(s_2)$. Then, by (b), $s_1 \mathscr{J} s_2$. Let $s_1, s_2 \in J$. Then, since φ is an α' homomorphism and J is regular, φ acts like an α homomorphism on J. From Fact 1.13, the α classes of S in J are in $1:1$ correspondence with the α classes of T in $\varphi(J)$. Hence, $s_1 \alpha s_2$. The converse is clear. The remaining assertion is easy to verify.

(e) This follows immediately from (c) and Fact 3.7. ∎

3.10 Definition. Let S be a semigroup. Let $\mathscr{P}(S, \gamma)$ be the collection of (φ, T) such that $\varphi : S \twoheadrightarrow T$ and φ is a γ homomorphism, i.e., φ restricted to any subgroup is $1:1$ (Definition 1.12). We write $\varphi : S \xrightarrow[\gamma]{} \!\!\!\!\rightarrow T$ if $\varphi \in \mathscr{P}(S, \gamma)$.

We now proceed to prove that S has a minimal homomorphic image with respect to $\mathscr{P}(S, \gamma)$.

3.11 Lemma. Let I be a maximal proper ideal of S, and suppose there exists $\varphi \in \mathscr{P}(S, \gamma)$ such that $\varphi(S) = \varphi(I)$. Let ψ be any homomorphism on S. Then ψ is a γ homomorphism iff ψ restricted to I is a γ homomorphism.

PROOF. Assume ψ restricted to I is a γ homomorphism. Let G be a nontrivial group in $S - I$. (If there are none, we are done.) Let $H = \varphi(G)$, and let S_1 be the subsemigroup $\varphi^{-1}(H)$. Then $\varphi(S_1) = H$, and, since $\varphi(I) = \varphi(S)$, we have $\varphi(S_1 \cap I) = H$; $S_1 \cap I$ is a nonempty ideal of S_1. Consider φ as the restriction of φ to S_1 from this point on. Let $K(S_1)$ denote the kernel of S_1. $K(S_1) \subseteq I$, and, since kernels go onto kernels under epimorphisms and a group is its own kernel, $\varphi[K(S_1)] = H$. Proposition 7.2.5 now tells us that each maximal subgroup of $K(S_1)$ is mapped onto H by φ. But, since φ is $1:1$ on subgroups, H is isomorphic to each maximal subgroup of $K(S_1)$.

Let G_1 be one of the maximal subgroups of $K(S_1)$, and let e be the identity of G_1. Define the map $g \to ege$ from G to $K(S_1)$. By Rees theorem and the properties of translations of 0-simple semigroups, $ege \in G_1$. Furthermore, this map is $1:1$, since, if $ege = ehe$, then $\varphi(g) = \varphi(h)$, which implies $g = h$.

Now $G_1 \subseteq I$, and so ψ is $1:1$ on G_1 by assumption. Let $g_1 \neq g_2 \in G$. Then $eg_1e \neq eg_2e \in G_1$. Thus, $\psi(eg_1e) \neq \psi(eg_2e)$, which implies $\psi(g_1) \neq \psi(g_2)$. Hence, $\psi \in \mathscr{P}(S, \gamma)$. The converse is clear. ∎

3.12 Proposition. A semigroup S has a minimal homomorphic image with respect to $\mathscr{P}(S, \gamma)$ which is denoted by S^γ and constructed as follows. If S is combinatorial, then $S^\gamma = \{0\}$. If S is noncombinatorial, let $J_1, \ldots, J_k$ be the k distinct noncombinatorial $\mathscr{J}$ classes of S, ordered so that, if $i < j$, then $J_j \nleqslant J_i$. Now we define a homomorphism ψ on S inductively. Let $\psi_1 = GM_{J_1}$. Now assume ψ_j has been defined. If ψ_j is $1:1$ on subgroups of J_{j+1}, let $\psi_{j+1} = \psi_j$. Otherwise, let $\psi_{j+1} = (\psi_j \times GM_{J_{j+1}})\Delta$. Let $\psi = \psi_k$. Then $\psi(S) = S^\gamma$.

PROOF. Since GM_{J_i} is $1:1$ on subgroups of J_i, $i = 1, \ldots, k$, it is trivial to verify that $(\psi, \psi(S)) \in \mathscr{P}(S, \gamma)$. Now, if $\varphi : S \xrightarrow[\gamma]{} T$, we must show that $\varphi(s_1) = \varphi(s_2)$ implies that $\psi(s_1) = \psi(s_2)$. Equivalently, we will show by induction that $\varphi(s_1) = \varphi(s_2)$ implies that $\psi_j(s_1) = \psi_j(s_2)$ for $1 \leqslant j \leqslant k$.

Suppose $\varphi(s_1) = \varphi(s_2)$. Let $x_1, x_2 \in J_1$. We first show that $x_1s_1x_2 \in J_1$ if and only if $x_1s_2x_2 \in J_1$. If $x_1s_1x_2 \in J_1$ and $x_1s_2x_2 \notin J_1$, then $x_1s_2x_2 \in B(J_1)$, and, since $\varphi(x_1s_1x_2) = \varphi(x_1s_2x_2)$, this implies $\varphi(J_1) \subseteq \varphi[B(J_1)]$, i.e., $\varphi[J_1 \cup B(J_1)] = \varphi[B(J_1)]$. But then by Lemma 3.11 a homomorphism that is a γ homomorphism on $B(J_1)$ is a γ homomorphism on $J_1 \cup B(J_1)$. $B(J_1)$ is combinatorial, and so the zero homomorphism is a γ homomorphism on $B(J_1)$, and hence is $1:1$ on subgroups of J_1, a contradiction. Thus, $x_1s_1x_2 \in J_1$ if and only if $x_1s_2x_2 \in J_1$ for all $x_1, x_2 \in J_1$.

We next show that, if $x_1s_1x_2 \in J_1$ (and $x_1s_2x_2 \in J_1$), then $x_1s_1x_2 = x_1s_2x_2$. By Rees theorem and the properties of translations of 0-simple semigroups (see Fact 7.2.14), $x_1s_1x_2 \mathscr{H} x_1s_2x_2$, and there exist $z_1, z_2, a_1, a_2 \in J_1$, so that $b_1 = z_1x_1s_1x_2z_2$ and $b_2 = z_1x_1s_2x_2z_2$ lie in the same maximal subgroup of J_1, and $a_1b_1a_2 = x_1s_1x_2$, $a_1b_2a_2 = x_1s_2x_2$. Now, since φ is $1:1$ on subgroups and $\varphi(b_1) = \varphi(b_2)$, we have $b_1 = b_2$, so that $x_1s_1x_2 = x_1s_2x_2$. Thus, for all $x_1, x_2 \in J_1$, either $x_1s_1x_2$ and $x_1s_2x_2$ both lie in $B(J_1)$, or $x_1s_1x_2 = x_1s_2x_2 \in J_1$. Hence, $\psi_1(s_1) = \psi_1(s_2)$.

Now by induction assume that $\varphi(s_1) = \varphi(s_2)$ implies $\psi_i(s_i) = \psi_i(s_2)$ for all i such that $1 \leqslant i \leqslant j < k$. We must show that $\varphi(s_1) = \varphi(s_2)$ implies $\psi_{j+1}(s_1) = \psi_{j+1}(s_2)$. If ψ_j is $1:1$ on subgroups of J_{j+1}, then $\psi_j = \psi_{j+1}$, and the induction step proceeds trivially. Hence, $\psi_{j+1} = (\psi_j \times GM_{J_{j+1}})\,\Delta$. Let $x_1, x_2 \in J_{j+1}$. We now show that $x_1s_1x_2 \in J_{j+1}$ if and only if $x_1s_2x_2 \in J_{j+1}$. Assume $x_1s_1x_2 \in J_{j+1}$ and $x_1s_2x_2 \notin J_{j+1}$. Then $x_1s_2x_2 \in B(J_{j+1})$, and $B(J_{j+1})$ is a maximal ideal of $B(J_{j+1}) \cup J_{j+1}$, and so $\varphi[B(J_{j+1})] = \varphi[B(J_{j+1}) \cup J_{j+1}]$. Then, by Lemma 3.11, since ψ_j is $1:1$ on the subgroups of $B(J_{j+1})$, ψ_j is $1:1$ on the subgroups of J_{j+1}, a contradiction. Then we can proceed as before to prove that $\psi_{j+1}(s_1) = \psi_{j+1}(s_2)$. ▮

3.13 Remark. (a) $S \xrightarrow[\gamma]{} \!\!\!\!\to T$ implies $S \xrightarrow[\gamma]{}\!\!\!\!\to T \xrightarrow[\gamma]{}\!\!\!\!\to S^{\gamma}$.

(b) Let $\varphi : S \xrightarrow[\gamma]{}\!\!\!\!\to T$, and let J be a regular $\mathscr{J}$ class of S. Then φ is $1:1$ when restricted to any $\mathscr{H}$ class of S in J. Thus, if S is a regular semigroup, then φ is a γ homomorphism iff φ is a $\gamma(\mathscr{H})$ homomorphism. This follows from 7.1.16.

(c) Let S be a 0-simple semigroup. Then $S^{\gamma} = GM(S)$.

(d) Let R be a subsemigroup of S, and let $\varphi : S \xrightarrow[\gamma]{}\!\!\!\!\to T$. Then φ restricted to R is a γ homomorphism. Thus, $R \xrightarrow[\gamma]{}\!\!\!\!\to \varphi(R) \xrightarrow[\gamma]{}\!\!\!\!\to R^{\gamma}$, and so $R^{\gamma} \mid S^{\gamma}$.

(e) It is *false* that $S \mid T$ implies that $S^{\gamma} \mid T^{\gamma}$, since $T \twoheadrightarrow S$ does not imply that $S^{\gamma} \mid T^{\gamma}$. Let $G \neq \{1\}$ be a group, and let $U_2 = \{0\}^I$ (see 5.2). Let $S = G \times U_2$. Then $S \to S^{\gamma}$ is given by $(g, x) \to (g, 0)$, and so $S^{\gamma} \cong G$. $G \times \{0\}$ is an ideal of S, and $S/(G \times \{0\}) \cong G^0$, so that $(G^0)^{\gamma} = G^0$ does not divide $S^{\gamma} = G$.

3.14 Definition. Define $\mathscr{P}(S, \gamma, \mathscr{J})$ to be the collection of (φ, T) such that φ is both a γ homomorphism and a $\mathscr{J}$ homomorphism. We call φ a $(\gamma + \mathscr{J})$ homomorphism.

3.15 Proposition. S has a minimal homomorphic image with respect to $\mathscr{P}(S, \gamma, \mathscr{J})$, denoted $S \twoheadrightarrow S^{\gamma+\mathscr{J}}$. We have two formulas for $S^{\gamma+\mathscr{J}}$.

(a) Let $\varphi : S \twoheadrightarrow S^{\gamma}$ and $\psi : S \twoheadrightarrow S^{\mathscr{J}}$. Let $(\varphi \times \psi)\,\Delta : S \to S^{\gamma} \times S^{\mathscr{J}}$. Then $(\varphi \times \psi)\,\Delta : S \twoheadrightarrow S^{\gamma+\mathscr{J}}$. Thus, $S^{\gamma+\mathscr{J}} \leqslant\!\leqslant S^{\gamma} \times S^{\mathscr{J}}$.

(b) Let S be regular. Then $S^{\gamma+\mathscr{J}} = S^{GGM}$.

(c) Let S be regular. $S \twoheadrightarrow T$ implies $S^{\gamma+\mathcal{J}} \twoheadrightarrow T^{\gamma+\mathcal{J}}$, and the following diagram commutes:

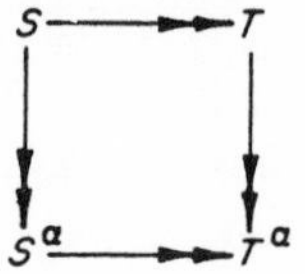

(d) Let S and T be regular. $T \mid S$ implies $T^{\gamma+\mathcal{J}} \mid S^{\gamma+\mathcal{J}}$.

PROOF. (a) Clearly, $(\varphi \times \psi)\Delta$ is a $(\gamma + \mathcal{J})$ homomorphism. Conversely, let Q_1 and Q_2 be the congruences on S induced by φ and ψ, respectively. Then $Q_1 \cap Q_2$ is induced by $(\varphi \times \psi)\Delta$. If $\theta : S \twoheadrightarrow S/Q$ is any $(\gamma + \mathcal{J})$ homomorphism, then $Q \subseteq Q_1$ and $Q \subseteq Q_2$, so that $Q \subseteq Q_1 \cap Q_2$. Thus, $(\varphi \times \psi)\Delta(S)$ is the minimal homomorphic image with respect to $\mathcal{P}(S, \gamma, \mathcal{J})$.

(b) Let $J_1, \ldots, J_n$ be the $\mathcal{J}$ classes of S. Since GGM_{J_i} is $1 : 1$ on subgroups of J_i, $i = 1, \ldots, n$, ΠGGM_{J_i} is a γ homomorphism. It is easy to see by the definition of GGM_J that ΠGGM_{J_i} is a $\mathcal{J}$ homomorphism. Hence, ΠGGM_{J_i} is a $(\gamma + \mathcal{J})$ homomorphism.

Let $(\varphi, T) \in \mathcal{P}(S, \gamma, \mathcal{J})$. We must show that, if $\Pi GGM_{J_i}(s_1) \neq \Pi GGM_{J_i}(s_2)$, then $\varphi(s_1) \neq \varphi(s_2)$. Now $\Pi GGM_{J_i}(s_1) \neq \Pi GGM_{J_i}(s_2)$ iff there exist a $\mathcal{J}$ class J of S and $x_1, x_2 \in J$ so that either (1) $x_1 s_1 x_2 \in J$ and $x_1 s_2 x_2 \notin J$, or (2) both $x_1 s_1 x_2$ and $x_1 s_2 x_2$ lie in J and $x_1 s_1 x_2 \neq x_1 s_2 x_2$. In case (1), since φ is a $\mathcal{J}$ homomorphism, we have $\varphi(x_1 s_1 x_2) \neq \varphi(x_1 s_2 x_2)$, and so $\varphi(s_1) \neq \varphi(s_2)$. In case (2), $x_1 s_1 x_2 \mathcal{H} x_1 s_2 x_2$, and so $\varphi(x_1 s_1 x_2) \neq \varphi(x_1 s_2 x_2)$, since φ is a $\gamma(\mathcal{H})$ homomorphism by Remark 3.13(b). Thus $\varphi(s_1) \neq \varphi(s_2)$. (c) and (d) follow immediately from Fact 3.7. ∎

3.16 Remark. Notice that, if S is regular, then

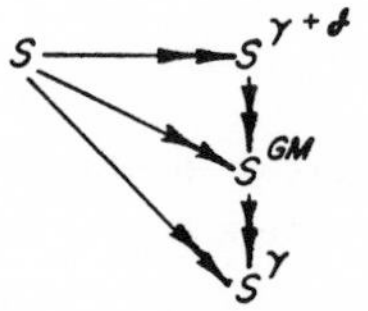

and the diagram commutes. This follows from the fact that $S^{\gamma+\mathcal{J}} \cong S^{GGM} \twoheadrightarrow S^{GM}$ and the way S^{γ} was defined.

The following proposition is very important in Chapter 9.

3.17 Proposition. Let S and $T_1, \ldots, T_n$ be union of groups semigroups, and let α be either $\gamma + \mathscr{J}$, $\mathscr{R}$, or $\mathscr{L}$. Then, if $S \leqslant\leqslant T_1 \times \cdots \times T_n$, and $\theta_i : T_i \twoheadrightarrow T_i^{\alpha}$, so that $\theta = \theta_1 \times \cdots \times \theta_n : T_1 \times \cdots \times T_n \twoheadrightarrow T_1^{\alpha} \times \cdots \times T_n^{\alpha}$, then $\theta(S) = S^{\alpha}$ and $S^{\alpha} \leqslant\leqslant T_1^{\alpha} \times \cdots \times T_n^{\alpha}$.

PROOF. θ restricted to S is an α homomorphism, since α homomorphisms are preserved under direct product and restriction. Thus, $\theta(S) \twoheadrightarrow S^{\alpha}$. On the other hand, let $p_i : S \twoheadrightarrow T_i$, so that $\theta_i p_i : S \twoheadrightarrow T_i^{\alpha}$. Now, since $S \twoheadrightarrow T_i$, we have $S^{\alpha} \xrightarrow{\varphi_i} T_i^{\alpha}$, so that, if $\psi : S \twoheadrightarrow S^{\alpha}$, then $\varphi_i \psi = \theta_i p_i$. Now

$$\begin{aligned}\theta(S) &= (\theta_1 p_1 \times \cdots \times \theta_n p_n)\, \Delta(S)\\ &= (\varphi_1 \psi \times \cdots \times \varphi_n \psi)\, \Delta(S)\\ &= (\varphi_1 \times \cdots \times \varphi_n)\, \Delta\psi(S)\\ &= (\varphi_1 \times \cdots \times \varphi_n)\, \Delta S^{\alpha}.\end{aligned}$$

Therefore, $S^{\alpha} \twoheadrightarrow \theta(S)$, and so $\theta(S) = S^{\alpha} \leqslant\leqslant T_1^{\alpha} \times \cdots \times T_n^{\alpha}$. ∎

3.18 Lemma. (a) Let $\varphi_i : S_i \twoheadrightarrow T_i$ for $i = 1, 2$ be a γ (respectively α') homomorphism, where $\alpha = \mathscr{L}$, $\mathscr{R}$, or $\mathscr{H}$. Then $\varphi = (\varphi_1 \times \varphi_2) : S_1 \times S_2 \twoheadrightarrow T_1 \times T_2$ is a γ (respectively α') homomorphism.

(b) Let $S = S^{\gamma}$ and $S = S^{\alpha'}$, where $\alpha = \mathscr{L}$, $\mathscr{R}$, or $\mathscr{H}$. Then $S = \{0\}$.

PROOF. (a) The proof of the statement for α' homomorphisms is easy. Let φ_i be a γ homomorphism for $i = 1, 2$, and G be a subgroup of $S_1 \times S_2$ such that $\varphi(G) = \{e\}$, where $e = (e_1, e_2)$ is an idempotent of $T_1 \times T_2$. Then $S_1' = \varphi_1^{-1}(e_1)$ and $S_2' = \varphi_1^{-1}(e_2)$ are combinatorial subsemigroups of S_1 and S_2, respectively, since φ_i is a γ map, and $G \subseteq S_1' \times S_2'$. Hence, $|G| = 1$.

(b) $S = S^{\gamma}$ implies $S = \{0\}$ or S has no nonzero combinatorial ideals, for, if I were a combinatorial ideal, $S \twoheadrightarrow S/I$ would be a γ map. Hence, let I be a 0-minimal ideal of S. Then $I - \{0\}$ is a regular $\mathscr{J}$ class of S whose $\mathscr{H}$ classes have order $\geqslant 2$. Now consider the congruence $\equiv$ on S defined by

$$s_1 \equiv s_2 \quad \text{iff} \begin{cases} s_1 = s_2 & \text{for all } s_1, s_2 \in S \\ s_1 \mathscr{H} s_2 & \text{if } s_1, s_2 \in I. \end{cases}$$

Then the homomorphism $S \twoheadrightarrow S/\equiv$ is a proper α' homomorphism for $\alpha = \mathscr{R}$, $\mathscr{L}$, and $\mathscr{H}$, contradicting $S = S^{\alpha'}$. Thus, $S = \{0\}$. ∎

The following proposition yields a weaker form of Theorem 1.14, the main result of Sect. 1. It is included here because the method of proof is essentially different from that used for Theorem 1.14.

3.19 Proposition. Let $\varphi : S \twoheadrightarrow T$, and let α be one of $\mathscr{L}$, $\mathscr{R}$, or $\mathscr{H}$. Then $\varphi = \varphi_n \cdots \varphi_1$, where $\varphi_1, \varphi_3, \ldots$ are γ homomorphisms and $\varphi_2, \varphi_4, \ldots$ are α' homomorphisms.

PROOF. Consider

$$S \twoheadrightarrow S^{\gamma} \twoheadrightarrow (S^{\gamma})^{\alpha'} \twoheadrightarrow (S^{\gamma\alpha'})^{\gamma} \twoheadrightarrow \cdots \twoheadrightarrow \{0\}. \tag{3.1}$$

Lemma 3.18(b) assures that this series reaches $\{0\}$. Let $\tilde{\Delta} : S \to S \times T$ be given by $\tilde{\Delta}(s) = (s, \varphi(s))$, and consider

$$S \xrightarrow{\tilde{\Delta}} S \times T \underset{\gamma}{\twoheadrightarrow} S^{\gamma} \times T \underset{\alpha'}{\twoheadrightarrow} (S^{\gamma})^{\alpha'} \times T \underset{\gamma}{\twoheadrightarrow} \cdots \twoheadrightarrow \{0\} \times T \cong T, \tag{3.2}$$

where the maps on T are the identity maps, and the maps on the first factor are given by the series (3.1). That these homomorphisms are alternately γ and α' homomorphisms follows from Lemma 3.18(a). Then the restriction of the series (3.2) to the images of S is

$$S \twoheadrightarrow S \underset{\gamma}{\twoheadrightarrow} S_1 \underset{\alpha'}{\twoheadrightarrow} S_2 \underset{\gamma}{\twoheadrightarrow} \cdots \twoheadrightarrow T, \tag{3.3}$$

since the restriction of a γ map is a γ map and the restriction of an α' map is a α' map. The composed homomorphism of (3.3) is $\varphi : S \twoheadrightarrow T$. ∎

3.20 Corollary. Let $\varphi : S \twoheadrightarrow T$ be an MPE (see Sect. 1). Then φ is either a γ homomorphism or an $\mathscr{H}'$ homomorphism. [In fact, from Sect. 1 we know that φ is either a $\gamma(\mathscr{H})$ homomorphism or an $\mathscr{H}$ homomorphism.]

3.21 Definition. Let $\varphi : S \twoheadrightarrow T$. Let $\{T_i : i = 1, \ldots, n\}$ be the set of all semigroups such that $S \xrightarrow{\alpha_i} T_i$ and $T_i \underset{\gamma}{\xrightarrow{\beta_i}} T$, where $\beta_i \alpha_i = \varphi$. Define the semigroup $T^{\gamma^{-1}}$ by

$$T^{\gamma^{-1}} = (\alpha_1 \times \cdots \times \alpha_n)\, \Delta(S).$$

3.22 Fact. (a) $T^{\gamma^{-1}} \twoheadrightarrow T$ is a γ homomorphism.

(b) Let T' be any semigroup such that $\varphi : S \twoheadrightarrow T' \xrightarrow[\gamma]{} T$. Then $T^{\gamma^{-1}} \xrightarrow[\gamma]{} T' \xrightarrow[\gamma]{} T$.

PROOF. (a) Using the notation of the definition, define $\theta : T_1 \times \cdots \times T_n \twoheadrightarrow T \times \cdots \times T$ by $\theta = \beta_1 \times \cdots \times \beta_n$. By Lemma 3.18, θ is a γ homomorphism since each β_i is. We prove $\theta(T^{\gamma^{-1}}) \cong T$, and this proves (a), since the restriction of a γ homomorphism is a γ homomorphism.

Any element of $T^{\gamma^{-1}}$ is of the form $[\alpha_1(s),\ldots, \alpha_n(s)]$, and so $\theta[\alpha_1(s),\ldots, \alpha_n(s)] = [\beta_1\alpha_1(s),\ldots, \beta_n\alpha_n(s)] = [\varphi(s),\ldots, \varphi(s)]$. Then identify $(t,\ldots, t)$ with $t \in T$. Thus, $\theta : T^{\gamma^{-1}} \xrightarrow[\gamma]{} T$.

(b) This is obvious from the definition of $T^{\gamma^{-1}}$. ∎

3.23 Remark. Let $\alpha = \mathscr{R}$, $\mathscr{L}$, or $\mathscr{H}$. Then, if $\varphi : S \twoheadrightarrow T$, $T^{\alpha'^{-1}}$ can be defined in exactly the same manner, and it has the same type of properties as $T^{\gamma^{-1}}$. This is true because α' goes under restriction [Fact 3.9(a)], because an element of a direct product of semigroups is regular iff each component is, and because two elements of a direct product are α-equivalent iff their components are. These concepts will be useful in the following sections. Note that $T^{\gamma^{-1}}$ and $T^{\alpha'^{-1}}$ make sense only with respect to a semigroup S and a homomorphism $\varphi : S \twoheadrightarrow T$.

The following proposition is the important source of $\mathscr{L}$, $\gamma(\mathscr{H})$, and γ homomorphisms.

3.24 Proposition. (a) Consider $(X_2, G) \text{ w } (X_1, S)$ where G is a left simple semigroup (e.g., a group) and S is a monoid. Let $p_1 : (X_2, G) \text{ w } (X_1, S) \twoheadrightarrow S$ be the natural projection homomorphism. Then p_1 is an $\mathscr{L}$ homomorphism.

(b) Consider $(X_2, C) \text{ w } (X_1, S)$ where C is a combinatorial semigroup and S is an arbitrary finite semigroup. Then

$$p_1 : (X_2, C) \text{ w } (X_1, S) \twoheadrightarrow S$$

is a $\gamma(\mathscr{H})$ homomorphism.

PROOF. (a) $(X_2, G) \text{ w } (X_1, C) \cong F(X_1, G) \times_Y S$, where $Y(1)$ is the identity endomorphism of G. Since $F(X_1, G) \cong G \times \cdots \times G$ ($|X_1|$ times), $F(X_1, G)$ is left simple, because left simple is preserved under direct products.

Hence, it is enough to prove the statement for $G \times_Y S \twoheadrightarrow S$, where $Y(1)$ is the identity endomorphism of G.

Let $p_1(s_2, s_1) = p_1(t_2, t_1)$ (i.e., $s_1 = t_1$). We have to show that, for all $s_2, t_2 \in G$, $(s_2, s_1) \mathscr{L} (t_2, s_1)$. Since G is left simple, $s_2 \mathscr{L} t_2$, and so, if $s_2 \neq t_2$, there exist $x, y \in G$ such that $xs_2 = t_2$ and $yt_2 = s_2$. Then $(x, 1)(s_2, s_1) = (x^1 s_2, s_1) = (t_2, s_1)$, and $(y, 1)(t_2, s_1) = (s_2, s_1)$, i.e., $(s_2, s_1) \mathscr{L} (t_2, s_1)$.

(b) We first show that $(X_2, C) \text{ w } (X_1, S) \xrightarrow{p_1} S$ is a γ homomorphism. $(X_2, C) \text{ w } (X_1, S) \cong F(X_1, C) \times_Y S$, and $F(X_1, C) \cong C \times \cdots \times C$ ($|X_1|$ times), and so $F(X_1, C)$ is combinatorial. Hence, it is sufficient to prove the statement for $C \times_Y S$. Let G be a subgroup of $C \times_Y S$, and let $G_1 = p_1(G)$, a subgroup of S. We know from the proof of Lemma 5.3.6 that there exists a subgroup $G_2 \subseteq C$ such that G is an extension of G_2 by G_1. But $G_2 = \{1\}$, since C is combinatorial, and so $G \cong G_1$. Therefore, p_1 is a γ homomorphism.

Now, to prove that p_1 is a $\gamma(\mathscr{H})$ homomorphism, it is enough to show that, whenever $(c_1, s) \mathscr{H} (c_2, s)$, then $c_1 = c_2$. Let H be the $\mathscr{H}$ class containing (c_1, s) and (c_2, s), and let $\mathscr{G}(H)$ be the (right) Schützenberger group of H. Then $\mathscr{G}(H)$ acts upon H in triangular form. For, let $\pi \in \mathscr{G}(H)$, and let $\bar{\pi} = (d_1, s_1)$ be a representative of π in $C \times_Y S$ (see the Notation of Fact 7.2.10). Then, for $(c, s) \in H$, we have

$$(c, s)\,\pi = (c, s)(d_1, s_1) = (c^s d_1, ss_1).$$

Thus, it is easy to see that $\pi \in C^1 \text{ w } S^1$, and so $\mathscr{G}(H) \subseteq C^1 \text{ w } S^1$. But C^1 is combinatorial, and so the projection map $q_1 : C^1 \text{ w } S^1 \twoheadrightarrow S^1$ is a γ homomorphism. Therefore, $q_1[\mathscr{G}(H)] \cong \mathscr{G}(H)$, and so the kernel of q_1 restricted to $\mathscr{G}(H)$ is exactly the identity of $\mathscr{G}(H)$.

Now let π be the element of $\mathscr{G}(H)$ such that $(c_1, s)\,\pi = (c_2, s)$. π acts like the identity on the first coordinate, and so $\pi \in \ker q_1$. Therefore, π is the identity of $\mathscr{G}(H)$, and $c_1 = c_2$. ∎

3.25 Fact. (a) If S is combinatorial, then $S^\gamma = \{0\}$ and $S^{GM} = \{0\}$. Thus, if S^γ is combinatorial, then $S^\gamma = \{0\}$, and, if S^{GM} is combinatorial then $S^{GM} = \{0\}$.

(b) Let S be a GGM semigroup with distinguished $\mathscr{J}$ class J. Let φ be a homomorphism on S which is $1:1$ on a maximal subgroup of J. Then φ is $1:1$ on S.

(c) S a GM semigroup implies $S^\gamma = S$.

(d) S a GGM semigroup implies $RLM(S) = S^{RLM} = S^{\mathscr{L}'}$.

(e) If S is both a GM and an RLM semigroup, then $S = \{0\}$.

PROOF. (a) $S^{GM} = \{0\}$ when S is combinatorial, since $GM_J(S) = \{0\}$ whenever J is a combinatorial $\mathscr{J}$ class. Hence, $S^{GM} = \{0\}$. The last statements follow because $(S^{\gamma})^{\gamma} = S^{\gamma}$ and $(S^{GM})^{GM} = S^{GM}$.

(b) Notice that φ is $\gamma(\mathscr{H})$ when restricted to J. Let $s_1 \neq s_2 \in S$. Since S is a GM semigroup, there exists $j_1, j_2 \in J$ such that $j_1 s_1 j_2 \neq j_1 s_2 j_2$. Then either (1) $j_1 s_1 j_2 = 0 \neq j_1 s_2 j_2$, or (2) $j_1 s_1 j_2 \mathscr{H} j_1 s_2 j_2$ in J. In case 1, since $\varphi(J) \neq \{0\}$ we have $\varphi(j_1 s_1 j_2) \neq \varphi(j_1 s_2 j_2)$. In case 2, since φ is $\gamma(\mathscr{H})$ on J we have $\varphi(j_1 s_1 j_2) \neq \varphi(j_1 s_2 j_2)$. Thus, in both cases, $\varphi(s_1) \neq \varphi(s_2)$ and φ is $1:1$ on S.

(c) Apply (b) and the construction of S^{γ}.

(d) $RLM(S) = RLM(S)^{RLM} = RLM(S)^{\mathscr{L}'}$. Thus it will suffice to prove that $S \twoheadrightarrow RLM(S)$ is an $\mathscr{L}'$ homomorphism, for $S \underset{\mathscr{L}'}{\twoheadrightarrow} T$ implies $S^{\mathscr{L}'} = T^{\mathscr{L}'}$.

From the proof of Proposition 2.17, $S \subseteq (G^0, G^0) \text{ w } (B^0, S') \cong F(B^0, G^0) \times_Y S'$, where $S' = \{f \in F_R(B^0) : f(0) = 0\}$, and $p_1 : F(B^0, G^0) \times_Y S' \twoheadrightarrow S'$ when restricted to S yields $p_1 : S \twoheadrightarrow RLM(S)$. Define the subsemigroup $T = \{(f_2, f_1) \in F(B^0, G^0) \times_Y S' : (b)f_1 = 0 \text{ iff } f_2(b) = 0\}$. We will show that p_1 restricted to T is an $\mathscr{L}$ homomorphism so that $p_1 : S \twoheadrightarrow RLM(S)$ is an $\mathscr{L}'$ homomorphism, since $S \subseteq T$.

We must show that any two elements of T with the same first coordinate are $\mathscr{L}$ equivalent. Let $(f_2, f_1), (g_2, f_1) \in T$. Let $B_1 = \{b \in B^0 : (b)f_1 \neq 0\}$. Define $(h_1, \bar{1})$ and $(h_2, \bar{1}) \in T$ by

$$(b)\bar{1} = \begin{cases} b & \text{if } b \in B_1 \\ 0 & \text{if } b \notin B_1 \end{cases}$$

$$h_1(b) = \begin{cases} g_2(b) f_2(b)^{-1} & \text{if } b \in B_1 \\ 0 & \text{if } b \notin B_1 \end{cases}$$

$$h_2(b) = \begin{cases} f_2(b) g_2(b)^{-1} & \text{if } b \in B_1 \\ 0 & \text{if } b \notin B_1 \end{cases}$$

Then $(h_1, \bar{1})(f_2, f_1) = (g_2, f_1)$ and $(h_2, \bar{1})(g_2, f_1) = (f_2, f_1)$ so $(f_2, f_1) \mathscr{L} (g_2, f_1)$ in T.

(e) Since S is a GM semigroup, either its distinguished $\mathscr{J}$ class is noncombinatorial or $S = \{0\}$. But since S is RLM, it cannot have a noncombinatorial distinguished $\mathscr{J}$ class. Hence $S = \{0\}$. ∎

3.26 Notation. The triple (J, G, N) of a semigroup S denotes that J is a $\mathscr{J}$ class of S, G is a maximal subgroup of J, and N is a normal subgroup of G (written $N \lhd G$).

3.27 Definition. (a) Let S be a semigroup, and let (J, G, N) belong to S. Represent J^0 by $\mathscr{M}^0(G; A, B; C)$. Define the semigroup $S/(J, G, N)$ by $S/(J, G, N) = [S/F(J)]/\equiv$, where $\equiv$ is the identity congruence on $[S/F(J)] - J$ and is given by the homomorphism $(g, a, b) \to (\omega(g), a, b)$ on J [see Proposition 7.2.5(c)], where $\omega : G \twoheadrightarrow G/N$ is the natural group homomorphism. It is easy to verify that, if any other coordinate system (with group G) $\mathscr{M}^0(G; A, B; P)$ is chosen for J^0, then the congruence $\equiv$ is unaltered. In other words, $S/(J, G, N)$ is independent of the coordinate system (with group G) chosen.

$S/(J, G, N)$ has a unique regular 0-minimal ideal, namely, the image of $J \cup F(J)$.

(b) Let S be a semigroup, and let (J, G, N) belong to S. Define the semigroup $GM(J, G, N)$ to be $GM[S/(J, G, N)]$.

(c) Let T be a semigroup with a unique regular 0-minimal ideal I. Let $\varphi : S \twoheadrightarrow T$ be given. Then we define *a kernel of* φ to be (J, G, N), where J is the unique minimal regular $\mathscr{J}$ class of S contained in $\varphi^{-1}(I^{\#})$, G is any maximal subgroup of J, and N is the (group) kernel of φ restricted to G [i.e., if 1 is the identity of G, then $N = \{g \in G : \varphi(g) = \varphi(1)\}$].

3.28 Proposition. Let φ be a homomorphism of a semigroup S onto a GM semigroup, and let (J, G, N) be a kernel of φ. Let $\mathscr{P}$ be the property of homomorphisms of S defined by

$$\mathscr{P} = \{(\psi, T) : \psi(J) \cap \psi[F(J)] = \phi \text{ and the group kernel of } \psi \text{ restricted to } G \text{ is contained in } N\}.$$

Then $(\varphi, \varphi(S))$ is the minimal homomorphic image of S with respect to $\mathscr{P}$.

PROOF. Notice first that $(\varphi, \varphi(S)) \in \mathscr{P}$. Now we must show that, if $\varphi(s_1) \neq \varphi(s_2)$ for some $s_1, s_2 \in S$, then $\psi(s_1) \neq \psi(s_2)$ for all $\psi \in \mathscr{P}$. Since $\varphi(S)$ is a GM semigroup with respect to the distinguished ideal $\varphi[J \cup F(J)]$, $\varphi(s_1) \neq \varphi(s_2)$ implies there exists $j_1, j_2 \in J$ such that $\varphi(j_1 s_1 j_2) \neq \varphi(j_1 s_2 j_2)$. If one, say $\varphi(j_1 s_1 j_2)$, equals zero, then $j_1 s_1 j_2 \in F(J)$, whereas $j_1 s_2 j_2 \in J$, so that $\psi(j_1 s_1 j_2) \neq \psi(j_1 s_2 j_2)$ for all $\psi \in \mathscr{P}$, which implies $\psi(s_1) \neq \psi(s_2)$.

So suppose $\varphi(j_1 s_1 j_2)$, $\varphi(j_1 s_2 j_2) \in \varphi(J)$. Then $j_1 s_1 j_2 \mathscr{H} j_1 s_2 j_2$, and so there exists $x, y \in S^1$ such that $x j_1 s_1 j_2 y$, $x j_1 s_2 j_2 y \in G$ and $\varphi(x j_1 s_1 j_2 y) \neq \varphi(x j_1 s_2 j_2 y)$. Let $j_1' = x j_1$, $j_2' = j_2 y$. Then $(j_1' s_1 j_2') N \neq (j_1' s_2 j_2') N$. Let K be the kernel of ψ restricted to G. Since $K \subseteq N$, we have $(j_1' s_1 j_2') K \neq (j_1' s_2 j_2') K$. In other words, $\psi(j_1' s_1 j_2') \neq \psi(j_1' s_2 j_2')$, and so $\psi(s_1) \neq \psi(s_2)$. ▌

3.29 Remark. An immediate corollary of Proposition 3.28 is the following: If (J, G, N) is a kernel of $\varphi : S \twoheadrightarrow T$, where T is a GM semigroup, then $GM(J, G, N) \cong T$.

Thus, for every GM homomorphic image of a semigroup S, there is an internal coding, namely, one of the kernels (J, G, N) of the homomorphism. And, no matter what kernel is picked, the GM semigroup can be recovered, for it is isomorphic to $GM(J, G, N)$.

3.30 Fact. (a) Let S be a semigroup, and let G_1 and G_2 be two maximal subgroups of S. Let e_1 and e_2 be the identities of G_1 and G_2, respectively. If $G_1 \mathscr{L} G_2$, then $G_1 = e_1 G_2$ and $G_2 = e_2 G_1$, and the map $G_i \twoheadrightarrow e_j G_i = G_j$, $i, j = 1, 2$, is an isomorphism. If $G_1 \mathscr{R} G_2$, then $G_1 = G_2 e_1$ and $G_2 = G_1 e_2$, and the map $G_i \twoheadrightarrow G_i e_j = G_j$, $i, j = 1, 2$, is an isomorphism.

(b) Let (J, G_1, N_1) belong to S, and consider $\varphi : S \twoheadrightarrow GM(J, G_1, N_1)$. Let $G_2 \mathscr{J} G_1$, and take the kernel of φ with respect to G_2, (J, G_2, N_2). Then $N_1 \cong N_2$. If $G_1 \mathscr{R} G_2$, then $N_1 = N_2 e_1$ and $N_2 = N_1 e_2$. If $G_1 \mathscr{L} G_2$, then $N_1 = e_1 N_2$ and $N_2 = e_2 N_1$.

PROOF. (a) Trivial.

(b) $N_1 = \{g_1 \in G_1 : \varphi(g_1) = \varphi(e_1)\}$, and $N_2 = \{g_2 \in G_2 : \varphi(g_2) = \varphi(e_2)\}$. Suppose $G_1 \mathscr{R} G_2$. Then $e_1 e_2 = e_2$ and $e_2 e_1 = e_1$. Consider $N_1 e_2$. Let $h \in N_1 e_2$; $h = g e_2$, with $g \in N_1$. $\varphi(h) = \varphi(g e_2) = \varphi(e_1)\varphi(e_2) = \varphi(e_2)$, and so $N_1 e_2 \subseteq N_2$. Similarly, $N_2 e_1 \subseteq N_1$, and so $N_1 e_2 = N_2$ and $N_2 e_1 = N_1$. When $G_1 \mathscr{L} G_2$, a similar proof yields the assertion. ▌

3.31 Definition. Given (J_1, G_1, N_1) of S, let $\theta : S \twoheadrightarrow RLM[GM(J_1, G_1, N_1)]$. Let J_2 be a regular $\mathscr{J}$ class of S with a maximal subgroup G_2. Let $1 \in G_2$ be the identity of G_2. We define

$$\begin{aligned}\ker[(J_1, G_1, N_1), (J_2, G_2)] &\equiv \{g \in G_2 : \theta(g) = \theta(1)\} \\ &= \text{the group kernel of } \theta \text{ restricted to } G_2 .\end{aligned}$$

Clearly, $\ker[(J_1, G_1, N_1), (J_2, G_2)] \lhd G_2$.

3.32 Remark. Another description of $N_2 = \ker[(J_1, G_1, N_1), (J_2, G_2)]$ can be given. Let X equal the set of $\mathscr{L}$ classes in the image of $J_1 \cup F(J_1)$ in $GM(J_1, G_1, N_1)$. Then G_2 is an operator group for X, i.e., $X \cdot G_2 \subseteq X$ under the definition $x \cdot g = x\theta(g)$, and $x \cdot (g_1 g_2) = (x \cdot g_1) \cdot g_2$. Let $R = X \cdot 1$. (Notice $X \cdot g = R$ for all $g \in G_2$.) G_2 permutes R, i.e., (R, G_2) is a (not necessarily faithful) transformation group. R is called the *range* of G_2.

Now X is the set of identified [under $S \twoheadrightarrow S/(J_1, G_1, N_1) \twoheadrightarrow GM(J_1, G_1, N_1)$] $\mathscr{L}$ classes of J_1^0, and R is the subset of these $\mathscr{L}$ classes which G_2 permutes. Consider the homomorphism φ on G_2 which makes the action of G_2 faithful on R. It is easy to see that $\varphi(G_2) = G_2/N_2$.

Therefore, $N_2 = \ker[(J_1, G_1, N_1), (J_2, G_2)]$ is that portion of G_2 which we can throw away and still know how G_2 acts on its range R in the identified $\mathscr{L}$ classes of J_1^0. These concepts will be used in Chapter 9.

3.33 Fact. Let J^0 be a 0-simple semigroup, and let X be a set. Suppose (X, J^0) is a (not necessarily faithful) transformation semigroup. Let G_1 and G_2 be maximal subgroups of J. Then G_1 and G_2 act on X. Let $R_1 = R_{11} \cup \cdots \cup R_{1n}$ and $R_2 = R_{21} \cup \cdots \cup R_{2m}$ be the ranges and transitive components of G_1 and G_2, respectively. Let $e_1 \in G_1$, $e_2 \in G_2$ be the identities of G_1 and G_2.

(a) If $G_1 \mathscr{L} G_2$, then G_1 and G_2 have the same range and transitive components. Let R be the range (or a transitive component) of G_1, and let $N_1 \lhd G_1$ be such that G_1/N_1 acts faithfully on R. Then G_2/e_2N_1 acts faithfully on R, and vice versa.

(b) If $G_1 \mathscr{R} G_2$, then the ranges and transitive components of G_1 and G_2 are in 1 : 1 correspondence. In fact, $R_2 = R_1e_2 = R_{11}e_2 \cup \cdots \cup R_{1n}e_2$, and $R_1 = R_2e_1 = R_{21}e_1 \cup \cdots \cup R_{2n}e_1$. Let R be the range (or a transitive component) of G_1, and let $N_1 \lhd G_1$ be such that G_1/N_1 acts faithfully on R. Then G_2/N_1e_2 acts faithfully on Re_2, and vice versa.

PROOF. (a) $R_1 = XG_1 = Xe_1G_2 \subseteq XG_2 = R_2$. Similarly, $R_2 \subseteq R_1$, so that $R_1 = R_2$. Let R_{1i} be a transitive component of G_1. Then there exists $x \in R_{1i}$ such that $R_{1i} = xG_1$. But $xG_1 = xe_1G_2$, and $xe_1 \in R_{1i}$, and so $R_{1i} = (xe_1)G_2$. Thus, every transitive component of G_1 is also a transitive component of G_2, and vice versa.

Let N_2 be the normal subgroup of G_2 which makes G_2 act faithfully on R. Now

$$N_i = \{g \in G_i : rg = r \text{ for all } r \in R\}, \qquad i = 1, 2.$$

Let $h \in e_2 N_1 \subseteq G_2$. Write $h = e_2 g$, $g \in N_1$. $rh = re_2 g = rg = r$ for all $r \in R$, and so $e_2 N_1 \subseteq N_2$. Similarly, $e_1 N_2 \subseteq N_1$, so that $e_2 N_1 = N_2$ and $e_1 N_2 = N_1$.

(b) In this case, $R_1 = XG_1 = XG_2 e_1 = R_2 e_1$, and $R_2 = XG_2 = XG_1 e_2 = R_1 e_2$. Let R_{2i} be a transitive component of G_2. Let $x \in R_1$. Then $xe_2 \in R_2$. Define $R_{1i} = xG_1$ and $R_{2i} = (xe_2)\, G_2$. Now $R_{1i} = xG_1 = xe_1 G_1 = xe_2 e_1 G_1 = (xe_2)\, G_1 = (xe_2)\, G_2 e_1 = R_{2i} e_1$. Similarly, $R_{2i} = R_{1i} e_2$.

Let $N_1 = \{g \in G_1 : rg = r \text{ for all } r \in R\}$, and let $N_2 = \{h \in G_2 : (re_2)\, h = re_2 \text{ for all } r \in R\}$. Then let $h \in N_1 e_2$, so that $h = ge_2$, where $g \in N_1$. Then $(re_2)\, h = rh = rge_2 = re_2$, so that $N_1 e_2 \subseteq N_2$. Similarly, $N_2 e_1 \subseteq N_1$, and so $N_1 e_2 = N_2$ and $N_2 e_1 = N_1$. ∎

Most of the results of this section are from Rhodes [5], Sect. 6. See Rhodes [6] for the relation of these results to the character theory of finite semigroups.

REFERENCES

1. J. Rhodes, A homomorphism theorem for finite semigroups, *Math. Systems Theory* **1**, 289–304 (1967).
2. M. P. Schützenberger, $\bar{\mathscr{D}}$ représentations des demi-groupes, *Compt. Rend. Acad. Sci. Paris* **244**, 1994–1996 (1957).
3. G. B. Preston, Matrix representations of semigroups, *Quart. J. Math. Oxford Ser.* **2**, 169–176 (1958).
4. K. Krohn and J. Rhodes, Complexity of finite semigroups, *Ann. of Math.* (in press).
5. J. Rhodes, Some results on finite semigroups, *J. Algebra* **3**, 471–504 (1966).
6. J. Rhodes, Complexity and characters of finite semigroups (to be submitted to *J. Comb. Theory*).

CHAPTER 9

Axioms for Complexity of Finite Semigroups[†,‡]

KENNETH KROHN
Krohn-Rhodes Research Institute, Washington, D.C.

JOHN L. RHODES[§]
University of California, Berkeley, California
Krohn-Rhodes Research Institute, Berkeley, California

BRET R. TILSON
University of California, Berkeley, California

The purpose of this chapter is to give methods for computing the (group) complexity of a given finite semigroup S or a given reduced finite state sequential machine M. Most of the results presented here are proved only for those machines whose semigroup is a union of groups. However, later papers will extend many methods to arbitrary finite semigroups. Nevertheless, the restricted results presented here go quite deep. This chapter depends heavily upon Chapters 1, 5, 6, 7, and 8.

We present a set of axioms and prove that exactly one function can satisfy them. Then we show that $\#_G$, when restricted to union of groups semigroups, satisfies the axioms. Finally, we use the axioms to develop several different methods for computing $\#_G$.

† The authors wish to thank Yale Zalcstein for his work on an earlier version of this chapter.

‡ This work was sponsored by the United States Air Force, Air Force Systems Command, Contract Number AF 33(615)-3893.

§ Alfred P. Sloan Research Fellow, 1967–1968.

1. The Axioms

1.1 Notation In the following, all semigroups are of finite order. $T \leqslant S$ denotes that T is a subsemigroup of S. We allow $S \leqslant S$. N denotes the set of nonnegative integers.

In this section, $\mathscr{S}$ will be a nonempty collection of finite semigroups closed under homomorphic images. Precisely, $S \in \mathscr{S}$ and $S \twoheadrightarrow T$ implies $T \in \mathscr{S}$.

We observe that S and S_1 isomorphic implies that $S \in \mathscr{S}$ iff $S_1 \in \mathscr{S}$. Also, $\{0\} \in \mathscr{S}$, since $S \twoheadrightarrow \{0\}$ for all S and $\mathscr{S}$. Finally, $S \leqslant\leqslant S_1 \times \cdots \times S_n$ and $S \in \mathscr{S}$ implies $S_j \in \mathscr{S}$ for $j = 1, \ldots, n$ (cf. 8.2.1).

Examples of collections of semigroups satisfying the foregoing are all finite semigroups, all regular finite semigroups, all finite semigroups that are a union of groups, and all finite abelian semigroups.

1.2 Definition (the $\mathscr{P}$ Axioms for Complexity). Let $\mathscr{P}$ be a property of semigroups (Definition 7.2.18), and let $\mathscr{S}$ be a collection of semigroups closed under homomorphic images. Then $\theta : \mathscr{S} \to N$ is a *G-complexity function for $\mathscr{S}$ with respect to $\mathscr{P}$* iff θ satisfies the following three axioms.

AXIOM I. Let $S \leqslant\leqslant S_1 \times \cdots \times S_n$. Then $\theta(S) = \max\{\theta(S_i) : i = 1, \ldots, n\}$.

AXIOM II. (Fundamental Lemma of Complexity). Let I be a combinatorial ideal of S.
Then $\theta(S) = \theta(S/I)$; $\theta(\{0\}) = 0$.

AXIOM III. Let $S \neq \{0\}$ be a GM semigroup. Then

$$\theta(S) = \begin{cases} \theta[RLM(S)] + 1 & \text{if } S \in \mathscr{P} \\ \theta[RLM(S)] & \text{if } S \notin \mathscr{P}. \end{cases}$$

1.3 Proposition. Let $\mathscr{S}$ and $\mathscr{P}$ be as just described. Then there exists at most one G-complexity function for $\mathscr{S}$ with respect to $\mathscr{P}$.

PROOF. Let θ_1 and θ_2 be G-complexity functions for $\mathscr{S}$ with respect to $\mathscr{P}$. Let S be a semigroup of smallest order in $\mathscr{S}$ such that

$$\theta_1(S) \neq \theta_2(S).$$

By Axiom II, $S \neq \{0\}$. Now, by Lemma 8.2.19, either (1) S has a UMPE; or (2) $S \leqslant\leqslant S_1 \times \cdots \times S_n$, where $| S_k | < | S |$ for $k = 1,\ldots, n$. Case 2 is impossible, since, by Axiom I,

$$\theta_j(S) = \max\{\theta_j(S_i) : i = 1,\ldots, n\} \qquad \text{for} \quad j = 1, 2,$$

and, by definition of S, $\theta_1(S_i) = \theta_2(S_i)$ for $i = 1,\ldots, n$. Thus, S has a UMPE, and so by Lemma 8.2.19 either S is a GM semigroup or S has a nonzero combinatorial ideal, I. The latter is impossible, since, by Axiom II, $\theta_j(S) = \theta_j(S/I)$ for $j = 1, 2$ and $\theta_1(S/I) = \theta_2(S/I)$ by definition of S.

Thus, S is a GM semigroup. Note that $| RLM(S)| < | S |$ when S is GM. Then $\theta_1[RLM(S)] = \theta_2[RLM(S)]$, and so, in either case of Axiom III, we have $\theta_1(S) = \theta_2(S)$, a contradiction. ▮

2. The Theorem

Uniqueness of a G-complexity function being assured by Proposition 1.3, we now concern ourselves with existence. The theorem of this section characterizes in several ways the G-complexity function for $\mathscr{S}$ with respect to $\mathscr{P}$, where $\mathscr{S}$ is the collection of all union of groups semigroups and $\mathscr{P}$ is the collection of all GM semigroups.

We begin by reviewing union of groups semigroups. *Throughout this section we assume all semigroups are union of groups.* Refer to Definition 7.2.23 and Proposition 7.2.24 for many results.

2.1 Summary of Results of Section 8.3 for Union of Groups Semigroups. (a) $\alpha = \alpha'$ for $\alpha = \mathscr{J}, \mathscr{R}, \mathscr{L}, \mathscr{H}$, and they all go under restriction.

(b) $S^{\mathscr{L}} = S^{RLM}$, $S^{\gamma+\mathscr{J}} = S^{GGM}$.

(c) Proposition 8.3.17 holds for $\gamma+\mathscr{J}$ and $\mathscr{L}$ (an important tool).

(d) $S^{\mathscr{J}}$ is a combinatorial semigroup, since $\mathscr{J}$ is a congruence when S is a union of groups.

2.2 Definition. A series $S_1 \twoheadrightarrow S_2 \twoheadrightarrow S_3 \twoheadrightarrow \cdots$ is said to *map onto* a series $T_1 \twoheadrightarrow T_2 \twoheadrightarrow T_3 \twoheadrightarrow \cdots$ iff there exist epimorphisms $S_i \twoheadrightarrow T_i$ for all $i = 1, 2, 3,\ldots$.

2.3 Remark. Let α and β be two operators on S such that $(S^\alpha)^\alpha = S^\alpha$ and $(S^\beta)^\beta = S^\beta$ (e.g., γ, $\gamma + \mathscr{J}$, $\mathscr{L}$, $\mathscr{J}$, GGM, etc.). Consider an alternating $\alpha - \beta$ series for S:

$$S \twoheadrightarrow S^\alpha \twoheadrightarrow (S^\alpha)^\beta \twoheadrightarrow S^{\alpha\beta\alpha} \twoheadrightarrow \cdots.$$

If an epimorphism in the series fails to be proper (proper means not $1:1$), then the series is constant thereafter. For, suppose $(T^\alpha)^\beta = T^\alpha$. Then $T^\alpha = (T^\alpha)^\alpha = T^{\alpha\beta\alpha}$, and $T^\alpha = T^{\alpha\beta} = (T^{\alpha\beta\alpha})^\beta$, etc.

We now define several integer-valued functions on the collection of semigroups that are unions of groups. The theorem of this section proves that they are all equal.

2.4 Definition. Let $S \in \mathscr{S}$, the collection of all union of groups semigroups.

(a) Define $\theta_a : \mathscr{S} \to N$ by $\theta_a(S) = \#_G(S)$, the G-complexity of S (see Definition 6.1.2).

(b) Consider the series

$$\{0\} \twoheadleftarrow \{0\}^{\gamma^{-1}} \twoheadleftarrow (\{0\}^{\gamma^{-1}})^{\mathscr{L}^{-1}} \twoheadleftarrow [(\{0\}^{\gamma^{-1}})^{\mathscr{L}^{-1}}]^{\gamma^{-1}} \twoheadleftarrow \cdots \twoheadleftarrow S. \qquad \text{(b)}$$

Define $\theta_b : \mathscr{S} \to N$ by $\theta_b(S) =$ the number of proper homomorphisms of the form $T^{\mathscr{L}^{-1}} \twoheadrightarrow T$ in the series.

(c) Consider the series

$$S \twoheadrightarrow S^{\gamma+\mathscr{J}} \twoheadrightarrow (S^{\gamma+\mathscr{J}})^{\mathscr{L}} = S^{(\gamma+\mathscr{J})\mathscr{L}} \twoheadrightarrow S^{(\gamma+\mathscr{J})\mathscr{L}(\gamma+\mathscr{J})} \twoheadrightarrow \cdots. \qquad \text{(c)}$$

Define $\theta_c : \mathscr{S} \to N$ by $\theta_c(S) =$ the number of proper $\mathscr{L}$ homomorphisms in the series.

(d) Consider the series

$$S \twoheadrightarrow S^{GM} \twoheadrightarrow (S^{GM})^{RLM} = S^{GM(RLM)} \twoheadrightarrow S^{GM(RLM)GM} \twoheadrightarrow \cdots. \qquad \text{(d)}$$

Define $\theta_d : \mathscr{S} \to N$ by $\theta_d(S) =$ the number of proper homomorphisms of the form $T \twoheadrightarrow T^{RLM}$ in the series.

(e) Consider the series

$$S \twoheadrightarrow S^\gamma \twoheadrightarrow (S^\gamma)^{\mathscr{L}} = S^{\gamma\mathscr{L}} \twoheadrightarrow S^{\gamma\mathscr{L}\gamma} \twoheadrightarrow \cdots. \qquad \text{(e)}$$

Define $\theta_e : \mathscr{S} \to N$ by $\theta_e(S)$ = the number of proper $\mathscr{L}$ homomorphisms in this series.

(f) Let $(GM)_i$ and $(RLM)_i$ represent GM and RLM semigroups, respectively. Consider all series of the form

$$S \twoheadrightarrow (GM)_1 \twoheadrightarrow (RLM)_1 \twoheadrightarrow (GM)_2 \twoheadrightarrow \cdots. \tag{f}$$

Let the *norm* of each such series be the largest integer n such that $(GM)_n \neq \{0\}$. Define $\theta_f : \mathscr{S} \to N$ by $\theta_f(S)$ = the maximum of the norms of all such series.

(g) Define $\theta_g : \mathscr{S} \to N$ by $\theta_g(S)$ = the largest integer n such that there exist $(J_1, G_1, N_1), \ldots, (J_n, G_n, N_n)$ of S satisfying the three followin gconditions:

(1) $J_1 < J_2 < \cdots < J_n$.
(2) $N_i \neq G_i$, $i = 1, \ldots, n$.
(3) $\ker[(J_i, G_i, N_i), (J_{i+1}, G_{i+1})] \leqslant N_{i+1}$, $i = 1, \ldots, n-1$.

(h) An *expansion* $\mathscr{E}$ *for* S is a function that assigns to each tuple $[(J_1, G_1, N_1), (J_2, G_2)]$, with $J_1 < J_2$ a nonempty set of tuples

$$\{N_{21}^{(\alpha)}, N_{22}^{(\alpha)}, \ldots, N_{2\alpha(2)}^{(\alpha)} : \alpha \in A, \text{ a nonempty set}\},$$

where each

$$N_{2j}^{(\alpha)} \lhd G_2$$

and

$$N_{21}^{(\alpha)} \cap \cdots \cap N_{2\alpha(2)}^{(\alpha)} = N_2 \equiv \ker[(J_1, G_1, N_1), (J_2, G_2)]$$

for each $\alpha \in A$. We write $N_2 \xrightarrow{(\mathscr{E},\alpha)} (N_{21}^{(\alpha)}, \ldots, N_{2\alpha(2)}^{(\alpha)})$. (See Remark 2.27 for examples of expansions.)

Let $\mathscr{E}$ be an expansion of S. Define $\theta_h^{(\mathscr{E})} : \mathscr{S} \to N$ by $\theta_h^{(\mathscr{E})}(S)$ = the largest integer n such that there exists $(J_1, G_1, N_1), \ldots, (J_n, G_n, N_n)$ satisfying the following three conditions:

(1) $J_1 < J_2 < \cdots < J_n$.

(2) Let $K_{i+1} = \ker[(J_i, G_i, N_i), (J_{i+1}, G_{i+1})]$, $i = 1, \ldots, n-1$. Then N_{i+1}, $i = 1, \ldots, n-1$, is a member of some tuple of the expansion $\mathscr{E}$:

$$K_{i+1} \xrightarrow{(\mathscr{E},\alpha)} (K_{(i+1)1}^{(\alpha)}, \ldots, K_{(i+1)\alpha(i+1)}^{(\alpha)}),$$

given by $[(J_i, G_i, N_i), (J_{i+1}, G_{i+1})]$. That is, $N_{i+1} = K^{(\alpha)}_{(i+1)j}$ for some $\alpha \in A$ and some j such that $1 \leqslant j \leqslant \alpha(i+1)$.

(3) $N_i \neq G_i$, $i = 1,..., n$.

(i) A semigroup S is *type I* iff $U_1 = \{r_0, r_1\}^r$ does not divide S^C, the maximal combinatorial image of S. Define $\theta_i : \mathscr{S} \rightarrow N$ by $\theta_i(S) =$ the length of the longest sequence of subsemigroups $(T_1, ..., T_n)$ of S satisfying

(1) T_1 is a noncombinatorial type I semigroup;

(2) T_j is a noncombinatorial type I subsemigroup of $IG(T_{j-1})$ for $i = 2,..., n$; and

(3) $IG(T_n)$ is combinatorial.

(j) Let $S \in \mathscr{S}$. See Curtis and Reiner [1] for the explanation of the following terminology. Let $\mathscr{C}(S)$ denote the character ring of S over $\mathbb{C}$, the complex number field. All representations considered are finite dimensional. Let $\mathscr{R}_1, ..., \mathscr{R}_n$ denote a complete set of inequivalent nonzero irreducible complex representations of S. Let $\chi_j = \chi(\mathscr{R}_j)$, $j = 1,..., n$, be the associated character. Thus, as is well known, $\chi_j \leftrightarrow \mathscr{R}_j$ is a well-defined one-to-one correspondence, and $\chi_1, ..., \chi_n$ form a vector space basis of

$$\mathscr{C}(S) = \left\{\sum_{i=1}^{n} a_i\chi_i : a_i \in \mathbb{C}\right\}.$$

Rhodes [2] proves that $\mathscr{R}_j(S)$ is a GGM semigroup, and thus we can consider the homomorphism $RLM\mathscr{R}_j$ or $S \twoheadrightarrow \mathscr{R}_j(S) \twoheadrightarrow RLM[\mathscr{R}_j(S)]$. Let $L_1, ..., L_n$ be the collection of $\mathscr{L}$ classes contained in the distinguished $\mathscr{J}$ class of $\mathscr{R}_j(S)$. For $s \in S$, let $M(s)$ be the $n \times n$ matrix with coefficients in $\{0, 1\}$ given by

$$M(s)(i,j) = \begin{cases} 1 & \text{iff } L_i s \subseteq L_j \\ 0 & \text{otherwise.} \end{cases}$$

Then clearly $RLM\mathscr{R}_j(s_1) = RLM\mathscr{R}_j(s_2)$ iff $M(s_1) = M(s_2)$. Define $\chi(RLM\mathscr{R}_j)$ by $\chi(RLM\mathscr{R}_j)(s) = \chi[M(s)]$, which equals the number of distinct L_i so that $L_i s \subseteq L_i$. $\chi(RLM\mathscr{R}_j)$ is the character of the matrix representation M, and thus

$$\chi(RLM\mathscr{R}_j) = \sum_{i=1}^{n} m_{ji}\chi_i,$$

where m_{ji} is a nonnegative integer.

Let $A : \mathscr{C}(S) \to \mathscr{C}(S)$ be the linear transformation defined by

$$A(\chi_j) = \chi(RLM\mathscr{R}_j) = \sum_{i=1}^{n} m_{ji}\chi_i .$$

Let $\mathscr{C}(S)^A = \{\chi \in \mathscr{C}(S) : A(\chi) = \chi\}$. Let $B : \mathscr{C}(S)/\mathscr{C}(S)^A \to \mathscr{C}(S)/\mathscr{C}(S)^A$ be the linear transformation induced by A. Rhodes [2] proves that B is nilpotent.

Then define $\theta_j : \mathscr{S} \to N$ by $\theta_j(S) =$ the index of B, with the usual convention that the index is zero iff $\mathscr{C}(S) = \mathscr{C}(S)^A$ and is the smallest *positive* integer n such that $B^n = 0$ otherwise.

2.5 Theorem. Let $\mathscr{S}$ be the collection of all finite semigroups which are union of groups semigroups, and let $\mathscr{P}$ be the collection of all GM semigroups. Then $\#_G$, the group complexity, is the (unique) G-complexity function for $\mathscr{S}$ with respect to $\mathscr{P}$. Writing θ for $\#_G$, we have

$$\theta = \theta_a = \theta_b = \cdots = \theta_j .$$

PROOF. We must prove that $\#_G$ satisfies Axioms I, II, and III (Definition 1.2). We have already shown in Chapter 6 that $\#_G$ satisfies Axiom I (see Fact 6.2.2(c)).

Now by a series of lemmas we prove that $\#_G$ satisfies Axiom III.

2.6 Notation. Recall the definition of the complexity of a semigroup S. In that notation $C(S) = (n, \mathbf{G})$, for example, meant that all minimal wreath product decompositions of S were of length n and had a group as the first coordinate (on the right). Suppose n is even. Then an equivalent notation for $C(S)$ would be $(\mathbf{C}, n)$; if n is odd, $C(S) = (\mathbf{G}, n)$. Thus we introduce $(\mathbf{C}, n)$, $(\mathbf{G}, n)$ and $(\mathbf{C} \vee \mathbf{G}, n)$ as follows:

$$(\mathbf{C} \vee \mathbf{G}, n) \equiv (n, \mathbf{C} \vee \mathbf{G}) \quad \text{for all} \quad n \geqslant 1$$

$$(\mathbf{C}, n) \equiv \begin{cases} (n, \mathbf{G}) & \text{if } n \text{ is even} \\ (n, \mathbf{C}) & \text{if } n \text{ is odd} \end{cases}$$

$$(\mathbf{G}, n) \equiv \begin{cases} (n, \mathbf{C}) & \text{if } n \text{ is even} \\ (n, \mathbf{G}) & \text{if } n \text{ is odd} \end{cases}$$

The change of notation carries with it the partial ordering previously defined.

Finally, we transfer the notion of addition of complexities to the new notation. Thus for example

$$(\mathbf{C}, 1) \oplus (\mathbf{G}, n) = (\mathbf{C}, n+1)$$
$$(\mathbf{C}, 1) \oplus (\mathbf{C}, n) = (\mathbf{C}, 1) \oplus (\mathbf{C} \vee \mathbf{G}, n) = (\mathbf{C}, n)$$
$$(\mathbf{G}, 1) \oplus (\mathbf{C}, n) = (\mathbf{G}, n+1)$$
$$(\mathbf{G}, 1) \oplus (\mathbf{G}, n) = (\mathbf{G}, 1) \oplus (\mathbf{C} \vee \mathbf{G}, n) = (\mathbf{G}, n)$$

2.7 Lemma. Let $S \neq \{0\}$ be a GM semigroup whose distinguished $\mathcal{J}$ class is a union of groups. If $S \neq G^0$ for some group G, then $C(S) = (\mathbf{G}, n)$ for some n. Of course, $C(G^0) = (\mathbf{C} \vee \mathbf{G}, 2)$.

PROOF. Let J be the distinguished $\mathcal{J}$ class of S. J is a union of groups, so by Fact 8.2.23(b), if S has a zero, the zero breaks off, so $S - \{0\}$ is a subsemigroup of S. Thus, in general, $S^{\#} \equiv S^0 - \{0\}$ is a subsemigroup of S. Notice that $S^{\#}$ is a GM semigroup with distinguished ideal J which is the kernel of $S^{\#}$.

We first prove that if $S \mid (X_2, C) \text{ w } (X_1, T)$ where C is a combinatorial semigroup, then $S^{\#} \mid T$. It is sufficient to assume $S \mid C \times_Y T$. Now $S^{\#} \mid C \times_Y T$, so let $C \times_Y T \supseteq S' \xrightarrow{\varphi} S^{\#}$.

Now we claim that $S^{\#} = (S^{\#})^{\gamma} \mid (S')^{\gamma}$. This follows from the construction of the minimal γ-homomorphic image (Proposition 8.3.12) and Proposition 8.3.4. From Remark 8.3.13(d) we have $R \subseteq S$ implies $R^{\gamma} \mid S^{\gamma}$. Combining these facts we see that $S^{\#} \mid (C \times_Y T)^{\gamma}$. But the projection map $p_1 : C \times_Y T \twoheadrightarrow T$ is a γ-homomorphism so $(C \times_Y T)^{\gamma} = T^{\gamma}$ and $S^{\#} \mid T^{\gamma} \mid T$.

Now it is easy to see that $C(S^{\#})$ must "end in a group," that is, $C(S^{\#}) = (\mathbf{G}, n)$ for some $n \geqslant 1$. Assuming otherwise leads to a contradiction. Now either $S = S^{\#}$ or $S = (S^{\#})^0$. But $C(S^{\#}) = C[(S^{\#})^0] = C(S)$ unless $S^{\#}$ is a group. ∎

2.8 Lemma. Let $S \neq \{0\}$ be an RLM semigroup. Then $C(S) = (\mathbf{C}, n)$ for some $n \geqslant 1$. In other words, RLM semigroups "end in a combinatorial."

PROOF. Suppose $C(S) = (\mathbf{G}, n)$ or $(\mathbf{C} \vee \mathbf{G}, n)$. Then there exists a transformation group (X_2, G) and a monoid T such that $S \mid (X_2, G) \text{ w } (X_1, T)$ where $C(T) = (\mathbf{C}, n-1)$. Then $p_1 : (X_2, G) \text{ w } (X_1, T) \twoheadrightarrow T$ is an $\mathcal{L}$-homomorphism; hence an $\mathscr{L}'$-homomorphism. (See Proposition 8.3.24.) Then $T \twoheadrightarrow [(X_2, G) \text{ w } (X_1, T)]^{\mathscr{L}'}$ and $S^{\mathscr{L}'} | [(X_2, G) \text{ w } (X_1, T)]^{\mathscr{L}'}$, so $S^{\mathscr{L}'} | T$. But $S^{\mathscr{L}'} = S^{RLM} = S$, since S is an RLM semigroup. Thus $S | T$, so assuming $C(S) \neq (\mathbf{G}, n)$ for some $n \geqslant 1$ leads to a contradiction. ▮

2.9 Lemma. Let $S \neq \{0\}$ be a GM semigroup which is a union of groups. Then $\#_G(S) = 1 + \#_G[RLM(S)]$.

PROOF. By Lemma 2.7, either S is a group with zero or $C(S) = (\mathbf{G}, n)$ for some $n \geqslant 1$. Suppose $S = G^0$ for some nontrivial group G. Then $C(S) = (\mathbf{C} \vee \mathbf{G}, 2)$ and $\#_G(S) = 1$. $RLM(S) = \{0\}^I$, so $\#_G[RLM(S)] = 0$, and the assertion is proven in this case.

Now assume $C(S) = (\mathbf{G}, n)$ for some $n \geqslant 1$. Let I be the distinguished ideal of S, and let $I^0 = \mathscr{M}^0(G; A, B; C)$. Then by Proposition 8.2.17(b) $S | (G^0, G^0) \text{ w } (B^0, RLM(S))$, so $C(S) \leqslant (\mathbf{C} \vee \mathbf{G}, 2) \oplus C[RLM(S)]$. Since $RLM(S)$ ends in a combinatorial we can obtain the inequality

$$C[RLM(S)] \leqslant C(S) \leqslant (\mathbf{G}, 1) \oplus C[RLM(S)].$$

Further, since $C(S) = (\mathbf{G}, n)$ for some $n \geqslant 1$, it is easy to see that $C(S) = (\mathbf{G}, 1) \oplus C[RLM(S)]$. Then $\#_G(S) = 1 + \#_G[RLM(S)]$. ▮

Thus $\#_G$ satisfies Axiom III. We now prove that $\#_G$ satisfies Axiom II, the Fundamental Lemma of Complexity.

The Fundamental Lemma of Complexity, critical to the theory of complexity, says that if I is a combinatorial ideal of S, then $\#_G(S/I) = \#_G(S)$. We give a proof here for the union of groups semigroup case, and this proof relies heavily upon the properties of that class of semigroups.

At first blush one might attempt to attack this theorem by proving that if I is an ideal of S, then $S | (X_2, I) \text{ w } (X_1, S/I)$. Then the theorem would follow immediately; in fact, the Prime Decomposition theorem itself would be a triviality. However, such a statement is not true. In fact, if I is combinatorial, $S | (X_2, C) \text{ w } (X_1, S/I)$ for *some* combinatorial semigroup C is *not true* in general. (See X.3.1.)

Preparatory to proving the theorem, we investigate the form and complexity of $PP(S^f)^S$, the semigroup of the partial product machine of S^f, in terms of S. (See Definition 5.3.10.)

2.10 *Remark.* Let $S_2 \times_Y S_1$ be a semidirect product of semigroups S_1 and S_2. Recall from Proposition 5.2.30 that

$$(S_2 \times_Y S_1)^f = (S_2^f \times S_1^{rf})\, h^\Gamma 2^\sigma_{S_2 \times S_1} (S_2^{rf} \times S_1^f)^\sigma$$

where

$$h[*, (s_2, s_1)] = (s_2, s_1)$$

and

$$h[(s_2, s_1), (t_2, t_1)] = (Y(s_1)\, t_2, t_1).$$

$PP[(S_2 \times_Y S_1)^f]$ can be written in a similar form. Namely,

$$PP[(S_2 \times_Y S_1)^f] = h_3(PP(S_2^f) \times S_1'^{rf})\, h_2^\Gamma 2^\sigma_{S_2' \times S_1'} (S_2'^{rf} \times PP(S_1^f))^\sigma\, h_1^\Gamma \tag{2.1}$$

where $S_i' = S_i \cup \{c\}$, $i = 1, 2$ and where

(1) h_1 is the identity on $S_2 \times_Y S_1$ and $h_1(c) = (c, c)$

(2) $h_2[*, (s_2, s_1)] = (s_2, s_1)$, $s_i \in S_i'$, $i = 1, 2$

and

$$h_2[(s_2, s_1), (t_2, t_1)] = \begin{cases} (c, c) & \text{if } (t_2, t_1) = (c, c) \\ (t_2, t_1) & \text{if } (s_2, s_1) = (c, c) \\ (Y(s_1)\, t_2, t_1) & \text{otherwise} \end{cases}$$

and

(3) h_3 is the identity on $S_2 \times_Y S_1$ and $h_3(c, c) = c$.

Notice that the c's occur only in pairs.

2.11 *Lemma.* Let S be a semigroup. Then

$$C[PP(S^f)^S] \leqslant (1, \mathbf{C}) \oplus C(S).$$

PROOF. The proof goes by induction on $\#(S)\ (\equiv \#(S^1, S))$. If $\#(S) = 1$, then S is either a group or is combinatorial. If S is a group, by the machine of the proof of Lemma 5.3.14(a) it follows that

$$C[PP(S^f)^S] \leqslant (2, \mathbf{G}) = (1, \mathbf{C}) \oplus C(S).$$

If S is combinatorial, then S divides a wreath product of U_3 semigroups. We will show that $PP(S^f)^S$ is combinatorial. Let the U_3-length of S be the smallest integer n such that $S \mid U_3 \le w \cdots w\, U_3$ (n times). Assume the U_3-length of S is 1. Then $S \mid U_3$ so $PP(S^f)^S \mid PP(U_3^f)^S$ by Lemma 5.3.14. Also by Lemma 5.3.14(b), $PP(U_3^f)^S$ is combinatorial, so $PP(S^f)^S$ is combinatorial in this case. Then by proceeding by induction on the U_3-length and using equation (2.1) it is easy to prove that $PP(S^f)^S$ is combinatorial iff S is combinatorial. Thus $C[PP(S^f)^S] = (1, \mathbf{C}) = (1, \mathbf{C}) \oplus C(S)$, and the assertion is true for $\#(S) = 1$.

Now assume the assertion is true for $\#(S) < n$, and let $\#(S) = n$. Then there exist semigroups S_1 and S_2 such that

$$S \mid (X_2, S_2) \text{ w } (X_1, S_1) = F(X_1, S_2) \times_Y S_1$$

and $\#(S_1) = 1$, $\#(S_2) = n - 1$. Let $T = F(X_1, S_2)$ and recall that $C(T) = C(S_2)$. Now $PP(S^f)^S \mid PP[(T \times_Y S_1)^f]^S$ and from equation (2.1) we have $PP[(T \times_Y S_1)^f]^S \mid C_2 \text{ w } PP(T^f)^S \text{ w } C_1 \text{ w } PP(S_1^f)^S$ where C_1, C_2 are combinatorial semigroups. By induction then we have $C[PP(S^f)^S] \leqslant (1, \mathbf{C}) \oplus C(T) \oplus (1, \mathbf{C}) \oplus C(S_1)$.

Now either $C(S_1) = (1, \mathbf{C})$, or $C(S_1) = (1, \mathbf{G})$ and $C(T) = (n - 1, \mathbf{C})$. In either case

$$C[PP(S^f)^S] \leqslant (1, \mathbf{C}) \oplus C(T) \oplus C(S_1) = (1, \mathbf{C}) \oplus C(S). \quad \blacksquare$$

2.12 Corollary. $\#_G[PP(S^f)^S] = \#_G(S)$.

PROOF. Since $S^f \mid PP(S^f)$, we have $\#_G(S) \leqslant \#_G[PP(S^f)^S]$. By Lemma 2.11 the opposite inequality is obtained. $\blacksquare$

2.13 Remark. We recall some important properties of union of groups semigroups. (Refer to Prop. 7.2.24.) Let S be a union of groups semigroup. Each $\mathcal{J}$ class of S is a simple semigroup, and the equivalence relation "$\mathcal{J}$" is a congruence. If $J_1, \ldots, J_n$ are the $\mathcal{J}$ classes of S, the epimorphism associated with the congruence "$\mathcal{J}$" can be represented as an epimorphism θ from S onto $M = (\{1, \ldots, n\}, *)$, where $*$ is defined by $a \in J_i$ and $b \in J_k$ implies $ab \in J_{i*k}$. M is a commutative band.

2.14 Definition. By a *combinatorial ideal* of a semigroup we mean an ideal whose maximal subgroups are trivial.

2.15 Theorem (Fundamental Lemma of Complexity). Let S be a union of groups semigroup with a combinatorial ideal I. Then

$$\#_G(S) = \#_G(S/I).$$

PROOF. In order to keep the notation clear, let K be the combinatorial ideal, instead of I. $S - K$ is a union of $\mathcal{J}$ classes of S;

index these $\mathscr{J}$ classes $J_1, \ldots, J_{n-1}$ so as to satisfy $J_i > J_j$ implies $i < j$. Then since each $\mathscr{J}$ class of S is a subsemigroup, it is easy to see that the ordered n-tuple $(J_1, \ldots, J_{n-1}, K)$ is a system for S. (Refer to Definition 5.4.2 and Remark 5.4.14.)

It is necessary to review the proof of Lemma 5.4.4. Using the action defined in that proof, define the machines $F_n : \Sigma S \to K^I$ and $F_i : \Sigma S \to J_i^I$, $i = 1, \ldots, n-1$, as follows: Let $\alpha = (s_1, \ldots, s_r) \in \Sigma S$. Then

$$(F_n(\alpha), F_{n-1}(\alpha), \ldots, F_1(\alpha)) \equiv (I, \ldots, I)\, \hat{s}_1 \cdot \hat{s}_2 \cdots \hat{s}_r .$$

For clarity we write out the explicit inductive definition. If $\alpha \in \Sigma S$ is length one, say $\alpha = s_1$, then for $i = 1, \ldots, n$,

$$F_i(\alpha) = \begin{cases} s_1 & \text{if } s_1 \in J_i \quad \text{(Case 2)} \\ I & \text{otherwise} \quad \text{(Cases 1 and 3)} \end{cases} \tag{2.2a}$$

Now let $\alpha_r = (s_1, \ldots, s_r)$ and $\alpha_{r-1} = (s_1, \ldots, s_{r-1})$. Then, for $i = 1, \ldots, n$,

$$F_i(\alpha_r) = \begin{cases} F_i(\alpha_{r-1}) & \text{if } s_r \in J_1, \text{ or } F_1(\alpha_{r-1})\, s_r \in J_2, \text{ or } \ldots \text{ or} \\ & F_{i-2}(\alpha_{r-1})\, F_{i-3}(\alpha_{r-1}) \cdots F_1(\alpha_{r-1})\, s_r \in J_{i-1} \quad \text{(Case 1)} \\ F_i(\alpha_{r-1})\, F_{i-1}(\alpha_{r-1}) \cdots & \text{if none of the above are true and} \\ \quad F_1(\alpha_{r-1})\, s_r & F_{i-1}(\alpha_{r-1}) \cdots F_1(\alpha_{r-1})\, s_r \in J_i \quad \text{(Case 2)} \\ I & \text{otherwise} \quad \text{(Case 3)} \end{cases} \tag{2.2b}$$

Notice that for $F_n(\alpha)$ Case 3 does not arise.

Now it is easy to verify the following machine equation.

$$S^f = h(F_n \times \cdots \times F_1)\, \Delta_n^\Gamma \tag{2.3}$$

where $\Delta_n : S \to S \times \cdots \times S$ (n times) is the diagonal map, that is $\Delta(s) = (s, \ldots, s)$, and $h : S \times \cdots \times S \twoheadrightarrow S$ is defined by $h(s_1, \ldots, s_n) = s_1 \cdots s_n$.

It follows immediately from (2.3) that

$$C(S) \leqslant LUB\{C(F_i^S) : i = 1, \ldots, n\}. \tag{2.4}$$

We now write a machine equation for F_n in terms of the ideal K and the machines $F_1, \ldots, F_{n-1}$, which is easy to verify.

$$F_n = K^{If} h^\Gamma 2_X [S^{rf} \times (F_{n-1} \times \cdots \times F_1)]^\sigma\, \Delta_n^\Gamma \tag{2.5a}$$

where $X = S \times (J_{n-1}^I \times \cdots \times J_1^I)$ and for $\alpha, \alpha_{r-1}, \alpha_r \in J_{n-1}^I \times \cdots \times J_1^I$

$$h(*, (s_1, \alpha)) = \begin{cases} s_1 & \text{if } s_1 \in K \\ I & \text{otherwise} \end{cases}$$

and

$$h[(s_{r-1}, \alpha_{r-1}), (s_r, \alpha_r)] = \begin{cases} S^{If}(\alpha_{r-1}) \cdot s_r & \text{if } \alpha_r = (I,..., I) \\ I & \text{otherwise.} \end{cases}$$

Then

$$F_n^S \mid K^I \mathrm{w}\, 2_X^S \mathrm{w}\, (S^r \times F_{n-1}^S \times \cdots \times F_1^S)$$

and since K^I, 2_X^S and S^r are combinatorial, we have

$$\#_G(F_n^S) \leqslant \max\{\#_G(F_i^S) : i = 1,..., n-1\}.$$

Therefore, by Eq. (2.4)

$$\#_G(S) \leqslant \max\{\#_G(F_i^S) : i = 1,..., n-1\}. \tag{2.5b}$$

We now proceed to the heart of the proof and show that

$$\#_G(F_i^S) \leqslant \#_G(S/K) \text{ for all } i = 1,..., n-1. \tag{2.6}$$

Then applying (2.6) to (2.5b) proves the theorem.

We now will construct combinatorial machines $\mathscr{M}_i$, $i = 1,..., n$ which keep track of the state of the machine F_i. More precisely, $\mathscr{M}_i : \Sigma S \to \{i,..., n, I\}$ will be a combinatorial machine that will, by the value of $\mathscr{M}_i(\alpha)$, determine which case of Eq. (2.2) $F_i(\alpha)$ satisfies ($\alpha \in \Sigma S$).

2.16 Definition. Let $M_i = \{i, i+1,..., n, I\}$ for $i = 1,..., n$. Define the machine $\beta_i : \Sigma M_i \to M_{i+1}$, $i = 1,..., n-1$ as follows:

$$\beta_i = h_{i3}([h_{i2} 2_{M_i}\{i,..., n\}^{rIf\sigma}] \times M_i^{rf})\, h_{i1}^{\Gamma}$$

where

(1) $h_{i1} : M_i \to M_i \times M_i$ with $h_{i1}(x) = (x, x)$

(2) $h_{i2} : (M_i \cup \{\ddagger\}) \times M_i \to M_{i+1}$ with

$$h_{i2}(\ddagger, j) = \begin{cases} I & \text{if } j = i \\ j & \text{otherwise} \end{cases}$$

and

$$h_{i2}(j_1, j_2) = \begin{cases} I & \text{if } j_2 = i \\ j_1 * j_2 & \text{if } j_1 = i \text{ and } j_2 \neq i \text{ or } I \\ j_2 & \text{otherwise} \end{cases}$$

where the operation "$*$" is the one described in Remark 2.13.

(3) $h_{i3} : M_{i+1} \times M_i \to M_{i+1}$ with

$$h_{i3}(j_1, j_2) = \begin{cases} I & \text{if } j_2 = I \\ j_1 & \text{otherwise.} \end{cases}$$

Clearly β_i is a combinatorial machine, i.e., β_i^S is a combinatorial semigroup.

We now define the machines $\mathcal{M}_i$. Let $i : S \to \{1,..., n\}$ be defined by $i(s) = k$, $1 \leqslant k \leqslant n - 1$ iff $s \in J_k$, and $i(s) = n$ iff $s \in K$, the ideal. Then define

$$\mathcal{M}_1 = \{1,..., n\}^{rf}\, i^{\Gamma}$$

and define

$$\mathcal{M}_i = \beta_{i-1} \cdot \beta_{i-2}^{\sigma} \cdots \beta_1^{\sigma} i^{\Gamma}, \qquad i = 2,..., n.$$

Equivalently, $\mathcal{M}_i = \beta_{i-1} \mathcal{M}_{i-1}^{\sigma}$, $i = 2,..., n$. (Notice that β_i is not involved in the definition of $\mathcal{M}_i$.) $\mathcal{M}_i$ is a combinatorial machine.

2.17 Lemma. Let $\alpha_1 = s_1$, $\alpha_2 = (s_1, s_2),..., \alpha_r = (s_1,..., s_r) \in \Sigma S$. Then the machine $\mathcal{M}_i$, $i = 1,..., n$, has the following properties: (for notational convenience, let $K = J_n$)

(a) $\mathcal{M}_1(\alpha_r) = k$ iff $s_r \in J_k$, $1 \leqslant k \leqslant n$.

(b) For $i = 2,..., n$, if $\mathcal{M}_i(\alpha_r) = I$, then $F_{k-1}(\alpha_{r-1}) \cdots F_1(\alpha_{r-1})\, s_r \in J_k$ for some k, $1 \leqslant k < i$.

(c) For $i = 2,..., n$, if $\mathcal{M}_i(\alpha_r) = k \in \{i,..., n\}$, then $s_r \notin J_1, F_1(\alpha_{r-1})\, s_r \notin J_2,..., F_{i-2}(\alpha_{r-1}) \cdots F_1(\alpha_{r-1})\, s_r \notin J_{i-1}$ and $F_{i-1}(\alpha_{r-1}) \cdots F_1(\alpha_{r-1})\, s_r \in J_k$.

In particular, for $i = 1,..., n$, if $\mathcal{M}_i(\alpha_r) = I$, then $F_i(\alpha_r)$ satisfies Case 1 (of Eqs. (2.2)). If $\mathcal{M}_i(\alpha_r) = i$, then $F_i(\alpha_r)$ satisfies Case 2. If $\mathcal{M}_i(\alpha_r) \in \{i + 1,..., n\}$, then $F_i(\alpha_r)$ satisfies Case 3.

PROOF. Part (a) is clear from the definition of $\mathcal{M}_1$.

We first investigate $\mathcal{M}_i(\alpha_r)$, $2 \leqslant i \leqslant n$. Let j_i be the largest integer such that $\mathcal{M}_i(\alpha_{j_i}) \neq I$ in the sequence $(\mathcal{M}_i(\alpha_1), \mathcal{M}_i(\alpha_2),..., \mathcal{M}_i(\alpha_{r-1})) =$

$\mathcal{M}_i^\sigma(\alpha_{r-1})$. In other words, $\mathcal{M}_i(\alpha_{j_i})$ is the last non-I in the sequence $\mathcal{M}_i^\sigma(\alpha_{r-1})$ (*not* $\mathcal{M}_i^\sigma(\alpha_r)$). By convention, we say $j_i = 0$ if it does not exist. Then investigating the definitions of the $\mathcal{M}_i$, $i = 2,..., n$ leads to the following formula:

$$\mathcal{M}_i(\alpha_r) = \begin{cases} I & \text{if } \mathcal{M}_{i-1}(\alpha_r) = i-1 \text{ or } I \\ \mathcal{M}_{i-1}(\alpha_r) & \text{if none of the above and } j_{i-1} = 0 \text{ or} \\ & \mathcal{M}_{i-1}(\alpha_{j_{i-1}}) \neq i-1 \\ (i-1) * \mathcal{M}_{i-1}(\alpha_r) & \text{if none of the above, i.e., if} \\ & \mathcal{M}_{i-1}(\alpha_{j_{i-1}}) = i-1 \text{ and} \\ & \mathcal{M}_{i-1}(\alpha_r) \neq i-1. \end{cases}$$

First, observe that it is easy to verify that (b) and (c) are true when α_r is a sequence of length 1. So assume $r \geqslant 2$. We proceed by induction on i of $\mathcal{M}_i$, first proving (b) and (c) for $\mathcal{M}_2(\alpha_r)$.

(b) If $\mathcal{M}_2(\alpha_r) = I$, then $\mathcal{M}_1(\alpha_r) = 1$, because $\mathcal{M}_1(\alpha_r)$ cannot be I. Thus $s_r \in J_1$.

(c) If $\mathcal{M}_2(\alpha_r) = k \in \{2,..., n\}$, then $\mathcal{M}_1(\alpha_r) \in \{2,..., n\}$; let $\mathcal{M}_1(\alpha_r) = k'$. Since $j_1 = n - 1$ we have two cases: (1) $\mathcal{M}_1(\alpha_{r-1}) \neq 1$ and $\mathcal{M}_1(\alpha_r) = k = k'$, and (2) $\mathcal{M}_1(\alpha_{r-1}) = 1$ and $1 * k' = k$.

CASE 1. $s_r \in J_k$, so $s_r \notin J_1$. $F_1(\alpha_{r-1}) = I$ since $\mathcal{M}_1(\alpha_{r-1}) \neq 1$, so $F_1(\alpha_{r-1})\, s_r \in J_k$.

CASE 2. $s_r \in J_{k'}$, so $s_r \notin J_1$. $F_1(\alpha_{r-1}) \in J_1$ since $\mathcal{M}_1(\alpha_{r-1}) = 1$, so $F_1(\alpha_{r-1})\, s_r \in J_{1*k'} = J_k$.

Thus assertions (b) and (c) are true for $\mathcal{M}_2(\alpha_r)$.

Assume (b) and (c) are true for integers less than i, and consider $\mathcal{M}_i(\alpha_r)$.

(b) If $\mathcal{M}_i(\alpha_r) = I$, then $\mathcal{M}_{i-1}(\alpha_r) = i - 1$ or I. By induction, $\mathcal{M}_{i-1}(\alpha_r) = i - 1$ implies $F_{i-2}(\alpha_{r-1}) \cdots F_1(\alpha_{r-1})\, s_r \in J_{i-1}$ and $\mathcal{M}_{i-1}(\alpha_r) = I$ implies $F_{k-1}(\alpha_r) \cdots F_1(\alpha_r) \in J_k$ for some $k < i - 1$. In either case, the assertion for $\mathcal{M}_i(\alpha_r)$ is proven.

(c) If $\mathcal{M}_i(\alpha_r) = k \in \{i,..., n\}$, then $\mathcal{M}_{i-1}(\alpha_r) \in \{i,..., n\}$. Let $\mathcal{M}_{i-1}(\alpha_r) = k'$. There are three possibilities: (1) $j_{i-1} = 0$; (2) $\mathcal{M}_{i-1}(\alpha_{j_{i-1}}) \neq i - 1$; and (3) $\mathcal{M}_{i-1}(\alpha_{j_{i-1}}) = i - 1$.

CASE 1. If $j_{i-1} = 0$, then $k' = k$ and $\mathcal{M}_{i-1}(\alpha_m) = I$ for each $m \leqslant r - 1$. This implies by induction that $F_{i-1}(\alpha_m)$ satisfies Case 1 for each $m \leqslant r - 1$, which in turn implies that $F_{i-1}(\alpha_{r-1}) = I$. Now, by induction, $\mathscr{M}_{i-1}(\alpha_r) = k$ implies $s_r \notin J_1, F_1(\alpha_{r-1})\, s_r \notin J_2, \ldots, F_{i-3}(\alpha_{r-1}) \cdots F_1(\alpha_{r-1})\, s_r \notin J_{i-2}$ and $F_{i-2}(\alpha_{r-1}) \cdots F_1(\alpha_{r-1})\, s_r \in J_k \neq J_{i-1}$. But then $F_{i-1}(\alpha_{r-1}) \cdots F_1(\alpha_{r-1})\, s_r \in J_k$, and (c) is satisfied for this case.

CASE 2. If $\mathscr{M}_{i-1}(\alpha_{j_{i-1}}) \neq i - 1$, then $k = k'$ and $F_{i-1}(\alpha_{j_{i-1}}) = I$, which implies $F_{i-1}(\alpha_{r-1}) = I$. Then we are in the same situation as Case 1 above, since $\mathscr{M}_{i-1}(\alpha_r) = k$, so (c) is satisfied for this case.

CASE 3. If $\mathscr{M}_{i-1}(\alpha_{j_{i-1}}) = i - 1$, then $(i-1) * k' = k$. By induction, $F_{i-1}(\alpha_{j_{i-1}}) \in J_{i-1}$, so $F_{i-1}(\alpha_{r-1}) \in J_{i-1}$. Since $\mathscr{M}_{i-1}(\alpha_r) = k' \in \{i, \ldots, n\}$, we have $s_r \notin J_1$, $F_1(\alpha_{r-1})\, s_r \notin J_2, \ldots, F_{i-3}(\alpha_{r-1}) \cdots F_1(\alpha_{r-1})\, s_r \notin J_{i-2}$, and $F_{i-2}(\alpha_{r-1}) \cdots F_1(\alpha_{r-1})\, s_r \in J_{k'} \neq J_{i-1}$, by induction. Then $F_{i-1}(\alpha_{r-1}) \cdots F_1(\alpha_{r-1})\, s_r \in J_{(i-1)*k'} = J_k$. ∎

We now proceed with the proof of the theorem. If $F_i(\alpha_r)$ is in Case 1, we know that it has not been changed; that is, $F_i(\alpha_r) = F_i(\alpha_{r-1})$. If $F_i(\alpha_r)$ is in Case 2, then we know that $F_i(\alpha_r) = F_i(\alpha_{r-1})\, F_{i-1}(\alpha_{r-1}) \cdots s_r$, and if $F_i(\alpha_r)$ is in Case 3, we know that $F_i(\alpha_r)$ has been reset to I and whatever was there previously $(F_i(\alpha_{r-1}))$ has been completely forgotten. These properties allow us to construct the next machine.

2.18 Remark. Let J be a $\mathscr{J}$ class of S. Recall the definition of the ideal $F(J)$, (see Notation 8.2.2). In the union of groups case, the zero breaks off of $S/F(J)$, so $S - F(J)$ is a subsemigroup of S. J is the kernel of $S - F(J)$.

For $i = 1, \ldots, n - 1$, it follows that $S - F(J_i) \subseteq S - K$ since $K \subseteq F(J_i)$, so $S - F(J_i) \subseteq (S - K) \cup \{0\} \cong S/K$. Write $S_i \equiv S - F(J_i)$, $i = 1, \ldots, n - 1$. Then $S_i \mid S/K$. Note that any element of a sequence $\alpha \in \Sigma S$ that belongs to $F(J_i)$ can play no role in the output of F_i.

Now using all the above information, including Lemma 2.17, it is not hard to verify the following machine equations for $i = 1, \ldots, n - 1$.

$$F_i = j_{i4}(J_i \cup \{c\})^{rIf}\, j_{i3}^{\Gamma}[M_i^{rf} \times PP(S_i^f)]^{\sigma}\, j_{i2}^{\Gamma}[\mathscr{M}_i \times (S_i \cup \{c\})^{rf}]^{\sigma}\, j_{i1}^{\Gamma} \qquad (2.7)$$

where

(1) $j_{i1} : S \to S \times (S_i \cup \{c\})$ with

$$j_{i1}(s) = \begin{cases} (s, s) & \text{if } s \in S - F(J_i) \\ (s, c) & \text{if } s \in F(J_i) \end{cases}$$

(2) $j_{i2} : M_i \times (S_i \cup \{c\}) \to M_i \times (S_i \cup \{c\})$ with

$$j_{i2}(l, x) = \begin{cases} (l, x) & \text{if } l = i \text{ or } I \\ (l, c) & \text{if } l \neq i \text{ or } I \end{cases}$$

(3) $j_{i3} : M_i \times (S_i \cup \{c\}) \to J_i^I \cup \{c\}$ with

$$j_{i3}(l, x) = \begin{cases} I & \text{if } l = I \\ x & \text{otherwise} \end{cases}$$

(4) $j_{i4} : J_i^I \cup \{c\} \to J_i^I$ with

$$j_{i4}(x) = \begin{cases} I & \text{if } x = c \\ x & \text{otherwise.} \end{cases}$$

From Eq. (2.7) we have

$$C(F_i^S) \leqslant (1, \mathbf{C}) \oplus C[PP(S_i^f)^S] \oplus (1, \mathbf{C}), \quad i = 1, \ldots, n-1$$

so $\#_G(F_i^S) \leqslant \#_G(S_i)$, $i = 1, \ldots, n-1$, by Corollary 2.12. Then since $S_i \mid S/K$, $i = 1, \ldots, n-1$, we have

$$\#_G(F_i^S) \leqslant \#_G(S/K), \quad i = 1, \ldots, n-1. \tag{2.6}$$

Now applying (2.6) to (2.5b) we obtain

$$\#_G(S) \leqslant \#_G(S/K).$$

But S/K is a homomorphic image of S so

$$\#_G(S) = \#_G(S/K).$$

This proves the Fundamental Lemma of Complexity (Theorem 2.15). ∎

We have now proved that $\theta = \theta_a = \#_G$. The remainder of the proof of Theorem 2.5 proceeds via another series of lemmas.

2.19 Lemma. $\theta_b = \theta_c = \theta_d = \theta_e$.

PROOF. First consider series (b) of Def. 2.4. Let $S_{-1} = \{0\}^{\gamma-1}$, $S_{-2} = (\{0\}^{\gamma-1})^{\mathscr{L}-1}$, etc., and notice that the series must reach S by virtue of Theorem 8.1.14 (or Proposition 8.3.19).

We claim that $S_{-1} = (\Pi\theta_j^{(1)})(S)$, where j runs over the collection of all epimorphisms such that

$$\theta_j^{(1)} : S \twoheadrightarrow T_j, \qquad T_j \xrightarrow[\gamma]{} \!\!\!\twoheadrightarrow \{0\},$$

$S_{-2} = (\Pi\theta_j^{(2)})(S)$, where j runs over the collection of all epimorphisms such that $\theta_j^{(2)} : S \twoheadrightarrow T_j$, and there exist epimorphisms so that $T_j \xrightarrow[\mathscr{L}]{} \!\!\!\twoheadrightarrow T_j' \xrightarrow[\gamma]{} \!\!\!\twoheadrightarrow \{0\}$, etc. To prove this, let $U_{-k} = (\Pi\theta_j^{(k)})(S)$. By definition of S_{-1}, $U_{-1} = S_{-1} = S^C$, the maximal combinatorial homomorphic image of S. Now, $S \twoheadrightarrow U_{-2} \xrightarrow[\mathscr{L}]{} \!\!\!\twoheadrightarrow U_{-1} \xrightarrow[\gamma]{} \!\!\!\twoheadrightarrow \{0\}$, since direct sums and restrictions of $\mathscr{L}$ and γ homomorphisms are $\mathscr{L}$ and γ homomorphisms, respectively. Since $S_{-2} = (S_{-1})^{\mathscr{L}^{-1}}$, we have $S_{-2} \twoheadrightarrow U_{-2}$. On the other hand, $S \twoheadrightarrow S_{-2} \xrightarrow[\mathscr{L}]{} \!\!\!\twoheadrightarrow S_{-1} \xrightarrow[\gamma]{} \!\!\!\twoheadrightarrow \{0\}$, and so $U_{-2} \twoheadrightarrow S_{-2}$. Thus, $U_{-2} = S_{-2}$. Continuing in this way, we prove $U_{-i} = S_{-i}$ for all $i = 1, 2, \ldots$. Let k be the smallest integer such that $S_{-k} = S$.

We now prove that the number of proper $\mathscr{L}$ homomorphisms in the series

$$S = S_{-k} \twoheadrightarrow S_{-k+1} \twoheadrightarrow \cdots \twoheadrightarrow S_{-2} \xrightarrow[\mathscr{L}]{} \!\!\!\twoheadrightarrow S_{-1} \xrightarrow[\gamma]{} \!\!\!\twoheadrightarrow \{0\} \qquad \text{(b)}$$

[i.e., $\theta_b(S)$] is less than or equal to the number of proper $\mathscr{L}$ homomorphisms in *any* alternating $\gamma - \mathscr{L}$ series of S starting with a γ-homomorphism.

Let k be even. Then series (b) starts with an $\mathscr{L}$ homomorphism. Suppose an alternating $\gamma - \mathscr{L}$ series of S starting with a γ got to $\{0\}$ in $k - 1$ steps. Then, by the preceding characterization of $S_{-(k-1)}$, we would have $S = S_{-(k-1)}$, a contradiction. If the series in question got to $\{0\}$ in $k - 2$ steps, then, by adding on the trivial map $\{0\} \xrightarrow[\gamma]{} \!\!\!\twoheadrightarrow \{0\}$ to the end, we have a series of length $k - 1$, again giving a contradiction. Thus the series must have length k or greater, and the assertion is true for this case.

Let k be odd, so that the series (b) starts with a γ-homomorphism. If the alternating series in question has length $k - 2$ or less, a contradiction again arises. So, in this case, the length of the series must be at least $k - 1$. But it is easy to see that the assertion holds for $\mathscr{L}$ homomorphisms here also, and so it is proved.

Now we apply the tools of Section 8.3 to get the commutative diagram in Fig. 1.

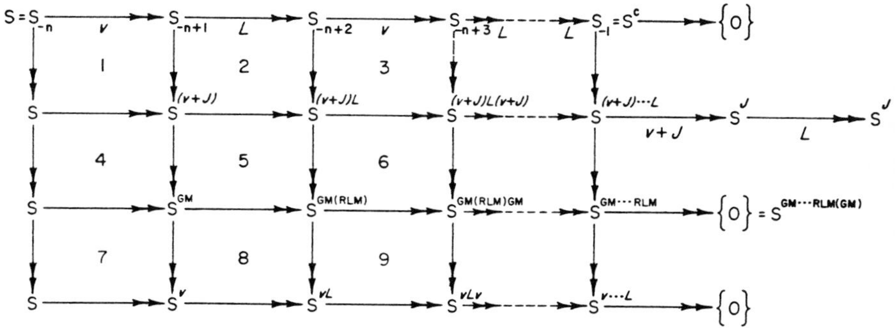

FIG. 1

If (b) starts in an $\mathscr{L}$ homomorphism, add the identity in the beginning so that it starts with a γ. Then notice that $S_{-1} = S^C \twoheadrightarrow S^{\mathscr{I}}$, since for union of groups $S^{\mathscr{I}}$ is combinatorial. Then every γ map except the last one is a $\gamma + \mathscr{I}$ map. Thus, square 1 commutes.

Since $S_{-n+1} \xrightarrow[\mathscr{L}]{} \!\!\!\!\!\twoheadrightarrow S_{-n+2}$, we have $S_{-n+1} \twoheadrightarrow S_{-n+2} \twoheadrightarrow S_{-n+1}^{\mathscr{L}}$. Using Proposition 8.3.2(b), square 2 commutes.

Since $S_{-n+2} \xrightarrow[\gamma+\mathscr{I}]{} \!\!\!\!\!\twoheadrightarrow S_{-n+3} \twoheadrightarrow S_{-n+2}^{(\gamma+\mathscr{I})}$, square 3 commutes by Fact 8.3.15. Continue in this manner on out the (b)–(c) ladder.

Now, by Remark 8.3.16, squares 4 and 7 commute. Since $S^{\mathscr{L}} = S^{RLM}$, squares 5 and 8 commute. For square 6, we have

$$\begin{array}{ccccc} S^{(\gamma+\mathscr{I})\mathscr{L}} & \twoheadrightarrow & S^{(\gamma+\mathscr{I})\mathscr{L}(\gamma+\mathscr{I})} & & \\ \downarrow & & \downarrow & & \\ S^{GM(RLM)} & \twoheadrightarrow & S^{GM(RLM)(\gamma+\mathscr{I})} & \twoheadrightarrow & S^{GM(RLM)GM}. \end{array}$$

For square 9, we have (by Fact 8.3.7)

$$\begin{array}{ccccc} S^{GM(RLM)} & \twoheadrightarrow & S^{GM(RLM)GM} & & \\ \downarrow & & \downarrow & & \\ S^{\gamma\mathscr{L}} & \twoheadrightarrow & S^{\gamma\mathscr{L}GM} & \twoheadrightarrow & S^{\gamma\mathscr{L}\gamma}. \end{array}$$

Continue in the same manner on out the diagram.

Now since S_{-1} is combinatorial, so are $S^{(\gamma+\mathscr{I})\cdots\mathscr{L}}$, $S^{GM\cdots RLM}$, and $S^{\gamma\cdots\mathscr{L}}$. We show that, if T is combinatorial, then $T^{(\gamma+\mathscr{I})} = T^{\mathscr{I}}$, $T^{GM} = \{0\}$, and $T^{\gamma} = \{0\}$.

The last two follow from Fact 8.3.25(a). For the first, recall that $T^{\gamma+\mathscr{J}} \leqslant\leqslant T^{\gamma} \times T^{\mathscr{J}}$. But $T^{\gamma} = \{0\}$. Hence, $T^{(\gamma+\mathscr{J})} \leqslant T^{\mathscr{J}}$ and $T^{(\gamma+\mathscr{J})} \twoheadrightarrow T^{\mathscr{J}}$, so they are isomorphic.

Now $S^{(\gamma+\mathscr{J})\cdots\mathscr{L}(\gamma+\mathscr{J})} = S^{(\gamma+\mathscr{J})\cdots\mathscr{L}\mathscr{J}}$ is isomorphic to $S^{\mathscr{J}}$, since every map in (c) is a $\mathscr{J}$-homomorphism. Clearly, $S^{\mathscr{J}\mathscr{L}} = S^{\mathscr{J}}$. Thus, we have justified the diagram (Fig. 1).

It is now clear that the number of proper $\mathscr{L}$ homomorphisms in (b) is greater than or equal to the number in (c), (d), or (e). That is,

$$\theta_b(S) \geqslant \theta_c(S) \geqslant \theta_d(S) \geqslant \theta_e(S).$$

But we have shown that $\theta_b(S) \leqslant$ the number of proper $\mathscr{L}$ homomorphisms in any alternating γ-$\mathscr{L}$ series of S, starting with a γ homomorphism and ending in $\{0\}$. [End (c) in zero by $S^{\mathscr{J}} \xrightarrow[\gamma]{} \{0\}$] Thus,

$$\theta_b(S) = \theta_c(S) = \theta_d(S) = \theta_e(S)$$

for all $S \in \mathscr{S}$. ∎

2.20 Lemma. $\theta = \theta_b = \theta_c = \theta_d = \theta_e$.

PROOF. We shall show first that θ_c satisfies Axiom I. Let $S \leqslant\leqslant S_1 \times \cdots \times S_n$. For each $k = 1,\ldots, n$, consider $S_k \twoheadrightarrow S_k^{\gamma+\mathscr{J}} \twoheadrightarrow S_k^{(\gamma+\mathscr{J})\mathscr{L}} \twoheadrightarrow \cdots \twoheadrightarrow S_k^{\mathscr{J}}$. Direct sum these series $(k = 1,\ldots, n)$, restrict to the diagonal, and take successive images. Then, by Proposition 8.3.17, the resulting series is series (c) for S. Now it is easy to see that θ_c satisfies Axiom I.

Next we prove θ_e satisfies Axiom II. $S \xrightarrow[\gamma]{} S/I$ iff I is a combinatorial ideal. Now, $S \xrightarrow[\gamma]{} S/I$ implies $S \twoheadrightarrow S/I \twoheadrightarrow S^{\gamma} = (S/I)^{\gamma}$; hence, the series (e) for S and S/I differ only by the first term and have the same length. This proves θ_e satisfies Axiom II.

Finally, we show θ_c satisfies Axiom III. Let S be a GM semigroup $\neq \{0\}$. Then $S \twoheadrightarrow RLM(S)$ equals $S \twoheadrightarrow S^{\mathscr{L}}$ by Fact 8.3.25(d). Also, S is GGM, and so $S = S^{GGM} = S^{\gamma+\mathscr{J}}$. Thus, series (c) for S is $S \twoheadrightarrow S^{\gamma+\mathscr{J}} = S \twoheadrightarrow RLM(S) = S^{\mathscr{L}} \twoheadrightarrow S^{\mathscr{L}(\gamma+\mathscr{J})} \twoheadrightarrow \cdots$, and hence $\theta_c(S) = \theta_c[RLM(S)] + 1$. ∎

2.21 Lemma. $S \in \mathscr{S}$, and $T \mid S$ implies $\theta(T) \leqslant \theta(S)$.

PROOF. $T \mid S$ implies $T^{GM} \mid S^{GM}$ implies $T^{GM(RLM)} \mid S^{GM(RLM)}$ implies $\cdots$, etc. Thus, when the series for S reaches $\{0\}$, the series for T must also have reached $\{0\}$ in at least the same number of terms. Hence, $\theta_d(T) \leqslant \theta_d(S)$. But $\theta = \theta_d$. ∎

2.22 Lemma. $\theta_f = \theta$.

PROOF. First note that, if S is a union of groups semigroup which is GGM but not GM, then $S = \{0\}^I$, for the distinguished ideal I of S must be combinatorial, and so $I^\# = A^l \times B^r$. But the requirement that S act faithfully on the left and the right of I forces $I^\#$ to be one element. Thus, $S = \{0\}^I$.

Now, if we replace the GM_i's from series (f) by GGM semigroups and define the norm of a series to be the largest integer n such that $(GGM)_n$ is noncombinatorial, then clearly the maximum of the norms of all these series equals $\theta_f(S)$.

Consider all series of this form, and add the trivial map $\{0\}^I \twoheadrightarrow \{0\}^I \twoheadrightarrow \cdots \twoheadrightarrow \{0\}^I$ to each so as to make them all the length of the longest. Then direct sum all these series. The number of GGM direct product terms that are noncombinatorial is clearly $\theta_f(S)$. Then restrict this series to the diagonal, and consider the first image. Clearly, it is $S^{GGM} = S^{(\gamma+\mathscr{I})}$, and S^{GGM} is a subdirect product of all the GGM_1 semigroups of all the series. Write this as

$$S^{(\gamma+\mathscr{I})} = S^{GGM} \leqslant\leqslant GGM_1^{(1)} \times \cdots \times GGM_1^{(k)}.$$

Now apply Proposition 8.3.17 to get

$$S^{(\gamma+\mathscr{I})\mathscr{L}} \leqslant\leqslant (GGM_1^{(1)})^{RLM} \times \cdots \times (GGM_1^{(k)})^{RLM}.$$

However, by transitivity of subdirect products, $S^{(\gamma+\mathscr{I})\mathscr{L}}$ is a subdirect product of the second term of the direct sum of all the series, since $(GGM_1^{(1)})^{RLM} \times \cdots \times (GGM_1^{(k)})^{RLM}$ is.

Write the second term $RLM_1^{(1)} \times \cdots \times RLM_1^{(k)}$. Then, applying Proposition 8.3.17 again, we get

$$S^{(\gamma+\mathscr{I})\mathscr{L}(\gamma+\mathscr{I})} \leqslant\leqslant RLM_1^{(1)GGM} \times \cdots \times RLM_1^{(k)GGM},$$

so that $S^{(\gamma+\mathscr{I})\mathscr{L}(\gamma+\mathscr{I})} \leqslant\leqslant GGM_2^{(1)} \times \cdots \times GGM_2^{(k)}$. Continue on in this manner.

We now use the following easily verified fact. Let $S \leqslant\leqslant S_1 \times \cdots \times S_n$. Then S is combinatorial iff each S_i is combinatorial, $i = 1,\ldots, n$.

If $\theta_f(S) = n$, then the first term of series (c) which could be combinatorial is the subdirect product of $RLM_n^{(1)} \times \cdots \times RLM_n^{(k)}$. If this is the case, series (c) ends after one more step at worst, since, if C is a combinatorial semigroup and $S \xrightarrow[\mathscr{I}]{} \!\!\!\!\!\rightarrow C$, then $C^{\gamma+\mathscr{I}} = S^{\mathscr{I}}$. In any case, the next term of (c) is combinatorial, since it is the subdirect of $\{0\}^I \times \cdots \times \{0\}^I$. Now, if $S \xrightarrow[\mathscr{J}]{\;\;\twoheadrightarrow\;\;} T \xrightarrow[\mathscr{J}]{\;\;\twoheadrightarrow\;\;} C = T^{(\gamma+\mathscr{J})}$ and C is combinatorial, then $C = S^{\mathscr{J}}$. So counting series (c) will yield n proper $\mathscr{L}$ homomorphisms. Thus, $\theta_f(S) = \theta_c(S)$ for all $S \in \mathscr{S}$. ∎

The following fact is a corollary of the foregoing proof. Let $S_{(n)}^{(\gamma+\mathscr{J})\cdots\mathscr{L}}$ denote the nth term of that form in a series (c) of S. Let $\theta(S) = n$. Take all the longest GGM-RLM series for S. Then we know that each GGM_n is the last GGM semigroup in the series which is not $\leqslant \{0\}^I$. RLM_n may or may not be $\leqslant \{0\}^I$. We give a necessary and sufficient condition that each $RLM_n \leqslant \{0\}^I$, which will be useful in proving $\theta_i = \theta$.

2.23 Fact.   Assume the above situation. Then some $RLM_n \not\leqslant \{0\}^I$ iff $U_1 \mid S_{(n)}^{(\gamma+\mathscr{J})\cdots\mathscr{L}}$.

PROOF.   First recall that $U_1 \mid S$ iff $U_1 \leqslant S$. The distinguished $\mathscr{J}$ class of an RLM semigroup is of the form A^r. If $\mid A \mid \geqslant 2$, then $U_1 \leqslant A^r$. If $\mid A \mid = 1$, then the RLM semigroup must be $\{0\}^I$ or $\{0\}$. Thus, $RLM_n \not\leqslant \{0\}^I$ iff $U_1 \mid RLM_n$.

Recall from the proof of Lemma 2.22 that $S_{(n)}^{(\gamma+\mathscr{J})\cdots\mathscr{L}}$ is a subdirect product of all RLM semigroups in the nth position of GGM-RLM series for S. If some $RLM_n \not\leqslant \{0\}^I$, then, since $S_{(n)}^{(\gamma+\mathscr{J})\cdots\mathscr{L}} \twoheadrightarrow RLM_n$, we have $U_1 \mid RLM_n \mid S_{(n)}^{(\gamma+\mathscr{J})\cdots\mathscr{L}}$. Conversely, suppose $U_1 \mid S_{(n)}^{(\gamma+\mathscr{J})\cdots\mathscr{L}}$. Then U_1 divides the direct sum of all the RLM semigroups heretofore mentioned. But U_1 is IRR, and so U_1 divides some RLM_n. Hence, $RLM_n \not\leqslant \{0\}^I$. ∎

2.24 Lemma. $\theta_g = \theta$.

PROOF.   Let

$$S \twoheadrightarrow GM_1 \twoheadrightarrow RLM_1 \to GM_2 \twoheadrightarrow \cdots$$

be a longest series of type (f), i.e., where, if GM_n is the last nonzero GM semigroup, then $n = \theta(S)$. Replace this series with the following series of *equal length*:

$$S \twoheadrightarrow GM_1 \twoheadrightarrow RLM(GM_1) \twoheadrightarrow GM_2 \twoheadrightarrow \cdots.$$

[This can be done, since $RLM(GM_j) = GM_j^{\mathscr{L}} = GM_j^{RLM} \twoheadrightarrow RLM_1$ by Fact 8.3.25(d).]

Let (J_i, G_i, N_i) be a kernel of $S \to GM_i$ [see Definition 8.3.27(c)]. Then we have the sequence $(J_1, G_1, N_1),\ldots, (J_n, G_n, N_n)$ satisfying

$J_1 < J_2 < \cdots < J_n$, for it is easy to see that, if $i < j$, then $S \twoheadrightarrow GM_j$ sends J_i to $\{0\}$. Furthermore, $N_i \neq G_i$, $i = 1,..., n$, since the maximal subgroups in the distinguished $\mathscr{J}$ classes of the GM_i are isomorphic to G_i/N_i, and by assumption these distinguished $\mathscr{J}$ classes are noncombinatorial, i.e., $| G_i/N_i | > 1$ for $i = 1,..., n$.

Let $K_{i+1} = \ker[(J_i, G_i, N_i), (J_{i+1}, G_{i+1})]$ (see Definition 8.3.31). Now K_{i+1} is the kernel of the homomorphism $S \twoheadrightarrow RLM(GM_i)$ restricted to G_{i+1}, and N_{i+1} is the kernel of the homomorphism $S \twoheadrightarrow RLM(GM_i) \twoheadrightarrow GM_{i+1}$ restricted to G_{i+1}. Thus, it is an easy result of group theory that $K_{i+1} \leqslant N_{i+1}$. Thus, the sequence $(J_1, G_1, N_1),..., (J_n, G_n, N_n)$ satisfies conditions 1–3 of the definition of θ_g. Thus, $\theta_g(S) \geqslant \theta(S)$ for all $S \in \mathscr{S}$.

Conversely, let $(J_1, G_1, N_1),..., (J_n, G_n, N_n)$ be a sequence satisfying 1–3, where $n = \theta_g(S)$. Let $S' = J_1 \cup \cdots \cup J_n$, so that S' is a subsemigroup of S, $J_1,..., J_n$ are the $\mathscr{J}$ classes of S', and $(J_1, G_1, N_1),..., (J_n, G_n, N_n)$ is a sequence for S' satisfying 1–3.

Consider $\varphi_1 : S' \twoheadrightarrow GM(J_1, G_1, N_1) \twoheadrightarrow RLM[GM(J_1, G_1, N_1)]$. Notice that K_2 equals the group kernel of φ_1 restricted to G_2, and $K_2 \leqslant N_2$ by assumption. Suppose $\varphi_1(J_2) \subseteq \varphi_1(J_1)$. $\varphi_1(J_1)$ is combinatorial, and so $\varphi_1(G_2) = G_2/K_2 = \{1\}$, a contradiction. Therefore, since $J_1 = F(J_2)$, we have $\varphi_1(J_2) \cap \varphi_1[F(J_2)] = \phi$. Thus, by Proposition 8.3.28, we have

$$S' \xrightarrow{\varphi_1}\!\!\!\twoheadrightarrow RLM[GM(J_1, G_1, N_1)] \twoheadrightarrow GM(J_2, G_2, N_2) \twoheadrightarrow$$
$$\twoheadrightarrow RLM[GM(J_2, G_2, N_2)].$$

Now continue on to construct a series of type (f). $GM(J_n, G_n, N_n) \neq \{0\}$, because $N_n \neq G_n$. Hence, $\theta_g(S) = n \leqslant \theta_f(S') = \theta(S') \leqslant \theta(S)$. Therefore, $\theta_g(S) = \theta(S)$ for all $S \in \mathscr{S}$. ∎

2.25 Fact. (a) Let (J, G, N) be given. Suppose $G/N \leqslant\!\leqslant G_1 \times \cdots \times G_n$ (i.e., there exist $N_i \lhd G$, $i = 1,..., n$ with $G/N_i = G_i$ and $N_1 \cap \cdots \cap N_n = N$). Then

$$GM(J, G, N) \leqslant\!\leqslant GM(J, G, N_1) \times \cdots \times GM(J, G, N_n).$$

(b) $\theta[GM(J, G, N] = \theta[GM(J, G, N_i]$ for some $i = 1,..., n$.

PROOF. (a) Since $N \leqslant N_i$, there exist homomorphisms $\varphi_i : GM(J, G, N) \twoheadrightarrow GM(J, G, N_i)$, $i = 1,..., n$. φ_i restricted to the maximal subgroup G/N of the distinguished $\mathscr{J}$ class of

$GM(J, G, N)$ is $G/N \twoheadrightarrow G/N_i = G_i$, and so $(\varphi_1 \times \cdots \times \varphi_n) \Delta$ is 1 : 1 on G/N. Then, by Fact 8.3.25(b), $(\varphi_1 \times \cdots \times \varphi_n) \Delta$ is 1 : 1 on $GM(J, G, N)$.

(b) This follows from Axiom I (Definition 1.2). ▌

2.26 Lemma. Let $\mathscr{E}$ be an expansion of S. Then $\theta_h^{(\mathscr{E})} = \theta$. Therefore, θ_h is independent of $\mathscr{E}$.

PROOF. Let $(J_1, G_1, H_1), \ldots, (J_n, G_n, H_n)$ be a longest sequence for S satisfying the condition of the definition of θ_g. Thus, $n = \theta(S)$. Let $S' = J_1 \cup \cdots \cup J_n$, as in the proof of Lemma 2.24.

Let $K_2 = \ker[(J_1, G_1, H_1), (J_2, G_2)]$. The following series is possible by Proposition 8.3.28:

$$S' \twoheadrightarrow GM(J_1, G_1, H_1) \twoheadrightarrow RLM[GM(J_1, G_1, H_1)] \twoheadrightarrow$$
$$\twoheadrightarrow GM(J_2, G_2, K_2) \twoheadrightarrow GM(J_2, G_2, H_2) \twoheadrightarrow \cdots.$$

Hence, we can conclude that $\theta[GM(J_2, G_2, K_2)] = n - 1$. Take an expansion for K_2:

$$K_2 \xrightarrow{(\mathscr{E}, \alpha)} K_{21}^{(\alpha)}, \ldots, K_{2\alpha(2)}^{(\alpha)}.$$

Then, since $K_2 = K_{21}^{(\alpha)} \cap \cdots \cap K_{2\alpha(2)}^{(\alpha)}$, there exists an integer j, $1 \leqslant j \leqslant \alpha(2)$, such that $\theta[GM(J_2, G_2, K_{2j}^{(\alpha)})] = n - 1$ by Fact 2.25. Furthermore, $GM(J_2, G_2, K_2) \twoheadrightarrow GM(J_2, G_2, K_{2j}^{(\alpha)})$. Let $N_2 = K_{2j}^{(\alpha)}$. Thus, there exists a series

$$S' \twoheadrightarrow GM(J_2, G_2, N_2) \twoheadrightarrow RLM[GM(J_2, G_2, N_2)] \twoheadrightarrow \cdots,$$

with $n - 1$ GM semigroup terms. Thus, taking a kernel of each $S \twoheadrightarrow GM$ in the series, we obtain a new sequence $(J_1, G_1, N_1 = H_1)$, (J_2, G_2, N_2), $(J_3, G_3, H_3'), \ldots, (J_n, G_n, H_n')$ for S' satisfying the conditions of the definition of θ_g.

Continuing on in this fashion, we obtain a sequence of length n satisfying conditions 1–3 of the definition of θ_h. Thus, $\theta_h^{(\mathscr{E})}(S) \geqslant \theta(S)$. Clearly, $\theta_h^{(\mathscr{E})}(S) \leqslant \theta(S)$ by Lemma 2.24, and so $\theta_h^{(\mathscr{E})}(S) = \theta(S)$ for every expansion $\mathscr{E}$ of S. ▌

2.27 Remark. (a) Let $N_2 = \ker[(J_1, G_1, N_1), (J_2, G_2)]$. Then the expansion $\mathscr{E}$ for the tuple $[(J_1, G_1, N_1), (J_2, G_2)]$ given by $N_2 \xrightarrow{\mathscr{E}} N_2$ is called the *trivial expansion*.

(b) The following expansion is of great importance. Let $[(J_1, G_1, N_1), (J_2, G_2)]$ be given, and let $N_2 = \ker[(J_1, G_1, N_1), (J_2, G_2)]$. Refer to Remark 8.3.32. There we saw that G_2 acts on the identified $\mathscr{L}$ classes of J_1. Let R be the range of G_2, and let $R = R_1 \cup \cdots \cup R_n$ (disjoint), where (R_i, G_2), $i = 1,\ldots, n$, are the transitive components of (R, G_2). Let the kernel of G_2 acting on R_i be N_{2i}. Then it is easy to see that $N_2 = N_{21} \cap \cdots \cap N_{2n}$. We let

$$N_2 \to N_{21}, \ldots, N_{2n}$$

be the only expansion associated with $[(J_1, G_1, N_1), (J_2, G_2)]$. We call this expansion the *transitive component expansion for S*.

2.28 Lemma. $\theta_i = \theta$.

PROOF. By the definition of θ_i, it is easy to see that $T \leqslant S$ implies $\theta_i(T) \leqslant \theta_i(S)$. Furthermore, the following two statements are true:

(a) Let $S \in \mathscr{S}$. Then

$$\theta_i(S) = \max\{\theta_i(T) : T \leqslant S \text{ and } T \text{ is type } I\},$$

where max of the empty set is zero.

(b) Let S be a noncombinatorial type I semigroup. Then

$$\theta_i(S) = \theta_i[IG(S)] + 1.$$

To prove (a), let $\theta_i(S) = n$, and let $(T_1, \ldots, T_n)$ be a maximal sequence satisfying (i) for S. Then $(T_1, \ldots, T_n)$ is a sequence for T_1 so that $\theta_i(T_1) \geqslant n = \theta_i(S)$. But $T_1 \leqslant S$, and so $\theta_i(T_1) = \theta_i(S)$.

To prove (b), let $\theta_i(S) = n$, and let $(T_1,\ldots,T_n)$ be a maximal sequence for S. Now $S \supseteq T_1 \supseteq IG(T_1) \supseteq T_2 \supseteq \cdots$, so that $IG(S) \supseteq IG(T_1)$, and so $(S, T_2, T_3, \ldots, T_n)$ is another maximal sequence for S, since S is type I. Then it is clear that $\theta_i[IG(S)] \geqslant n - 1$, since it has a sequence $(T_2, \ldots, T_n)$. However, if $\theta_i[IG(S)] > n - 1$, then $\theta_i(S) > n$, a contradiction. So $\theta_i[IG(S)] + 1 = \theta_i(S)$.

Now suppose statements (a) and (b) were also true for θ. Then we claim $\theta = \theta_i$. We proceed by induction on $|S|$. Suppose the statement is true for all semigroups S such that $|S| \leqslant n - 1$. Let S have order n.

Suppose S is not type I. Then every semigroup in $\{T : T \leqslant S$ and T is type $I\}$ is a proper subsemigroup of S, so that $\theta_i(T) = \theta(T)$ for each T, by induction. Hence, $\theta(S) = \theta_i(S)$ by (a).

Suppose S is noncombinatorial type I. Now $IG(S) < S$, since (b) is true for θ_i. Hence, $\theta_i[IG(S)] = \theta[IG(S)]$, and so by (b) $\theta_i(S) = \theta(S)$.

Hence it suffices to prove (a) and (b) for θ. We do this in the next two lemmas.

2.29 Lemma. Let $S \in \mathscr{S}$. Then

$$\theta(S) = \max\{\theta(T) : T \leqslant S \text{ and } T \text{ is type } I\},$$

where max of the empty set is zero.

PROOF. We shall construct a subsemigroup T of S such that $\theta(T) = \theta(S)$ and T is type I.

Take the transitive component expansion, $\mathscr{E}$, for S. Let $\theta(S) = n$, and let $(J_1, G_1', N_1'),\ldots, (J_n, G_n', N_n')$ be a maximal sequence satisfying conditions 1–3 of the definition of $\theta_h^{\mathscr{E}}$. First we construct a new sequence $(J_1, G_1, N_1),\ldots, (J_n, G_n, N_n)$ that also satisfies these conditions. Let $G_n = G_n'$ and $N_n = N_n'$, and let Y_{n-1} be the transitive component of G_n determined by N_n. Y_{n-1} is a union of $\mathscr{L}$ classes of J_{n-1}. Let G_{n-1} be a maximal subgroup of J_{n-1} which is $\mathscr{R}$-equivalent to G_{n-1}' and is contained in Y_{n-1}. Then let $(J_{n-1}, G_{n-1}, N_{n-1})$ be a kernel of $S \twoheadrightarrow GM(J_{n-1}, G_{n-1}', N_{n-1}')$. By Fact 8.3.30, if e_{n-1} is the identity of G_{n-1}, then $N_{n-1} = N_{n-1}' e_{n-1}$. Since $GM(J_{n-1}, G_{n-1}, N_{n-1}) \cong GM(J_{n-1}, G_{n-1}', N_{n-1}')$, N_n is a member of the transitive component expansion for $[(J_{n-1}, G_{n-1}, N_{n-1}), (J_n, G_n)]$.

Since N_{n-1}' codes a transitive component of G_{n-1}' in J_{n-2}, by Fact 8.3.33 $N_{n-1} = N_{n-1}' e_{n-1}$ codes a transitive component for G_{n-1} in J_{n-2}. Call it Y_{n-2}. Choose a maximal subgroup $G_{n-2} \leqslant Y_{n-2}$ such that $G_{n-2} \mathscr{R} G_{n-2}'$. Then let $(J_{n-2}, G_{n-2}, N_{n-2})$ be a kernel of $S \twoheadrightarrow GM(J_{n-2}, G_{n-2}', N_{n-2}')$. As before, N_{n-1} is a member of the expansion for $[(J_{n-2}, G_{n-2}, N_{n-2}), (J_{n-1}, G_{n-1})]$. Continuing on in this manner yields the new sequence.

Let Y_i, $i = 1,\ldots, n-1$ be the transitive component of G_{i+1} just described. Let $y_i \in Y_i$. Then $J_i y_i$ is the $\mathscr{L}$ class containing y_i, and $Y_i = J_i y_i G_{i+1}$.

We now proceed to construct T inductively. Let $T_1 = G_n \equiv X_n$. Clearly, T_1 is a type I semigroup.

Let $X_{n-1} = Y_{n-1}$, and let $T_2 = X_n \cup X_{n-1}$. T_2 is a semigroup, since $G_n J_{n-1} \subseteq J_{n-1}$, and T_2 has two $\mathscr{J}$ classes, X_n and X_{n-1}, with $X_{n-1} < X_n$. It is easy to see that $\ker[(X_{n-1}, G_{n-1}, N_{n-1}),$

$(X_n, G_n)] \leqslant N_n$, and the sequence $(X_{n-1}, G_{n-1}, N_{n-1}), (X_n, G_n, N_n)$ for T_2 satisfies the conditions of the definition of θ_g, and so $\theta(T_2) = 2$.

Now, to show that T_2 is type I, we must show that $U_1 \not\leqslant T_2{}^C$. Equivalently, we must show that any congruence on T_2 which contains the $\mathscr{H}$ classes (i.e., shrinks them to a point) must shrink the $\mathscr{R}$ classes of T_2 to single points. Then each $\mathscr{J}$ class of $T_2{}^C$ will be of the form A^l, and $U_1 \not\leqslant T_2{}^C$. Let φ be the homomorphism associated with such a congruence. Then $\varphi(X_n)$ is a single element, and $\varphi(X_{n-1}) = \varphi(J_{n-1}y_{n-1})\, \varphi(G_n)$. $J_{n-1}y_{n-1}$ is an $\mathscr{L}$ class, and so $\varphi(J_{n-1}y_{n-1})$ is of the form A^l. But, since $\varphi(G_n)$ is one element, $\varphi(X_{n-1})$ is of the form A^l. Therefore, T_2 is a type I semigroup.

We now construct T_3. Let $X_{n-2} = J_{n-2}y_{n-2}X_{n-1}$. Since $G_{n-1} \subseteq X_{n-1}$, we have $Y_{n-2} \subseteq X_{n-2}$. Let $T_3 = X_n \cup X_{n-1} \cup X_{n-2}$. Clearly, T_3 is a semigroup with three $\mathscr{J}$ classes, $X_{n-2} < X_{n-1} < X_n$. By the same reasoning as before, $\ker[(X_{n-2}, G_{n-2}, N_{n-2}), (X_{n-1}, G_{n-1})] \leqslant N_{n-1}$. Therefore, we have a sequence of length three for T_3 satisfying the definition of θ_g, so that $\theta(T_3) = 3$.

As before, let φ be any homomorphism on T_3 which collapses the $\mathscr{H}$ classes to a point. We must show that $\varphi(X_{n-2}) = \varphi(J_{n-2}y_{n-2})\, \varphi(X_{n-1})$ is of the form A^l. Since $J_{n-2}y_{n-2}$ is an $\mathscr{L}$ class, $\varphi(J_{n-2}y_{n-2})$ is in that form, and we already know that $\varphi(X_{n-1})$ has that form. We know that $J_{n-2}y_{n-2}$ is in the range of G_{n-1} and, by Fact 8.3.33, in the range of every maximal subgroup that is $\mathscr{L}$ equivalent to G_{n-1}. This means that every idempotent in the $\mathscr{L}$ class containing G_{n-1} fixes $J_{n-2}y_{n-2}$. Let that set of idempotents be denoted $\{e_i\}$. Then it is easy to see that $\varphi(X_{n-1}) = \varphi(\{e_i\})$. Thus,

$$\varphi(X_{n-2}) = \varphi(J_{n-2}y_{n-2})\, \varphi(\{e_i\}) = \varphi(J_{n-2}y_{n-2}),$$

so that $\varphi(X_{n-2})$ is of the form A^l, and T_3 is a type I semigroup.

By continuing the same procedure, we construct $T \equiv T_n$, which is a subsemigroup of S which is type I and is such that $\theta(T) = n$ ∎

2.30 Lemma. Let $S \in \mathscr{S}$ be a noncombinatorial type I semigroup. Then

$$\theta(S) = \theta[IG(S)] + 1.$$

To prove this lemma, we need the following facts.

2.31 Fact. (a) Let $S \in \mathscr{S}$ be a *GGM*, *RLM*, or *LLM* semigroup. Then $IG(S)$ is a *GGM*, *RLM*, or *LLM* semigroup, respectively.

If S is a GM semigroup, then $IG(S)$ is a GM semigroup iff S is not a group with zero.

(b) Let $S \in \mathscr{S}$ be type I. Consider a longest alternating GGM-RLM series for S. This series ends in $\{0\}^I$ or $\{0\}$. The last term of the series which is $\not\leq \{0\}^I$ is a GGM term that is either a group or a group with zero.

(c) Let $S \in \mathscr{S}$, and suppose $IG(S) = S$. Consider a longest alternating GGM-RLM series for S. The last term of the series which is $\not\leq \{0\}^I$ is a (combinatorial) RLM semigroup.

PROOF. (a) Let S be a GGM semigroup with distinguished $\mathscr{J}$ class J. Since S is a union of groups, $J \cap IG(S)$ is a $\mathscr{J}$ class of $IG(S)$. Call it J'. Then J' is the unique minimal nonzero $\mathscr{J}$ class of $IG(S)$. Let $s_1 \neq s_2 \in IG(S)$. Since S is a GGM semigroup, there exists $j \in J$ such that $js_1 \neq js_2$. Let e be the identity for j. Then $jes_1 \neq jes_2$, which implies $es_1 \neq es_2$. Since $e \in J'$, we see that $IG(S)$ acts faithfully on the right of J'. Similarly, $IG(S)$ acts faithfully on the left of J'. Thus $IG(S)$ is a GGM semigroup. The proofs are identical for RLM and LLM semigroups.

Let S be a group with zero. Then $IG(S) = \{0\}^I$, and hence not GM. Conversely, let S be a GM semigroup, and suppose $IG(S)$ is not GM. From the foregoing, it is clear that, if S is a GM semigroup, then $IG(S)$ will be a GM semigroup iff J' is noncombinatorial or $IG(S) = \{0\}$.

Hence J' is combinatorial, which means that $J' = E(J) = \{$the identities of the maximal subgroups of $J\}$. Thus, there exists a Rees matrix representation of J, $\mathscr{M}(G; A, B; C)$, with $C(b, a) = 1$ for all $(b, a) \in B \times A$. But, since S is GM, the structure matrix C can have no proportional rows or columns (see Fact 8.2.22), so that $J = G$. But, by the Schützenberger representation for GM semigroups [see Lemma 8.2.17(b)], we have $S = G$ or G^0. But since $IG(S) \neq \{0\}$, $S = G^0$.

(b) The RLM semigroup after the last noncombinatorial GGM semigroup must be combinatorial. Call it T. Then $S \twoheadrightarrow S^C \twoheadrightarrow T$. If $T \not\leq \{0\}^I$, then $U_1 \mid T \mid S^C$, a contradiction. Hence, the last term $\not\leq \{0\}^I$ is GGM, and thus a GM semigroup. Call it S_1, and let J be its distinguished $\mathscr{J}$ class. We claim that J is left simple, for, if it is not, then $U_1 \leq RLM_J(S_1)$, a contradiction. But the Schützenberger representation for GM semigroups shows us that, if S_1 is left simple, then $S = G$ or G^0.

(c) Suppose not. Then, by the proof of (b), the last term $T = G$ or G^0. But, if $IG(S) = S$ and $S \twoheadrightarrow T$, then $IG(T) = T$. Since $IG(G) = \{0\}$ and $IG(G^0) = \{0\}^I$, we have a contradiction. ∎

PROOF OF LEMMA 2.30. Let $\theta(S) = n$. Then there exists a GGM-RLM series for S:

$$S \twoheadrightarrow GGM_1 \twoheadrightarrow RLM_1 \twoheadrightarrow \cdots \twoheadrightarrow GGM_n \twoheadrightarrow \{0\}^I \text{ or } \{0\} \tag{2.8}$$

where $GGM_n = G$ or G^0 [by Fact 2.31(b)]. If $\varphi : S \twoheadrightarrow T$, then $\varphi[IG(S)] = IG(T)$. Hence the restriction of (2.8) to $IG(S)$ yields

$$IG(S) \twoheadrightarrow IG(GGM_1) \twoheadrightarrow \cdots \twoheadrightarrow IG(GGM_{n-1}) \twoheadrightarrow IG(RLM_{n-1}) \twoheadrightarrow \{0\}^I \text{ or } \{0\}$$

and each $IG(GGM_i)$, $i = 1, \ldots, n-1$, is a GM semigroup by Fact 2.31(a). Thus, $\theta[IG(S)] \geqslant \theta(S) - 1$.

Now suppose $\theta[IG(S)] = n$. Then there exists a series for $IG(S)$ with n GGM semigroups which ends in $RLM_n \not\leqslant \{0\}^I$ [Fact 2.31(c)]. By Fact 2.23, $U_1 \mid [IG(S)]_{(n)}^{(\gamma+\mathscr{I})\cdots\mathscr{L}}$. But $[IG(S)]_{(n)}^{(\gamma+\mathscr{I})\cdots\mathscr{L}} \mid S_{(n)}^{(\gamma+\mathscr{I})\cdots\mathscr{L}}$, and so this implies there exists a series for S with the nth RLM term $\not\leqslant \{0\}^I$, which is a contradiction, since $\theta(S) = n$ and all maximal series for S must end in GGM. Thus, $\theta[IG(S)] \neq n$, and $\theta(S) = \theta[IG(S)] + 1$. ∎

2.32 Lemma. $\theta_j = \theta$.

PROOF. Let $X \subseteq \mathscr{C}(S)$. Let $p(X) = \{\chi_i :$ there exists $x \in X$ such that $x = \sum_{j=1}^{n} a_j \chi_j$ with $a_i \neq 0\}$. Let $H(X) : S \twoheadrightarrow T = H(X)(S)$ be defined by $H(X) = \Pi\{\mathscr{R}_i : \chi_i \in p(X)\}$. Let $RLM(X) = \Pi\{RLM\mathscr{R}_j : \chi_j \in p(X)\}$. Now $RLM\mathscr{R}_j(S) = \mathscr{R}_j(S)^{\mathscr{L}} = \mathscr{R}_j(S)^{RLM}$, and thus, by Proposition 8.3.17,

$$\varphi H(X) = RLM(X), \tag{2.9}$$

where $\varphi : H(X)(S) \twoheadrightarrow [H(X)(S)]^{\mathscr{L}}$.

It was proved by Rhodes [2] that

$$H[\mathscr{C}(S)](S) = S^{\gamma+\mathscr{I}}. \tag{2.10}$$

Let $\mathscr{R}$ be a matrix representation of S (which is not necessarily completely reducible). Then it is proved by Rhodes [2] that $H[\chi(\mathscr{R})](S) = [\mathscr{R}(S)]^{\gamma+\mathscr{I}}$. It then follows from Proposition 8.3.17 that, if $\{\mathscr{R}\}$ is a collection of matrix representations of S and $\chi\{\mathscr{R}\} = \{\chi(\mathscr{R})\}$, then

$$H(\chi\{\mathscr{R}\})(S) = ([\Pi\{\mathscr{R}\}](S))^{\gamma+\mathscr{I}}. \tag{2.11}$$

It is also proved by Rhodes [2] that $\mathscr{C}(S)^A$ is the linear span of $p[\mathscr{C}(S)^A]$, and

$$H[\mathscr{C}(S)^A](S) = S^{\mathscr{I}}, \tag{2.12}$$

and, furthermore, if $X \subseteq \mathscr{C}(S)$ is such that $X \supseteq \mathscr{C}(S)^A$, then $H(X)$ is a $\mathscr{I}$-homomorphism, and

$$H(X) : S \twoheadrightarrow S^{\mathscr{I}} \qquad \text{iff} \quad X = \mathscr{C}(S)^A. \tag{2.13}$$

From the definition of $A : \mathscr{C}(S) \to \mathscr{C}(S)$, it is easily verified that for $X \subseteq \mathscr{C}(S)$

$$p[A(X)] = p(\chi[RLM(X)]). \tag{2.14}$$

We now prove $\theta_j = \theta_c$. By (2.10), $H[\mathscr{C}(S)] : S \twoheadrightarrow S^{\gamma+\mathscr{I}}$, and by (2.9), $RLM[\mathscr{C}(S)] = S \twoheadrightarrow S^{\gamma+\mathscr{I}} \twoheadrightarrow S^{(\gamma+\mathscr{I})\mathscr{L}}$. Furthermore by (2.11),

$$H(\chi RLM[\mathscr{C}(S)]) : S \twoheadrightarrow S^{\gamma+\mathscr{I}} \twoheadrightarrow S^{(\gamma+\mathscr{I})\mathscr{L}} \twoheadrightarrow S^{(\gamma+\mathscr{I})\mathscr{L}(\gamma+\mathscr{I})}.$$

But (2.14) yields $p(A[\mathscr{C}(X)]) = p(\chi RLM[\mathscr{C}(S)])$, and thus

$$H(\chi RLM[\mathscr{C}(S)]) = H(A[\mathscr{C}(S)]) \qquad \text{or} \qquad H(A[\mathscr{C}(S)]) : S \twoheadrightarrow S^{\gamma+\mathscr{I}} \to S^{(\gamma+\mathscr{I})\mathscr{L}} \twoheadrightarrow S^{(\gamma+\mathscr{I})\mathscr{L}(\gamma+\mathscr{I})}.$$

Now, by continuing in this fashion to compute $H(A^k[\mathscr{C}(S)])$ and using (2.12)–(2.14), we find the first integer n so that $H(A^n[\mathscr{C}(S)])(S) = S^{\mathscr{I}}$ (so that $\theta_c(S) = n$) is equal to the first integer n, so that $A^n[\mathscr{C}(S)] \subseteq \mathscr{C}(S)^A$. But this last integer is the index of B. Thus, $\theta_j(S) = \theta_c(S)$. This proves Lemma 2.32 and completes the proof of Theorem 2.5. ∎

3. Corollaries of the Theorem

We denote the unique G-complexity function for union of groups semigroups with respect to GM semigroups by $\#_G : \mathscr{S} \to N$. In this section, all semigroups are union of groups *unless otherwise specified.*

3.1 Corollary (Continuity of Complexity with Respect to Homomorphisms).

(a) $\varphi : S \xrightarrow[\gamma]{} T$ implies $\#_G(S) = \#_G(T)$.

(b) $\varphi : S \xrightarrow[\mathscr{L}]{} T$ implies $\#_G(T) \leqslant \#_G(S) \leqslant \#_G(T) + 1$.

(c) Let $\varphi : S \twoheadrightarrow T$ be an epimorphism, and let $\#_G(S) = n$ and $\#_G(T) = k$. Then there exist epimorphisms $S = S_n \twoheadrightarrow S_{n-1} \twoheadrightarrow \cdots \twoheadrightarrow S_k = T$, so that the composite epimorphism is φ, and $\#_G(S_j) = j$ for $j = k, \ldots, n$.

PROOF. (a) If $S \xrightarrow[\gamma]{} T$, then $S^\gamma = T^\gamma$. Thus, series (e) for T is identical to series (e) for S after the first γ map. Hence, $\theta_e(S) = \theta_e(T)$.

(b) Let

$$S \twoheadrightarrow GM_1 \twoheadrightarrow RLM_1 \twoheadrightarrow GM_2 \twoheadrightarrow \cdots$$

be a longest series of this type for S. Now, since $S \xrightarrow[\mathscr{L}]{} T$, we have

$$T \twoheadrightarrow T^{\mathscr{L}} = S^{\mathscr{L}} = S^{RLM} \twoheadrightarrow RLM_1,$$

so that

$$T \twoheadrightarrow RLM_1 \twoheadrightarrow GM_2 \twoheadrightarrow \cdots$$

is a series of type (f) for T. Then $\#_G(T) = \theta_f(T) \geqslant \#_G(S) - 1$. On the other hand, $\#_G(T) \leqslant \#_G(S)$.

(c) Since $\varphi : S \twoheadrightarrow T$ can be decomposed into alternating γ-homomorphisms and $\mathscr{L}$-homomorphisms (Theorem 8.1.14), the assertion follows immediately from (a) and (b). ∎

3.2 Corollary (Continuity of Complexity with Respect to Subsemigroups).

(a) If T is a maximal proper subsemigroup of S, then $\#_G(T) \leqslant \#_G(S) \leqslant \#_G(T) + 1$.

(b) Let $T \leqslant S$, with $k = \#_G(T) \leqslant \#_G(S) = n$. Then there exist subsemigroups $T = S_k \leqslant S_{k+1} \leqslant \cdots \leqslant S_n = S$, so that $\#_G(S_j) = j$ for $j = k, \ldots, n$.

PROOF. (a) Consider a longest series for S of the form

$$S \twoheadrightarrow GM_1 \twoheadrightarrow RLM_1 \twoheadrightarrow GM_2 \twoheadrightarrow \cdots \twoheadrightarrow \{0\}.$$

Since $RLM(GM_k) = GM_k^{RLM} \twoheadrightarrow RLM_k$, replace each RLM_k by $RLM(GM_k)$. The new series will be the same length, i.e., there are $\#_G(S)$ nonzero GM semigroups in the series. Restrict to T, and take successive images to get

$$\begin{array}{ccccccccc} S & \twoheadrightarrow & GM_1 & \twoheadrightarrow & RLM(GM_1) & \twoheadrightarrow & GM_2 & \twoheadrightarrow \cdots \twoheadrightarrow & \{0\}, \\ \cup\!| & & \cup\!| & & \cup\!| & & \cup\!| & & \\ T & \twoheadrightarrow & T_{11} & \twoheadrightarrow & T_{12} & \twoheadrightarrow & T_{21} & \twoheadrightarrow \cdots \twoheadrightarrow & \{0\}. \end{array} \quad \begin{array}{c}(3.1)\\ \\ (3.2)\end{array}$$

Since T is a maximal proper subsemigroup of S, T_{k1} and T_{k2} are maximal subsemigroups of GM_k and $RLM(GM_k)$, respectively. By Prop. 7.3.3, a maximal subsemigroup contains at least all but one $\mathcal{J}$ class of the semigroup. Let I_{k1} and I_{k2} be the distinguished $\mathcal{J}$ classes (with respect to being GM and RLM semigroups) of GM_k and $RLM(GM_k)$, respectively.

If I_{11} is contained in T_{11}, then it is the unique minimal nonzero $\mathcal{J}$ class of T_{11}, and T_{11} acts faithfully on the left and right of it. In other words, T_{11} is a GM semigroup $\neq \{0\}$. Since I_{12} is the image of I_{11}, I_{12} is contained in T_{12}, and T_{12} is an RLM semigroup. Continue on in this manner. If $I_{k1} \subseteq T_{k1}$ for every k, then series (3.2) has the same number of nonzero GM semigroups as does series (3.1). Thus, since series (3.2) is of form (f), we have $\#_G(T) = \#_G(S)$.

Suppose, then, that $I_{j1} \not\subseteq T_{j1}$ for some j, $1 \leqslant j \leqslant \#_G(S)$. Pick the smallest such j. Then $GM_j - I_{j1} \subseteq T_{j1}$. Let $\varphi : GM_j \twoheadrightarrow GM_{j+1}$. Then $GM_{j+1} - \varphi(I_{j1}) \subseteq T_{(j+1)1}$. But we claim $\varphi(I_{j1}) = \{0\}$. For its image in $RLM(GM_j)$ is combinatorial and 0-minimal, and yet $I_{(j+1)1}$ is noncombinatorial, and so $\varphi(I_{j1}) = \{0\}$. Thus, $T_{(j+1)1} = GM_{j+1}$ or $GM_{j+1} - \{0\}$. Thus, the remainder of series (3.2) is identical to series (3.1) except for a zero, maybe.

Thus series (3.2) can be written in form (f) as

$$T \twoheadrightarrow \cdots \twoheadrightarrow T_{(j-1)2} \twoheadrightarrow T_{(j+1)1} \twoheadrightarrow \cdots \twoheadrightarrow \{0\}.$$

So, in this case, $\#_G(T) \geqslant \#_G(S) - 1$.

(b) This follows immediately from (a). ∎

3.3 Corollary (Continuity of Complexity with Respect to Division). Let $T \mid S$, with $k = \#_G(T) \leqslant \#_G(S) = n$. Then there exist $T = T_k \mid T_{k+1} \mid \cdots \mid T_n = S$ such that $\#_G(T_j) = j$ for $j = k, \ldots, n$.

PROOF. This follows immediately from Corollaries 3.1 and 3.2. ∎

3.4 Corollary. Axioms I and II of Definition 1.2 are equivalent to Axiom I and the following.

AXIOM II′. $S \xrightarrow[\gamma]{} \!\!\!\!\rightarrow T$ implies $\#_G(S) = \#_G(T)$, where S is an arbitrary finite semigroup.

PROOF. Clearly, I and II′ implies I and II. Conversely, suppose Axioms I and II are given. Let $\varphi : S \twoheadrightarrow T$ be a γ-homomorphism, and write $\varphi = \varphi_n \varphi_{n-1} \cdots \varphi_1$, where φ_i, $i = 1, \ldots, n$, is an *MPE*. Clearly, each φ_i is a γ-homomorphism, and so it will suffice to prove that $\#_G(S) = \#_G[\varphi(S)]$ when φ is a γ-*MPE*.

Now by Lemma 8.1.18 there exists a $\mathscr{J}$ class J of S such that φ is $1:1$ on $S - J$ and φ separates $(J \cup F(J))$ and its complement in S. If J is regular, then φ is a $\gamma(\mathscr{H})$ homomorphism on J.

If J is null, let $\psi : S \twoheadrightarrow S/F(J)$. Then $(\varphi \times \psi)\,\Delta$ is $1:1$ on S.

If J is regular, define $\psi : S \twoheadrightarrow [S/F(J)]/\equiv$, where $\equiv$ is the congruence on $S/F(J)$ given by $s_1 \equiv s_2$ iff $s_1 = s_2$ or, if $s_1, s_2 \in J$, then $s_1 \mathscr{H} s_2$. Then ψ is an $\mathscr{H}$-homomorphism on $S/F(J)$. Then it is easy to verify that $(\varphi \times \psi)\,\Delta$ is $1:1$ on S.

We pause to note that Axiom I alone implies that, if $\varphi : S \twoheadrightarrow T$, then $\#_G(S) \geqslant \#_G(T)$. For $(\varphi \times Id)\,\Delta$ is $1:1$ on S, and so $\#_G(S) = \max[\#_G(S), \#_G(T)]$ by Axiom I. Thus, $\#_G(S) \geqslant \#_G(T)$.

Now we return to the proof. Since $(\varphi \times \psi)\,\Delta$ is $1:1$ on S, by Axiom I we have

$$\#_G(S) = \max(\#_G[\varphi(S)], \#_G[\psi(S)]). \tag{3.3}$$

φ is $1:1$ on $S - J$, and so there exist $\varphi(S) \twoheadrightarrow S/[J \cup F(J)]$. Furthermore, $S/[J \cup F(J)] \twoheadrightarrow \psi(S)/\psi[J \cup F(J)]$, and so $\varphi(S) \twoheadrightarrow \psi(S)/\psi[J \cup F(J)]$. Then $\#_G[\varphi(S)] \geqslant \#_G(\psi(S)/\psi[J \cup F(J)])$. But $\psi[J \cup F(J)]$ is a combinatorial ideal of $\psi(S)$, and so $\#_G[\psi(S)] = \#_G(\psi(S)/\psi[J \cup F(J)])$ by Axiom II. Thus $\#_G[\varphi(S)] \geqslant \#_G[\psi(S)]$, and by (3.1) we have $\#_G(S) = \#_G[\varphi(S)]$. ∎

Exercises and Extensions

X3.1. Show that the semigroup of all functions on three letters, $F_R(X_3)$, *never* divides $C \,\mathrm{w}\, [F_R(X_3)/K]$, where K is the combinatorial kernel of $F_R(X_3)$ consisting of the three constant functions, and where C is any combinatorial semigroup.

[Hint: First show that $F_R(X_3)$ is regular with three $\mathscr{J}$ classes, $J_3 = SYM_R(X_3)$, $J_2 \cong \mathscr{M}^0(\mathbf{Z}_2\,;\, X_3\,,\, X_3\,;\, C) - \{0\}$, where $\mathbf{Z}_2 = \{1, -1\}$ is the cyclic group of order two, and where

$$C = \begin{pmatrix} 0 & 1 & 1 \\ 1 & 0 & -1 \\ 1 & 1 & 0 \end{pmatrix},$$

and $J_1 = K \cong X_3^r$. Then assume

$$F_R(X_3) \twoheadleftarrow T \leqslant C' \times_Y [F_R(X_3)/K]$$

where C' is combinatorial. Let $K(T)$ be the kernel of T, let p_1 be the projection homomorphism on the semidirect product, and consider $p_1[K(T)]$. Then either (1) $p_1[K(T)] \leqslant J_3$, (2) $p_1[K(T)] \leqslant J_2$, or $p_1[K(T)] = \{0\}$. If case (1) holds, then

$$F_R(X_3) | \; C' \times_Y J_3 ,$$

which implies

$$IG[F_R(X_3)] | \; IG[C' \times_Y J_3].$$

But $IG[C' \times_Y J_3]$ is combinatorial since J_3 is a group, so $IG[F_R(X_3)]$ is combinatorial, a contradiction. If case (3) holds, then $(t, x) \to Y(0)\, t$ is a homomorphism of T onto $T' \leqslant C'$ that separates the $\mathscr{L}$ classes of $K(T)$. Thus $F_R(X_3) | \; T' \mid C'$, a contradiction. (See Fact 5.3.19.) If case (2) holds, prove that $p_1[K(T)]$ is a subsemigroup of $\mathbf{Z}_2 \times \{1, 2\}^r$ or $\mathbf{Z}_2 \times \{1, 2\}^l$, using the structure of C. Thus conclude that $p_1(T)$ is a subsemigroup of a union of groups semigroup with two $\mathscr{J}$ classes, D_1 and D_2, where $D_2 \leqslant J_3$ and $D_1 = p_1[K(T)]$. Then show $p_1(T) | \; C_1 \le G_1$ with C_1 a combinatorial semigroup and G_1 a group. Thus $F_R(X_3) | \; C_2 \le C_1 \le G_1$ so $IG(F_R(X_3))$ is combinatorial, a contradiction.]

X3.2 (Allen). Let $\mathbf{Z}^+$ be the semigroup of positive integers under addition. Show that there exists a $Y : \mathbf{Z}^+ \to \mathrm{Endo}_L(\mathbf{Z}^+)$ such that any finitely generated semigroup divides $\mathbf{Z}^+ \times_Y \mathbf{Z}^+$.

[Hint: First show that $\Sigma\{0, 1,..., n\}$ is isomorphic to a subsemigroup of $\Sigma\{0, 1\}$ for all $n = 1, 2,...$, so that every finitely generated semigroup divides $\Sigma\{0, 1\}$. Define Y by $Y(k)(z) = 2^k \cdot z$, and verify that $t \to [n_2(t), n_1(t)] \in \mathbf{Z}^+ \times_Y \mathbf{Z}^+$ is a $1:1$ homomorphism, where $t \in \Sigma\{0, 1\}$, $t = (t_1 ,..., t_k)$ and $n_1(t) = k$, $n_2(t)$ is the positive integer with binary expansion $t_k \cdots t_1$.]

NOTES AND REFERENCES

This chapter is recent, previously unpublished research by Rhodes, except for the proof that $\theta_a \equiv \#_G$ satisfies the axioms, which is proved in Krohn and Rhodes [3]. In fact, more is proved there, namely that $C(S) \leqslant (\mathbf{C}, 1) \oplus C(S/I)$, where S is a union of groups semigroup and I is a combinatorial ideal.

That θ_b through θ_j satisfy the axioms depends very heavily on Rhodes [4], Sect. 6 (or Sects. 2 and 3 of Chapter 7 of this volume) and on Rhodes [2].

For recent results extending some of the methods of this chapter to regular and arbitrary finite semigroups, see Tilson [7], Rhodes and Tilson [6], and Rhodes [8]. For a generalization of the Rees theorem, see Allen [5].

1. C. W. Curtis and I. Reiner, "Representation Theory of Finite Groups and Associative Algebras." Wiley (Interscience), New York, 1962.
2. J. Rhodes, Complexity and characters of finite semigroups (to be submitted to *J. Comb. Theory*).
3. K. Krohn and J. Rhodes, Complexity of finite semigroups, *Ann. of Math.* (to appear).
4. J. Rhodes, Some results on finite semigroups, *J. Algebra* **3**, 471–504 (1966).
5. D. Allen†, "Relations between the local and global structure of finite semigroups." Ph. D. Thesis, University of California, Berkeley (1968).
6. J. Rhodes and B. Tilson, Lower bounds for complexity of finite semigroups (submitted to *Math. System Theory*).
7. B. Tilson, Ph. D. Thesis, University of California, Berkeley (to appear).
8. J. Rhodes, A proof of the fundamental lemma of complexity-weak version (to appear).

† Present address: Bell Telephone Labs., Holmdel, New Jersey.

CHAPTER 10

Expository Lectures on Topological Semigroups

JANE M. DAY[†]
The Institute for Advanced Study, Princeton, New Jersey

The study of topological semigroups began about 1950, and Professor A. D. Wallace is known as the founder. He has originated and contributed heavily to most of the major areas of research, and most people in the field are his mathematical descendants.

The purpose of this chapter is to convey some of the flavor and techniques of topological semigroups, rather than to give a representative or detailed survey of the literature. Many of the results stated here are not given in complete generality, and many results of much interest are not discussed at all, among the most important of which are those on the cohomology of compact connected semigroups, due to Wallace [W 1, 4, and 5], many of which appear in one work [W 8]. We include some shorter proofs, especially those which display techniques of interest.

Most of the interesting theorems to date about semigroups concern the compact, locally compact, or discrete cases, and most of the discussion that follows deals with compact semigroups. By discrete we mean algebraic, for it is true that an algebraic semigroup is Hausdorff in the discrete topology (every set is open), hence is naturally a topological semigroup with all functions defined on it continuous. In particular, a finite semigroup is naturally a compact topological semigroup.

For general information about topological semigroups, see the new book by Hofmann and Mostert [H-M], the excellent expository dissertation of Paalman-de Miranda [P-de M], and Wallace [W 8].

Insofar as topology is concerned, we depart some from customary notation in that we prefer A^*, $A\backslash B$, and $\square$ for the closure of a set,

[†] Present address: College of Notre Dame, Belmont, California.

set difference, and the empty set, respectively, and we do not distinguish between x and $\{x\}$. Where there may be no confusion of meaning, topological usage will take preference over algebraic.‡ Thus, to say a set is *closed* is to mean that it is closed in the topology and *not* that it is a subsemigroup. The general topology we use can be found in the references [H-Y, Hu, Ke].

Definitions. A *semigroup* is a nonempty Hausdorff topological space S, together with a continuous associative multiplication

$$S \times S \to S,$$

which usually remains anonymous and is denoted by juxtaposition. S is called the *underlying space* of the semigroup, and, when there can be no confusion about the multiplication, we say "S is a semigroup." In all the following, let S and W denote semigroups.

For $A, B \subset S$, AB denotes $\{ab \mid a \in A, b \in B\}$ and A^2 denotes $\{aa' \mid a, a' \in A\}$. Two facts from topology which are fundamental in all that follows are that the product of compact spaces is compact and the continuous image of a compact space is compact. Therefore, if A and B are compact in S, then AB is compact, and, in particular, if A is compact, then xA and Ax are compact for each $x \in S$.

In topology, a *homeomorphism* is a function that is onto, continuous, and whose inverse is a continuous function. In semigroups, an *iseomorphism* is a function that is both an isomorphism and a homeomorphism.

The minimal ideal of S is customarily denoted by $K(S)$. For a compact semigroup S, $K(S)$ exists and its structure is completely known; in the language of algebraic semigroups, $K(S)$ is completely simple [C-P]. In particular, $K(S)$ is compact and is the disjoint union of a family of compact groups (see Theorem 3.9).

The set of all idempotents of S is customarily denoted by $E(S)$. A *subgroup* of S is a subset G of S which is algebraically a group with its inherited multiplication. The multiplication in a subgroup G is clearly continuous, and, if G is locally compact, inversion is also

‡ Editor's note: In this chapter alone, all semigroups will be topological. It is our belief that many of the results developed for finite semigroups and machines in previous chapters will soon be extended to topological semigroups and machines; and it is our hope that the juxtaposition of Dr. Day's elegant exposition with this material may hasten such developments. Her papers with Professor Wallace [D-W] may be viewed as the first chapters of a theory of topological machines.

continuous, so that G is a topological group [E]. For each idempotent $e \in E(S)$, there is a maximal group in S with e as identity (see Lemma 1.6).

A *bing* is a compact connected semigroup, and a *clan* is a bing with identity. Shown in Fig. 1 are some simple examples of semigroups, all with their usual multiplication: the real interval [0, 1], the unit disk D in the complex plane, and, for fixed $n \geqslant 1$, any convex subset of D which contains the nth roots of unity $\{\alpha_1, \ldots, \alpha_n\}$. (We sketch an illustration of this for $n = 3$.) Observe that each of these semigroups is actually a clan.

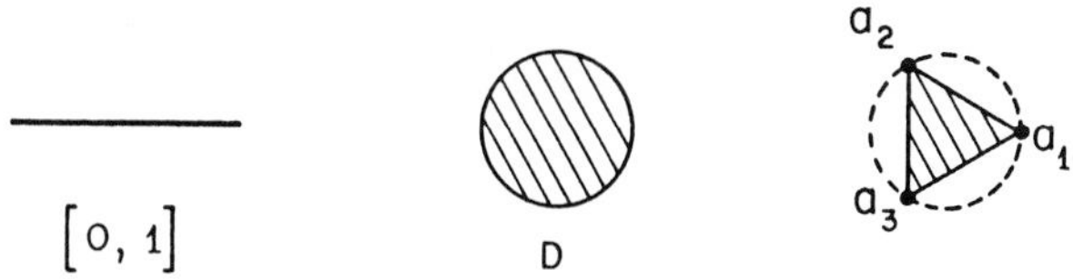

FIG. 1

1. Arcs and Semigroups

A *thread* is a semigroup whose underlying space is an *arc*, a Hausdorff continuum in which every point is a cutpoint except two points, called endpoints. (A closed real interval $[a, b]$ with $a < b$ is an arc with endpoints a and b.) A *standard thread*, or *I-semigroup*, is a thread for which one endpoint is a zero and the other is an identity.

The structure of threads is of considerable interest in its own right and also because quite a lot is known about the existence of threads, especially I-semigroups, in larger semigroups. Faucett [F 1] proved that an I-semigroup with no interior idempotents must be homeomorphic to the real interval [0, 1]. (However, in general, I-semigroups need not be metric; they can be "too long.") Faucett obtained further results that went a long way toward characterizing I-semigroups, and the job was completed by Mostert and Shields [M-S 1], where they used the information in their study of certain clans on compact manifolds with boundary (see 2.3). Independently, Clifford obtained more general results on threads which completely described threads with idempotent endpoints [Cl 1, 2], and Cohen and Wade characterized metrizable threads with zero and identity [C-W]. One of the most important facts about I-semigroups is that they are all abelian; we shall describe their structure, but first we need some definitions.

1.1 Definitions. (1) A *unit thread* is a semigroup iseomorphic to [0, 1] with its usual real multiplication.

(2) A *nil thread* is a semigroup iseomorphic to $[\frac{1}{2}, 1]$ with multiplication defined by $xy = \max\{\frac{1}{2}$, usual product of x and $y\}$ [see Example 2.2(1)].

(3) An arc with its cutpoint order and multiplication defined by $xy = \min\{x, y\}$ is a *min thread.* (On an arc A, the *cutpoint order* is defined as follows: choose one endpoint, a, and, for $x, y \in A$, define $x \leqslant y$ iff $x = a$ or $x = y$ or x separates a and y in A. It is proved in [H-Y] that this is a linear order.)

1.2 Theorem [M-S, Cl 1, C-W, F]. Let S be an I-semigroup, and give S its cutpoint order, letting the zero be the minimal element. Then $E(S)$ is closed, and, for $x, y \in E(S)$, $xy = \min\{x, y\}$; the complement of $E(S)$ is the union of disjoint open intervals, and, if P is one of these, P^* is a subsemigroup of S which is a unit thread or a nil thread; and, finally, if $x \in P$ and $y \notin P$, $xy = \min\{x, y\}$. In particular, S is abelian.

Not all threads are abelian, even those with idempotent endpoints, as shown by the following.

1.3 Example. Let S be the subset of the plane defined by

$$S = ([0, 1] \times 0) \cup (0 \times [0, 1])$$

(see Fig. 2) and define multiplication in S by

$$(x, y)(x', y') = (xx', xy' + y).$$

This is a nonabelian thread with identity but no zero; however, each element p in the vertical segment is a *left zero*, i.e., $pS = p$. Note that the horizontal segment is a unit thread.

According to Theorem 1.2, a thread with just two idempotents, the endpoints (i.e., an I-semigroup with no interior idempotents), is

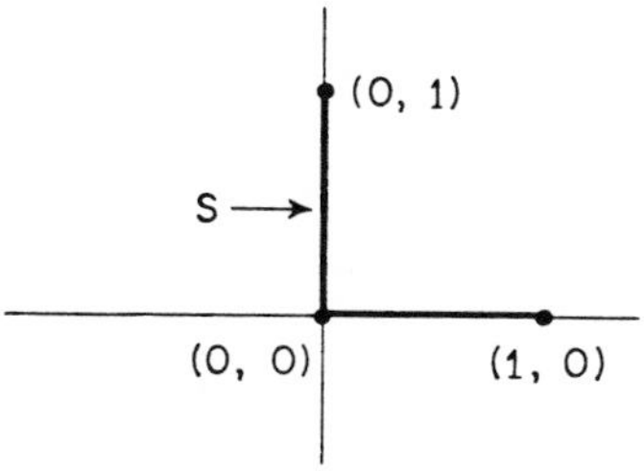

FIG. 2

either a unit or nil thread. Wallace inquired about higher dimension cells, but practically nothing is known.

1.4 Major Problem [W]. What is the semigroup structure, if any, of an n-cell for $n > 1$ if one requires that the set of idempotents equal the boundary? In particular, does a 2-cell admit such a semigroup?

In Example 2.2(3), we give an example of a semigroup on a 2-cell with the boundary plus one interior point as idempotents, but no standard technique will eliminate the interior idempotent in that semigroup. In general, to define a semigroup with desired geometric properties on a space S is very difficult; it is usually relatively easy to define continuous functions $S \times S \to S$ with the properties, but getting associativity is hard. Thus, new examples are usually built from already known semigroups, by techniques such as those described under Section 2.

In passing, we mention that a theorem of Cohen and Krule [C-K] implies that a nontrivial homomorphism from a real I-semigroup preserves dimension, although in general semigroup homomorphisms have little respect for dimension; there are examples of homomorphisms from compact semigroups onto semigroups of higher dimension, whereas this cannot happen with groups. (This follows from results in Montgomery and Zippin [M-Z]). By dimension we mean inductive, or topological, dimension [H-W]. For more information about dimension and semigroups, see Anderson and Hunter [A-H].

1.5 Definition. A *one-parameter semigroup* in S is a function $\sigma : [0, 1] \to S$ which is continuous, 1-1, and which satisfies

$\sigma(x + y) = \sigma(x)\,\sigma(y)$ whenever x, y, $x + y \in [0, 1]$. σ ([0, 1]) is an arc, as a subspace of S, since [0, 1] compact, S Hausdorff, and σ continuous and 1-1 imply that σ is a homeomorphism into S. Informally, we speak of the image of [0, 1] under σ as being the one-parameter semigroup. Observe that this image need *not* be a subsemigroup of S, since [0, 1] is not closed under addition. As an example of a one-parameter semigroup that is not a subsemigroup, take the closed interval $[\frac{1}{2}, 1]$ on the real axis, where S is the unit disk in the plane with usual complex multiplication (see Fig. 3).

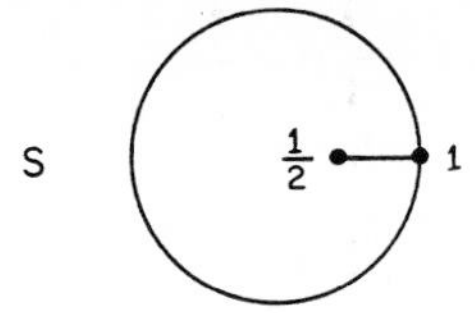

FIG. 3

1.6 Lemma. If $e \in E(S)$, there exists a maximal subgroup of S, $H(e)$, containing e, and

$$H(e) = \{x \in eSe \mid xx' = e = x'x \text{ for some } x' \in eSe\}$$
$$= \{x \in S \mid x \cup xS = e \cup eS \text{ and } x \cup Sx = e \cup Se\}.$$

In 1960, Mostert and Shields [M-S 2] published the following theorem, which continues to be a major tool in the study of semigroups. The first version of the theorem, which required that $H(1)$ be a Lie group, appeared in 1957 [M-S 1]. Let us say that an arc A in S *emerges from an idempotent* $e \in S$ iff $A \cap H(e) = e$. The example of a one-parameter semigroup given in Sect. 1.5 is also an example of an arc emerging from an idempotent.

1.7 Theorem [M-S 2]. Let S be locally compact with identity 1, suppose that there is a compact subgroup G of $H(1)$, open in $H(1)$ but not open in S, and suppose there exists a neighborhood of 1 containing no other idempotents. Then S contains a one-parameter semigroup emerging from 1.

This theorem remains difficult to prove, although it has been almost ten years since the first version of it appeared. Mostert and Shields remark that, if they did not need their one-parameter semigroups to emerge, then they could use Gleason's theorem on the existence of one-parameter groups in locally compact groups, which is easier to prove (see [M-Z]). Mostert and Shields' theorem naturally causes one to wonder whether there is an arc or one-parameter semigroup emerging from a nonisolated idempotent, and whether a one-parameter semigroup in S is a subset of a thread in S. The answers are no, as shown by the examples below, although it is true that a bing must be reasonably well behaved about an idempotent outside $K(S)$, since Koch [K 2] proved that each neighborhood of such an idempotent contains an arc. However, these arcs need not contain the idempotent, and they need not be subsemigroups of S or even one-parameter semigroups.

1.8 Definition. The *semigroup product* of S and W is the Cartesian product $S \times W$ with coordinatewise multiplication, i.e., $(x, y)(x', y') = (xx', yy')$.

1.9 Examples. Let $I = [0, 1]$ with usual real multiplication, and let C be the unit circle and D the unit disk in the complex plane with usual complex multiplication.

(1) $I \times C$ is a hollow cylinder semigroup with identity (1, 1) and minimal ideal $0 \times C$. Let

$$S = (0 \times C) \cup \{(e^{-t}, e^{2\pi it}) \mid 0 \leqslant t < \infty\},$$

so that S is the base circle $0 \times C$, together with an infinite spiral winding down on it (see Fig. 4). Observe that S is a clan with identity (1, 1), and $K(S) = 0 \times C$. Any arc in S emerging from (1, 1) is a one-parameter semigroup, but the smallest subbing containing such an arc is all of S; hence, no such arc can be extended to a thread in S. We will call S the single spiral semigroup.

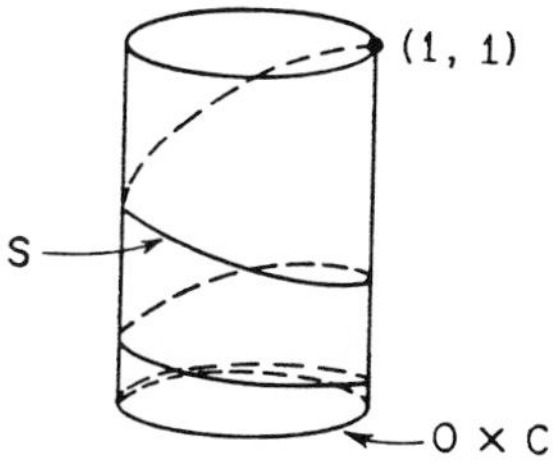

FIG. 4

(2) $I \times D$ is a solid cylinder semigroup with identity (1, 1) and minimal ideal (0, 0). The spiral semigroup S defined in (1) is a subsemigroup of $I \times D$, and $T = S \cup (0 \times D)$ is also a subsemigroup. T is a spiral winding down on the boundary of a 2-cell, together with the 2-cell (see Fig. 5). Observe that T is a clan with identity (1, 1) and zero, $K(T) = (0, 0)$. Here again we see that any arc emerging from (1, 1) is a one-parameter semigroup, but none can be extended to a thread in T.

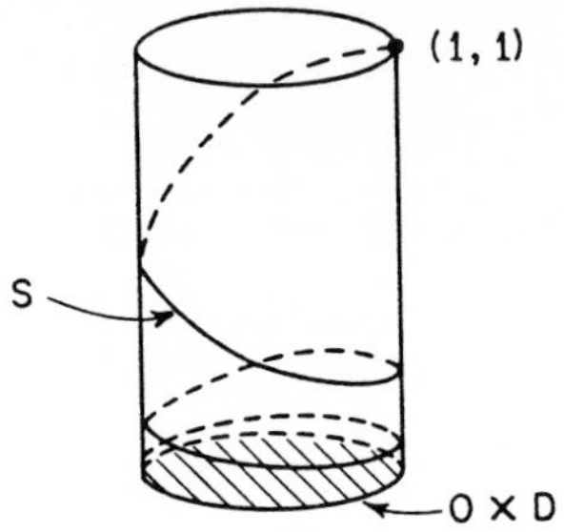

FIG. 5

(3) This example, due to Hunter [Hn 3], is a clan T' in which no arc emerges from the identity, and, in fact, the identity lies on no arc at all. It is, of course, not open in $E(T')$. In E^3, let D_i be the disk defined by $x^2 + y^2 \leqslant (1/i)$ and $z = 1 - (1/i)$, for $i = 1, 2, 3,\ldots$, so that the disks D_i converge to the point $u = (0, 0, 1)$. From the center of D_{i+1}, start a half-line A_i that stays within the cone determined by the center of D_{i+1} and the boundary of D_i and that winds upon the boundary of D_i as in (2). Let $T_i = A_i \cup D_i$, and give T_i the multiplication defined on T, in (2), for each $i = 1, 2, 3,\ldots$, so that the center of D_i is the zero for T_i. Let $T_\infty = u$ and $T' = \bigcup \{T_i \mid i = \infty, 1, 2, 3,\ldots\}$. Complete the definition of multiplication in T' as follows: define ∞ to be greater than any integer, and, if $x \in T_i$, $y \in T_j$, and $i < j$, define $xy = yx = x$. Then T' is a clan with zero, $K(T) = (0, 0)$, and identity, u, and no arc in T' contains u (see Fig. 6). One has, of course, to check continuity of multiplication at $T_i \cap T_{i+1}$ for each i, and associativity on T'. This multiplication would not be continuous if one started the spiral of T_i at the identity of D_{i+1} rather than at its zero. Observe that T' is made from single spirals in a similar fashion to the way

I-semigroups are built up of unit, nil, and min threads (see 1.2 and 1.11). Also observe that there are nondegenerate *connected* groups in every neighborhood of u (the boundaries of the disks), and intuitively these appear to be the obstructions to constructing an arc emerging from u. This is actually true and is due to Koch; the theorem follows.

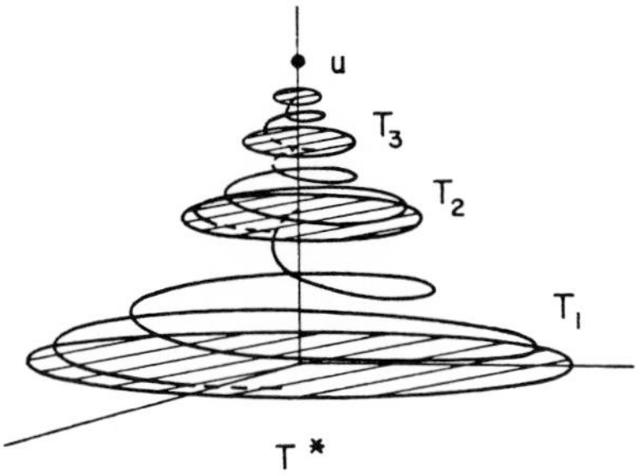

FIG. 6

1.10 Theorem [K 4]. If S is a bing in which each subgroup is totally disconnected, then for each idempotent $e \in S \backslash K(S)$, there is a subsemigroup I of S which has e as identity, meets $K(S)$, and is an I-semigroup.

One tool that Koch uses in his proof is the Mostert-Shields one-parameter semigroup theorem (see 1.7).

1.11 Definition. An *irreducible semigroup* is a clan T that contains no proper subcontinuum containing the identity of T and meeting $K(T)$, which is also a subsemigroup.

It is possible for an irreducible semigroup not to be *topologically irreducible* between its identity and minimal ideal, i.e., there could be a proper subcontinuum joining the two, even though no proper continuum subsemigroup joins them. For example, S, T, and T' in Example 1.9 are each irreducible, but T and T' are not topologically irreducible. The significance of this distinction is that it was conjectured long ago that irreducible semigroups had to be abelian; many attempts were made to prove it, and Koch and Wallace showed [K-W 2] with the tools of point-set topology that a topologically irreducible clan is abelian. However, it has been proved only recently by Hofmann and Mostert [H-M] that an irreducible semigroup is abelian, and the proof is not elementary. We state their main theorem below. For an expository discussion of their work, see Mostert [M].

The semigroup T' in Example 1.9(3) shows that irreducible semigroups can be considerably more complicated than threads or single spirals; they are actually built up of basic building blocks, which Hofmann and Mostert call *cylindrical semigroups*, put together in a way more complicated but similar to the way I-semigroups are built up of unit, nil, and min threads.

The structure of irreducible semigroups is of special significance, since "most" bings contain them, according to the following.

1.12 Lemma. If S is a bing and $e \in S \backslash K(S)$, S contains an irreducible semigroup with e as identity that meets $K(S)$.

The proof of this is easy: observe that $\{eSe\}$ is a family of clans that contain e and intersect $K(S)$, and the family is linearly ordered by inclusion. (This family has only one member.) By Zorn's lemma, there is a maximal such family, and then its intersection is an irreducible semigroup as required.

The following very beautiful theorem is the heart of Hofmann and Mostert's work on irreducible semigroups.

1.13 Theorem [H-M]. An irreducible semigroup is abelian, and the irreducible semigroups are clans for which $S/\mathscr{H}$ is naturally an I-semigroup, where $\mathscr{H}$ is the equivalence relation on S defined by

$$\mathscr{H} = \{(x, y) \in S \times S \mid x \cup Sx = y \cup Sy \text{ and } x \cup xS = y \cup yS\}.$$

The relation $\mathscr{H}$ defined here is one of the *Green equivalences* on S (Sect. 4), and, according to Def. 1.8, the maximal subgroup $H(e)$ containing an idempotent e is the $\mathscr{H}$-class of e. $S/\mathscr{H}$ is the space obtained by identifying the points of each $\mathscr{H}$-class so that, in particular, the subgroups of S are shrunk to points, and $S/\mathscr{H}$ contains no nondegenerate connected group.

For example, consider the single spiral S of Example 1.9(1). The $\mathscr{H}$-class of each $x \in S \backslash (0 \times C)$ is just x, and the only other $\mathscr{H}$-class is the base circle. Thus, $S/\mathscr{H}$ is S with its base circle shrunk to a point, which is obviously an arc. Similarly for T of Example 1.9(2): the $\mathscr{H}$-classes of S are as just described, and each circle in $0 \times D$ of radius r about $(0, 0)$, $0 \leqslant r \leqslant 1$, is an $\mathscr{H}$-class (see Fig. 7).

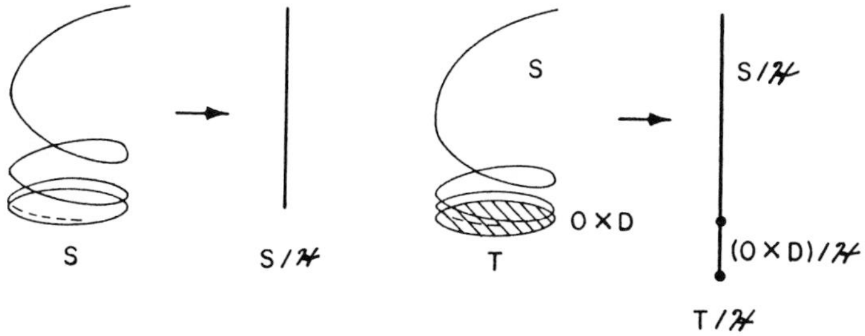

FIG. 7

It is clear that $\mathscr{H}$ can be defined and will be an equivalence relation for any semigroup S, so that $S/\mathscr{H}$ is a well-defined space, and, if S is compact, then $S/\mathscr{H}$ is Hausdorff. (There are somewhat weaker conditions than compactness [Hu].) However, in general, $S/\mathscr{H}$ is not a semigroup naturally; in other words, the product (in S) of two $\mathscr{H}$-classes need not be contained in another $\mathscr{H}$-class. Put yet another way, $\mathscr{H}$ need not be a *congruence* (see Theorem 2.5 for formal definition). If S is *normal*, meaning $xS = Sx$ for each $x \in S$, then $S/\mathscr{H}$ will be naturally a semigroup. Obviously, if S is abelian, then S is normal, and this is one important reason why it is so very useful to know if a semigroup is abelian. For example, Hunter proved in 1960 [Hn 1] that, if S is a normal irreducible semigroup, then $S/\mathscr{H}$ is an I-semigroup, but it was not known for arbitrary irreducible semigroups until Mostert and Hofmann proved them abelian. These and other people have gained much insight into the structure of compact semigroups from this work of Hunter and from the ingenious examples which appear in his papers and those of Hunter and Anderson and Rothman and Hunter (see for instance [A-H], [Hn 1, 2, 3], and [H-R]).

2. Constructing New Semigroups from Old

The semigroup product defined in Def. 1.8 is one basic way to construct new semigroups from old. Another basic idea is to replace part of a given semigroup with something else, as described in 2.1 and 2.6.

2.1 Definition of Rees Quotient. Let S be a compact semigroup, and let I be a *closed* ideal. Let S/I denote the usual quotient space obtained by identifying all points of I, and let $\phi : S \to S/I$ be the natural map. Then S/I is a semigroup with multiplication defined by $\phi(x)\,\phi(y) = \phi(xy)$, and such a quotient semigroup is called a *Rees quotient*.

Because I is an ideal, the multiplication is well defined. Compactness of S and closure of I are used to prove S/I Hausdorff and the multiplication continuous (see 2.5).

2.2 Examples of Rees Quotients. (1) A nil thread is a Rees quotient of a unit thread; precisely, the usual nil thread defined in Def. 1.1(2) is $[0, 1]/[0, \frac{1}{2}]$, where $[0, 1]$ is the usual unit thread.

(2) A disconnected semigroup can be made into a connected one if there is a closed ideal intersecting all components. For example, let W be a finite semigroup with n elements and $I = [0, 1]$ be the usual unit thread. Then $W \times I$ is compact and has n components; $W \times 0$ is a closed ideal intersecting them all, and $W \times I/W \times 0$ is a connected fan. We sketch the case $n = 2$ in Fig. 8.

FIG. 8

(3) Let S^1 be a semigroup on the one-sphere, let $I = [0, 1]$ be an I-semigroup, and let $T = S^1 \times I$ be the semigroup product. Then T is a hollow cylinder, $I_r = S^1 \times [0, r]$ is an ideal of T for $r \in [0, 1)$, and the Rees quotient T/I_r is topologically a 2-cell with its bounding sphere a subsemigroup (see Fig. 9).

One can generalize this by using S^{n-1}, $n \geqslant 2$, instead of S^1, to get semigroups on n-cells that have the bounding $(n - 1)$ sphere as a subsemigroup. There is a theorem due to Mostert and Shields which implies that a clan on an n-cell with zero and the boundary as a subsemigroup must be such a Rees quotient of a cylinder. Their theorem, which we state below, is actually much more general and is stated for *L-semigroups*, which are, by definition, clans on compact

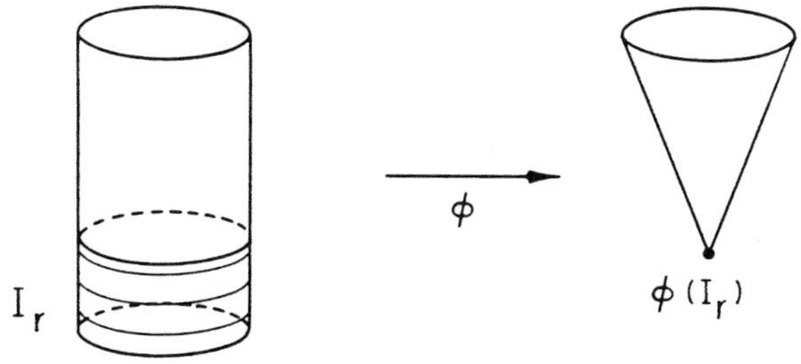

FIG. 9

manifolds with boundary such that the boundary is a subbing. It was to prove this theorem that Mostert and Shields completed Faucett's work on I-semigroups and proved the first version of their one-parameter semigroup theorem, both of which we have mentioned earlier.

2.3 Theorem [M-S]. If S is an L-semigroup with boundary B, then B is a compact Lie group; B acts on S by left translation, and the space of orbits S' is an I-semigroup; and there is an I-semigroup J in S such that J is a cross section for S', hence $S = JB$. If S has a zero, then S is iseomorphic to $(J \times B)/K$, where K is an ideal of $J \times B$. The multiplication in S is differentiable iff S' is a unit thread.

As an example, it is easy to see that the usual complex disk is $(I \times C)/K$, where I is the usual unit thread, C is the circle group, and $K = 0 \times C$. (See Fig. 4.)

This theorem provided partial answers to the following questions, which had been asked by Wallace.

2.4 Questions [W]. Suppose S is a semigroup on a compact manifold with boundary that is a subsemigroup. To what extent is the multiplication of S determined by that of B? When is the multiplication differentiable?

Little is known about the structure of such semigroups if there is no identity, except that Hudson [H] showed that, in case S is a closed n-cell and the bounding sphere B is a left trivial subsemigroup of S ($xB = x$ for each $x \in B$), then either S is left trivial or $(S \backslash K(S))^* = BT$ for some I-semigroup T contained in S.

In Def. 2.1, we indicated why it is all right to squeeze a closed ideal to a point, in other words, why the Rees quotient space turns out to be a semigroup. Formally, a Rees quotient of a compact semigroup is a special case of the general technique of dividing out a closed congruence, which yields a semigroup according to the following proposition. The correspondence between congruences and homomorphisms is of basic importance, and so we state the proposition in full generality. As indicated, it is true if one reads "discrete" instead of "compact" and "compact Hausdorff."

2.5 Theorem. Suppose that S is a compact (discrete) semigroup and $\mathscr{C}$ is a closed equivalence relation on S, and let $\phi : S \to S/\mathscr{C}$ be the natural map. Then $S/\mathscr{C}$ is compact Hausdorff (discrete) in the quotient topology, which is defined by letting U be open in $S/\mathscr{C}$ iff $\phi^{-1}(U)$ is open.

If $\mathscr{C}$ is also a congruence, then $S/\mathscr{C}$ is naturally a semigroup, meaning that ϕ is a homomorphism. Thus, a closed congruence on S induces a homomorphism from S onto another semigroup.

Conversely, if $f : S \to T$ is a homomorphism from S onto T, then

$$\mathscr{C} = \{(s, s') \in S \times S \mid f(s) = f(s')\}$$

is a closed congruence on S, and $S/\mathscr{C}$ is iseomorphic to T, via $\bar{f} : S/\mathscr{C} \to T$, defined by $\bar{f}\phi = f$:

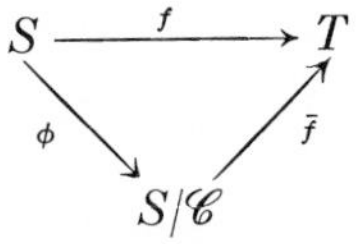

The following construction is, like the Rees quotient, an application of Theorem 2.5, but a more sophisticated one. The Rees quotient replaces an ideal by a point, whereas the Borsuk Paste Job describes conditions under which a subsemigroup can be replaced by another semigroup. This is a simple variation of K. Borsuk's well-known technique of pasting with a continuous function.

2.6 Borsuk Paste Job. Let S be a compact semigroup, let A be a closed subsemigroup of S, and let $f : A \to T$ be an onto homomorphism. Let $\Delta(S) = \{(x, x) \mid x \in S\}$, the diagonal of S. Let $\mathscr{E} = \Delta(S) \cup \{(a_1, a_2) \in A \times A \mid f(a_1) = f(a_2)\}$. Then $\mathscr{E}$ is a closed equivalence relation on S, and, if $\mathscr{E}$ is a congruence, then $S/\mathscr{E}$ is a semigroup and looks like S with A cut out and T pasted in according to the rule f. If A is an ideal of S, then $\mathscr{E}$ will be a congruence in case $f(xa_1) = f(xa_2)$ and $f(a_1x) = f(a_2x)$ for each $x \in S$.

2.7 Examples. (1) Rees quotient. Let A be a closed ideal of a compact semigroup S, let T be a one-point semigroup, and let f map A to T.

(2) A clan on the Möbius strip. Let C and I be as in Example 1.9, and let $S = I \times C$, $A = 0 \times C$, and $T = C$. Define $f: A \to T$ by $f(0, z) = z^2$. One easily sees that the pasting merely identifies opposite points on the base circle of S and leaves the rest of S unchanged. To see geometrically that the paste space is actually a Möbius strip, one can (i) cut S in half vertically and slide the front half down; (ii) rotate the front half 180°; (iii) paste the two adjacent edges together, which gives a 2-cell and amounts to identifying opposite points on the base circle of S, except for the corner points; and (iv) rejoin the cut edges of S as they were originally, which completes the identification of opposite points of the base circle of S so that one has the paste space now, and which is the usual way of getting a Möbius strip from a cell (see Fig. 10).

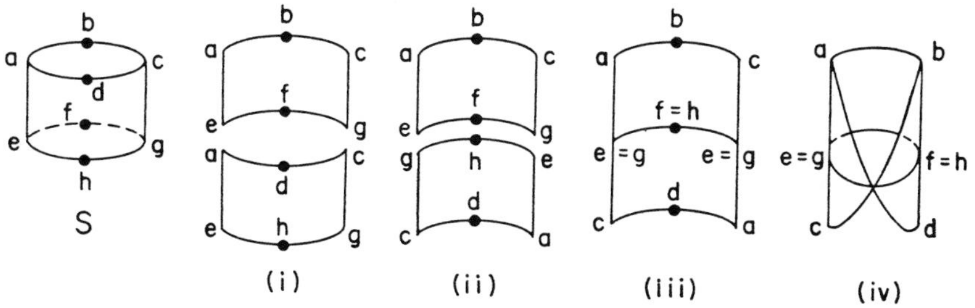

FIG. 10

(3) A clan on an umbrella. Let D be as in Example 1.9, $A = \{z \in D \mid |z| \leqslant \frac{1}{2}\}$, $T = [0, \frac{1}{2}]$ with real multiplication, and define $f: A \to T$ by $f(z) = |z|$ (see Fig. 11).

(4) Let S be the single spiral of Example 1.9(1), and let $\{a, b\}$ be a two-element semigroup. (For example, the multiplication could be left trivial, (see 2.4); or $\{a, b\}$ could be the cyclic group of two elements.) Let T denote the base circle of S, and let $W = \{a, b\} \times S$

FIG. 11

be the usual semigroup product (see Def. 1.8). W is compact, since $\{a, b\}$ and S are. Let $A = \{a, b\} \times T \subset W$, and define $f: A \to T$ to be projection. Then the hypotheses of Theorem 2.6 are satisfied, and the paste space is a double spiral (see Fig. 12). Since, for any finite (or, more generally, compact) semigroup X, $X \times S$ is compact, one can paste cardinal X number of spirals in the same way. Compare this example with Example 2.2(2).

FIG. 12

In all the foregoing examples, one must check each time that the equivalence relation induced by f is a closed congruence.

3. Some Useful Tools of Compact Semigroups

The topics discussed in this section are elementary but among the most frequently used facts about compact semigroups. There are a few simple but important things from topology which one needs to know, and we state them without proof.

3.1 Background Topology. Let X, Y and Z denote Hausdorff spaces.

(1) If $A, U \subset X$ and U is open, then $A^* \cap U \neq \square$ implies $A \cap U \neq \square$.

In (2) and (3), let $\mathscr{A}$ be a nonempty family of subsets of X which is a *tower*, i.e., for each $A, B \in \mathscr{A}$, either $A \subset B$ or $B \subset A$, and let $\cap\, \mathscr{A}$ denote $\cap\{A \mid A \in \mathscr{A}\}$.

(2) If each $A \in \mathscr{A}$ is compact and nonempty, then $\cap \mathscr{A}$ is compact and nonempty.

(3) Let $f : X \to Y$ be continuous; then $f(\cap\mathscr{A}) \subset \cap\{f(A) \mid A \in \mathscr{A}\}$, and, if each $A \in \mathscr{A}$ is compact, then $f(\cap\mathscr{A}) = \cap\{f(A) \mid A \in \mathscr{A}\}$. Thus, if X is a semigroup and $\mathscr{A}$ is a tower of compact subsets of X, then $x(\cap\mathscr{A}) = \cap\{xA \mid A \in \mathscr{A}\}$ for each $x \in X$.

(4) For any continuous function $f : X \to Y$ and $A \subset X$, $f(A^*) \subset f(A)^*$, and, if A is compact in X, then $f(A^*) = f(A)^*$. Thus if A and B are subsets of a semigroup, then $A^*B^* \subset (AB)^*$, and if A^* and B^* are also compact, then $A^*B^* = (AB)^*$.

(5) If $A \subset X$, if A is compact and if $z \notin A$, there is an open set W such that $A \subset W$ and $z \notin W$.

(6) If A and B are compact, $A \times B \subset X \times Y$, $f : X \times Y \to Z$ is continuous and $f(A \times B) \subset W$, W open, then there are open sets U and V such that $A \subset U$, $B \subset V$, and $f(U \times V) \subset W$. Thus, if $X = Y = Z$ is a semigroup and $AB \subset W$, W open, there are open sets U and V such that $A \subset U$, $B \subset V$, and $UV \subset W$.

3.2. Definition. For $x \in S$, let $\Gamma_n(x) = \{x^p \mid p \geqslant n\}^*$, $\Gamma(x) = \Gamma_1(x)$, and $N(x) = \cap\{\Gamma_n(x) \mid n \geqslant 1\}$.

The following theorem was discovered by Koch and by Numakura [N].

3.3 Theorem. If $x \in S$ and $\Gamma(x)$ is compact, then $N(x)$ is an ideal of $\Gamma(x)$ and is a group. Thus, for an element x in a compact semigroup, the powers of x cluster at some idempotent, and, in particular, a compact semigroup contains an idempotent.

PROOF. A closed subset of a compact space is compact, so $N(x)$ is the intersection of a nonempty tower of nonempty *compact* sets. Therefore, $N(x)$ is compact and nonempty by Proposition 3.1(2). The nonempty intersection of subsemigroups of a semigroup is again one, so $N(x)$ is a semigroup.

To prove that $N(x)$ is an ideal of $\Gamma(x)$, we shall show that $x^rN(x) = N(x)$ for each $r \geqslant 1$, hence $\{x^r \mid r \geqslant 1\}\, N(x) \subset N(x)$; then, by Proposition 3.1(1) and (4), $\Gamma(x)\, N(x) \subset N(x)$. Dually, $N(x)\, \Gamma(x) \subset N(x)$. So let $r \geqslant 1$, and compute: $x^rN(x) = x^r(\cap\{\Gamma_n(x) \mid n \geqslant 1\})$, and, by Proposition 3.1(3), this equals $\cap\{x^r\Gamma_n(x) \mid n \geqslant 1\}$; by Proposition 3.1(4), $x^r\Gamma_n(x) = (x^r\{x^p \mid p \geqslant n\})^*$, which clearly equals $\{x^{r+p} \mid p \geqslant n\}^* = \Gamma_{r+n}$.

Thus,

$$x^r N(x) = \cap \{\Gamma_{r+n}(x) \mid n \geqslant 1\} = \cap \{\Gamma_n(x) \mid n \geqslant r+1\},$$

which equals $N(x)$, since $\Gamma_{r+1}(x) \subset \cdots \subset \Gamma_1(x)$.

Since $N(x)$ is a semigroup, to prove it is a group it suffices to show that $yN(x) = N(x)\,y = N(x)$ for each $y \in N(x)$. We showed previously that $x^r N(x) = N(x)x^r = N(x)$ for each $r \geqslant 1$, and intuitively the x^r's "converge" to the points of $N(x)$, and so this ought to imply the equalities we need. It does, but one needs compactness to get it. The following is a proof. Let $A = \{a \in \Gamma(x) \mid aN(x) = N(x)\}$; if we knew $A^* \subset A$, then, because $\{x^r \mid r \geqslant 1\} \subset A$, we would have $\Gamma(x) \subset A^* \subset A$ and, in particular, $N(x) \subset A$, as desired. To prove $A^* \subset A$, let $y \in A^*$, and suppose, by way of contradiction, that $y \notin A$. Then $yN(x) \not\subset N(x)$, so there is $z \in N(x) \backslash yN(x)$. Since y and $N(x)$ are compact, so is $yN(x)$, hence, by Proposition 3.1(5), there is an open set W such that $z \notin W$ and $yN(x) \subset W$. [Note $N(x) \not\subset W$.] By Proposition 3.1(6), there are open sets U and V such that $y \in U$, $N(x) \subset V$, and $UV \subset W$. But, by Proposition 3.1(1), since $y \in U \cap A^*$, there is some $a \in U \cap A$; $a \in U$ implies $aN(x) \subset UV \subset W$, and $a \in A$ implies $aN(x) = N(x)$, so we have a contradiction. Therefore, it is false that $y \notin A$, hence $A^* \subset A$.

By a dual argument, $A' = \{a \in \Gamma(x) \mid N(x)a = N(x)\}$ is closed and hence $\Gamma(x) \subset A'$; therefore,

$$\Gamma(x) \subseteq A \cap A' = \{a \in \Gamma(x) \mid aN(x) = N(x)a = N(x)\},$$

and, in particular, $N(x) \subset A \cap A'$. ▮

Before continuing, observe that the proof that A is closed depends only on the compactness of $N(x)$, and one can prove in the same way that, for any compact subset N of a semigroup S, $\{x \in S \mid xN \supset N\}$, $\{x \in S \mid xN \subset N\}$, $\{x \in S \mid Nx \subset N\}$, and $\{x \in S \mid Nx \subset N\}$ are closed.

3.4 Definition. An *act* is a semigroup S, a space X, and a continuous function

$$S \times X \to X,$$

which usually remains anonymous and whose values are denoted by juxtaposition, such that

$$t_1(t_2 x) = (t_1 t_2)\, x$$

for each t_1, $t_2 \in S$ and $x \in X$.

People familiar with machine theory will recognize that an act is just a continuous machine. Acts have been used when convenient, such as in the Swelling Lemma (Lemma 3.5), for a number of years. However, direct study of them began only recently ([B, S, D-W 1, 2]; also see 3.6 and 3.7).

The following lemma is an extremely useful tool due to Wallace; it should be called The Nonswelling Lemma; however, it has become known as the Swelling Lemma.

3.5 The Swelling Lemma. [W 3]. Suppose S acts on X, $x \in S$ and $\Gamma(x)$ is compact, and A is a compact subset of X such that $xA \supset A$. Then $xA = A$, and, for each $y \in \Gamma(x)$, $a \to ya$ is a homeomorphism of A onto A; thus, the idempotent in $\Gamma(x)$ is an element acting as the identity on A.

PROOF. Since $xA \supset A$, $x^2A \supset xA \supset A$, and, by induction, $x^nA \supset A$ for all $n \geqslant 1$. Thus, $\{x^n \mid n \geqslant 1\} \subset \{y \in S \mid yA \supset A\}$, and the latter set is closed (see remark after proof of 3.2), hence $\Gamma(x) \subset \{y \in S \mid yA \supset A\}$. By Theorem 3.3, since $\Gamma(x)$ is compact, there is an idempotent $e \in N(x)$, and, by the previous sentence, $eA \supset A$. This implies $ea = a$ for each $a \in A$ (because $x \in eS$ implies $x = ey$ for some $y \in S$, hence $ex = e^2y = ey = x$). Therefore $a \to ea$ is the identity map of A, and, in particular, $eA = A$.

To see that $yA = A$ for any $y \in \Gamma(x)$ we have yet to prove $yA \subset A$. So observe that $yA = yeA$, $ye \in N(x)$ since $N(x)$ is an ideal of $\Gamma(x)$, and $N(x)$ is a group, so that there exists $(ye)^{-1} \in N(x)$ such that $(ye)(ye)^{-1} = e$. We know that $(ye)^{-1}A \supset A$, hence $(ye)(ye)^{-1}A \supset yeA$, i.e., $A \supset yA$. Therefore, $yA = A$. Finally, $a \to ya$ is the same map as $a \to yea$, and this is a homeomorphism because it maps A onto A and has a continuous inverse, $a \to (ye)^{-1} a$. ∎

3.6 Applications of the Swelling Lemma. (1) Suppose S is a compact semigroup, $T = S \times S$ is the usual Cartesian product, and multiplication in T is defined by $(x, y)(x', y') = (xx', y'y)$.

(Observe that this is not the usual semigroup product, defined in Def. 1.8; this multiplication often provides a cheap way to get two-sided objects from one-sided theorems, as follows.) T is a compact semigroup, and, because of the particular multiplication we gave T, T acts on S via the function $[(x, y), s] \to xsy$.

If A and S are compact, $A \subset S$, and, if $xAy \supset A$ for some $x, y \in S$, then $x'Ay' = A$ for each $(x', y') \in \Gamma(x, y)$ [i.e. $\Gamma((x, y))$ for $(x, y) \in T$], and, in particular, S contains left and right identities for A.

PROOF. T is compact since S is, and so, by the Swelling Lemma, $(x', y')\, A = A$ for each $(x', y') \in \Gamma(x, y)$, i.e., $x'Ay' = A$. If (e, f) is the idempotent in $\Gamma(x, y)$, $eAf = A$ implies $eA = A = Af$ so that e and f are left and right identities for A, respectively. [This depends on the fact that e and f are idempotent, and, in general, $xAy = A$ does not imply $xA = A$ or $Ay = A$. Also, $\Gamma(x, y)$ is only a subset of $\Gamma(x) \times \Gamma(y)$, so one cannot conclude that $x'Ay' = A$ for each $x' \in \Gamma(x)$, $y' \in \Gamma(y)$.] ▮

(2) A compact semigroup S is *stable*, i.e., $baS \supset aS$ implies $baS = aS$, and $Sab \supset Sa$ implies $Sab = Sa$ for all $a, b \in S$. (Stability implies that the Green relations $\mathscr{D}$ and $\mathscr{J}$ on S are equal [K-W 1].)

(3) If S is a compact semigroup and $xS = S$ for some $x \in S$, then S has a left identity, the idempotent in $\Gamma(x)$.

(4) [W 7] If S is a compact semigroup, $x \in A = A^* \subset S$, and $xA \supset A$, then $\Gamma(x)$ is a group contained in A. The most interesting aspect of this is that A *need not be a subsemigroup.*

PROOF. $x \in A$ implies $x^2 \in xA$, which equals A by the Swelling Lemma; hence, $x^2 \in A$. By induction, $x^n \in A$ for all $n \geqslant 1$; by hypothesis, A is closed, hence $\Gamma(x) \subset A$. Therefore, by the Swelling Lemma, $e\Gamma(x) = \Gamma(x)$, where e is the idempotent in $\Gamma(x)$. But $e\Gamma(x) \subset N(x)$ since $N(x)$ is an ideal of $\Gamma(x)$, so $\Gamma(x) = N(x)$; hence, $\Gamma(x)$ is a group. ▮

The next lemma is a useful tool in case one is studying compact semigroups with cutpoints or compact semigroups acting on continua with cutpoints.

3.7 Lemma. [W 6, D-W 1, 2]. Let S be compact and let S act on a continuum X. If H is a subset of S with nonempty boundary $F(H)$ and if H^* contains a point x such that $Sx \subset H^*$, then, for some $p \in F(H)$, $Sp \subset H^*$.

Intuitively this says that, if any point in H^* is taken inside H^* by S, however far inside H^* that point may be, it pulls the image under S of some boundary point of H, i.e., some "outer" point, inside H^* also. This is obviously convenient to use when H has just one boundary point, and is an important tool in the proofs of Property 3.8(1) and (2).

The proofs of Propositions 3.7 and 3.8(1) are relatively lengthy, and we omit them; 3.8(1) generalizes a theorem of Faucett [F 2].

3.8 Applications of Lemma 3.7. (1) [D-W 1, 2]. Let $S \times X \to X$ be an act, with S and X compact. Let J be maximal with respect to $\square \neq J \subset X$ and $SJ \subset J$. If $C \subset X \backslash J$ and C is the intersection of continua with one-point boundaries, then C contains at most one point.

This proposition, in turn, is an important tool for Day and Wallace [D-W 1, 2], where acts $S \times X \to X$ are studied for which X is a continuum with *open dense half-line*, i.e., X contains a homeomorphic copy of (0, 1] which has closure equal to X (is dense) but "sticks out" (is open). Every point in the image of (0, 1) is a cutpoint. The single spiral in Example 1.9(1) is an example of a continuum with open dense half-line.

(2) [B]. Let S be a compact semigroup acting on $I = [0, 1]$, with $S0 = 0$. Then the set of zeros for the action, $\{x \in I \mid Sx = x\}$, equals $[0, c]$ for some $c \in [0, 1]$.

PROOF. Let $Z = \{x \in I \mid Sx = x\}$, and let z be the least upper bound of Z, which exists since $Z \neq \square$ $(0 \in Z)$ and Z has an upper bound, 1. Since S is compact, one can prove that Z is closed (see proof of Lemma 3.5), hence, $z \in Z$. Thus, $Z \subset [0, z]$ and $0, z \in Z$. Suppose $x \in (0, z)$, so that x is the boundary in I of both $[0, x]$ and $[x, 1]$. Let $H = [0, x]$, and apply Lemma 3.7 to conclude that $Sx \subset [0, x]$, since $S0 = 0$. Let $H = [x, 1]$ and apply Lemma 3.7 again to conclude that $Sx \subset [x, 1]$, since $z \in [x, 1]$ and $Sz = z$. Therefore, $Sx = x$, hence $x \in Z$, which is to say, $(0, z) \subset Z$. Therefore, $[0, z] = Z$. ▮

The following proposition contains information that is used very frequently. In the terminology of algebraic semigroups, it says that the minimal ideal of a compact semigroup is completely simple, and in fact the proof is largely algebraic. After using compactness to prove the existence of minimal left, right, and two-sided ideals, topology is not used again, and the proof proceeds just as in the completely simple case (see 1.1.7 and Chapter 7).

3.9 Theorem. If S is a compact semigroup, S has a compact minimal ideal $K(S)$, and, if $\hat{L}$ and $\hat{R}$ are the families of all minimal left and minimal right ideals of S, respectively, then

$K(S) = \cup\hat{\mathcal{L}} = \cup\hat{\mathcal{R}}$. Furthermore, if $L \in \hat{\mathcal{L}}$ and $R \in \hat{\mathcal{R}}$, then $LR = K(S)$ and $L \cap R = H(e)$ for some idempotent e; hence $K(S)$ is the union of disjoint groups. If $x \in K(S)$, the minimal left ideal containing x is Sx and the minimal right ideal containing x is xS.

PROOF. S is a compact ideal of S, so there is a nonempty maximal tower of compact ideals, $\mathscr{T}$, by Zorn's lemma. By Proposition 3.1(2), $K = \cap\mathscr{T}$ is compact and nonempty, so K is a minimal compact ideal of S. K is a minimal ideal since, for any $x \in K$, SxS is compact, is an ideal, and is a subset of any ideal containing x. Similarly, S contains minimal left and right ideals. K is unique, for, if K' were another minimal ideal, $\square \neq KK' \subset K \cap K'$, hence $K \cap K'$ is an ideal, so $K \cap K' = K = K'$.

$\bigcup\hat{\mathcal{L}} \subset K$ since if $L \in \hat{\mathcal{L}}$, because L is a left ideal and K is an ideal, we have both that $KL \subset L \cap K$ and KL is a left ideal, hence $KL = L \subset K$. Obviously $\bigcup\hat{\mathcal{L}}$ is a left ideal, so, if we prove it is a right ideal, then it must equal K. To do it, first observe that $Lx \in \hat{\mathcal{L}}$ for each $L \in \hat{\mathcal{L}}$ and $x \in S$ (for Lx is obviously a left ideal, and, if M were a left ideal contained in Lx, then $\{y \in L \mid yx \in M\}$ is a left ideal contained in L, hence equals L, hence M equals Lx). Therefore $(\bigcup\hat{\mathcal{L}})S = \bigcup\{LS \mid L \in \hat{\mathcal{L}}\} = \bigcup\{Lx \mid L \in \hat{\mathcal{L}},\ x \in S\} \subset \bigcup\hat{\mathcal{L}}$, so that $\bigcup\hat{\mathcal{L}}$ is a right ideal and $K = \bigcup\hat{\mathcal{L}}$. Dually, $K = \bigcup\hat{\mathcal{R}}$.

Let $L \in \hat{\mathcal{L}}$ and $R \in \hat{\mathcal{R}}$. Clearly, LR is an ideal and $LR \subset K$, hence $LR = K$. Next observe that, if $x \in L$, $Lx \subset L^2 \subset L$ and $Lx \in \hat{\mathcal{L}}$ imply $Lx = L$; dually, $x \in R$ implies $xR = R$. One can see that $R \cap L$ is a group as follows: clearly, $\square \neq RL \subset R \cap L$ and RL is a semigroup; if $x \in RL$, then $Lx = L$ and $xR = R$ by the previous observation, hence $xRL = RLx = RL$, so that RL is a group. Finally, $R \cap L = (R \cap L)\,e \subset RL$, where e is the idempotent in RL, hence $R \cap L = RL$, and thus $R \cap L$ is a group.

Let $x \in K$, and choose $L \in \hat{\mathcal{L}}$ such that $x \in L$. Clearly Sx is a left ideal, and also $Sx \subset SL \subset L$; hence $Sx = L$. Dually, $x \in xS \in \hat{\mathcal{R}}$. ▮

4. Relative Green Relations

4.1 Introduction. The usual Green relations are defined for a topological semigroup S just as for an algebraic semigroup ([C-P]; also see Chapter 7). They are equivalences, are closed if S is compact, and are fundamental tools for studying the structure of both topological and algebraic semigroups. Recall the Hofmann-Mostert theorem

(Theorem 1.13), for example; also beautiful are the structure of the minimal ideal of a compact semigroup, analyzed as a $\mathscr{D}$-class (see 4.5 and 4.6), and M. Schützenberger's theorem about the $\mathscr{H}$-classes in a general $\mathscr{D}$-class (see 4.7). Wallace [W 6, 7, 8] defined *relative ideals* and *relative Green relations* and generalized many theorems to the relative, topological case.

Let S be a semigroup and $T \subset S$ in the remainder of these notes. Observe that, in general, T is *not* a subsemigroup of S.

4.2 Definitions. For $x, y \in S$, define $(x, y) \in \mathscr{L}_T$ iff $T^1x = T^1y$; $(x, y) \in \mathscr{R}_T$ iff $xT^1 = yT^1$; $(x, y) \in \mathscr{J}_T$ iff $T^1xT^1 = T^1yT^1$; $\mathscr{H}_T = \mathscr{L}_T \cap \mathscr{R}_T$; and $\mathscr{D}_T = \mathscr{L}_T \circ \mathscr{R}_T$. The relations thus defined, $\mathscr{L}_T$, $\mathscr{R}_T$, $\mathscr{H}_T$, $\mathscr{J}_T$, and $\mathscr{D}_T$, are called *relative Green relations* of S. If $T = S$, they are the usual Green relations defined by Clifford and Preston [C-P]. The subscript is not customary, but we use it here for emphasis. For $x \in S$, let R_x, L_x, D_x, and H_x denote the $\mathscr{R}_T$-class, $\mathscr{L}_T$-class, $\mathscr{D}_T$-class, and $\mathscr{H}_T$-class containing x, respectively.

According to the following lemma, the classes of a relative relation provide decompositions of the usual Green classes, which indicates one of the reasons why relative Green relations should be useful; so far, there have been no significant applications of the relative relations, but they are probably potentially powerful tools. Most theorems about the usual Green relations generalize if one takes $T = T^*$ and sometimes also $T^2 \subset T$. We omit the proof of Lemma 4.3 because it is a simple computation and proofs of Theorems 4.4, 4.7, and 4.8 because of length.

4.3 Lemma. For any $T \subset S$, each equivalence class of the usual Green relation $\mathscr{L}_S$ is the union of $\mathscr{L}_T$-classes; i.e., $\mathscr{L}_T \subset \mathscr{L}_S$. Similarly, $\mathscr{R}_T \subset \mathscr{R}_S$, $\mathscr{J}_T \subset \mathscr{J}_S$, $\mathscr{H}_T \subset \mathscr{H}_S$, and $\mathscr{D}_T \subset \mathscr{D}_S$.

4.4 Theorem. [W 7]. If $x, y \in S$ and $xy \in R_x \cap L_y$, then $R_y \cap L_x = H_e$ for some $e \in E$, and H_e is a subgroup of S. Also, $H_xH_y = H_{xy} = R_x \cap L_y$.

If also $T^2 \subset T$ and $xT \cup Ty \subset T$, then the Clifford egg-box diagram shown in Fig. 13 is valid, rows denoting $\mathscr{R}_T$-classes, columns denoting $\mathscr{L}_T$-classes, and the total diagram a subset of a $\mathscr{D}_T$-class. Conversely, but with no assumptions on T, if $e \in E$, $x \in L_e$, and $y \in R_e$, then $xy \in R_x \cap L_y$.

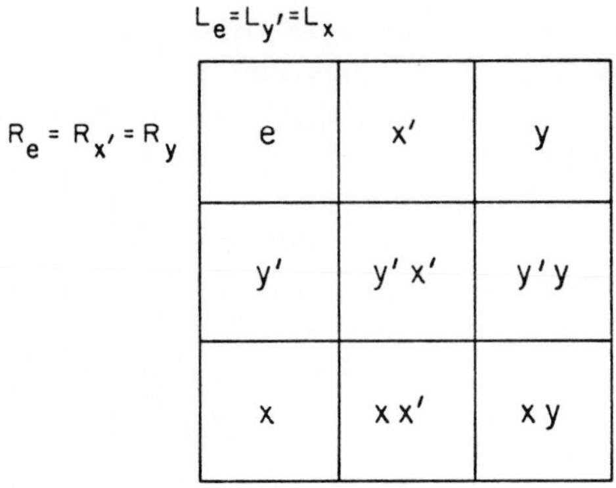

FIG. 13

4.5 Theorem. [W 8]. Let S be compact and T closed. The space $Z = S \times S \times S$ with multiplication defined by $(x, y, z)(x', y', z') = (x, yzx'y', z')$ is a semigroup, $f : Z \to S$ defined by $f(x, y, z) = xyz$ is a homomorphism, and, if $e \in E(S)$ and $Z_e = (L_e \cap E) \times H_e \times (R_e \cap E)$, then $f \mid Z_e$ is a homeomorphism into S; hence $f \mid Z_e$ is an iseomorphism into S.

Let $H = \bigcup\{H_f \mid f \in E(S)\}$ and $M_e = \{x \in S \mid ex, xe \in H\}$. Define $u : H \to E$ by letting $u(x)$ be the identity of H_f, the $\mathscr{H}_T$-class containing x. Then u is continuous, hence $g : M_e \to Z$ defined by $g(x) = [u(xe), exe, u(ex)]$ is continuous, and $g \mid f(Z_e)$ is the inverse of f.

If Z_e is a subsemigroup, and it will be if $D_e \subset H$, then $f \mid Z_e$ is an isomorphism.

4.6 Corollary: Rees-Suschkewitz Theorem. [C-P, W 2, 7, 8]. If S is compact and $e \in E \cap K$, then K is iseomorphic with $(Se \cap E) \times eSe \times (eS \cap E)$ with multiplication defined by $(x, y, z)(x', y', z') = (x, yzx'y', z')$, and K is a retract of S, as are $K \cap E$, $eS \cap E$, eSe, and $Se \cap E$.

PROOF. By Theorem 3.9, $eS \cup Se \subset K$ and $K \subset H$, hence $M_e = S$. Also by Theorem 3.9, since $e \in K$, $L_e = Se$ and $R_e = eS$ so, by definition of $\mathscr{H}$, $H_e = eS \cap Se$. Since $e = e^2$, $eS \cap Se = eSe$, and so from Theorem 4.5 we have that

$$Z_e = (Se \cap E) \times eSe \times (eS \cap E),$$

Z_e has the required multiplication, and $f \mid Z_e$ is an iseomorphism onto $(Se \cap E)\, eSe(eS \cap E)$, which equals K by the following argument. Since $eS = eSeS = eSe^2S$, $e(eS \cap E) = eS \cap E$, and $(Se \cap E)\,e = Se \cap E$, we see that

$$(Se \cap E)\,eSe(eS \cap E) = (Se \cap E)(Se)(eS)(eS \cap E) = (L \cap E)\,LR(R \cap E),$$

where $L \in \hat{L}$, $R \in \hat{R}$. From Theorem 3.9, $(L \cap E)\,L = L$, $R(R \cap E) = R$, and $LR = K$.

Also, $fg : S \to K$ is a retraction of S onto K, and $ufg : S \to E \cap K$ is a retraction of S onto $E \cap K$. Composing g with projections onto the respective factors of Z_e gives retractions of S onto $Se \cap E$, eSe, and $eS \cap E$. ▮

4.7 Schutzenberger Theorem. [C-P, W 7, 8] Let S be compact, $T = T^*$, and, for $a \in S$, define $P_a = \{x \in S \mid xH_a = H_a\}$ and

$$\mathscr{C}_a = \{(x, y) \in P_a \times P_a \mid xa = ya\}.$$

If cardinal $H_a > 1$, then P_a is a closed subsemigroup, $\mathscr{C}_a$ is a closed congruence on P_a, and there exists an analytic diagram as follows:

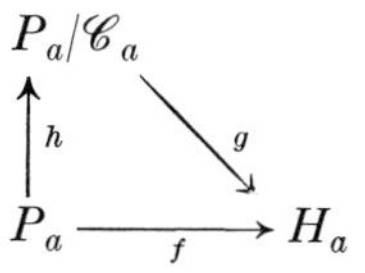

where h is canonical, $f(x) = xa$, g is a homeomorphism, and $P_a/\mathscr{C}_a$ is a compact group. If $a^2 = a$, then f is a homomorphism and g is an iseomorphism. Whether or not $a^2 = a$, there is a single group G homeomorphic with H_b for every $b \in D_a$ and iseomorphic with H_b if H_b contains an idempotent.

Another structure theorem that is of interest is the following. For $T \subset S$, J is a *maximal proper T-ideal* if $\square \neq J \neq S$,

$$T^1JT^1 \subset J,$$

and J is maximal with respect to being a subset of S with these properties. The following, which is due to Wallace, generalizes to T-ideals, when $T^2 \subset T$, a theorem in Faucett *et al.* [F-K-N] about the structure of the complement of a maximal proper ideal. It would be useful if there were an analog of this theorem for T not necessarily a subsemigroup.

4.8 Theorem. [W 8, B-W]. Let S be compact, let T be a closed subsemigroup, let J be a maximal proper T-ideal, and let $A = S\backslash J$. Suppose cardinal $A > 1$.

(i) If $TST \subset J$, then either $S = J \cup Ta$ and $A = L_a$ for each $a \in A$ or $S = J \cup aT$ and $A = R_a$ for each $a \in A$.

(ii) If $TST \not\subset J$, then $S = J \cup TaT$, $J_a = A$, $L_a = Ta \cap A$, and $R_a = aT \cap A$ for each $a \in A$.

(iii) If $T \cap A \neq \square$, then either $T \cap J$ is a maximal proper ideal of T or $T = A$ and T is simple.

For more information about relative ideals, see Bednarek and Wallace [B-W, W 6, 7, 8].

REFERENCES

[A-H] L. W. Anderson and R. P. Hunter, Homomorphisms and dimension, *Math. Ann.* **147**, 248–268 (1962).

[B] R. Balman, "Continua acting on the unit interval," Thesis, Univ. of Florida (1966).

[B-W] A. R. Bednarek and A. D. Wallace, Relative ideals and their complements, *Rev. Math. Pures Appl.* **21**, 13–22 (1966).

[Cl] A. H. Clifford, [1] Connected ordered topological semigroups with idempotent endpoints I, *Trans. Amer. Math. Soc.* **88**, 80–98 (1958);
[2] Connected ordered topological semigroups with idempotent endpoints II, *Trans. Amer. Math. Soc.* **91**, 193–208 (1959).

[C-P] A. H. Clifford and G. B. Preston, The algebraic theory of semigroups I, *Amer. Math. Soc. Surveys* **7**, Providence, Rhode Island (1961).

[C-K] H. Cohen and I. S. Krule, Continous homomorphic images of real clans with zero, *Proc. Amer. Math. Soc.* **10**, 106–109 (1959).

[C-W] H. Cohen and C. I. Wade, Clans with zero on an interval, *Trans. Amer. Math. Soc.* **88**, 523–535 (1958).

[D-W] J. M. Day and A. D. Wallace, [1] Semigroups acting on continua, *J. Austral. Math. Soc.* (to be published);
[2] Multiplication induced in the state space of an act, *Math. Systems Theory* (to be published).

[E] R. Ellis, A note on the continuity of the inverse, *Proc. Amer. Math. Soc.* **8**, 372–373 (1957).

[F] W. M. Faucett, [1] Compact semigroups irreducibly connected between two idempotents, *Proc. Amer. Math. Soc.* **6**, 741–747 (1955);
[2] Topological semigroups and continua with cut-points, *Proc. Amer. Math. Soc.* **6**, 748–756 (1955).

[F-K-N] W. M. Faucett, R. J. Koch, and K. Numakura, Complements of maximal ideals in compact semigroups, *Duke Math. J.* **22**, 655–661 (1955).

[H-M] K. H. Hofmann and P. S. Mostert, "Elements of Compact Semigroups." Merrill, Columbus, Ohio, 1966.

[H-Y] J. G. Hocking and G. S. Young, "Topology." Addison-Wesley, Reading, Massachusetts, 1961.

[H] A. L. Hudson, Some semigroups on an n-cell, *Trans. Amer. Math. Soc.* **99**, 255–263 (1961).

[Hu] S. T. Hu, "Elements of General Topology." Holden-Day, San Francisco, California, 1964.

[Hn] R. P. Hunter, [1] Certain upper semicontinuous decompositions of a semigroup, *Duke Math. J.* **27**, 283–290 (1960);
[2] Note on arcs in semigroups, *Fund. Math.* **49**, 233–245 (1961);
[3] On the structure of homogroups, *Fund. Math.* **52**, 69–102 (1963).

[H-R] R. P. Hunter and N. J. Rothman, Characters and cross sections for certain semigroups, *Duke Math. J.* **29**, 347–366 (1962).

[H-W] W. Hurewicz and H. Wallman, "Dimension Theory." Princeton Univ. Press, Princeton, New Jersey, 1941.

[Ke] J. L. Kelley, "General Topology." Princeton Univ. Press, Princeton, New Jersey, 1955.

[K] R. J. Koch, [1] On monothetic semigroups, *Proc. Amer. Math. Soc.* **8**, 397–401 (1957);
[2] Arcs in partially ordered spaces, *Pacific J. Math.* **9**, 723–728 (1959);
[3] Ordered semigroups in partially ordered semigroups, *Pacific J. Math.* **10**, 1333–1336 (1960);
[4] Threads in compact semigroups, *Math. Z.* **86**, 312–316 (1964).

[K-W] R. J. Koch and A. D. Wallace, [1] Stability in semigroups, *Duke Math. J.* **24**, 193–196 (1957);
[2] Admissibility of semigroup structures on continua, *Trans. Amer. Math. Soc.* **88**, 277–287 (1958).

[M] P. S. Mostert, The structure of topological semigroups revisited, *Bull. Amer. Math. Soc.* **72**, 601–618 (1966).

[M-S] P. S. Mostert and A. L. Shields, [1] On the structure of semigroups on a compact manifold with boundary, *Ann. of Math.* (2) **65**, 117–143 (1957);
[2] One parameter semigroups in a semigroup, *Trans. Amer. Math. Soc.* **96**, 510–517 (1960).

[M-Z] D. Montgomery and L. Zippin, "Topological Transformation Groups." Wiley (Interscience), New York, 1955.

[P-de M] A. B. Paalman-de Miranda, "Topological Semigroups." Mathematisch Centrum, Amsterdam, 1964.

[N] K. Numakura, On bicompact semigroups, *Math. J. Okayama Univ.* **1**, 99–108 (1954).

[S] D. Stadtlander, "Semigroup actions on topological spaces," Dissertation, Pennsylvania State Univ. (1966).

[W] A. D. Wallace, [1] On the structure of topological semigroups, *Bull. Amer. Math. Soc.* **61**, 95–112 (1955);

[2] The Rees-Suschkewitsch structure theorem for compact simple semigroups, *Proc. Nat. Acad. Sci. U.S.A.* **42**, 430–432 (1956);

[3] Inverses in Euclidean mobs, *Math. J. Okayama Univ.* **3**, 23–28 (1953);

[4] The Gebietstreue in semigroups, *Indag. Math.* **18**, 271–274 (1956);

[5] Acyclicity of compact connected semigroups, *Fund. Math.* **50**, 99–105 (1961);

[6] Relative ideals in semigroups I, *Colloq. Math.* **9**, 55–61 (1962);

[7] Relative ideals in semigroups II, *Acad. Sci. Hungary* **14**, 137–148 (1963);

[8] "Project mob," Univ. of Florida (1965).

CHAPTER 11

The Syntactic Monoid of a Regular Event[†]

ROBERT MCNAUGHTON
Rensselaer Polytechnic Institute, Troy, New York

SEYMOUR PAPERT
Massachusetts Institute of Technology, Cambridge, Massachusetts

In this chapter, we shall present the basic conceptual apparatus for the use of monoids and semigroups in the study of a finite automaton. These concepts, important and fundamental as they are for the theory of finite automata, seem to lack an adequate elementary exposition anywhere in the literature. This exposition will not be completely elementary, in that we assume that the reader knows some algebra as well as the rudiments of automata theory. But he need have no previous knowledge of the algebraic theory of machines, nor need he have any professional facility for algebra or for automata theory. The Rabin-Scott paper [1] contains an admirably clear account of some of these ideas. Written in 1957, however, it does not go far enough for present needs. More recent research papers fail to accommodate the uninitiated reader.

Although we presuppose some knowledge of algebra, we begin by

† Work reported herein was supported by Project MAC, an M.I.T. research program sponsored by the Advanced Research Projects Agency, Department of Defense, under Office of Naval Research Contract Number Nonr-4102(01). Reproduction in whole or in part is permitted for any purpose of the United States Government. This chapter was written as a section of a larger paper, "On Noncounting Events," not yet complete. We are indebted in many ways to M. P. Schützenberger.

reviewing the definition of a semigroup and monoid. A semigroup is a set of elements S together with a binary product on these elements (the product of a and b being written ab) satisfying the following two stipulations:

(1) For $a, b \in S$, $ab \in S$.

(2) $(ab)c = a(bc)$ for all $a, b, c \in S$.

If, in addition there is an identity (or neutral element) e such that

(3) $ea = ae = a$ for all $a \in S$,

then S is a *monoid*. The difference between monoids and semigroups is trivial, and it seems wasteful to have two words for concepts that are so nearly alike. It would appear that the *monoid* is the more useful of the two concepts for the study of events, and we shall henceforth omit reference to semigroups altogether. This decision, however, does not separate us from those who talk of semigroups in their algebraic approach to automata theory.

We shall use the same notation for the set of elements of a monoid as for the monoid itself. Thus, when we say "let M be a monoid," we shall also use M to represent the set of elements of this monoid, a common and convenient ambiguity that never causes trouble among knowledgeable users.

It will be recalled that, in these terms, a *group* is a monoid whose every element a has an inverse a^{-1} such that $a^{-1}a = aa^{-1} = e$. It turns out that an important technique in the algebraic theory of automata involves the subgroups of a given monoid, i.e., those submonoids that are groups.

The set Σ^* of all words over the alphabet Σ is a free monoid whose identity (neutral element) is the null word λ, concatenation of words being the monoid product, which is clearly associative. By an *event* (or language) over the alphabet Σ, we shall mean any subset of Σ^*. Of particular interest will be the *regular* events, which are associated with finite automata, and may be characterized by homomorphisms of Σ^* onto certain finite monoids.

We shall say a word about notation. Let γ be a mapping such that, for any word $W \in \Sigma^*$, $\gamma(W)$ is an element of a monoid M. To say that γ is a homomorphism is to say that $\gamma(WV) = \gamma(W)\gamma(V)$, for all W and $V \in \Sigma^*$. For any set A of words in Σ^*, $\gamma(A)$ is the precise set of all elements m in M such that, for some word $W \in A$, $\gamma(W) = m$. $\gamma^{-1}(m)$ is the set of all words that map to m under γ. And, for any subset S of M, $\gamma^{-1}(S)$ is the precise set of words in Σ^* which map to members of S under γ.

Note that, if γ is a homomorphism of Σ^* *onto* a monoid, then of necessity $\gamma(\lambda) = e$. The importance of the null word λ is what makes it essential that any semigroup used be a monoid. The theory of regular events could have been developed without the use of the null word, but the inclusion of the null word has made for a much smoother theory. For this reason, we find it convenient to dispense with those semigroups that are not monoids in our study of events.

Generally, when we start with an event E, we are interested only in homomorphisms γ for which E is *closed* under $\gamma^{-1}\gamma$, in other words, those for which $E = \gamma^{-1}\gamma(E)$.

For any γ that maps Σ^*, let us say that W_1 is *congruent* to W_2 *modulo* γ [or $W_1 \equiv W_2(\text{mod}\, \gamma)$] if $\gamma(W_1) = \gamma(W_2)$. Let us also say that W_1 is *congruent* to W_2 modulo E [or $W_1 \equiv W_2(\text{mod}\, E)$] if, for all words V and X, $VW_1X \in E$ if and only if $VW_2X \in E$. It is important to keep in mind that these are two distinct concepts of congruence. But, although they are distinct, their relationship is the key to the use of the concept of monoid in the study of events.

We make use of the partition of Σ^* into congruence sets, and note the relationships between these partitions for different congruence relations. A *congruence set* of words (modulo γ or modulo E) is a nonempty set having, with any member, all and only all the words congruent to it (modulo γ or modulo E, respectively). Congruence sets are commonly called "congruence classes," but we prefer to use the word "set" for sets of words and "class" for classes of sets.

Of all homomorphic mappings of Σ^*, there is one that is preëminent for studying an event E, namely, the mapping to the *syntactic monoid* of E, or $S(E)$. The elements of $S(E)$ are the congruence sets modulo E. The homomorphism simply maps a word onto the congruence set modulo E of which that word is a member; it is a many-one mapping, because every word over Σ is a member of one and only one congruence set modulo E.

To make $S(E)$ a monoid, we must introduce a product and establish that it is associative. To this end, we note that, if A and B are congruence sets, then, for some congruence set C, $AB \subseteq C$. That is to say, the congruence set C contains all words of the form WW', where $W \in A$ and $W' \in B$. (However, since there may be words in C other than those of this form, we cannot say, in general, that $C = AB$.) This observation gives us the product operation; thus, the product of two congruence set A and B is defined as that congruence set C such that $AB \subseteq C$. That this operation is associative follows from the fact that concatenation is associative.

(Actually, it takes a bit of reflection to verify the last sentence. A bit more reflection is required in the foregoing to establish that all words of AB are in a common congruence set; the reader who is new to these ideas must go back to the definition of "congruence modulo E" and construct the proof himself, which is straightforward.)

The syntactic monoid is so called because its definition is in terms of the notion of congruence of words modulo an event.

1.1 Theorem. If γ is the homomorphism of Σ^* to $S(E)$, then E is closed under $\gamma^{-1}\gamma$; furthermore, for any words W and W', $W \equiv W'(\text{mod } \gamma)$ if and only if $W \equiv W'(\text{mod } E)$.

PROOF. To justify the first clause, it suffices to prove that any two words W and W' mapping to the same element under γ are either both in E or both outside of E. But, if W and W' map to the same element, they must be congruent modulo E; thus, $W = \lambda W \lambda \in E$ if and only if $W' = \lambda W' \lambda \in E$. The second clause of Theorem 1.1 is simply a restatement of the definition of "syntactic monoid." ▮

However, there are other such homomorphisms γ of Σ^* such that E is closed under $\gamma^{-1}\gamma$. The relationship between the image monoids of these and the syntactic monoid is important. The following is a generalization of Theorem 1.1.

1.2 Theorem. A necessary and sufficient condition that E be closed under $\gamma^{-1}\gamma$, where γ is a homomorphism, is that, for all W and W', $W \equiv W'(\text{mod } \gamma)$ implies $W \equiv W'(\text{mod } E)$.

PROOF. Sufficiency: Assume the condition. For any $W \in \Sigma^*$, let A_W be the set of words congruent to W modulo γ. Then, for any W, $\gamma^{-1}\gamma(A_W) = A_W$. Taking $B = \bigcup_{W \in E} A_W$, it follows that $\gamma^{-1}\gamma(B) = B$. We can accomplish our objective of showing that $\gamma^{-1}[\gamma(E)] = E$ by showing that $E = B$, which we now do.

That $E \subseteq B$ follows immediately from the definition of B. Suppose now that W is an arbitrary word of B. There is a $W' \in E$ such that $W' \equiv W(\text{mod } \gamma)$, implying that $W' \equiv W(\text{mod } E)$. But then $W \in E$ also (for $W' = \lambda W' \lambda \in E$, which implies by the definition of "congruence" that $\lambda W \lambda = W \in E$).

Necessity: Assume that $\gamma^{-1}[\gamma(E)] = E$. We must prove that, for every W and W', $W \equiv W'(\text{mod } \gamma)$ implies $W \equiv W'(\text{mod } E)$. Assume that $W \equiv W'(\text{mod } \gamma)$, which means that $\gamma(W) = \gamma(W')$. To show that $W \equiv W'(\text{mod } E)$, we must show that, for every V and X, $VWX \in E$ if and only if $VW'X \in E$. But note that $\gamma(VWX) = \gamma(V)\,\gamma(W)\,\gamma(X)$, and $\gamma(VW'X) = \gamma(V)\,\gamma(W')\,\gamma(X)$, since γ is a homomorphism; since $\gamma(W) = \gamma(W')$, $\gamma(VWX) = \gamma(VW'X)$. But this implies that $VWX \in \gamma^{-1}[\gamma(VW'X)]$ and $VW'X \in \gamma^{-1}[\gamma(VWX)]$. But, since $\gamma^{-1}[\gamma(E)] = E$, $VWX \in E$ if and only if $VW'X \in E$. ▮

Let us reflect on the significance of Theorem 1.2. Both the homomorphism and the event E partition Σ^* into congruence sets. Theorem 1.2 says that a necessary and sufficient condition that E be closed under $\gamma^{-1}\gamma$ is that the γ partition be *finer* than or equal to the E partition, in other words, that every congruence set modulo γ is a subset of some congruence set modulo E. Thus, the partition of the homomorphism to the syntactic monoid is the coarsest partition of any homomorphism γ such that $\gamma^{-1}\gamma(E) = E$. Theorem 1.3 establishes a fundamental relationship between an arbitrary such monoid and the syntactic monoid. The reader may be interested in comparing the role of the syntactic monoid among the class of all monoids such that $\gamma^{-1}\gamma(E) = E$ (where γ is the homomorphism to the respective monoid) with the role of the reduced state graph among the class of state graphs for the event. As is well known, an arbitrary graph for an event is homomorphic to the reduced state graph.

Indeed, we can think of a state graph as partitioning Σ^* into sets of words, each set corresponding to one of the states and being precisely the set of words spelled out by paths beginning at the initial state and ending at the given state. As exposited by Rabin and Scott [1], such sets can be characterized mathematically by saying they are the equivalence sets of a right-invariant equivalence relation; an equivalence relation rel over words is *right*-invariant if W rel W' implies WU rel $W'U$. Taking the obvious analogous definition of "left invariant relation," they define "congruence relation" to be an equivalence relation that is both left invariant and right invariant. The congruence relations discussed by us are examples of these.

1.3 Theorem. If $\gamma^{-1}\gamma(E) = E$, where γ is a homomorphism, then the monoid $M = \gamma(\Sigma^*)$ can be mapped homomorphically onto $S(E)$.

PROOF. Recall that the elements of $S(E)$ are congruence sets (mod E) of words. By Theorem 1.2, each congruence set modulo γ is a subset of some congruence set modulo E. Let η be the mapping of M onto $S(E)$ such that, for each $s \in M$, $\eta(s)$ is the congruence set modulo E of which $\gamma^{-1}(s)$ (a congruence set modulo γ) is a subset. Clearly, the mapping is *onto*. We need only prove that η is a homomorphism, in other words, that, for each s_1 and $s_2 \in M$, $\eta(s_1 s_2) = \eta(s_1)\,\eta(s_2)$. But, since every element in M is the image under γ of some word in Σ^*, it suffices to show that, for all words W_1 and W_2,

$$\eta[\gamma(W_1)\,\gamma(W_2)] = \eta[\gamma(W_1)]\,\eta[\gamma(W_2)]. \tag{1}$$

Since γ is a homomorphism, $\gamma(W_1 W_2) = \gamma(W_1)\,\gamma(W_2)$; to prove (1), therefore, it suffices to prove

$$\eta[\gamma(W_1 W_2)] = \eta[\gamma(W_1)]\,\eta[\gamma(W_2)], \tag{2}$$

or, in other words, that $\eta\gamma$ is a homomorphism.

But $\eta\gamma$ simply maps each word to its congruence set, which the reader can verify by examining the definition of η. And this mapping has already been shown to be a homomorphism in the discussion of the construction of the syntactic monoid of an event. ▌

All the foregoing applies whether the monoid $\gamma(\Sigma^*)$ is finite or infinite. We are interested in this paper only in regular events, and the following theorems tell us that we can confine our attention to those γ for which $\gamma(\Sigma^*)$ is finite.

A *finite state graph* over an alphabet Σ has a finite number of nodes or *states* indicated by circles, from each of which radiates one arrow for each letter of Σ, the head of the arrow reaching some state. One state is singled out as *initial*; others may be dubbed *terminal* states. In Fig. 1, $\Sigma = \{0, 1\}$, and there are three states. Terminal states are double circles, and a single unlabeled arrow points to the initial state. Such a graph may be regarded as diagramming the state changes of a finite automaton with input set Σ.

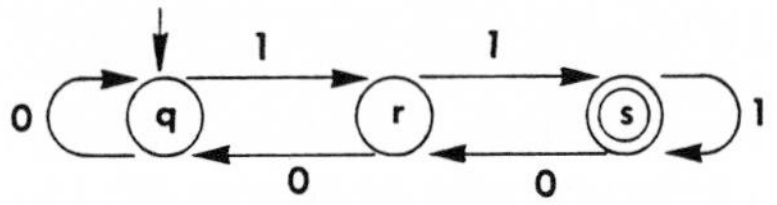

FIG. 1. G.

In such a graph G, let $G(s, W)$ be the state reached by a path beginning at s and spelling out W. $G(s, W)$ always exists uniquely in a state graph. Let $G(W)$ be $G(s_0, W)$ where s_0 is the initial state. Thus, $G(\lambda)$ is the initial state itself. We trust that the use of the letter G both for the graph and in this functional manner will not cause confusion.

We say an event E contained in Σ^* is a *regular event* if there is a finite state graph G with initial state s_0 and set T of terminal states such that

$$E = \{W \in \Sigma^* \mid G(W) \in T\},$$

It is well known that the regular events are precisely those that can be denoted by *regular expressions* in that they may be expressed in terms of singleton sets by a finite number of applications of the union, complex product ($A \cdot B = \{ab \mid a \in A \text{ and } b \in B\}$) and iterate operation ($A^* = \{a_1 \cdots a_n \mid n \geqslant 0, \text{ each } a \in A\}$). (Ginsburg's chapter places these notions in a somewhat broader context, whose algebraic setting is then provided by Shamir.)

A *reduced state graph* G for a regular event E is one in which (1) for every state s of G there is a word W such that $s = G(W)$, and (2) for every pair of states s and s' such that $s \neq s'$, there is a W such that either $G(s, W)$ is a terminal state and $G(s', W)$ is not a terminal state or vice versa.

1.4 Theorem. Every regular event E has a reduced state graph that is unique up to isomorphism, has fewer states than any other state graph for E, and is algorithmically determinable from any of the usual ways a regular event is given (such as an arbitrary state graph or a regular expression).

The proof of this well known theorem is omitted. We assume that the reader is familiar with the theorem if not the proof [1].

1.5 Theorem. Two words W and W' are in the same congruence set modulo a regular event E if and only if, for every state s in the reduced state graph G for E, $G(s, W) = G(s, W')$.

PROOF. Suppose first that W and W' are in the same congruence set modulo E, in other words, that, for all V and X, $VWX \in E$ if and only if $VW'X \in E$. Let s be any state. There is a path from the initial state to s; suppose the path spells out V. Suppose that $s_0 = G(s, W) \neq G(s, W') = s_1$. Then there is an X such that either $G(s_0, X)$ is a terminal state and $G(s_1, X)$ is not, or vice versa. Then $VWX \in E$, but $VW'X \notin E$, or vice versa, contradicting the assumption that $W \equiv W'(\text{mod } E)$. It follows then that $G(s, W) = G(s, W')$.

Suppose now that, for every s in G, $G(s, W) = G(s, W')$. Then, for every V, $G(VW) = G(VW')$ and, hence, for every X, $G(VWX) = G(VW'X)$. Hence, $VWX \in E$ if and only if $VW'X \in E$. ▌

Given a graph G, we may associate each word W with that mapping on the states of G which sends s to $G(s, W)$. Theorem 1.5 says congruent words modulo E are those which induce the same functions on the reduced state graph G for E. Noting that, if G has n states, there are at most n^n mappings on the states of G, we may recall Theorem 1.3 to obtain the following important corollary.

1.6 Corollary. An event E on the alphabet Σ is regular if and only if the syntactic monoid $S(E)$ is finite and, thus, if and only if there is a homomorphism γ of Σ^* onto a finite monoid S such that $E = \gamma^{-1}\gamma(S)$. ▌

Theorem 1.5 gives us a useful computational method for getting the syntactic monoid, which we shall present by example. Consider the state graph G of Fig. 1, clearly reduced. In order to keep track

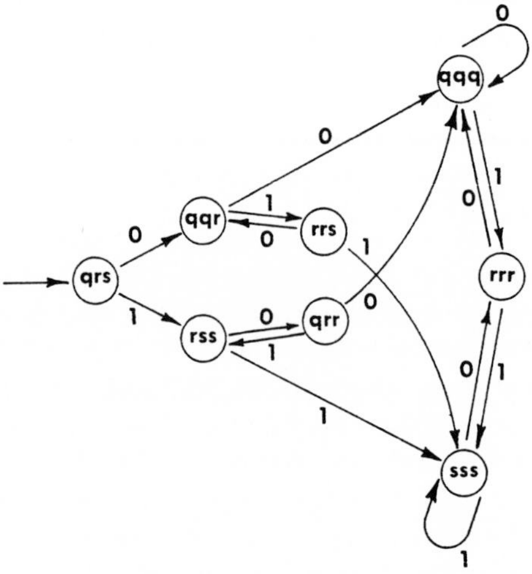

FIG. 2. G'.

of congruence sets of words, we must see what happens when each word is applied to each of the states. Construct a new state graph G' whose initial state is labeled qrs and such that, for each word W, $G'(W) = G(q, W)\, G(r, W)\, G(s, W)$. G' is constructed in a step-by-step fashion, noting that $G'(0) = qqr$, $G'(1) = rss$, $G'(00) = qqq$, $G'(01) = rrs$, etc. The result is Fig. 2.

Each state of G' represents a congruence set of words of the event given by G. For any state s', the congruence set is the set of all words W such that $G'(W) = s'$. Thus, the set corresponding to qrs is the unit set of λ; qqr is the set $0(10)^*$, etc. By the construction method and Theorem 1.5, it should be clear that $G'(W) = G'(W')$ if and only if $W \equiv W'(\text{mod } E)$. Thus, G' represents the syntactic monoid of G. If we let representative words in each congruence set be names for the classes, except for using m for rrr, the multiplication table for this monoid is as shown in Table I.

TABLE I

	λ	0	1	01	10	00	11	m
λ	λ	0	1	01	10	00	11	m
0	0	00	01	m	0	00	11	m
1	1	10	11	1	m	00	11	m
01	01	0	11	01	m	00	11	m
10	10	00	1	m	10	00	11	m
00	00	00	m	m	00	00	11	m
11	11	m	11	11	m	00	11	m
m	m	00	11	m	m	00	11	m

This multiplication table can be identified with the monoid, and any small semigroup can be practically presented in this form. But note that the state graph of Fig. 2 also presents the same information; the multiplication of any two elements can be obtained in a scan that is almost as easy as a look at the table. For example, if we wish to find the product of the element (10) with (m), we note that $m = 110$ and then trace out 10110 from the initial state and land at the circle marked rrr. We then recall that rrr represents $110 = m$, and we have completed the multiplication. In order to facilitate this process, we relabel the state graph of Fig. 2 as Fig. 3 and call it "the monoid graph." This will be the manner of presenting the syntactic monoid of a regular event, and it will be assumed below that the reader

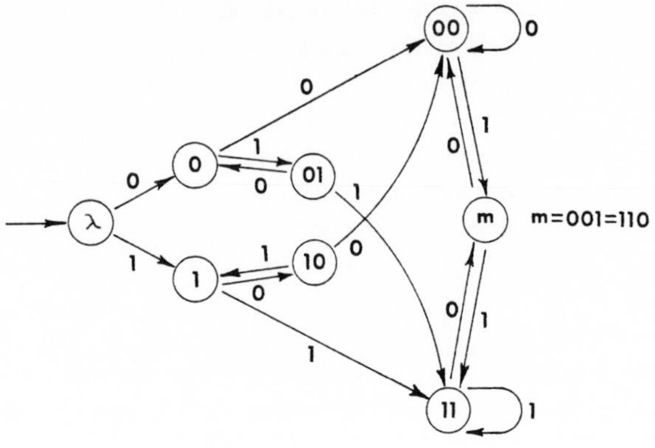

FIG. 3

knows how to construct it from a reduced state graph and how to use it as a representation of the syntactic monoid. (It should be noted that many contemporary group theorists make fruitful use of such graphs for representing groups.)

Two more examples follow. Figures 4a and 5a are reduced state graphs for two events, and Figs. 4b and 5b are their respective syntactic monoids. A two-headed arrow labeled 1 (or 0) means that a 1 (or 0) goes from each state to the other.

Many questions about a finite automaton can be resolved if we know the subgroup structure of its syntactic monoid. The reader of the chapters on the Krohn-Rhodes decomposition theory has already

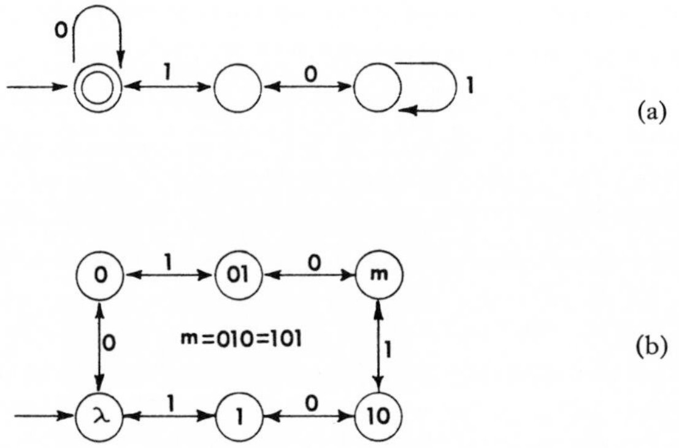

FIG. 4a, b

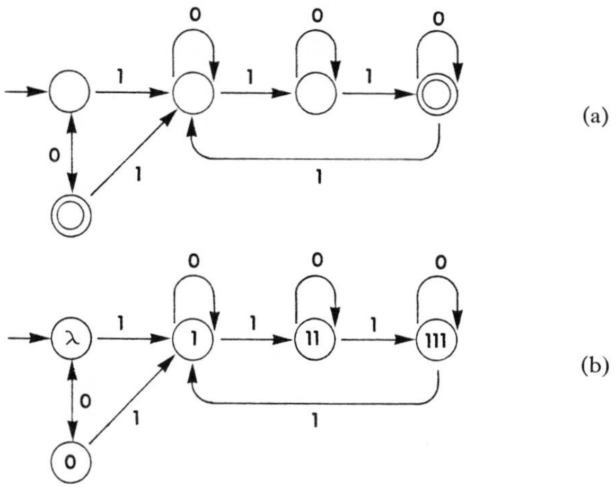

FIG. 5a, b

seen the playoff in mode of decomposition between subgroups of a monoid and the "group-free" parts. In our research on noncounting events, we have discovered (as a result of reading Schützenberger [2]) that, if the syntactic monoid of an event has no nontrivial subgroups, many things can be said about the event which have no apparent relationship to algebra. Such an event, for example, can be expressed as a variant of the regular expression, in that it can be expressed in terms of singleton sets by a finite number of applications of union, intersection, complementation (with respect to the set of all words over the alphabet), and complex product, but without any application of the iterate operation (or asterisk). Furthermore, as Schützenberger proves [2], such are precisely the events that can be described in a certain system of symbolic logic. The expressive power of closely related systems of symbolic logic can be inferred from this result. Since 1962 (with the appearance of the Krohn-Rhodes theory), it has become increasingly apparent that the algebraic approach to automata theory is most powerful. And the deepest applications all necessitate an examination of the subgroup structure. It is for this reason that we devote the remainder of this chapter to the presentation of a working algorithm for finding the maximal subgroups of a finite monoid.

A *subgroup* of a monoid is a subsemigroup that turns out to be a group. In other words, it is a set of elements (1) that is closed under the product operations, (2) that has an identity, and (3) that has an inverse for each of its members. The identity i of the subgroup need not be the identity of the original monoid. What must be true is that $i^2 = i$, in other words, that i be an idempotent. Conversely, every idempotent of the monoid is the identity of some subgroup of the monoid, even though it may be just the trivial group (i.e., the group of order 1) consisting of the idempotent all by itself.

Given a subgroup G whose identity is i, we shall say that G is a subgroup *around* the idempotent i. It turns out that every idempotent of a monoid has a maximal group around it, which will follow from Theorem 1.11. We shall assume that our problem is that of finding these maximal subgroups, since all other subgroups of the monoid are subgroups of these.

Note that, in the monoid of Fig. 3, all the elements are idempotents except 0 and 1. The monoid of Fig. 5b has the two idempotents λ and 111, whereas monoid of Fig. 4b has just λ, the monoid identity, as an idempotent. As we shall see presently, the plethora of idempotents in Fig. 3 reflects the fact that that monoid has only trivial subgroups. On the other hand, the monoid of Fig. 4b is a group. Figure 5b is between these two extremes; it has nontrivial subgroups, but it is not a group itself. To avoid leaving a false impression, we must admit that it is possible for a monoid to have few idempotents and yet have only trivial subgroups. Such is the monoid given as Fig. 6, which has just two, and yet (as we shall see) no nontrivial subgroups.

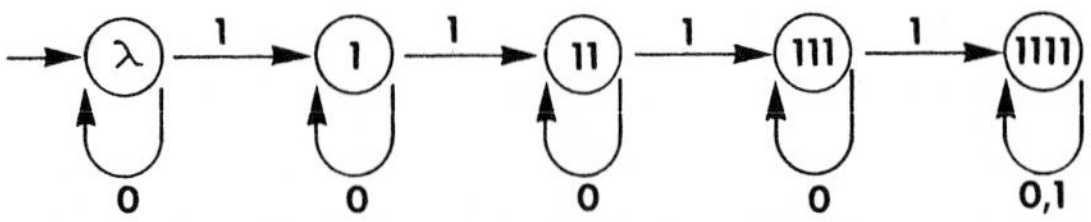

FIG. 6

(By the way, we leave it to the reader to verify that Fig. 6 is the graph of a monoid. One method to check a state graph to see if it is a monoid graph is to treat it as a reduced state graph for an event and construct the syntactic monoid graph for it. Then the original graph is a monoid graph if and only if it is isomorphic to the graph that results by this construction. The proof of this last statement is left as an elementary exercise for the reader.)

Each element a of a finite monoid M determines a power series

$a, a^2, a^3, \ldots$. Since M is finite, there can be only finitely many distinct elements in this power series. Let $n(a)$, $q(a)$, and $m(a)$ be positive integers defined as follows: $n(a)$ is the smallest positive integer such that, for some $y > n(a)$, $a^{n(a)} = a^y$. Then $q(a)$ is the smallest positive integer such that $a^{n(a)} = a^{n(a)+q(a)}$. Finally, $m(a)$ is that multiple of $q(a)$ such that $n(a) \leqslant m(a) \leqslant n(a) + q(a) - 1$. These three integers determine powers of a which play an important role in determining the maximal subgroups of a monoid, and we shall now prove some theorems about them.

1.7 Lemma. The elements $a^{n(a)}, a^{n(a)+1}, \ldots, a^{n(a)+q(a)-1}$ are pairwise distinct.

PROOF. Suppose $a^{n(a)+i} = a^{n(a)+j}$, $0 \leqslant i < j \leqslant q(a) - 1$. Since $a^x = a^y$ implies $a^{x+z} = a^{y+z}$, for any x, y, and z, we get $a^{n(a)+i+q(a)-j} = a^{n(a)+q(a)} = a^{n(a)}$, which contradicts the definition of $q(a)$ since $i + q(a) - j < q(a)$. ▮

1.8 Theorem. $a^{m(a)}$ is an idempotent and the only idempotent among the powers of a.

PROOF. Note that, since $a^{n(a)} = a^{n(a)+q(a)}$, for all $x \geqslant n(a)$,

$$a^x = a^{x+q(a)}. \tag{3}$$

Since $m(a)$ is a multiple of $q(a)$, $a^{m(a)} = a^{m(a)+q(a)} = a^{m(a)+2q(a)} = \cdots = a^{2m(a)}$, which shows that $a^{m(a)}$ is an idempotent.

Suppose now that a^x is an idempotent, in other words, that $a^{2x} = a^x$. x cannot be less than $n(a)$, since $a^{n(a)}$ is the smallest power of a equal to a higher power. Suppose that $x - n(a) \equiv i_1[\mathrm{mod}\ q(a)]$ and $2x - n(a) \equiv i_2[\mathrm{mod}\ q(a)]$, where $0 \leqslant i_1 \leqslant q(a) - 1$ and $0 \leqslant i_2 \leqslant q(a) - 1$. By (3), $a^x = a^{n(a)+i_1}$ and $a^{2x} = a^{n(a)+i_2}$. By the lemma, the only way for a^x and a^{2x} to be equal is for i_1 and i_2 to be equal, which would imply that $x \equiv 2x[\mathrm{mod}\ q(a)]$, which can be true only if x is a multiple of $q(a)$. But then $a^x = a^{m(a)}$, which proves that $a^{m(a)}$ is the only idempotent among the powers of a and concludes the proof of Theorem 1.8. ▮

1.9 Theorem. $\{a^{n(a)}, a^{n(a)+1}, \ldots, a^{n(a)+q(a)-1}\}$ is a cyclic subgroup with identity $a^{m(a)}$ and generated by $a^{m(a)+1}$.

PROOF. Note that $a^{m(a)+1}a^{m(a)+1} = a^{m(a)+2}$, since $m(a)$ is a multiple of $q(a)$. Indeed, for any i, $(a^{m(a)+1})^i = a^{m(a)+i}$; also, if

$$m(a) + i > n(a) + q(a) - 1,$$

then $a^{m(a)+i} = a^{m(a)+i-q(a)}$. Thus, the set generated by $a^{m(a)+1}$ is identical to $\{a^{n(a)}, a^{n(a)+1},..., a^{n(a)+q(a)-1}\}$. In particular, $(a^{m(a)+1})^{q(a)} = a^{m(a)}$, and $(a^{m(a)+1})^{q(a)+1} = a^{m(a)+1}$, and so, by elementary group theory, it is a cyclic group of order $q(a)$ with identity $a^{m(a)}$. ▮

1.10 Theorem. Any power a^x of a is in a subgroup of the monoid if and only if $x \geqslant n(a)$.

PROOF. Theorem 1.9 gives us one half of Theorem 1.10, and so let us assume that $x < n(a)$. By elementary group theory, if a^x were in a finite group, then a^x would generate a cyclic subgroup of that group, and, for some $y > 1$, $a^x = (a^x)^y = a^{xy}$. This would contradict the stipulation that $a^{n(a)}$ is the smallest power of a equal to one of its higher powers. Thus, a^x cannot be in any subgroup of the monoid. ▮

The significance of Theorem 1.10 is that, once we have determined $n(a)$ and $q(a)$, we have determined which powers of a are in subgroups and which are not, and how many of each kind there are.

1.11 Theorem. The set-theoretic union of all cyclic groups around an idempotent is a group and contains every subgroup around that idempotent as a subgroup.

PROOF. Let G_u be the closure under the product operation of the set-theoretic union of all cyclic subgroups around the idempotent u. Thus G_u as defined is a submonoid; and, for any element $a \in G_u$, $a = c_1c_2 \cdots c_n$, where the c's are elements of respective cyclic subgroups around u. $a^2 = c_1c_2 \cdots c_nc_1c_2 \cdots c_n$ is then also in G_u, as are all powers of a, of which there are finitely many. For each i, there is a $c_i^{-1} \in G_u$ such that $c_i^{-1}c_i = c_ic_i^{-1} = u$. Now $a^{-1} = c_n^{-1}c_{n-1}^{-1} \cdots c_1^{-1}$ is in G_u, and all powers of a^{-1}, of which there are finitely many. Clearly, $aa^{-1} = a^{-1}a = u$. The set consisting of u, all powers of a, and all powers of a^{-1} is thus a finite group with u as identity, since it clearly satisfies all the axioms; this group must be identical to its cyclic subgroup generated by a. And so we have proved that every element of G_u is in a cyclic subgroup with u as identity.

Hence G_u is the set-theoretic union itself. That G_u is a group is easily verified.

Now consider an arbitrary subgroup G around u. For every $a \in G$, the cyclic subgroup of G generated by a has u as its identity and must be a subgroup also of G_u. But, since G is the union of such cyclic subgroups, G is a subgroup of G_u. ∎

1.12 Theorem. Subgroups around distinct idempotents are nonoverlapping.

PROOF. Suppose G_1 and G_2 are groups around idempotents u_1 and u_2, $u_1 \neq u_2$ and $a \in G_1$ and $a \in G_2$. This is absurd, for many reasons, not the least of which is that u_1 and u_2 would both have to be powers of a, contradicting Theorem 1.8. (Theorem 1.12 is still true for infinite monoids. The proof is left for the reader.) ∎

We now describe a computation procedure for obtaining all the maximal subgroups of a finite monoid, justified by Theorems 1.8–1.12. Start with an arbitrary member a of the monoid. Determine $n(a)$, $q(a)$, and $m(a)$, which yields the information that $a^{n(a)}, \ldots, a^{n(a)+q(a)-1}$ are distinct elements in the maximal subgroup around the idempotent $a^{m(a)}$, and that $a, a^2, \ldots, a^{n(a)-1}$ are not in any subgroup at all.

Next, take an arbitrary element b not among the powers of a, and do the same for b, finding a cyclic group around an idempotent among the powers of b. This idempotent may or may not be identical to the previously discovered idempotent and, if so, it may be that some, all, or none of the other elements of the cyclic subgroup are among those of the previous cyclic subgroup.

We continue this way until all elements of the monoid are exhausted, keeping track of which maximal group, if any, each element belongs to. The result is the division of the monoid into its maximal subgroups, and the miscellaneous collection of elements not in any subgroup.

Applying this procedure to the monoid of Fig. 5b, taking $a = 0$, we get the power series $0, 0^2, 0^3 = 0$; thus, $n(0) = 1$, $q(0) = 2$; the idempotent is $0^2 = \lambda$, and the cyclic group is $\{0, \lambda\}$ around λ. Then, taking $b = 1$, the power series is $1, 1^2, 1^3, 1^4 = 1$ and $n(1) = 1$, $q(1) = 3$. The cyclic group is $\{1, 11, 111\}$ around the idempotent 111. This exhausts the monoid; it consists of two maximal subgroups, which are themselves cyclic groups, and no elements outside of these.

Note that, if our procedure is applied to Fig. 4b, the same idempotent λ would turn up each time. There are four distinct cyclic groups $\{\lambda, 0\}$, $\{\lambda, 1\}$, $\{\lambda, m\}$, $\{\lambda, 01, 10\}$. No elements are outside the one maximal subgroup around λ, which means that the monoid as a whole is a group. The reader familiar with group theory would not have to use the computation procedure to ascertain that fact, but would see immediately that Fig. 4b is the symmetric permutation group on three objects.

In applying this procedure to the monoid of Fig. 3, we might start with 0, getting $0, 0^2, 0^3 = 0^2$, with $n(0) = 2$, $q(0) = 1$. Thus, 0 is not a member of any subgroup, and we have the trivial subgroup of the idempotent 0^2. Similarly, 1 is not part of any subgroup, but it generates the trivial subgroup around 11. Continuing, we find that each of the remaining elements is an idempotent, and there are no nontrivial subgroups.

REFERENCES

1. M. Rabin and D. Scott, Finite automata and their decision problems, *IBM J. Res. Develop.* **3**, 114–125 (1959); reprinted in "Sequential Machines, Selected Papers" (E. F. Moore, ed.), pp. 63–91. Addison-Wesley, Reading, Massachusetts, 1964.
2. M. P. Schützenberger, "On a Family of Sets Related to McNaughton's *L*-Language," *in* "Automata Theory" (E. R. Caianiello, ed.), pp. 320–324. Academic Press, New York, 1966.

CHAPTER 12

Lectures on Context-Free Languages

SEYMOUR GINSBURG†

System Development Corporation, Santa Monica, California

In the mathematical theory of languages, we view a language as a subset L of the set Σ^* of all finite sequences (words, strings) on some finite alphabet Σ, together with some method of description. Speaking informally, we may single out three main modes of description:

(1) *Generation.* We have a set of rules, called a *grammar,* for generating exactly those words of Σ^* which belong to L.

(2) *Acceptance.* We have a device—some sort of finite-state machine with auxiliary storage—such that, if we start it in its initial state and feed in a string from Σ^*, the final state will belong to a designated set (in which case we say the string is *accepted*) iff the string belongs to L.

(3) *Algebraic.* Given a basic family of sets and a list of algebraic operations, we might consider each subset of Σ^* built up from the basis by a finite number of the operations to be a language. Given such a language, we might then look for a grammar or acceptor that also characterizes it.

† Editor's note: Dr. Ginsburg gave five lectures at Asilomar, based on his book "The Mathematical Theory of Context-Free Languages," McGraw-Hill, New York, 1966. He has kindly permitted me to rework my notes from these lectures into a chapter for this book, as a service to readers who may find the combinatorial theory a necessary background for the algebraic theory given by Dr. Shamir in the next chapter. Proofs were not supplied in the lectures, and so those given here are my own.

We warn the reader that our technical use of the word "word" may well correspond to "sentence" or "complete utterance" in talking of a natural language.

In 1955, Chomsky[†] introduced four models of language in an attempt to formalize natural language. In 1959, he specialized one of these models to obtain the family of context-free languages. It is this family that will attract most of our attention in what follows.

We emphasize that the context-free languages are just a formal approximation to natural languages. However, in 1960, it was noted that the bulk of ALGOL could be treated as a context-free language; that it was not entirely so was due in a large part to the presence of so-called "semantic" rules for handling declaration statements, etc. As a result, there is now much interest in context-free languages as models of programming languages, part of a theory of data-processing. Concepts, and unifying ideas, have come out of this, but as yet the theory has not yielded any effective measures for assessing the relative value of different computer languages.

1. Grammars and Ambiguity

We now present one formalization of the intuitive notion of a grammar just discussed. We use e to denote the empty word, of length 0.

1.1 Definition. A *phrase-structure grammar* is a 4-tuple

$$G = (V, \Sigma, P, \sigma),$$

where

(i) V is a finite nonempty set: the *total vocabulary*.

(ii) $\Sigma \subseteq V$: the set of *terminal symbols*. (We shall be interested in languages over Σ and may think of $V - \Sigma$ as grammatical symbols.)

(iii) P is a finite set of ordered pairs (u, v) with u in $(V - \Sigma)^* - \{e\}$ and v in V^*. We usually write (u, v) as $u \to v$ and call it a *production* or *rewriting rule*. (Note that v may be e.)

(iv) $\sigma \in V - \Sigma$ is the initial symbol.

[†] For references to, and fuller treatment of, any material discussed in this chapter, we refer the reader to Ginsburg's book. Thus [G, p. 7] will refer to page 7 of that book, etc.

Elements of $V - \Sigma$ are called (*metalinguistic*) *variables*, or *auxiliary* symbols.

Given a grammar G, we write $y \Rightarrow z$, and say y *directly generates* z, if y and z are words on V for which we can find u, u_1, u_2 and v such that (u, v) is in P and $y = u_1 u u_2$ and $z = u_1 v u_2$.

We use $\Rightarrow^*$ to denote the transitive closure of $\Rightarrow$, i.e., if y and z are in V^*, $y \Rightarrow^* z$ just in case $y = z$, or there is a sequence $z_1, z_2, \ldots, z_k$ in V^* such that $y = z_1 \Rightarrow z_2 \Rightarrow z_3 \Rightarrow \cdots \Rightarrow z_{k-1} \Rightarrow z_k = z$. We call such a sequence $z_1, \ldots, z_k$ a *derivation* or *generation* of z from y (by the rules of the grammar G).

1.2 Definition. $L \subseteq \Sigma^*$ is called a *phrase structure language* if there exists a phrase structure grammar $G = (V, \Sigma, P, \sigma)$ such that

$$L = L(G) = \{w \in \Sigma^* \mid \sigma \Rightarrow^* w\}.$$

It turns out that the phrase structure languages form the largest class of effectively generable subsets of Σ^*.

1.3 Theorem. A set of words is a phrase structure language iff it is recursively enumerable.†

PROOF OUTLINE. Certainly every phrase structure language is recursively enumerable; one either believes this from Turing's hypothesis (alias Church's thesis), or else applies standard techniques for proving sets recursively enumerable.

Conversely, one associates with a recursively enumerable set S a Turing machine Z that produces the nth element of the set when started in state q, scanning the left-most symbol of a string of n 1's, and halts when and only when it reaches state q_s. One then simulates Z by a phrase structure grammar

$$G_Z = (V, \Sigma, P, \sigma),$$

where $V = \Sigma \cup \{\sigma\} \cup Q$, where Σ is the alphabet of Z, and Q its set of states, and where P has appropriate productions for each quintuple of Z, plus productions

$$\sigma \rightarrow \sigma 1, \qquad \sigma \rightarrow q_1$$

† The reader unacquainted with recursively enumerable sets, recursive sets, and Turing machines may consult [BMM] (M. A. Arbib, "Brains, Machines, and Mathematics," McGraw-Hill, New York, 1964), especially Sects. 1.5-6 and 5.3 for an elementary exposition and references to more detailed accounts.

to set up the initial complete configurations, and

$$q_s \to e$$

to remove the halt state from a terminal complete configuration. Then clearly $S = L(G_Z)$. ▮

This theorem tells us that the class of phrase structure languages is too broad for it to serve as a model for programming languages, for we would like a programming language to be recursive so that a computer can tell whether or not a string of symbols constitutes a valid program. However, the collection of recursive sets is still too broad, for we cannot tell whether a set is recursive or not. We seek subfamilies of the recursive sets to which we can give a grammar formulation.

1.4 Definition. A *context-sensitive grammar* is a phrase-structure grammar for which each production (u, v) satisfies $l(u) \leqslant l(v)$.† L is a context-sensitive language if $L = L(G)$ for some context-sensitive grammar G.

1.5 Theorem. Every context-sensitive language is a recursive set.

PROOF OUTLINE. Given v, we use the length condition to see that there are only finitely many derivations that yield distinct strings of length $\leqslant l(v)$, and we check all of these effectively to see if v is itself derivable. ▮

1.6 Fact. No context-sensitive language contains e.

The notion of *context* in this discussion refers to the context of a *single letter*. This motivates the following definition.

1.7 Definition. A *context-free grammar* is a phrase structure grammar in which each production $u \to v$ has the property $l(u) = 1$; i.e., each rule has the form $u \to v$ with $u \in V - \Sigma$, $v \in \Sigma^*$. L is a *context-free language* (C.F. language; C.F.L.) if $L = L(G)$ for some C.F. grammar G.

1.8 Fact. e may be in a C.F.L.

1.9 Fact. L context-free implies $L - \{e\}$ context-sensitive.

PROOF. See [G, Theorem 1.8.1.] ▮

† For each word z, $l(z)$ denotes the length of z.

1.10 Example. If $\Sigma = \{a, b\}$, $V = \{a, b, \sigma\}$, $P = \{\sigma \to a\sigma b, \sigma \to ab\}$ then $L(G) = \{a^n b^n \mid n \geqslant 1\}$, which is thus a C.F.L.

Unfortunately, it is not usually possible to obtain so explicit a description of a language defined implicitly by a C.F. grammar.

1.11 Example. Let $G = (V, \Sigma, P, \xi_1)$, with $\Sigma = \{a, b, c, d\}$, $V = \{\sigma, \alpha, \beta, \gamma, a, b, c, d\}$, and

$$P = \{\sigma \to a\alpha, \alpha \to \beta\alpha, \alpha \to \beta, \beta \to dc, \beta \to bb\gamma, \gamma \to cc\}.$$

Then the derivation $\sigma \Rightarrow a\alpha \Rightarrow a\beta\alpha \Rightarrow a\beta\beta \Rightarrow a\beta dc \Rightarrow abb\gamma dc \Rightarrow abbccdc$ may be "graphed" by a tree known as the *generation tree*, in which the word generated is given by the terminal nodes, read from left to right, a structure reminiscent of the parsing tree of "grade-school"† English.

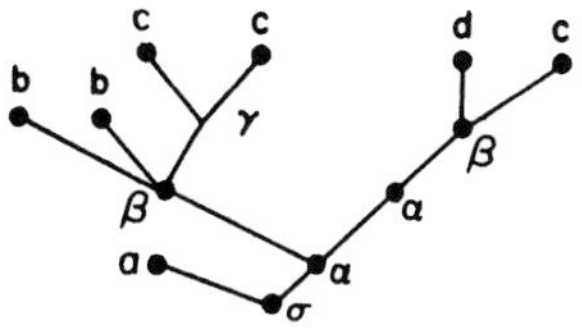

Now this same generation tree corresponds to several different derivations, but, since all these derivations yield the same tree, we want to regard them as corresponding to the same "parsing" of the derived word. We may avoid this diversity of derivations for a tree, by associating with the tree the *leftmost derivation*, i.e., that in which, at each stage, a production is applied to the leftmost variable; this is always possible, since all replacements are context-free. For instance, the leftmost derivation for the foregoing tree is

$$\sigma \Rightarrow a\alpha \Rightarrow a\beta\alpha \Rightarrow abb\gamma\alpha \Rightarrow abbcc\alpha \Rightarrow abbcc\beta \Rightarrow abbccdc.$$

We may now embody the notion of a grammar as being ambiguous if there are words of the language which can be parsed in different ways.

1.12 Definition. A C.F. grammar is *unambiguous* if each word in $L(G)$ has exactly one generation tree (i.e., exactly one leftmost derivation). Otherwise, G is called *ambiguous.*

† An Americanism.

We repeat that this notion is one of *syntactic* ambiguity. In data-processing, a word in the language encodes a program. A compiler must be able to break the program down uniquely into its components. Of course, a language might be ambiguous syntactically and yet unambiguous semantically in that, no matter how many different ways an ambiguous string was compiled, it would yield a program that would cause a computer to compute the same function. But such notions of semantic ambiguity are outside the scope of the present subject.

The reader may readily convince himself every C.F.L. has infinitely many C.F. grammars. Thus, given an ambiguous grammar for a language, we may seek unambiguous grammars for the language. Such a search may or may not succeed.

1.13 Definition. A C.F.L. is said to be *inherently ambiguous* if every grammar generating it is ambiguous.

That there do exist inherently ambiguous languages was first shown by Parikh, who provided the example

$$\{a^i b^j a^k b^l \mid j = l \text{ or } i = k;\, i, j, k, l \geqslant 1\}.$$

An ambiguous grammar (V, Σ, P, σ) for this set is

$$V = \{a, b, c, \sigma, \sigma_1, \sigma_2, \sigma_1', \sigma_2'\}, \qquad \Sigma = \{a, b, c\},$$

$$P = \{\sigma \to \sigma_1\sigma_1', \sigma \to \sigma_2\sigma_2', \sigma_1 \to a\sigma_1 a, \sigma_1 \to \sigma_1', \sigma_1' \to b\sigma_1' \;\; \sigma_1' \to b, \sigma_2 \to a\sigma_2,$$
$$\sigma_2 \to a, \sigma_2' \to b\sigma_2' b, \sigma_2' \to \sigma_2\}.$$

However, to prove that *every* grammar for this set is ambiguous is a difficult task, and the reader is referred to [*G*, Chapter 6] for the many details.

2. Acceptors and Languages

We now introduce a version of finite automata apropos for the study of formal languages.

2.1 Definition. A *finite state acceptor* (f.s.a.) is a quintuple

$$A = (K, \Sigma, \delta, q_0, F),$$

where

K is a finite nonempty set: the set of *states*;
Σ is a finite nonempty set: the set of *inputs*;
$\delta : K \times \Sigma \rightarrow K$ is the *transition* or *next-state* function;
$q_0 \in K$ is the *start state*; and
$F \subseteq K$ is the set of designated *final states*.

As usual, we extend δ to $K \times \Sigma^*$ by requiring $\delta(q, xa) = \delta[\delta(q, x), a]$ and setting $\delta(q, e) = q$. We interpret A as a system, which, if in state q at time t and receiving input x, will at time $t + 1$ be in state $\delta(q, x)$.

For the f.s.a. $A = (K, \Sigma, \delta, q_0, F)$, we call

$$T(A) = \{w \in \Sigma^* \mid \delta(q_0, w) \in F\}$$

the set of tapes accepted by A. We call sets of the form $T(A)$, where A is an f.s.a., *finite-state-acceptable*, or *finite-state languages*.

For two subsets D and E of Σ^*, we defined their *product*, or *complex product*, to be

$$D \cdot E \text{ (or } DE) = \{de \mid d \in D \text{ and } e \in E\},$$

and we define the *closure* or *iterate* of D to be

$$D^* = U_{i=0}^{\infty} D^i,$$

where $D^0 = \{e\}$ and $D^{i+1} = D^i D$. D^* is thus the subsemigroup of Σ^* generated by D, and Σ^* is indeed Σ^*.

We say a subset of Σ^* is *regular* if it is a finite set, or can be obtained by a finite number of applications of the set-theoretic union, complex product, and iterate operations. We owe to Kleene the following theorem.

2.2 Characterization Theorem. A set is finite-state acceptable iff it is regular.

PROOF. See, e.g., [BMM, Sect. 1.7]. ∎

We now turn to devices that are, in a sense, multivalued in operation; at each stage, we allow any one of several stated transitions to occur. We do not attach weights to these transitions, and so we may consider the machines to be "possibilistic," rather than probabilistic.

With these devices, we accept a sequence if at least one of its possible transition sequences leads to a designated final state; we pay off if there is any success, without worrying about the multitude of failures.

2.3 Definition. A *nondeterministic f.s.a.* (ndfsa) is a quintuple

$$A = (K, \Sigma, \delta, q_0, F),$$

where δ is a function from $K \times \Sigma$ onto 2^K (the set of subsets of K) and K, Σ, q_0 and F are as before.

2.4 Definition. If $A = (K, \Sigma, \delta, q_0, F)$ is an ndfsa, then $T(A)$, *the set of tapes accepted by* A, comprises those $x_1 \cdots x_k$ (each $x_i \in \Sigma$) for which there exists a sequence $q_1, \ldots, q_k$ of states from K such that

$$q_i \in \delta(q_{i-1}, x_i), \qquad 1 \leqslant i \leqslant k, \tag{1}$$

$$q_k \in F. \tag{2}$$

2.5 Theorem. If A is an ndfsa, then $T(A)$ is regular.

PROOF. Note that $T(A)$ is accepted by the fsa

$$A' = (2^K, \Sigma, \delta', \{q_0\}, F'),$$

where, for $K' \subseteq K$, $\delta'(K', x) = \cup\{\delta(q, x) \mid q \in K'\}$ and $F' = (K' \subseteq K \mid K' \cap F \neq \phi)$. ▮

Thus, nondeterminism introduces no new sets in the study of fsa's. However, we shall see that the notion plays a vital role in the study of C.F.L.'s.

2.6 Theorem. The collection of regular sets is closed under set intersection and complementation.

PROOF. Let $E = T(A)$, where $A = (K, \Sigma, \delta, q_0, F)$ is an f.s.a. Then $\Sigma^* - E$ is $T(A')$, where $A' = (K, \Sigma, \delta, q_0, K - F)$, and so is also regular. If E and H are regular, then, by what we already know, so is $E \cap H = \Sigma^* - [(\Sigma^* - E) \cup (\Sigma^* - H)]$. ▮

These properties are much harder to verify from the inductive characterization of regular sets.

2.7 Definition. A CF grammar $G = (V, \Sigma, P, \sigma)$ is said to be *right-linear* if each production in P is of the form $\xi \to u$ or $\xi \to u\alpha$, where u is in Σ^* and α is in $V - \Sigma$.

2.8 Theorem. A set $R \subseteq \Sigma^*$ is regular iff $\exists$ some right-linear grammar G such that $R = L(G)$. Furthermore, G can be assumed to be unambiguous.

PROOF. Let $A = (K, \Sigma, \delta, q_0, F)$ be an fsa that accepts R, and let $G = (V, \Sigma, P, \sigma)$, where $V = \Sigma \cup \underset{\sim}{Q} \cup \{\sigma\}$, and let P contain (i) a production $\sigma \to q_0$; (ii) and for each $q, q' \in K$ and $x \in \Sigma$ such that $\delta(q, x) = q'$ a production $q \to xq'$; (iii) and for each q in F a production $q \to e$. Then G is unambiguous, and $L(G) = R$.

A somewhat modified reversal of this construction yields the converse. ▮

Thus, the regular sets are all C.F.L.'s. However, not all C.F.L.'s are regular, an example of one that is not regular being $\{a^i b^i \mid i \geqslant 1\}$.

We shall show that we may define a class of acceptors, more general than the f.s.a.'s, that do, in fact, accept only and all C.F.L.'s. The appropriate notion is a nondeterministic pushdown acceptor, which was first introduced as a tool for mechanical translation, and as a programming concept.

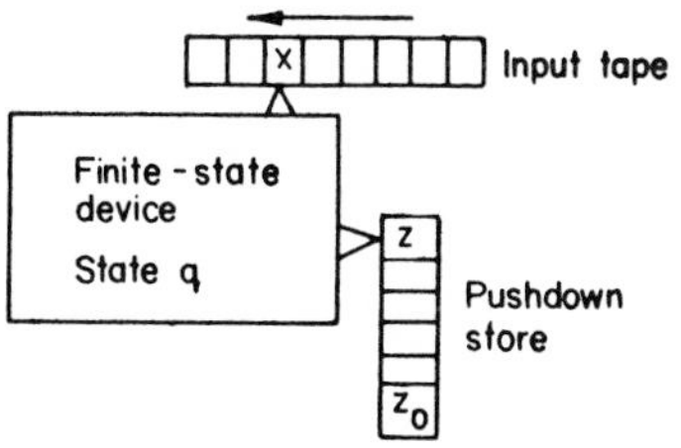

Our picture is of a finite-state device, to which is adjoined a pushdown store—a finite but expandable tape, only the topmost square of which may be read by the machine at any time. Inputs come in from the right.

The device may either scan the input symbol x, in which case the input tape is advanced one space, and the triple (q, x, z) of state, input, and top pushdown square determine possible next-states q', and possible strings γ, with which to replace z, in which case the machine completes the cycle scanning the rightmost (i.e., topmost) square of γ (unless $\gamma = e$, which gives an erase, and the machine ends scanning the square below z). Alternatively, the machine may only use q and z to determine (q', γ), in which case the input tape is not advanced. Thus, the action is nondeterministic.

The pushdown store is a FILO store: first in, last out.

The machine halts if the pushdown store is emptied, and so we introduce a special symbol z_0 to mark the end of its tape; computation always starts with just z_0 in the pushdown store.

2.9 Definition. A *pushdown acceptor* (pda)† is a septuple

$$M = (K, \Sigma, \Gamma, \delta, z_0, q_0, F),$$

where

K, Σ, Γ are finite nonempty sets (the *states*, *inputs*, and *pushdown symbols*, respectively),

$z_0 \in \Gamma$ is the *pushdown start symbol*,

$q_0 \in K$ is the *start state*,

$F \subseteq K$ is the set of designated *final states*, and

δ is a mapping from $K \times (\Sigma \cup \{e\}) \times \Gamma$ into the finite subsets of $K \times \Gamma^*$.

Given a pda M, let $\overset{*}{\vdash}$ be the relation on $K \times \Sigma^* \times \Gamma^*$ defined as follows. For z in Γ, x in $\Sigma \cup \{e\}$, write $(p, xw, \alpha z) \vdash (q, w, \alpha\gamma)$ if $\delta(p, x, z)$ contains (q, γ). Note that x may be empty. Write $(p, w, \alpha) \overset{*}{\vdash} (p, w, \alpha)$. Furthermore, for each β in Γ^* and x_i in $\Sigma \cup \{e\}$, $1 \leqslant 1 \leqslant k$, write $(p, x_1 \cdots x_k w, \alpha) \overset{*}{\vdash} (q, w, \beta)$ if there exists $p = p_1, p_2, \ldots, p_{k+1} = q$ in K, and $\alpha = \alpha_1, \alpha_2, \ldots, \alpha_{k+1} = \beta$ in Γ^* such that $(p_i, x_i \cdots x_k w, \alpha_i) \vdash (p_{i+1}, x_{i+1} \cdots x_k w, \alpha_{i+1})$ for $1 \leqslant i \leqslant k$.

2.10 Definition. A word $w \in \Sigma^*$ is *accepted* by a pda M if

$$(q_0, w, z_0) \overset{*}{\vdash} (q, e, \alpha)$$

for some $q \in F$ and some α in Γ^*. The set of all tapes accepted by M is denoted by $T(M)$.

We then have the theorem, whose proof is given in [*G*, Sect. 2.5].

2.11 Characterization Theorem. A set L of words is a context-free language iff $L = T(M)$ for some pda M.

This theorem is an important tool in showing that we may prove a language C.F. by exhibiting a pda that accepts it. Unfortunately, this

† The nondeterministic pda is so important that we omit the label and only make special comment if a pda is deterministic.

task may be a hard one; it is usually easy to prove that all strings of a language are accepted by a suitable pda, but hard to show that the pda accepts no other strings.

2.12 Example. Let $\Sigma = \{a, b\}$, and let L be the set of words with exactly as many occurrences of a as occurrences of b. Consider the pda M that reads an input symbol at a time and deletes the top letter from the pushdown store if it is the "opposite" of the input letter, whereas we add the input letter to the store if it is equal to that atop the store. At the first step, of course, we must add whatever input is scanned. Let the device be in its final state if the symbol z_0 is atop the pushdown store. Then it may be proved that $L = T(M)$. Thus, L is C.F.

A *deterministic pda* is one in which δ is single-valued, and with the further restriction that, if $\delta(q, e, z)$ is defined, then $\delta(q, a, z)$ is defined for *no* a in Σ. The sets accepted by deterministic pda's are called *deterministic C.F.L.'s*. The deterministic C.F.L.'s form a proper subset of the class of all C.F.L.'s.

2.13 Example. The set of palindromes is a C.F.L. that is not deterministic. It is easy to build a nondeterministic pda that accepts just the palindromes by writing half the string in the pushdown store, and then checking off symbols as the second half is read in; nondeterminism enters in "guessing" when the halfway point is reached. However, one may show that no deterministic pda can accept precisely the palindromes.

The next two theorems are proved in [G, Sect. 2.6].

2.14 Theorem. If L is a deterministic C.F.L., then $L = L(G)$ for some unambiguous grammar G.

However, there do exist unambiguous languages that are not deterministic; roughly speaking, unambiguous L's are those for which there exists a pda that accepts each string of L in only one way.

2.15 Theorem. If L is a deterministic C.F.L., then $\Sigma^* - L$ is also a deterministic C.F.L.

On the contrary, the class of all C.F.L.'s is *not* closed under complementation (see below). Deterministic C.F.L.'s are not easy to prove theorems about but are, of course, better objects to program with than general C.F.L.'s.

3. Operations

We now turn to questions like the following: If f is an operation on languages and L is a C.F.L., is $f(L)$ also a C.F.L?

3.1 Example. $\{a^n b^n b^n \mid n \geqslant 1\}$ is not a C.F.L. (For proof, see [G, p. 84].)

3.2 Fact. The class of C.F.L.'s is not closed under intersection.

PROOF. $L_1 = \{a^i b^j c^j \mid i, j \geqslant 1\}$ and $L_2 = \{a^i b^i c^j \mid i, j \geqslant 1\}$ are both C.F.L.'s, but $L_1 \cap L_2$ is *not* a C.F.L. ▮

3.3 Theorem. The class of C.F.L.'s is closed under the $\cup$, $\cdot$, and $*$ operations.

PROOF. Given grammars for L_1 and L_2, replace them by grammars with disjoint sets of metalinguistic variables to obtain

$$G_1 = (\Sigma^1 \cup \Sigma, \Sigma, P_1, \sigma_1), \qquad G_2 = (\Sigma^2 \cup \Sigma, \Sigma, P_2, \sigma_2).$$

It is then easy to verify that G_3 is a grammar for $L_1 \cup L_2$, G^4 is a grammar for $L_1 \cdot L_2$, and G_5 is a grammar for L_1^*, where

$$G_3 = (\Sigma^1 \cup \Sigma^2 \cup \Sigma \cup \{\sigma\}, \Sigma, P_1 \cup P_2 \cup \{\sigma \to \sigma_1, \sigma \to \sigma_2\}, \sigma),$$

$$G_4 = (\Sigma^1 \cup \Sigma^2 \cup \Sigma \cup \{\sigma\}, \Sigma, P_1 \cup P_2 \cup \{\sigma \to \sigma_1\sigma_2\}, \sigma),$$

$$G_5 = (\Sigma^1 \cup \Sigma, \Sigma, P \cup \{\sigma \to e, \sigma \to \sigma\sigma_1\}, \sigma).$$ ▮

3.4 Corollary. The class of C.F.L.'s is not closed under complementation.

PROOF. If it were, the foregoing theorem would then imply it was closed under intersection. ▮

3.5 Theorem. If L is a C.F.L. and R is a regular set, then $L \cap R$ is also a C.F.L. Furthermore, if L is unambiguous, then so is $L \cap R$.

PROOF. [G, p. 88]. ▮

This theorem has many applications in the study of C.F.L.'s.

3.6 Example. Suppose L is C.F., and let L_n be the set of all words in L whose length is divisible by n. Then $L_n = L \cap R_n^*$, where R_n is the set of words of length n. Thus, L_n is a C.F.L.

3.7 Definition. A *generalized sequential machine* (*gsm*) is a sextuple

$$S = (K, \Sigma, \Delta, \delta, \lambda, q_0),$$

where

K, Σ, and Δ are finite nonempty sets (the *states*, *inputs*, and *outputs*),
$q_0 \in K$ is the *start state*,
$\delta : K \times \Sigma \rightarrow \Sigma$ is the *next-state function*, and
$\lambda : K \times \Sigma \rightarrow \Delta^*$ is the *output function*.

Note that a single input may yield no output, a single output symbol, or a whole string. If $\lambda(K \times \Sigma) \subseteq \Delta$, we obtain our familiar finite automata (also known as complete sequential machines, etc.).

If S is a gsm and $w \in \Sigma^*$, we set $S(w) = \lambda(q_0, w)$.

3.8 Theorem. If L is C.F. and S is a gsm, then $S(L)$ is also a C.F.L.

PROOF. [G, Sect. 3.3]. ▮

3.9 Example. Let L be a C.F.L. Let $f(a_1 a_2 \cdots a_k) = a_2 a_4 \cdots$ for each word with $a_i \in \Sigma$. Clearly, f is a gsm mapping, and so $f(L)$ is also a C.F.L.

3.10 Definition. Given Σ, for each a in Σ, let Σ_a be a finite nonempty set. For each a in Σ, specify a subset $\tau(a)$ of Σ_a^*. We then extend τ to Σ^* by letting

$$\tau(e) = \{e\}, \qquad \tau(a_1 \cdots a_k) = \tau(a_1) \cdots \tau(a_k).$$

Such a τ is called a *substitution mapping.*

If L is C.F. and τ is an unrestricted substitution mapping, we cannot expect $\tau(L)$ to be C.F. Just take $\tau(a)$ to be a non-C.F. language, and set $L = \{a\}$. However:

3.11 Theorem (the Substitution Theorem). If L is C.F. and τ is a substitution mapping with $\tau(a)$ C.F. for every a in Σ, then $\tau(L)$ is C.F.

PROOF. This is an easy exercise of the type undertaken to prove Theorem 3.3. ▮

3.12 Example. For each set of words X, let $\text{Init}(X) = \{u \neq e \mid \exists w$ with uw in $X\}$. We show that, if L is C.F.L., then so is Init(L). For each a in Σ, set $\tau(a) = \{a, ac\}$ with $c \notin \Sigma$. Then $\tau(L) \cap \Sigma^* c \Sigma^*$ is still C.F. Now, let S be the gsm that acts like an identity until it reaches a c, and then just "emits" e. Clearly, $\text{Init}(L) = S[\tau(L) \cap \Sigma^* c \Sigma^*]$ and so is a C.F.L.

3.13 Theorem. Given Σ, there exists an alphabet Σ', a C.F. language D, and a homomorphism $H:(\Sigma')^* \twoheadrightarrow \Sigma^*$ such that, for each C.F. language $L \subseteq \Sigma^*$, one can find a regular set $R \subseteq (\Sigma')^*$ such that

$$L = h(D \cap R).$$

PROOF. [G, Sect. 3.7]. D is called a Dyck language. ▮

4. Decision Problems

If we are given two C.F.L.'s L_1 and L_2, we may ask if there exists a gsm that maps L_1 onto L_2. Clearly, the answer is no if $|L_1| < |L_2|$, and yes if $L_1 = L_2$. We may ask if there is a *decision procedure*—given L_1, L_2, is it *effectively solvable*† whether or not there exists a gsm S such that $S(L_1) = L_2$?

4.1 Theorem. Each C.F.L. L is a recursive set; i.e., given a C.F. grammar for L, we can effectively decide of a word w whether or not it is in L.

PROOF. This is a corollary of Theorem 1.5, using Fact 1.9. ▮

4.2 Theorem. Given arbitrary C.F. grammars G_1 and G_2, it is not effectively decidable whether or not

(a) $L(G_1) = L(G_2)$;
(b) $L(G_1) \subseteq L(G_2)$;
(c) $L(G_1) = \Sigma^*$;
(d) $L(G_1) \cap L(G_2) = \phi$; or
(e) there exists a gsm S such that $S[L(G_1)] = L(G_2)$.

† For background on this, cf. [BMM], Sects. 5.2 and 5.3.

PROOF. [G, Sects. 4.1 and 4.2]. ▮

Given L_1 and L_2, we can always use a constant map to get $S(L_1) \subseteq L_2$. But (cf. [G, Theorem 4.3.2]):

4.3 Theorem. If L_1 and L_2 are infinite C.F.L.'s, it is recursively unsolvable to tell whether or not there exists a gsm S such that $S(L_1) \subseteq L_2$ and $S(L_1)$ is infinite.

4.4 Theorem. It is recursively unsolvable to tell for an arbitrary C.F. grammar G whether or not it is ambiguous.

PROOF. [G, p. 139]. ▮

Ginsburg and Spanier have intensively studied a subfamily of the C.F.L.'s—the *bounded context-free languages*—which have much better behavior with respect to operations and decision problems than the family of all C.F.L.'s. We refer the reader to Chapter 5 of [G] for a full treatment of these languages.

CHAPTER 13

Algebraic, Rational, and Context-Free Power Series in Noncommuting Variables†

Eliahu Shamir
The Hebrew University, Jerusalem, Israel

1. Introduction

A context-free grammar‡ with n auxiliary symbols $\xi_1, \ldots, \xi_n$ generates n languages $L_1, \ldots, L_n$ over the terminal alphabet A; L_j is determined by the choice of ξ_j as the initial symbol. The productions of the grammar are recursive rules for computing increasingly longer words of $L_1, \ldots, L_n$. From another point of view, spelled out in Sect. 2, the grammar is a system of n polynomial equations with union and product of sets of words as basic operations. This system of equations is satisfied by the n-tuple $(L_1, \ldots, L_n)$. This point of view is apparent in the "Backus notation," which was originally used to describe the syntax of ALGOL 60.

It was observed by Schützenberger [1, 2] that there is much to gain and nothing to lose if, instead of languages, one considers formal power series in noncommuting variables. These objects are simply functions from A^* to Z (the integers). Each power series (ps) is determined by assigning an integral coefficient to each word $u \in A^*$. The collection of all ps is a ring,§ and the equations of the grammar

† The research leading to the writing of this chapter was partially supported by the Office of Naval Research, Information Systems Branch, under Contract NR62558-4695.

‡ Cf. Chapter 12 for notation and terminology.

§ We assume the reader knows the definition and simplest algebraic properties of rings.

become honest polynomial equations in this ring, equations that are satisfied by the n-tuple of ps $(f_1, \ldots, f_n)$. Again, the equations give recursive rules whereby $f_j(u)$, the coefficient of f_j at u, is expressed as a polynomial in the "lower" coefficients $f_k(v)$ of subwords v of u. The complete solution $(f_1, \ldots, f_n)$ is constructed by successive approximation.

Thus, a context-free grammar is, in fact, a system of algebraic equations. If the variables $a \in A$ stand for commuting (say numerical) variables, the system becomes an ordinary algebraic system that is solved by the functions $f_1, \ldots, f_n$ (functions of the variables $a \in A$), which can be shown to be algebraic functions. Context-free systems are special in two respects. The first is a technical restriction [cf. (2.1)] that insures unique solvability. The second restriction is that the coefficients of all the monomials in the system are 0 or 1. This restriction is essential and is responsible for the combinatorial flavor of the theory of context-free grammars and languages. The coefficients of the solutions $f_1, \ldots, f_n$ are necessarily nonnegative. They are restricted to 0 or 1 only if the grammar is unambiguous. In any case, $f_j(u)$ is the number of distinct generations (or "trees") of u from ξ_j. This number is called the *degree of ambiguity of u with respect to ξ_j*.

We shall focus the attention here on algebraic systems with *arbitrary* numerical coefficients. More generally, we let the coefficients belong to an arbitrary commutative ring with identity. Together with the algebraic systems, it is useful to consider the subclass of rational systems that arise from finite-state grammars (i.e., finite automata) by allowing arbitrary ring coefficients.

It turns out to be quite useful to consider an algebraic system of equations as a grammar in which the productions have certain "weights" taken from the ring of coefficients. Indeed, many combinatorial arguments and constructions, originally devised for context-free grammars, carry over to the new situation. Most of Schützenberger's results [1, 2] can be obtained in this way, and the proofs will seem familiar to readers acquainted with the context-free theory.

2. Algebraic and Rational Power Series

Let A be a finite set of symbols and A^* the free monoid generated by the symbols of A and with the identity (empty string) e. Let R

be a commutative ring with identity 1. A function $f : A^* \to R$ is called a power series (ps) and is also expressed as a formal sum

$$f = \Sigma_{x \in A^*} \langle f, x \rangle\, x, \qquad \langle f, x \rangle = f(x) \in R.$$

The collection of all ps is a ring with identity under the operations

$$\langle f + g, x \rangle = \langle f, x \rangle + \langle g, x \rangle,$$
$$\langle fg, x \rangle = \Sigma_{uv=x} \langle f, u \rangle \langle g, v \rangle.$$

This ring is denoted by $R[A]$.

The *support* of f is the set $\{x \mid f(x) \neq 0\}$. A finite [singleton] supported ps is a *polynomial* [*monomial*]. For any monoid S, the polynomials $p = \Sigma \langle p, s \rangle s$ form a ring with identity $R_{\text{pol}}[S]$ (the monoid ring). In the case $S = A^*$ is free over A, we denote it by $R_{\text{pol}}[A]$. It is a subring of $R[A]$.

Let $X = \{\xi_1, \ldots, \xi_n\}$ be a set of symbols ("variables") disjoint from A, and let $p_j \in R_{\text{pol}}[X \cup A]$. We assume that

$$\langle p_j, \xi_i \rangle = 0, \qquad p_j(e) = 0, \qquad 1 \leqslant i, j \leqslant n. \tag{2.1}$$

An *algebraic system* is then a system of equations

$$\xi_j = p_j, \ 1 \leqslant j \leqslant n \qquad [p_j = p_j(\xi_1, \ldots, \xi_n, a_1, a_2, \ldots), a_i \in A]. \tag{2.2}$$

The solution $\xi_1 = f_1, \ldots, \xi_n = f_n$, $f_j \in R[A]$ of the system is the one obtained as follows: let $f_1^{(0)} = \cdots = f_n^{(0)} = 0$ and

$$f_j^{(k+1)} = p_j(f_1^{(k)}, \ldots, f_n^{(k)}, a_1, a_2, \ldots), \qquad 1 \leqslant j \leqslant n.$$

Then $f_j = \lim_{k \to \infty} f_j^{(k)}$ exist; in fact, the coefficients of strings of length r in $f_j^{(k)}$ are independent of k for $k > r$ [because of (2.1)]. Clearly, $(f_1, \ldots, f_n)$ is a solution of (2.2). Moreover, it is easily shown to be the unique solution satisfying

$$\langle f_j, e \rangle = 0, \qquad 1 \leqslant j \leqslant n. \tag{2.3}$$

A component of the solution of an algebraic system is called an *algebraic* ps.

REMARK. Consider polynomial systems $q_j = 0$ which, instead of (2.1), satisfy the more general elimination condition: if $\Sigma \alpha_{ij} \xi_i$ is the linear part of q_j, then the matrix (α_{ij}) is invertible in R. Such a system is easily seen to be equivalent to a system satisfying (2.1); hence its solution consists of algebraic ps.

An algebraic system is *rational* (and its solution consists of *rational* ps) if all the monomials of p_j are of the form $\alpha x \xi_i$ or αx, $x \in A^*$.

An algebraic [rational] ps in which all the nonzero coefficients are 1 is a context-free [finite-state] system. The solution components are context-free [finite-state] ps. Their supports are (and exhaust all) context-free [finite-state] languages. These systems are usually described by productions instead of equations; thus, if $p_j = z_{j1} + \cdots + z_{j\pi(j)}$, $1 \leqslant j \leqslant n$, then the productions of the grammar are

$$\xi_j \to z_{j1}, \ldots, \xi_j \to z_{j\pi(j)}, \qquad 1 \leqslant j \leqslant n.$$

The coefficient $\langle f_j, x \rangle$ of the context-free ps f_j is the number of different generation (trees) from ξ_j to x in the defining grammar. This is the degree of ambiguity of x (with respect to ξ_j and the given grammar).

It is useful to describe any algebraic system in a grammar form. Here, if $p_j = \alpha_{j1} z_{j1} + \cdots + \alpha_{j\pi(j)} z_{j\pi(j)}$ (in a collected form), then

$$\xi_j \to \alpha_{j1} z_{j1}, \ldots, \xi_j \to \alpha_{j\pi(j)} z_{j\pi(j)}, \qquad 1 \leqslant j \leqslant n \tag{2.4}$$

are the productions of the system. The coefficient α_{ji} is the *weight* of the corresponding production. The *underlying (context-free) grammar* is obtained by setting all nonzero weights to 1. If Γ is a generation tree from ξ_i to x in the underlying grammar, then $\omega(\Gamma)$, the weight of Γ, is the product of the weights of all productions occurrences in Γ. The following proposition is easily established by induction.

2.1 Proposition. Let $f_1, \ldots, f_n$ be the solution of an algebraic system $\xi_j = p_j$, $1 \leqslant j \leqslant n$. Let $\Gamma_1, \ldots, \Gamma_r$ be all the different generation trees from ξ_j to a given $x \in A^*$ in the underlying grammar. Then

$$\langle f_j, x \rangle = \Sigma_{i=1}^{r} \omega(\Gamma_i). \tag{2.5}$$

This is 0 if there are no trees from ξ_j to x. [If all weights are 1, the context-free case, then (2.5) is the number of distinct trees.]

Now let $R_{\text{rat}}[A]$ denote the collection of rational ps and $R_{\text{alg}}[A]$ the algebraic ps over A. Both are subrings of $R[A]$.

2.2 Proposition (Closure under Kleene's Operations). Both $R_{\text{rat}}[A]$ and $R_{\text{alg}}[A]$ are rings. They are rationally closed, i.e., closed under the quasi-inverse operation $f^* = f + f^2 + f^3 + \cdots$. [This converges because of (2.3).] Moreover, $R_{\text{rat}}[A]$ is the least rationally closed subring of $R[A]$ containing all $a \in A$.

2.3 Proposition (Closure under Substitution)

Let $P_j \in R_{\text{pol}}[\xi_1, ..., \xi_n, b_1, b_2, ...]$, and consider the system

$$\xi_j = p_j(\xi_1, ..., \xi_n, g_1, g_2, ...) \tag{2.6}$$

obtained by substituting the algebraic [rational] ps $g_1, g_2, ... \in R[A]$ for $b_1, b_2, ...$. The solution of (2.6) (where the right-hand sides are not necessarily polynomials over A) exists and is algebraic [rational].

The proof of both theorems can be carried out as the corresponding theorems for grammars, indicated in the subsections, namely, Theorems 2.2, 3.3, and 3.11 of Chapter 12.

Let $(f_1, ..., f_n)$ be the solution of an algebraic [rational] system. By adding variables, we can obtain that $(f_1, ..., f_n, f_{n+1}, ..., f_r)$ is the solution of an algebraic [rational] system in which all polynomials p_j are quadratic (of order $\leqslant 2$). This is achieved exactly as for grammars. Each production

$$\xi \to b_1 \cdots b_{q+2}, \qquad q > 0, \quad b_j \in A \cup X$$

is replaced by the $(q + 1)$ productions

$$\xi \to b_1\eta_1, \ \eta_1 \to b_2\eta_2, \ ..., \ \eta_q \to b_q\eta_{q+1}, \ \eta_{q+1} \to b_{q+1}b_{q+2},$$

where $\eta_1, ..., \eta_{q+1}$ are new variables. The process preserves rationality. Thus, a rational ps solves a system whose productions are of the form

$$\xi_i \to \alpha a \xi_j \qquad \text{or} \qquad \xi_i \to \alpha a, \qquad a \in A.$$

Such a system can be interpreted as a (nondeterministic) automaton with states ξ_i, with αa effecting a transition from ξ_i to ξ_j. (If $\xi_i \to \alpha a$, then ξ_i is a final state.) As for deterministic or probabilistic automata (i.e., Markov processes), this leads quite easily to a matrix representation, found by Schützenberger:

2.4 Proposition. $f \in R_{\text{rat}}[A]$ if and only if there is a natural n and a homomorphism $\Gamma : A^* \to R_n$ (the ring of $n \times n$ matrices over R) such that

$$\langle f, x \rangle = \Gamma(x)_{1n} \qquad \text{(the } 1n \text{ entry of this matrix).} \tag{2.7}$$

The *Hadamard product* of $f, g \in R[A]$ is given by $\langle f \circ g, x \rangle = \langle f, x \rangle \langle g, x \rangle$. It is obviously commutative, and, if R has no zero divisors, the support of $f \circ g$ is the intersection of support f with support g.

2.5 Proposition. If f is a rational ps and g is an algebraic [rational] ps, then $f \circ g$ is algebraic [rational].

Schützenberger's proof uses his representation result (Proposition 2.4). However, using the remarks preceding that proposition (namely, that a rational system can be viewed as an automaton with coefficients in R) and Proposition 2.1, we can repeat the proof for the intersection of context-free and finite-state languages (Theorem 3.5 of Chapter 12). We shall presently indicate a similar (but more complex) proof for preservation of algebraic ps by R-transductions.

3. Transductions and Assignments

An R-transduction will be a map $\tau : R[A] \to R[B]$. The values $\tau(x)$ for $x \in A^*$ will be in $R_{\text{pol}}[B]$. Any such map satisfying this condition has a unique extension (by linearity) to a map $R[A] \to R[B]$. An R-transduction is determined by a quadruple $T = (W, Q, Q_I, Q_F)$, where Q is a finite set, $Q_I \subset Q$, $Q_F \subset Q$, and

$$W : Q \times A^* \times B^* \times Q \to R$$

is a function with finite support D. W is essentially a labeled directed graph with set of nodes Q (Q_I initial nodes, Q_F terminal nodes) and the possible transitions $(q, u, v, q') \in D$ (from q to q') having weights in R (the values of W). An R-transduction is *proper* if $(q, e, v, q') \notin D$. A path ρ is a string of D^* of the form

$$\rho = (q_0, u_1, v_1, q_1)(q_1, u_2, v_2, q_2) \cdots (q_{k-1}, u_k, v_k, q_k), \tag{3.1}$$

and $q_0 \in Q_I$, $q_k \in Q_F$. We also set

$$\pi_1(\rho) = u_1, \ldots, u_k, \qquad \pi_2(\rho) = v_1, \ldots, v_k, \tag{3.2}$$
$$\omega(\rho) = \Pi_{i=1}^{k} W(q_{i-1}, u_i, v_i, q_i),$$

where $\omega(\rho)$ is the *weight* of the path ρ. We set $\omega(\rho) = 0$ if $\rho \in D^*$ is not a path. Then

$$\Sigma\omega(\rho)\,\rho \in R_{\text{rat}}[D], \tag{3.3}$$

as one easily verifies. Now for $x \in A^*$ we define

$$\langle \tau x, y\rangle = \Sigma\omega(\rho), \text{ sum over all } \rho \text{ with } \pi_1(\rho) = x,\ \pi_2(\rho) = y.$$

For a proper transduction, this sum is always finite, and it is zero for all but a finite number of y. Hence, τx is a polynomial over B^*, and τ can be extended to $R[A]$. The underlying absolute transduction of a given R-transduction is the one where all nonzero weights are replaced by 1. This is essentially the concept studied by Ginsburg [3], which can be achieved by a gsm (Definition 3.7 of Chapter 12) transforming a string reading it from left to right, the result being again transformed by a second gsm reading it from right to left. If $|\tau|$ is obtained as τ, but by setting every nonzero value of W equal to 1, we clearly have

$$|\tau|\, x = \Sigma_y y \cdot (\text{the number of paths } \rho \text{ with } \pi_1(\rho) = x,\ \pi_2(\rho) = y). \tag{3.4}$$

For τx itself, we have to replace in (3.4) "the number of paths" by the weighted sum over paths. Finally, if $f = \Sigma\langle f, x\rangle\, x$, then $\tau f = \Sigma_y \langle f, x\rangle \cdot$(the weighted sum over paths ρ with $\pi_1(\rho) = x$, $\pi_2(\rho) = y$).

3.1 Proposition. If f is an algebraic [rational] ps and τ is defined by a proper R-transduction, then τf is algebraic [rational].

PROOF. (Similar to the absolute case, part of which, by our foregoing comment, follows from Theorem 3.8 of Chapter 12 and the fact that the family of context-free languages is closed under reversal of all strings.) We first replace the given transduction by an equivalent one for which $(q, u, v, q') \in D$ implies that u is a single symbol. Next we observe that, for a fixed $q_0 \in Q_I$, $q_k \in Q_F$,

$$f(u_1 \cdots u_k)(q_0, u_1, v_1, q_1)(q_1, u_2, v_2, q_2) \cdots (q_{k-1}, u_k, v_k, q_k) \quad (3.5)$$

is algebraic [rational] over D; the system defining it is easily obtained from the one defining f. We take the Hadamard product of (3.3) and (3.5) and sum over all pairs in $Q_I \times Q_F$. The result is still algebraic [rational]. Finally, we substitute $(\cdot, u, v, \cdot) \to v$ (using Proposition 2.3, for instance) and obtain τf, as one easily checks. ∎

The *converse* transduction $\tau^\wedge : R[B] \to R[A]$ is obtained by taking $W(q, v, u, q') = W(q, u, v, q')$. It is proper if $(q, u, e, q') \notin D$.

An *assignment* is a homomorphism $\nu : A^* \to R_{\text{pol}}[B]$ such that its value on the generator $a \in A$ satisfies $\nu a \neq e$, $\nu a \neq 0$. By extension to $R[A]$, we obtain a transduction ν that is moreover proper and a one-state transduction. If $\langle \nu a, e \rangle = 0$, i.e., the transduction is never erasing, then the converse $\nu^\wedge$ of an assignment is a proper R-transduction.

For $|\nu|$, we have $|\nu|\, a = v_1 + \cdots + v_k$, $v_j \in B^*$. We say that v_j are *assigned* to a. If $|\nu|\, a' = v_1' + \cdots + v_k'$, then $|\nu|\, aa' = \Sigma_{ij} v_i v_j'$. So aa' is assigned all the strings $v_i v_j'$ (and so on, for longer strings). These same strings $v_i v_j'$ will appear with suitable weights in $\nu aa'$. It is easily seen now that, for $y \in B$,

$$|\nu|^\wedge y = \Sigma_x x \cdot (\text{the number of times } |\nu|\, x = y) \quad (3.6)$$

(or "the weighted number of times," in case of ν). Finally, if $K \subset B^*$ and k is its characteristic function, then

$$\langle \nu^\wedge k, x \rangle = \text{the weighted number of times } \nu x \in K. \quad (3.7)$$

4. A Representation Result and Some Consequences

It is natural at this point to ask whether all algebraic ps over R can be obtained from context-free ps by R-transductions. The answer is positive. Actually, all algebraic ps over R are obtained by transductions $\nu^\wedge$ (converses of assignments) from one special type of context-free ps: the characteristic functions of modified Dyck sets, which we proceed to define.

Let Δ be a set of $2m$ elements that come in pairs: $\delta, \bar{\delta}, \delta', \bar{\delta}'$, etc. Let $S = S_\Delta$ be the monoid generated by the symbols of Δ and the relations $\delta\bar{\delta} = e$, for all pairs in Δ. (If we add the relations $\bar{\delta}\delta = e$, we get a free group.) The set $K_\gamma = \{x \in \Delta^* \mid x \text{ represents } \gamma \text{ is } S_\Delta\}$ is called a *modified Dyck set.*

Let us note that K_γ differs in two respects from a customary Dyck set [1], which consists of all x representing the identity (instead of γ) in the free group (instead of S_Δ).

4.1 Theorem. Let $\nu' : A^* \to R_{\text{pol}}[S]$ be a monoid homomorphism of A^* into the monoid ring of S. We assume that $\langle \nu'(a_i), e\rangle = 0$, but $\nu'(a_i) \neq 0$. Let γ be any element of S. The ps f given by

$$\langle f, x\rangle = \langle \nu'(x), \gamma\rangle \qquad x \in A^* \tag{4.1}$$

is algebraic (and context-free if the coefficients of $\nu'(a)$, $a \in A$ are all 1).

PROOF. ν' is determined by $\nu'(a)$, $a \in A$. Let each $\nu'(a)$ (i.e., each monomial) be represented in reduced form by a polynomial νa of $R[\Delta]$. This determines by extension a homomorphism $\nu : A^* \to R_{\text{pol}}[\Delta]$ and $\nu : R[A] \to R[\Delta]$ (ν is the "lifting" of ν' from $R[S]$ to $R[\Delta]$). By our assumptions, both ν and the converse $\nu\hat{}$ are proper R-transductions. ν is moreover a one state transduction. Let $K_\gamma \subset \Delta^*$ be the set of all strings representing $\gamma \in S$, and k_γ the characteristic function of K_γ. It is well known (and easily proved) that K_γ is a nonambiguous context-free language, i.e., k_γ is context-free, in particular, algebraic. Now

$$\begin{aligned}\langle f, x\rangle = \langle \nu'(x), \gamma\rangle &= \text{the weighted number of times } \nu x \in K_\gamma \\ &= \langle \nu\hat{}k_\gamma, x\rangle,\end{aligned} \tag{4.2}$$

by (3.7). By proposition 3.1, f is algebraic and clearly context-free in the case $\nu = |\nu|$. ∎

REMARK. The theorem remains true (with the same proof) if S_Δ is replaced by a free group.

Our main result is a strong converse of theorem 4.1. To this end, we introduce a particular set of elements of S_Δ :

$$C = \{\text{all elements of the form } \delta, \delta\bar{\delta}', \delta\bar{\delta}'\bar{\delta}''\}.$$

Let T be the subsemigroup of S_Δ generated by C. (T does not contain the identity.) In C^*, we have the natural equivalence relation $x \equiv y$ if both represent the same element of S_Δ. In order to be able to use the arithmetic of categories of Bar-Hillel et al. [5], we introduce in C^* another (nonsymmetric, partial-order) relation "x cancels to y" which implies $x \equiv y$ if $y = \delta$ (but not always). It is convenient here to use the notation

$$\delta,\ \delta\backslash\delta',\ \delta\backslash\delta'\backslash\delta'' \qquad \text{for} \quad \delta,\ \delta\bar{\delta}',\ \delta\bar{\delta}'\bar{\delta}'', \text{ respectively.}$$

We say that $x \in C^*$ *directly cancels* to $y \in C^*$ iff $x = u\delta\delta\backslash\delta' v$, $y = u\delta' v$ or $x = u\delta\delta\backslash\delta'\backslash\delta'' v$, $y = u\delta'\backslash\delta'' v$. Now we take the ancestral relation, i.e., x *cancels* to y if there exist $x = z_0, z_1, \ldots, z_r = y$ such that z_i directly cancels to z_{i+1}, $1 \leqslant i \leqslant r$.

4.2 Lemma. For $x \in C^*$, $x \equiv \delta$ iff x cancels to δ.

PROOF. Obviously, x cancels to y implies $x \equiv y$. Now let $y = \delta$ and $x = c_1 \cdots c_m$, $c_k \in C$. We use induction on m. If $m = 1$, x must be δ. If $m > 1$, let k be the first index such that $c_k = \delta'\backslash\delta''$ or $c_k = \delta'\backslash\delta''\backslash\delta'''$. Clearly, $k > 1$, and c_{k-1} must be δ'. Thus, x directly cancels (and $\equiv$) to an x' of smaller length. Now $x' \equiv \delta$, and so by induction x' cancels to δ; hence, x itself cancels to δ. ∎

The set C with the relation "cancels to" on C^* was called restricted categorical system by Bar-Hillel *et al.* [5]. The main result there dealt with "categorical grammars" of the following type. To each $a \in A$, we assign a finite number of "categories" from C. This is, in fact, a one-state absolute transduction ν discussed at the end of Sect. 3. Then each $x \in A^*$ is assigned by ν several categories-strings, i.e., elements of C^*. If one of these cancels to a particular element of $\delta \in C$, then x is accepted by the grammar. It was proved by Bar-Hillel *et al.* [5] that each context-free grammar is equivalent to a categorical grammar of the type just described, and vice versa.

Theorem 4.3 extends this result to algebraic systems. As expected, ν will assign to each $a \in A$ weighted categories.

4.3 Theorem. Let $\xi_1 = p_1, \ldots, \xi_n = p_n$ be an algebraic system with $f_1, \ldots, f_n \in R[A]$ its standard solution. It is possible to construct a set Δ containing, in particular, $\xi_1, \ldots, \xi_n$ and a homomorphism $\nu' : A^* \to R_{\text{pol}}[S]$ of the type described in Theorem 4.1 such that

$$\langle f_j, x\rangle = \langle \nu'(x), \xi_j\rangle, \qquad 1 \leqslant j \leqslant n.$$

More precisely, we can choose $\nu'(a)$ as a finite combination of elements in C (weighted categories). If ν is the lifting of ν' to $R_{\text{pol}}[C]$, we can set a 1-1 weight-preserving correspondence between generation trees Γ from ξ_j to x and the strings of categories assigned to x by ν which cancel to ξ_j.

The last assertion proves the whole theorem, since by Proposition 2.1 $\langle f_j, x\rangle$ is the sum of weights of the trees from ξ_j to x, whereas by formula (4.2) $\langle \nu'(x), \xi_j\rangle$ is the sum of weights of the corresponding category strings. Proof of that assertion is given by Shamir [6].

4.4 Corollary. Every context-free language L is given as $|\nu|\hat{}K_\gamma$, where $|\nu|$ is a one-state, nonerasing absolute transduction (operating here on sets instead of their characteristic functions). Moreover, $|\nu|\,a$ can be taken as a set of elements in C.

K_γ is here, as in the proof of Theorem 4.1, the set of all strings in Δ^* representing the element $\gamma \in \Delta$ in the above monoid S_Δ. This is a variant of the one-sided Dyck set [3] (in which γ is replaced by the identity).

Another way to express this result is to consider inside C^* all the strings that (as strings in Δ^*) represent γ. Call this set M. Then L is obtained from M by substituting $A_c \subset A$ for each $c \in C$, where

$$A_c = \{a \in A \mid \text{the category } c \text{ is assigned to } a\}.$$

We are able to present now a simple proof of Parikh's theorem [3, 7]. Let $n_a(x)$ denote the number of a's occuring in x. For $x \in C^*$, $[n_c(x)]_{c\in C}$ is a vector with nonnegative integral coordinates, provided C is ordered in some fixed way. This vector is the *commutative image* of x. The (commutative) image of a set is the set of images.

4.5 Lemma. Let Δ have $2m$ elements. Then the commutative image of the set of M just defined is characterized by m linear equations for n_c, $c \in C$, with coefficients 0, 1, or 2. The equations characterizing the commutative image of L are then obtained by substituting $\Sigma_{a\in A_c} n_a$ *for* n_c.

This is the Parikh theorem. To prove the lemma, we observe that every $x \in M$ belongs to K_γ, as an element of Δ^*. We write now m linear relations for n_c expressing the fact that, in x, (1) the number of δ = the number of $\bar{\delta}$, $\delta \in \Delta$, $\delta \neq \gamma$; and (2) the number of γ = the number of $\bar{\gamma} + 1$. These relations are necessary for belonging to the image of M, but they are easily seen to be sufficient (using induction). Since each $c \in C$ contains at most two δ or $\bar{\delta}$, the coefficients are 0, 1, or 2. The last assertion of the lemma is clear. ▌

We conclude this section with another proof of Proposition 2.5, starting now from the representation theorems as definitions of rational and algebraic ps. Indeed, let $\langle f, x\rangle = \mu(x)_{1n}$ as in (2.7) and $\langle g, x\rangle = \langle \nu'(x), \gamma\rangle$ as in (4.1). Let $h = f \circ g$, the Hadamard product of f and g. We adjoin to the set Δ (see the beginning of the section) the symbols $1, 2, \ldots, n, \bar{1}, \bar{2}, \ldots, \bar{n}$. Define

$$\lambda(a) = \sum_{i,j=1}^{n} \mu(a)_{ij} \bar{\imath} \nu'(a) j.$$

We claim that $\langle \lambda(x), \bar{1}\gamma n\rangle = f(x) \cdot g(x) = h(x)$; hence, $h(x)$ is again algebraic. Indeed, let $x = a_1 \cdots a_r$. Then, if $c_1 \cdots c_r$ is a string of categories assigned to x which multiplies to γ (and only then),

$$(\bar{1}c_1 i_2)(\bar{\imath}_2 c_2 i_3) \cdots (\bar{\imath}_r c_r n) \qquad \text{multiplies to} \quad \bar{1}\gamma n.$$

The weight of this string is $\omega(c_1 \cdots c_r)\, \mu(a_1)_{1i_2}\, \mu(a_2)_{i_2 i_3} \cdots \mu(a_r)_{i_r n}$. Summing over all $i_2, \ldots, i_r$, we get $\omega(c_1 \cdots c_r)\, \mu(x)_{1n}$; summing over all $c_1 \cdots c_r$ multiplying to γ, we get $\langle \nu'(x), \gamma\rangle\, \mu(x)_{1n}$.

The result shows, in fact, that, instead of taking weights in R, we can take weights in the ring of matrices over R. We still get algebraic ps.

In principle, we have now a fairly good knowledge of the class of algebraic ps, provided we know well the context-free ones and the rational ones. Still, it is difficult to establish nontrivial necessary conditions for a ps f to be algebraic, or to exhibit an f that is not algebraic. (One such example is the characteristic function of the set $\{a^n b^n c^n\}$, which is not algebraic over the integers.)

In this connection, we mention that the useful result about the properties of the Hadamard product (Proposition 2.5) has a "commutative" analog. Moreover, if R is a finite field, the Hadamard product of two algebraic functions is algebraic [8]. It would be interesting to know whether the same result holds for noncommutative variables. Indeed, it would imply the commutative version, although there is no direct connection between the Hadamard products in the two cases. Questions about algebraic and rational power series over finite fields and rings would seem to fit in well with the theory of finite sequential machines and finite semigroups.

REFERENCES

1. N. Chomsky and M. P. Schützenberger, The algebraic theory of context-free languages, *in* "Computer Programming and Formal Systems" (F. Braffort *et al.*, eds.). North-Holland Publ., Amsterdam, 1963.
2. M. P. Schützenberger, On a theorem of R. Jungen, *Proc. Amer. Math. Soc.* **13**, 885–890 (1962).
3. S. Ginsburg, "The Mathematical Theory of Context-Free Languages." McGraw-Hill, New York, 1966.
4. C. C. Elgot and J. E. Mezei, On relations defined by generalized finite automata, *IBM J. Res. Develop.*, 47–68 (1965).
5. Y. Bar-Hillel, C. Gaifman, and E. Shamir, On categorial and phrase structure grammars, *Bull. Res. Council Israel Sect. F* **9**, 1–16 (1960).
6. E. Shamir, A representation theorem for algebraic and context-free power series in non-commuting variables, *Information and Control* **11**, 1–2 (1967).
7. R. J. Parikh, "Language generating devices," Quart. Progr. Rept. 60, Res. Lab. of Electronics, M.I.T., pp. 199–212 (January 1961).
8. H. Furstenberg, Algebraic functions over finite fields, *J. Algebra* **7**, 271–277 (1967).
9. Y. Bar-Hillel, M. Perles, and E. Shamir, On formal properties of simple phrase structure grammars, *Z. Phonetik, Sprachwiss. Kommunikationsforch.* **14**, 143–172 (1961).
10. J. Lambek, The mathematics of sentence structure, *Amer. Math. Monthly* **6**, 154–170 (1958).
11. J. Rhodes and E. Shamir, Complexity of grammars by group theoretic methods, *J. Combinatorial Theory* (to be published).
12. M. P. Schützenberger, On the definition of a family of automata, *Information and Control* **4**, 245–270 (1963).
13. M. P. Schützenberger, "Certain elementary families of automata," Symp. on the Mathematical Theory of Automata. Brooklyn Polytechnic Inst., Brooklyn, New York, 1962.

Appendix

The material in this volume by no means exhausts the wealth of topics now being studied in theories of machines, languages, and semigroups. In addition to the expository lectures that have expanded into the present volume, some 56 research papers were presented at the Asilomar Conference. The reader may well wish to consult these papers, and so we refer him to the three main repositories. Other papers from the Conference will be found in other issues of these journals, as well as in the *Journal of the Association for Computing Machinery*.

Mathematical System Theory **1**, No. 3 (1967) *et seq.*

A. R. Bednarek and A. D. Wallace, "A relation-theoretic result with applications in topological algebra."

J. M. Day and A. D. Wallace, "Multiplication induced in the state-space of an act."

R. Graham, "Subsemigroups of 0-simple semigroups."

A. Heller, "Stochastic transformations and automata."

J. Rhodes, "A homomorphism theorem for finite semigroups."

E. Tully, "A class of finite commutative archimedean semigroups."

L. A. M. Verbeek, "Congruence separation."

T. G. Windeknecht, "Mathematical systems theory: causality."

H. P. Zeiger, "Yet another proof of the cascade decomposition theorem for automata."

Information and Control **11**, Nos. 1 and 2 (1967)

M. A. Arbib, "Automaton automorphisms."

L. Falb, "Infinite-dimensional filtering."

P. Fischer, "Turing machines with a schedule to keep."

N. Hibbard, "Scan limited automata and context limited grammars."

H. Ibarra, J. Gray, and M. Harrison, "Two-way pushdown automata."

R. McNaughton, "The loop complexity of pure group events."

J. Mezei, "Algebraic automata and context-free sets."

A. Paz, "Minimization theorems and techniques for sequential stochastic machines."

E. Shamir, "A representation theorem for algebraic and context-free power series in non-commuting variables."

R. E. Stearns, "A regularity test for push-down languages."

J. Ullian, "Partial algorithm problems for context free languages."

H. P. Zeiger, "Ho's algorithm, commutative diagrams and the uniqueness of minimal linar systems."

Journal of Computer and System Sciences **1**, No. 2 (1967)

Y. Give'on, "On some properties of the free monoids with applications to automata theory."
J. Hartmanis and W. A. Davis, "Homomorphic images of linear machines."
R. Langer, K. Krohn, and J. Rhodes, "A theory of finite physics with an application to the analysis of metabolic systems."
D. S. Scott, "Some definitional suggestions for automata theory."
J. D. Ullman and J. E. Hopcroft, "Non-erasing stack automata."

Glossary of Symbols

$\langle a \rangle$, 3
A, automaton, 57 ff.
A^l, 4
A^r, 4
A^*, free monoid over A, i.e., set of sequences on set A, including empty sequence (similarly U^*, X^*, etc.), 19, 38, 64, 330
  closure of event A, 319
  topological closure of set A, 269
$A \cdot B$, 4
$A \backslash B$, set difference, 269
A, transformation automaton, 68
$B(J)$, 151
$cl(S)$, 179
C, cover, 70
$\mathrm{C}_{(n,m)}$, 107
$C(S)$, 135
$C(X, S)$, 133
$(\mathbf{C}, n)$, $(\mathbf{G}, n)$, and $(\mathbf{C} \vee \mathbf{G}, n)$, 239
CF, context free, 316
CFL, context free language, 316
$\mathscr{C}\mathscr{M}(n, G)$, 8
$\mathscr{C}(S)$, 238
D_X, delay machine, 48
D_A, D_1, 98
$\mathscr{D}$, $\mathscr{D}_T$, D_x, Green relation and class, 291
e, empty string, 298, 314, 330
ef, f a machine, 107
$E(S)$, set of idempotents of S, 8, 270
Endo(S), endomorphisms of S, 42
Endo$_L(S)$, 82
f_i, input-output function with initial state q_i, 17
f^S, semigroup of function f, 39, 81
f^{S1f}, etc., 86
f^σ, 86
f^Γ, 5
f^{Sf}, 81, 82
$f|g$ and $f|g$ (lp), 86, 87
$f \times g$, f and g machines, 89
$\langle f, x \rangle$, coefficient of x in ps f, 331
$f \odot g$, Hadamard product of ps f and ps g, 334
fsa, finite-state acceptor, 318
F, block of states, 75
$F(H)$, boundary of H, 288
$F(J)$, 182
$F(A, B)$, 6
$F(S, S')$, arbitrary maps from S to S', 43
$F(A)$, $F_R(A)$, $F_L(A)$, 6
$FN(n, c)$, 182
$\mathscr{F}$, $\mathscr{F}^S$, 82
gsm, generalized sequential machine, 325
$GM(J, G, N)$, 228
GLB or glb, 4
GGM_J, GM_J, 202
$\mathscr{G}(H)$, $\mathscr{G}(J)$, 166, 167
$H(e)$, group around idempotent e, 274, 278
$\mathscr{H}$, $\mathscr{H}_T$, H_x, Green relations and class, 278, 291
$IG(S)$, 8
IRR$_{SD}$, 103
IRR, IRR(S), 102
j_f, h_f, 86
(J, G, N), 228
$\mathscr{J}$, $\mathscr{J}_T$, Green relation, 291
J_S, L_S, R_S, and H_S, 150
$J_a \leqslant J_b$, $R_a \leqslant R_b$, $L_a \leqslant L_b$, 151
J^0, J a $\mathscr{J}$ class, 151

$\mathscr{J}$, $\mathscr{L}$, $\mathscr{R}$, $\mathscr{H}$ and $\mathscr{D}$, 150

ker[$(J_1, G_1, N_1), (J_2, G_2)$], 229

$K(S)$, minimal ideal of S, 9, 270

$K(\mathscr{S})$, $K_i(\mathscr{S})$, 101

$l(v)$, length of string v, 316

L_x, left translation operator, 16, 38
class of Green relation, 291

L_α, 101

$L(G)$, language generated by grammar G, 315

$L(s)$, $R(s)$, $J(s)$, 150

$L : S \to F_L(S^1)$, $R : S \to F_R(S^1)$, 6

LLM_J, RLM_J, 201

LUB or lub, 4

$\mathscr{L}$, $\mathscr{L}_T$, Green relation and class, 291

M, machine, 37

M_q, input-output function, 38

$M(f)$, reduced machine of function f, 38

$M|M'$, machine division, 39

$M' \times_Z^\eta M$, cascade of M and M', 40

MPE, 191

$M_X^R\, M_X^L$, 166

$\mathscr{M}(G; A, B; C)$, 8

$\mathscr{M}^0(G; A, B; C)$ or $S_{mn}(G, C)$, 7, 8

(mod R), R a relation, 4

$(n, \mathbf{C})$ $(n, \mathbf{G})$ $(n, \mathbf{C} \vee \mathbf{G})$, 133

N_J, 199

N_n, 148

$N(x)$, $\cap \{\Gamma_n(x) \mid n \geqslant 1\}$, 285

$NF(f)$, 88

pda (nondeterministic) pushdown acceptor, 322

ps, power series, 329

P, partition, 66

P_X, 121

PPf, f a machine, 107

$\mathscr{P}(S, P)$, 194

$\mathscr{P}(S, \alpha')$, 217

$\mathscr{P}(S, \gamma, \mathscr{J})$, 221

$\mathrm{Perm}_R(X)$, $\mathrm{Perm}_L(X)$, $\mathrm{Perm}(X)$, 181

PRIMES, PRIMES(S), PRIMES($\mathscr{S}$), 102

Q, set of memory states, 16, 37

Q_f, $[\ ]_{Q_f}$, and $\equiv_{Q_f}$, f a machine, 92

$Q_1 \vee Q_2$, Q_i congruences, 214

$Q(GM)$, $Q(GGM)$, $Q(RLM)$, $Q(LLM)$, 216

$r(S)$, 6

$\mathscr{R}_T$, R_X, Green relation and class, 291

R^{-1}, R a relation, 4

$R[A]$, ring of power series with variables A and coefficients in R, 331

$R_{\mathrm{pol}}[A]$, subring of polynomials in $R[A]$, 331

$R_{\mathrm{rat}}[A]$, subring of rational ps in $R[A]$, 333

$R_{\mathrm{alg}}[A]$, subring of algebraic ps in $R[A]$, 333

RM, LM, RLM, LLM, GGM, GM, 204

RM_J, LM_J, 199

$RI(X)$, $LI(X)$, $I(X)$, 166

$RI_T(X)$, $LI_T(X)$, $I_T(X)$, 166

$RT(S)$, $LT(S)$, 171

REP, 141

$RLM[GM_J(S)]$, etc., 205

$\mathscr{RM}(n, G)$, $\mathscr{CM}(n, G)$, 8

s^{-1}, 2, 178

s^n, 2

$[s]$ or $[s]_\equiv$, 5

S_M, finite machine semigroup, 20

S^C, 250

$(S^{f\sigma})^n$, 121

S^P, (e.g., $S^{\mathscr{L}}$, $S^{\mathscr{R}}$, etc), 194

$S^{\alpha-1}$, 224

$S^{\alpha'}$, 218

S^γ, 220

$S^{\gamma+\mathscr{J}}$, 221

$S\#$, 205

S^{GM}, S^{GGM}, S^{RLM}, S^{LLM}, 216

S^f, S^{fS}, 82

S^1, S^0, S^I, 5, 6

$S_{(n)}^{(\gamma+\mathscr{J})\cdots\mathscr{L}}$, 254

$S(E)$, syntactic monoid of E, 299

S, T, semigroups, $S \leqslant T$, 234

(S, P), 88

$(S_1, P_1) \equiv (S_2, P_2)$, 88

(S^1, S), 90

$(S, \cdot)$, 2

S/I, I an ideal, 147, 280

$S/\equiv$, $\equiv$ a relation, 5

$|S|$, 2

$S \mid S'$, semigroup division, 40, 87

$(S, i) \mid (S', i')$, division of semigroup with output, 40

$(S_1, P_1) \mid (S_2, P_2)$, 88

$S_1 \times \cdots \times S_k$, 7
$S_2 \times {}_{\varphi}S_1$, 82
$S_2 \times {}_Z S_1$ semidirect product of semigroups, 42
S' w S, wreath product of semigroups, 44, 95, 96
$SP(\mathscr{F})$, $SP_i(\mathscr{F})$, 95
$S \underset{P}{\twoheadrightarrow} T$, 87
$S \underset{a'}{\twoheadrightarrow} T$, 217
$S \underset{\gamma}{\twoheadrightarrow} T$, 219
$\mathrm{SIS}_R(X)$, $\mathrm{SIS}_L(X)$, 6
$\mathrm{SYM}_R(A)$, $\mathrm{SYM}_L(A)$, 6
$\mathscr{S}, \mathscr{S}^f$, 82
${}^{S}t$, 82
$T(A)$, set accepted by device A, 319, 320, 322
U, input set, 59
$U_3^{(n)}$, 121
U_0, U_1, U_2, U_3, the UNITS, 98
UMPE, 207
UNITS, 102
v, element of U^*, 64
w^*, 174
$W(\mathscr{S})$, 95
$\bar{W}(\mathscr{S})$, $\bar{W}_i(\mathscr{S})$, 95
$\hat{W}(\mathscr{S})$, $\hat{W}_i(\mathscr{S})$, 96
X, state set, 59
input alphabet, 16, 37
X_n, 85
$\langle X \rangle$, 3
$(X, \tilde{S})$ or $(X, S^{\sim})$, 115
(X, S), $(S^1, R(S))$, 83
$(X, S) \times (Y, T)$, 90
(X, S) w (Y, T), 84
$(X, S) \mid (Y, T)$, 90
$(X, S) \wr (Y, T)$, 84
$(X, S) \subseteq (Y, T)$, 90
Y, output set, 16, 37, 59
$(Y, T) \xrightarrow{(\theta, \varphi)} (X, S)$, 90
2_A, 98
2^X, 4
$\not{C}$, 238
β, output function, 37
γ, $\gamma(a)$, 194, 195
δ, next-state function, 16, 37
$\eta_{\equiv}$, $\equiv$ a congruence, 5
$\eta_I : S \twoheadrightarrow S/I$, 148
λ, output function, 16
$\varphi_1 \times \cdots \times \phi_{n'}$, ϕ_i homomorphism, 197
(φ, T), 191
$(\varphi_1, T_1) \leqslant (\phi_2, T_2)$, 192
$\Delta: S \to S \times \cdots \times S$, 197
$\Gamma_n(x)$, $\{x^p \mid p \geqslant x\}$, 285
$\Gamma(x)$, $\Gamma_1(x)$, 285
$\Pi\varphi_i$, φ_i, homomorphisms, 197
$\Pi\{X_a : a \in A\}$, 7
Σ, input alphabet, 298
ΣX, semigroup generated by X, i.e., nonempty sequences on X, 5, 17
$\oplus$, 135
Λ, empty string, 38
$\lhd$, normal subgroup, 49
$\square$, empty set (Chapter 10 only), 269
$\emptyset$, empty set (except Chapter 10), *passim*
$\to$, produces, 314
$\twoheadrightarrow$, 3
$\Rightarrow$, direct derivation, 315
$\overset{*}{\Rightarrow}$, derivation, 315
$\leqslant \leqslant$, 197
$\cong$, 3, 83
$\vdash$, pda direct derivation, 322
$\overset{*}{\vdash}$, pda derivation, 322
$\#(S)$, 242
$\#_G(S)$, 129
$\#_{G^a}(M)$, 129
$\#_{G^b}(S)$, 129
$\#_{G^c}(X, S)$, 130
$\#(X, S)$, 133

Author Index

Numbers in parentheses are reference numbers and indicate that an author's work is referred to, although his name is not cited in the text. Numbers in italics show the page on which the complete reference is listed.

A

Allen, O., 132, 212, 266, *267*
Anderson, L. W., 273, 279, *294*
Arbib, M. A., 49(2, 3), *54*, 145, *343*
Assmus, E. F., 50

B

Backus, J., 329
Balman, R., 287(B), 289(B), *294*
Bar-Hillel, Y., 338, *341*
Bayer, R., 50
Bednarek, A. R., 294, *294*, *343*
Borsuk, K., 282
Burnside, W., 106

C

Caianiello, E., 312, 314
Chomsky, N., 329(1), 330(1), 337(1), *341*
Clifford, A. H., 1, 51, *54*, 105, *145*, 160, 177, 183, *189*, 270, 271, 272(Cl 1, 2), 289, 290(C-P), 291, 292(C-P), 293 (C-P), *294*
Cohen, H., 272, 273, *294*
Cowan, J. D., 34(4), *35*
Curtis, C. W., 238, *267*

D

Davis, W. A., *344*
Day, J. M., 270(D-W), 287(D-W 1, 2), 288(D-W 1, 2), 289, *294*, *343*

E

Elgot, C. C., *341*
Ellis, R., 271, *294*

F

Falb, L., 54, *343*
Faucett, W. M., 271, 272(F), 281, 289, 293, *294*, *295*
Fischer, P., *343*
Florentin, J. J., 50
Frobenius, 77, 79
Furstenberg, H., 340(8), *341*

G

Gaifman, C., 338(5), *341*
Galois, E., 79
Ginsburg, S., 313, 314, 327, 335, 339(3), *341*
Ginzburg, A., 80
Give'on, Y., *344*
Gleason, A., 275

Graham, N., 189, *189*
Graham, R., 189, *189*, *343*
Gray, J., *343*
Green, J. A., 150, 153, 155, 160, *189*

H

Hadamard, J., 334, 336
Hall, M., 51, *54*, 76, *80*
Harrison, M., *343*
Hartmanis, J., 61, 70, 73, *80*, 120, *125*, *344*
Heller, A., *343*
Hibbard, N., *343*
Hocking, J. G., 270(H-Y), 272, *295*
Hofmann, K. H., 269, 277, 278(H-M), 279, 290, *295*
Hopcroft, J. E., *344*
Hu, S. T., 270(Hu), 279(Hu), *295*
Hudson, A. L., 281, *295*
Hunter, R. P., 273, 276, 279, *294*, *295*
Hurewicz, W., 273(H-W), *295*

I

Ibarra, H., *343*

J

Jordan, C., 79

K

Kalman, R. E., 54
Kautz, W. H., 33(3), *35*
Kelley, J. L., 270(Ke), *295*
Kleene, S. C., 333
Koch, R. J., 275, 277(K 4), 284, 285(K 1), 288(K-W 1), 293(F-K-N), *295*
Krohn, K. B., 17, 21, 27, 28, *35*, 46, 48, *54*, 77, 101, 103, 113, 120, 125, *125*, 130, 132, 143, 145, *145*, 212, 213, *231*, 266, *267*, 307, *344*
Krohn, K. B., 17, *35*
Krule, I. S., 273, *294*

L

Lambek, J., *341*
Langer, R., 130, *145*, *344*
Liu, C. L., 70, *80*

M

McNaughton, R., 297, 312, *343*
Markov, A. A., 334
Mateosian, R., 1, 101, 120, *125*, 143, 145, *145*
Mezei, J. E., *341*, *343*
Montgomery, D., 273, 275(M-Z), *295*
Moore, E. F., 312
Mostert, P. S., 269, 271, 272(M-S), 274(M-S 1), 275, 277, 278(H-M), 279, 281, 290, *295*
Munn, W. D., 51, 183, *189*

N

Numakura, K., 285, 293(F-K-N), *295*, *296*

P

Paalman-de Miranda, A. B., 269, *295*
Papert, S., 297
Parikh, R. J., 318, 339, *341*
Paz, A., *343*
Perles, M., *341*
Perry, Y., 80
Preston, G. B., 1, *54*, *145*, 160, 183, *189*, 199, 212, *231*, 270, 289, 290(C-P), 291, 292(C-P), 293(C-P), *294*

R

Rabin, M., 297, 301, 303(1), *312*
Redei, L., 51, *54*
Rees, O., 157, 160, 189
Reiner, I., 238, *267*
Rhodes, J., 17, 21, 27, 28, *35*, 46, 48, *54*, 77, 101, 103, 113, 120, 125, *125*, 130, 132, 140, 143, 145, *145*,

183, 189, *189*, 197, 212, 213, 231, *231*, 238, 239, 261, 262, 266, *267*, 307, *341*, *343*, *344*
Rothman, N. J., 279, *295*
Rounds, W., 144

S

Schützenberger, M. P., 166, 183, *189*, 199, 212, *231*, 307, *312*, 329, 330, 334, 337(1), *341*
Scott, D., 297, 301, 303(1), *312*, *344*
Shamir, E., 80, 338(5), 339, *341*, *343*
Shields, A. L., 271, 272(M-S), 274 (M-S 1), 275, 277, 281, *295*
Stadtlander, D., 287(S), *296*
Spanier, E., 327
Stearns, R. E., 61, 70, 73, *80*, 120, *125*, *343*

T

Tilson, B. R., 132, 266, *267*
Tully, E., *343*

U

Ullian, J., *343*
Ullman, J. D., *344*

V

Verbeek, L. A. M., 54, *343*

W

Wade, C. I., 272, *294*
Wallace, A. D., 269, 270, 273(H-W), 277, 281, 285, 287(D-W 1, 2), 288(D-W 1, 2)(K-W 1)(W 6, 7), 289, 290, 291, 292(W 8), 293, 294(B-W), *294*, *295*, *296*, *343*
Wallman, H., 273
Windeknecht, T. G., *343*
Winograd, S., 34(4), *35*

Y

Young, G. S., 270(H-Y), 272, *295*

Z

Zalcstein, Y., 132, 233
Zeiger, H. P., 25, 26, 27, *35*, 113, 115, 120, *125*, 145, *145*, *343*
Zippin, L., 273, 275(M-Z), *295*

Subject Index

A

Abelian group, 21
Accepted, 313, 320
Act, 285
Action (right), 83
  faithful, 83
ALGOL, 314, 329
Algebraic systems, 330 ff.
Ambiguity, 317
  degree of, 330
  inherent, 318
  syntactic, 318
Arc, 271
Assignment, 62, 336
Automaton, 55
  continuous, 285
  cyclic, 47
  cyclic semigroup, 28, 34
  errors, 34
  group, 21, 22, 75
  left simple semigroup, 28
  linear, 31, 33
  Mealy, 17
  Moore, 17
  permutation, *see* Group
  permutation-reset, 25, 27
  quotient, 68
  reset-identity, 26, 28
  standard semigroup, 20, 22, 25
  state-output, 37
  sub-, 69
  transformation, 68
Auxiliary symbols, 315
Axiom I, 234
Axiom II, 234
Axiom II′, 265
Axiom III, 234
Axioms for complexity, 234

B

Band, 8
Bing, 271
Boolean matrices, 16
Boundary, 288
Breaks off, 10

C

Cartesian product, 7
Cascade, 55
  form, 55
  of machines, 40
  related to semigroups, 48
  related to series-parallel, 48
  wreath products and, 46
Categorial grammar, 338
Character ring, 238
Church's thesis, 315
Clan, 271
Closed set, 270
Closure, 319
  under homomorphism, 299
Coarser, 72
Coding function, 21, 23–25
Collapser map, 21, 27, 30
Column monomial matrix, 8

Commutative diagram, 59
Commutative image, 339
Compact semigroup, 269
Completely simple semigroup, 289
Complex product, 319
Complexity, 79, 133, 140
  addition of, 135, 240
  existence, 139, 140
  main theorem, 239
  number, 133, 242
  of semigroups, 135, 239
  of transformation semigroups, 133
Component, 62
Composition
  factors, 78, 159
  series, 78
    ideal, 159
Computation of complexity, 235
Concatenation, 298
Congruence, 4
  left, 5
  right, 5
  on semigroup, 49, 279, 282, 299, 301
Construction of semigroups, 174
Context free grammar, 316, 329 ff.
Context free language, 316, 329 ff.
  characterisation theorem, 322
  closure properties, 324
  decision problems, 326–327
  deterministic, 323–326
Context free system, 329 ff.
Context-sensitive
  grammar, 316
  language, 316
Continuity of complexity
  with respect to division, 265
    to homomorphisms, 263
    to ideals, 143, 144
    to subsemigroups, 263
Continuous machine, 285
Converse of transduction, 336
Coordinate map
  for any $\mathscr{J}$ class, 162
  for 0-simple semigroups, 158
  for regular $\mathscr{J}$ class, 162
Coordinatewise multiplication, 7
Coordinatized (or egg box) (or Green-Rees) picture, 155
Covers, 55, 70, 71
Cross section, 281
Cutpoint order, 272
Cyclic machine, 47
Cyclic point, 85
Cyclic semigroup machine, 28, 34
Cylindrical semigroup, 278

D

Decomposition, 23–25, 28, 55
Derivation, 315
  left most, 317
Diagonal map, $\triangle$, 197
Dimension, 273
Direct product, 7
  of transformation semigroups, 90
Discrete semigroup, 269
Division
  length preserving machine, 87
  of machines, 39, 86
  of semigroups, 40, 87
  transformation semigroup, 90
Dual, 7
Dyck set, 326, 336–7

E

Emerge from idempotent, 274
"End in a combinatorial," 240
"End in a group," 240
Endomorphism, 82
Epimorphism (= onto homomorphism), 3
  α ($\alpha = \mathscr{J}, \mathscr{L}, \mathscr{R}, \mathscr{H}$), 194
  α'($\alpha = \mathscr{J}, \mathscr{L}, \mathscr{R}, \mathscr{H}$), 217
  $\gamma(\alpha)$ ($\alpha = \mathscr{J}, \mathscr{L}, \mathscr{R}, \mathscr{H}$), 195
  γ, 194
  $\gamma + \mathscr{J}$, 221
  maximal proper (MPE), 195
  natural, 147
  unique maximal proper (UMPE), 207
Equivalence
  of machines, weak, 39
  right (-invariant), 301

Errors in machines, 34
Event, 298
Expansion, 237
  transitive component, 257
  trivial, 256
Extension of semigroup
  by congruence, 49
  ideal, 51
  Schreier, 50–52
  by semigroup, 49

F

Feedback, 16, 30
Finite-state
  acceptor, 318
  system, 332
Free
  group, 337
  monoid, 330
Fundamental Lemma of Complexity, 234, 243

G

G-complexity function, 234
  θ_a, 236
  θ_b, 236
  θ_c, 236
  θ_d, 236
  θ_e, 236
  θ_f, 237
  θ_g, 237
  θ_h, 237
  θ_i, 238
GC-decomposition, 128
Generalized embedding theorem, 140
Generalized sequential machine, 325, 335
Generation, 315
  tree, 317, 332
Grammar, 313
Graph, 334
Green relations, 150, 153, 278, 288, 290
  relative, 290
Group, 2
  abelian, 21
  cyclic of order n, 5
  machines, 21, 22
  simple, 21, 24, 28
  torsion, 11
Group-complexity, 127, 129
  existence, 139, 140
  of machine, 129
  main theorem, 239
  of semigroup, 129
  of transformation semigroup, 130

H

$\mathscr{H}$ class, 150
Hadamard product, 334, 336
Hazards, 15, 34
Homeomorphism, 270
Homomorphic image, 3
Homomorphism, 3, 57, 191, 299 ff., *see also* Epimorphism
  α ($\alpha = \mathscr{J}, \mathscr{L}, \mathscr{R}, \mathscr{H}$), 194
  α' ($\alpha = \mathscr{J}, \mathscr{L}, \mathscr{R}, \mathscr{H}$), 217
  γ, 194
  $\gamma(\alpha)$ ($\alpha = \mathscr{J}, \mathscr{L}, \mathscr{R}, \mathscr{H}$), 195
  $\gamma + \mathscr{J}$, 221
  generalized group mapping with respect to *J* (GGM_J), 202
  group mapping with respect to *J* (GM_J), 202
  left letter mapping with respect to *J* (LLM_J), 201
  left mapping with respect to *J* (LM_J), 199
  length preserving, 86
  local, 160
  one to one, 3
  onto, 3
  P, 87, 194
  partial, 161
  right letter mapping with respect to *J* (RLM_J), 201
  right mapping with respect to *J* (RM_J), 199
  unique extension of map to a, 86

I

I-semigroup, 271
Ideal, 9
  combinatorial, 243
  distinguished, 205
  left, 9
  maximal, 143
  maximal proper, 293–294
  minimal, 270
    left, 9, 289
    right, 9, 289
  nearly maximal, 143
  0-minimal, (left, right), 9
  principal (left, right), 150
  relative, 291, 293–294
  right, 9
Idealizer, 166
  left, 166
  right, 166
Idempotent, 2, 270, 308 ff.
Identity, 2
  left, 2
  right, 2
Independence of coordinates, 60
Index
  of cyclic semigroup, 11
  of nilpotent linear transformation, 239
Initial block of cover, 74
Initial state of graph, 302
Input-output functions, 15, 18, 31, 38
Inverse element
  group inverse, 2
  semigroup inverse, 178
Inverse function, 3
IRR, 102
  IRR(S), 102
Irreducibility
  of machines, 41
    related to semigroups, 46
  s-irreducibility, 46
  of semigroups, 42
  topological, 277
Iseomorphism, 270
Isomorphic, 3, 83, 192
Isomorphism, 3, 58

J

$\mathscr{J}$ class, 150
  combinatorial, 202
  distinguished, 205
  noncombinatorial, 202
  null, 152
  regular, 152
  θ-singular, 196

K

Kernel
  of semigroup, 9
  of semigroup homomorphism, 228
Kleene's operations, 319, 333
Krohn-Rhodes decomposition theorem, 28

L

$\mathscr{L}$ class, 150
L-semigroup, 280
Left simple semigroup machine, 28
Left trivial semigroup, 281
Left zero, 272
Linear machine, 31, 33
Linked equation (Eq. 7.2.8 and X7.2.15), 172
Local multiplication, 157
Locally compact semigroup, 269
Logical design, 15, 21, 31

M

Machine, 81, *see also* Automaton
  basic combinatorial, 128
  combinatorial, 128
  delay, 98
  fundamental expansion of, 86
  group, 128
  group-free, 128
  identity-reset, 128
  natural extension of, 86
  normal form of, 88
  *n*th iteration of, 121
  parallel composition, 89

partial product, 107
permutation, 128
prime decomposition theorem of, 103
proposition concerning, 93
REP(T), 141
semigroup of, 81
series composition, 89
2_A, 98
Maximal (minimal) homomorphic image
with respect to being group, 193
with respect to property, 192
Mealy machine, 17
Min-thread, 272
Minimal γ homomorphic image, 219, 220
Möbius strip, 283
Monoid, 2, 298, *see also* Semigroup
computation procedure for finding maximal subgroups, 311
Monomial map, 106
Monomorphism, 3
Monothetic semigroup, 284
Moore machine, 17

N

Nil thread, 272
Nilpotent class, 179
Norm, 237
Normal, 279
modes, 79
Normalization of structure matrix, 158, 159
Nondeterministic fsa, 320

O

One-parameter semigroup, 273
Open dense half-line, 289
Orbit, 281

P

Parikh's theorem, 339
Pascal array, 124
Path, 335
Partition, 61, 62
pair, 63
preserved, 61
Period (of cyclic semigroup), 11
Permutation automaton, 75
Permutation-reset, 25, 27
Permuter, 181
left, 181
right, 181
Phrase-structure
grammar, 314
language, 314
Physics, finite, 130
Pointwise multiplication, 7
Polynomial, 331
Power series (ps), 329 ff.
Precedes, of blocks of cover, 74
Preserved partition, 61
Prime decomposition theorem, 101, 103, 113
PRIMES, 102
(S), 102
($\mathscr{S}$), 102
Principal ideal factors, 149
Principal ideal series, 149
Principle of induction for combinatorial semigroups, 120
Product (of sets), 319
Production, 314, 329, 332
Property
local, 175
of homomorphisms, 191
of semigroups, 175
Proportional
on left rows, 208
on right columns, 208
Pushdown acceptor (pda), 322
deterministic, 323

Q

Quasi-inverse, 333

R

$\mathscr{R}$ class, 150
Races, 15, 34

Range, 78, 230
Rank, 78
Rational system, 332
Reachable, 38
Recursive set, 316
Recursively enumerable set, 315
Reduced
  form, 38
  state graph, 303
    as representation of syntactic monoid, 306
Rees quotient semigroup, 51, 280
Rees-Suschkewitsch theorem, 292
Rees theorem, 147, 157
Redei-Schreier theorem, 53–54
Regular event, 298, 303, 319
  characterization theorem, 319
Regular semigroup element, 175
Relation, 4
  equivalence, 4
  greatest lower bound of (GLB or glb), 4
  Green, 150
  identity, 4
  least upper bound of (LUB or lub), 4
  reflexive, 4
  symmetric, 4
  transitive, 4
  transitive closure of, 4
Relative ideal, 291, 293–4
Representation
  character of, 238
  irreducible, 238
  left regular, 6
  left Schutzenberger (alias LM_J), 199
  Rees matrix (= coordinate map), 157
  right regular, 6
  right Schutzenberger (alias RM_J), 199
  Schutzenberger-Preston, 199
Reset, 25, 72
Reset-identity machine, 26, 28
Response, 57
Retract, 66
  lemma, 66
Rewriting rule, 314
Right-linear CF grammar, 321
Row monomial matrix, 8

S

Schutzenberger group, 166, 167
Schützenberger theorem, 291, 293
Semidirect divisor closure of semigroups, 101
Semidirect product, 82
  of semigroups, 42
    Schreier extensions and, 52
Semigroup, 1, 2
  abelian, commutative, 2, 132
  band, 8
  combinatorial, 120, 180
  compact, 269
  completely simple, 289
  congruence, 49
  cyclic, 3
  cylindrical, 278
  discrete, 269
  free, 5
  free nilpotent of class c on n generators, 182
  of function, 39
  generalized group mapping (GGM), 204
  group mapping (GM), 204
  I-semigroup, 271
  inverse, 132, 178
  irreducible, 102, 103
    with respect to semidirect products, 103
    topological, 277
  L-semigroup, 280
  left letter mapping (LLM), 204
  left mapping (LM), 204
  left trivial, 281
  locally compact, 269
  machine of, 82
  mapping, 83
  monothetic, 284
  nilpotent, 179
  normal, 279
  null, 9
  0-simple (left, right), 9
  one-parameter, 273
  PRIME, 102
  quotient, 147

Rees matrix, 7
regular, 175
regular Rees matrix, 8
reverse, 6
right letter mapping (*RLM*), 204
right mapping (*RM*), 204
simple (left, right), 9
single spiral, 275
standard null, 148
subdirectly indecomposable, 207
symmetric inverse, 6
syntactic monoid, 299
topological, 270
topologically irreducible, 277
torsion, 3
transformation (= mapping), 83
type I, 238
union of groups, 177, 235
UNIT, 102
Semigroup product, 275
Semilocal theory, 197
Series
α-β, 236
(b), 236
(c), 236
(d), 236
(e), 236
(f), 237
Series mapping onto series, 235
Series-parallel, 22, 30
cascades and, 48
Series parallel closure of machines, 95, 100
Similar, blocks of cover, 74
Simple group, 21, 24, 28
Simulation, 39
Single spiral semigroup, 275
Solution of algebraic system, 331
Stable, 288
Standard semigroup machine, 20, 22, 25
Standard thread, 271
State, 56
diagram, 16
transformation, 64
transition, 16, 17, 20 ff.
State graph, 302
reduced, 303
State-output automaton, 37
Structure matrix, 7
Subautomaton, 69
Subdirect product, 197
Subdirectly indecomposable, 207
Subgroup, 3
maximal proper, 3
of monoid, 308 ff.
of topological semigroup, 270
Subsemigroup, 3
cyclic, 3
generated by set, 3
inverse, 178
main proposition, 184
maximal combinatorial, 183
maximal proper, 3, 183
unitary (left, right), 181
Substitution, 333
mapping, 325
theorem, 325
Successor, 57
Support of power series, 331
Swelling lemma, 287
Syntactic monoid, 299
System, 114

T

Terminal state of graph, 302
symbol, 314
Thread, 271
min, 272
nil, 272
standard, 271
unit, 272
Topological semigroup, 270
Topologically irreducible, 277
Transduction, 334 ff.
Transformation automaton, 68
Transformation (or mapping) semigroup, 83
abstract semigroup determined by, 83
left, 174
right, 83
Translations, 171
left, 171
left translation of free semigroup, 101
linked, 171

right, 171
Turing machine, 315
Turing's hypothesis, 315

U

U_0, U_1, U_2, U_3, 98
Unambiguous, *see* Ambiguity
Unique minimal P homomorphic image, 87
Uniqueness lemma, 70
Unit thread, 272
UNITS, 102

V

Variable
metalinguistic, 313
Vocabulary, 314

W

Weights, 332, 335
Wreath divisor closure of semigroups, 95, 96, 100
Wreath product, 83, 84
of abstract semigroups, 44
machine cascades and, 45
of semigroups, 96
of transformation semigroups, 84

Z

Zero, 2
left, 2, 272
right, 2
Zorn's lemma, 278, 290